PRAISE FOR

Ella Baker and the Black Freedom Movement

"[This] book is an exemplar of intellectual history, social history, women's and gender history, and organizational history. The biography also reads as an organizing guide for current and future activists interested in grassroots activism. . . . It has fundamentally altered how historians and activists understand past movement work and future movement strategies."—*Chronicle of Higher Education*

"Baker kept a low profile, which makes Barbara Ransby's complex, crisply written biography more impressive for its vivid rendering of an elusive character."—*Wall Street Journal*

"The strength of Ransby's work is in her detailed accounting of Baker's political life, accompanied by an analysis of Black struggle in the twentieth century."—*The Crisis*

"Ransby, a historian of indisputable talent and skill, provides numerous intricate, heretofore unknown facts and details of Ella Baker's life while growing up in the South and the path that led her to involvement in civil and human rights efforts. . . . This is a superb book."—*Encounter*

"An intriguing and nuanced biography. . . . Ransby's treatment of Baker's life is not so much intent upon installing her name on the civil rights marquee as it is concerned with distilling the principles that Baker advocated and conveying her approach to social change."—*Progressive*

"Ensures that all who wish to know about Baker's tireless work can find a detailed account in one volume."—*Black Issues Book Review*

"Ransby offers the grit and gleam of Baker's practical humanist vision of participatory democracy. . . . A remarkable biography worthy of her remarkable subject."—*Library Journal*

"The definitive biography of one of America's most important civil rights leaders in the twentieth century."—*Religious Studies Review*

Ella Baker

AND THE BLACK FREEDOM MOVEMENT

The Gender and American Culture series, guided by feminist perspectives, examines the social construction and influence of gender and sexuality within the full range of American cultures. Books in the series explore the intersection of gender (both female and male) with such markers of difference as race, class, and region. The series presents outstanding scholarship from all areas of American studies—including history, literature, religion, folklore, ethnography, and the visual arts—that investigates in a thoroughly contextualized and lively fashion the ways in which gender works with and against these markers. In so doing, the series seeks to reveal how these complex interactions have shaped American life.

A complete list of books published in Gender and American Culture is available at https://uncpress.org/series/gender-and-american-culture.

Ella

Baker

and the Black Freedom Movement

A RADICAL VISION

Barbara Ransby

Second Edition

With a new preface by the author and a new foreword by
Robin D. G. Kelley.

THE UNIVERSITY OF NORTH CAROLINA PRESS   *Chapel Hill*

Set in Charter and Meta types by Keystone Typesetting, Inc.
Manufactured in the United States of America
Excerpt from Mississippi Goddam by Nina Simone
© 1964 (renewed) WB Music Corp. All rights reserved.
Used by permission of Warner Bros. Publications U.S., Inc., Miami, FL 33014.
Cover art © George Ballis / Take Stock / TopFoto.

978-1-4696-8134-4 (pbk.: alk. paper)
978-1-4696-8135-1 (epub)
978-1-4696-8136-8 (pdf)

The Library of Congress has cataloged the original edition of this book as follows:
Ransby, Barbara.
Ella Baker and the Black freedom movement: a radical democratic
vision / Barbara Ransby.
p. cm.—(Gender and American culture)
Includes bibliographical references (p.) and index.
ISBN 978-0-8078-2778-9 (cloth: alk. paper)
ISBN 978-0-8078-5616-1 (pbk: alk. paper)
ISBN 978-0-8078-6270-4 (ebook)
1. Baker, Ella, 1903–1986. 2. African American women civil rights
workers—Biography. 3. Civil rights workers—United States—Biography.
4. Civil rights movements—United States—History—20th century.
5. African Americans—Civil rights—History—20th century. 6. National
Association for the Advancement of Colored People—Biography.
7. Mississippi Freedom Democratic Party—Biography. 8. Southern
States—Race relations. 9. United States—Race relations. I. Title.
II. Series: Gender & American culture
E185.97.B214 R36   2003
323′.092—dc21   2002153275

CONTENTS

ILLUSTRATIONS

FOREWORD

Vincent Harding was a giant in the Black Freedom Movement. Born and raised in Harlem, he earned degrees from City College and Columbia University and a PhD in history from the University of Chicago. He and his wife, Rosemarie Freeney-Harding, moved to Atlanta in 1960 to become full-time movement workers. They worked with the Student Nonviolent Coordinating Committee, the Congress of Racial Equality, and the Southern Christian Leadership Conference, where Vincent occasionally drafted speeches for Dr. Martin Luther King Jr., including his iconic "Beyond Vietnam: A Time to Break Silence" speech, declaring King's opposition to the Vietnam War. Yet when Harding's daughter, noted anthropologist Rachel Harding, asked him decades later to talk about his initiation into the movement, he replied, "The first name that comes to mind is Ella Baker."

In an interview published in the summer 1997 issue of *Callaloo*, Harding continued,

> [She] was one of those people who was obsessed with democracy. She really believed in the possibilities of democracy. And she was especially concerned that every opportunity be taken to teach democracy in the course of the Freedom Movement itself. . . . I remember especially, some very exciting time, I think it was in Albany, Georgia, at a mass meeting. I was supposed to be speaking at the mass meeting, and one of the things she said to me was, "Vincent, never go in front of this many people who really want to do something with themselves and for themselves unless you are ready to teach. Have something that you can teach in the situation." Ella Baker's model of a democratic teacher was very, very important to me. I would consider her one of my major supporters, teachers, encouragers in this whole area of a truly democratic kind of life.[1]

Harding's anecdote beautifully distills Ella Baker's radical democratic vision and offers an apt summary of Barbara Ransby's magnificent account of Baker's life, work, and thought. Published twenty years ago, *Ella Baker and the Black Freedom Movement* remains the finest movement biography we have, matched only by George Lipsitz's *A Life in the Struggle*.[2] By movement biography I am referring to work that critically examines a life as a window into insurgent social movements, revealing the dynamic relationship between thought and action, praxis and power. Baker is a unique figure in that she passed through so many different movements as organizer, leader, strategist, and teacher but either shunned the limelight or was pushed aside by male leaders. However, her impact was much greater than her public visibility.

Baker left a scattered and uneven archive compared to the men in the movement. This book is even more remarkable given that Ransby had to build and structure the archive as she wrote. Baker's papers were available to her but not organized at the time. Her commitment to knowing not only what Baker did but how she *thought* is outstanding. Ransby drew upon interviews, organizational records, and Baker's private papers. In doing so she demonstrates that Baker's radical humanism and her ideas about community organizing grew out of her youth, community and kin networks, a rooted Black culture, formative political experience, collective memory, the improvisational nature of solving day-to-day problems, astute observations of the political terrain, deep listening, and education.

Simply put, Baker was more interested in freedom than fame. More than a posture or an ethical principle, her critique of the charismatic, media-savvy leader was foundational to her radical democratic vision. She rejected top-down leadership. She told feminist historian Gerda Ray Lerner in 1970 that she "felt it was a handicap for oppressed peoples to depend so largely upon a leader, because unfortunately in our culture, the charismatic leader usually becomes a leader because he has found a spot in the public limelight. . . . Such a person gets to the point of believing that he is the movement."[3] Instead, she believed in the capacity of ordinary people to lead and make decisions through participatory democracy.

Ransby breaks down what participatory democracy actually meant to Baker and for actual movement building. Anyone with a rudimentary understanding of the civil rights movement knows about the legendary "endless meetings" held by the Student Nonviolent Coordinating Committee. But as Ransby demonstrates, those long meetings were not simply about consensus building but rather were also about forms of knowledge production, collective interrogations into problems or challenges ahead, and the development of strategies to address them. Within the Student Nonviolent Coordinating Committee, members pushed each another's ideas to the limit until there was some level of transformation. This was the genius of Baker's radical democratic vision and the basis for her theory of change.

Organizing, she believed, begins with showing up, making connections, building trust, and then asking people to define their issues rather than presenting them with an agenda. Campaigns should emerge organically from the needs and experiences of the community, be nondogmatic, flexible, willing to shift directions, and prepared to create permanent structures with rooted leaders.

Among Ransby's numerous contributions is her decision to cast Baker as an "organic intellectual." Unfortunately, for many U.S. scholars the phrase has come to mean activists with limited formal education whose ideas are drawn from experience or folk wisdom. But this is not what Antonio Gramsci meant by "organic intellectual," and Barbara Ransby knows it.[4] What made Baker an organic intellectual was her rootedness in movements and communities attempting to challenge the forces that constrained their lives, denied them of basic rights and freedom, and made them vulnerable to premature death. To be grounded in movements usually means developing new modes of thought in struggle and in the service of revolution. As Ransby so eloquently put it, "[Baker] redefined the meaning of radical and engaged intellectual work, of cross-class and interracial organizing, and of a democratic and humanistic way of being in the world, all the while trying to mold the world around her into something better."

These words could have been used easily to describe Barbara Ransby. She may hold a distinguished chair at the University of Illinois Chicago, but social movements have always been her primary home. She wrote *Ella Baker and the Black Freedom Movement* not for tenure, not for glory, not for the awards and accolades it received but to share the lessons for the present held in Baker's life. Ransby embodies Baker's radical democratic practice. She is especially fond of what became Baker's signature opening question: "Who are your people?" Ransby immediately understood that the question was intended to "locate an individual as a part of a family, a community, a region, a culture, and a historical period. Baker recognized that none of us are self-made men or women; rather, we forge our identities within kinship networks, local communities, and organizations." Ransby grew up in a working-class neighborhood in Detroit where knowing one's people was essential for community cohesion and political solidarity. She attended Rosary High School, a predominantly white Catholic school on Detroit's west side, and as a freshman became the first—and only—African American elected student body president. But her orientation was always toward the Black community.

Ransby really *knew* her people. In 1971, at age fourteen, she wrote a regular column for the Black-owned *Michigan Chronicle* called "Teens about Town," covering the activities of local Black youth. She reported on graduations, awards, couples, college acceptances, sweet sixteen parties, the hippest fashions, youth-oriented community organizing, all the "boss" bands, the hottest musicians, and the budding poets. ("We have turned to poetry as a way to release our thoughts, our fears, our aspirations and convictions," Ransby once wrote.) Taken together, these columns reveal the depths of social networks among kids and portray a vibrant, striving, close-knit community. Anyone who has attended Black church services knows that preceding the sermon are announcements—deaths, graduations, births, the sick who need visiting and prayers, and so forth. In many ways, "Teens about Town" did this work but with a political purpose, an eye to the future, and always a sense of loving pride and joy. It contained the kind of information every organizer needs.

In July 1972, Ransby wrote about the campaign Keep Detroit Beautiful Teens, which recruited young people to wage an "all-out campaign to combat litter"—a precursor to Detroit Summer launched exactly twenty years later by Jimmy and Grace Lee Boggs, legendary radical thinkers and organizers committed to transforming the city. Before heading off to New York, Ransby organized against police violence and spent much of her time in various political study groups—including one led by the Boggses. As a student at Columbia University, she quickly emerged as a principal leader of the anti-apartheid movement, and as a graduate student at the University of Michigan, Ransby, along with fellow graduate students Cathy Cohen, Tracye Matthews, and Premilla Nadasen, organized the Free South Africa Coordinating Committee. In 1987 when Black student protests against racism erupted across the country, they formed the United Coalition Against Racism. When I joined the faculty at the University of Michigan, Ransby and her comrades were a force to be reckoned with. They had just won an extraordinary demand to create the Ella Baker–Nelson Mandela Center for Anti-Racist Education, an activist space for critical engagement and study open to everyone, including non-university working-class residents. While completing her doctoral dissertation on Baker, Ransby moved to Chicago and continued to work on a dizzying number of local and national campaigns, such as the Black Radical Congress, the Chicago Committee in Solidarity with Southern Africa, and African American Agenda 2000, formed in response to the gender exclusion and conservatism of the Million Man March. More recently, she helped launch the Movement for Black Lives, founded and directs the Social Justice Initiative at University of Illinois Chicago, and is a founding member of The Rising Majority.

The point of sharing this all-too-brief capsule history of Ransby's activism is to suggest that wherever she went, whatever she did, she brought Ella Baker with her. She helped transform Chicago into what is arguably the nation's hub of Black organizing. Similar to Baker, she has played a critical role as a supporter of, and mentor to, many Black youth-oriented movements, including Black Youth Project 100, We Charge Genocide, Assata's Daughters, #LetUsBreathe Collective, and Ella's Daughters. Launched in 2008, Ella's Daughters embraced "the humanist democratic radical tradition" of its namesake. According to its founding principles, humanist meant affirming "the dignity and worth of all people"; democratic entailed "collective thinking and decision-making"; and to be radical was "to get to the root cause of things." Its members opposed "racism, patriarchy, heterosexism, misogyny, imperialism, homophobia, xenophobia, economic exploitation, zero-sum politics, militarism, and any other system of domination that seeks to rob people of their right to life, agency, and pleasure."[5] Although the organization no longer exists, its impact on movement circles still reverberates. Thanks to Barbara Ransby, Ella Baker and the profound knowledge she left us still live.

There is still more to discover from Baker's extraordinary life and Ransby's telling. Only Barbara Ransby could have written this book. Ransby has managed to extract the core lessons from her work and, above all, from her vision guiding her work, and turn them into a compass for all of us. She has lived what Harding called "a truly democratic kind of life."[6] She believes in the capacity of people to make their own history but understands that changing history requires a radical democratic vision and organization. And she believes in freedom, not as a far-off destination or utopian dream but as a remolding of life-worlds, relations of power, and thought by people in a constant struggle. And as Ella's most astute daughter, she knows we cannot rest until it comes.

Robin D. G. Kelley
Los Angeles
International Women's Day, March 8, 2024

· · · · · ·

NOTES

1. Rachel E. Harding and Vincent Harding, "Biography, Democracy, and Spirit: An Interview with Vincent Harding," *Callaloo* 20, no. 3 (Spring 1997): 684.

2. George Lipsitz, *A Life in the Struggle: Ivory Perry and the Culture of Opposition* (Philadelphia, PA: Temple University Press, 1988).

3. Ella Baker, "Developing Community Leadership," in *Black Women in White America*, ed. Gerda Lerner (New York: Random House, 1972), 351.

4. Antonio Gramsci, *Selections from the Prison Notebooks*, ed. Quintin Hoare and Geoffrey Nowell Smith (New York: International Publishers, 1971).

5. "What Is Ella's Daughters?—Ella's Daughters Mission Statement," *Ella's Daughter National Planning Committee* (blog), April 2008, https://ellasdaughters.wordpress.com/about/.

6. Harding and Harding, "Biography, Democracy, and Sprit," 684.

PREFACE

When *Ella Baker and the Black Freedom Movement* was published in 2003, the United States had not yet elected its first Black president or experienced the right-wing and racist calamity of the Trump years.[1] The devastating financial crisis of 2008, which caused many people to question some of the basic tenets of capitalism, was not yet on the horizon, nor had the Occupy Wall Street movement launched its full-scale indictment of capitalism. The mass movement against racist police violence under the banner of Black Lives Matter—sparked by the police murders of Michael Brown, George Floyd, Breonna Taylor, and so many others—had not yet been inscribed into our consciousness, nor had it exploded into the headlines and onto the streets. The massive nationwide protests of 2020 had yet to bring 20 million people to the streets, disrupting traffic on major highways, staging vigils in opposition to Floyd's murder and related acts of state violence, and demanding racial justice—all of this in the middle of a historic global pandemic.

In June 2007, I went to Atlanta with my friend Lisa Yun Lee to attend the U.S. Social Forum, a light on the political horizon at that time. Organizers migrated from all over the country to celebrate, coalesce, and conspire for freedom. The gathering of thousands of activists was a part of the larger World Social Forum that began in Porto Alegre, Brazil, when the new socialist governments of Latin America were on the rise. It was an exhilarating and historic political event. A surprising highlight came when a stranger approached me and thanked me profusely for the Ella Baker book. Then another did the same. Then another. This was my first time receiving such compliments for my scholarship in an activist space. Another similar encounter happened a few years later in Chicago. At that time a young organizer who had just returned from a United Nations event in Geneva, where, as part of the We Charge Genocide delegation, she had testified about police violence against Black youth in Chicago, offered her own praise for the book. At a welcome home event for the delegation, she said to me that the Ella Baker biography was the reason she became an organizer. I was floored. In that moment, I felt the book was serving the special purpose for which it was intended.

Another exceptionally memorable experience with teaching the book came during my brief stint as a volunteer instructor for the Prison + Neighborhood Arts Project at Stateville Correctional Center, a maximum security prison in central Illinois. My incarcerated students took the civil rights movement class, and the book on Baker, very seriously. It was the most vigorous and rigorous discussion of Baker's life I have ever had in a classroom setting. My students at Stateville came into our stark, windowless classroom each week with their dog-eared, heavily highlighted copies of the book, with many comments and questions scribbled in the margins. They fell in love with Ella Baker and her tough, principled, no-nonsense approach to politics. Those qualities appealed to them, as did her loyalty to those most left out of the equation when rights and resources are being doled out. The students were among that sector of the population that Baker was most concerned about and committed to.

I was honored to serve as a conduit for conveying Ella Baker's story and her political vision and values. It is not the book, per se, but Ella Baker's powerful example that touches people so deeply. The book has earned numerous awards and recognitions from professional historical organizations for which I am enormously grateful, but it is the tribute from movement organizers that has moved me the most and serves as a poignant and treasured affirmation.

Ella Baker's relevance to students, organizers, civil rights movement historians, and our incarcerated neighbors and family members is clear, but I often ask myself, after the long journey she and I have traveled together, What does she mean to me? What does Ella Baker's legacy and lessons demand of me? In partial response to those persistent questions, I have carried Ella Baker's words and example with me through my various organizing efforts over the past two decades. In 2007 I cofounded a group called Ella's Daughters by reaching out to the many amazing women who were agitating, organizing, and writing for justice, and whose work and way of working reminded me of Baker. This was how we described our group: "Ella's Daughters is an international network of women working in the humanist democratic radical tradition of Ella Jo Baker. We oppose racism, sexism, imperialism, homophobia, xenophobia, and economic exploitation. We support full empowerment of the disabled. We advocate respect for, and protection of, the natural environment, robust democratic participation, and full human rights for all people . . . as the cornerstone of a just society."[2] Over its five or so years of active engagement, Ella's Daughters involved an intergenerational network of over 200 women, many of us still in touch and still carrying on in Baker's tradition in one way or another. It is always a delight when I run into one of Ella's daughters at a demonstration, conference, or meeting. I am reminded in those instances that her political spirit is still very much alive.

I am also reminded of that enduring spirit of intergenerational solidarity when I think of the work that my dear friend the political scientist Cathy J. Cohen is doing. She helped to launch the Black feminist group Black Youth Project 100, and she now works to amplify the voices of young people through her engaged scholarship and intellectual leadership of the GenForward Survey research project at the University of Chicago. This project captures the opinions and political views of young people of color: voices that other prominent surveys routinely overlook.

· · · · · ·

People from the Student Nonviolent Coordinating Committee used to say Ella Baker was legendary within social movement circles but relatively unknown outside of them. But her legacy has deepened and elongated over the past twenty years. Two markers of Baker's increased visibility today are evidenced by a very different set of claims to fame. In 2021, when Joe Biden was nominated as the Democratic Party candidate for president, he began his acceptance speech by making a surprise mention of Ella Baker, calling her a "giant of the civil rights movement" and championing her grassroots approach to leadership by quoting her words, and one of my book chapter titles: "Give people light and they will find a way."[3] Biden is not a part of Ella Baker's political tribe or tradition, but someone in his circle was informed enough to know that mentioning her name and reputation might engender good feelings among historically conscious and progressive voters.

During Black History Month the following year, I was invited to be part of an Instagram conversation with popular hip hop artist, performer, and social media celebrity Big Freedia, who composed a song for the occasion, appropriately titled "The Ella Baker Shaker." The title is a nod to the fact that Baker so often shook things up as an organizer and internal movement agitator. These mentions of Baker speak to very different audiences but also reflect her wide and eclectic appeal over time.

With broader audiences and with the passage of time, it is easy for Baker's politics and practices to get diluted and distorted in the popular imagination. Given that, I want to reiterate some important facts and clarify some misunderstandings that come up from time to time. First, Baker was not an advocate of leaderlessness. She embraced and embodied a particular type of leadership, as sociologist Charles Payne argued long before my book did. Hers was a kind of group-centered leadership that decentered singular charismatic (usually male) leaders who took on messianic or prophetic roles. People who teach following as the only way of fighting have done a disservice to our movements, she insisted. Each of us must step up in our own way to fuel, steer, and propel our struggles forward. That is what she taught us.

The second misreading of Baker is more general. There is a folksy way that older women in social movements are often discussed. I tried my best to liberate Baker from that stereotype, to portray her as the savvy strategist and movement intellectual that she was. Still, she is sometimes cast as this kindly nurturing elder who simply cheered on the youth. She did indeed believe in working with and supporting the leadership of young people, but she did not fetishize youth as a political category. If they were serious, sharp, and radical enough, she was with them. But she did not assume that age, either hers or theirs, dictated political leanings.

Finally, the depth and nature of Baker's political beliefs and ideological groundings often get collapsed and sanitized. She not only opposed Jim Crow segregation, racial disenfranchisement, unequal pay, and other forms of discrimination but also railed against patriarchal authority, imperialism, colonialism, war, and capitalism itself. Her politics were not vague: they were specific and radical. She was a democratic socialist and one of the founders of the short-lived Mass Party Organizing Committee, an explicitly socialist formation. That commitment was incubated in Harlem in the 1930s when she worked with the cooperative movement and taught and organized alongside communists and leftists of various stripes. She also spoke out on behalf of Puerto Rican independence and against the Vietnam War. Never dogmatic. Never sectarian. But always clear in her convictions.

· · · · · ·

Two events in 2023 reminded me of the import of Baker's legacy. One was the annual Socialism Conference in Chicago, hosted by my friends at Haymarket Books. At that conference I was privileged to share the stage with my daughter, Asha Ransby-Sporn, a respected community organizer and movement strategist who began organizing at age seventeen. In a conversation focused on the book, we reflected on how Baker had impacted each of us. For Asha, the solid commitment to grassroots organizing and movement building as a vocation is something she and Baker shared in common.

For me, the intergenerational nature of Baker's work for most of her life resonated. I have worked with various youth-led and intergenerational organizations: African American Women in Defense of Ourselves, the Movement for Black Lives, and Rising Majority, among others. I say half-jokingly in those spaces that I try to model Ella Baker and participate as a well-behaved elder—not as one that "scolds and molds," as one young activist quipped about another less well-behaved elder who visited Ferguson, Missouri, during the 2014 youth-led uprising.

The second important event commemorating Ella Baker in 2023 was a conference in New York hosted by the Barnard Center for Research on Women and its director, my longtime sister-scholar, Professor Premilla Nadasen. Premilla was a leader of the student anti-apartheid movement and later the director of the Ella Baker–Nelson Mandela Center for Anti-Racist Education, which we formed as student activists at the University of Michigan in the late 1980s. Talking about Baker decades later felt like a homecoming. Respected colleagues, beloved friends, and treasured comrades gathered at Barnard College in December 2023, a week or so before what would have been Baker's 120th birthday, to celebrate the book and its subject. But it was more than that. It was also a test of our convictions to the injustices of our own time. The most glaring and gut-wrenching event on the world stage at that moment was the genocidal Israeli bombardment of Palestinians in Gaza. After a terrible and violent attack on Israeli civilians on October 7, the right-wing government of Israel launched a military assault and invasion of the Gaza Strip, mercilessly killing entire families and leaving their homes—and some of their bodies—in the rubble. The world was outraged by Israel's excessive retaliation, but the United States sided with Israel, giving only lip service to the massacre of thousands of Palestinians. Columbia University, the larger institution of which Barnard is a part, had just suspended two student groups that were rightly calling for an immediate cease-fire in Gaza. The students in turn called for a boycott of the university. Our event was quickly given an exemption by the student activists because of its purpose and content. We had a WWED (what would Ella do) moment: as a gesture of solidarity, we invited speakers from Students for Justice in Palestine and Jewish Voice for Peace, two progressive groups that oppose the Israeli occupation, to address the crowd at the opening session. This was an issue close to our hearts since Premilla and I had gone on an Indigenous and Women of Color Feminists delegation to Palestine in 2011 and seen firsthand the suffering of the Palestinian people. The students were passionate, eloquent, and smart. Ella would have been proud.

And so, this is the work of the book and the power of radical histories: not simply to tell stories of the past that then lay dormant or conjure nostalgic images of earlier struggles for freedom but that serve as examples and inspiration for how we carry on, flaws, frailties, and mistakes notwithstanding.

· · · · · ·

As I look back at the very long acknowledgments in the original edition of this book, I can safely say I am still grateful to all those people for their support, love, and collegiality both before and after the book's publication. Some of them, including my parents-in-law, have passed on. Their love and secular spirits remain with us. The memory of my own parents and grandparents sustains me every day. One person I would like to uplift here, whose name did not appear in the very first printing of the book due to an editorial oversight on my part, is Professor Thomas C. Holt. Tom was my advisor, mentor, and patient teacher during my graduate school years at the University of Michigan and after. He gave me the encouragement and confidence to embark upon my dissertation writing at a time when I had many doubts and competing obligations. Now retired, he continues to be a shining example of a brilliant historian and an all-around stellar human being. In addition to Tom, I am grateful to a whole host of new friends, colleagues, and comrades who came into my life since 2003, too many to list here. I do, however, as always, want to thank my immediate family: Peter, Asha, and Jason. They continue to be the center of my world in every way, and I am forever grateful for their anchoring love and unwavering support. The newest member of our family, born a few months before the twentieth anniversary of this book, is our grandniece, Nina Veronica Sanchez. She is the precious embodiment of our hopes and dreams for a brighter and more just future for her and for the world. We hope that one day she will live in the kind of world that Ella Baker, and many of us, have dreamed of and fought for.

· · · · · ·

NOTES

1. "Black" is capitalized in the new foreword and preface of *Ella Baker and the Black Freedom Movement* to underscore the reference to a people. It is conventionally capitalized when referring to ethnic and national groups. "Black" refers to a diverse multinational, multiethnic people with shared African roots. To capitalize "Black," distinguishes references to Black people from the simple adjective "black." This usage is informed by Black liberation movements that have resisted the erasure and denigration

of Black peoples, cultures, and narratives. See Mike Laws, "Why We Capitalize 'Black' (and Not 'White')," *Columbia Journalism Review*, June 16, 2020, www.cjr.org/analysis /capital-b-black-styleguide.php#:~:text=The%20first%20is%20broad%20adherence ,suspended%20if%20"a%20particular%20author.

2. "What Is Ella's Daughters?—Ella's Daughters Mission Statement," *Ella's Daughter National Planning Committee* (blog), April 2008, https://ellasdaughters.wordpress .com/about/.

3. "Transcript: Joe Biden's DNC speech," CNN, last modified August 21, 2020, 6:36, www.cnn.com/2020/08/20/politics/biden-dnc-speech-transcript/index.html.

ACKNOWLEDGMENTS

This book has taken me on a long and circuitous path, which began in 1989 when I chose to research the life of Ella Baker as a dissertation topic. Since that time I have encountered many wonderful fellow travelers, and experienced difficult detours along the way. One of my children grew up, another was born, and both my parents passed away. Political struggles and personal commitments repeatedly pulled me away from the task of research and writing.

If it takes a community to raise a child, it certainly takes a community to produce a book. Many people have contributed to this book directly and indirectly, and it would be disrespectful to Ella Baker's memory if I did not take time and space to recognize them. I must first express my appreciation to Ella Baker's family, especially her niece Jackie Brockington, who died months before the book was published, who, along with Joanne Grant, gave me early and extensive access to Ella Baker's papers when they were still housed at her old apartment in Harlem. Jackie never said, "No," to anything I asked for—photographs, copies of documents, or a few hours of her time. I was touched that she always asked about my family and trusted me with the precious memories of hers. She exemplified those fine qualities for which others praised her beloved aunt Ella. I regret terribly that she did not live to see the completion of the book. I am also deeply indebted to Joanne Grant, whose documentary *Fundi* brought Ella Baker to life for my generation and whose own biography of Baker made a vital contribution. Joanne was a friend and colleague throughout the writing of my dissertation. In the spirit of Ella Baker, we chose to cooperate and coexist rather than compete in our efforts to tell her story in our own words. We agreed early on that there was certainly room for two Ella Baker biographies.

I have had the benefit of quite a number of amazing readers and researchers who have made invaluable contributions to this project. Cathy Cohen, my dear friend and adopted sister, has been a glowing inspiration and an unwavering source of support. During our morning phone conversations, at our respective computers, she often began with the question, "How's Ella?"—as if checking in on an ailing family member. She read large portions of the manuscript and opened her home and her heart at critical junctures. Tracye Matthews, friend, colleague, reader, research associate, fellow activist, and birthing coach, read, edited, and dug up details to help move this book along. The photo of Ella Baker that she gave me has hung above my computer for six years now. My dear friend Premilla Nadasen schlepped down to the Municipal Archives in New York and maneuvered her way around bureaucratic hurdles to get access to Ella Baker's divorce records. She and her family then welcomed me into their Mount Vernon, New York, home for a weeklong writing retreat in the summer of 2001 to finish one round of revisions on the book. Thanks to Billy Gladstone for keeping the coffee brewed and Tyler Kiran for being a delightful distraction during my stay.

Gerald Horne is a generous colleague who, when I asked him to read 500 pages in a week, responded that he would be honored. Timothy Tyson and John Dittmer were also extremely knowledgeable and thoughtful readers and continue to be treasured colleagues, who remind me with their own sterling examples that we can love our subjects and still write damn good history books. And I will be ever grateful to the amazing Charles Payne, whose own work helped to bring Ella Baker to a wider audience and who nudged me along for years with hugs, gentle criticism, profound insights, and words of reassurance.

Martha Biondi took time away from her own book-writing to read and comment on my manuscript. Her comments have strengthened the final product, and her professional and political example continues to strengthen my resolve. I would also like to thank scholar-activist Leith Mullings for her generous reading of several chapters. Colleagues of mine at the University of Illinois at Chicago—Sue Levine, Bill Ayers, Amanda Lewis, John D'Emilio, and Eric Arnesen—read the manuscript carefully and provided enormously helpful suggestions and comments. John and I have had many wonderful Ella and Bayard lunches to talk about our tandem biographies. We all anxiously await what promises to be the definitive biography on Bayard Rustin.

Aldon Morris introduced me to Ella Baker in his civil rights seminar fifteen years ago, and I am ever grateful. He continues to be a friend, mentor, and colleague. Clayborne Carson, Susan Carson, Stewart Burns, and the staff at the King Papers Project were enormously helpful to me at the early stages of this project during the week I spent at Stanford. They provided advice, information about historical documents and obscure archives, and a friendly and intellectually stimulating environment. Daniel Holliman aided me in digging up information in George Schuyler's papers at Syracuse University at a moment when timing was everything. Herbert Hill welcomed me into his home, fed me a fine meal, and shared important insights and recollections. On a separate occasion in another city, Lenora Taitt-Magubane did the same thing. Other researchers have sent me little treasures—letters, news clippings, and interviews—to fatten my already engorged Ella Baker files. For these contributions, I thank John Bracey, Jerry Markowitz, Andrea Vasquez, John Thornbery, Julius Scott, Pam Sporn, Archie Allen, Wendy Plotkin, and Kathleen Cleaver. Penny Von Eschen and Kevin Gaines have also been wonderful colleagues and supportive friends. Vincent Harding's support is also much appreciated.

I owe still another enormous debt to historians Nell Painter, Linda Kerber, and Linda Gordon, all notoriously busy women who took time out to read my manuscript and offer suggestions and kind words of encouragement. Nell went the extra mile to help me grapple with the vexing issue of Baker's private life by providing me with a rich reading list of psychological studies on the social meanings of privacy and identity, which I have tried to weave into the text.

Through their own pioneering work, the following scholars have created an academic and a popular audience for black women's history, and each of them in different ways has supported and inspired my work: Darlene Clark Hine, Elsa Barkley Brown, Tera Hunter, Deborah Gray White, Stephanie Shaw, Tiffany Patterson, Rosiland Terborg-Penn, Ula Taylor, Chana Kai Lee, Stanlie James, Angela Davis, Evelyn Brooks Higginbotham, Joy James, Sharon Harley, Paula Giddings, and Beverly Guy-Sheftal.

And Robin D. G. Kelley is in a category all his own. He has always been there for me. My brother-friend-comrade-mentor. His encouragement, advice, solidarity, and remarkable example of a brilliant scholar and a fundamentally humane person have sustained my optimism about unraveling the past and shaping the future. Tom Holt, a brilliant historian, was my dissertation chair and much more. He was a political ally, role model, and my intellectual compass from the start. Earl Lewis and Michael Dawson offered priceless insights and encouragement along the way.

The time Ella Baker spent with the Student Nonviolent Coordinating Committee in the 1960s was some of her most rewarding work. Meeting and getting to know the remarkable collection of people associated with SNCC was for me one of the most rewarding aspects of researching this book. SNCC activists Judy Richardson, Connie Curry, and Ivanhoe Donaldson read the entire manuscript and put up with numerous follow-up queries as acts of solidarity and generosity. Judy went out of her way to provide me with a copy of an excerpt from Judith Rollins's *All Is Never Said* that mentions Ella Baker. I thank them from the bottom of my heart, as well as all of the other SNCC people who allowed me to interview them (their names are listed in the bibliography); they have warmly welcomed me into the SNCC family and included me in reunions, reminiscences, and sometimes a little bit of movement gossip. I am humbled by their friendship and kindness, especially that of my first SNCC friend, Martha Prescod Norman. Each one of them, as well as the admirable and indefatigable Anne Braden, gave me the dual gifts of time and trust. Even those I did not formally interview—Bill Strickland, Charles McDew, Michael Thelwell, Cleveland Sellers, Zohara Simmons, Gloria House, Julian Bond, Larry Fox, and others—informed my reading of Ella Baker's life through their public remarks and in private conversations. I hope this book is some small measure of repayment. The contribution of Kwame Ture (Stokely Carmichael) to this project was heroic even though we only spent a few hours together. Despite terminal cancer, he persevered in the freedom struggle until the end. I interviewed him at his bedside during his last visit to the States. Despite the frailness of his body, his mind was sharp and his words clear. He spoke to me like a man with a stake in both the past and the future. Other individuals whom I interviewed have passed on, including Conrad Lynn, John Henrik Clarke, Jackie Brockington, Prathia Hall (Wynn), Marvel Jackson Cooke, and Gloster Current. Their memories and contributions live on in these pages and beyond.

And what would I have done without excellent editors, researchers, and librarians? Grey Osterud, a fine wordsmith with a keen eye, helped me through the last phase of writing, chapter by chapter. From her desk in rural Massachusetts to my desk in Chicago, she offered ideas, questions, and suggestions. Interspersed between revisions, we digressed to learn about one another's backgrounds, politics, religious views, and children. I jokingly called her my book therapist because she cheered me on as much as anything else and reminded me that what often felt large and unwieldy could be harnessed and completed.

Kate Torrey, the director of the University of North Carolina Press, has given new meaning to the words "patience" and "grace." Although my early manuscript was in a very unpolished state, she saw potential in this project and nurtured and nudged it and me along every step of the way. A skilled editor, and an all-around fine human being, she has most importantly given me the space, time, and encouragement needed to bring this book to fruition. Two other capable editors, Paul Betz and Pamela Upton, have seen me through the final stages.

A small battalion of graduate and undergraduate students has contributed bits and pieces to this project over the decade. Some dug up obscure articles in the library, while others traveled with me to archives to excavate more pieces of the Ella Baker puzzle. With one exception, most of them worked for short stints, ranging from a few hours to a couple of months, but all of their labors are appreciated; they include Jasmine Patel, Emily Mann, Jeff Helgeson, Greg Simmons, David Brewer, Rachel Caidor, Gareth Canaan, David Levine, and Rychelle (Kitty) Hooper (who was one of the stalwarts). John Santiago, Deva Woodly, Brandi Adams, Lisa Jones, Quincy Mills, and Anne McCarthy also contributed. No words can express the gratitude I feel for Sarah Wood, my first research assistant, who stumbled with me through the early days of this project, diligently tracked down information and individuals, and served as a sounding board for ideas; an impeccable young colleague, she was also a devoted friend. She then came back to help me in the final stages despite her own hectic schedule as she prepared to move to Pennsylvania. Ella belongs to her as much as to anyone.

Numerous librarians, archivists, and photographers have provided me with priceless resources. I am immensely grateful to Howard Dodson, Diane Lachatanere, and Andre Elizee at the Schomburg Center for Research in Black Culture in New York City for allowing me to plow through Baker's unprocessed papers once they were deposited there. Also deserving of special thanks are the photographers Harvey Wang and Charmian Reading and the staffs at the State Historical Society of Wisconsin, the North Carolina Collection at the University of North Carolina at Chapel Hill, the Martin Luther King Jr. Papers Project, the Library of Congress, and the Moorland-Spingarn Research Center at Howard University.

There are others who have never read a line of this book as of yet but who live in its pages because for me they represent a continuation of Ella Baker's tradition. For much of the time I was conceiving of this book, I was engaged in various political struggles, attempting to learn from and apply Ella Baker's lessons as I went. In the process, I worked alongside some extraordinary people who embodied Baker's democratic values and radical humanist vision. The members of African American Women in Defense of Ourselves, especially Elsa Barkley Brown and Deborah King, took Baker's ideas and put them directly into practice; they continue to be an inspiration to me. Bill Fletcher, with whom I worked for five years on the Black Radical

Congress, stands out as a model of the selfless organizer—enormously wise, profoundly humane, often underappreciated. Manning Marable, Leith Mullings, Abdul Alkalimat, Fran Beal, Lisa Brock, Cheryl Harris, Humberto Brown, Jarvis Tyner, Prexy Nesbit, Ajamu and Rukiya Dillahunt, and Jean Carey Bond are other activists from whom I have learned a great deal as well. Tanaquil Jones was a dear friend and close ally for years as I struggled to hear Ella Baker's political voice and find my own. Much of the reason I decided to write this book in the first place has to be attributed to my political family at the University of Michigan in the 1980s, who sat in with me at the administration building to demand an honorary degree for Nelson Mandela, picketed during the dead of winter for the Martin Luther King Jr. holiday to be recognized by the university, and helped establish the Ella Baker–Nelson Mandela Center for Anti-Racist Education. Those not already mentioned include Hector Delgado, Michael Wilson, Roderick Linzie, Lillien Waller, Rajal Patel, Nikita Buckhoy, Lannis Hall, David Maurasse, David Fletcher, Jocelyn Sargent, Emery Smith, Kimberly Smith, Regina Freer, Anthony Vivasis, Brett Stockdill, and too many more to name. A. Sivanandan, Jenny Bourne, Hazel Waters, and Liz Fekete at the Institute for Race Relations in London have provided me with a political home away from home during my visits there. Back home in Chicago, my friends at the Crossroads Fund have buoyed my optimism in bleak political times.

There are those whose contributions were professional or political, and then there are those whose contributions were entirely personal. Arlene Branscomb, my daughter Asha's caregiver for five years, may not even remember the topic of this book. However, Arlene gave me the most precious gift a mother can hope for, peace of mind that my child was in capable and loving arms when I was working. Her kindness and warmth reminded me daily of the care and interdependency that holds families and communities together. Jacqui BassiriRad too was a surrogate mom for Asha many afternoons during the final stage of the book's preparation, and Hormoz BassiriRad kept us well fed with Persian delicacies. Laura Henderson at the Buzz Café in Oak Park kept me fueled with caffeine as I sat and wrote for hours.

Beth Richie sent me flowers and good wishes during an especially intense period of work. Other friends—Aisha Ray, Linda Hillman, Lynette Jackson, Lisa Yun Lee, Kim and Mary Byas, and Bernardine Dohrn—have sustained me in many ways as I juggled my various responsibilities in order to complete this book. Linda took time out to pull herself away from her potter's wheel to read and give feedback on the text on three occasions. Her skills as a writer and editor were enormously helpful.

Finally, the members of my immediate family, to whom this book is dedicated, have loved me unconditionally and welcomed Ella Baker into our home and our lives as if she were one of us. They have endured my intermittent need to shut myself off from the world and write, and they have pulled me out of my seclusion to remind me that there is a larger world beyond this book and my computer. Despite his own extremely demanding career, my husband, Peter Sporn, has been my anchor in the storm for nearly half of my life, and I could not have written this book without his love and his unrelenting support. My daughter, Asha, reminds me day in and day out of the power of a creative imagination to remake things from what they are into something better. I am in awe of her energy and determination. Like Ella, she will be her own woman and demand that the world make a place for her. My son, Jason, the budding activist/philosopher took off for his first year at Brown University just as this book was being sent to the publisher. In the summer of 2002, he was both my research assistant and my political comrade. His honest observations and probing questions pushed me to dig deeper and think harder about the meaning of Ella Baker's legacy for his generation. Jason's wit and wisdom made this book a better product, and his love and friendship have made me a better person.

My extended family—Jo and Paul Sporn, Pam Sporn, Paul Foster, Lelanie Foster, and Papito Foster—have loved and tolerated me through the writing of this book. Paul Sporn has served as a writing coach and everloving confidant for which I thank him. My parents and grandparents—Charlie and Ethel Ransby, Rosia and Henry Pittman, and John and Queenie Fallens, all of whom have passed on—never read this book. Even if they had been alive, they might not have done so. My mother had the most formal education in the family, and she never finished high school. They were sharecroppers in Newnan, Georgia, and Greenwood, Mississippi, who migrated north to become factory workers and maids in Detroit, Michigan. They were the kind of strong, hard-working, generous, astutely aware ordinary people that Ella Baker valued so much. Perhaps that is what initially attracted me to her story and her ideas. It is certainly my memory of them and their example of the best humanity has to offer that inspires me to persevere as a historian and an activist.

ABBREVIATIONS

ACMHR: Alabama Christian Movement for Human Rights
AFL: American Federation of Labor
CIO: Congress of Industrial Organizations
COFO: Council of Federated Organizations
CORE: Congress of Racial Equality
CP: Communist Party
ILGWU: International Ladies Garment Workers Union
MFDP: Mississippi Freedom Democratic Party
MIA: Montgomery Improvement Association
MPOC: Mass Party Organizing Committee
NAACP: National Association for the Advancement of Colored People
PRSO: Puerto Rican Solidarity Organization
SCEF: Southern Conference Education Fund
SCHW: Southern Conference on Human Welfare
SCLC: Southern Christian Leadership Conference
SDS: Students for a Democratic Society
SNCC: Student Nonviolent Coordinating Committee
TSCC: Temporary Student Coordinating Committee
UAW: United Auto Workers
UCMI: United Christian Movement Inc.
UNIA: Universal Negro Improvement Association
VEP: Voter Education Project
WEP: Workers Education Project
WPA: Works Progress Administration
YMCA: Young Men's Christian Association
YNCL: Young Negroes Cooperative League
YPF: Young People's Forum
YWCA: Young Women's Christian Association

Ella Baker

AND THE BLACK FREEDOM MOVEMENT

INTRODUCTION

In order for us as poor and oppressed people to become a part of a
society that is meaningful, the system under which we now exist has to be
radically changed. This means that we are going to have to learn to think in
radical terms. I use the term radical in its original meaning—getting down
to and understanding the root cause. It means facing a system that does not
lend itself to your needs and devising means by which you change that system.
Ella Baker, 1969

Ella Baker spent her entire adult life trying to "change that system." Somewhere along the way she recognized that her goal was not a single "end" but rather an ongoing "means," that is, a process. Radical change for Ella Baker was about a persistent and protracted process of discourse, debate, consensus, reflection, and struggle. If larger and larger numbers of communities were engaged in such a process, she reasoned, day in and day out, year after year, the revolution would be well under way. Ella Baker understood that laws, structures, and institutions had to change in order to correct injustice and oppression, but part of the process had to involve oppressed people, ordinary people, infusing new meanings into the concept of democracy and finding their own individual and collective power to determine their lives and shape the direction of history. These were the radical terms that Ella Baker thought in and the radical ideas she fought for with her mind and her body. Just as the "end" for her was not a scripted utopia but another phase of struggle, the means of getting there was not scripted either. Baker's theory of social change and political organizing was inscribed in her practice. Her ideas were written in her work: a coherent body of lived text spanning nearly sixty years.

Biography is a profoundly personal genre of historical scholarship, and the humbling but empowering process of finding our own meanings in another person's life poses unique challenges. As biographers, we ask questions about lives that the subjects themselves may never have asked outright and certainly did not consciously answer. Answers are always elusive. We search for them by carefully reading and interpreting the fragmented messages left behind. Feminist biographers and scholar-activists like myself face particular challenges. It is imperative that we be ever cautious of the danger inherent in our work: imposing our contemporary dilemmas and expectations on a generation of women who spoke a different language, moved at a different rhythm, and juggled a different set of issues and concerns. The task of tailoring a life to fit a neat and cohesive narrative is a daunting one: an awkward and sometimes uncomfortable process of wading barefoot into the still and often murky waters of someone else's life, interrogating her choices, speculating about her motives, mapping her movements, and weighing her every word. No single descriptor ever seems adequate to capture the richly nuanced complexity of a life fully lived. Every term is inherently inadequate, each one loaded with someone else's meanings, someone else's baggage. How can a biographer frame a unique life, rendering it full-bodied, textured, even contradictory, yet still accessible for those who want to step inside and look around?

My journey into Ella Jo Baker's world has been a personal, political, and intellectual journey, often joyous and at times painful. It has taken me in and out of some twenty cities and to numerous libraries, archives, county courthouses, kitchen tables, front porches, and a few dusty attics. This long journey has been marked by periods of difficult separation followed by hopeful reunions. In the process I have revisited the faces, experiences, and southern roots of my own mother, father, grandparents, aunts, uncles, and cousins: Mississippi sharecroppers, domestic and factory workers, honest, generous, hard-working, resilient black people. Most importantly, in the process I have developed an intense and unique relationship with my subject. I have chatted, argued, commiserated, and rejoiced with Ella Baker in an ongoing conversation between sisters, one living and one dead. In this book, I have tried to tell Ella Baker's story partly as she would have told it and partly the way I—a historian and an activist of a different time and place—felt it had to be told.

There are those who insist that biographical writing is compromised and tainted by an author's identification and closeness with her subject. This does not have to be the case. I do not apologize for my admiration for Ella Baker. She earned it. I admire her for the courageous and remarkable life she led and for the contributions she made without any promise of immediate reward. I admire her for the ways in which she redefined the meaning of radical and engaged intellectual work, of cross-class and interracial organizing, and of a democratic and humanistic way of being in the world, all the while trying to mold the world around her into something better.

· · · · · · ·

I first came upon Ella Baker's story through my search for political role models, not research subjects. As an anti-apartheid and antiracist student activist at Columbia University and the University of Michigan in the 1980s and as a black feminist organizer thereafter, I was drawn to the example of Ella Baker as a woman who fought militantly but democratically for a better world and who fought simultaneously for her own right to play more than a circumscribed role in that world. As an insurgent intellectual with a passion for justice and democracy, Ella Baker held an affinity for the most oppressed sectors of our society. So, my first connection to Ella Baker was a political one. This connection has enhanced rather than lessened my desire to be thorough, rigorous, and balanced in my treatment of her life and ideas. For me, there is more at stake in exploring Ella Baker's story than an interesting intellectual exercise or even the worthy act of writing a corrective history that adds a previously muted, black, female voice to the chorus of people from the past. To understand her weaknesses as well as her strengths, her failures as well as her triumphs, her confusion as well as her clarity is to pay her the greatest honor I can imagine. To tell her life truths with all their depth and richness is to affirm her humanity and all that she was able to accomplish, because of and at times in spite of who she was. There are vital political and historical lessons to be gleaned by looking back in time through the lens of Ella Baker's life.

Ella Josephine Baker's activist career spanned from 1930 to 1980, touched thousands of lives, and contributed to over three dozen organizations. She was an internationalist, but her cultural and political home was the African American community. So it is within the Black Freedom Movement in the United States—the collective efforts of African Americans to attain full human rights, from the nadir of segregation at the turn of the twentieth century through the peak of the civil rights movement in the 1960s and beyond—that I locate her story. For Baker, as for W. E. B. Du Bois, racism was the litmus test for American democracy and for international human rights. Both were convinced that racism had infected every major social problem of the twentieth century: colonialism and imperialism, war and fascism, the oppression of women, the politics of crime and punishment, and the exploitation of labor; both recognized that very little progress could be made without tackling the political cargo of race. Baker organized for democratic rights for over fifty years, from Harlem to Mississippi, in interracial coalitions and African American organizations, and (unlike Du Bois) she lived to see the day when ordinary black folks enjoyed some of the fruits of freedom. But she died knowing that the process of struggle and social transformation would continue.

Ella Baker played a pivotal role in the three most prominent black freedom organizations of her day: the National Association for the Advancement of Colored People (NAACP); the Southern Christian Leadership Conference (SCLC); and the Student Nonviolent Coordinating Committee (SNCC; pronounced "snick"). She worked alongside some of the most prominent black male leaders of the twentieth century: W. E. B. Du Bois, Thurgood Marshall, George Schuyler, Walter White, A. Philip Randolph, Martin Luther King Jr., and Stokely Carmichael. However, Baker had contentious relationships with all these men and the organizations they headed, with the exception of SNCC during its first six years. For much of her career she functioned as an "outsider within." She was close to the centers of power within the black community, but she was always a critical and conditional insider, a status informed by her gender, class loyalties, and political ideology. Baker criticized unchecked egos, objected to undemocratic structures, protested unilateral decision making, condemned elitism, and refused to nod in loyal deference to everything "the leader" had to say. These stances often put her on the outside of the inner circle.

While her most public political associations were with men, some of Ella Baker's most significant and sustaining relationships were with a group of women activists, some of them not very well-known, who were her friends and co-workers over many years. These women provided the sisterly support that allowed Baker to fight all of the battles she did, both inside and outside the Black Freedom Movement. Ella Baker was part of a powerful, yet invisible network of dynamic and influential African American women activists who sustained civil rights causes, and one another, across several generations. Her life intersected with such notable black women as Anna Arnold Hedgeman, Dorothy Height, Nannie Helen Burroughs, Pauli Murray, Mary McLeod Bethune, Septima Clark, and Fannie Lou Hamer. She was dear friends with NAACP legends Ruby Hurley and Lucille Black. As Diane Nash and Eleanor Holmes Norton suggest, women like Ella Baker were laying the foundation for contemporary black feminists even before the term was invented. This earlier generation of women lived the politics others have since written about, challenging treatment that belittled the seriousness of their contributions, resisting models of organizing that placed men and men's work at the center, and carving out public identities as leaders, strategists, and public intellectuals—identities that were generally reserved for men.

A creative and independent thinker and doer, Baker operated in a political world that was, in many ways, not fully ready for her. She inserted herself into leadership situations where others thought she simply did not belong. Her unique presence pioneered the way for fuller participation by other women in political organizations, and it reshaped the positions within the movement that they would occupy. At each stage she nudged the movement in a leftward, inclusive, and democratic direction, learning and modifying her own position as she went.

For Ella Baker, anchoring her activism within the black freedom struggle was not simply a matter of identity but rather a part of a political analysis that recognized the historical significance of racism as the cornerstone of an unjust social and economic order in the United States extending back to slavery. A movement for black freedom, defined broadly, she thought, would inevitably be a movement against economic exploitation and the oppressive conditions faced by other groups within American society as well. At least it had that potential. African Americans and, in a complex variety of ways, other peoples of color were excluded from basic access to the political process, marginalized socially, and super-exploited economically for the better part of the twentieth century. If this contradiction could not be confronted, Baker felt, there was no hope for American society as a whole. More precisely, she felt that to push and challenge political and economic leaders on this question would expose some of the society's fundamental flaws and serve as an impetus for transformative social change on multiple fronts.

An aging and irascible Virginia Durr, the legendary white civil rights activist from Montgomery, once confronted me at a conference to remind me that "Ella Baker didn't just belong to black people." She was right. Baker's work, influence, and political family extended well beyond the confines of the African American community and the struggle against racism. She had strong ties to the more democratic tendencies within the white left. She worked closely with the multiracial labor and cooperative movements, while at the same time championing struggles against colonialism and imperialism around the world.

Ella Baker was concerned with the plight of African Americans, but she was also passionately committed to a broader humanitarian struggle for a better world. Over the course of her life, she was involved in more than thirty major political campaigns and organizations, addressing such issues as the war in Vietnam, Puerto Rican independence, South African apartheid, political repression, prison conditions, poverty, unequal education, and sexism. Still, because of who she was—a daughter of the Jim Crow South and a granddaughter of slaves—and because of the political analysis she formulated early in her career, which was centered on antiracist politics, Baker's primary frame of reference was the African American experience and the struggle for black freedom.

Baker identified with and helped advance a political tradition that is radical, international, and democratic, with women at its center. She critiqued black separatism as a narrow, dead-end strategy, yet she did not hesitate to criticize the chauvinism and racism of white colleagues in multiracial coalitions all the while stressing the importance of black leadership. Her own political ideology and worldview was a result of the cross-fertilization of the vibrant black Baptist women's movement of the early twentieth century, the eclectic and international political culture of depression-era Harlem, and the American tradition of democratic socialism—a variegated mix of northern and southern, religious and secular, American and global, left and liberal elements.

Ella Baker's life gives us a sense of the connections and continuities that link together a long tradition of African American resistance. Each intergenerational organization she joined, each story she told, each lesson she passed on was a part of the connective tissue that formed the body politic of the Black Freedom Movement in the United States from the 1930s into the 1980s. Following Baker's path back through the years, trying to look at national and world events from her vantage point, takes us to different sites of struggle, opens up different windows of conversation, and pushes us into different people's lives than if we were to have someone else as our guide.

Finally, Ella Baker was a skilled grassroots organizer and an "organic" intellectual—one who learned lessons from the street more than from the academy and who sought to understand the world in order to change it. Many other activists looked to her, especially during the last half of her life, for her strategic and analytical insights and guidance. Her radical, democratic, humanistic worldview, her confidence in the wisdom of the black poor, and her emphasis on the importance of group-centered, grassroots leadership set her apart from most of her political contemporaries. Her ideas and example influenced not only SNCC in the 1960s, but also the leaders of Students for a Democratic Society (SDS) and the embryonic women's movement of the late 1960s and the 1970s.[1] Baker was a role model and mentor for an entire generation of activists who came of age politically in the 1960s. Within progressive circles, even those who did not know her knew of her.

Ella Baker was a movement teacher who exemplified a radical pedagogy, similar to that of Latin American educator and political organizer Paulo Freire. She sought to empower those she taught and regarded learning as reciprocal. Baker's message was that oppressed people, whatever their level of formal education, had the ability to understand and interpret the world around them, to see that world for what it was and to move to transform it. Her primary public constituency was the dispossessed. She viewed a democratic learning process and discourse as the cornerstone of a democratic movement.

Ella Baker's private life was as unconventional as her public one. For example, many of her political colleagues never knew that she had, at one time, been married. She deemphasized her married life, never took her husband's name, and traveled extensively over the course of her nearly twenty-year marriage. Throughout the marriage, her principal passion was politics; after her divorce, she was singularly devoted to her first love.

Some aspects of Ella Baker's private life remain a mystery, not because I have not snooped and pried with the voyeuristic appetite of a private detective, but because she was so consciously and thoroughly discreet about personal affairs and protective of her family and domestic life. One of my chief frustrations as a biographer has been the difficulty of attempting to follow the trail of a woman who, in many respects, tried not to leave one. There is no memoir or diary, nor are there boxes of intimate personal correspondence. What remains is, for the most part, her public voice and presence as documented in over thirty archival and manuscript collections of organizations and individuals across the country. Her own personal papers, which chronicle only part of the story, are now deposited at the Schomburg Center for Research in Black Culture in Harlem. I have spent untold hours pouring over the documents there. I have interviewed dozens of people who knew her and tracked down letters, papers, and photographs in the most out-of-the-way places. Yet there is much we may never know.

A part of interpreting and revisiting Ella Baker's life has involved a series of oral history interviews with friends, family members, and co-workers who knew her over the years. These conversations gave me not only the facts about Baker's life but the feel of it as well. While these excavated memories helped me add movement and fluidity to otherwise still-life snapshots of Baker, I also appreciate the limits of our recollective powers. I have tried in every instance possible to find more than one source to substantiate particular individual assertions. In other instances I have qualified those assertions as speculative or remembered. I also realize that written documents can be misleading, so I do not mean to privilege them without condition. All of the sources are used as pieces of a larger puzzle, reinforced by other parts as they fit or don't fit what is already known. In addition to the recollections and observations of others, I have tried to tap Ella Baker's own words as much as possible. Even when speaking for herself, however, in the dozen or so interviews that have been preserved, Baker is more often than not speaking with the benefit and the blurred vision of hindsight, years and in some cases decades after the fact. As honest and straightforward a person as she was, and as lucid as she was until the early 1980s, I cannot always afford to take her at her word. Memories fade, ideas change, and thus what we thought we felt or did at the time is filtered through the lens of our ongoing sense of ourselves. In reconstructing her political views, however, I gave Ella Baker and myself greater license than when reconstructing a series of events largely because I am as concerned about where she ended up politically and philosophically as I am with how she got there. Her conclusions and self-representation are critical elements in summing up her life's work and her ideas.

Psychologists have written about the complex ways in which public individuals, especially women, demarcate the boundaries between public and private lives as a form of psychological protection. Ella Baker guarded her privacy. Her refusal to talk about certain aspects of her past, while being wholly open about others, resembles "the culture of dissemblance" that historian Darlene Clark Hine talks about. In analyzing the silence surrounding black women and rape, Hine writes: "By dissemblance I mean the behavior and attitudes of black women that created the appearance of openness and disclosure but actually shielded the truth of their inner lives and selves from their oppressors."[2] In the case of Ella Baker, the shielding was from public view and scrutiny, not only from her oppressors, but often from friends and colleagues as well. Shielding their private lives from public view provided a margin of protection for black women of Ella Baker's generation, who were vilified and stereotyped by whites and often circumscribed to a limited sphere of activity by black men. According to her friend Lenora Taitt-Magubane, Ella Baker never wanted to be "pigeon-holed." The less known about the complex person she was, perhaps the less likely she was to be sized up and assigned an identity with narrow borders. Bernice Johnson Reagon once observed that Baker was the first woman she met who would not allow a discussion of her marital status. This was liberating for Reagon and other young women because they then felt personal and romantic relationships could be left at the door when they went into a meeting, which better enabled them to participate on their own terms regardless of who they were or were not dating at the time. Hine concludes that "a secret, undisclosed persona allowed the individual black woman to function, to work effectively as a domestic in (sometimes hostile) white households."[3] I would add that it may have allowed Ella Baker and many of her female counterparts to function more effectively—although not without a psychological price—within predominately male civil rights leadership circles. Still, all was not shielded from public view. And from literally thousands of documents, articles, interviews, flyers, letters, and FBI reports emerges the story of Ella Baker's amazing and incandescent life.

· · · · · ·

This biography surveys Ella Baker's long and rich political career in an effort to explain the unique political and intellectual contributions she made to the movement for radical democratic change in America. Like most biographies, it begins by exploring the familial and educational experiences that were the foundation of her public political life. Baker's childhood and schooling through college are covered in chapters 1 and 2. Baker's well-read and deeply religious mother was her moral anchor in her early years, providing her with intellectual training and a sense of social responsibility that she would carry with her always. Her time in boarding school and college at Shaw Academy and University in Raleigh, North Carolina, was a period of intellectual and political growth. Baker had a stellar academic career and organized her first protest against what she perceived as an unjust exercise of authority by college administrators. Chapter 3 explores Ella Baker's eye-opening cultural and political encounters in Harlem in the late 1920s and 1930s, a time when she secularized her childhood values and embraced the radical democratic vision of social change that she would modify and build on for the next half century. In chapter 4 I survey Ella Baker's six-year tenure as a part of the national staff of the NAACP from 1940 to 1946, first as a field secretary and then as the national director of branches. During the intense period of World War II, Ella Baker traveled throughout the minefield of the American South, organizing local branches, encouraging local leaders to be more active, and building up a network of contacts that she would rely on for years to come. In her capacity as the NAACP's director of branches, Baker sought to democratize the organization by empowering local and regional leaders and by deemphasizing legal battles and giving more attention to grassroots struggles. Chapter 5 focuses on Baker's work concerning school reform and police brutality in New York City in the 1950s; these struggles occurred against the backdrop of mounting anticommunist and Cold War policies and rhetoric. Baker herself had a curious and ambivalent relationship to the communist question, one that evolved and changed over time.

The second half of the book deals with the period of the modern civil rights and black power movements, the apex of Baker's political sojourn. Chapters 6 and 7 chronicle Ella Baker's work with the SCLC in the mid- to late 1950s and specifically her concentrated work with the more active SCLC affiliates in Shreveport, Louisiana, and Birmingham, Alabama. Chapter 6 offers a perspective on Baker's complicated and conflicted relationship with Martin Luther King Jr. and the tensions between them, which revolved largely around their divergent views on leadership and organization. Chapters 8 and 9 detail Baker's pivotal role in the founding of SNCC and her capacity as mentor and adviser to the young activists of that group from 1960 to 1966. Chapters 10 and 11 focus on SNCC's work in Mississippi in the 1960s, her work with the Mississippi Freedom Democratic Party (MFDP) and the rise of black power. Chapter 11 ends with a discussion of Ella Baker's political involvement in the 1970s and 1980s after the collapse of SNCC. During the final years of her life, Ella Baker spoke out passionately against political repression and in support of anticolonial struggles, most notably in connection with the Free Angela Davis campaign and the Puerto Rican Independista Movement. For several years she also lent her name and her dwindling energies to an effort to create an independent third political party to the left of the Democrats through the Mass Party Organizing Committee.

The book concludes, in chapter 12, by outlining Ella Baker's political philosophy as it relates to both historical and contemporary contexts, offering a living legacy to all of us who share her vision of a more just and democratic society, not as an event in history but as an ongoing process around which to organize our lives and work.

· · · · · ·

On Saturday, December 13, 1986, precisely eighty-three years to the day after her birth, Ella Jo Baker died quietly in her sleep in the modest Harlem apartment she had occupied off and on for nearly forty years. The end of her life did not come as a surprise to those close to her. She had been sick for some time, and her health had been spiraling downward rapidly in the months preceding her death. But as natural and uneventful as her passage may have seemed, it represented the end of a rich and influential political career, and even the end of an era. Those who gathered to mourn her death the following Friday symbolized in their diversity the breadth and depth of Ella Baker's influence on American politics for the better part of the twentieth century.

It was a cold and rainy day in New York City and a week before Christmas when the overflow crowd piled into Harlem's historic Abyssinian Baptist Church to remember and to celebrate a woman who had touched more lives than she herself could have realized. Those who came to honor Ella Baker wore fur coats, African prints, Islamic kufis, and yarmulkes. They were young with dreadlocks and elderly with graying temples and receding hairlines. They were black and white and a myriad of shades in between, men and women, rich and poor, those formally educated and those self taught. Among those who gathered were politicians, religious leaders, entertainers, and renowned scholars. Crowded in among the celebrities were those whom Ella Baker sometimes referred to as the little people: people without credentials or titles, but people she had valued and respected in her life, and who now honored her in death. They were neighbors, local merchants, and even those who didn't know Ella Baker personally but knew her enough by reputation that they came to pay their respects. This is what Ella Baker had done for decades. If a child was born or if someone in her extended family passed away, she found time to acknowledge the importance of that singular life. Harlem activist Yuri Kochiyama, an internment camp survivor who was on the speaker's platform with Malcolm X when he was assassinated, remembered fondly Ella Baker's kindness toward her family when her son, Billy, died in 1975. Ella Baker did not know Billy Kochiyama, really. He had gone to Mississippi in 1965 as an act of solidarity with the growing Black Freedom Movement, and they crossed paths briefly. When he died tragically ten years later, Baker sent a telegram and made a phone call to Billy's parents to express her condolences. Yuri Kochiyama, who had admired Baker from a distance, and met her only once, treasured the gesture. Yuri Kochiyama in turn paid her respects that rainy December day in Harlem.[4]

Throughout much of her life Ella Baker was a radical humanist and a consummate coalition builder, connecting young and old, black and white, neophytes and veterans, and staunch leftists and ambivalent moderates. Gathered together in the Abyssinian church that day was the eclectic and sometimes fractious group of people Baker had claimed as her political family. Crowded shoulder to shoulder, they found their political differences receding in their shared admiration for a fallen comrade, sister, teacher, and mother. Ardent nationalists, orthodox Marxists, establishment politicians, and free-floating radicals—people with long-standing antagonisms, some of whom hadn't spoken to each other in years—mingled in a slow common procession. Only Ella Baker could convene such a gathering. There were touching moments that suggested her political children had actually internalized her belief that in the end the politics are only as important as the real human beings with and for whom we struggle. Standing at Baker's graveside in the frigid December air, white activist Bob Zellner found himself positioned between his two old friends, Jamil Al-Amin (H. Rap Brown) and Kwame Ture (Stokely Carmichael): two men who had come to symbolize "Black Power" and had been associated with militant black nationalist rhetoric. There they stood, the three of them together. Al-Amin draped his coat around the ill-clad Zellner, and Ture quietly shared his umbrella. No words were exchanged.

The voice that echoed most powerfully through the cavernous church where Ella Baker's funeral was held was that of Bernice Johnson Reagon, one of Ella Baker's political daughters and founder of the black women's a cappella group Sweet Honey in the Rock. Her commanding voice drew attention to every line of Ella Baker's favorite movement song, "Guide My Feet." "Guide my feet, while I run this race, . . . because I don't want to run this race alone . . . because I don't want to run this race in vain." And Ella Baker did neither. She ran long, she ran hard, and she ran with a diverse assortment of folks over some fifty years. Ella Baker did not represent any single tendency of the American left or a particular wing of the Black Freedom Movement; rather, she forged a hybrid political vision and an inclusive style of democratic leadership. The long-term goal, for which she admittedly had no blueprint, was simply a more democratic, egalitarian, and humane world. Baker's values and her deeply felt ideals guided her feet over variegated and difficult terrain. In the race, she was not a sprinter but a long distance runner.[5]

NOW, WHO ARE YOUR PEOPLE?

NORFOLK, VIRGINIA, AND LITTLETON,
NORTH CAROLINA, 1903–1918

· · · · · ·

I was young when I became active in things and I became active in things
largely because my mother was very active in the field of religion.
Ella Baker, 1979

Black Baptist women encouraged an aggressive womanhood that felt personal
responsibility to labor, no less than men, for the salvation of the world.
Evelyn Brooks Higginbotham, 1993

In the early 1980s Paula Giddings, the writer and historian, went to Ella
Baker's modest Harlem apartment to interview the legendary activist for a
book Giddings was writing on African American women's history. At that
meeting Giddings had hoped to learn more about the half century of history Ella Baker had witnessed and helped shape: her role in the Works
Progress Administration and the cooperative movement in Harlem during
the 1930s; her dangerous organizing work for the NAACP in the South during the 1940s; her collaboration with and criticisms of Dr. Martin Luther
King Jr. in the 1950s; and her pivotal role in the founding of the Student
Nonviolent Coordinating Committee in the 1960s. A few minutes into the
visit, Giddings realized that the exchange she had hoped for was not to be.
Instead of responding to Giddings's questions about the past, Baker kept
asking her a single question: "Now, who are your people?" Giddings regret-
fully concluded that, after all the battles Ella Baker had fought and won
over the course of her fifty-year political career, she was losing the fight
with Alzheimer's and was no longer able to provide the information and
insights she sought. To Giddings, it seemed as if Baker were groping for a

cognitive anchor in the conversation.[1] Yet Baker's desire to know and place her visitor was characteristic of what had been important to her throughout her life. The question "Now, who are your people?" symbolizes Baker's approach to life-history as well. Who one's people were was important to Ella Baker, not to establish an elite pedigree, but to locate an individual as a part of a family, a community, a region, a culture, and a historical period. Baker recognized that none of us are self-made men or women; rather, we forge our identities within kinship networks, local communities, and organizations.

Ella Baker's family, her childhood experiences in Norfolk, Virginia, and Littleton, North Carolina, and her secondary and college education at Shaw University in Raleigh and her transformative political encounters in Harlem during the Great Depression all contributed to her evolving identity as a woman, an activist, and an intellectual, and set the stage for the years of political activism that would follow.

So, who were Ella Baker's people? She was born on December 13, 1903, in Norfolk, Virginia, and grew up from the age of seven in the small town of Littleton, North Carolina. Ella Jo was the middle of three surviving children; she had an older brother, Blake Curtis, and a younger sister, Maggie. Her parents, Georgianna (Anna) Ross Baker and Blake Baker, raised their children to be upstanding members of the rural community where they themselves had grown up. Her maternal grandparents, Mitchell and Josephine Elizabeth Ross, owned their own farm, and her grandfather was a noted Baptist clergyman. Her paternal grandparents, Teema and Margaret Baker, were landless tenant farmers.[2] Both sets of grandparents had grown up under slavery, and their differing educational and economic positions reflected both the obstacles that faced freedmen and freedwomen and the achievements of black families in the rural South after Reconstruction. Baker's parents attended secondary school and sought to better their position, moving to the city of Norfolk in search of opportunity and then returning to Littleton in search of security. Blake's job as a waiter on a Norfolk steamer line required him to travel, while Anna presided at home and played a prominent role in the Baptist church.

During her childhood in Littleton, Ella Baker was nurtured, educated, and challenged by a community of strong, hard-working, deeply religious black people—most of them women—who celebrated their accomplishments and recognized their class advantage, but who also pledged themselves to serve and uplift those less fortunate. Anna Ross Baker was the single most influential force in Ella's early life. Ella described her mother as a stern and pious woman who believed in discipline almost as much as she believed in God: "My mother was a . . . very positive and sort of aggressive woman."[3] Ella grew up in a female-centered household, surrounded by a community of Christian women actively engaged in uplifting their families and communities. These women were as much concerned with enlightening the mind as they were with saving the soul. At a statewide convention of Baptist women, the local group to which Anna belonged urged members to "do all in our power to foster education."[4] Trained as a teacher herself, Anna instructed all three of her own children in grammar, writing, and speech before they entered school.

For Anna Ross Baker's daughters, it was important to be ladylike as well as to be learned. Female respectability was coveted and cultivated by middle-class black women of her generation. Ella and her sister, Maggie, were tutored in etiquette, proper grooming, and deportment. They were expected to conform to conventional standards of female respectability as they pursued their studies and practiced their religion. At the same time that Baker was encouraged to strive to be exceptional, she was also constantly reminded that humility and service to others were Christian virtues incumbent upon those who enjoyed academic opportunities and middle-class status. In the early-twentieth-century South, women like Anna and Ella were imbued with the conviction that their relative privilege carried with it a fundamental obligation to work for the improvement of their race and, especially, to better the condition of the many women and children who were denied such advantages.

The Ross-Baker family belonged to that stratum of black people who saw themselves as representatives of the race to the white world and as role models for those less fortunate within the black community. To borrow the historian Glenda Gilmore's term, they were the "best men" and "best women."[5] Many black people who occupied positions of some class advantage received what the historian Stephanie Shaw has called a "mixed message—rendering a person part of and apart from the group."[6] Ella Jo Baker's life is marked by the working-out of this paradoxical position: she drew on the strengths of her childhood community, rejected the strictures of middle-class womanhood and the dominant ideologies of her society, and affiliated herself with the poor black people whom she saw as the most oppressed and the most able to transform the world through collective action. Formed by who her people were when she was a child, Ella Baker ultimately chose her own people. In the years after she left North Carolina, Ella Baker embraced some aspects of her early socialization and rejected others, yet she carried vivid memories of her childhood with her and rein-terpreted their meaning as she grew and changed. To understand the com-plex social environment that nurtured Baker's early social conscience and her evolving identity as a woman, an intellectual, and a political activist, this chapter and the next explore central themes in her childhood and education. These themes include the central role of religion in women's sense of self and in their mission in the world; intraregional southern migration in search of economic opportunity and to escape Jim Crow in its most virulent, urban form; the importance of language and education; and the multiple meanings of family and community. The chapter takes up these themes that Ella Jo Baker encountered and interprets them in rela-tion to her development, but it does not present them entirely from her point of view. Rather, the facts of her life are set in historical context, and the way in which Baker remembered the past is sometimes juxtaposed with my own historical perspective.

. . . . . .

SPREADING THE FAITH AND UPLIFTING THE RACE

Religion, specifically black southern Baptist religion, was a major force in Anna Ross Baker's life, and consequently it became a major force in Ella Baker's life. "I was young when I became active in things and I became active in things largely because my mother was very active in the field of religion," Baker reflected at the age of seventy-five.[7] Anna's strong belief in God went hand in hand with her conviction that faith must be translated into deeds. At a statewide convention of her Baptist women's group, she admonished others to "let Christ take the first place in your vocation and life. Inquire of the Lord what he would have us do. Let us stay on the job for Christ."[8] In a more general sense, the church was one of the social and ideological bedrocks of the rural southern black community in which Ella Baker grew up. Religion was important to her family in particular, and it was a defining feature of the community and culture of which they were a part. According to Eric Anderson, a historian of North Carolina, in the Sec-ond Congressional District, which included Littleton, "Protestant Chris-tianity . . . permeated the district, touching people's lives more steadily than any other institution. . . . The very pervasiveness of religion obscured its boundaries with politics, society, and work."[9]

The Baker children were deeply immersed in the black Baptist tradition. Although Ella and her two siblings were never required to attend church services more than once a week, as many other devout southern Baptist families were accustomed to doing, they were drawn into the wider religious world in which the Ross family played an active leadership role.[10] Anna's family was so religious that all of her six brothers were named after Christ's disciples: Luke, Mark, John, Peter, Paul, and Matthew.[11] Ella's uncle Luke was president of the Warren County Sunday School Association, and her maternal grandfather, Mitchell Ross, served as a minister.[12]

Ella and her siblings frequently accompanied their mother to local and regional missionary meetings. "My mother was an ardent church worker . . . and the women had developed a state conference and [they] had regular meetings, and I had been to all these kinds of things," Baker recalled.[13] Ella actually participated in the programs on several occasions, reciting poems and reading from biblical texts. These auxiliary associations had been formed, Baker explained, in order for "the women . . . to be able to have some identity of their own."[14] At these meetings she observed not simply ritualistic expressions of faith but also the business of applying religious principles, particularly the principle of Christian charity, in the real world. The missionary association sponsored an orphanage, aided the sick and elderly, funded scholarships for black college students, and provided aid to local, church-affiliated grammar schools.[15] Ella witnessed this important work being organized and carried out by confident, competent, and committed African American women. These women's groups operated with a considerable amount of autonomy. Women conducted their own meetings, managed their finances, and made policy decisions. Many members drew their daughters into these activities, Baker recalled; "they also would carry their young who could articulate."[16] These women's collective example of strength and activism had a profound effect on Ella Baker.

Anna Ross Baker and her sisters in the church preached and practiced an activist, woman-centered faith, which was similar to the Social Gospel doctrine being espoused by white Protestant denominations around the same time.[17] Although they were predominately middle class and imbued with a maternalist, missionary objective to "Christianize" their less fortunate brethren and sistren, these devout black Baptist women were more than elitist charity workers. Through home visits and reading groups called "Bible bands," they forged personal, cross-class relationships with the poor and illiterate members of their communities. They did not confine their work to prayerful study and community service; they extended their mission to secular affairs, advocating antilynching legislation, crusading for temperance, and challenging segregation. Theirs was an activist religion that urged women to act as positive agents for change in the world.[18]

Ella Baker's mother was a part of a generation of educated southern black women who, in the late nineteenth and early twentieth centuries, began actively to assert themselves as a group to be reckoned with inside the black Baptist Church. The National (Black Baptist) Woman's Convention, formed in 1900, reflected the consolidation of local and regional efforts by black Baptist women, many of them missionaries, to play a more active role in the life of their church and community. The North Carolina Convention, to which Anna Ross Baker belonged, was affiliated with the Woman's National Convention and sent two delegates to its annual meetings.[19] According to the historian Evelyn Brooks Higginbotham, their collective mission and worldview constituted a type of feminist theology, one that "challenged the 'silent helpmate' image of women's church work and set out to convince the men that women were equally obliged to advance not only their race and denomination, but themselves. . . . Within a female-centered context, they accentuated the image of woman as saving force, rather than woman as victim. They rejected a model of womanhood that was fragile and passive, just as they deplored a type preoccupied with fashion, gossip, or self-indulgence. They argued that women held the key to social transformation."[20] This description fits Anna Ross Baker perfectly.

Ella Baker's mother was intimately involved in this movement; she identified with its activist, woman-centered philosophy and strove to instill in her daughters the desire to mold themselves in the images of strong, intelligent, and socially engaged black women. Ella deeply admired her mother's fortitude and compassion. Years later, in the secular context of the political and civil rights organizations with which she worked, she emulated her mother's example of zealous and selfless service on behalf of those victimized by injustice and social inequity, albeit in a different language and with expanded political objectives.

The southern black Baptist women's missionary movement embodied the "lift as we climb" approach to community service, as did the National Association of Colored Women's Clubs founded in 1896.[21] As some members of the race excelled and progressed, it was their duty to help others along and to contribute to the welfare of those less able and fortunate than themselves. This responsibility to serve the community was derived as much from a sense of class distinction as from a sense of moral duty. Yet for African American women the relationship between class status and moral obligation was a reciprocal one; indeed, staunch religious faith and selfless service to others was one way in which a woman and her family could attain a respectable, even elevated position within the community. Embedded in uplift ideology was a certain degree of elitism, along with a sense of class prerogative on the part of middle-class blacks who felt they should act as race ambassadors toward white society and as moral police and social workers inside the black community.[22]

Elitism coexisted with a commitment to equality, so black women's organizations could support cross-class relationships as well as reinforce class distinctions. While Anna Ross Baker's sisters in the church saw themselves as distinct from ordinary black folk, they rejected elitism in their rhetoric.[23] Leaders of the black Baptist women's movement often railed against individuals for whom charity work was an avocation rather than a vocation. Nannie Helen Burroughs, a leader of the black women's convention movement, condemned the socialite who "smoothes her well-gloved hand while she studies the 'wonderfully interesting slum problem' as a diversion."[24] Instead, they embraced the masses of less fortunate black people and made sacrifices, both material and personal, in order to provide assistance. Missionary women who were advocates of temperance, modesty, and propriety also embraced the principle of providing aid to the downtrodden, irrespective of their status, their sins, or their inadequacies. This was a concept that Ella Baker accepted, internalized, and carried with her for the rest of her life.

The women's missionary movement stressed the importance of hands-on service to those in need; their approach was one of active intervention. This orientation was consistent with the ethos of mutual aid that had shaped black communities since slavery and Reconstruction. Ella Baker remembered her mother being called upon late at night to come to the aid of other members of the community: "Mama was always responding to the sick."[25] According to the mores of the southern black Baptist women's movement, the duty to help others was serious, immediate, and practical. Anna Ross Baker exemplified that view.

The value that Baker's mother placed on concrete service to others is illustrated in two stories that Ella Baker later told about her childhood. The Powell family rented a farmhouse on land that Baker's family owned in Littleton. The mother had died, and the father was too overwhelmed and impoverished to care for the children properly. So it was Ella's responsibility to visit the children's home regularly, bathe them, comb their hair, and bring their dirty clothes back for her mother to wash.[26] This hands-on approach to service required an intimate identification with those being served. In the second story, those who suffered were regarded as neighbors even though they lived on the other side of town. Ella was restless, curious, and a bit of a wanderer, so she often drifted far from home despite her mother's disapproval. On one such roaming adventure Ella encountered Mandy Bunk, whose parents were mentally ill and who lived in squalid conditions on the outskirts of Littleton. As Ella was walking past the Bunks' house, she noticed that Mandy was standing on her porch bleeding. Ella went home immediately and retrieved her mother to help: "She needed medical attention. So what do you do? I mean, she was a person. You couldn't just pass by her and say, 'oh, that's just Mandy Bunk, you see, who also raised her pig in one room and herself in the other room.' You don't do that."[27] The lesson Ella Baker took from these experiences was that the poor and afflicted were not a caste of contaminated or contaminating "untouchables." They were not some reified and depraved "other," but rather an extension of self, a concept she articulated quite eloquently in later years.

While black Baptist missionary women at the turn of the century defended their place in the public sphere and in the work of the church, they accepted and valued women's primary roles as mothers, homemakers, and wives.[28] Like other women's groups, black women's organizations sometimes described their public, political work as an extension of their role in the household. One piece of literature declared metaphorically: "The task of our Baptist women is like a housewife, a hard piece of work. We are to continue humming until the Lord says 'enough done.'"[29] For southern black women, this perspective was more than a justification of their public role; it was also an expression of the extent to which family, kinship, and community overlapped in African American society. Ties of extended family and fictive kinship helped bond Ella Baker's childhood community together and shaped her family's interdependent relationship with a larger network of neighbors and friends. Collective parenting was a commonplace practice. Ella's mother did not hesitate to feed, clothe, and discipline other people's children when the need arose. And Ella's aunt Eliza unofficially adopted and raised several children who were not biologically her own but were in need of parenting.[30] This practice is an example of what Patricia Hill Collins, a feminist sociologist, describes as the African American concept of "other mothers," whereby a child is nurtured by female relatives or neighbors when the child's biological parents cannot do so.[31] According to Baker, family was defined broadly rather than narrowly. She "had a family who placed a very high value on people. We were the kind of family that was not just my mother and her brood, but if somebody came by who needed something, you got something."[32]

Ella Baker's most enduring image of her mother was as an unbending tower of strength. Anna Ross Baker was very conscious of presenting herself as a "lady"—poised, graceful, and precise in her speech—but ladylike behavior did not mean feigning weakness or frailty. It meant, instead, asserting and defending her dignity. In a 1974 interview, Baker described her mother as a "feminist."[33] Five years later, she remarked that her mother "would have been very much at home leading a feminist movement," and she described Anna Ross Baker as a firm, authoritative person who commanded respect from those around her.[34] In many references to her mother, Baker stressed that she was a "precise-spoken" woman with a large "ego."[35] In using the term "ego," Baker did not appear to suggest that her mother was self-centered or vain. Rather, she was strong, determined, and unwavering in her self-confidence. She carried herself with dignity and self-respect and insisted that others treat her in a similar manner. One story Baker told epitomizes her mother's attitude. Once, when a white salesman came to the Bakers' door and, in a paternalistic gesture that was common in those days, referred to Anna Ross Baker as "aintie," she sharply corrected him, pointing out that they were certainly not related. "I didn't know my brother had a son like you," she snapped.[36] As far as Ella Baker could remember, her mother showed no deference to white authority and very little deference to male authority. Baker's mother was the strong-willed disciplinarian of the family who did not mince her words or tolerate disrespect from her children. Her father was quiet and nurturing, a reversal of conventional gender attributes.[37]

Another influential female role model for Ella Baker during her childhood in North Carolina was her maternal grandmother. Josephine Elizabeth Ross, called Bet for short, was a rebellious spirit who, despite a very arduous life, lived to be nearly ninety-six years old. Ella Josephine Baker, called Ella Jo for short, was her grandmother's namesake. Baker recalled being told that her maternal grandmother, who had been born into slavery, was named after two queens, Josephine and Elizabeth. Baker remembered her grandma Bet as a feisty, fun-loving person who always enjoyed the company of children and was ever ready to engage her grandchildren in a game of catch ball or a lively discussion. This demeanor was in contrast to Ella Baker's mother, who was always very sober and serious.[38]

According to Ross family lore, as a slave Bet had actively resisted attempts by her owners to deny her autonomy as a person and specifically as a woman. She was herself the product of an illicit sexual encounter between a master and one of his young female slaves. Indeed, Bet's mother was allegedly poisoned by the master's wife because she was jealous of the liaison that had taken place between her husband and his slave, of which the young Bet was a constant reminder.[39] The sexual violation of enslaved black women by white men, which was often repeated from one generation to the next, was a central fact of American slavery. How enslaved women and their kin responded to and remembered such acts is deeply revealing of their stance toward personhood and womanhood. As the story was passed down in the Ross family, Bet was raised by her own grandmother. When she was old enough to go to work, she was assigned to the master's house, where her duties would be less physically grueling than the field work performed by the majority of the slaves. However, Bet's life was hardly devoid of the oppressive conditions faced by her darker-skinned counterparts in the field. One specific event illustrates her vulnerability and the fact that, even though she was the master's biological child, she was first and foremost a slave. According to Ella Baker, "[W]hen she [Bet] was of marriageable age, . . . the mistress wanted to have her married to a man whom we knew as Uncle Carter. . . . And she didn't like Carter. And so when she refused to concur with the wishes of the mistress, the mistress ordered her whipped, but the master, who was still her father, refused to have her whipped. . . . But he did put her out on the farm and she even had to plow . . . she would plow all day and dance all night. She was defiant."[40] After she refused to marry Carter, Bet chose Mitchell Ross instead. Even under the abject conditions of slavery, Bet pushed against the will of her slave mistress and master to define her own humanity. She took great pride in retelling this story to her grandchildren.

Bet Ross shared many stories with her grandchildren. Baker remembered her grandmother's powerful tales of the suffering and struggle she had witnessed over her long life. She was a "raconteur," Baker recalled, "recounting what took place during her period of slavery."[41] The tales of slavery and Reconstruction passed down by the Ross and Baker families instilled in the young Ella the value of personal and political resistance and impressed on her the fact that chattel slavery was not ancient history but a mere generation away. What Baker remembered about her grandmother's stories was not the brutality and degradation of enslavement but the resistance and the triumphs.[42] Although the Ross and Baker families attempted to shelter their children from the harsh realities of racism that surrounded them, they did not deny or attempt to conceal the more brutal aspects of the past. Instead, they passed on stories of defiance in the defense of dignity. What was instilled in young Ella Baker by the family's storytelling tradition was not only that she was the descendant of slaves; but that she came from a long line of militant fighters.

· · · · · ·

THE PROMISE AND PERILS OF LIFE IN NORFOLK

Blake Baker and Anna Ross were married in 1896,[43] the same year that the Supreme Court's historic *Plessy v. Ferguson* decision upheld the constitutionality of racial segregation and enshrined the "separate but equal" justification for Jim Crow. In the wake of this decision, color lines were drawn in what many thought was indelible ink, inscribed by a battery of local ordinances and regulations that penetrated virtually every aspect of life. In 1903, the year of Ella Baker's birth, the scholar-activist W. E. B. Du Bois wrote, "[T]he problem of the Twentieth Century is the problem of the color-line."[44] Ella Baker's parents began their married life at the nadir of race relations in the post-Reconstruction South, and they raised their children amid the harsh realities of segregation, political disenfranchisement, and racist violence.

Both of Ella Baker's parents were natives of eastern North Carolina. The Rosses lived in Elams, a riverside community just outside Littleton, and the Bakers lived in the nearby county seat of Warrenton.[45] Blake and Anna met in secondary school in Warrenton, struck up a friendship, and began to court. Although both came from large families, were the offspring of former slaves, and were the eldest son and daughter in their respective families, their backgrounds were otherwise quite different. Blake's parents were illiterate and landless,[46] while Anna's parents were literate land-owners.

Blake and Anna were ambitious for themselves and for their children. They dreamed of a better life than white Americans thought they, or their children, deserved. They studied, worked hard, relocated, and endured painful separations in order to realize a small part of that dream. They were by no means members of the "black bourgeoisie," a group that the sociologist E. Franklin Frazier characterized as coveting their privilege and distancing themselves from the mass of ordinary black folk.[47] But the Bakers were not poor either. They persisted in their optimism, despite an often bleak social climate, that they would make some progress in their own lives and benefit the race in the process. To a certain extent, they did both.

As the agricultural base of the South shrank in the early 1900s, tens of thousands of African Americans migrated from farms to cities, leaving behind their plows and hoes for jobs as Pullman porters, service workers, and domestic servants. Ella Baker's parents were among them. Like many others from eastern North Carolina, both black and white, the Bakers migrated to the bustling port city of Norfolk, Virginia, because it was the nearest "big" city to their home, with a population of over 50,000 in 1900.[48] By the turn of the twentieth century, the city had become the heart of commercial activity in the region. "With a deep harbor and a strategic location at the confluence of the Chesapeake Bay and the Atlantic Ocean, the city's fortunes as a commercial center were on the rise" after the Civil War. Between 1880 and 1900, capital investment increased tenfold, and the labor force quintupled. Hundreds of trains and boats passed through Norfolk's harbor and along its roadways, transporting cotton, coal, and other commodities from the South to the markets and manufacturing centers of the North. Many of those who came to work in the city were African American. The city's black population had risen to nearly 46 percent by 1870.[49]

Norfolk was a place very much in flux when Blake and Anna Baker arrived. The racial politics of the city were undergoing a dynamic transformation as the economy boomed and its population grew. Norfolk was a mecca for new migrants because of its vital commercial base and many employment opportunities. However, for black residents, what may have looked like a promised land from afar looked quite different close up. Norfolk's neighborhoods became increasingly segregated, and the black and white communities became more polarized and insular. Three factors made the climate in the city more difficult for blacks after the turn of the twentieth century: the imposition of a strict system of Jim Crow segregation; the move toward black disenfranchisement in the wake of Reconstruction; and dramatic incidents of racist vigilante violence.

Between 1890 and 1910, according to historian Earl Lewis, "Jim Crow society slowly enveloped daily life." City ordinances mandating the segregation of public accommodations were passed one after another, circumscribing and even eliminating black residents' access to public facilities. For example, a 1906 ordinance enforced segregated seating on city streetcars.[50] Imposing the new Jim Crow laws and extracting the subservience they demanded from black men and women in Norfolk was not an easy task. A 1910 newspaper headline read, "Judge Fines Insolent Negro $25" for "insulting" a white woman on a public bus. City ordinances required blacks to defer to whites in all aspects of public life, and humiliating treatment was routinely meted out to those who resisted.[51] None of these developments was unique to Norfolk; the city's policies paralleled the evolution of racial politics throughout the South in this period.[52]

White Norfolkians also took steps to minimize black political participation. The 1901–02 Virginia state convention passed an "understanding clause," which required that voters prove their understanding of the Constitution as a condition of suffrage and that prospective voters pay a poll tax. Both measures were designed to limit the black electorate, and they did. In 1901, 1,826 African Americans voted in Norfolk. By 1904 the number was down to 504, and by 1910 only forty-four blacks paid the tax required to vote. Moreover, between 1904 and 1908 white reformers eliminated the city's ward system, which weakened the voting base of black politicians and effectively eliminated African American candidates from local politics.[53]

The physical exclusion and political marginalization of African Americans in Norfolk was underwritten by frequent public incidents of antiblack mob violence. Race riots were quite common in southern cities; Atlanta and Charleston also experienced major riots during the first decade of the twentieth century. Norfolk experienced its worst race riot in 1910, when whites randomly attacked black residents as retribution for the victory of the black prizefighter, Jack Johnson, over a white contender.

During that Fourth of July weekend, while some of Norfolk's white citizens celebrated the ideals of freedom and independence, its African American residents feared for their lives. Incensed by the black heavyweight boxer's triumph, enraged whites took to the streets to vent their anger and indignation and reaffirm by collective violence the sense of white superiority that had been lost in the ring. Blacks were pulled from streetcars and beaten mercilessly. Others were chased down alleyways and pummeled by jeering crowds. Most of the trouble was apparently initiated by white sailors whose ships were docked in the Norfolk harbor. Local newspapers reported that "every boat brought fresh batches of sailormen looking for trouble. Negroes were being attacked and mauled everywhere." The riot left forty people injured and over 200 in jail. Similar outbreaks of antiblack violence occurred in several other cities in the wake of the Johnson victory.[54]

The Baker family moved to Norfolk in search of economic opportunity, as did many other African Americans from rural areas, and they witnessed the increasingly violent efforts that white residents made to maintain white supremacy in the city as its black population swelled. Blake Baker moved to Norfolk in about 1895, a year before he and Anna were married.

As was the pattern with many black migrant families, one person went ahead to secure a job and a place to live before sending for the rest of the family. Blake initially found a job as a boatman and got a room in a house at 85 St. Paul Street.[55] Two of Anna's brothers, Peter and Matthew, also migrated to Norfolk around the same time. Matthew and Blake moved in together, sharing a small house at 102 Scott Street, around the corner from where Blake had lived the year before.[56] Peter set out on his own and eventually established a successful dairy farm just outside town.[57] Within a few years, Blake was able to find a better paying job as a waiter on a steamship run by one of the many steamship companies based in Norfolk. He earned a decent wage and enjoyed what was, at the time, considered a relatively comfortable standard of living. The only disadvantage of the job was that Blake had to be out of town several nights a week as the steamer shuttled back and forth between Norfolk and Washington, D.C.

Blake and Anna were wed in 1896. She left her teaching job and her family in North Carolina and moved to Norfolk to settle down with her new husband in the small house on Scott Street. The neighbors were a diverse group of black Norfolkians. With the exception of the white grocer down the block and a few other white-owned small businesses, the entire community was black. The people who lived in the Baker family's neighborhood included Mr. Jordan, a barber who lived two doors down; Nelson Darden, a longshoreman; Joe Stokes, a carpenter; and Mr. Petty, a shoemaker. Norfolk was a growing community, and between 1897 and 1900 several new houses were constructed on the Bakers' block.[58]

Starting a family was not easy for the Bakers; the three children who survived infancy were born over a period of seven years. Anna experienced at least two unsuccessful pregnancies before the birth of Ella's older brother, Blake Curtis, on December 23, 1901. Two Decembers later, Ella Josephine arrived. A second son, Prince, died in infancy when Ella was about three. Anna had at least two other unsuccessful pregnancies, ending in miscarriage or stillbirth, over the years. The Bakers' youngest child, Margaret Odessa (Maggie), was born in 1908.

By 1910, the growing family had moved into a bigger house, which they rented, on the corner of Lee and O'Keefe Streets.[59] This neighborhood, where Ella lived until the age of seven and which she remembered most vividly, was a newly developed, "colored" section of town called Huntersville. Most of her neighbors there were educated and owned their own property. They were skilled workers, professionals, and small entrepreneurs.[60] There was also a concentration of maritime workers, like Ella

Baker's father, who worked as porters and waiters for various shipping companies based in the port city. Baker remembered Huntersville as a more middle-class neighborhood than the older section of town where the family had previously lived.[61]

One neighbor in particular made a strong impression on young Ella Baker. Known as "the Black Money King," he was probably Dennis Alston, a North Carolinian who, like Ella's parents, had relocated to Norfolk.[62] Baker remembered him as a dignified man who was very dark-skinned and was coincidentally one of the most prosperous African Americans in town. "He was a very proud and very well-groomed man, [with] sharp features. I guess he struck me as a Zulu might, a strong, tall type."[63] This combination of qualities had great appeal to Ella Baker.

One day while young Ella was swinging on her front gate, as was her habit, she saw the impressive Mr. Alston passing by, and they began to chat. A friendly, assertive, and precocious child, Ella was always looking for a good conversation. She described herself in retrospect as "one of these talking children . . . one who insisted on being able to talk to people."[64] And she liked talking to Dennis Alston. She liked him so much she decided to ask him to become her godfather, even though her family was devoutly Baptist and he was not. He reminded her of her beloved grandfather, Mitchell Ross, who had recently died. Like her grandfather, "he prided himself on being black."[65] Later Baker likened Alston to the regal African statesman Jomo Kenyatta of Kenya.[66] Ella Baker's adoration of Alston's dark complexion suggests a type of black pride that seems to have been typical in her family. This appreciation for African characteristics is significant because at that time a disproportionate number of well-to-do blacks were light-skinned, and in some circles light skin and straight hair were celebrated as marks of superiority and beauty. Ella's notion of beauty was clearly different.

When Alston approached Ella Baker's mother regarding the possibility of her becoming his godchild, Anna was not impressed with Alston's good looks or regal demeanor. She was outraged that a Presbyterian would ask a Baptist to change denominations. Becoming Alston's goddaughter would have meant that Ella would be baptized, and the practice of baptizing infants and children violated Anna's religious convictions. Her response bespoke her pride and was a reflection of what Ella repeatedly referred to as her mother's "ego." Anna told Alston in no uncertain terms that her own father "would turn over in righteous indignation in his grave if he thought that any of his children or his children's children had gone from the Baptist

Church to the Presbyterian." Baker described this kind of response as characteristic of her mother: "You see, her ego was just as great as his, as the man who wanted me as his god-child but [wanted me] christened in his church."[67] Anna Ross Baker was a woman of strong opinions who did not hesitate to express those views. Her eldest daughter displayed this very same trait as she matured. Throughout her childhood, Ella observed her mother carry herself with dignity and a strong sense of self-confidence in her interactions with blacks and whites alike.

Anna Ross Baker's strength and determination notwithstanding, the years in Norfolk were not easy ones for the Baker family. Blake was away from home a lot, and Anna missed North Carolina. The five tragic losses of children that Ella's parents experienced took their toll, both physically and emotionally. One of the saddest events in Ella's youth was the death of her infant brother, Prince. "This was the first death I knew of in the family," Baker later recalled. "I remembered it in particular because my father was the only one who went to wherever the internment was taking place. And it was a carriage, and I was very eager to be in the carriage, but they didn't permit me to go."[68] Anna Ross Baker suffered from a respiratory ailment, most likely chronic bronchitis, which grew worse during the family's years in Virginia. Ella herself was not always healthy either. When she was about six years old, she was afflicted with typhoid fever and suffered a long and difficult recovery.[69]

Anna Ross Baker never felt quite at home in the city. Baker recalled: "My mother didn't like Norfolk."[70] Even with a steady stream of guests visiting from North Carolina, she was still homesick. Most summers, Anna would take the children back to North Carolina for an extended vacation lasting several months, and they would return to Norfolk in the fall.[71] This seasonal shuttle between city and country was typical of many recent migrants; it reflected their ambivalent feelings about leaving behind the calm pace, familiarity, and sense of community associated with rural and small-town life for the hectic impersonalism of the city. The same ties of kinship and friendship that brought blacks to the city to settle or just to visit also took them back to the country, where their "people" were an anchor and support in times of personal tragedy and illness, as well as during economic difficulties and vigilante violence.

Anna did not work outside the house after she moved to Norfolk, which may have intensified her sense of isolation. Baker recalled that her mother did not even consider resuming her teaching career, largely because Blake did not want her to. Like many men of his generation, black and white, he wanted to feel that he could provide for his family without his wife having to work.[72] African American men not only accepted the prevailing notion that breadwinning was central to masculinity but also worried about the insults their wives might encounter in working for whites. While it was not socially acceptable for middle-class women to go out to work, most black families needed the income that married women's employment could provide. So it was acceptable for wives to take in boarders as a way to supplement the family income. And this is what Anna did. Boarders were a constant presence in the Baker home. Keeping boarders added significantly to Anna's burden of household labor at a time when she was often unwell and occupied with the care of young children.

In 1910 the Baker family—with the significant exception of Ella's father—packed up and moved back to North Carolina. There were at least three reasons for the family's decision, one explicit and two implicit. Anna Ross Baker was determined that the children receive the best education available to them, a reason for the move that she communicated clearly to Ella. The 1910 race riot not only jeopardized the immediate security of black people but also signaled their increasingly bleak prospects in Norfolk; although Baker never discussed the race riot, it may have figured in her parents' decision. Third, the family was drawn back to North Carolina by continuing ties of obligation to kinfolk at home, which became more pressing after the death of Mitchell Ross. Blake Baker kept his job on the steamship line that sailed out of Norfolk, so he visited his family when he could on weekends and holidays.

Anna Ross Baker was critical of the schooling available to black children in Norfolk, and she felt that her own native state could provide her children with a better education and a richer cultural experience.[73] Education was an especially significant arena of contest in the Jim Crow South, as African Americans' academic opportunities were increasingly limited by white elites' determination to confine blacks to menial, manual jobs. Anna's father, Mitchell Ross, had taught himself to read and had instilled in his children the importance of education as a stepping stone to social advancement. Anna's training and experience as a teacher meant that she had high standards for what education should provide. Curtis and Ella enrolled in public school in Norfolk, and Ella was in first grade by the time the family moved. In 1910 Norfolk had some thirty-eight public schools, eight of them designated for colored children of all ages.[74] There is no evidence to suggest that Norfolk's public schools were any better or worse than schools in North Carolina. Comments Baker made later in life, however, suggest that her mother felt more comfortable with the grammar school in Littleton because she knew the teachers and the principal and therefore had greater confidence in her ability to oversee her children's education.

The second likely reason for the family's move back to North Carolina was the racial violence that increasingly plagued Norfolk during the early twentieth century. In her recollections of the family's years in the city, Baker never mentioned the 1910 race riot. It is unclear whether any members of Ella's family were directly affected by the riot, but some of their friends and neighbors certainly were. Much of the rioting took place in downtown Norfolk at the streetcar depot, where black shipyard workers congregated to catch the trolley back to their homes after work. It is fair to assume that some of Blake's co-workers witnessed or were victims of the violence. Everyone was aware of the race riot, even if they were not personally involved and did not live in the affected neighborhoods. The mayhem and bloodshed were headline news in Norfolk papers for over a week.[75] Since Anna and the children customarily spent their summers in North Carolina, they may not have been in the city when the riot took place, but the adults in the family were surely well aware of the violence. With Blake away from home so often, even the confident and capable Anna Baker may have felt vulnerable.

The death of Mitchell Ross, Ella Baker's maternal grandfather, around 1909 was also a likely factor in the family's move back to Littleton. Anna's elderly mother, Bet, was living alone. In the Ross family, as with many southern farm families, black and white, there was a serious set of intergenerational obligations. It is likely that, as the eldest daughter, Anna felt a duty to be closer to her mother.

· · · · · ·

COMING HOME TO LITTLETON

Ella Baker's parents navigated the treacherous terrain of the American South in the early 1900s in search of the best possible life and fullest range of opportunities for themselves and their children. The family's move to Littleton meant a greater physical and emotional distance between the children and their father. Blake visited the family on holidays, and Anna would occasionally pack up the children, mainly Ella and Maggie, and make the trek back to Norfolk to spend a few days with Blake.[76] The children did not see much of their paternal grandparents, Teema and Margaret Baker, because they lived over a day's ride away, and Teema Baker died when Ella was still quite young.

Ella Baker's mother and maternal relatives were the main adult influences in her life after the family came home to Littleton. They moved into a house owned by one of Anna Ross Baker's sisters, who had recently moved to Philadelphia, and were closely connected with other members of the Ross family. This was a woman-centered world. Ella Baker had vivid childhood memories about growing up with her mother, her maternal grandmother, and her aunts.[77] In the small towns of Littleton and Elams, which was just across the river, Ella Jo Baker's maternal relatives were pillars of the black community. The Rosses were not wealthy people, but they were better off than most. Anna was one of a dozen siblings, and her circle of extended kin was even larger. Mitchell Ross, the reigning patriarch of the family until his death, had been a prominent Baptist minister and farmer in Elams.

On January 24, 1888, Mitchell Ross and several of his male relatives were able to realize the dream shared by black freedpeople throughout the South in the wake of emancipation: they purchased their own land. With it they purchased a greater margin of self-respect, independence, and social mobility for their children and grandchildren. It was a memorable day in the Ross family's history when Mitchell Ross made the final installment of the $250 he had contracted to pay for a fifty-acre plot of land, which was most likely a portion of the plantation he had once lived on as a slave.[78] Two of his relatives, Everett and Plummer Ross, made similar purchases of smaller, adjacent plots as a part of the disposition of the estate of William D. Elams, the landowner who may have been the Rosses' former master. These transactions occurred nearly twenty years before Ella Baker was born, but the story remained an integral part of her family's oral tradition for many decades. Ella Baker was still recounting a version of it nearly a hundred years later.[79] The land was a great source of family pride. Baker sent home a portion of her first paycheck after she moved to New York to pay off back taxes and to keep the land from being sold.[80]

Over the years, the Rosses became successful independent farmers, escaping the trap of sharecropping that ensnared so many others. They grew cotton, wheat, and corn and raised chickens and cattle. Their farms provided them with a certain degree of insulation from the fluctuations in the economy, since they were always assured of having food on the table. In recollecting her frequent visits to her grandfather's farm when she was a young child, Baker remarked that he "had developed an orchard, . . . and he had lots of cattle, . . . [and] a big garden."[81] Land ownership also offered a bulwark against the very real possibility of economic reprisals from whites, a constant threat faced by black tenant farmers and sharecroppers. Although Mitchell Ross's children and grandchildren occasionally worked on the land, picking cotton and tending to the livestock, his main objective was that they secure an education. Formal schooling was a luxury the Rosses, unlike many of their less fortunate counterparts, could afford.[82]

The school that Ella Baker and her siblings attended in Littleton was a two-room grammar school attached to the South Street Baptist Church and run by Mr. Lonzie (Alonzo) Weaver.[83] Weaver was a stern disciplinarian who led the children in daily prayers and insisted on strict adherence to school rules and regulations. Although Weaver was clearly in charge, the two teachers were women: Bertha Palmer, who moved from Warrenton to Littleton to teach there, and Susie Grundy, a Littleton native. Church funds helped to establish the school, which was free to those who attended.[84] One of Baker's fondest memories of her schooling in Littleton was playing on the school baseball team. She reminisced: "I would rather play baseball than to eat . . . we had a mixed team of boys and girls, some much bigger than I, and I played baseball at recess. I'd take my lunch with me and eat it on the way to school, rather than bother with having to eat during lunch time."[85]

Ella, Curtis, and Maggie attended Lonzie Weaver's modest school for several years until Ella, apparently the most academically oriented of the three children, was sent away to Shaw boarding school in Raleigh in 1918. Curtis enrolled in Greensboro Agricultural and Technical College, and Maggie went away briefly to another, less prestigious, boarding school.[86] "Maggie was the wild one," the more frivolous and fun-loving of the two sisters, recalled Maude Solomon, a girlhood friend of Maggie's.[87] Ella was serious and studious. Maggie eventually dropped out of school, while Ella went on to earn her college degree with honors.

The fact that Ella Baker and her siblings attended school year-round and went on to secondary school and even college was in stark contrast to the experiences of many of their peers who were the sons and daughters of impoverished sharecroppers. Jenny Newell, one of Ella's childhood classmates in Littleton, remembered that "we went to school when we could, but papa was on somebody else's land so we had to work the fields when he needed us. . . . Ella Jo [Ella Baker's nickname] and them went to school regular though, and their mama taught them at home too."[88] Plantation owners discouraged and, in some cases, forbade black farmers and their children from obtaining an education. The system of debt peonage that bound so many black peasants depended on their illiteracy, since share-cropping contracts and accounting were often fraudulent.[89] For tenant farmers' children, such as Jenny Newell, economic necessity meant that work was a higher priority than schooling. Ella Baker was well aware that "the tenant farmer class . . . were bound more or less by what their owner needed and if it was cotton picking time, the children picked cotton."[90] Most black youths were not able to go to high school, not to mention college. The Ross children and grandchildren enjoyed exceptional advantages.

Ella Baker's family was characterized by a certain flexibility in gender dynamics, male and female roles, and masculine and feminine attributes. Although domestic responsibility and childcare fell largely on her mother and wage-earning fell primarily on her father, her parents did not exhibit or inculcate the behaviors and attitudes conventionally associated with males and females. This fluidity may have contributed to Ella Baker's own construction of a gender identity that was less than conventional.

As children, Ella and her older brother, Curtis, did not conform to the expectations that were commonly held for boys and girls. Ella was always more aggressive and adventuresome. Baker described her brother as "thin, tall, and not too combative, whereas I was the opposite as far as being combative."[91] The way Baker remembered her childhood role and persona, she was a tomboy who stood up to playground bullies and defended her shy and timid older brother when she had to. Baker proudly described herself as a tough little kid who rarely backed down from a fight: "I wasn't big enough to challenge anybody, but I never ran." She added, "I was neither girl nor boy in certain ways."[92]

Although Blake Baker was the main income-earner and discouraged his wife from continuing her work as a teacher, Anna was an equal decision-maker and authority figure in the family. In fact, some of the key decisions about the family seem to have been made primarily by Anna, in particular the decision to return to North Carolina for the sake of the children's schooling. Moreover, given Blake's virtual absence from the household for most of the year, she was the principal disciplinarian as well.[93] Baker described her mother as having "a sort of matriarchal approach to young people or to anybody because she was very positive. She didn't do much playing with you." She described her father, in contrast, as mild-mannered and tolerant.[94] "He didn't insist on too many things, because after all he wasn't home except on every other day," she recalled. He must have been even less of a presence once the family moved back to Littleton.[95]

At the same time that Ella Baker admired her mother's strength and her father's gentleness, she had a clear sense of the constraints placed on her mother because she was a woman. Ella seemed determined not to succumb to the burdens and limitations women suffered as a result of their sex. In Baker's retrospective view, her mother was an able and talented woman who had suppressed her own personal ambitions because of her domestic responsibilities and the sexism she encountered in society. In recounting her mother's life story, Baker observed: "She was a very bright woman . . . and at the time, of course, that she came along, there were only certain things that women, especially black women, could do . . . and so she taught . . . she never worked after she married. And then of course children started coming."[96] Ella Baker was intent on not following the same path. She refused to teach, declined to have children, and opted for a rather unconventional marriage. Perhaps Baker's lack of interest in having children had to do, in part, with her mother's painful experience. Anna was pregnant eight times, suffered four miscarriages or stillbirths, and lost one child in infancy.[97] For many women of her generation, pregnancy and childbirth were painful and dangerous.

It is possible that Ella's memories of her mother's painful losses and unrealized ambitions dimmed any romantic notions of motherhood and marriage she might otherwise have harbored. When asked why she never had children of her own, she confessed: "I wasn't interested, really, in having children, per se."[98] Reflecting with regret on her mother's unfulfilled aspirations, Baker remarked: "Had she not been female, she probably would have gone on into something else. But the time was not yet right for being female and not married . . . and so she married and I came along."[99]

Baker herself never fully conformed to the dominant society's prescription for what a woman, especially a black woman, ought to be. In conversations and interviews, she often downplayed gender issues, yet in her personal and political life she consciously violated most of the social conventions that dictated proper feminine behavior. Although she married during the 1930s, she did not center her life around her husband. While she never sought the limelight in political organizations and criticized many of her male colleagues who did, she also refused to play the role of the silent helper to the prominent male leaders with whom she was associated, from Walter White in the NAACP during the 1940s to Martin Luther King in the

Southern Christian Leadership Conference during the 1950s. Ella Baker was an assertive, outspoken woman of strong opinions. These traits sometimes made her male colleagues uncomfortable, but they would have made Anna Ross Baker quite proud.

· · · · · ·

CLASS AND COMMUNITY

Ella Baker developed a special relationship with her maternal grandfather, Mitchell Ross, during her extended summer visits to the family farm in North Carolina while she was still living in Norfolk. Although he died when she was about six or seven, just before the family returned home, his influence continued, both because of the close bond they had developed and because of his enduring imprint on the Ross-Baker family's position in the church and community. Mitchell Ross became a great source of inspiration in Baker's life.

A prominent Baptist minister in Warren County, Ross often traveled to nearby communities to deliver guest sermons, and sometimes he served several churches at once. His influence and reputation extended beyond his immediate congregation. Ella was his favorite grandchild. She would often travel with Reverend Ross in his horse-drawn buggy, and she was sometimes allowed to sit in a deacon's chair behind the pulpit while her grandfather preached, a practice that the more socially conservative Anna Ross Baker thought entirely inappropriate for a young child.[100] But the precocious little girl beamed at the elevated status she temporarily enjoyed. Ella also liked hearing her grandfather preach. Ross's preaching style distinguished him from many other southern black Baptist preachers of his era. According to Baker, he discouraged his congregation from "screaming and shouting" during his religious services. "My grandfather didn't care too much for noise in the church . . . [T]he story goes that if they began to do a lot of shouting and throwing their arms, he'd call them by name and tell them to sit down and keep quiet. And if they didn't, then he had his sons . . . go and take them up and sit them outside the church, let them cool off."[101] This practice may have reflected Ross's disdain for the loud and lively expressions of religious enthusiasm commonly associated with poor and uneducated blacks, as well as his emphasis on the substantive content of the sermon. Ella Baker viewed her grandfather's preaching style as a more genuine mode of conveying moral teachings than the drama and theatrics that many popular black Baptist ministers employed. Mitchell Ross had a special affection for young Ella. Perhaps he saw a bit of himself in this articulate and willful child, who was insatiably curious, always spoke her mind, and never backed down from a fight. Although she was no more than seven, he referred to her as the "grand lady."[102] For the rest of her life, she strove to live up to his grand expectations.

An independent, hard-working farmer and devout preacher of the Gospel, Ross was a recognized community leader who was reputed to have been active in Reconstruction-era politics in North Carolina. He was an ardent proponent of equal rights and black suffrage and was sometimes called on to defend those convictions, both verbally and physically. Ella described her grandfather as a "man who had the nerve to fight back . . . and he identified with the struggles of his people. The thing that was passed on was not subservience. It was always fighting back. It was said that when [black people] went up to register to vote . . . if they [white segregationists] interfered, he and his sons would go up and stand by the folks if necessary. . . . This is what fed the lifeline of our family."[103] Baker took pride in her grandfather's defense of black citizenship, just as she took pride in her grandmother's defiance of her owners' attempts to violate her autonomy while she was enslaved.

Mitchell Ross rejected many of the cultural practices that reminded him of the humiliation and degradation of slavery. Baker said that "he did not believe in eating certain things that he had eaten during slavery. He could not eat cornbread as such . . . and he wouldn't let his wife force the children to eat cornbread [either]."[104] In this respect, as with his preaching style, Ross seemed to disassociate himself from many popular black cultural traditions as an affirmation of pride and a symbol of his own social progress. Ross clearly had compassion for the mass of poor black people. However, as is the case with many poor people who achieve a modicum of success, there is a dialectic of affinity and distance relative to whom and what they have left behind. These tensions reflect Ross's status as a leader who was part of the people and at the same time apart from the people; indeed, he may have viewed himself and been perceived by his kinfolk as slightly above the people. Ella Baker seems never to have acknowledged these contradictions in the position of her grandfather, whom she loved without reservation.

Mitchell and Bet Ross continued to fight the injustices faced by black freedpeople just as they had resisted, on the very same terrain, the indignities of slavery. The personal and economic choices they made in the post-Reconstruction years demonstrate their commitment to the community. For example, the Rosses never regarded the land they purchased in 1888 as private property in the strict sense of the term. They viewed it not only as a resource for the economic well-being of their immediate family but also as a source of stability for the entire community. Land could serve as a weapon in the struggle against the white planters' attempts to dominate and control the African American population. According to Baker, one of the first schools for Negro children in the Littleton-Elams area after Emancipation was built on land that Mitchell and Bet Ross donated for that purpose. A small parcel of the land was allocated to the Roanoke Chapel, which became an important black religious institution in Elams.[105] County records show that in 1888 Bet and Mitchell Ross donated a parcel of land to the Roanoke Chapel Baptist Church, some of which may have been designated for the building of a church school for black children from the surrounding area.[106] During hard economic times, the Ross family felt called on to make even greater sacrifices. Land not only represented capital but could also serve as collateral. Baker recalled that the family farm was mortgaged more than once during the late nineteenth century, and the money the family borrowed was used to help feed other families in the community who were less fortunate than the Rosses. There is no evidence to corroborate Baker's recollections of the aid her family provided to neighbors; such acts were not written down in public or church records, however deeply they were inscribed in the memories of both donors and recipients. But county records do show that the Ross family's land was mortgaged twice, in 1889 and 1890.[107]

Cooperation, the sharing of resources, and a strong community spirit were fundamental values among African Americans. Ella Baker's extended family was part of a larger network of black farmers in Warren County, North Carolina, who emphasized self-help and mutual aid as strategies for survival and the betterment of the race. The cooperative ethos that permeated Baker's childhood was deeply implicated in prevailing notions of family and community; it connoted groups of individuals banding together around shared interests and promoting a sense of reciprocal obligation, not of individualism and competition.[108] For example, African American farmers exchanged goods, services, and other resources among themselves. Expensive farm equipment was purchased collectively or used communally; Baker remembered a wheat-threshing machine being used cooperatively. "There was a deep sense of community that prevailed in this little neck of the woods," she once observed. "It wasn't a town, it was just people. And each of them had their twenty-, thirty-, forty-, fifty-acre farms, and if there were emergencies, the farmer next to you would share in something to meet that emergency. For instance, . . . if there was a thresher around, you didn't have each person having his own. So you came to my farm and threshed."[109] Baker retained positive memories of the cooperative spirit evident in Littleton and Elams.

As an adult, Baker said that the socialist principle—to each according to need, from each according to ability—was very much in operation in her childhood community. She "grew up out of more or less kind of a Socialistic bit of thinking . . . [but it was] not called such."[110] The sociologist Charles Payne argues that much of Baker's political work in her later years was an attempt to rekindle and recapture some of the communal values and feelings of group solidarity that she so fondly remembered from her childhood in North Carolina.[111] But this is more a reflection of Baker's values as she looked back than a reflection of the values that fully characterized her childhood community. By all indications, members of the Ross family were fair-minded people with a great deal of compassion for others. Yet Baker's recollections do not account for the very real class differences that existed within the black community itself. The cooperative farming practices she described so vividly were self-help strategies that could only be employed by those who shared the advantage of land ownership. This network of mutual aid did not encompass the majority of blacks, who were bound to the land as tenant farmers. Although poor black tenants' struggle for survival also led them to adopt a cooperative ethos, they faced much greater obstacles with fewer material resources than landowning families like the Rosses did.

Ella Baker's childhood perceptions of her hometown community were also shaped by its distinct demographic and political history. The towns of Littleton and Elams were situated in the historic Second Congressional District of eastern North Carolina. From the 1870s, when the state's congressional districts were reconfigured, until the early 1900s, when most black citizens were disenfranchised, the Second District was referred to contemptuously by white southern Democrats as the "Black Second" because it was one of the few congressional districts in the nation with a majority-black electorate. Warren County, where the Rosses and Bakers lived, was considered the "blackest" county in the district; African Americans made up nearly 70 percent of the population.[112] The formation of the district in 1872 was the work of racist southern Democrats who gained control of the state legislature in 1870 and moved to isolate black Republicans by lumping a large number of them in one congressional district, hoping to insure Democratic victories in the remaining districts of the state. As a result, the Second District was a Republican stronghold for most of the late nineteenth and early twentieth centuries.[113] The black electorate of the Second District wielded considerable political power, especially relative to their counterparts in other parts of the state.

The young Ella Baker benefited from a social climate in which the adults in her immediate circle, in spite of the racism in the larger society, were able to function on a daily basis with a certain margin of confident self-determination. Her childhood memories, for the most part, are devoid of images of enforced black subservience: of the humiliating gestures of deference exacted from southern blacks in the form of bowed heads and "yes ma'am" and "yes sir" in the presence of whites. Instead, Baker recalled a community of proud black people, a number of whom were educated property owners actively engaged in local and state politics. These impressions shaped Ella's assumptions about racial equality and boosted her confidence in herself and black people in general. While Baker's recollections of life in Littleton were not representative of the experiences of the majority of black people, they left powerful impressions in her own mind and therefore contributed concretely to the formation of her social conscience.

Taken as a whole, the childhood memories that Ella Baker shared with interviewers later in life characterize Littleton as a rather idyllic southern town. Her most salient memory of racial conflict during her childhood involved a young white boy who dared to call her "nigger" when she was walking through downtown Norfolk with her father at Christmastime. She turned around and began punching the boy before her father could intervene. In Littleton, a white sheriff's son who made the mistake of hurling a racial epithet her way was also made to regret the error. Ella threw rocks at the boy and chased him off her street. Baker rarely mentioned specific, personal encounters with racism during her early childhood, in contrast to her vivid and accurate recollections of many other childhood events.[114]

Baker herself concluded that her parents had successfully protected her from the brunt of southern racism: "The manner in which we lived sheltered us from the bad aspects of race."[115] This protection created a space within which Ella Baker's self-esteem and confidence could flourish. Her parents had fashioned a life for their children that allowed them to avoid routine contact with whites. Baker recalled: "We did not come in contact with whites too much. . . . I was shielded from having contact with them at an early age. . . . This was a complete black community to a large extent. Even the store on the corner, it was Mr. Foreman's store, he was black. Even the ice cream store was owned by Mr. Evans. . . . So, this is the kind of insulation that was provided by the black people themselves . . . you didn't have to run afoul of a lot of insults."[116] The Bakers' residence in an all-black neighborhood with black-owned stores insulated the children from racism in their daily lives.

Although most black families endeavored to protect their children from the humiliation of racial epithets and second-class treatment by whites, few could afford the luxury. Most black children in the early twentieth century had to work for wages as field hands or domestics; so contact with whites could hardly be avoided. Ella Baker's grandfather had insisted that his children and grandchildren not work for white people;[117] they worked with and under the supervision of their parents and other family members. The Ross-Baker family could afford to keep their young people at home, providing them another layer of insulation from racism.

When "whites only" signs began to pollute Norfolk's public space and increasing racial violence threatened blacks' physical and psychological well-being, Anna Ross Baker collected up her children and fled home to her own people. In the black middle-class section of Littleton, Ella and her siblings must have been aware of racism, but their daily lives and formative identities were not strongly shaped by it. Their mother saw to that. The children read, played music, participated in church programs, and vigorously pursued their studies at home and at school. Their contact with whites was limited, and most of those in their circle of close friends and extended family were educated and relatively comfortable materially.

The majority of blacks in Littleton were not as protected from the impact of racial subordination as the Ross-Baker children were. In Littleton, as in many other small towns throughout the South, black subservience to white authority was enforced through legislation, intimidation, and force. Anti-black violence, although not on the same scale as the urban riots of the day, was a long-standing feature of the racial order and political tradition of eastern North Carolina. In his study of racial terror in the North Carolina Piedmont region during Reconstruction, Paul Escott indicates that, while Warren County was not one of the hardest-hit areas, Alamance and Caswell Counties, only short distances away, were the scenes of hundreds of acts of vigilante violence during the mid- to late nineteenth and early twentieth centuries.[118] It is likely that on a day-to-day basis race relations in Littleton were quite civil—as long as African Americans stayed in their place, kept their distance, and did not violate the established conventions of white supremacy.

Whites praised those whom they perceived as the "good Negroes" of Littleton. In 1892, the local newspaper made this comment about Henry P. Cheatham, the "Black Second's" black congressman: "He is a polite gentleman and is thought well of by everybody. Some of our colored citizens should take pattern after him. We wish we could speak as complimentary of all of his color who hold federal offices in this state."[119] Those colored citizens who were not as "gentlemanly" as Mr. Cheatham met with a very different response. In a lengthy syndicated column reprinted in a local Littleton paper, one writer defended lynching as a necessary bulwark against what he perceived as widespread black lawlessness.[120]

In 1897, the Littleton paper described an incident in which two black men approached the house of Captain J. W. Dempsey, presumably a captain in the former Confederate army, and asked his wife for food. She turned them away, and when Mr. Dempsey heard of this "outrage," he chased the two men down and beat them both with the butt of his rifle. The paper recounts the incident as if Dempsey were a hero and his actions perfectly justified. The article concludes: "They [the two Negro men] had been convinced [by Dempsey's actions] that it was un-gentlemanly and was not permissible to visit a lady in her home, insult her and demand food."[121] This incident and the report published in the newspaper reflects the way in which white racism was inflected by sexuality; any interracial encounter, especially involving a black man and a white woman, was regarded as a specifically sexual violation of racial boundaries, and white men's reactions were potentially explosive. If black men overstepped the limits of the deferential behavior whites expected, they were targeted for violent retribution.

Race was not the only dividing line in Littleton. Although a strong web of interdependent relationships bound the African American community together, it was by no means a homogeneous community free of class tensions. Baker's recollections on this score deny any internal conflict among blacks arising from class distinctions: "Where we lived there was no sense of hierarchy in terms of those who have, having the right to look down upon . . . those who didn't have," she once commented.[122] By other accounts, however, there were palpable class differences between the haves and have-nots in her hometown. Families who lived on East End Avenue, the main residential street, were generally thought to be better off than the majority of townspeople. East End Avenue is a small, narrow street by contemporary standards and remains unpaved to this day, but then it was considered a prestigious address. About 1911, Ella Baker's family rented a big white house on East End Avenue, with a large, inviting front porch and a pecan tree in the front yard. Their neighbors included the Brown, Davis, Hill, and Hawkins families.[123]

Baker recognized that her closest neighbors, as well as her own family, enjoyed a higher socioeconomic status than most of their black contemporaries. She explained:

> There was this section where we lived where the blacks, our neighbors, each had their own place. Next to us was the Reverend Mr. Hawkins, who in addition to being a minister was a bricklayer. And [other] men were artisans, like brick plastering and so forth. And somebody else was a carpenter. So you had at that time an intermixture. All of the heads of the families and their wives who lived in the section we called East End were at least literate. They had been to school somewhere, and many of them had been to what might have been considered college or an academy.[124]

Like their neighbors, the Bakers "lived in a six-room two-story house . . . [with] a dining room, and dining room furniture, and silver."[125] The sound of the children playing the piano and the sight of Ella's mother reading in the living room were well-understood signs of their middle-class status.[126]

The view from the other side of town was strikingly different. "They were big-shot Negroes," recalled Maude Solomon; "some of them were so biggity they didn't want their wives to go and work for the white folks like the rest of us." Solomon saw her own situation in stark contrast to that of the Ross-Baker clan and their East End Avenue neighbors. She was born out of wedlock and lived with her mother in a small, two-room house on Ferguson Street, in a run-down section of town.[127] The Baker children were clearly among the "haves" of Littleton's black community, and Maude Solomon was one of the "have-nots." As a child, Ella must have perceived this class difference and the social distance it involved, even though her parents and grandparents did not dwell on the advantages that distinguished them from other black people.

Relationships among African Americans of different socioeconomic classes in early-twentieth-century Littleton were not static mirror images of class relations in the dominant white society. Despite visible differences in wealth, status, and consciousness, the black community was not sharply polarized along class lines. Living on the poor side of town did not prevent Maude Solomon from becoming friends with Maggie. Baker's childhood experiences encompassed the dual class realities that characterized most

African Americans' lives during the early twentieth century. On the one hand, there was a clear distinction between the small, elite group of educated black artisans and landowners and the majority of blacks, who were illiterate or semiliterate, landless, and relatively impoverished.[128] On the other hand, the two groups generally lived in close proximity and were linked together in their day-to-day activities and by their shared condition of racial oppression.

Ella Baker's family and friends straddled this class divide. While the Ross-Baker children and their Ross relatives enjoyed certain class privileges, Ella was constantly reminded that others did not share their good fortune. Members of her extended family, as well as her schoolmates and neighbors, suffered the brunt of economic hardship. And those people were almost as much a part of Ella's life and consciousness as were her more affluent friends and relatives. "I've been identified over a long period of time with people, a lot of whom had nothing," Baker recalled, "although in terms of my immediate family, we have never lived out in the streets."[129]

Most people on Blake Baker's side of the family were uneducated and relatively poor. In a social context in which land and literacy were the two most significant determinants of class status, Ella Baker's paternal grandparents were clearly at the bottom of the socioeconomic hierarchy. Her father's name was a tacit symbol of his own proximity to slavery days. He was named after his father's former master, Blake Baker, a prominent North Carolina planter and Confederate war veteran. County estate records that list Teema as an item of property in the inventory of the white Blake Baker's estate are a chilling reminder of the circumstances of bondage from which Ella Baker's family had emerged.[130] Even though Ella did not spend much time with her father's family, they were still very much a part of her consciousness and her sense of family heritage. Baker was well aware that she was only two generations removed from slavery and only one generation removed from the poverty and illiteracy that trapped so many southern blacks. All of these factors helped to mold Ella Baker's sense of morality, justice, and social obligation.

· · · · · ·

Ella Baker's class privilege and the way in which her parents conceptualized the meaning of that privilege were key factors in shaping her class analysis of society and her model for political leadership within movements for social change. Baker's family internalized and inculcated the notion that from those to whom much is given, much is expected. Moreover, as good Christians steeped in the African American tradition of mutual aid, they felt that because they had been "blessed" with good fortune they were obliged to reach out to those who were less successful and provide assistance when and where they could. In Baker's words: "Your relationship to human beings was more important than your relationship to the amount of money you made."[131] Her family emphasized the importance of sharing what they had with others. Baker's recollections move from sharing food to other forms of solidarity: "[My family was] never hungry. They could share their food with people. So, you shared your lives with people."[132] To Ella Baker, this became a matter of moral obligation. A certain degree of elitism remained within her parents' and maternal grandparents' ethos of Christian charity. Implicit in this philosophy is the idea that the disadvantaged are not fully capable of helping themselves. Ella Baker later rejected this assumption outright, as she came to see what she described as the hidden inner strength within people and communities that on the surface appeared to be without resources or recourse.

Baker's parents' and maternal grandparents' sense of community service seems to have been based on the contradictory notions of duty to and distinction from the masses of the black poor. The characteristics of which the Ross-Baker family were most proud were not those things that linked them to the majority of their fellow African Americans; they took pride, instead, in what most set them apart: land ownership, education, and Mitchell Ross's ministerial work. They were landowners at a time when tenant farming trapped most southern blacks in economic conditions that resembled slavery. They were literate and educated when most were not. Their style of religious worship, under Ella's grandfather's tutelage, consciously distinguished them from the "screaming and shouting" of most black Christians.[133] This is not to suggest that members of the Ross-Baker family were not genuine in the help they provided to their disadvantaged neighbors, or that they had different criteria for success than most of their contemporaries. But their class consciousness nonetheless stands in clear contrast to the radical egalitarianism that Ella Baker embraced in her work and life, and that contrast underscores the evolution that occurred in her own thinking over time.

As she matured personally and politically, Ella Jo Baker departed from her family's characteristic posture vis-à-vis the poor and downtrodden. She eventually adopted the notion that the more privileged, educated, and articulate members of the African American community were not only duty-bound to come to the aid of their less fortunate brothers and sisters, but also had to humble themselves in order to create the social space necessary for the more oppressed people in the community to speak and act on their own behalf. Ella Baker built on, but moved beyond, the religious teachings of her youth. The values of charitable giving, sacrifice, and communalism that she internalized as a child became a part of her more secular world view as an adult. She ultimately identified with the plight of the poor and the working class, not as a gesture of Christian charity, but as an act of political solidarity. The choices she made over the course of her life distanced her from her relatively advantaged class background and merged her own consciousness and material self-interest with the concerns of the have-nots. In economic terms, she "eked out an existence" most of her adult life.[134]

Although Ella Baker's childhood experiences did not mold her into the radical political activist and intellectual she later became, they form an important foundation and context for our understanding of her grassroots, group-centered leadership style, her egalitarian vision for a renewed society, and, perhaps most important, her unwavering confidence that, as an African American woman, she had both the capacity and the obligation to be a powerful force for social change. What that change should be and how it should be enacted were open questions she grappled with for many years. Ella Baker's upbringing, rooted in a tradition of pride, resistance to oppression, a deep sense of community cooperation, and a strong sense of her strength as a woman left an indelible mark on her character and helped to shape her values, priorities, and convictions. Her family background instilled a bedrock commitment to community service, a sense of the usefulness of cooperative—as opposed to competitive and individualistic—survival strategies, an awareness of the pitfalls of self-aggrandizement, and the notion that women, as well as men, had both a right and a duty to be actively engaged in struggles to make the world a better place. Ella Baker left Littleton at the age of fourteen to attend Shaw Academy, a private, church-run boarding school in Raleigh, North Carolina. Although she never went back to live there permanently, she remained tied to her hometown for the rest of her life. Her family continued to own land there, and Baker often retreated to the house where her mother had lived to work or write—and to reconnect herself with "her people" and the place that provided her with important political and personal groundings.[135]

A RELUCTANT REBEL AND
AN EXCEPTIONAL STUDENT

SHAW ACADEMY AND SHAW UNIVERSITY,
1918–1927

. . . . . .

I didn't break the rules, but I challenged the rules.
Ella Baker, 1977

Awake youth of the land and accept this noble challenge of salvaging
the strong ship of civilization by the anchors of right, justice and love.
Ella Baker, valedictorian speech, 1927

From 1918 to 1927, Ella Baker lived, worked, and learned on the campus of Shaw University, a Baptist boarding school and college in Raleigh, North Carolina. She matured socially, intellectually, and politically in this environment. Next to the church, Shaw was the most influential institution in Ella Baker's early life. Anna Ross Baker selected the school because it met her academic and moral standards. She anticipated that Shaw would groom her eldest daughter to be both learned and ladylike. Such qualities would serve her well in the teaching career that Anna Baker had planned for her upon graduation. The expectation was that Ella's achievements at Shaw would serve not only her own best interest but also the interests of her family and community, promoting the advancement of the race. Ella Baker eventually fulfilled her obligation of service a thousand times over, but not in the way that her parents anticipated when they sent her off to school.

Shaw nurtured Ella Baker's intellectual growth at the same time that it inadvertently fueled her rebellious spirit. Her curiosity about the larger world deepened as she was exposed to new ideas and broadened her intellectual horizons. When she was a senior in high school, Baker had her first confrontation with an authority to which she found it impossible to defer. The student protests in which she was involved during her later years at Shaw centered on campus concerns, including the dress code and the required course in religion. The articulate young woman became a spokesperson for her peers as they challenged the teachers and administrators whom they had been taught to respect and not to question. These formative years marked the beginning of Ella Baker's self-identification as a rebel and her lifelong work as an intellectual and a political organizer.

Ella Baker did not need to go to college to learn the value of community service, humility, and a strong love of knowledge. The Ross-Baker family had emphasized all of these virtues for as long as Ella could remember. Language was especially important to Anna Ross Baker, who taught all three children how to read before they entered public school. She passed on her talent as a public speaker and her passion for the spoken word to Ella, coaching her in elocution and tutoring her in spelling and grammar. Baker recalled that her mother "had a great appreciation for, and almost a bias for, how people were able to speak and write."[1] Anna Ross Baker's emphasis on the accurate use of standard English represented a public expression of the family's class status and educational achievements.

Anna was so concerned that Ella be adequately prepared to enter Shaw that she had Ella spend an additional year at a local school working closely with a tutor.[2] Few teachers could meet Anna Ross Baker's high standards. Baker recalled: "The year before high school was spent largely with an old time teacher who would fit her [Anna's] appreciation . . . I went through all this business with grammar, all the things you learn in grammar that I couldn't even articulate now . . . [but] that teacher was just like my mother. She fit my mother's needs in terms of how she carried me through all the declensions. She carried me through all the parts of speech and how they are used."[3]

Although Ella Baker sometimes questioned whether Anna Ross Baker's obsession with proper language was "a good thing or not," since it emphasized class distinctions among African Americans, she recognized that her own proficiency in spoken language and her polished use of the written word, which were largely a result of the tutelage her mother provided, gave her a certain power and self-confidence that many others did not have. ". . . And I had a big voice to start with," Baker reflected.[4] Over the course of her life others often admired and sometimes were intimidated by Ella Baker's use of language. She wielded words, big and small, as political tools: to make complex ideas simple, to deliver a cutting-edge criticism, to thwart an attack from the opposition, or to inspire a comrade to struggle a little harder. One of her young protégés in the 1960s commented admiringly, "I so much wanted to be as articulate and eloquent as she [Ella Baker] was. Her words were always powerful."[5] Anna Ross Baker's passion for language led Ella to become a skilled speaker and an effective communicator. But Baker saw rhetorical ability as a potentially double-edged sword. The ability to impress others with words did not necessarily mean that the speaker had something substantive to say or that he or she was prepared to translate those fancy words into deeds. In describing the exaggerated emphasis placed on speaking and preaching ability in the black church, Baker observed that orators were unduly "lionized" because of their verbal prowess.[6] Yet Baker's ability to articulate ideas and convictions, both for herself and for others, enabled her to defend the rights and interests of those who were less educated and to hold her own against whoever was standing in the way of the changes she sought.

. . . . . .

Shaw Academy and University, like other black colleges, universities, and normal schools in the South, was founded during the Reconstruction era in order to promote the advancement of African Americans.[7] These institutions received most of their initial financial support from the Freedmen's Bureau, northern religious organizations such as missionary societies, and individual white philanthropists. Shaw was founded in 1865 by the American Baptist Home Mission Society.[8] From the outset, African Americans themselves, despite their obvious economic disadvantage as freed people, managed to contribute economically to black educational institutions like Shaw. The North Carolina State Baptist Convention and local black churches and missionary associations routinely raised funds for Shaw. This type of self-help activity was typical of the postemancipation era. Historian Herbert Gutman emphasizes that "the former slaves themselves played the central role in building, financing and operating these schools. . . . Postwar educational efforts by blacks built upon a firm base of educational activism during slavery."[9] The Ross family exemplified this tradition. In addition to paying tuition while Ella was a student at Shaw, Anna Ross Baker participated in fund-raising campaigns to support the school years after her daughter graduated, as part of her work with the Women's Auxiliary Progressive Baptist Missionary Association.[10] Most black people in the late nineteenth and early twentieth centuries saw education as a pathway to their goals of freedom and empowerment and were prepared to make sacrifices to support both elementary and higher education.

Like most black colleges, Shaw was a fairly conservative institution controlled by paternalistic northern white benefactors. As Baker put it, "Shaw was founded by the New England white Christians."[11] Northern missionaries and reformers saw education as a vehicle for preparing ex-slaves to assume their new roles as hard-working, law-abiding American citizens. From the end of radical Reconstruction through the institutionalization of Jim Crow, white administrators of black colleges accepted segregation and promoted accommodationist views. Whites with close ties to northern contributors continued to run these colleges even when a second generation of well-educated African Americans was prepared to lead them. In fact, Shaw did not appoint its first African American president until 1931, four years after Ella graduated.[12] According to Wilmoth Carter, who documented Shaw's history, the institution enjoyed several notable distinctions. It was "the oldest [historically black] institution of higher learning founded in the South, [and] the first Negro institution in America to open its doors to women."[13] The tensions between the views and practices of paternalistic white administrators and the aspirations of students, their families, and the school's supporters in the black community were intensified by the fundamental contradiction between the first-rate education offered to students and the second-class positions they would be forced to occupy after graduation.[14] Institutions like Shaw communicated mixed messages. Although Shaw's administrators emphasized humility and Christian service, they reinforced many elitist assumptions about social class. The exceptional status of its students was a given.

As Evelyn Brooks Higginbotham points out in her discussion of southern Baptist missionaries in this period, institutions like Shaw had both a radical and a conservative impulse.[15] A coeducational classical curriculum, parallel to curricula at white colleges and universities, implied that African American men and women were as intellectually capable as their white counterparts. At the same time, the enforcement of a strict, middle-class code of conduct created visible markers that distinguished those who were educated from the majority of the race. At Shaw, the rejection of notions of innate black inferiority merged with elitist assumptions about the moral and cultural superiority of those with education and class advantage. This elitism was tempered, however, by a strong sense of moral obligation to aid and uplift those who were less able and to do so with a humble spirit.

A commitment to Christian service was integral to Shaw's mission as an institution. At Shaw, as at most private colleges, religious instruction was required by the school's core curriculum. Bible class and daily attendance at chapel were mandatory. The catalog read: "As Shaw University is a Christian school, the study of the English Bible is a part of the regular curriculum. The work is so arranged as to give a comprehensive knowledge of both the Old and New Testaments."[16] The official school motto was "For Christ and humanity."[17] Not surprisingly, all of the school's presidents up to the 1920s were either former missionaries or ministers.

Shaw's philosophy represented a mix of intellectual elitism and social conservatism, with a heavy emphasis on selfless Christian service. This aspect of Shaw's philosophy was consistent with the religious values and teachings of the Ross-Baker family. The school deemphasized individualism and stressed community service and Christian charity instead. "Where I went to school . . . you went there to give . . . the best of yourself to other people, rather than to extract from other people for your own benefit," Baker recalled.[18] The moral training she received at Shaw encouraged her to be modest and self-effacing. "My not pushing myself, as I saw it, came out of the Christian philosophy," she remarked.[19] Selfishness and self-promotion were vices not to be tolerated. Shaw was the kind of school where students "sang, 'Others, Lord, yes, others, and none of self for me. Help me to live for others that I might live like thee.'"[20]

The contradiction between Shaw's philosophy of Christian service and its intellectual and class elitism is epitomized in a statement by its president, Joseph Leishman Peacock, quoted in the college newspaper in 1925: "college life . . . includes the opportunity to associate with minds and hearts of the highest type."[21] Although Shaw's philosophy discouraged crude displays of snobbery, its administrators and faculty clearly thought of their students as exceptional, distinct from and, to some extent, better than the masses of ordinary black people. While most African Americans saw academic learning as a passport to full citizenship, the northern white missionaries who directed and supported schools like Shaw viewed black education as a source of both racial uplift and social control.[22] They hoped to produce a group of moderate race leaders who would temper black protest and help to instill the Protestant work ethic in their less-educated counterparts. Members of the educated black elite regarded themselves both as advocates for and as educators of their people. They lobbied for resources and rights at the same time that they urged poor and working-class blacks to uphold dominant standards of morality in order to demonstrate their worthiness for citizenship.

The mission of black Baptist colleges like Shaw, according to Evelyn Brooks Higginbotham, was to produce members of what W. E. B. Du Bois called the "Talented Tenth," a highly educated cadre of race leaders who would tutor, lead, and act as ambassadors for the larger black community.[23]

> Through the Talented Tenth, northern white Baptists hoped to trans-form—albeit indirectly—the illiterate and impoverished black masses into American citizens who valued education, industriousness, piety, and refined manners. . . . Through the black educated elite, the de-graded masses would be introduced to the values of white, middle-class Protestant America. . . . It was the men and women of the Talented Tenth who assured race management—that is, control of the masses—and consequently the well-being of the nation. . . . From the north-ern Baptists' perspective, a well-educated black vanguard constituted a buffer between white society and the black masses. . . . In the event of rebellion, the Talented Tenth would serve as a critical mediating force between several million oppressed blacks and white America.[24]

Du Bois's conceptualization of the Talented Tenth was distinct from the visions of white missionaries and other black leaders like Booker T. Wash-ington, who primarily advocated industrial, manual training for blacks and accommodation in matters of civil rights. In Du Bois's view, a classical liberal arts education for a black leadership class could serve as a means of achieving civil rights for the entire black community. He rejected segrega-tion and the assignment of all black people to positions of subordination in the economic, social, and political life of the country.[25] The missionary spirit and the concept of the Talented Tenth embodied both a genuine commitment to community service and the improvement of the race and a strong dose of elitism and social conservatism. Consistent with the school's philosophy, Shaw's administrators dictated and enforced a very rigid code of conduct for its students and faculty. Their behavior was to be exemplary enough to earn them leadership status, a badge of respectability, and mem-bership in the middle class. Such behavior would supposedly demonstrate their civility to whites and legitimate their fuller inclusion in the dominant society. It was also intended to distinguish them from black common folk who were untutored and unpolished. The school's philosophy was consis-tent with the view articulated by Du Bois in the first decade of the twentieth century: "developing the Best of the race so that they may guide the Mass away from the contamination and death of the Worst, in their own and other races."[26] Since it was considered a privilege to be accepted at the school, students were expected to be grateful and to behave accordingly.

In order to be admitted to Shaw during the late nineteenth and early twentieth centuries, an applicant had to be of "unblemished moral character."[27] Shaw's rules were designed to ensure that students remained morally above reproach, even as they traversed the dangerous years of adolescence. The college strictly regulated behavior and deportment, prohibiting dancing, card playing, and the use of tobacco, which were common leisure activities among poor and working-class African Americans. Dress and appearance were especially important marks of class and sexual respectability for young women. Female students were not allowed to wear "evening dresses, French heels, [or] ear rings."[28] Dating and socializing were strictly supervised.[29] Students were reprimanded and disciplined for the slightest violations of school protocol. Those who left campus without permission or missed chapel services were routinely disciplined and might even be expelled.[30] Students had to make formal requests to be late or absent from classes or school events, and "no frivolous conversations or attention to trivial matters or visiting in each others rooms, lounging upon beds or loitering upon the grounds" were allowed.[31] The school bulletin warned that "only those students who are willing to comply cheerfully with reasonable rules and regulations are desired at this institution."[32]

Shaw offered a comparable list of course offerings to both male and female students, and classes were mixed rather than segregated by sex. Still, the school's philosophy held that women's responsibilities centered on their homes and families, and residential life was organized to ensure that female students practiced domestic skills. A section of the catalog titled "Special Requirements for Girls" reads: "A period of work will be required daily of each girl, under the supervision of a matron, for which no compensation will be given. . . . Each girl is required to have aprons suitable for house and laundry work, and those who wait tables must have waitresses aprons."[33] The middle-class image of black womanhood did not preclude public or professional activity, but creating and maintaining order in the home was seen as a core feature of female respectability.[34]

The etiquette that governed interaction between male and female students at Shaw was quite rigid, and its rules were firmly enforced. School-sponsored social events were formal and heavily chaperoned. According to Effie Yergan, a classmate of Ella's, school parties were "more like banquets than dances."[35] At religious services, "the boys marched in one line and the girls in another," and female students occupied the center aisle while the male students sat on either side.[36] Sex-segregated seating at chapel was presumably intended to prevent informal contact that might distract young people from their prayers. There were some covert romantic interludes between students, Yergan said, but these were rare. Students who married secretly were—if caught—penalized by immediate expulsion.[37]

Shaw students were forbidden from socializing with the black community in Raleigh, except in the formal capacity of charity workers under the supervision of school authorities. Students who were learning to lead and serve their race had to have some contact with their uneducated counterparts, but school officials evidently thought that their interaction had to be closely controlled in order to prevent the masses from influencing the elite rather than vice versa. Administrators frowned on casual contact with Raleigh residents, seeing it as detrimental to the cultivation of respectable, middle-class alumnae. The 1881–82 catalog states that "no young man or woman from the city, without any legitimate business, will be allowed to visit the students in their rooms or mingle with them upon the grounds."[38] The 1927 catalog reads: "Boarding girls are expected to come directly to school from the train, and to return directly to their homes at the close of school . . . [and] are not allowed to visit in the city during the session."[39] Female students were even forbidden from visiting family members in the city without express permission from the University's president, and their monthly shopping trips were chaperoned.[40] These rules drew sharp lines of demarcation—reflected in appearance and deportment as well as formal learning—between Shaw's middle-class academic community and the common people of Raleigh. After her years at Shaw, Ella Baker spent much of her life trying to break down such divisions.

· · · · · ·

COMING INTO HER OWN

Ella Baker moved from the secure and somewhat sheltered environment of home to begin her journey into adulthood at Shaw Academy against the backdrop of a rapidly changing and increasingly dangerous world. In the wake of World War I, the meaning of American democracy, especially as it applied to African Americans, was hotly contested. Wartime rhetoric called on all Americans to do their part to "make the world safer for democracy." And many African Americans did. Two hundred thousand black men served in the war, a fourth of them in combat, and all of them in segregated units.[41] Blacks remained disenfranchised at home, and racial violence was on the rise; attacks on black soldiers in uniform were soon followed by racist violence against black urban-dwellers. The "Great Migration" of southern blacks to northern and western cities began during the war and accelerated through the 1920s. Race leaders debated what strategies ought to be adopted at such a perilous yet potentially transformative time.[42]

In office from 1913 to 1921, Woodrow Wilson was the first southerner to be elected to the presidency since Reconstruction, and he saw no contradiction between racial inequality and American democracy. Indeed, he was an unapologetic segregationist; he applauded the racist film *Birth of a Nation* and imposed segregation in federal offices in the nation's capital. There were advances for some and setbacks for others. In 1920, women finally won access to the ballot. Baker was sixteen years old and in her third year of high school. Still, millions of African American women were excluded from the political process, as were most African American men. Ella Baker began to develop her personal ambitions and to define her own worldview at a time when the citizenship rights of women and African Americans were at an important crossroads.

Of all the southern cities where Ella Baker could have ended up, with perhaps the exception of Atlanta, Raleigh was probably better than most. Two famous North Carolinians who came of age in Raleigh a decade ahead of Baker were Sarah and Elizabeth Delany, two black middle-class sisters who late in life became the subject of an award-winning book, *Having Our Say*. The Delany sisters, older siblings of the Harlem-based black jurist Hubert Delany, with whom Ella Baker was to become acquainted, recalled Raleigh as "a center for education," with two premiere black colleges to its credit, Shaw and St. Augustine. The Delany sisters described Raleigh as "a good place for a Negro of the South to be living, compared to most places at that time."[43] Shaw's environment was fairly insular, but when students were allowed to venture out, the environment was less hostile than in other cities in the Jim Crow South.

Shaw University opened new intellectual horizons for Ella Baker, exposing her to a myriad of ideas and experiences she had never previously encountered. The institution's litany of rules, elitist social milieu, and fairly conventional notions about gender expressed the values, views, and aspirations that had shaped Ella's education at home; yet being away at boarding school and college gave her the opportunity to define herself, to develop an independent identity, and to take a stand on the controversial questions of the day. Above all, as a first-rate, comprehensive institution of higher education, Shaw offered Baker ample opportunity to discover and explore the world of ideas. She took full advantage of the scholarly expertise and resources made available to her there, and she excelled academically. Her curiosity was insatiable. She read the works of Kant, Socrates, Aristotle, and Carter G. Woodson and studied the lives of Frederick Douglass, Harriet Tubman, and Sojourner Truth.[44] Baker was already a voracious reader who was enamored of books and delighted in the exchange of ideas when she came to Shaw. There, as a member of the debate team, she honed her oratorical skills and grappled with current social issues. Effie Yergan, her classmate, recalled that Ella "had a heavy voice, and helped to win a lot of trophies and honors for the school."[45]

Ella Baker's most important mentor at Shaw was Professor Benjamin Brawley. Although Baker enjoyed good relationships with several faculty members, Brawley had the most profound impact on her thinking. In addition to teaching a course on Shakespeare, he coached the debate team and advised the campus newspaper, the *Shaw University Journal*, on which Ella also worked. Brawley exemplified the highest standards of academic excellence, especially in writing for and speaking to the public.

A meticulous scholar and prolific writer, Brawley wrote some seventeen books during his life.[46] He demanded perfection from his students and deplored mediocrity. Perhaps it was his high standards of scholarship that attracted him to the bright and articulate Ella Baker. She was an exceptional student, and he was a serious scholar. But there was another side of Brawley that may have particularly impressed young Ella Baker. A sensitive man, he was committed to racial equality and community service. He spoke out against racial discrimination and the second-class status imposed on African Americans of his generation. Although he came from an upper-middle-class black Atlanta family, Brawley chose to spend a semester after college working as a teacher in a one-room schoolhouse in an impoverished black community in rural Florida. He often shared memories from that experience with his students at Shaw.[47] His stories had a lasting effect on Ella Baker.

Brawley was a legendary figure at Shaw, thoroughly bourgeois in his manner and a bit of an eccentric. Prim and proper himself, he insisted on strict adherence to school rules and protocol. He would lock his classroom door and refuse admittance to students who were more than a few minutes late.[48] One observer remarked that most "students stood in awe of Brawley. He was precise and exacting in class, immaculate in dress, frowned on men who said 'hello' to women, [and] refused to attend basketball games because the male players were not sufficiently clad."[49] He always left his office door open when meeting with female students to circumvent any possible assumptions of impropriety. Reminiscing about her college education at Shaw, Effie Yergan characterized Professor Brawley as "uptight and rigid,"[50] two words that no one who knew Ella Baker later in her life would ever have associated with her. Yet, despite their contrasting styles and personalities, Baker developed a fairly close relationship with Brawley. Perhaps he reminded her of her mother, who had many of the same qualities, especially a sharp wit and a love of ideas. In her reminiscences, Baker gently mocked Brawley's elitism and formality, observing that he was "Hah-vahd" educated and "classic-al-ly inclined." He was so prudish, Baker recalled critically, that he even forbade students from reading what she termed "all the nice salacious things that were in Shakespeare."[51] But Brawley was a rigorous and compassionate intellectual, and this distinguishing feature won Ella Baker's enduring admiration. The two kept in touch long after Ella left Shaw. In the 1930s, when Baker was living in New York, she invited her old teacher to speak at an event held by the Young Negroes' Cooperative League (YNCL), which she was organizing at the time, and Brawley agreed.[52]

Extracurricular activities were nearly as important to Ella Baker's intellectual development as her classroom experiences. She began her journalism career at Shaw in her freshman year of college, when she was the youngest student contributor to the campus newspaper.[53] She then became associate editor of the *Shaw University Journal*, a student publication established in 1924. In 1925 she took over as editor; her mentor, Professor Brawley, served as the faculty adviser.[54] Since she was curious about all kinds of subjects, journalism became a way for Ella to raise questions that she otherwise might not have had the opportunity to ask. She received As and Bs in all of her English and composition classes, and she seems to have been almost as good a writer as she was a public speaker.[55] These communications skills came in handy when Baker began her work as a political organizer. Over the years, she would contribute to such important African American periodicals as *The Crisis*, the *Amsterdam News*, the *Norfolk Journal and Guide*, the *National News*, and the *West Indian News*.[56]

Ella Baker's education and experience at Shaw gave her skills and self-confidence that she drew on throughout her life, especially as a woman operating in meetings and organizations dominated by men. In reflecting on what experiences helped to prepare her for her later political activism, Baker recalled: "My man-woman relationships were on the basis of just being a human being, not a sex object. As far as my sense of security, it had been established. . . . I had been able to compete on levels such as scholarship. . . . And I could stand my own in debate. And things of that nature. I wasn't delicate."[57] So, despite the conservative norms regarding gender that Shaw tried to inculcate in students, Ella Baker's education was a source of empowerment that enabled her to feel confident relating to men as an equal rather than as a sexual subordinate.

There is no indication Baker took a serious romantic interest in anyone while she was at Shaw, although she reportedly met her future husband, T. J. Roberts, when she was enrolled there.[58] She was also rumored to have had a crush on a football player.[59] According to her classmate Effie Yergan, Ella Baker was popular. "She was friendly to everyone, but I don't think she ever had a steady beau . . . you know how men were at that time, and some of them still today, they wanted you to be beautiful and dumb. [She] was too intelligent for that. The boys were probably intimidated."[60] Yergan's reminiscences suggest that during her college years Baker cultivated a persona that enabled her to associate with men on a collegial basis, keeping them at a certain personal distance and creating a space in which she could be forthright and assertive.

Shaw provided Ella Baker with a window on the wider world. The social and intellectual atmosphere of the Shaw campus was enhanced by the presence of international students and by visiting speakers who discussed their work as foreign missionaries and world travelers. According to historian Wilmoth Carter, "Many foreign students came from Canada, Mexico, South Africa, Liberia, Sierra Leone, the Congo, Jamaica, Trinidad, British Guiana, the Canal Zone, the Philippines and Puerto Rico." There were no white students at the school until after 1954.[61] Meeting a diverse mix of students from around the world must have been quite an experience for students from small towns in the South, many of whom had never traveled outside the state, much less outside the country.

Ella savored the taste of the world that Shaw offered her. Two people in particular encouraged her to think of the world in global terms: Max Yergan, a 1914 Shaw graduate who spent seventeen years in Africa working for the Young Men's Christian Association (YMCA), and his wife, who was a teacher at Shaw. Max Yergan later became a close ally of Paul and Essie Robeson and lobbied for the decolonization of Africa through the Council on African Affairs, which he and the Robesons founded.[62] A radical opponent of imperialism, Yergan was also a socialist during the 1930s.[63] In 1922, when Baker was still in high school, he visited the campus and talked about his travels in Africa.[64] A wide-eyed Ella Baker was in the audience. As she was to recall in about 1980: "Max Yergan was the first person that I met who had been to South Africa. . . . I was in school and his wife was a teacher there. . . . And they went to South Africa under the aegis of the YMCA as missionaries. And when they got back they told stories of South Africa that some people are just getting for the first time now." Baker added that her own interest in the situation in South Africa was "long since imbedded in me from that input which was their experience."[65] Her curiosity about the world was piqued by her relationship with the Yergans.

In the 1920s Ella Baker herself contemplated a career as a medical missionary, an ambition influenced both by role models like Max Yergan and by her mother.[66] During her college years, Ella engaged in projects that closely resembled Anna Ross Baker's missionary activities back home. In her junior year, for example, Ella worked with the Student Friendship Fund, which raised money for "students in other lands who are struggling bravely amid difficult and adverse circumstances to prepare themselves for future service."[67] This group supported Shaw's missionary work to establish schools and churches in Africa and elsewhere. In the winter of 1925, Baker raised $25.50 for the fund, an impressive sum at the time.[68] She also belonged to Shaw's YWCA; although her Y affiliation never took her as far as Max Yergan's had, she was selected as a delegate to attend a YWCA meeting held at the Commodore Hotel in Manhattan.[69] That was Baker's first visit to New York City, and it may have influenced her decision to move there after graduation.[70]

When she was still in high school at Shaw Academy, Ella Baker wrote an eloquent essay praising the role of the church in African American history. Titled "The Negro Church, the Nucleus of the Negroes' Cultural Development," the paper concluded that the church had "cradled the aesthetic tendencies of the race."[71] Ella paid homage to the preacher's leadership role within the church, describing him as "the spiritual leader, the teacher, the lawyer, and general adviser of his congregation."[72] She observed that many ministers were political as well as spiritual leaders; like her beloved grandfather, Mitchell Ross, they used the pulpit to advocate for the race. At the same time, the essay apologized for the gradualist approach to reform that many church leaders embraced, explaining that a more radical approach was not realistic: "The group's economic resources would not be adequate to carry out a radical program."[73] Therefore, one could not justifiably blame those moderate leaders who called for patience and slow progress. This is certainly a far cry from the expectations and criticisms Ella Baker would direct at apolitical church leaders a generation later.

· · · · · ·

A POLITE DISSIDENT AND A RELUCTANT REBEL

During her years at Shaw, Ella Baker always asked questions. As a senior in high school and as a college student, she challenged the school's conservative dress code, criticized the paternalistic racism of its president, and protested its methods of teaching religion and the Bible. Ella was ambivalent about exactly how confrontational she was willing to be, especially given the high price she might be required to pay for dissent. Students who broke the rules and persisted in their defiance of authority were expelled from school, dimming their prospects and disappointing their parents. The three known protest activities in which Ella Baker was involved over the course of her years at Shaw offer a portrait of her as a tentative young activist, a polite dissident, and a reluctant rebel.[74] As she reflected years later, "I did not break the rules [at Shaw], but I challenged the rules."[75]

Interestingly, the first issue on which Ella Baker took a strong stand was one in which she personally had very little at stake. When she was a high school senior, she was asked by a group of older female students to be their spokesperson in requesting permission to wear silk stockings on campus. The 1923 bulletin declared that "fancy, colored or silk hose . . . will not be allowed. If brought or sent they will be returned."[76] The specificity of this rule and the explicit statement of the consequences for breaking it suggest that violations had, in fact, occurred. A group of female students, most of whom were in college, sought to change this policy. Although Ella was not very fashion-conscious and did not even own a pair of silk stockings, she was asked to be the leader and spokesperson for the group because of her reputation for being assertive and articulate. According to Baker, the other girls "didn't have guts enough, or maybe a combination of guts and articulation, to deal with [their grievance] . . . and they came to me."[77]

Ella Baker wrote a letter on behalf of the students petitioning the school to relax the dress code, and the group presented its request to the dean of women students.[78] After all, it was the twenties. Magazines were filled with sketches and photographs of well-dressed ladies wearing silk stockings, and the young women of Shaw felt they had every right to dress as stylishly as the next person. The dean was not persuaded. Not only did the dean reject their petition, but "after this the girls had to go to chapel every night" as punishment.[79] Indeed, the dean became so upset by this bold and willful affront to the authority of the school administration that she called Ella Baker into her office to pray that she would see the error of her ways. Strong-willed Ella, of course, had no regrets, even though she was threatened with expulsion.[80] Baker recalled that the dean became so distraught over this unapologetic defiance that she fainted to the floor of her office during one of their conversations. "I didn't seem particularly penitent, and she [the dean] was very disturbed about it. But it didn't bother me because I felt I was correct."[81]

On one level, it appears as though the protesters simply wanted to be able to conform to changing standards of fashion by wearing silk hose. On another level, however, especially for someone like Ella, for whom the issue was purely a matter of principle rather than a personal objective, there were larger things at stake. Fashion was an important cultural arena of struggle for competing gender constructs in the 1920s: the so-called flappers challenged conventional femininity. Young, single, urban women, through their dress, dance, and demeanor, contested prevailing standards of womanhood and morality, projecting an assertive, self-confident, and consciously sexual public image. Conflicts about how respectable women of this generation ought to comport themselves were expressed in the popular media and from the pulpit. While Shaw women did not aspire to become flappers, they were asserting their right to be expressive and creative through their dress. And, since wearing silk stockings likely meant wearing shorter skirts, they were also rejecting the commonly held assumption that proper ladies had to keep their legs covered as a sign of respectability. As Baker put it, "I felt it was their right to wear stockings if they wanted to."[82] Although the dean of women did not back down in the face of this challenge, the rule against silk hose was removed from the dress code by the time Ella graduated four years later.[83] In this incident, the nineteen-year-old Ella stood her ground against authority, but she did not pursue the issue when the group she represented accepted its defeat.

The next time Ella Baker challenged the school administration, she did so alone. When the president of the university entertained northern white guests on campus, it was his custom to invite some students to perform. "They'd want you to sing spirituals," Baker remembered. "Many students resented" this, but went along with it out of either fear or respect for the school's chief administrator.[84] Ella found such practices demeaning and would not go along. She "had a strong voice," but she adamantly refused to participate in what she perceived as an undignified performance. Such an act of defiance by an undergraduate student, Baker concluded, must have "irked" the president.[85] For the rest of her life, as a matter of principle, Baker resisted any inclination to ingratiate herself with people in power.

During her junior year in college, Ella Baker once again confronted university officials. This time she was part of a large group of protesters who took a firm stance with a mild tone. On February 1, 1926, Ella Baker joined with fifty-seven other juniors and seniors in refusing to take the required Bible examination as it was administered by a particular faculty member, claiming that the test was being administered unfairly.[86] Students objected specifically to the fact that the professor had demanded they memorize their readings and lectures and had forbade the use of note-books during the exam, which was apparently a customary practice. Students submitted a formal letter of protest to the faculty council of the university indicating their refusal to sit for the exam and voicing their complaints about the way the course had been taught. The tone of the letter was mild, almost obsequious. The students stressed that they were not trying to be antagonistic, but they claimed disingenuously that they simply were unable to grasp the subject as it had been presented.[87]

After receiving a negative response from the administration, the majority of the students backed down, acquiesced to the admonitions of the administration, and took the exam at the designated time under threat of expulsion. A few stood fast. Ella Baker was not among them. It is unclear exactly why she made this decision. The fact that she was likely to be expelled if she persisted in her opposition was probably a formidable consideration. She may have contacted her parents and been advised to comply with the school's directive. She may have reconsidered the situation on her own and decided that, if she were going to take a stand on principle, this was not the right time or the right issue.

Significantly, Ella Baker had encountered serious difficulties in Bible class the year before. Her sophomore transcript shows a C− in religion, the lowest grade of her entire nine years at Shaw and a striking aberration in her otherwise stellar record.[88] Baker's problems with religion courses at Shaw may have involved simple incompatibility with particular instructors, but they may well have represented something more substantive. As the daughter of a devoutly religious woman and the granddaughter of a minister, Ella had been immersed in biblical teachings as a child. Neither her near-failing grade in her sophomore Bible class nor her near-refusal to take the exam in her junior Bible class reflected ignorance or an inability to comprehend the material. Perhaps she was beginning to ask questions about religion in a way that was not encouraged at Shaw. As Effie Yergan recalled, "There wasn't much room for discussion or debate in Bible class. They taught it like a history course, that's all."[89] Memorizing names, dates, and sequences of events was a far cry from contemplating complex theological issues or considering the contemporary implications of Christianity. Ella had been inquisitive even as a child, and in college she was an avid debater; she was not comfortable accepting things at face value. The method of religious instruction at Shaw apparently did not suit her intellectual or personal sensibilities.

· · · · · · ·

By the time Ella Baker completed her college education at Shaw, she had begun to carve out her own path. Most important, she chose not to pursue education as a professional career. In doing so, she rejected what was expected of well-educated, middle-class black women and what her mother had wanted for her. Baker later explained that she resented the fact that, in her mother's generation and her own, teaching was regarded as "inevitable"; she had a "rebellious streak," which led her to resist conformity.[90] Through her years at Shaw, Baker had developed a political critique of black educational institutions. Since schools were still largely under white control, teachers had to be conservative and subdued in order to get and keep their jobs. Women "couldn't teach unless somebody in the white hierarchy okayed your teaching," Baker complained. It was "a demeaning sort of thing, and I resented this, and I refused to teach."[91] "I had seen generations of graduates also go out and teach. And sometimes there had been people who had shown spirit fighting back in school but after they taught they came back and they were nothing. They had no spirit."[92] So, although Ella had several "good offers" of teaching jobs, she adamantly refused to accept any of them.[93] She was intent on preserving her own fighting spirit; she saw the socialization that women went through to become teachers and the resulting subordinate position they came to occupy as a threat to that spirit.

During her years at Shaw, Ella Baker was a rebel but not yet a radical, tactically prepared to question but not to defy the rules, and philosophically ready to argue against the limitations of the dominant authority but not to challenge its fundamental validity. Ella Baker retained a basic faith in the major institutions of American society, even as she recognized the existence of injustice and discrimination. She clung to the belief that, through her own individual effort, education, hard work, and faith, she could help to uplift the race and, by extension, all of humanity. Baker recalled that, at the tender age of twenty-three, she felt that "the world was out there waiting for you to provide a certain kind of leadership and give you an opportunity."[94]

Graduation day in April 1927 was a shining moment in Ella Baker's life. As the culmination of her sterling academic career, she was chosen valedictorian, one of two student speakers at commencement. Her proud parents sat in the audience, no doubt beaming at what she and they had accomplished. Ella's graduation address reflected her oratorical skill, her commitment to social justice, her youthful idealism, and her religiosity. In her words there is clear evidence that she was the progeny of deeply religious people and that she shared their faith. There is also a hint of the determined activist she soon became: "Awake youth of the land and accept this noble challenge of salvaging the strong ship of civilization, by the anchors of right, justice and love. . . . let us resolve that for the welfare of the whole, for the good of all, for the uplift of the fallen humanity, for the extension of Christ's kingdom on earth . . . there shall be no turning back . . . we will strike against evil, strife and war until the echo shall resound in the recesses of the earth and . . . the waters of the deep."[95] These words were indeed prophetic, although perhaps not precisely in the way Ella intended at the time. The optimism she expressed in 1927 was soon challenged by the onset of the Great Depression. The harsh realities of poverty and discrimination, coupled with her exposure to a whole array of left-wing political groups, radicalized her views and reoriented her thinking. As she moved from a religious to a more secular stance, the critical questioning and rebelliousness that marked her youth deepened and broadened. Ella Baker became a radical intellectual and activist with a vision of a new social order.

HARLEM DURING THE 1930S
THE MAKING OF A BLACK RADICAL ACTIVIST
AND INTELLECTUAL

• • • • •

[Harlem] is the fountainhead of mass movements. From it flows the progressive vitality of Negro life. Harlem is, as well, a cross-section of life in Black America—a little from here, there and everywhere. It is at once the capital of clowns, cults and cabarets, and the cultural and intellectual hub of the Negro world.

Roi Ottley, 1943

. . . a hotbed of radical thinking.

Ella Baker, 1977

When Ella Baker arrived in New York City in 1927, she walked up and down the streets of Harlem in sheer amazement. The intoxicating sounds of jazz floated in the air, competing with police sirens, domestic arguments, and soapbox speakers. The congestion, intensity, and excitement of urban life were all around her. At every turn Baker realized that she was further from home than she had ever been before: away from the South, from the sheltered confines of the Shaw campus, from her protective hometown community, and from the restrictive authority of her mother.[1]

Unlike others who had consciously chosen to move to Harlem because of its reputation as a center of modern African American cultural life, Ella Baker arrived there somewhat by chance. Her original plan when she finished college was to attend the University of Chicago, one of Professor Brawley's alma maters, to pursue graduate studies in sociology or medicine in preparation for a career as a medical missionary. She was all "gung ho" for the idea, but her family's finances were limited, and the Ross-Bakers had no relatives in Chicago to cushion the transition, either financially or socially. Anna Ross Baker was also reluctant to let her elder daughter get too far away from her supervision or at least from the watchful eye of someone she trusted. In New York there was cousin Martha Grinage, a woman slightly older than Ella, whom Anna had helped raise in North Carolina. This familial connection provided assurance that even if Ella did not find a job right away, she would at least have a roof over her head and food in her stomach, not to mention a respectable home to shelter her from the vices of the big city.

Ella got a taste of the real world the summer after she left Shaw and before she landed in New York. That summer she worked at a New Jersey resort hotel, what she termed a "roadhouse," that served food and provided entertainment for guests. She especially enjoyed the camaraderie of her fellow workers. For her, the job was temporary, but for some of her coworkers it was the only kind of job they could look forward to. This introduction to the world of work broadened Ella Baker's perspective. She recalled that she did not hesitate to stand up for herself: "If something came up that I didn't like, I'd react to it. I retained what I called my essential integrity . . . I neither kowtowed nor felt the need to lord over anyone else."[2]

The hotel employees were from diverse backgrounds. "We were all mixed up in nationality," Baker was to recall.[3] The mix also included show business types, aspiring actors, black and white students, and some Europeans. "That particular summer I met a very interesting group of young people," she commented years later.[4] This wild and irreverent crew in no way resembled the model of respectability that her parents and teachers had tried to cultivate. The owner was a wealthy eccentric who enjoyed mingling with the guests, whom Baker mockingly called the local "royalty." She took a liking to Ella because she was talkative and friendly. "I had to wait on the table of the owner of the place. . . . She wanted me to wait on her table because she had these royalties at the table and I talked. I'm not the court jester but one of the court's better spoken servers."[5] This summer job may have represented only a moment of youthful adventure, but it took Ella Baker far from home and brought her into contact with a colorful and eclectic group of people. Although the political culture was very different, it resembled the bohemian communities she would soon encounter in Greenwich Village and Harlem.

There was another development in Ella Baker's life at this juncture that likely did not please her mother. During her last year of college at Shaw, after an impressive academic career with few distractions other than an occasional protest, Ella had fallen in love with a smart, gentle-spirited, handsome young man named T. J. Roberts (also known as T. J. Robinson).[6] The relationship progressed rapidly, and by the time Baker was due to leave North Carolina for New York, it was quite serious.[7] But her romantic interest in one man was not enough to lessen the seductive lure of the big city. By all indications, Roberts himself was looking for a way to move north, and the two lovers would soon be reunited.

When Ella Baker did finally arrive in New York, she was seduced, not by Harlem's fiery nightlife, but rather by its vibrant political life. During the late 1920s and the 1930s, Baker came of age politically and began to formulate the worldview and theoretical framework that influenced her organizing work for the next fifty years. In this historic decade, she evolved from an idealistic and tentative young rebel into a savvy and determined organizer committed to achieving justice through radical social change. In Harlem, Baker debated passionately with left-wing men and embraced a community of dynamic young women whom her friend Pauli Murray later described as black feminist foremothers.[8]

Ella Baker was among the tens of thousands of African Americans who migrated to the North during the 1920s. Hopeful migrants followed their dreams of a better life to such urban hubs as New York and Chicago, contributing to one of the most dramatic interregional migrations in this nation's history. Although few of those who participated in the Great Migration found the promised land they were looking for, they dramatically transformed the social landscape they encountered, forging a new sense of community, creating a dynamic culture, and developing new strategies for resistance to racial oppression and economic exploitation.[9]

What emerged in the African American capital of Harlem during the decades following World War I was a discourse and practice based on the politics and vision of fundamental social transformation, that is, a semi-autonomous black left. The development of this heterogeneous political community was fueled by several factors: the rise of a black intelligentsia consciously critical of conservative accommodationism, liberal uplift ideology, and narrow black nationalism; the influx of blacks from the diaspora who helped to internationalize and radicalize the ideas and politics of U.S.-born blacks; and finally, the increasingly independent voice of black women activists, artists, and writers.

Ella Baker's new-found community was now a distinctly international one. Harlem's new residents came not only from the farms and fields of the

U.S. South, but also from Jamaica, Barbados, Antigua, Guyana, Trinidad, and, in smaller numbers, various parts of Africa. By 1930, 55 percent of all foreign-born blacks in the United States lived in Harlem. Among them were W. A. Domingo, Claudia Jones, Cyril V. Briggs, Otto Huiswood, Grace Campbell, and Richard Moore, all of whom became key forces in shaping Harlem's black left community from the 1910s through the 1930s.[10]

Baker recalled fondly that Harlem during the years of the Great Depression was "a hotbed of radical thinking."[11] The political and cultural rumblings of the late 1910s and early 1920s had infused a new spirit of resistance and intellectual energy into the community. The cultural revolution known as the Harlem Renaissance, the black pride movement led by the Jamaican-born Marcus Garvey, and the agitation and education carried on by a small group of black socialists known as the Harlem radicals had effectively re-colored and revitalized Harlem's political and cultural landscape a decade before Ella Baker's arrival. These developments, coupled with the economic suffering caused by the onset of the depression in 1929 and socialist rumblings increasingly heard around the world, laid the foundation for the "unprecedented explosion of protest activity" that occurred during the 1930s.[12] For Ella Baker and many others, Harlem was a politically and intellectually invigorating place to be. Intense political debates raged everywhere, spawning militant protests in the streets. There were rent strikes, picket lines, marches, street corner rallies, and the famous Harlem riot of 1935, which was triggered by an incident of alleged police brutality. Looking back during the late 1970s on the vibrant and volatile political climate that she had encountered in Harlem almost fifty years before, Baker remarked that "I was filling my cup"; "I drank of the 'nectar divine'."[13]

· · · · · ·

THE EDUCATION OF A RADICAL INTELLECTUAL

Ella Baker's first task in New York City, after her summer stopover in New Jersey, was finding a job. Searching for work that paid enough to enable her to support herself provided her with a radically new kind of education, even before the depression was in full swing. Baker quickly realized that, as a black woman, her career options were sorely limited. Even her coveted college diploma was not much help. On her arrival in the city, Ella moved in with her cousin Martha and worked at whatever odd jobs she could find.[14] She knocked on the doors of employment agencies all over town and was unable to find work. She was even turned down for a job addressing envelopes because there were so many others competing for the low-paying job.[15] Baker's situation was not unusual. African American women in general were concentrated at the bottom of the economic hierarchy.[16] This discovery came as a shock to the wide-eyed young woman. Baker had left North Carolina with great ambitions and high hopes, believing that great opportunities awaited her.[17] The reality she encountered shattered her naive optimism. She had only seen glimpses of the world beyond her sheltered childhood community and the gated campus of Shaw, but in New York City, largely on her own, she confronted the harshness of the larger society head-on.

One of the first full-time jobs Ella Baker found in the city was waitressing at New York University's Judson House restaurant in Greenwich Village. The work was hard and the pay low, but the job offered other rewards. Since she worked only the busy lunch and dinner hours, Ella could spend her free time exploring the neighborhood. Like Harlem, the Village was a vital center of political and cultural activity during the late 1920s. Left-wing meeting places, coffeehouses, and bookstores in Greenwich Village provided almost as much stimulation for Baker as did the black intellectual and arts community uptown. During her afternoon breaks, she would visit the public library or stroll through Washington Square Park. She especially enjoyed the spring, when the park was being groomed for the summer season; the smell of freshly plowed soil reminded her of the farm community of her youth.[18] It was in Greenwich Village that she first heard about the ideas of socialism and communism.

Still as eager as she had been as a child to engage strangers in conversation, Ella would meet people on the streets of New York and begin a discussion. Quite by accident one day, she struck up a conversation with a young man who, she quickly learned, was a Russian Jew eager to exchange ideas about the Bolshevik revolution and socialist movements in general. As she recalled the encounter, "I was just standing there looking at pigeons or whatever else and this chap starts talking and he began to try to recruit me into one party or the other."[19] They talked for what seemed like hours. Baker was fascinated. She didn't join his party because she "didn't have the burning need to just jump into an organization," but she became curious about socialism, Marxist theory, and subjects she "had not heard of before."[20] But the chance meeting in the park had sparked her interest, and she began to read more about radical ideas on her own. According to one friend and co-worker during the 1930s, "Ella Baker was a student of Marx and we used to debate that often."[21]

Baker had an insatiable urge to learn as much as she could about politics and world affairs, so she took advantage of every opportunity to attend lectures and engage in discussions about these subjects. Two vital Harlem institutions became important intellectual training grounds for Baker and her friends. One was the 135th Street library, later renamed the Schomburg Center for Research in Black Culture, and the other was the Harlem Branch YWCA (close in proximity and function to the YMCA). Both institutions were teeming with political activity, hosting regular forums on issues ranging from socialism to segregation. They became key gathering places for many young Harlem artists, intellectuals, and activists. On his arrival in New York in 1921, the poet Langston Hughes recounted: "I came up out of the subway at 135th and Lenox into the beginnings of the Negro Renaissance. I headed for the Harlem YMCA down the block, where so many new, young dark . . . arrivals in Harlem have spent their early days. The next place I headed to that afternoon was the Harlem Branch Library just up the street."[22] These two institutions were the dual pillars of Harlem's intellectual and political life for over two decades.

Her intellectual curiosity and growing passion for politics led Baker to spend more and more time at the Harlem library, where she met and befriended white librarian Ernestine Rose, twenty years her senior. Beginning in 1925, Rose oversaw the founding and expansion of the Negro Division within the library and mentored a young interracial staff to maintain the collection.[23] At the library, Baker helped establish the first Negro History Club, which met regularly to discuss historical and contemporary events relevant to blacks. The group routinely sponsored forums and other educational events for the Harlem community. Sometimes heated discussions would spill over into the street; interested discussants would gather around an able orator perched atop a crate, or standing on a stepladder, as she or he preached about colonialism, the class struggle, or American racism. The library occasionally even paid some soapbox speakers for their oratory, a political tradition that was imported to Harlem by Caribbean immigrants.[24] Baker recalled, "If you hadn't stood on the corner of 135th and & 7th Avenue [protesting and debating] . . . you weren't with it."[25] There is no evidence that Baker herself ever climbed on one of these makeshift stages to display her oratorical abilities, but in May 1936 she helped organize a street-corner discussion on lynching sponsored by the library.[26]

Baker joined the library's Adult Education Committee around 1933. The Harlem Adult Education Experiment, as it was called, sponsored forums, lectures, and debates on a wide range of topics.[27] According to Elinor Des

Verney Sinette, who wrote a history of the Harlem library, it was "especially innovative in the character and breadth of its activities. In addition to the traditional library services, the Harlem Experiment used the library and its resources to offer courses in the graphic and performing arts, to sponsor lectures and book discussions for local residents and to make its facilities available for community forums."[28] Baker's involvement in the Adult Education Experiment was evidence of her profound interest in African American social and political history and of her commitment to spreading that knowledge to as wide an audience as possible. Up to this point in her life, knowledge had been a source of personal empowerment; now, as she became more political, she came to see education and knowledge as tools in the struggle against oppression. From her perspective, reading, discussions, forums, and lectures were as important to a movement for social change as mass protests, boycotts, and strikes.

Baker became an employee of the Harlem branch library in January 1934, when she was hired to coordinate an educational and consciousness-raising program for Harlem youth and young adults, aged sixteen to twenty-six. She "organized and developed the Young People's Forum (YPF) in 1936 and later worked with the adult Education Committee on its summer programs for mothers in Colonial and St. Nicholas Avenue Parks."[29] According to Baker's supervisor, she "successfully formed an active organization, which she brought in touch with other youth groups in the neighborhood and city."[30] As early as the 1930s, Baker served as a catalyst linking together different sectors of the black community, breaking down generational barriers and facilitating exchanges of skills and resources. In the YPF, she introduced Harlem teenagers to an impressive roster of prominent speakers, emphasizing the need for active participation by the youth themselves. As Baker exposed many young people to the world of books and ideas, she sought to instill in them a sense of their own power to think critically, analyze events, and articulate their opinions and beliefs. The YPF included discussions about "social, economic, and cultural topics," as well as library-sponsored debates on various controversial issues of the day.[31] In her work with the YPF and in many other contexts, Ella Baker was a teacher without a traditional classroom. The belief that education and the exchange and dissemination of ideas could make a difference in people's lives was to remain central to her life's work.

The 137th Street YWCA was another important gathering place, attracting many strong-minded, young, single women who were seeking the excitement, intellectual freedom, and the cultural stimulation that only Harlem could provide. Pauli Murray, who later became a prominent civil rights lawyer, religious leader, and feminist poet, rented a room at the Y in 1929. Murray described the Harlem YWCA as a focus of political and social activity, and a "heady" place to be at that time. On its staff were such bright and determined black women as Dorothy Height, later the head of the National Council of Negro Women, Anna Arnold Hedgeman, the YWCA's membership secretary, Viola Lewis Waiters, and Margaret Douglass; all went on to illustrious careers as professionals, public figures, and political activists.[32] According to Murray, "None of these women would have called themselves feminists in the 1930's, but they were strong independent personalities who, because of their concerted efforts to rise above the limitations of race and sex, and to help younger women do the same, shared a sisterhood that foreshadowed the revival of the feminist movement in the 1960s."[33] Baker spent many hours in the Y cafeteria and meeting rooms. In this thriving community of black women, she found the inspiration and intellectual challenges that aided her in defining her own personal and political identity.

Pauli Murray, Ella Baker, and the friends who congregated at the YWCA represented a new model of black womanhood in this era. Untrammeled by attachments to either birth families or husbands, these women were adventuresome, educated, and ambitious. The social climate of the times and the abysmal conditions of suffering created by the depression helped to channel much of their energy and ambition into radical political activity. Some of them worked with the Communist and Socialist Parties but many more of them were "fellow travelers" in a loosely connected circle of oppositional forces. If there was a rally about the Scottsboro case to defend young black men against trumped-up charges of raping two white women on a train, they called up one another and went as a group. If there was a picket line organized by the "Don't Buy Where You Can't Work" campaign, which used consumer boycotts to persuade stores with black customers to hire black employees, leaflets would be dropped off at the Y for distribution. This was a loose, informal network of women activists, many of whom did not join or pledge allegiance to any of the organized left factions but were actively engaged with a wide range of issues.[34]

Women were integral to Harlem's political life, both as individuals and in organized groups. Some organizations, such as the Harlem Housewives League and the Domestic Workers Union, represented collective action around the common interests of women. In her study of African American women's political activism, the historian Deborah Gray White argues convincingly that "seldom did African American women organize across class lines."[35] In the unique political environment of depression-era Harlem, however, such cross-class unity was indeed attempted and occasionally achieved. Maids, cooks, and unemployed workers bonded with leftist, middle-class teachers in adult education classes. Ordinary Harlem residents worked with journalists and other professionals in the cooperative movement. And the library, the YMCA and YWCA, and the street corners were democratic public spaces where community members, either formally educated or self-taught, gathered, debated, and collaborated. In all these venues, women were central participants.

Pauli Murray stood out among this group of smart and spirited young women. She was articulate, well read, witty, and fiercely interested in politics and social justice. She and Ella Baker became fast friends. Their lives had interesting parallels. Both women grew up in North Carolina; both migrated to Harlem around the same time; and both obtained jobs in the Workers Education Project of the Works Progress Administration. Both were involved in the Jay Lovestone political faction during the 1930s and affiliated with the (Lovestone-influenced) Liberal Party during the 1940s and 1950s. Years later, when Baker was working for the NAACP and the Student Nonviolent Coordinating Committee, Murray lent support and sang the praises of her old friend.[36] After she left Harlem, Murray attended Howard University Law School, taught law at Yale and Brandeis, eventually entered the ministry, and wrote four books. The two women remained in touch off and on for over forty years.

Baker's political awakening was stimulated by the lively social and intellectual community she encountered in Harlem, and her close comradeship with other women activists such as Murray nurtured her political maturation. Her development as a radical intellectual took place through a systematic educational process that went on both inside and outside cultural institutions. Baker later described herself as one of the "ignorant ones" when she first arrived in Harlem with her college degree in hand.[37] In retrospect, she felt that she had gained a clearer understanding of the world around her and of how to go about changing it through her political education by activists, many of whom had less formal education than she. In lauding Baker's credentials in a 1932 article in the NAACP's magazine, *The Crisis*, her mentor, George Schuyler, underscored the learning process that occurred through Baker's participation in the low-wage work force. "By force of circumstances," he observed, "her 'post graduate' work has included domestic service, factory work and other freelance labors, to which 'courses' she credits her education."[38] Baker learned many valuable lessons about history, politics, and people through her experiences as a political organizer, journalist, worker, and teacher, as well as through her discussions and interactions with other activists in a wide array of settings.

• • • • • •

The streets of Harlem provided a cultural and political immersion like no other. At no other time in twentieth-century African American history was there a more vibrant black public sphere than in Harlem in the 1920s and '30s, infused as it was with the exciting intellectual rhythms of the black diaspora. The serious exchange of ideas, cultural performances, and political debates flowed out of classrooms, private homes, meeting halls and bars onto the neighborhood thoroughfare of Lenox Avenue.

As historian Irma Watkins-Owens writes: "From World War I through the 1930's, the unclaimed terrain of the Harlem streetcorner became the testing ground for a range of political ideologies and a forum for intellectual inquiry and debate." These self-styled orators are sometimes described as "soapboxers," but because of their choice of political platform Watkins-Owens calls them "stepladder speakers."[39] Among them were well-known Harlem radicals like Baker's friend Frank Crosswaith of the Harlem Labor Center and Hubert Harrison, a socialist and onetime Marcus Garvey supporter. Women participating on the stepladder circuit included Audley "Queen Mother" Moore, Grace Campbell, Williana J. Burrroughs, and Elizabeth Frederickson. The struggle to determine Harlem's public culture was as much a class and ethnic struggle as a struggle over which speakers and ideas would predominate. Respectable Harlemites saw the sometimes raucous crowds that gathered as a source of embarrassment; preachers looked down on the crude language that was sometimes expressed; and police actually arrested several speakers for disturbing the peace. Still, the tradition continued.[40] Streetcorner discussions were an informal site of Ella Baker's political education in the 1930s, but there were more formal courses of study as well.

In 1931, Baker spent a semester at the Brookwood Labor College in Katonah, New York. There she had an opportunity to learn about theories and models of social change, as well as the history of working people. Brookwood, where Pauli Murray had also spent time, was established in 1921 by a group of socialists and pacifists in order to offer union organizers and other progressives a socially relevant curriculum.[41] It was one of a number of worker education schools set up around that time to train labor organizers. The teachers at Brookwood went far beyond their stated mission. They were radical, not only in what they taught but also in how they taught, experimenting with new teaching methods and encouraging students to think and speak for themselves. In her book on the Brookwood educators and their cohorts, the historian Susan Kates describes how these teachers sought "to enact forms of writing and speaking instruction incorporating social and political concerns in the very essence of their pedagogies."[42] This was Baker's first encounter with an open, democratic approach to formal education. She saw enormous transformative potential in democratic and nontraditional learning environments like Brookwood. She took ideas, theoretical paradigms, and philosophies seriously, and she spent much of her adult life mastering ways of how to pass that knowledge on to others and empower them in the process.

Ella Baker's political work from the late 1930s onward was consistent with a worldview that she constructed from the wide range of ideologies and traditions she had engaged with over the years. She combined the black Baptist missionary values of charity, humility, and service with the economic theories of Marxists and socialists of various stripes who advocated a redistribution of society's wealth and a transfer of power from capitalist elites to the poor and working classes. Added to the mix was Baker's popular democratic pedagogy, which emphasized the importance of tapping oppressed communities for knowledge, strength, and leadership in constructing models for social change.

In many respects, Baker herself was what Gramscian theorists refer to as an "organic intellectual." Her primary base of knowledge came from grassroots communities and from lived experience, not from formal study. She was a partisan intellectual, never feigning a bloodless objectivity, but always insisting that ideas should be employed in the service of oppressed people and toward the goal of social justice. In the 1930s, New York was her classroom, and Baker was both student and teacher.

In his biographical study of Ivory Perry, a St. Louis activist, George Lipsitz offers a useful definition of an organic intellectual in practice:

> Traditional intellectuals can distinguish themselves purely through the originality of their ideas or the eloquence of their expression, but organic intellectuals must initiate a process that involves people in social contestation. . . . Organic intellectuals try to understand and change society at the same time. . . . Organic intellectuals generate and circulate oppositional ideas through social action. They create symbols and slogans that expose the commonalities among seemingly atomized experi-

ences, and they establish principles that unite disparate groups into effective coalitions. Most significantly, they challenge dominant interests through education and agitation that expose the gap between the surface harmonies that seem to unite society and the real conflicts and antagonisms that divide it.[43]

This description characterizes much of the public intellectual work that Ella Baker did, beginning with the Harlem Adult Education Experiment and the Young People's Forum and continuing with the Young Negroes' Cooperative League and with the Workers Education Project later in the decade. By the time she was thirty, she had become a radical intellectual committed to teaching and learning from the people in movements for social change, an approach that would continue to distinguish her political work.

· · · · · ·

THE YOUNG NEGROES' COOPERATIVE LEAGUE
AND THE DREAM OF A NEW SOCIAL ORDER

In the early 1930s, grim economic realities, the looming threat of a second world war, and the rise of European fascism had a strong, sobering effect on the young activists and intellectuals Ella Baker associated with. Their debates about politics, economics, and social change took on timely relevance and had concrete implications for the lives of the masses of black Harlemites. The historic backdrop of the depression era imbued their exchanges with a new sense of urgency.

The Great Depression hit Harlem hard. Forced evictions of entire families in the dead of winter were common sights, as were the hungry faces of poverty-stricken children and long lines of desperate job-seekers. Anna Arnold Hedgeman, who was on the staff of the Harlem YWCA that Baker frequented, recalled:

With the financial collapse in 1929, a large mass of Negroes was faced with the reality of starvation and they turned sadly to public relief. A few chanted optimistically, "Jesus will lead me, and Welfare will feed me," but . . . meanwhile men, women and children searched in garbage cans for food, foraging with dogs and cats. Many families had been reduced to living below street level . . . in cellars and basements that had been converted into makeshift flats. Packed in damp, rat-ridden dungeons, they existed in squalor not too different from that of the Arkansas sharecroppers.[44]

Seeing black people living in southern-style poverty in the North's most modern city shook many Harlemites' assumptions about which pathways would lead to progress for the race. These scenes of suffering had a tremendous impact on Baker's evolving political consciousness.

Baker's political journalism reveals her responses to the depression. An article she coauthored in 1935 with African American communist Marvel Cooke, vividly describes the abysmal plight of black New Yorkers. Titled "The Bronx Slave Market," the article highlights the connections among wage labor, slavery, race, and sex. Baker documented the humiliating experiences of black domestic workers who huddled together on designated street corners in the early morning hours, waiting for white middle-class women to look them over and choose a lucky one to hire for the day. Baker, who, according to a friend, had worked briefly as a maid herself, posed as a job seeker in order to get an insider's view of what these women were going through. The humiliation that such self-exposure entailed was compounded, so Baker found, by the desperate act that some women were driven to: that of selling their bodies to the highest bidder:

> The Simpson Avenue block exudes the stench of the slave market at its worst. Not only is human labor bartered and sold for slave wage, but human love also is a marketable commodity. . . . Rain or shine, cold or hot, you will find them there—Negro women, old and young, sometimes bedraggled, sometimes neatly dressed—but with the invariable paper bundle, waiting expectantly for Bronx housewives to buy their strength and energy for an hour, two hours, or even for a day. . . . If not the wives themselves, maybe their husbands, their sons, their brothers, under the subterfuge of work, offer worldly-wise girls higher bids for their time.[45]

Baker and Cooke's vivid account of these scenes illustrates how deeply both women were affected by the depression and its dehumanizing impact on poor black women.[46]

"The Bronx Slave Market" reflects Ella Baker's lucid assessment of the complex realities of race, gender, and class in the lives of African American women. The women Baker observed on Simpson Avenue were victimized by their position as blacks, as workers, and as women. Baker's description meshes these analytical abstractions together in the intricate web of lived human experience. Although poor black women were sexually exploited as women, there was no magical, raceless and classless sisterhood between them and the white female employers, who were just as eager to use them for their muscle as their husbands were to use them for their sexual services. The economic rigors of the depression had intensified all forms of oppression, pushing many black women from the lower rungs of the wage labor force back to day work and even into occasional prostitution. When Baker and Cooke wrote their article, the modern concept of feminism was still a foreign notion to most Americans, black and white. Yet the black feminist notion of intersecting systems of oppression as a cornerstone of black women's collective experience was an observable reality, and in their article Cooke and Baker came close to articulating it as a theory.[47]

Ella Baker and Marvel Jackson Cooke traveled in overlapping political and social circles. They knew one another by reputation and through mutual friends but had not formally met until they were asked by an editor at *The Crisis* to coauthor an article on the plight of poor black women in the Bronx. Over the course of several weeks, as the two women researched, discussed, and wrote their story, they got to know one another and gradually became friends. After the publication of "The Bronx Slave Market," Baker and Cooke were on a few panels together and saw one another from time to time at social and political events in Harlem.[48] They developed a mutual respect and admiration for one another that, according to Cooke's recollections decades later, continued despite their political differences. Ella Baker spoke quite fondly of Marvel in an interview as late as the 1970s.[49]

Marvel Jackson Cooke, the daughter of black Debsian socialists from Minnesota, came to New York in 1927, the same year that Baker did, and quickly landed a job as W. E. B. Du Bois's secretary and assistant. Her mother had known Du Bois previously and thus helped her to secure the job. Du Bois introduced Marvel Jackson (later Marvel Cooke) to a whole array of political ideas, and according to his biographer, David Lewis, also may have made unwanted sexual advances toward the naive young woman.[50] She made other political and personal connections on her own, and she eventually chose to join the underground section of the Communist Party (CP). She became a "mainstay" of the "popular front" publication the *People's Voice* and grew to be very close to Paul and Essie Robeson and other well-known CP members and sympathizers who congregated in Harlem. Cooke lived in the popular 321 Edgecomb Avenue apartment building that was at one time or another the home of George and Josephine Schuyler, the journalist Ted Poston, and NAACP executives Walter White and Roy Wilkins.[51] Her sister's marriage to Wilkins could have connected Cooke to a wider network of people, but she and her brother-in-law were at odds politically; so the relationship was never close. Cooke's clandestine party membership circumscribed her involvement in other political activities, a fact that she regretted many decades later.[52] Her closest friends were, for the most part, her party comrades.

The differences as well as the connections between Baker and Cooke are revealing. The two women were close in age, lived nearby, and shared a left-leaning political orientation and passion for ideas. Yet their social and political lives were not analogous. While Cooke associated primarily with other members of the Communist Party, Ella Baker's circle was much broader and more eclectic. She maintained close relationships with some cp members, and she worked with many others on particular campaigns. Baker did not confine her associations to people of a single ideological stripe or political party. In the early 1930s, she admittedly had more questions than answers. She sought out people with whom she could study social conditions and political strategy and places where wide-ranging discussion and debate flourished. This curiosity inescapably brought Baker into contact with not only communists and socialists but also the followers of Marcus Mosiah Garvey, who were a visible and vocal force on the Harlem political scene, despite Garvey's deportation the year Ella Baker arrived there. A Jamaican immigrant and admirer of Booker T. Washington, Garvey arrived in Harlem in 1916 and began recruiting members to his Universal Negro Improvement Association (unia). His message of African pride and economic self-sufficiency for blacks, coupled with his flamboyant pageantry, won him thousands of followers and the ire of both the federal government and black political leaders like W. E. B. Du Bois, who saw his politics as escapist and self-promoting. Ella Baker's close friend William Pickens, an naacp official, was one of Garvey's most ardent critics. But unia's popularity piqued Ella Baker's interest: she regularly read the organization's paper, the *Negro World*, and, according to Conrad Lynn, even attended public forums organized by the group.[53] Baker spent much of her early years in Harlem in public venues soaking up the culture, the politics, and the intellectual fervor. She even enjoyed dining at the restaurant run by Father Divine's organization on occasion, because it was another lively site for political and intellectual engagement with ordinary Harlem residents.[54]

For most of the 1930s, however, Ella Baker's closest political ally was the iconoclastic writer and activist George Schuyler, a socialist, philosophical anarchist, and critic of Soviet-style communism. He became a mentor to Baker, and through him and his wife, Josephine, a young, white artist from Texas, Baker was absorbed into a lively community of writers, artists, and radical intellectuals from across the nation and around the world who were living in Harlem at the time. Baker and Schuyler were introduced to each other by a mutual friend, L. M. Cole, a reporter for the *Baltimore Afro-American*, and the two hit it off right away. Schuyler was a smart, creative, provocative, and critical thinker who, according to Baker, impressed her because he "would raise questions that weren't being raised."[55]

Baker soon became a regular member of the circle that gathered at the Schuylers' home, which was large, lively, and exceptionally open, as Marvel Cooke recalled. People would bring friends or acquaintances without a specific invitation from the hosts.[56] In this setting, Baker found others who were grappling with the same moral, philosophical, and political dilemmas that she was wrestling with at the time. She enjoyed their company, but, she later recalled, she "didn't care as much about the socializing as the exchange of ideas, or at least being exposed to the debate."[57] The Schuylers' apartment, like the YWCA cafeteria, the forums at the library, and the public parks and street corners of Harlem, was a site for an animated discourse that helped define African American public life. In these venues, politics and culture were debated and areas of consensus were formed and reformed.[58] The activists, writers and artists who convened regularly at the Schuylers' apartment had a certain romantic appeal about them. They were young, creative, bold, witty, and cosmopolitan. Some were known to be pretty "snappy dressers," too.[59] Their spirited conversations often lasted until dawn, and participants left intellectually energized and physically exhausted. Ella Baker took part in many of these late-night parlays, enjoying the stimulating company, provocative conversations, and elegant hospitality. The Schuylers resided at one of Harlem's more prestigious addresses, in the "Park Lincoln Apartments on Edgecomb Avenue on what Harlemites called the upscale area of 'Sugar Hill.'" A reporter described the building as one "where a rich canopy runs out to the sidewalk, and where a liveried footman in gold braid must announce a visitor before he is permitted to go up in the automatic elevator."[60] In other words, the group's criticisms of capitalist decadence were made in very comfortable surroundings.

Despite this obvious material contradiction, most members of Schuyler's circle were not simply armchair radicals; they were organizers as well. Schuyler was as much of a doer as he was a talker and a writer. By all indications, he was genuinely committed to improving the conditions of the poor, even though he had managed to secure a fairly cushy lifestyle for himself.

A belligerent and colorful character in Harlem politics during the 1920s and 1930s, Schuyler became even more controversial thereafter.[61] Born in

Providence, Rhode Island, in 1895, he served in the army during World War I and then settled in New York City. In 1923 he joined the staff of the Harlem-based socialist magazine the *Messenger*, working alongside Chandler Owen and A. Philip Randolph; the latter became one of the country's best-known labor leaders as head of the Brotherhood of Sleeping Car Porters and then as a founder of the Congress of Industrial Organizations.[62] Schuyler became contributing editor of the magazine after Owen's departure in the winter of 1923. As a protégé of Randolph, Schuyler was pulled into a circle of black radical intellectuals that included Frank Crosswaith, a black labor leader; Robert Bagnall, an NAACP official; and J. A. Rogers, a journalist and self-taught historian. These Harlem leftists were united by their opposition to the separatist nationalism of Marcus Garvey. Under the banner of the short-lived organization the Friends of Negro Freedom, the group met weekly at Randolph's apartment to discuss contemporary politics, history, and philosophy. Those Sunday gatherings made quite a strong impression on Schuyler, who recalled that nothing "escaped the group's probing minds and witty shafts."[63] By the late 1920s, the *Messenger* had ceased to exist, the group had disintegrated, and Schuyler had begun writing a popular column, "Views and Reviews," for the nationally circulated African American newsweekly the *Pittsburgh Courier*. The column surveyed domestic politics and race issues and occasionally commented on foreign affairs.

Ella Baker and George Schuyler became very close friends despite their very distinct personalities. Schuyler was an arrogant, irreverent, and sometimes ostentatious young writer, who took particular pleasure in intellectual sparring matches with worthy opponents. He was a close friend and admirer of the iconoclastic, white editor of the *American Mercury*, H. L. Mencken; in fact, he was sometimes referred to as the black Mencken.[64] Schuyler took great delight in ridiculing groups and individuals that he deemed corrupt, backward, or inept. His targets covered the gamut from black ministers and petit bourgeois black entrepreneurs to Communist organizers. According to his longtime colleague A. Philip Randolph, Schuyler took few things seriously.[65] In contrast, Baker was pensive and unassuming. Despite her wit and good-natured humor, she took everything seriously, and, as one friend recalls, she always "seemed mature beyond her years."[66]

By the early 1930s, Ella Baker was no longer a devoutly religious person, but she still appreciated the cohesive role of the church as a spiritual and material resource for black people.[67] In contrast, Schuyler was an avowed and outspoken atheist who saw Christianity and religion as stumbling blocks to black progress. At times, his criticisms of the black church were so ruthless and relentless that anyone who was uncritical of organized religion on some level would have been unable to work closely with him. Presumably, Baker had developed her own doubts and criticisms of the church as an institution by this time.[68] Her doubts later evolved into a more developed critique of the mainstream black church in general and of the black clergy in particular. Yet, despite or perhaps because of their contrasting characteristics, Schuyler and Baker were the best of friends and the closest of comrades for several years. They complemented each other in their joint political endeavors, with Baker guaranteeing that business matters were taken care of and Schuyler serving as a figurehead and spokesperson for the cause. In her relationship with Schuyler, Baker took on a role she continued to play for much of her political life, that of a behind-the-scenes organizer who paid attention to the mechanics of movement building in a way that few high-profile charismatic leaders did, or even knew how to do.

Ella Baker was frequently a resource for the Schuylers in personal as well as political matters. When the Schuylers' daughter, Phillipa, was born in 1932, George was, as usual, away on business, and he asked Ella to assist his wife. Ella stayed with Josephine for a few days after the baby was born, keeping her company and helping her with chores around the apartment.[69] Ella and Josephine became very good friends. Baker recalled that the wives of many of Schuyler's black colleagues disapproved of his interracial marriage, which was quite uncommon in those days, and did not welcome Josephine into their social circle.[70] For Baker, that was simply not an issue.

But there were other issues in the Schuylers' marriage that caused her some difficulty.[71] Much later, Baker hinted that George may have had extramarital affairs and further intimated that she had kept George's philandering a secret from his wife. Her disapproval and silence reflected Ella Baker's complicated and often conflicted relationship with black men in leadership positions. She was close enough to their day-to-day lives to witness the backstage drama, the character flaws, the sexism, and the contradictions between their high ideals and their imperfect, even duplicitous actions. Although she was often critical, her criticism may have been muted by the political goals she shared with her colleagues. Baker acquiesced to the permeable and artificial divide between the personal and the political only with regard to sexual matters.[72] She was aware that Schuyler, and later some of her colleagues in the Southern Christian Leadership Conference, were cheating on their wives and professing moral rectitude according to conventional standards, but she did not expose their behavior or frame it in political terms, even though she clearly viewed it as an expression of male sexual privilege, an option not socially acceptable for their wives or, for that matter, for Baker herself. Despite George Schuyler's male chauvinism and adulterous behavior behind closed doors, Ella Baker was still willing to work with him politically.[73] Many years later, she revealed his secrets, but even then she was not explicit: "Of course George was male and had opportunities to exercise his maleness by traveling. I wouldn't claim that George was a saint and all."[74] Still, she accepted him as a flawed person, yet a reliable colleague.

The idea of forming black consumer cooperatives as a strategy to combat the economic devastation being wreaked by the depression and to educate black people about socialism galvanized the group of intellectuals and activists that gathered around Schuyler. He proposed the idea in his column in the *Pittsburgh Courier* and received a positive response from readers. In the spring of 1930, Schuyler issued a call to young blacks interested in the "economic salvation" of the race through cooperative economics to come forth and establish a new organization for the purpose of studying the idea and "carrying the message to all corners of Negro America."[75] He emphasized that the young recruits had to be "militants, pioneers, unswerved by the defeatist propaganda of the oldsters, and the religious hokum of our generally . . . parasitic clergy."[76] By November, he had only received a handful of responses. Undeterred, Schuyler joined forces with Ella Baker and called a meeting of those who were interested in the idea. The Young Negroes' Cooperative League (YNCL) was formed in 1930. In October 1931, the group held its first annual conference at the YMCA in Pittsburgh, with Robert Vann, publisher of the *Pittsburgh Courier*, delivering the introductory remarks. The event was attended by thirty delegates "who paid their own carfare to come" from as far away as Washington D.C. and South Carolina.[77] Despite the small number of official delegates, the conference's opening session drew a capacity crowd of over 600 people. Baker shared the speaker's platform with Schuyler and Vann, addressing the important role of black women in the emerging cooperative movement. Schuyler became the first president of the YNCL, and Baker was unanimously elected to serve as its national director.[78]

The YNCL was a coalition of local cooperatives and buying clubs loosely affiliated in a network of nearly two dozen affiliate councils scattered throughout the United States. Each council functioned independently but contributed funds for the national office, which was based in New York City. The YNCL circulated a newsletter, served as a clearinghouse for information, attempted to bolster the cooperative concept through national publicity efforts, and offered workshops and training sessions for co-op leaders. In her capacity as executive director of the organization, Baker staffed the national office and traveled around the country consulting with local council leaders and promoting the value of cooperative ventures, for which she received a salary of $10 a week.[79] As the masthead of the group's stationery proclaimed, its principal purpose was to "gain economic power through consumer cooperation."[80] Baker emphasized her own commitment to that mission in 1932, when she stated: "We accept with zest the opportunity which is now ours to prove to ourselves and others that the Negro can and will save himself from economic death."[81]

The founding statement of the YNCL reflected many of the principles of grassroots democracy and group-centered leadership that Ella Baker advocated for the rest of her political life. The coalition pledged itself to the full inclusion and equal participation of women. An explicit emphasis on gender equality was unusual for any political organization, black or white, during this period; this commitment suggests that Baker's remarks about the vital role women could play in the cooperative movement were well received, and it certainly underscores the group's inclusive and egalitarian orientation. The YNCL took steps to ensure the full participation of its rank and file in decision making and leadership. Since membership in individual co-ops had to be purchased through the buying of shares, larger shareholders could conceivably have wielded greater influence in determining the priorities of the co-ops than smaller shareholders. To avoid such inequalities, the YNCL adopted the position that each member was allotted only one vote, regardless of the number of cooperative shares he or she owned. In a pamphlet titled "An Appeal to Young Negroes," George Schuyler declared the organization's commitment to grassroots democracy: "We are ultra democratic and all power rests in the hands of the rank and file. All officers serve only during the pleasure of the electorate."[82] This emphasis on participatory democracy is all the more significant in a political climate where the major organizations trying to organize among blacks— the NAACP, the CP, and the UNIA—were under fire for elitist, authoritarian, or messianic leadership styles.

Another founding principle of the YNCL was that young people should be in the forefront of the struggle for social change. If the energy, optimism, and rebelliousness of youth could be harnessed and directed into constructive political channels, the black movement would be revitalized. The YNCL restricted its membership to young adults thirty-five years old and younger. Older adults could be admitted only after a two-thirds vote of approval by the local membership. The group's founder, George Schuyler, was already thirty-five years old when the organization was established; Ella Baker was twenty-seven. Schuyler commented at the time, "This measure is designed to keep the control of the organization in the hands of young people. We consider most of the oldsters hopelessly bourgeois and intent on emulating Rockefeller and Ford on a shoestring budget."[83] To ensure that its autonomy would remain uncompromised, the YNCL refused to accept financial support from churches or charitable foundations.[84]

While Ella Baker and the other leaders of the YNCL held no great reverence for older, established leaders, they did not assume that the mantle of leadership should pass to them automatically because of their youth. In the tradition of the young intellectuals known as the Harlem radicals in the 1920s, a group to which Schuyler had belonged, the YNCL placed great emphasis on internal discussion and education among its members. The founding statement declared that "each council should follow a well-planned educational program, emphasizing at all times the inclusiveness and far-reaching effects of Consumers Co-Operation on the Negro's social and economic status."[85] Rank-and-file members were offered an analysis of the cooperative movement as it related to larger national and international issues as part of their orientation to the cooperative movement. The organization's founders insisted "we must be trained before trying to lead people" and that therefore in the first year "each council [will be] engaged in extensive educational work."[86] The key role of mass education in grassroots organizing was another principle Baker pushed for time and again in the decades that followed.

In 1930, the YNCL envisioned an ambitious five-year plan, which, according to Schuyler, was inspired by the Bolsheviks' five-year economic plan. It included the goals of training 5,000 co-op leaders by 1932, establishing a cooperative wholesale outlet by 1933, and financing an independent college by 1937. Although most of these heady plans were never realized, the YNCL's membership did grow steadily in its first few years. Starting with a core group of thirty in December 1930, the organization boasted a membership of 400 two years later, with local councils in some twenty-two cities from California to New York.[87] Two of the more successful ventures were a grocery store employing four full-time workers and "doing a business of

$850 a week" in Buffalo, New York, and "a co-operative newsstand and stationery store" in Philadelphia.[88]

The organization faced financial difficulties from the outset. In January 1932, Ella Baker, as executive director of the organization, oversaw the kick-off of a three-month "Penny a Day" campaign urging YNCL supporters to set aside a penny each day to invest in cooperative projects in the hope of revitalizing the cooperative movement and saving the fledgling national office of the YNCL. The campaign was timed to coincide with three dates of historic significance: Abraham Lincoln's birthday, Negro History Week, and the signing of the Emancipation Proclamation. The second annual conference was held in Washington, D.C., in April 1932. By September of that year, however, the national office was forced to close because of the lack of financial support from local councils. Without any guarantee of steady income, Baker continued to serve as unpaid executive director of the YNCL, answering correspondence, accepting speaking engagements, and coordinating weekly meetings of the New York council, which were held at the offices of the Urban League.[89] At the height of the organization's financial crisis, Baker urged her comrades to remain optimistic: "remember, every movement has started as our movement has started."[90]

Ella Baker's determination in the face of such formidable obstacles was due, in large part, to her having begun to develop a long-range view of political struggle. The founders of the YNCL had a vision of social change and racial uplift that extended well beyond the immediate benefits resulting from the establishment of buying clubs and cooperative enterprises. They viewed the cooperative movement as much more than a survival strategy to ameliorate the suffering of a handful of black participants; it was a vital, practical proving ground for the socialist principles of communalism and mutual aid. To them, the concepts of cooperation and collective action were the ideological pillars on which this larger movement was to be built. The cooperative movement was thus a microcosm of a new social order and embodied the idealistic vision held by many of its proponents.

Cooperatives offered an alternative to the cut-throat, unbridled competition that many felt had led to the 1929 stock market crash and the ensuing depression. In describing the mission of the cooperative movement, Baker declared: "Ours is an unprecedented battle front. We are called upon to . . . be in the vanguard of the great world movement toward a new order."[91] An article distributed by the YNCL explains the mission of the more radical wing of the 1930s cooperative movement as follows: "The consumer coop is an evolutionary movement, whereby the people . . . hope to obtain full control of the supply and distribution of the necessities of life, thereby eliminating the profit motive from trade. . . . Consumer cooperation is revolutionary, for its ultimate aim is to create a better social structure by making unnecessary the present form of government which is operated by and for the privileged class."[92]

Baker and her idealistic young comrades saw the building of cooperative economic institutions as the first step toward a peaceful transformation of society from capitalism to a more egalitarian, socialist alternative. Buying cooperatives would, they hoped, demonstrate on a small scale the efficiency of collective economic planning and simultaneously promote the values of interdependency, group decision making, and the sharing of resources. As sociologist Charles Payne points out, this vision echoes the memories Baker treasured from her childhood in North Carolina during the early 1900s. She often spoke fondly of a time when mutual obligation and shared resources were the ties that bound small southern black communities together and brought out the best in the individual members of those communities.[93] The plan of the organization was that all profits earned by shareholders would be "used for the common good"; profits were to be reinvested in "clinics, libraries, and cooperative housing to combat slums."[94] In a 1935 article for the *Amsterdam News*, Baker articulated her hope that the new cooperative ventures would be harbingers of "the day when the soil and all of its resources will be reclaimed by its rightful owners—the working masses of the world."[95] In her 1935 view of the world, a redistribution of wealth had to be a part of any radical reorganization of society.

The YNCL was not formally linked to any socialist or communist party, and its founders were harshly critical of the weaknesses of much of the organized left. Yet the YNCL's leaders had their own vision, however elusive, of how their efforts could transform society and eradicate capitalism. George Schuyler was firm and outspoken in his condemnation of the evils of modern capitalism, and Ella Baker shared that critique. This conviction was central in Schuyler's call for the formation of consumer cooperatives. In a 1930 column, Schuyler identified capitalism as the cause of much of the suffering experienced by African American people. He responded sharply to an anticommunist critic:

> [W]hen the best minds of the age are questioning how long an economic system can last that exploits its slaves and does not even protect

them from hunger and the elements; when we see capitalistic governments advocating many policies that were suggested by Socialists 50
years ago, and finally, when capitalism has been the greatest factor in
the ravishing of Africa and the degradation of her transplanted sons and
daughters, it sounds strange to hear a smug little Negro editor criticize
other Negroes because they have the intellectual courage, ability and
vision to study socialism and bolshevism.[96]

Linking economic exploitation, enslavement, and colonialism, Schuyler
proclaimed that only a left-wing analysis could adequately address the
problems facing the race. The progress of the race depended on a clear-
sighted critique of the class dynamics of American capitalism. Schuyler
outlined the YNCL's long-term objectives in terms that stressed the group's
unique combination of revolutionary goals with an evolutionary process of
social transformation:

> Co-operative democracy means a social order in which the mills,
> mines, railroads, farms, markets, houses, shops and all the other neces-
> sary means of production, distribution and exchange are owned cooper-
> atively by those who produce, operate and use them.
>
> Whereas the Socialists hope to usher in such a Utopia society by the
> ballot and the Communists hope to turn the trick with the bullet, the co-
> operator (who is really an Anarchist since the triumph of his society will
> do away with the state in its present form—and I am an Anarchist) is
> slowly and methodically doing so through legal, intelligent economic
> cooperation or mutual aid.[97]

Schuyler claimed to be an anarchist in part to be provocative. He identified
with a freer form of radicalism that rejected the strictures of a Soviet-style
state or the centralized hierarchy of a Bolshevik-type vanguard party. He
seems to have embraced socialist ideals, not socialist or communist parties.

Baker did not share all of Schuyler's views, but she did share his optimism about the cooperative movement, proclaiming that "from economic
planning must spring our second emancipation."[98] For the rest of her life
she challenged the inequities inherent in a capitalist society. In an article
published in 1970, for example, Baker argued that "only basic changes in
the social structure of the country will be adequate to the needs of the poor,
both black and white," given that "in the midst of such great wealth, millions are impoverished."[99]

The YNCL and the concept of economic cooperation enjoyed a very broad base of support that spanned the spectrum of African American political thought during the early 1930s. Such moderate black leaders as newspaper publisher Robert Vann, Howard University president Mordecai Johnson, and Benjamin Brawley of Shaw, expressed support for the organization, although none of them were socialists, much less philosophical anarchists. These unlikely associations suggest two things. First, cooperative economics was rooted in the long-standing tradition of black self-help, mutual aid, and uplift, so it had wide appeal to both small entrepreneurs and socialists. Cooperatives could be viewed as a way of navigating the racist stumbling blocks within American capitalism; alternatively, they could be seen as a direct challenge to its legitimacy. Second, in a time of systemic economic crisis, many small business people were eager to try any methods they could, however unorthodox, to keep their businesses afloat. For blacks in particular, the repertoire of survival strategies included the pooling of resources and a willingness to at least temporarily substitute cooperation for competition.

Baker and Schuyler were heirs to a long tradition of mutual aid in the African American community, and many black organizers had seen cooperatives as an avenue for economic improvement. During the 1920s and 1930s, several organizations and leaders, including, most notably, W. E. B. Du Bois, advocated similar strategies. According to historian Manning Marable, Du Bois's commitment to all-black cooperative ventures was consistent with his deepening socialist vision and simply took into account the reality of American racial politics in the Jim Crow era. Du Bois, in Marable's words, "firmly believed that the Negro middle class could lead black workers to a moderate socialist program. In a series of articles in the *Pittsburgh Courier,* Du Bois explained that the entire working class could 'make one assault upon poverty and race hate.' But to begin this process, black Americans had to build their own separate organizations along cooperative lines."[100] Du Bois held the view, Marable concludes, that "the rise of black cooperativism would ultimately establish a unity between workers of both races."[101] In other words, African Americans had to initiate a transitional strategy toward socialism that made political sense within the confines of Jim Crow. Toward this end, Du Bois "supported the development of black cooperatives."[102]

Varied political tendencies can be identified under the rubric of the cooperative movement. Du Bois represented one strain, while Father Divine represented quite another. A flamboyant and controversial messianic religious leader who professed no socialist aspirations whatsoever, Divine adopted cooperative methods and rhetoric in building his religious empire. He organized soup kitchens, stores, and nurseries by calling on his followers to pool their meager resources and labor together under the banner of self-help. Divine's cooperative enterprises did help many poor black people to survive during hard times. Contrary to the YNCL's policy of channeling profits into community projects, however, Divine siphoned off a good chunk of the excess to support his own lavish lifestyle.[103] Some supporters of cooperatives had more straightforward, pragmatic goals. Many small business people entered into partnerships and joint, bulk-buying arrangements to minimize their costs and maximize their profits. Although advocates of "black capitalism" supported cooperatives, most of them strongly disapproved of the YNCL. For example, in 1933 the YNCL was sharply criticized by the conservative Colored Merchants Association and the National Negro Business League. Schuyler predictably reacted with biting criticisms of his own.[104]

The YNCL was a short-lived experiment in collective black self-determination. Like many economic cooperatives, it was unable to survive the concrete pressures of a dominant social and economic system antithetical to its aims or to sustain a mass base of committed supporters. It proved especially difficult to hammer out a daily practice to implement the group's long-term goals. The organization was plagued by monetary woes from its inception and eventually collapsed under the weight of financial obligations that could not be met. Schuyler's biographer, Michael Peplow, attributes the failure of the YNCL not only to the lack of capital and financial support but also to the fact that Schuyler's inflammatory remarks about the black church and the black middle class had made him too many enemies.[105]

Rooted in the idealism of the utopian socialist communities of the nineteenth century, cooperatives held out the illusory hope of creating an oasis of economic democracy in the midst of a capitalist society, an objective rife with pitfalls and contradictions from the outset. Schuyler traveled to England and met with organizers of the famous British cooperative movement to garner lessons to ensure the longevity and stability of the YNCL, but the odds were against the venture.[106] Cooperatives needed capital, which few black people had even during the best of times. In the depths of the Great Depression, the minimum funds required to sustain stable buying co-ops were simply unavailable. Cooperatives were not a short-term solution to economic woes; they needed considerable time to demonstrate progress. In such urgent and uncertain times, most people were not confident or patient enough to allow them to work. The co-ops that did succeed were absorbed into the dominant economy.

Still, the cooperative movement held a special appeal for Ella Baker. Given the range of political organizations based in New York City during the early 1930s, why did she choose to dedicate her efforts to the YNCL? One reason is that the cooperative philosophy resonated with many of the ideals that were instilled in her as a child. She brought her memories and ideals of community solidarity in the rural South to bear on the predicament in which she found oppressed black people in the urban North.

Judging from the political views that the mature Ella Baker articulated during the 1960s, there are other ways in which the YNCL must have appealed to and influenced her as well. Baker's political philosophy called for challenging the laws and institutions of society in order to eliminate discrimination and inequity, but at the same time she felt strongly that any movement for social change must transform the individuals involved—their values, priorities, and modes of personal interaction. Baker expressed this viewpoint as early as the 1940s, and it remained a constant theme in her politics thereafter. The cooperative movement offered organizers a way of working with people on a protracted, day-to-day basis. The process of setting up co-ops, establishing common priorities for those involved, solidifying democratic methods of decision making, and building communications networks encouraged people at the grassroots to engage in social change and transformation, changing themselves, each other, and the world around them simultaneously. Unlike such singular events as voting on election day or attending a political rally, involvement in cooperatives and buying clubs enabled people to redefine the ways in which they related to neighbors, friends, and co-workers. For Baker, political struggle was, above all, a process, and she insisted that the structure of political organizations had to allow for the process of personal and political transformation to occur.

In many respects, the YNCL experiment foreshadowed a very similar organization with which Baker would be closely affiliated some thirty years later, the Student Nonviolent Coordinating Committee (SNCC). Both organizations were decidedly independent of more moderate black leadership. Both embraced the concept of leadership at the grassroots as opposed to a top-down model. And both focused on youth as a cutting-edge force for social change. The two groups certainly had different goals and emerged from distinctly different historical contexts. But parallels are clear: both the YNCL and SNCC were distinguished from other contemporary organizations by their focus on grassroots education, democratic decision-making, and a step-by-step, transformative process of working toward long-term goals. The connection between the YNCL and SNCC in Baker's own life history illuminates the carryover of strategies for resistance and change, which were passed on through conduits like Ella Baker from generation to generation. Since the YNCL was so crucial in shaping Baker's own political thinking, she presumably drew on many of the lessons and mistakes of that experience in the efforts to launch and sustain SNCC during the early 1960s.

Her years in the YNCL left Baker with a wealth of political experience, but her lack of any real material wealth took its toll. Throughout the depression, she suffered bouts of unemployment and was in a perpetual state of financial instability. Her predicament was shared by many other educated people, both black and white, but her commitment to voluntary political organizing kept her poorer than some. To make ends meet, Baker took short-term jobs whenever they were available, often finding them through friends. In the summer of 1934, she worked with the World's Fair Boosters and Friends of Africa, in their offices on 135th Street, to promote black attendance at the fair and coordinate the Negro exhibits. She worked briefly, along with John Henrik Clarke, on the Youth Committee of 100 against Lynching; with Lester Granger at the New York Urban League; with Harlem's Own Cooperative; and with the Brotherhood of Sleeping Car Porters.[107] Some of this was volunteer work, and some provided her with a nominal salary. She also did freelance writing for a wide variety of periodicals and worked as office manager for the *National News*, a short-lived publication edited by Schuyler that was geared toward a black readership. Finally, Les Granger told her about job openings at the Works Progress Administration (WPA). Baker immediately "went down and signed up."[108]

· · · · · ·

THE WORKERS EDUCATION PROJECT

In October 1936, Baker began working as a consumer education teacher for the Workers Education Project (WEP) of the WPA, based initially in offices on Broadway across from City Hall and later on 14th Street in lower Manhattan.[109] Her experience in coordinating and conducting education programs in the cooperative movement qualified her for this assignment. The WPA was one of numerous New Deal agencies set up during the depression by President Franklin D. Roosevelt to combat massive unemployment through the creation of government-funded jobs. Employment programs designed specifically for educated workers aimed to use their talents for the public good: artists created murals and sculptures for public buildings; the Federal Theatre hired actors and directors to stage plays for popular audiences; the Federal Writers Project compiled guides to states and collected historical documents. Black leaders close to the Roosevelt administration made sure that black artists, writers, and teachers were not denied access to employment programs for educated workers, and some projects documented and supported African American culture.[110]

The WEP consisted of 1,000 teachers nationwide who were sympathetic with the militant forces within the burgeoning trade union movement, specifically the Congress of Industrial Organizations (CIO). The project's official purpose was to "cooperate with union officials and community leaders in organizing and conducting classes in workers' and consumers' problems."[111] WEP teachers held classes in settlement houses, union halls, churches, and workplaces, and discussions ranged from practical questions about the social security program to the growth of fascism abroad.[112] The New York City office had a staff of about eighty and was supervised by Isabel Taylor, "a mild-mannered woman whose background included settlement house work in the tradition of Jane Addams, and working with coal mining families in Pennsylvania."[113] Initially, according to Baker's friend and WEP co-worker Conrad Lynn, "the government felt we [in the WEP] should be neutral in the struggle between capital and labor . . . but we won the right to study the history of the labor movement," which soon became a primary focus of the group's work.[114] Lynn recalled how prolabor WEP teachers tried to infuse radical politics into their classes. "We ferreted out instances of exploitation of workers, educating them about instances such as the famous Triangle Shirtwaist fire in which dozens of workers were killed due to the unsafe conditions they were forced to work under." Such lessons, Lynn admitted, were intended to motivate workers to join the growing trade union movement.[115] Baker's long-time friend Pauli Murray, who also worked with the WEP, made the case for partisanship even more strongly in a 1938 report on how to improve the project's efforts. In her view, teachers needed to bolster workers' confidence so that they would not be "satisfied with things as they are." She felt that the WEP should encourage black workers, in particular, to overcome feelings of "inferiority and timidity" and to "see the world as theirs and from which they have a right to take what rightfully belongs to them."[116]

Ella Baker was recognized as a successful educator within the WEP. Soon after joining the WPA, she was promoted to assistant project supervisor in the Manhattan office of the WEP. There, Baker coordinated and conducted workshops on consumer issues for church, labor, and community groups. She was also the author of several publications, including a study guide on consumer issues that was distributed nationwide.[117] Like Lynn and Murray, Baker strove to politicize the content of her work and radicalize her students by linking the problems of consumers with larger issues of inequality and the need for social change. A flyer announcing one of Baker's consumer education workshops read: "Some consumers organize to save money, others to save the world—what does consumer education mean to you?"[118] Her syllabi posed such questions as "Why so much poverty in so rich a country as America?" and "What role can organized and dynamic consumer action play in issuing in a new social order?"[119]

Baker undertook concerted efforts to make consumer education available and accessible to black Americans, who might otherwise not have seen WEP programs as relevant to them. She conducted workshops in Harlem, holding classes in old storefronts and at workplaces, and created an educational exhibit on consumer issues in Harlem Hospital to accommodate hospital employees, especially nurses who might not have otherwise attended.[120] Pauli Murray shared Baker's goal of making the WEP more accessible to black workers and supported her efforts, praising Baker's work in Harlem and urging the office to lend more publicity to the work.[121]

The WEP provided a serious political education for the teachers it employed. "We had few guidelines and we learned as we taught, pooling our experiences," recalled Murray. "We also had to familiarize ourselves with the immediate problems of clothing workers, Pullman car porters, domestic workers, transport workers, sales clerks, the unemployed, or whatever groups we were assigned to. We had to be well informed on contemporary social, economic and political issues to satisfy the demand among workers for discussions of political events."[122] The WEP teachers learned from their dialogues with adult students and from their debates with one another. They studied, argued, and grappled on a day-to-day basis with the most pressing economic and political problems of the time. Looking back decades later, Conrad Lynn was convinced that he had encountered "some of the best political minds collected under one roof" while working there.[123] In the WEP, young radical intellectuals hammered out together new approaches to social change.

The WEP was host to virtually every sector of the American left, from proponents of labor union organizing and independent socialists to members of the Communist Party. Baker recalled their passionate debates with pleasure: "You had every spectrum of radical thinking on the WPA. We had a lovely time. . . . Boy it was good, stimulating."[124] In this intellectually dynamic environment, where theories were tested against the experiences of working adults as well as against alternative points of view, many of the amorphous ideals that had attracted Baker to the YNCL were challenged and refined. The YNCL had introduced Baker to progressive politics; in the WEP, her ideas were forged into a coherent political analysis.

Baker also studied and taught in the workers' education program at the Rand School for Social Science, located on East 15th Street in Lower Manhattan. In 1936, while she was working for the WEP, Baker attended classes at the Rand School, and by 1937 she was teaching consumer issues at the school's weekly afternoon classes for women.[125] Founded in 1906 by members of the American Socialist Society and funded by Carrie Sherfey Rand, a wealthy Iowa radical and former abolitionist, the school offered courses on socialist theory, economics, and labor history and hosted such notable intellectuals as John Dewey, Bertrand Russell, and Charles Beard. By the 1930s the school's cafeteria, classrooms, and bookstore were hangouts for an interracial crowd of young radical thinkers and activists.[126] Her experience as a student and teacher at the Rand School was another part of Baker's deepening involvement in and exposure to leftist politics in New York City.

In the WEP office where Baker worked, there were constant debates and discussions about such topics as the future of socialism, the relationship of the communist movement to the struggle for Negro rights, how to structure organizations democratically, the rise of fascism in Europe, and the future of colonialism in Africa. Her coworkers included Conrad Lynn, a lawyer for the Young Communist League; Agnes Martuoucci, a member of the Socialist Party; and Pauli Murray, who supported the independent socialist faction led by Jay Lovestone. "You had every splinter of the CP," Baker recalled, as well as a variety of socialists and independent radicals. In describing the backgrounds of her co-workers at the WEP, Baker remembered that many of her white colleagues were so-called red diaper babies who had been brought up in leftist families, but who "had become disillusioned with the bringing in of the socialist order through the CP, and yet who couldn't leave the idea."[127] They were actively looking for socialist alternatives. Lynn echoed Baker's assessment: the WEP staff "were men and women committed to the cause of labor, and they represented every party and tendency of the left. For the first time Trotskyists, Lovestoneites, Stammites, Socialists, Anarchists, and Henry Georgeites mingled with orthodox Communists."[128]

In this new environment, Baker clarified her thinking about class, and began to put her ideas about education and social change into practice. The philosophy of education that she expressed during her work for the WEP reflects some key features of her larger political vision. One of the main goals of workers' education, according to Baker, was to provide the worker with "a more intelligent understanding of the social and political economy of which he is a part."[129] For Baker, consumer issues were not apolitical matters that affected everyone regardless of their economic position. She pointed out that although "everyone is a consumer . . . here, we are primarily concerned with the wage earner whose income fails to satisfy the needs and desires of himself and his family . . . and who can find small comfort and little hope in our present economy."[130] In describing her approach to consumer education, Baker insisted that "the aim is not education for its own sake, but education that leads to self-directed action."[131] Consumer politics were one aspect of a larger class struggle between the haves and have-nots. Baker saw consumers as workers at the other end of the production process and struggle over consumer power as analogous to the struggle for workers' power on the factory floor. As she put it in her syllabus: "All work is but a means to the end of meeting consumer demands. The 'real wage' is what the pay envelope will actually buy. The wage-earner's well-being is determined as much at the points of distribution and consumption as at the point of production. . . . Since recurrent 'business slumps' and the increased mechanization of industry tend to decrease the primal importance of the worker as producer, he must be oriented to the increasingly more important role of consumer."[132]

In other words, organization at the point of consumption was potentially as important as the Marxist strategy of organization at the point of production. By acting collectively as consumers and as workers, ordinary people could influence the economy and improve the condition of their lives. In her WEP course syllabus, Baker raised fundamental questions about the economic injustice of American capitalism and suggested that an independent, aggressive consumer movement had an important role to play in changing that system.[133] She clearly saw her work as a part of a bigger process of social and economic change along socialist lines.

The WEP exposed Baker to the entire spectrum of leftist political ideologies and factions. She was a careful observer and critic of the left and had many close friends in opposing organizations and parties. In her opinion, the Communist Party "was the most articulate group for social action. [It] may not have been well organized all the time, but it was articulate."[134]

Charles Payne points out that Baker also admired the localized "cell structure" of the CP, which could be interpreted any number of ways, but, given
the trajectory of Baker's politics after the 1930s, it is likely that she simply
valued the localized process of intensive small-group discussion and planning that a "cell" structure composed of small units that worked closely
together would allow for.[135] Baker respected the CP's leadership in organizing white and black industrial workers during the 1930s, and its white
members were some of the staunchest antiracists around. However, her
criticisms of the party, which she did not write down, seem to have outweighed her praise.[136] Baker's relationships with CP members were not
governed by the politically expedient notion of "live and let live." Rather,
she constantly struggled with her friends and comrades around points of
disagreement. Conrad Lynn, one of her closest CP friends, recalled that
Baker often "shoved reading material under my nose critical of the Communist Party." Yet the two remained lifelong friends.[137] Even though Baker
was more closely associated with the socialists, rather than the communists, in Harlem, she never endorsed the "militant anticommunism" of
some of her friends, such as A. Philip Randolph, who, according to historian Mark Naison, took the position that "communism represented a 'Fifth
Column' in American life that had to be destroyed at all costs."[138]

Among all the various and competing leftist organizations active in New
York during the 1930s, Baker was particularly sympathetic to the Lovestonites, an independent socialist faction named after its leader, Jay Lovestone, who had split from the Community Party during the late 1920s.[139] In
interviews, John Henrik Clarke and Conrad Lynn agreed about Baker's
Lovestonite affiliation.[140] The fact that one of Baker's closest friends, Pauli
Murray, supported Lovestone adds weight to Lynn's and Clarke's recollections.[141] Lovestone and his followers were critical of the Communist Party's
view of the Bolshevik revolution as a virtual blueprint for socialist revolutions worldwide. As proponents of a brand of American exceptionalism,
they believed that the United States had to follow its own path toward
socialism. Lovestone had been general secretary of the Workers (Communist) Party during the late 1920s, when the so-called Negro question was
being hotly debated within party circles. Before he was ousted in 1929,
Lovestone and his black and white allies within the party opposed the
notion of black self-determination founded on the idea of a southern-based
Negro "nation within a nation," which was introduced at the Sixth Congress of the Communist International in Moscow in 1930. Lovestone had
little confidence in organizing in the agrarian South and thought that the

party should urge blacks to migrate to the industrial North instead.[142] Lovestone advocated interracial organizing on the basis of common class interests. One of his strongest black supporters within the party was Lovett Fort-Whiteman, who coauthored an internal party document that called for the abolition of the party-run American Negro Labor Congress on the grounds that it unfairly segregated black workers coming into the party. Those on the other side of the debate countered that critics of the American Negro Labor Congress and the self-determination position were minimizing race and suggesting that it was marginal to the class struggle.[143] Lovestone recognized that racism was a problem within the party as well as in the nation as a whole, and he maintained that the party should fight "white chauvinism" and upgrade "Negro work."[144]

According to historian Paul Buhle, the Lovestonite faction, after its expulsion from the Workers (Communist) Party, encouraged "a rethinking of communist policies in a more open fashion" while promoting an aggressive agenda, including the development of a Worker's School headed by Bertram Wolfe.[145] The group, in Buhle's assessment, maintained a "small but vital intellectual following" in the early thirties.[146] Baker may have been drawn to the Lovestonites' lively intellectual debates and emphasis on radical education. The group's interracial composition and its commitment to understanding the connections between racial injustice and class inequality would also have appealed to her. Whatever the attraction to the controversial group, Baker's affiliation with Lovestone was a loose one at best.

Baker was well informed about left political theory and questioned all the viewpoints. She read and debated Marxist ideas regularly with her coworkers in the WEP, but she was never known to toe a "party line" of any type. Indeed, she was a vigorous opponent of sectarianism, regarding organizational splits over abstractions as destructive to organizing for change. Baker's interest in Marxism was an extension of her open-minded exploration of a wide spectrum of political views. According to some of her friends, she was fairly promiscuous in her political associations during and after the 1930s. It did not matter whether she dealt with communists, Lovestonites, socialists, or ardent Garveyites; she was eager to engage them all. This openness to diverse political views and ideologies characterized much of her political life. Anyone concerned with social and economic justice, civil rights, and human progress was a potential ally—or at least worthy of a hearty debate. Even at this early stage of her political career, Baker was a catalyst for bringing people together. She was a common denominator among the varied and often contentious segments of Harlem's progressive political community. "Characters of all the various political stripes would drop by Ella's apartment, just for the political challenge of it. She would argue her point one day," John Henrik Clarke recalled, "and see you on the street and hug you the next. Principled disagreements were not a basis to shut anybody out."[147]

· · · · · ·

INTERNATIONALISM AND THE BLACK DIASPORA

Moving from the provincial South to metropolitan Harlem opened Baker's eyes to the variety of black diasporic cultures and politics. One of the things Baker loved about New York was its global character, a multinationalism that permeated the political and cultural life of the city. Baker marveled that "if ever there was any ferment across the ocean in terms of social action and development of political parties like communist, socialist, etc., New York became the place where it birthed and blossomed most."[148] During the 1930s, Baker, like many African Americans, took a greater interest in world affairs and U.S. foreign policy. As John Henrik Clarke put it, "black took on a bigger meaning and freedom took on a global character."[149]

In 1932, Baker worked as a reporter for the *West Indian News* and familiarized herself with Caribbean politics and culture; she also became acquainted with the Caribbean socialist Richard Moore.[150] In January 1937, when England sent troops to suppress a strike by oil workers in the British colony of Trinidad and Tobago, Baker took a stand in support of the striking workers. She had lengthy conversations with her friend Conrad Lynn about the incident, firing him up so much that he disrupted a meeting of the New York City Committee of the Communist Party by demanding that they funnel aid to the embattled black strikers.[151] The CP committee refused, and Lynn walked out of the meeting threatening to resign his membership in protest. Lynn recounted this dramatic incident in his autobiography, *There Is a Fountain*, but only years later did he mention that his conversations with Ella Baker were the impetus for his actions.[152]

During 1934–35, when the Italian dictator, Mussolini, moved to annex the African nation of Ethiopia, thousands of Harlemites mobilized to protest the violation of Ethiopia's autonomy and to support the Ethiopian resistance. Ella Baker lent her voice in support of this international campaign, marching in demonstrations, attending meetings, and circulating petitions under the organizational banner of the American League against War and Fascism.[153] The league held a major march through Harlem on

August 3, 1935, which brought out nearly 25,000 people.[154] Baker's close relationship with one of the key leaders of the Ethiopian aid campaign, Rev. William Lloyd Imes, suggests that she may have played more of a role in this effort than extant documents indicate.[155] In "Light on a Dark Continent," an unpublished article on the richness of African history written by Baker in the late 1930s, she directly challenged the bias of Eurocentric histories, pointing out that, in fact, the so-called Dark Continent of Africa was the birthplace of the human species.[156] These words and activities indicate that Baker's politics were framed by a much larger internationalist perspective and included a particular concern with the issues of African colonialism and independence.

Pan-Africanism linked the liberation of people of African descent throughout the diaspora to the struggle for self-determination on the continent of Africa. W. E. B. Du Bois was one of its major proponents within the United States, advocating solidarity among black people around the world but rejecting any type of narrow, racial separatism at home. Baker's internationalist stance and her critique of black nationalism went hand in hand as well. She was indubitably a "race woman," unapologetic about her love and affinity for black people, and she situated herself politically and personally within a diverse and sometimes fractious black community. She lived her entire adult life in the historically and culturally rich black enclave of Harlem out of choice rather than necessity. But her affinity and sense of community did not stop there. Baker's class analysis and political perspective suggested the need for cooperation and coalition building with other oppressed people, regardless of race. The Young Negroes' Cooperative League was the only all-black organization with which Baker was affiliated, and the YNCL maintained amicable relations with nonblack organizations, especially cooperatives, that had similar economic and political goals. Baker never worked with organizations that espoused narrow nationalist ideas or advocated Garvey-style separatism. Her views on these questions closely resembled those of Du Bois. They both recognized that, in a historical period defined by Jim Crow segregation, all-black organizations were necessary modes of self-help and group empowerment, yet they did not preclude working with predominantly white or multiracial organizations simultaneously or in the future.[157] In the economic crisis of the depression, African Americans had to take immediate steps to resist oppression and ensure their survival. They could work toward establishing principled, enduring coalitions with whites and with other people of color, especially on issues of economic justice, but coalition-building was a protracted process and was most effectively conducted from a strong, autonomous base.

Baker saw the necessity of forming alliances across racial lines and national boundaries on pragmatic political grounds. In response to remarks made by a Philadelphia minister urging blacks to pull themselves up by their bootstraps, that is, without allies, she argued in an unpublished essay written around 1940:

> I could but think "how true and yet how false." True that a new economic order must be built, but false to hope that it can be built by the Negro alone on any policy of racial isolation. True that the Negro's future will be determined by his own efforts, but false to expect . . . that it can be achieved by . . . racial isolation. While we are tugging at our own bootstraps, we must realize that our interests are more often than not identical to that of others. We must recognize the identity of interests, work with other groups . . . [and yet not sacrifice our interests to that of the larger cause]. A difficult but unavoidable task.[158]

Baker, like Du Bois, combined a commitment to self-determination with a vision of social and political transformation in which African Americans would work alongside other oppressed groups to establish a new social and economic order. The international perspective that enabled Du Bois and Baker to link black Americans' struggles with those of Africans and others against colonialism was key to their ability to untie the knot that, within the United States, too often made self-determination and multiracial organizing look like antitheses rather than compatible, even mutually necessary goals.

Baker's internationalism and her commitment to coalition-building remained steadfast throughout her long political life. She connected racial and economic injustice and looked to other oppressed groups as potential allies. In 1968, for example, Baker observed: "The logical groups for the black masses to coalesce with would be the impoverished whites, the mis-represented and impoverished Indians, and the alienated Mexican-Americans. These are the natural allies in my book."[159] Baker later expressed her internationalist views by her involvement in the Puerto Rican solidarity movement, the struggle against colonialism in Africa, and the anti–Vietnam War movement. She also made deliberate efforts to expose civil rights activists to struggles in other parts of the world. Although Baker never traveled outside the United States, her universal vision of politics and human rights encompassed the globe and linked her with individuals from the Caribbean to the African continent. The foundations of this internationalist perspective were laid in Harlem during the 1930s.

· · · · · ·

A MOST UNCONVENTIONAL MARRIAGE

Some time in the early 1930s, there are conflicting accounts on exactly when, Ella Baker moved out of her cousin's apartment and into a place of her own, located across from a small park on St. Nicholas and West 133d Streets.[160] This was a bold and unconventional act. Baker was aware that "for black women from nice homes"—"[n]ice religious homes"—to be living alone in a big city like New York was frowned on.[161] But she was not overly concerned about what other people thought of her choices. The new apartment afforded her privacy, space enough to gather with groups of friends, and the ability to come and go as she pleased. When asked years later if her mother, Anna, had approved of the move and her New York lifestyle, Baker responded that it really didn't matter, since she was too far away to do anything about it.[162]

Baker's early years in New York City were dominated by professional and political activities, though she did have a few personal friends, including the Schuylers. She occasionally got together with Emma Lance, who worked on the WPA-sponsored Federal Theatre Project, to "drink a few beers and talk over matters of 'Affairs of State,' as well as romance."[163] In a very frank and detailed letter to Ella after the two women had not seen one another in some time, Emma confided irreverently that she was dating two men at the same time but was still working too hard to devote proper attention to either one. Her level of candor and disclosure suggests that the two women were quite close. A male friend, Freeman Hubbard, also confided in Baker about his love life and other personal matters, at one point chastising "busy little Ella" for not keeping in closer touch.[164]

Soon after Ella arrived in New York, her boyfriend from back home, T. J. Roberts, or Bob as she called him, began sending telegrams declaring his affection and longing to be with her. Addressing her as "darling" and "sweetheart," Bob promised Ella that he was "still loving you" despite their distance.[165] The two kept up an active correspondence, augmented by phone calls between 1927 and 1930. At times, Bob complained that Ella had not responded quickly enough to his previous telegram or call; it appears that on other occasions Bob had let the communication between them lag. They professed their love for one another, and both expressed a desire to be together. Eventually, after years of separation punctuated by her visits home and his visits to New York, they decided to get married.[166] Roberts and Baker shared the apartment on St. Nicholas Avenue in Harlem for nearly twenty years.

The marriage was anything but traditional. Baker never assumed her husband's surname, an unusual act of independence during the 1930s. When Baker was visiting her family in Littleton, one of her cousins asked what had possessed her to keep her own last name after she married. "I had it all this time, I just figured I would keep it," she explained matter-of-factly.[167] Nor did she stay home in Harlem to perform whatever wifely duties might have been expected of women of her generation. From her first years as an organizer and educator for the YNCL, she had traveled wherever her work took her. Baker did not change this pattern when she married; in 1941, she accepted a job as a field organizer for the NAACP that required her to be away for weeks at a time. Roberts was a quiet and gentle man who did not interfere with Ella's principal passion, which was politics. Indeed, he kept such a low profile that when the FBI was spying on Baker during the 1940s they assumed he was a female relative living with her and apparently had no idea she was married.[168] Many close friends were also unaware of what Baker later referred to as her "domestic arrangement."[169]

Although Baker was married to Roberts for many years, she seems never to have treated him as an integral part of her life or as an influencing force in her thinking. In interviews conducted over many years, she repeatedly minimized the importance of her married life, denied that it had any relevance to her political work, and declined to answer probing questions that attempted to unravel her marital mystery. Student activists with whom Baker worked during the 1960s remember her being open and frank about almost everything except her marriage. "It was one of the few things she just wouldn't talk about," recalled Bernice Johnson Reagon.[170] "When I asked her about her husband she would say, 'oh no, it's not important,'" remembers Joyce Ladner.[171] Baker bluntly told an interviewer not to "get too personal" when she broached the subject of marriage.[172] "Many people didn't even know Miss Baker had ever been married; she was explicitly *Miss Baker*" to most of her political associates.[173]

Ella Baker's deliberate silence about her married life makes it difficult for a biographer to do more than document the fact of her marriage and acknowledge this gap in the story she told about her life. Yet her papers and her friends' observations of her and her husband during these years do offer some clues about the relationship. Although Roberts was never as politically active as Baker, he was a fighter in his own way, refusing to accept indignities meted out routinely to blacks and demanding fair treatment when and where he could. When Roberts was treated rudely by a clerk in a Miami, Florida, railway station while he was traveling, he wrote a strong letter of complaint to the railway company insisting on an apology.[174] During the 1940s, Roberts was active in the tenants' rights group in their Harlem apartment building at 452 St. Nicholas Avenue,[175] one of the few contexts in which the twosome had an open, public identity as a married couple.[176] Roberts was willing to fight when issues had an immediate impact on him and his loved ones. He left the larger political battles to Baker.

John Henrik Clarke, who met Ella Baker through the Committee of 100 against Lynching, knew the couple well during the 1930s and frequently visited their apartment. According to Clarke, the marriage was not a union of equals. Roberts "was out of his league with Ella," Clarke observed. "She took him in like a little puppy out of the rain. I think she sort of felt sorry for him."[177] "He had his interests and she had hers," recalled another close friend.[178] Despite their differences, the couple stayed together and weathered some difficult years. They were often separated by the demands of their jobs: Baker's work for the NAACP required extensive travel, and Roberts's work in the refrigeration business also took him on the road quite a bit. Undoubtedly, being apart so much put a strain on their relationship. After a period of separation and an attempted reconciliation, which included marital counseling from a Harlem pastor, the marriage was not salvageable and finally ended in divorce in 1958.[179] Years later, Baker and her niece, Jackie Brockington, who had lived with the couple for several years, attended Bob Roberts's funeral to pay their respects.[180] Even after the marriage ended, connections and obligations remained. Just as she didn't write off political friends, she was not prepared to write Bob off either, even if they were no longer a couple.

The late 1930s were especially difficult years for Baker personally and financially. On December 11, 1938, two days before Ella's thirty-fifth birthday, her father died, leaving her mother alone and economically vulnerable. Ella had developed an independent identity during her years in Harlem, but now she was recast as an adult daughter with significant responsibility for her aging mother. Ella had always been the responsible one, not Maggie, so the burden fell on her shoulders. It was difficult for Ella to contribute to the support of her kin when it was so hard to find paid work herself. Her marriage did not improve her financial situation, since both she and Roberts had difficulty keeping jobs. This problem was so common during the depression that many couples postponed marriage for years because of financial uncertainty. By 1939, Baker and her new husband were nearly destitute. Bob Roberts answered a *New York Times* classified ad for a couple to work as janitors, an indication of just how desperate they were.[181] Ella Baker wrote letters to the New York Housing Authority, the American League for Peace and Democracy, and other organizations inquiring about possible employment, all to no avail. In 1940, she applied unsuccessfully for an emergency loan from a New York charity, pointing out that she did so only as "a last resort" after an extended period of unemployment.[182] John Henrik Clarke recalled that "Ella was always broke and always borrowing money from one friend or another."[183]

Money was never important to Baker. She focused on her political work and thought about money only when there was none. In 1938 she applied for a job as youth coordinator for the NAACP. Two years later, they hired her as an assistant field secretary, which launched another phase of her political career as a grassroots organizer and guaranteed a steady income at least for a while.

Baker was always a fiercely independent soul who routinely shunned convention and refused to be corralled into the prescribed roles that others wanted her to play. In college, she was a rebel, albeit a reluctant one, who defied the rigid rules and bureaucratic hierarchy of Shaw's administration. During her early years in Harlem, she quickly evolved from a curious and naive young rebel to a serious and committed left-wing radical. Reflecting on her arrival in Harlem, Baker recalled: "I, perhaps at that stage, had the kind of ambition that others may have . . . the world was out there waiting for you to provide a certain kind of leadership and give you the opportunity. But with the Depression, I began to see that there were certain social forces over which the individual had very little control. It wasn't an easy lesson. It was out of that context that I began to explore more in the areas of ideology and theory regarding social change."[184]

This realization was a turning point in Baker's life. After nearly a decade in Harlem, working in various political organizations and studying a wide range of ideas about social change, she rejected much of the middle-class "grooming" she had received at home and at Shaw and instead became a radical activist and grassroots organizer. Baker forfeited many of the class privileges that her education and talents might have afforded her. She chose instead to struggle on behalf of the oppressed. Her rewards were not material ones.

FIGHTING HER OWN WARS

THE NAACP NATIONAL OFFICE, 1940–1946

. . . . . .

We must have the "nerve" to take the Association to people wherever they are.
Ella Baker, 1941

Give people light and they will find a way.
Ella Baker, 1944

In December 1940, as fascism swept across Europe and North Africa and the United States vacillated about entering the conflict, Ella Baker enlisted in another war—the war against American racism—by joining the staff of the National Association for the Advancement of Colored People (NAACP), one of the fastest-growing black freedom organizations.

After two years of trying to get her foot in the door at the NAACP, Baker had landed a job as assistant field secretary, earning $29 a week.[1] She was ecstatic. What could be better than getting paid to fight the system? Throughout the remainder of the decade, as the predominantly male spokespersons for black America made pronouncements about the war, federal legislation, and world affairs, organizers like Ella Baker were fighting in the trenches of southern battlefields for social and economic justice for African Americans. Through their actions, they were making real the national black freedom slogan of "double victory," victory against fascism abroad and racism at home. Their courageous efforts laid the basis for the postwar struggle over the very meaning of American democracy, a meaning that inescapably hinged on the issue of race. For Baker and many of her closest allies, the struggle had another layer as well. By the 1940s, Baker was convinced that how one fought was as important as what one was fighting for; the key to change lay in the process of movement building. Therefore she lobbied to make the structure and practices of the NAACP more inclusive and egalitarian and to infuse a greater spirit of activism and militancy into its local campaigns as a strategy for grassroots empowerment. During her years with the NAACP, Baker honed her skills as a rank-and-file organizer and began to explore ways of implementing her evolving ideas about democratic mass action.

Throughout her nearly six-year tenure with the NAACP's national staff, first as a field secretary and then as the national director of branches, Baker traveled into the bowels of the American South, suffering the insults of Jim Crow segregation and often putting her own life in danger in order to support local antidiscrimination campaigns and recruit new members to the association. Although antiracist whites still served on the NAACP's board of directors and belonged to branches in some northern cities, the strict segregation that pervaded every aspect of life in the South meant that local branches were composed almost entirely of African Americans. In many southern cities and small towns, the NAACP was the only black freedom organization on the scene, and joining it was a militant gesture. In doing field work for the NAACP, then, Baker was organizing black people to confront white supremacy. This was a physically grueling and emotionally stressful job, and Baker was only able to do it because of the support she received from a network of close friends and colleagues, most of whom were women.

In the NAACP, as in other political organizations, women were indispensable but underappreciated. The association had never elected a woman as its executive secretary, and women were often excluded from the informal inner circle of decision makers.[2] On the other hand, women formed the backbone of many of the most active local branches, as well as of the national office staff itself. Women's contributions had to be acknowledged, even if they did not translate into formal positions of power. Both field secretaries and local branch leaders had a certain amount of autonomy, and—despite the national leadership's preoccupation with control—the day-to-day organizing work they did in the field was crucial to the association's success. In the final analysis, the NAACP provided an opportunity for women like Ella Baker to wield considerable influence at the local level and to a lesser extent nationally. At times, Baker had to defend her authority and her autonomy, but the respect she earned from her co-workers and from local activists and the skills she brought to her assigned tasks meant that even those who disliked her outspoken and assertive style had to put up with it, at least for a while.

· · · · · ·

FIELD WORK FOR THE NAACP

Founded in 1909–10 by the prominent scholar-activist W. E. B. Du Bois as an interracial organization committed to achieving racial equality, the NAACP experienced considerable growth and success over its first thirty years. Fighting its battles largely in the legal arena, the NAACP won a number of key victories, recruited a cadre of bright and talented young black activists and lawyers to its staff, and earned a reputation as the preeminent black rights organization of the day.

Emerging out of the all-black Niagara Movement, the NAACP was as much a challenge to the conservative political tendencies among African American leaders as it was a response to the unabashed racism and vigilante violence of white society. In 1909, Booker T. Washington was the reigning patriarch of black American politics. Although a radical black tradition had existed through slavery, Reconstruction, and beyond, Washington's accommodationist stance, which advocated self-help instead of protest, set the tone for the era. The NAACP's demand for racial equality seemed radical in comparison to Washington's politics, especially in the hostile climate of the early twentieth century. In the beginning the association's leadership, embodied in its board of directors, was predominately white and middle class, and its rank-and-file membership was relatively small. After a series of legal victories regarding voting rights in the 1910s and 1920s, including a 1915 Supreme Court decision that struck down the discriminatory grandfather clause and another in 1927 that outlawed the all-white primary in Texas, the organization grew considerably in prominence and visibility. In 1920, the Harlem Renaissance writer James Weldon Johnson, who was an associate of Ella Baker's during the 1930s, became the first black to head the organization. He was succeeded by the controversial and flamboyant Walter White, who took over as the second black executive secretary in 1930.[3]

The NAACP came of age during the Great Depression and World War II. Its aggressive attack on lynching and other forms of racial violence, its fight against discrimination in the armed forces and war industries, and finally its campaign against inequality in public education put the organization on the national map. There were internal changes as well. By the onset of the depression, the NAACP's leadership had an increasing black presence, and the organization enjoyed tremendous growth. Over the course of Baker's years with the association's national office, from 1940 to 1946, its membership mushroomed from 50,000 in 1940 to almost 450,000 by 1945.[4] The NAACP became a nationwide organization with a significant presence in southern small towns as well as in northern cities. Baker worked for the association at a pivotal moment in its development as a leading force within the Black Freedom Movement.

The NAACP's growth was promoted by its active national staff. By the 1940s, this cadre of educated young, predominately black professionals were increasingly influencing the association's programs and policies. As the group expanded, internal debates and struggles over its politics and policies became more frequent. One of the palpable tensions Baker observed was generational as well as political, foreshadowing some of the political differences that later manifested themselves in the civil rights movement of the 1960s. At the time Baker was hired, she later recalled, the NAACP had entered "a period when there were young people who were joining the staff and who were demanding certain kinds of opening up, which meant primarily going down and working with people, not just having a great big mass meeting and collecting the membership."[5] They were challenging what they perceived to be the more moderate and elitist practices of their elders.[6]

The push to widen the organization's base was linked to an ongoing effort to expand its agenda. During the depression, economic issues came to the fore in the NAACP, as was true in other African American organizations. The clamor for change peaked in 1933 at a conference held in Amenia, New York, at the estate of Joel Spingarn, a longtime white backer of the NAACP. The gathering included young radical black intellectuals, such as E. Franklin Frazier, Ralph Bunche, and Abram Harris, who demanded that the group become more oriented toward mass action and more focused on labor and economic issues. While their specific proposals for change were rejected by the national leadership, many staff members still hoped to push the organization in that general direction. Some of these young activists became Ella Baker's allies and role models during the 1940s, as the association continued to grapple with questions about what kind of organization it should be and what work should be given priority.

Black politics at that time, perhaps even more so than today, were dominated by personalities, a fact that Ella Baker spent a great deal of her life trying to change. The two personalities who dominated the NAACP during the 1930s and 1940s were W. E. B. Du Bois, founder and editor of the association's monthly magazine, *The Crisis*, and Walter White, its executive secretary. Du Bois was a Harvard-trained scholar who had studied in Berlin and published works of history, sociology, political analysis, and autobiography. By the 1940s he had an international reputation as an outspoken opponent of American racism and of colonialism worldwide, and he was a leading advocate of Pan-Africanism, a philosophy that called for the decolonization and unification of Africa.[7] Walter White also was an author and longtime civil rights crusader, but he was never as erudite or politically sophisticated as Du Bois. Their relationship was permeated by competition and conflict. White had a great sense of his own importance, which he liked to flaunt. His egotism offended many black people, especially those who believed that his arrogance stemmed from misplaced pride in his striking physical features: he was blonde, blue-eyed, and very light complected. But White's commitment to the struggle for racial justice was as clear as his own racial appearance was ambiguous.

Personal tensions and political differences put Du Bois and White on a collision course. According to his supporters, Du Bois, who had no pint-sized ego himself, was engaged in a push to democratize the association during the 1930s and 1940s, seeking to open up decision making and conduct more mass campaigns. White, on the other hand, felt that Du Bois was using *The Crisis* to put forth his own political views, some of which were at variance with the official policies of the NAACP. Most notably, Du Bois clashed with White and others on the board over his support for all-black economic initiatives during the 1930s, a position they felt undermined the association's commitment to full integration. To some, however, the conflict between the two men was largely a clash of egos and personalities. Neither man won a decisive victory. Du Bois initially resigned from the NAACP in 1935, but he continued to enjoy strong support and returned to the national office in 1944. White finally fired him in 1948. Ironically, it was the ousted Du Bois who left the more enduring legacy, as others carried on the principles he had articulated.

Ella Baker respected Du Bois, shared many of his left-wing sentiments, and felt that the NAACP could "use his many and varied talents." Yet she was not comfortable with either White's or Du Bois's leadership style. She described Du Bois as aloof and both men as having a great sense of ego and self-importance.[8] Neither of them was the kind of organizer Baker modeled herself after; such high-profile, public figures did not draw her to the association and keep her there. It was the brave and unheralded local people scattered in NAACP branches throughout the country, along with her few close friends in the New York office, who earned Baker's respect, loyalty, and perseverance.

An interesting and eclectic supporting cast of characters staffed the NAACP offices in New York during the 1940s, ranging from sophisticated and articulate young lawyers to quiet but tireless secretaries and office workers. Although the most visible NAACP leaders during the 1940s were male, a number of tough, creative, and hard-working women were indispensable to the daily operations of the New York office and the grassroots field organizing that sustained it. W. E. B. Du Bois's future wife, Shirley Graham, was one of them. Graham, a novelist, playwright and left-leaning activist who worked briefly for the NAACP as a field organizer in 1943, expressed enormous respect for Baker as a democratizing force within the organization. Five years after her own departure from the staff, Graham, by then married to Du Bois, wrote a scathing letter protesting her husband's ouster and linking his criticisms about the lack of democratic accountability with the grievances that Baker had expressed at the time of her own resignation in 1946.[9] Other women that Baker respected and worked closely with included Lucille Black, Charlotte Crump, Ruby Hurley, and Daisy Lampkin, all of whom she relied on for sisterly support.

Baker was one of four field secretaries when she joined the staff in 1940. Daisy Lampkin, the eldest and most experienced of the group, immediately took Ella under her wing. The job of field secretary required long hours, hard work, and extensive travel. The field secretaries were the direct links between the NAACP national leadership and the association's rank-and-file members. Field workers traveled several months out of the year assisting branch leaders in setting up and conducting membership and fundraising drives. Those who were so inclined also helped branches to pursue local campaigns on issues they regarded as important. Field secretaries were the front-line troops whom Madison Jones, a national staff member, once jokingly called the "field hands" of the organization, underscoring the distinction between those who did tough, direct organizing and those who worked from their desks in the New York office.

As a part of her orientation as a new field secretary, Baker was asked to accompany Lampkin on a visit to the Washington, D.C., branch, which was holding its annual membership drive. Walter White hoped that Baker would "be able to observe Daisy's techniques in putting over a campaign."[10] Baker admired Lampkin's savvy as an organizer, although in many respects the two women were quite different. Lampkin was nearly twenty years Baker's senior, with a decade of service at the NAACP and long experience in African American women's politics. Lampkin had been an advocate of woman suffrage, had lobbied for the passage of the Nineteenth Amendment, and was active in both the National Association of Colored Women and the National Council of Negro Women, two prominent black women's organizations. She was also vice president of the African American newspaper the *Pittsburgh Courier* and a close associate of Robert Vann, the paper's publisher, who had supported Ella Baker's efforts in the cooperative movement during the 1930s. Lampkin was a legendary organizer of NAACP branches and served as something of a role model for Baker when she was first hired.[11]

Baker was grateful to get the job with the NAACP and eager to prove herself. Branch officials in Washington, D.C., were quite impressed by her performance. Herbert Marshall, the branch president, wrote to Walter White commending Baker's skills and insights as an organizer: "I predict for her a very brilliant future as a member of our NAACP family."[12] In September 1941, her colleague E. Frederic Morrow, who later served in the Eisenhower White House, concluded that Baker's "success in the past few months with the Association has been phenomenal."[13]

In March 1941, Ella Baker began traveling on her own. Her first stop was Birmingham, Alabama, where she launched a major membership drive.[14] Many new organizers would have been intimidated by the prospect of venturing, all alone, into so notorious a place. By the 1940s, Birmingham already had a formidable reputation for racism and repression. Anne Braden, who spent part of her childhood in Alabama, commented that "Birmingham was so bad that race and union organizers were snatched off the streets and beaten nearly half to death in the 1930's, and racist police chief Bull Connor was doing his dirty work in the 40's as well," meaning that he was openly encouraging antiblack violence.[15] Martin Luther King Jr. once described Birmingham as the "most thoroughly segregated city in the United States."[16] After a systematic campaign by Alabama's white elites to suppress civil rights organizing, the NAACP was banned from the state in 1956.[17] Birmingham remained a pivotal site of civil rights struggles for the next two decades.

In this dismal climate of repression and racial violence, Baker met some tough and courageous people. She viewed the branch president, Rev. J. W. Goodgame Jr., as a "doer," and she described local activists, particularly Mr. and Mrs. J. J. Green, as "people who endeared themselves to me to an unusual degree."[18] The friendships forged through her work in Birmingham made it, ironically, one of Baker's favorite cities. Despite its virulent racism and vigilante violence, she once described it as "one of the places in the South where I felt at ease." Whenever she took time out for a few days of leisure during her extended travels, she stopped in Birmingham. Baker liked "shopping in the big department stores there"—probably buying hats, which was one of her few and favorite indulgences.[19] She loved hats. Perhaps it was a quick way for someone as busy as she was to add a little pizzazz to her outfit without much fuss. She had a sense of style but never much time or patience for makeup, fancy hairdos, and the like. Her hats were her fashion statement, and she was very upset when on at least two occasions during her travels in the 1940s her hatboxes were left behind on trains. She dispatched letters to just about everyone concerned to locate the prized possessions, which eventually she did.[20]

In the spring of 1941, during the Birmingham campaign, Baker went to great lengths to drum up support for the NAACP. Working with Rev. Goodgame, she frequented neighborhood gathering places to try to reach the common folk. On one particular day, they "spent the morning visiting barber shops, filling stations, grocery stores and housewives, getting people to work."[21] Baker was not above resorting to material incentives to motivate people to recruit new members for the NAACP. She was pleased to report that "with the announcement of cash prizes, we have been able to get the pastors of most of the leading churches to agree to act as captains and accept 100 members as their quota."[22] The membership drive was a resounding success. During a stay of nearly two weeks, Baker helped enlist dozens of new members and raised thousands of dollars for the NAACP.

Baker wanted to build as large a base for the NAACP as she could. She conveyed to Assistant Secretary Roy Wilkins her ideas for "increasing the *Crisis* circulation and bolstering my campaign efforts [by visiting] some of the pool-rooms, boot black parlors, bars and grilles," with the aim of "having a *Crisis* made available to regular patrons of the business."[23] These forays into traditionally male domains—obvious gender transgressions—exemplify Baker's habit of pushing the boundaries of acceptable behavior for a respectable, middle-class, married woman during the 1940s. In her letter to Wilkins, she described this activity as the result of her strong "desire to place the NAACP and its program on the lips of all the people . . . the uncouth MASSES included."[24] Baker used this expression sarcastically: in her thinking, the masses were not "uncouth"; rather, they were central to her political vision for change. Her style of organizing always focused on how she could make a campaign, an issue, or an organization have greater appeal to the mass of ordinary people.

Baker had a way of appealing to ordinary people by making herself accessible, speaking in a familiar language that people could readily understand, and interacting with them in a way that made them feel they were important to her. She nurtured and cultivated this unassuming manner. Baker recognized that aspects of her background—her class privilege, higher education, residence in New York City, and close contact with prominent national leaders—made her different from many of the uneducated folk she worked with in the South. Nevertheless, she did not want those differences to overshadow their commonalities. Baker was fond of telling a story about a woman who said to her after a meeting in some small southern town that the two of them were wearing the same dress. Such an encounter would be a society woman's nightmare, but Ella Baker delighted in it: "I've had women come up to me and say, 'Your dress is just like mine.' And that's an identification. See, they don't know how to deal with the verbal part, but they are identifying with you. And instead of you turning up your nose to turn them off, you can say something that shows that that's good. We've both got good dresses."[25] Baker interacted with the woman in a way she thought would make the woman feel most comfortable. She did not view the comment as petty; rather, she tried to read between the lines to understand why the woman had approached her. The woman's comment about the piece of clothing they had in common suggested that the woman had also identified with what Baker had said in her speech, although the woman was uncertain about how to express it. Other NAACP leaders had come to town in the past wearing expensive clothing. Baker approached people in a different manner. "They didn't have to worry about me wearing any minks," Baker joked later; "I didn't own any—didn't want any."[26] Her remarks underscore the point that she was straightforward and unpretentious. This down-to-earth quality enabled her to rapidly develop a rapport with people, especially poor and working-class people.

This story gives us insight into Baker's personal organizing style. In an interview many years later, Baker described how she approached her NAACP work in the South. Over the years, she had arrived at the conclusion that political participation was not mainly about high-powered leaders like White or Du Bois but rather about the ways in which ordinary people could transform themselves and their communities. This process was both profoundly political and deeply human. She explained it this way:

There're some people in my experience, especially "the little people" as some might call them, who never could explain the NAACP as such. But they had the knack of getting money from John Jones or somebody. They might walk up to him: "Gimme a dollar for the NAACP." And maybe because of what they had done in relationship to John Jones, he'd give the dollar. They could never tell anybody what the program of the Association was. So, what do you do about that. You don't be [sic] demeaning to them. You say, well here is Mrs. Jones, Mrs. Susie Jones, and remember last year Sister Susie Jones came in with so much. . . . Now, somewhere in the process she may learn some other methods, and she may learn to articulate some of the program of the Association. But whether she does or not, she *feels* it. And she transmits it to those she can talk to.[27]

In Baker's political philosophy, personal relationships were the building blocks that led to solidarity and collective action. Sociologist Belinda Robnett suggests that emotions are also critical variables in mobilizing and organizing people for action. It is important that people *feel* as well as think about what they are involved in.

The process of individual politicization described by Baker resembles the theories developed by feminist social scientists and historians such as Karen Brodkin Sacks, Chana Kai Lee, Bernice Johnson Reagon, and Temma Kaplan, who, like Robnett, argue that women's social relationships are critical resources in community-based political mobilization. For example, Sacks's study of a hospital workers' unionization drive focuses on the web of personal and political relationships sustained largely by women workers, whom she terms "centerwomen." She concludes that "political activism is embedded in, and flowers from, everyday inter-personal and social experiences."[28] Ella Baker armed herself with this understanding as she marched across the South doing battle with Jim Crow racism in the fall of 1941, and as she battled to change the organizational culture of the New York office.

Baker's next campaign, in Virginia, was almost derailed even before it began. Here she had to prove herself not only as a new organizer but also as a woman capable of doing what others perceived as a man's job. She agreed at the last minute to conduct Virginia's annual membership campaign because her colleague Fred Morrow was unable to go as scheduled.[29] A few days before her arrival, John M. Tinsley, the Richmond branch president and state chairman, dispatched a letter to Walter White containing the following message:

Our branches in Virginia need guidance, organization, information, and inspiration. But we feel it will be too much of a hardship upon any woman to undertake to do this. In many communities the only time at which a meeting can be held when a large number of people will be free to attend is late at night or on certain Sundays. In some parts of the state personal accommodations will be comfortable, but we cannot say that for every locality. For all of these reasons we recommend a young man who can easily adjust himself to all of these conditions to cover Virginia.[30]

By the time Tinsley's letter reached Walter White's desk, it was too late to intercept Baker and send a man instead. But it is unlikely that White would have tried to make this kind of substitution, and it is even more unlikely that Baker would have accepted such a change without a fight. She showed up on Tinsley's doorstep a few days later, unaware that he preferred a man.

Tinsley was a dentist, and he and his wife Ruth had long been active in the Richmond branch. He was one of those black professionals who, as Baker put it, "had an income separate and apart from the establishment."[31] Many of his patients were his fellow NAACP members, so he had a bit more economic insulation than those whose employers were white segregationists. Some southern NAACP leaders, like other civil rights activists, relied on their relative economic independence to protect them from reprisals. A small, thin man whom Baker described as "tiny"—not much bigger than herself—Tinsley was a fighter and a good organizer.[32] Over the course of her eleven-day stay, the two worked side by side. By the time she left Richmond, Tinsley was an enthusiastic Ella Baker fan. His sexist assumptions about a woman's limited capabilities had been shattered. In his follow-up letter to White, Tinsley described Baker in glowing terms: "One of the most important and wonderful things that has happened to Richmond was the presence of the national field worker, Miss Ella J. Baker. . . . Never during her stay in Richmond did she slacken the pace. She was going from the time of her arrival until the time she left. . . . She has demonstrated to the people of Richmond and over the State of Virginia one characteristic very few people have and that is the wonderful and outstanding quality of mixing with any group of people and trying to help solve their problem[s]."[33] One of the lessons Baker took away from these early experiences was the importance of patience and process. People without confidence to express themselves could grow into that confidence if given the time and space to do so, and people skeptical of women's leadership could be won over, occasionally even without major confrontations.

Richmond was one of the NAACP's largest branches. During the membership drive, Baker met with virtually all of the major black organizations in town, including the city's Baptist Ministers Conference, the Independent Order of St. Luke, the North Carolina Mutual Life Insurance Company, and students and faculty at Virginia Union University. Through Baker's efforts, the chapter raised over $1,000 and recruited more than 1,500 new members.[34] But Baker was not satisfied. She observed that "as successful as the Richmond campaign was . . . there were many more people who could have joined the NAACP had there been sufficient campaign workers to contact them."[35] Perhaps she was thinking of the "uncouth masses"—the poor, illiterate, or semiliterate people who were sometimes given low priority in membership drives. She was equally concerned about the lack of involvement in branch activities. Richmond had an impressive membership roster, but most members were not in the habit of actually participating in the work of the organization. Baker found this problem in a number of the NAACP's larger branches. Her goal was to get more people actively engaged in local campaigns, confronting local elites, talking to one another in meetings, and feeling a greater sense of ownership of the organization. Popular participation was the first step in making the association a more democratic and mass-based organization. The NAACP had to belong to the masses, and they had to claim it as their own, she insisted.[36]

After leaving Richmond, Baker ventured into the more rural parts of the state where Tinsley feared conditions would be too difficult for her, visiting such places as Danville, Nottaway County, Farmville, and Martinsville. Although the smaller towns had many fewer members than the Richmond branch, she gave serious thought and attention to the particular circumstances in each locale, and she welcomed the opportunity "to work in areas and with branches that are in need of intensive organizational efforts."[37] Baker found her efforts in these communities both challenging and rewarding. Tinsley accompanied her on some of the trips that did not require an overnight stay. "He had a big car. And he was a bad driver," Baker, who herself never learned to drive, recalled, "but I rode with anybody."[38] This tour cemented the friendship between the dentist and the activist. One Christmas, the Tinsleys sent Baker a Virginia ham as a gesture of their affection, one that she deeply appreciated.[39] The kind of relationships Baker created during her tenure with the NAACP were not just business or professional relationships; they were profoundly personal ones.

In her work with NAACP branches, Baker went well beyond the national leadership's preoccupation with collecting membership dues to fund the legal department's litigation against discrimination. Like the other members of the younger cohort on the national staff, she wanted to see members engage actively in local struggles. In Baker's view, the field organizer had to forge friendships, earn the trust and confidence of members at the branch level, and mobilize people on the basis of the relationships that held communities together. Baker recognized that familial and personal relationships were the foundation of any sustained local organizing campaign and that it was the job of any outside organizer to identify and build on that foundation. In order to further this aim, Baker stayed in the South for longer periods of time. Although she complained that her visits to most branches were not nearly long enough, she stayed longer than her predecessors had. Previously, according to Baker, "the pattern" was for "a well-known person [to] come in and speak at a meeting and leave the next day."[40] Baker would stay in one place for up to two weeks and make extended tours through the region. She generally left New York in September and did not return until November, and she went out "into the field" again for a month or two in the spring. These extended visits allowed her to get to know local activists, to build greater rapport with them, and to become familiar with the issues and problems that concerned them most. The lengthy absences from home did little for her marriage, but the local NAACP branch work benefited from her sacrifice.

Baker contended that field secretaries had to know the issues and culture of each locale in order to organize a campaign. It was only through this type of attention to detail that serious programs of action could be developed, and Baker understood this better than anyone. In Danville, she noted that the principal issues were "police brutality and getting Negroes to qualify and vote." In Farmville, "qualifying voters, teachers' salaries and school busses [were] the immediate concerns of the branch." And in Nottaway, "voting seem[ed] to strike the most responsive chord."[41] Baker's hard work and enthusiasm in both the Alabama and Virginia campaigns were applauded by the people she met and commended by her superiors in the NAACP hierarchy. During her first few months as an NAACP field secretary, she made an impressive debut.

In the fall of 1941 Baker undertook another series of membership drives for the association, reporting that "with the exception of two days in October and two days in November, the period from September 6th to November 25th was spent in the field." She delivered some sixty-three speeches in seven cities.[42] It was an exhausting itinerary. Baker was anxious to do more outreach and to explore ways of more actively engaging members in practical work. She was optimistic that "the masses of Negroes [were] ready for the program of the Association," and she was determined to bring it to them.[43] Ella chided her colleagues to be more creative and aggressive in their outreach efforts: "We must have the 'nerve' to take the Association to people wherever they are. As a case in point, the mass-supported beer gardens, night clubs etc., in Baltimore were invaded on a small scale during the membership campaign there. And with considerable success. . . . We went in, addressed the crowds and secured memberships and campaign workers. With the results that are well summed up in a comment overheard in one club, 'you certainly have some nerve coming in here, talking , but I'm going to join that doggone organization.' "[44]

Despite her enthusiasm about her work, Baker's job was not an easy one. While on the road she worked every day almost to the point of collapse. In October 1941, she complained she was in the NAACP office in Baltimore as late as 9:30 at night "after weeks of nothing but work."[45] She often doubted whether the time and energy she invested was actually paying off in results. In another letter to Walter White, Baker lamented: "I must leave now for one of those small church meetings which are usually more exhausting than the immediate returns seem to warrant but it's a part of the spade work, so let it be."[46] Travel was difficult, office space and supplies were limited, and the frenzied pace was often taxing on her health and spirits. But Baker was on a mission and therefore comfortable accommodations were a secondary consideration. She admitted that she would sleep almost anywhere and eat almost anything. Traveling mostly by train, she would typically leave one town on Sunday morning after a weeklong visit, only to have another series of meetings with local officials on her arrival in the next town, followed by speeches at up to five churches on a given Sunday afternoon.[47] The seemingly boundless enthusiasm Baker had brought with her to the job was finally being tested by the grueling work regimen that was demanded of her.

· · · · · ·

FRIENDSHIP AND FRICTION IN THE NAACP FAMILY

Although Ella Baker occasionally vented to Walter White about the frustrations of organizing in the field, she never got much sympathy. White was more obsessed with his own image and ego to bother with such matters. "He was very much in love with himself," Baker once snipped.[48] A travel itinerary as hectic as Baker's did not leave much time for family life. But Ella rarely mentioned Bob in her correspondence with friends and co-workers. Roberts was also on the road much of the time during this period, trying to make a go of his refrigeration business. He suffered several illnesses, and during the late 1940s he spent time receiving medical care in North Carolina.[49] Baker interrupted her travel itinerary at least two times to check on him.

One of the most nurturing and supportive relationships Baker formed while working at the NAACP was with Lucille Black, the national membership secretary. Black began working for the association in the early 1940s and continued her affiliation more than thirty years. A superficial look at Lucille Black's career might give the impression that she was a loyal, hardworking staff member, but otherwise not terribly interesting. Such a characterization would not do her justice. Lucille was an intellectual, a voracious reader, and a bit of an eccentric. She was lively, colorful, and a savvy political organizer. Apparently, she was also quite attractive. One former lover described her as "a tall voluptuous brown-skinned woman," with a sharp wit and a deep commitment to social justice. Lucille loved jazz and bourbon, hated cooking, read Kafka, and chose never to marry, despite having been asked repeatedly.[50] She was Ella Baker's dear friend and confidante for many years. The two women enjoyed long phone conversations, meals together, and occasionally evenings out. Their relationship was anchored in politics, a sisterhood steeped in struggle. "Lucille was probably Ella's closest friend in the office," an NAACP staffer observed.[51]

Baker let her guard down with Black, complaining about her problems and confessing her doubts and insecurities. While traveling alone, Baker would routinely sit down at the end of a busy day and write Lucille a rambling, cathartic, and often witty rendition of the day's events. In one letter Ella complained to Lucille: "Today, I am worn to a frazzle. Train connections are not so good . . . [and the situation] leaves me quite frayed."[52] In another letter to Black, she confessed: "The outlook for this trip does not appear rosy. I am constantly challenged to 'pass a miracle' which will demonstrate how small, isolated, and rural communities can initiate active branches in the absence of some major tragedy. . . . The best I can do is try to jolt or scare them into action, and make an effort to maintain it through correspondence long enough to bring the branch membership up to at least fifty members. But such are the trials of those who must act as Mother Confessor to the Little Folk. So let it be."[53] These letters were an important outlet for Baker to express her frustrations and disappointments as she undertook the difficult work of grassroots organizing in the South.

Baker's letters to Black eloquently express her analysis of the class politics within the organization and the black community and clearly articulate her own egalitarian sensibilities. Ella had great distaste for the petit-bourgeois lifestyles and snobbery displayed by some of the local branch leaders. She felt that their elitism and pompous attention to social, rather than political, events were obstacles to more militant mass action. Even in the stifling atmosphere of the Jim Crow South, especially in the cities, black professionals and entrepreneurs had carved out a niche within the confining walls of the racial order. Within those confines, there was an ever-present struggle over issues of resistance and accommodation.

The letters to Black complained about the middle-class socialites who had a stranglehold on some local branches. She did not hide her contempt for the pettiness she encountered in these circles. She wrote to Lucille about a visit she was compelled to make in Georgia: "I am stopping at the home of three women of leisure whose major past time[sic] is idle chatter . . . [and] who were too busy to attend the meeting last night."[54] From Florida, Ella wrote: "The campaign chairman is experiencing a slight let down in that I am not a social elite, and cannot join her in a game of bridge or golf at the 'Country Club.' "[55]

Baker felt that the class hierarchy within the black community was a major obstacle to creating more active and effective branches that would be able to reach out to every sector of the African American community. In Baker's opinion, some of the middle-class black professionals who ran local branches "had attitudes that were not particularly helpful in terms of change. For instance, . . . they would be against the idea of going to battle for the town drunk who happened to have been brutalized when being arrested, because who was he?"[56] Baker referred to this hypothetical scenario of police brutality toward the town drunk repeatedly, and it reveals her fundamental criticism of the vision of change embodied by the black elite. In essence, some middle-class black leaders felt that only those blacks who conformed to the dominant culture's notion of social respectability should be held up as deserving of civil rights and full citizenship. This was not always the position they articulated publicly, but it was implicit in their actions. Baker felt that this viewpoint had to be rooted out and challenged, first, as a matter of principle and, second, in order to mobilize the support and participation of poor and working-class members of the black community who were, after all, the overwhelming majority.[57]

Another source of personal support in her dealings with others was Baker's friendship with Charlotte Crump, a young woman who worked as the NAACP's coordinator of publicity and promotions in the early 1940s.

Crump was friendly, easygoing, and perhaps a little lonely, since her husband was stationed elsewhere with the military. She and Baker often went out to lunch or dinner together at a nearby restaurant called the Starlight, where they would relax and, as Crump described it, "gripe about this or that."[58] One of Crump's main gripes concerned her run-ins with her male supervisors, White and Wilkins. Despite the fact that she worked weekends, holidays, and some evenings, both White and Wilkins complained that she did not work hard enough and threatened to have her punch a time clock to ensure that she was in the office by 9:30 every morning.[59] In 1945, when Baker was no longer in White's good graces, very similar complaints would be lodged against her as well. At this point, however, Baker served as a sounding board for her friend Charlotte.

Much of the correspondence between Baker and Crump was business-related, since Crump coordinated the publicity for Baker's visits to various branches. However, their exchanges always had a personal tone. Crump signed her letters "affectionately" or "faithfully" and jokingly chastised Ella to "get a little rest because we don't want to have to carry you into Fifth on a stretcher when you return."[60] Crump's concern and affection for Baker are apparent in these details. Baker was known for overworking and pushing herself to the limit. Friends and colleagues like Crump constantly reminded her to take it easy and take better care of herself, although she rarely took their advice.[61]

The NAACP women seemed to look out for one another. They knew the difficulties of navigating the internal dynamics of the organization as well as the dangers and inconveniences associated with being on the road. Many of their letters back and forth are punctuated with admonitions to "take care of yourself" and "don't let [it] get you down."[62] Baker took a special interest in the hardships that her friend Ruby Hurley experienced while traveling on NAACP business in Norfolk in 1943, soon after Baker had assumed the post of director of branches. She made suggestions about how Hurley might arrange more comfortable accommodations during her stay and then assured her that she would try to attend a meeting on youth in Harlem in the wake of the 1943 "riot" in order to convey some of Ruby's concerns, which are not specified in the letter. Given the demands on Baker's schedule this was a generous gesture, and she concluded the letter jokingly, "now ain't I a friend."[63] Both Hurley and Baker also stayed in touch with their mutual friend, Pauli Murray, who also remained very much involved in NAACP activities. Pauli wrote to Ruby when she was considering law school. When Ruby wrote back to encourage her, she updated her on how hard Ella was working and concluded, "in the meantime, good luck from both of us."[64]

Not all of Baker's relationships in the NAACP were so amicable, and not all of her female colleagues were sisterly. She made friends and enemies alike. Her first major conflict within the NAACP "family" was with the formidable Lillie Jackson, an unapologetic socialite who headed the Baltimore branch.[65] Baker made no secret of her disdain for the pretenses and self-aggrandizing behavior of those who were overly concerned with status and appearance. These sensibilities immediately put her on a collision course with Jackson.

The two women are a study in opposites. Jackson basked in the spotlight and insisted on deference from those around her. Although she came from humble origins, she went to great lengths to demonstrate the wealth she and her family had acquired and their rank as one of Baltimore's most prominent black families. Baker, on the other hand, was self-assured but modest. She dressed plainly and spoke with a simple elegance that endeared her to educated and uneducated audiences alike. Jackson's identity was very much that of a respectable, married woman. Baker was an ambiguously married woman, if in fact her marital status was known, and she flirted with the limits of respectability with her aggressive organizing style. No one would accuse Lillie Jackson of being an appendage of her husband or anyone else, but she did harbor some very conventional notions about marriage and the proper role of married women. Her status as Mrs. Jackson was important to her, a value she passed on to her daughter, Juanita, who, in her own words, "resigned [her post with the NAACP] to marry my prince."[66] Baker saw herself as a fiercely independent woman and defied the conventions that restricted the activities of married women simply by ignoring them.

Personalities, class biases, and divergent gender identities all contributed to the problems between Baker and Jackson, which developed in September 1941, when Baker went to Baltimore to help conduct the annual membership drive. There had already been conflict between the national office and the branch leadership before she arrived. Baltimore had requested a paid secretary to help handle branch business; the national officers apparently felt no such position was needed; and the branch leaders had threatened to withhold dues and hire someone themselves.[67] Other national staff members had complaints about Lillie Jackson as well. When field secretaries visited Baltimore, Jackson treated them as a part of her personal staff. She was accustomed to planning their schedules and mediating their contacts with other branch members. One staff member recalled that Jackson would have "scheduled our trips to the bathroom, if she could have."[68]

Even though Baker was still new to the association, she had no intention of catering to the whims of the branch president. Baker went around Jackson to meet directly with rank-and-file members, including those with grievances about how the branch was being run. Jackson viewed this as a direct affront to her leadership. The very day that Ella Baker left Baltimore for another campaign in Norfolk, Lillie Jackson dispatched a letter to Walter White harshly criticizing Baker and alleging incompetence and a "bad attitude" on her part. Baker's "attitude has been discourteous and contemptible, and is not conducive to the best interests of all concerned." Jackson accused Baker of trying to disrupt the Baltimore branch by fomenting dissension and of being "antagonistic" and uncooperative.[69] Jackson took the view that "there are always a few disgruntled people in every organization. Certainly campaign directors should not encourage dissension and confusion in a branch. That, however, is precisely what Miss Baker has done."[70] Baker disapproved of Jackson, and she said so in her reports to her supervisors in the national office. In her view, Jackson dominated the Baltimore group in such a way as to stifle its growth and to engender bad feelings among potential new members.[71] What Jackson described as Baker's "bad attitude" was probably reflective of her negative view of the way in which the branch was being directed. In Baker's opinion, the branch was being run by a group of short-sighted, self-serving bureaucrats who were roadblocks to progress. Although the Baltimore branch boasted nearly 3,000 members, they were members in name only; they had signed up and paid their dues, but they were asked to do little else. In one of her monthly field reports, Baker observed: "The need for greater membership participation in the larger branches was emphasized when in Baltimore a functioning publicity committee and speaker's bureau were not obtainable."[72] Baker confided to Roy Wilkins that she thought the Baltimore branch leaders were petty and arrogant, and they used "almost blackmail" techniques in persuading others to support the branch financially. Even more seriously, she accused the Jackson family of nepotism and favoritism in the exercise of their political power. She noted specifically that one or another of Lillie Jackson's relatives had repeatedly "won" trips to the national NAACP conferences, to the exclusion of other members.[73] Even though Jackson's persistent and vindictive attacks undoubtedly bothered Baker, she was more deeply troubled by the heavy-handed and undemocratic style of leadership that Jackson personified. The Baltimore branch had only the appearance of a strong local organization. The branch leadership had not cultivated a group of local leaders or developed a serious program for action; instead, the chapter was run like an exclusive social club.

Fortunately for Baker, both Walter White and Roy Wilkins defended her against Jackson's criticisms and deflected blame for the conflict away from Baker and back on the branch leaders themselves. According to Wilkins, "The Jackson family will find fault with every national officer who does not conform to their personal ideas. They do not like Mrs. Lampkin; they spend a lot of time trying to smear me; Morrow has never been there; and now they are trying to smear Ella. I think a good rule from now on would be to let them conduct their own campaigns and probably hoist themselves by their own petard."[74] White expressed astonishment at the allegations from Baltimore, pointing out to Lillie Jackson that her complaints about Ella Baker were "at such variance with the reports from every other branch with which she has worked that I am convinced that there must be some basic misunderstanding."[75] Although tensions between Baker and Jackson persisted for some years, this controversy blew over without any apparent damage to Baker's political career or her reputation within the NAACP. She was promoted to director of branches less than two years later. But the road Baker traveled was indeed a difficult and, at times, a dangerous one. In order to do the work to which she had committed herself, she had to face challenges more serious than those presented by the likes of Lillie Jackson.

. . . . . .

DANGERS ALL AROUND

Although Baker was never arrested or beaten during her NAACP days, it was certainly not because she traveled in a safe environment. There were dangers all around her, and she escaped harm only through a combination of blind luck and constant awareness. When threats were apparent, Baker maneuvered carefully. Her refusal to always conform to the conventions of Jim Crow meant she had many close calls. One day in December, 1942, while she was riding a bus in Georgia, she braced herself for a confrontation.

> I got on a bus [and] . . . it was crowded and it had a lot of whites on it, service people, and there was only one other black person and I could tell that she was one of the ladies who paid payroll. But I could see that she was not going to be pushed around either. So I said, "well, we'll see here today" because they [bus drivers] had the habit of demanding that

you get up and let them [white passengers] sit down. But they didn't do it that day. Because I was prepared to not get up and I could tell she was not going to be moved.[76]

When Baker and her quietly defiant ally did not relinquish their seats, they were subjected to a litany of verbal abuse. She recalled that she sat and "listened to two white sailors [standing above her] talking about how they had killed a black woman." Baker, understanding the volatility of the situation, regretted that she "couldn't confront them," but she wisely decided not to in this instance.[77]

Another time, a bus driver refused to let Baker and other blacks board a bus in Florida because a white sailor was sprawled out on a seat in the back of the bus designated for "colored" passengers. Baker just stood there and watched the bus pass by.[78] She endured a number of similar humiliating experiences. Baker was known for being tough and confrontational if she had to be, but she was also practical. She chose her battles carefully and assessed what was at stake and the likely outcome of a fight before she entered into it. Her own survival strategy dictated that she had to tolerate certain insults and abuses, garner her anger and her strength, and bring them to bear under more favorable conditions. However, there were times when she simply could not avoid confrontation.

For Ella Baker, the fight for social justice waged through the NAACP became a personal as well as political crusade. She had been told since she was a young child that she was inferior to no one, and she believed it. But her confidence routinely rubbed against the reality of Jim Crow segregation. Baker's struggle against racism was as much about standing up for herself as it was about lending her strength to struggles initiated on behalf of others. There were numerous instances over the course of her life when she personally tested the limits of America's racial policies, vented her anger, and affirmed her own humanity in the process. One such instance occurred in the spring of 1943, when she was traveling by train from Mobile, Alabama, to Jacksonville, Florida.

On May 4, 1943, hungry and tired, Baker entered the dining car of the train at about 5:45 P.M. to have her supper. Initially, she had no intention of challenging the company's Jim Crow policy. She entered the diner and proceeded to take a seat in the section designated for "colored" passengers. However, four white soldiers were already seated there. When Ella Baker took a seat near the white soldiers' table, the white steward nervously ran over to her and insisted that she could not sit there because it violated state law, which required separate eating facilities for white and "colored" diners. Baker pointed out to him that she had complied with state law and sat in the designated section. If he were so concerned about enforcing segregated eating facilities, he should "request that the four white soldiers move forward, since there was ample space in the section reserved for whites." When the steward declined to act on Baker's suggestion, she took it upon herself to ask the soldiers to move, which, much to her surprise, they did. In the waiter's version of the incident, Baker was "insulting and abusive." He contended that white passengers were so outraged at Baker's behavior that they offered to use physical force to remove her from the diner, but the steward nobly intervened to avert a confrontation. Baker was eventually served her dinner at the table she had originally occupied.[79]

Three weeks later, on the last leg of the same trip, Baker confronted a very similar situation. This time, perhaps feeling emboldened by her earlier victory, she stood her ground with even greater resolve, but her defiance was met with violence. On May 29, while she was heading home to New York from Jacksonville, she entered the dining car of the train for a meal at about 1:45 P.M. No curtain was in place to divide the white and "colored" sections of the diner, as was the custom. She sat down at a booth near the kitchen, which was usually reserved for "colored" people, and waited for service. A white steward then confronted Baker, insisting that she leave the car and come back later when the white passengers were finished eating. It had been a long and tiring trip. Her blunt response was that "I was hungry and I preferred eating then."[80] Baker reminded the steward that, while segregation was the law in Florida, there were also laws that provided for first-class passengers to be served at their convenience. The steward was so flustered and offended by the willful self-confidence of this dignified, middle-aged Negro woman that he immediately summoned two military policemen who were also traveling on the train to assist him in removing her from the diner. Baker had no intention of going peacefully. She described the rest of the incident as follows:

Two white military police immediately rushed to where I was sitting, one snatched me up by my arm, bruising my leg in two places, and told me to "get out of there." I reminded the M.P. that he was overstepping his bounds. He disregarded this remark. I then spoke louder and appealed to the house and said "this man is overstepping his authority." This seemed to shock him into realizing that he was manhandling me without any right to do so. He freed my arms and he, the other M.P. and the steward rushed out of the car in search, I presume, of the train conductor. When they returned, I was leaving the dining room and the M.P. who had manhandled me was remarking, "but I have no jurisdiction over her."[81]

Baker was so insulted by the treatment she had received that she ate dinner in her seat that evening instead of going back to the dining car, and she skipped breakfast altogether on Sunday morning.[82] When she arrived back in New York she immediately filed a complaint with the railway company. Her friend and colleague Thurgood Marshall, the future Supreme Court justice, who was then on the NAACP's legal staff, submitted the complaint on her behalf.[83] Baker did not make it easy for railway workers—or anyone else for that matter—to treat her as a second-class citizen.

The historic struggle for fair treatment on public transportation was a particularly powerful and symbolic issue for African American women, and Baker's actions in 1943 had implications for both race and gender politics. Ida B. Wells, the famed advocate of black and women's rights, had thrown down the gauntlet nearly twenty years before Ella Baker's birth when she sued the Chesapeake and Ohio Railway company for ejecting her from the "ladies coach" of a passenger train in 1884 in Tennessee. While Wells was very much a lady, she was black and therefore not eligible for the courtesies afforded white womanhood. Instead of the more comfortable "ladies coach," she was required to ride with the rough-and-tumble, predominantly male crowd in the smoking car.[84] Wells was not alone in her protest. Many African American women took similar, though less publicized, stances against demeaning treatment on public transportation. Over a half century later, Rosa Parks, Joanne Gibson Robinson, and thousands of African American women in Montgomery, Alabama, became the decisive force in winning the famed Montgomery bus boycott, an event cited as the spark that ignited the postwar Black Freedom Movement. In all of these confrontations, as black women demanded respectful treatment on public trains and busses, they struggled to define the parameters of race relations, class distinctions, and gender identity that manifested themselves in the ebb and flow of daily life. Ella Baker and other black women who engaged in similar protests were laying claim to the privileges afforded to their white counterparts. They were rebelling against social custom by insisting on being treated as "ladies" in a culture that much more readily cast them as "mammies" or "aunties."

In this instance, Baker relied on her knowledge of the law to defend herself from being "manhandled," as she put it. Such an assertion crossed other boundaries as well. Here she was, a black woman speaking with great clarity and confidence, asserting her rights as a citizen, invoking the law, and publicly reprimanding white men—soldiers, no less. In this exchange, Baker not only insisted on courtesies usually reserved for white women but also spoke in an authoritative language more associated with white men than with black or white women. Baker defied society's expectations of who and what a Negro woman ought to be. Her defiance of the conventions defining black womanhood permeated her life, extending beyond white racist views to the expectations that prevailed within her own family and community. Her wrestling with the white military police on the train who attempted unsuccessfully to "put her in her place" was paralleled by her wrestling with the circumscribed role prescribed for her by her family and with the supportive, sometimes deferential role most of her male colleagues in the NAACP expected her to play. She was determined to stand up for herself at the same time that she stood up for her sex, her race, and those at the bottom of the social and economic hierarchy. This type of willful self-assertion was an act of both personal empowerment and political intervention.

Assertive actions characterize Baker's years of work with the NAACP. In standing up for herself, she confronted the contradictions embedded in dominant assumptions about the proper role of black women of her generation. On the one hand, they were expected to be engaged in improving the condition of the race, and many, out of necessity, were employed outside their homes. These activities located black women, including respectable middle-class women, in the public arena as social reformers and as workers. Yet the culture was permeated with the idea that a woman's primary role was to be a mother and a homemaker. There was indeed a tension between the celebrated contributions of women like Ida B. Wells-Barnett, Nannie Helen Burroughs, and Mary McCleod Bethune—Baker's activist foremothers—and criticisms of them as encroaching on leadership roles reserved for black men. Although black women's activism was encouraged, it was circumscribed by what Evelyn Brooks Higginbotham terms the "politics of respectability," an attempt to represent the prevailing model of female propriety and ladylike behavior while still participating in strategies for racial progress and social reform.

The dangers facing a militant black woman in the Jim Crow South were undeniable, perhaps incalculable. Baker traveled long stretches alone, making her a vulnerable target. And she traveled with the label of NAACP organizer hanging over her head, which was a red flag to white vigilantes throughout the South. Ku Klux Klan members were known to attack people who distributed African American newspapers simply because the publications advocated black suffrage and desegregation. When Baker visited a given locale, her presence was announced through flyers, handbills, and the black press. Headlines blazoned: "Hear This Dynamic Speaker"; "Look Who is Here—Ella Baker"; "Join Now, This Is Your Fight Too—Hear Ella Baker."[85] The intervention of militant "outside agitators" must have enraged the likes of Bull Conner, the racist sheriff of Birmingham, and other avowed white supremacists. But, remarkably, Baker was able to ease in and out of southern communities for six years relatively unscathed.

Not all of her colleagues were so lucky. During the 1940s, Ella Baker worked closely with Harry T. Moore, a teacher and high school principal in Mims, Florida. Moore was a steadfast organizer who coordinated the NAACP branches statewide. He spearheaded a campaign to equalize the salaries of white and black teachers, and helped organize other black educators in Florida. Baker and Moore were in regular correspondence during the mid-forties, and she spent time with him and his family during her frequent Florida visits on behalf of the department of branches. On Christmas night in 1951, Moore and his wife Harriet were murdered when dynamite was thrown under their home.[86] Murder was the ultimate fear of NAACP leaders throughout the South in the postwar period, as public lynching had been for earlier generations. Lethal violence lurked just below the surface of southern race politics. Baker understood this minefield and navigated it with caution.

At the same time that Baker worried about the threat of white vigilante violence, the federal government worried about the alleged "danger" that she represented. Throughout the World War II period and the Cold War years that followed, Baker was under constant surveillance by the Federal Bureau of Investigation and by Military Intelligence. They monitored her moves, speculated about her motives, and compiled reams of reconnaissance data on her public activity and her private life. FBI informants called Baker on the phone to obtain information about her whereabouts, feigned interest in her politics to get a closer view of her day-to-day activities, and pumped her friends and associates to amass a profile of a woman they deemed potentially subversive.[87]

Most of the FBI agents who spied on Baker from the 1940s through the 1970s did not know what to make of this middle-aged hell-raiser who defied categorization. She led an unconventional life, made enormous sacrifices for the causes and campaigns to which she devoted herself, and asked for very little material reward or recognition in return. She maintained an eclectic circle of friends of various ages, races, and political affiliations, yet she herself never belonged to any one organization for very long. Reading between the lines of the FBI's individual reports on Baker's activities, one can almost hear the agents' queries, pregnant with all the biased stereotypes the agency held about dissidents: What is she up to? Who does she work for? What is her hidden agenda? The agents' own inability to answer such basic questions led one of them to conclude that Baker was "unstable."[88] It was the very way that she looked at the world that made her difficult to label. Since she saw revolution as a process, as a living experiment in creative vision and collaboration, very little, in her opinion, could be predetermined. No blueprint could be rigidly adhered to. There was an organic interaction between the people involved in social change and those opposed; among different sectors, generations, and regions of the movement; between what we know and what we dare to dream. Although Baker had a definite worldview, which she articulated, enacted, and defended, there was fluidity and flexibility in the positions she took and the alliances she formed. Even the FBI could not pin her down.

Despite the hectic pace, long hours, and dangers inherent in her job, Baker loved her work as a field organizer for the NAACP. Perhaps she even enjoyed certain aspects of the solitary, nomadic lifestyle that the job afforded her. During long train rides between cities she was alone with her thoughts, and at those times she must have struggled to make meaning out of the work she was doing ten to twelve hours a day. How far had she traveled from her own origins in the South? In some ways she was a world apart, and in other ways she had come full circle. Over twenty years after leaving Littleton and abandoning her mother's missionary zeal, and over a decade after renouncing her own missionary ambitions in order to pursue a more secular path, here she was with her little, dusty, tattered suitcase living a missionary's existence: traveling from one town to another preaching the "Gospel" of racial justice, and at times attempting, as she herself put it, to "pass a miracle."[89] Baker admitted, "I was the missionary type—I was on a crusade to save something."[90] But what was that "something"? And how would she ever succeed against such enormous odds?

The South could seem comfortable and familiar at times, but at other times Baker must have felt like a foreign visitor. In the decade and a half since she left Shaw University in Raleigh, she had become a New Yorker. She made friends from places most small-town southerners had never heard of; she related to whites in the bohemian arts and leftist political communities in ways that would make most black southerners fear for their lives; and she adopted a secular political language for discussing right and wrong, which would have made her mother cringe. One friend from North Carolina told Baker admiringly, "You are a lady of the world [now]," underscoring the divergent paths the two women's lives had taken since Ella Baker had left her hometown, while the friend had remained in North Carolina.[91]

As worldly and cosmopolitan as Baker had become during her years in New York, she still maintained close ties to her family in the South. One of her cousins, Helen Gilchrist, recalled: "Ella would swing through here with her little typewriter and spend a few days. She loved my cooking and she'd come over to my house and get a good home-cooked meal, and then she'd be off again."[92] Baker remained especially close to her mother. Even though she had rejected the two things her mother wanted most for her in life, a teaching career and a life in the church, she still found a way to make Georgianna Ross Baker proud. When Ella conducted membership drives in North Carolina or Virginia, not only would she always find time to visit and spend time in Littleton, but she also would frequently arrange to have her mother attend one of the public meetings at which she was scheduled to deliver the keynote address. Even though later in life Ella would question the value of eloquent oratory as a tool for political mobilization, during her NAACP campaigns she was known as a powerful public speaker. Having served as Ella's childhood "speech coach," Anna Baker must have taken great satisfaction in the fact that her daughter's oratorical skills were being put to good use. On at least one occasion, Ella indicated she would "delegate my mother to represent me" at an NAACP event in Warrenton, North Carolina.[93] Ella had been trained in pronunciation and diction by her perfectionist and proper mother, but she developed her own speaking style that was itself quite effective. One of her friends and NAACP co-workers, Odetta Harper Hines, described her speaking style this way: Baker was "a powerful speaker who talked without notes from her heart to the hearts of her audience. Very forceful, with a strong voice that projected even without a microphone. Her speeches weren't full of statistics, nor were they anecdotal. They were to the point [but still] . . . very human and warm."[94]

CLASS, GENDER, AND PERSONAL POLITICS

World War II unsettled the class, gender, and racial order of the United States, creating a new sense of possibility for women, working people, and African Americans. Women went into the factories in large numbers, and civil rights activists forced the government and businesses to open up defense industry jobs to black men and women. New forms of mass mobilization developed along with new modes of political action. Ella Baker followed her own path amid these exciting possibilities, linking the NAACP's civil rights agenda to the labor movement, pushing for greater gender equity within the association, and emphasizing the need for rank-and-file organizing built on preexisting community networks as a model for the NAACP.

In Baker's view, the struggle against racism was deeply embedded in an overarching class struggle between the haves and the have-nots. Influenced by the egalitarian ethos of her childhood community, the socialist milieu of Harlem in the 1930s, and her close association with labor union organizers in the Workers Education Project, Baker was strongly sympathetic to the growing trade union movement, regarding it as a natural ally for the NAACP. In a 1943 memo, she pointed out that "branches should be made more and more aware that the fight for Negro rights is but one aspect of the larger fight for social and democratic gains . . . for instance, the fight for up-grading of Negro workers might well gain support if a given local branch would also take the leadership in support of the labor movement's fight against anti-labor legislation."[95] Baker saw the complementary goals of interracial labor organizing and civil rights activism as the basis for potential coalitions among groups or even for a unified economic and political initiative within the African American community.

During 1942 and 1943, Ella Baker became increasingly involved in the labor movement, which was spearheaded by left-wing unions of the Congress of Industrial Organizations (CIO). Founded in 1936 to organize workers in entire mass-production industries rather than on the basis of their particular skills, the CIO emphasized the mobilization of unskilled and semiskilled workers. Considerable numbers of African Americans worked in such positions, especially after wartime labor shortages opened up employment opportunities in mines, steel plants, auto factories, shipyards, and other essential industries.

In contrast to the CIO, the more established American Federation of

Labor (AFL) had a long history of exclusionary and segregationist practices. Earlier in 1942 the United Auto Workers (UAW), the CIO's largest member union, had taken an unequivocal stand in support of civil rights for African Americans in Detroit in a conflict that erupted over black families' access to the Sojourner Truth public housing project, a struggle that erupted into a full-scale riot in 1943. The UAW's position in the controversy won it the respect and support of local black leaders and prospective union members and the attention of antiracist activists in the NAACP. On the national level, CIO leadership had taken a firm stand against antiblack hate strikes initiated by white segregationists within the union. The CIO represented a stronger commitment to interracial union organizing than any other major labor organization of its day.[96]

In November 1942, Baker became involved in the CIO's efforts to organize shipyard workers in Newport News, Virginia. She believed strongly in linking economic and social justice issues and, for her, civil rights and labor were a perfect fit. The AFL, which had unionized skilled workers in particular trades, competed with the CIO for the allegiance of less-skilled workers and laborers, many of whom were black. As Baker described that struggle:

> The CIO is here to organize the southeastern shipyard and the local branch is playing ball with the organizers and both CIO and NAACP are expecting to win through the contact. Yesterday several hours were spent in conference with reps of the International Longshoremen's Association, which is the one bona fide Negro group in the AF of L here; and the AF of L is attempting to use them as a buffer between the Negro and the damaging CIO policies of non-discrimination. Hence I am trying to aid the branch in avoiding an appearance of partisanism in this growing labor dispute; and yet at the same time make membership gains in both fields. This is not easy because the President [of the local NAACP branch] and many of the officials have already gone on record as being more CIO than AFL.[97]

Despite her public profession of neutrality, Baker revealed her partisan support for the CIO in a letter to Lucille Black: "The CIO is moving in, organizing everything. . . . I wish I could stay here several months. It is just the time to do a real piece of organizing for the NAACP, but as usual, I can only linger long enough to stir up sufficient interest to increase the membership by a few hundred and collect a few dollars. . . . I am rushing to a CIO meeting."[98] Baker appreciated the mass appeal of the labor movement, especially that of the CIO during its initial organizing campaigns. In her view, the mobilization of African Americans in the workplace and in the community were inextricably related, and the NAACP as well as the CIO would gain from the upsurge in activism. She had, after all, worked with the Brotherhood of Sleeping Car Porters in New York, as an extension of her community organizing work on racial and economic justice in the 1930s.

The CIO was also trying to organize in the sugar, laundry, and paper box industries.[99] Allegations of racism in the AFL and charges of communist involvement in the CIO escalated the level of antagonism between the rival organizations, which peaked when a black CIO organizer was beaten up, presumably by AFL supporters, and "a free for all fight ensued."[100]

The allegations concerning the CIO's ostensible ties to communism prompted Baker to defend the union. It is unclear whether she believed that the political affiliation of union organizers should not matter or whether she thought that the allegations were unfounded. Based on her later wavering on the issue, it is most likely that she leaned toward the latter position. She reported to Walter White that she chastised AFL leaders for using the "red scare" to try to deter black workers from joining the CIO. In 1943, the so-called red scare had a different historical meaning than it would just a few years later when Cold War anticommunism permeated the culture. This issue would polarize the NAACP in the postwar years, with the national leadership taking a firmly anticommunist position and purging members who had communist affiliations. In 1943, Baker was condemning a practice that would later take hold in her own organization and to which she would briefly consent. In any case, she was pleased to report that "the best-thinking Negroes have not been brought into the picture on the side of the status quo. To the contrary, the most articulate community leaders are definitely pro-CIO. This includes the president of our branch, and most of the members of the executive board."[101] In her official statements, however, Baker "neither lauded the CIO or damned the AFL; but stressed the greater need for Negroes to be on guard to protect their special interests within and outside of the organized labor movement."[102] As an official NAACP representative, she felt compelled to express a neutral position publicly, so as to not "expose the NAACP to the criticism of being partisan."[103]

Ella Baker's support for the CIO was tempered by an awareness of some of its internal weaknesses. Above all, she worried that the CIO's animus against the AFL might cause conflicts among black workers themselves. For example, she deplored the fact that a young black man named Elijah Jackson "was so definitely anti-AFL that he could barely be civil in company with Negro AFL members."[104] A number of black workers in the shipyard industry, especially in the building trades, were in AFL-affiliated unions.[105] Baker wanted to be able to bring the entire black community and its allies together around the shared concern for racial and social justice, and she saw sectarianism of any kind, including within the labor movement, as an obstacle to that objective. This inclusive, democratic sensibility persisted throughout her career as an organizer, as did her commitment to militant trade union activism. In a 1947 speech in Atlanta, she admonished black civil rights workers to "identify themselves with the labor fight, as well as other fights of oppressed people everywhere."[106]

Ella Baker's work alongside southern labor activists was yet another example of her willingness to venture into a predominantly male terrain. Nearly all of the union members mentioned in her correspondence were men. Since the shipbuilding and steel industries with which she had the most contact employed a predominantly male work force, it is likely she was the only woman in many of the meetings she attended. But this did not deter her; she seemed to not even notice the gender aberration her presence represented.

Baker was not naive about sexism, but her approach was to simply plow ahead as if she expected no one to stop her—and, more often than not, no one did. But she did not try to ignore sexism in the hope that it would just go away. She pushed for broader inclusion and fairer treatment of other women and took opportunities to make women feel valued within the organization, including women whose main roles in life were those of wife and mother. In one instance, she publicly commended an Alabama woman for her intention to take out NAACP memberships for each of her five children. Citing her as an example of "progressive motherhood," Baker invited the woman to have a picture taken for an NAACP publication in order to inspire other mothers to do likewise.[107] This was her way of demonstrating that there was a place in the organization for everyone, homemakers as well as wage workers.

Like workers, women were another underutilized group that Baker saw as integral to the NAACP's efforts. When asked by a new member about the prospect of starting up a separate women's auxiliary to one of the existing branches, Baker scoffed at the idea. It would, she felt, marginalize women and circumscribe their participation, excluding them from the mainstream of the organization. In direct response to this suggestion, Baker noted: "It is my opinion that any woman who wishes to contribute to the welfare of the Association can find opportunity to do so through the regular branch program. . . . From our experience we have found that women who become members of the women's auxiliary tend to isolate themselves from the main program of the Association and to forget that money-raising, as important as it is, can never take the place of the purpose for which the NAACP was organized."[108] Perhaps not surprisingly, the person inquiring about the establishment of a separate women's auxiliary was a man, not a woman.

Although Baker had been politically mentored in the all-female environment of the black Baptist missionary movement, she felt that the NAACP's relative openness to women's participation should be exploited and expanded. When she assumed her post as director of branches, she emphasized explicitly that women and men should be considered equally for all jobs.[109] Such measures, she believed, would enhance the strength of the larger struggle by enhancing the personnel base from which the group could draw to carry out its programs. Moreover, she did not want to see women who wanted to play a role in the movement have their aspirations eclipsed because of sexism.

One important aspect of Baker's efforts to recruit more active members, men and women, into the ranks of the NAACP was her personalized approach to political work. At the same time that she sought to recruit large numbers of people to join the NAACP, she still tried to recognize and affirm the value of each individual. This type of personalism or humanism became Ella Baker's trademark as an organizer. In her travels throughout the South on behalf of the NAACP, she met hundreds of ordinary black people and established enduring relationships with many of them. She slept in these people's homes, ate at their tables, spoke in their churches, and earned their trust. And she was never too busy, despite her intense schedule, to send off a batch of personal thank-you notes, sending regards to those she did not contact directly and expressing gratitude for the support and hospitality she had received. In a follow-up letter to local activists in Birmingham, she wrote: "I enjoyed my stay in the Magic City, I enjoyed working with Mr. Green in his official capacity as President of the branch, and most especially I remember the pleasant hours spent in your home and your presence. . . . Please give my regards to Mereva, and Aunt and Uncle Guice." She also promised to "write a little note to all of the key workers" to encourage them in their recruitment efforts.[110] This was typical of her warm, personal correspondence with many branch leaders.

Baker encouraged her male colleagues to follow her example of forging stronger personal ties with individual activists on the branch level. For example, she advised Walter White that the NAACP could be strengthened by "paying some attention to the human interest angle of correspondence from branches, such as the recognition of the illness and death of branch officers and workers."[111] Baker often intervened in order to maintain good relationships between the national office and the organization's constituency. On one occasion, White had neglected to respond to a request for support from the Newport News branch regarding a dispute in which a veterans hospital had recruited black nurses from Tuskegee and neglected to provide housing for them. Baker reminded the executive secretary that "sometime ago the Newport News branch wrote you for advice on the Kecoughtan Veterans Facility. . . . They are quite anxious to hear from you at your earliest convenience." Baker covered for White by telling the branch leaders that he was "unusually busy," but she promised that she "would call the matter to [his] attention," which she promptly did.[112]

A keen judge of character, Baker used her insights into human behavior to work effectively with others. In one instance, while negotiating with an older NAACP member who had decided to deed her estate to the organization on her death, Baker was careful not to seem too eager and push for a more immediate contribution in the form of a life membership, "les[t] she thinks . . . I think of her as a gift horse."[113] Baker was very sensitive about how she came across to the people in the communities where she did outreach work. An organizer did not have to have the perfect political strategy but did have to have the respect and trust of those he or she struggled alongside. This was Baker's contention.

. . . . . .

GIVE PEOPLE LIGHT AND THEY WILL FIND THE WAY

In 1943, Ella Baker became the director of branches, supervising the field secretaries and coordinating the national office's work with local groups. As the highest-ranking female staff member, she had greater influence over national policy, although never as much as she would have liked. The post put her in a better position to pursue her agenda for a more democratic, inclusive, and action-oriented organization. But the way in which she was appointed to the post was itself an example of the kind of dictatorial style that Baker was anxious to undo.

While working on a membership drive in Mobile, Alabama, in the spring of 1943, she received a rather terse letter from Walter White announcing her new appointment. She was floored. Since the post had been left vacant for nearly two years after William Pickens left the organization in 1941, Baker wondered why there was such a rush to fill it now. When Baker resigned the position three years later, she recalled her appointment as an example of the organization's internal problems. In her words: "[T]he manner in which I was appointed or rather "drafted" as Director of Branches indicated a thought pattern that does not lend itself to healthy staff relations. . . . At no time had we [White and Baker] discussed the directorship either in respect to myself or to anyone else. . . . [M]y right to an opinion in the matter was completely discounted."[114] Although Baker was pretty sure that her friends Thurgood Marshall and Bill Hastie had influenced White to choose her for the post, the timing and awkward process led her to believe that White was trying to make an impression or cover up some past oversight. Baker never got over the way in which she had been shuttled into leadership without consultation or consent.

Baker's reply to White's letter of appointment indicated that she was flattered as well as surprised. She asked to discuss the implications of the new assignment before she gave him her answer. White had not anticipated the possibility that Baker would decline the post, and he had issued statements to the press at the same time that he sent her the letter "offering" her the job.[115] Such presumptuous arrogance, which was not unusual for White, demonstrated that he viewed Baker as more of a pawn than a peer. She accepted the new title with some trepidation, viewing it as an opportunity to effect some of the changes she felt were sorely needed in the NAACP.

A top priority for the new director of branches was to lessen the organization's bureaucracy and White's dominating role in it. Baker was disturbed by the fact that "the program was more or less channeled through the head [the executive secretary and the national office] and not the people out in the field."[116] While working as a field secretary, Baker had lobbied for a regional or state structure that would reduce the rigid hierarchy within the association and place more power in the hands of capable and heroic local leaders like her friend Harry Moore in Florida.[117] In one letter to Wilkins, Baker reminded him that "regional secretaries are an imminent need."[118] Baker also advocated giving greater responsibility and autonomy to local branches. In 1942, she urged the development of "neighborhood units" on the model of Birmingham. These would not be "separate branches, but in the neighborhood there is a chairman and a co-chairman, and various committees." The value of such a substructure, she contended, "is that you have more people participating in branch work and you are able to contact more persons who perhaps will never get to the general branch meeting but will attend little neighborhood meetings."[119] Her goal was to make the organization more accessible to people at every level of involvement. Baker suggested that branch supervision be "decentralized," allowing field workers to work more closely with individual branches.[120]

Ella Baker's strong commitment to local leadership persisted through-out her career as an activist. She once commented that "persons living and working in a community are in a better position to select leadership for a community project than one coming into the community."[121] As far as Baker was concerned, that observation applied as much to NAACP branches during the 1940s as it did to SNCC in the Mississippi Delta during the mid-1960s. By 1942, Baker had become quite vocal in her criticisms of bureaucratic leadership. She insisted that the strength of an organization grew from the bottom up, not the top down. "The work of the National Office is one thing, but the work of the branches is in the final analysis the life blood of the Association," she argued.[122] In many respects, Baker's criticisms of the organization closely resembled Du Bois's. In 1946, the year Baker resigned from her post as director of branches, Du Bois argued that "power and authority" were too tightly concentrated "among a small tight group which issues directives to the mass of members." Like Baker, Du Bois concluded that the association had to "hand down and distribute authority to regions and branches."[123]

A fundamental commitment to democratic practice distinguished Ella Baker's progressive politics. She despised elitism and placed her confi-dence in the many rather than the few, however talented and enlightened they might be. Moreover, she had come to recognize that the bedrock of any serious social change organization is not the eloquence or expertise of its top leaders; it lies, instead, in the commitment and hard work of the rank-and-file membership and the willingness and ability of those mem-bers to engage in a vibrant and reciprocal process of discussion, debate, and decision making. Baker carried this viewpoint with her into her orga-nizing efforts with the Southern Christian Leadership Conference during the 1950s. She felt that the national NAACP relied too heavily on its lawyers and educated spokesmen and neglected its branch structure. Legal initia-tives were fine; but, without mass campaigns waged in tandem, the victo-ries were shallow and short-lived.

Baker was well aware that NAACP branches were floundering because of a lack of direction or a lack of channels through which to contribute to the larger struggle—or, worse still, they were stifled by the narrow, self-serving agendas of bureaucratic branch leaders. In Baker's view, there was no excuse for local branches simply to serve as cheerleaders and fund-raisers for the national office. Programs of action were key to the vitality and relevance of local branches. In a letter to Lucille Black written from Rome, Georgia, she remarked: "Rome manifests all the expected symptoms of a branch that has had the same president for 24 years; and of a community that thinks nothing can be done in the South that would challenge the status quo."[124] Bringing in new leadership and challenging the black community's resignation in the face of Jim Crow were, in Baker's mind, closely related; only people who refused to become accustomed to things as they were had the determination to act for change.

One of Ella Baker's first goals as director of branches was "to increase the extent to which the present membership participates in national and local activities."[125] She also pledged "to transform the local branches from being centers of sporadic activity to becoming centers of sustained and dynamic community leadership."[126] Toward that end, she organized a series of regional leadership conferences designed to cultivate leadership at the grassroots level. Initially, her idea for regional gatherings met with opposition.[127] But she mobilized the Committee on Branches, which she had put together, to support the idea, and pressured Walter White to allow her to proceed.

Interestingly, and probably not wholly by chance, Ella's old friend Pauli Murray, the leftist lawyer who was then living in California, added her voice to those supporting the leadership training initiative. In the summer of 1944, just as Baker was making her case for the proposal, Murray wrote to Walter White and Roy Wilkins endorsing a very similar concept. In a witty and humorous letter to White, she demanded to know "when you burn out fifty years from now, who is going to take your place? When I burn out much sooner, who is going to be the gadfly getting into people's hair and urging them to get things done? . . . The NAACP needs a carefully worked out NAACP leadership training program . . . where young men and women would sit down for several weeks and discuss with you, Roy, Dean Hastie, Ella Baker and countless others the problems and techniques of organization."[128] In her follow-up letter to Wilkins, Murray stressed the need for such training on the branch level: "In trotting over the country in my vagabond fashion, I am appalled at the lag between the sure-fire fighting techniques developed by the national office staff members and the slow, inefficient methods of local volunteer officers. Race-relations has become a profession and its workers should be technically trained. Who is more capable to lead off in the training process than the national staff?"[129] There is no paper trail indicating that Ella Baker had requested Pauli Murray's timely intervention, but it is likely that the two women were in touch, as they had been on and off for over a decade. Murray singled out Baker for praise in her letter to White: "I've seen Ella in action and they don't come finer."[130]

Ella Baker's leadership conferences were an enormous success; and when she left the association in 1946, Roy Wilkins remembered them as one of her main contributions to the national organization.[131] The first regional leadership conference was held in New York City on November 11–12, 1944. The purpose of the conference was "to emphasize the basic techniques and procedures for developing and carrying out programs of action in the branches."[132] Over 150 delegates from seventy-three branches and six states attended the two-day conference, which addressed such topics as individual and mass protest, political pressure, education and propaganda, legal action, and cooperation and collaboration with other groups.[133] Baker was very concerned with the mechanics of movement building. She thought that, rather than simply telling people to develop a program, the association should impart to them the skills and information necessary to carry out such a task effectively and with confidence.

Between 1944 and 1946, under Baker's direction, leadership conferences were held in Shreveport, Tulsa, Atlanta, Jacksonville, Chicago, Easton (Pennsylvania), and Indianapolis.[134] Baker pulled in top officials to deliver lectures, offer welcoming remarks, and conduct workshops. Roy Wilkins, Thurgood Marshall, and Walter White all participated at one time or another.[135] For the conference held in New York, Gloster Current, president of the Detroit branch, and Leslie Perry of the Washington Bureau, which focused on lobbying and litigation, were flown in to speak. Baker also drew on the expertise of people outside the official structure of the association; for example, she invited Grace Hamilton of the Atlanta Urban League and Dorothy Homer of the New York Public Library. Ministers in towns where the conferences were convened were always asked to participate.[136] At the conference held at the Mt. Zion Baptist Church in Indianapolis in January 1945, both the city's mayor and Indiana's governor delivered welcoming addresses; Ella Baker and Thurgood Marshall represented the national NAACP.[137] At the Atlanta conference held in March, Baker and Marshall were accompanied by the national membership secretary, Lucille Black, and an assistant field secretary, Donald Jones. Building on the lessons of the two previous conferences, the Atlanta meeting had a much more detailed agenda. An evening session led by Marshall focused on such concrete issues as "police brutality; discrimination in public facilities, city parks and playgrounds; segregation in Inter-State Transportation; job discrimination;

the G.I. Bill of Rights . . . and the Negro Veteran; and . . . Labor Legislation."[138] Venues were chosen to maximize attendance: after daytime proceedings at Atlanta's Butler Street YMCA, evening mass meetings were held at Bethel Church.

Two residents of Montgomery, Alabama, who attended the Atlanta meeting later played decisive roles in the civil rights movement. E. D. Nixon, an organizer for the Brotherhood of Sleeping Car Porters, and Rosa Parks, a local NAACP activist, became key figures in the momentous Montgomery bus boycott of 1955–56. Parks confided in Baker some time later that this was the first time she had traveled outside the Montgomery area, and the experience made a lasting impression.[139] "I know Ella Baker had a profound effect on Rosa Parks," observed an activist who knew both women.[140] Years later, Parks agreed.[141]

In preparation for the leadership conferences, Baker sent out questionnaires asking what topics participants wanted to discuss at the gatherings. She tried to set an agenda that did not assume that the experts and national leaders were there to enlighten the masses. The title of the leadership conferences Baker coordinated was "Give People Light and They Will Find the Way." This title, drawn from one of Baker's favorite hymns, captures the essence of what she was trying to accomplish. She believed that people did not really need to be led; they needed to be given the skills, information, and opportunity to lead themselves.

· · · · · ·

TIME TO MOVE ON

The view that common people were capable of identifying the problems they faced and learning how to address them was shared by some of Baker's NAACP colleagues, but not by all. As she began to assert herself in the leadership of the NAACP, Baker made Walter White more and more uneasy. She was outspoken in executive staff meetings, criticized White when she thought he was wrong, and insisted on being either consulted about decisions affecting the branches or left alone to follow her own course. The association's resistance to engaging in mass mobilizations and grassroots organizing, coupled with the lack of internal democracy that prevented internal dialogue about such issues, contributed to Baker's decision to resign her post as director of branches in 1946.

Some of her NAACP colleagues found Baker's manner abrasive and her straightforward style annoying. A common word used to describe her was "difficult."[142] The ways in which she often described herself are consistent with the notion that she was deliberately "difficult." That is, she did not ingratiate herself with those in high positions, and she did not hesitate to speak her mind even when her ideas were controversial. To men like Walter White, this made her difficult. Baker was really never much of a team player, in the affable, conformist sense of the term. One problem was that she said what others thought but were more discreet about. She gave concrete meaning to the slogan "Speak truth to power." For example, there seems to have been an almost universal consensus among the New York staff that Walter White was egotistical, vain, and short-sighted. People whispered about him in the hallway, and many of his staff criticized him in private.[143] Baker recalled White as someone who went out of his way to remind everyone around him how important he was. For example, he would keep visitors waiting to give them the impression that he was too busy with more urgent matters to see them at the agreed-upon time. He would also walk into the middle of the office where the telephone switchboard was located to confer with the operator in a loud voice about the calls he was expecting from one important person or another.[144] His motives were transparent to most observers. However, most staff members discreetly kept their negative opinions of White to themselves. According to Herbert Hill, an NAACP staff member during the years shortly after Baker's tenure and later the architect of the NAACP's labor programs, "Ella made no secret of her contempt for Walter White."[145] Neither did Du Bois. As a result, both Baker and Du Bois were nudged out of the organization.

Baker realized that her days on the national staff were numbered when she and her friend Ruby Hurley openly defied Walter White's leadership at an Administrative Committee meeting in the winter of 1944. Hurley and Baker abstained from a vote endorsing a letter White wanted to send the mayor of New York City regarding a controversy that was brewing at Harlem's Sydenham Hospital. White, who was not at the meeting himself, was offended by his subordinates' independence and sent off a terse memo reprimanding Baker and Hurley and asking for an explanation of their actions. Baker cited this incident two years later in her letter of resignation, indicating that she "knew then that independent thinking was not to be tolerated on the staff."[146] She also knew that she could not operate comfortably for very long in such an environment.

The relationship between Baker and White grew more tense over the next year. He was not accustomed to anyone questioning his administrative decisions and viewed it as an affront to his leadership. For example, when White finally moved to implement Baker's suggestion that regional secretaries be hired to coordinate branch work, she applauded the decision but challenged the procedure as unfair, pointing out that there should be more detailed discussion throughout the organization before such important changes were made. She added that, before new staff were hired from the outside, present staff should be given an opportunity to apply for the new positions.[147]

The more Baker pushed for accountability regarding administrative decisions, the more White prodded her for alleged infractions of office procedure. White's charges seem petty or even fabricated. In November 1945, he dictated a stinging memo complaining that Baker was not working hard enough. He asserted that "throughout your time with the Association you have been out of the office on personal matters more than any other executive to the detriment of your work and office morale."[148] By all other indications, Baker was a tireless worker. On several occasions, she ignored her own health and came into the office against doctor's orders to perform some of the seemingly never-ending tasks associated with her job.[149] Baker's grueling itinerary for the years she was with the NAACP belies Walter White's suggestion that she was not pulling her weight in the organization. Moreover, it was only because White took the time to calculate Baker's days off over a five-year period that he was able to assert that she had taken more time off than any of her co-workers. Such research had to have been undertaken with a precise motive in mind. Even if Baker was off sick more than others, she certainly was not shirking her responsibilities, as White argued, since her calendar indicated that she worked evenings, weekends, and holidays throughout her tenure with the association. It was probably no coincidence that White's reprimand of Baker came only a week after Baker's criticism of White's unilateral action regarding the regional secretaries.

White's criticism of Baker for taking too much personal time was particularly callous and insensitive given the fact that Baker had just suffered a bereavement. The main reason she had requested personal time off during the months leading up to White's memo was the prolonged, terminal illness of her cousin Martha Grinage, whom she regarded as a sister. Martha had grown up with Ella in North Carolina, moving in with Ella's family after her own mother's death, and Ella had stayed with Martha when she first came to New York in 1927. Ella felt closer to Martha than she did to her own sister, Maggie. Martha was seriously ill and in and out of the hospital throughout the summer and fall of 1945. On several occasions, Ella rearranged her travel and meeting schedules in order to visit and help care for Martha.[150] After Martha died on October 16, Walter White did not even attend the funeral; he sent an impersonal telegram instead.[151]

Later that winter, Baker's family responsibilities expanded again as she adopted her nine-year-old niece, Jackie. In January 1946, Ella's brother, Curtis, wrote to her that Jackie "was asking about her relatives up north."[152] Jackie was the daughter of Ella's younger sister, Maggie. Since Maggie was unable to care for the child, the responsibility had fallen to Ella's mother and brother. Maggie had always been known as the wild and wayward child.[153] "My sister wasn't going to be very responsible [for the child] anyway," Ella admitted, "so, mama and papa [before his death] took the baby."[154] By the mid-1940s, Anna Ross Baker was aging and less able to care for Jackie, and Curtis, who was unmarried, may have been reluctant to become her primary caregiver. So Ella Baker agreed to take responsibility for the child, and Jackie moved from Littleton, North Carolina, to New York City to live with her aunt. Baker's new family commitment was a secondary factor contributing to her decision to resign from her administrative post with the NAACP. She anticipated that she would need to be closer to home for a while and feared that the time and travel commitments required by the job might be incompatible with her new parental responsibilities. At age forty-two, for all intents and purposes, Baker became a mother, a role she had not planned for herself, but one she embraced after it was thrust on her.

A conventional mother she was not. Jackie later recalled: "I had to move fast to keep up with her. I would sit in the back of meetings and do my homework many a night."[155] Ella relied on her husband and a female neighbor to assist with child-rearing. Baker recollected that "we could depend on Miss Lena being there to look out the window at the right time, and then [Jackie] would go upstairs to her place and be fed . . . she went to Miss Lena's regularly because I frequently had night meetings."[156] Bob seems to have filled in as well. One friend observed that "he did help look after the child, he helped Ella in that way."[157] Although Baker remained closer to home after Jackie came to live with her, she did not confine her work to a regular eight-hour day. She relied on others to help care for Jackie and tried to keep up an active pace of work.

Baker was already looking for another job when she decided to adopt Jackie. She responded to White's reprimand immediately by looking for other employment. In November 1945, she contacted Mary McLeod Bethune, the prominent civil rights activist, to inquire about job possibilities. Baker and Bethune were not friends, but they were acquainted. Bethune, nearly thirty years Baker's senior, had gone to a boarding school in North

Carolina, had contemplated becoming a missionary, was fiercely independent, and was deeply committed to community service and political activism—although of a somewhat different sort than Ella Baker's grassroots community organizing. Bethune was an educator and founder of Bethune-Cookman College, a friend of Eleanor Roosevelt, adviser to President Roosevelt, and leader of the black women's club movement.[158] She was certainly one of the most high-profile and politically influential black women of her generation. She knew of Ella Baker's work and respected her reputation as an organizer. Bethune responded cordially to Baker's inquiry, acknowledged her skills and talents, but no job offer was ever made.[159]

When Ella Baker left the NAACP's national staff in May 1946, it was not primarily because she was a new parent, although that was a contributing factor. She left mainly because she had little confidence that the national organization would make room for dissenting opinions or differing political views:

> My reasons for resigning are basically three—I feel that the Association is falling short of its present possibilities; that the full capacities of the staff have not been used; that there is little chance of mine being utilized in the immediate future. Neither one nor all of these reasons would induce me to resign if I felt that objective and honest discussion were possible and that remedial measures would follow. Unfortunately, I find no basis for expecting this. My reactions are not sudden but accumulative, and are based upon my own experience during the past five years and the experience of other staff, both present and former.[160]

Although Baker was characteristically honest in voicing her strong criticisms of the way the organization operated, she confined her opinions this time to a letter sent directly to the executive secretary and declined to make her criticisms a public issue at the NAACP's national convention, a move that Gloster Current, her colleague, successor, and sometime nemesis, saw as a "gracious gesture."[161] It was probably more practical and strategic on Baker's part than anything else. She understood that the NAACP was still a powerful and in many ways effective black freedom organization, although hampered by its internal weaknesses. She did not want to discredit the organization publicly, and she had every intention of continuing to work with the NAACP on terms more to her liking.

Baker's departure from the national staff came as such a blow to many of her associates at the branch level that she was inundated with letters expressing gratitude for her assistance and pleading with her to stay on.

After learning of her resignation, her friend John Leflore, a labor organizer and NAACP leader in Mobile, wrote: "All of us here and people throughout the country whom we have talked to, and who know you, have nothing but praise [for your work] . . . we have grown to love you."[162] Baker appreciated the words of praise and thanks she received from branch members, and she assured friends like Leflore that, while she was stepping down as director of branches, she was by no means resigning from the struggle. Baker's reputation and personal ties were strong enough that some NAACP branch leaders continued to treat her as if she were an official of the organization. Long after she had left the national office, Baker received a steady flow of invitations to speak at NAACP branch events across the South. For example, in January 1947, she went to Atlanta to help launch the annual membership drive at Big Bethel Church. The newspaper account of her visit reported that she "electrified" the audience, giving them both a history lesson and a political directive. Slaves were not given their freedom by Abraham Lincoln, Baker claimed; black soldiers fought and died for their freedom in the Civil War. The 1940s were no different, she insisted. Before stepping down from the podium, Baker called on her listeners to ally themselves with "the cause of oppressed people everywhere."[163] As she had told John Leflore, her commitment to the more activist and militant forces of the NAACP did not depend on her being on the payroll of the national office.

Although Ella Baker had developed a national network through her role as director of branches, she spent the last few years of her tenure cultivating ties to progressive individuals and organizations in New York as well. It was through this network that Baker was able to find employment. In the late 1940s and early 1950s, she managed to piece together an income through a series of odd jobs with several civil rights and community service organizations. Her longest employment stint was with the New York Cancer Committee, where she coordinated a public health education program. This was important work, but it was not her life's calling. It was not long before she plunged back into politics.

In the early 1950s, Baker would turn her attention from the national political stage to the local one in Harlem and New York City. The northern-based black freedom struggle was long overlooked, Baker felt; so, after her departure from the NAACP's national staff, she would ground herself in the struggles that burdened the lives of her own neighbors, friends, and family in New York. She soon realized that a local focus still could not keep at bay national politics and even global rivalries.

COPS, SCHOOLS, AND COMMUNISM
LOCAL POLITICS AND GLOBAL IDEOLOGIES—
NEW YORK CITY IN THE 1950S

· · · · · ·

I came into the social justice movements at the height of the repression of the Cold War
period. . . . Organizations seeking civil rights, peace and justice had been crushed
everywhere. . . . And although I discovered in those years that there was always a
resistance movement, many people did indeed fall into silence. . . . But the one thing
that could not be crushed was a burning desire of African Americans to be free.
Anne Braden, 1999

In 1952, Ella Baker was elected president of the large New York City NAACP
branch, becoming its first woman president. She had been active in the
branch for several years working with the youth council and several other
projects, but her new post provided her with the latitude and authority to
orchestrate some of the kinds of political campaigns she had long envisioned. After traveling around the country for two decades aiding grassroots groups to develop activist campaigns for change, she now had an
opportunity to shape and direct such a movement in the heart of New York
City. Her base of operations was Harlem, where she had long experience
and manifold ties with diverse groups of black and white political activists
and progressive intellectuals. Actually, she moved branch headquarters
from offices downtown to the heart of the black community in Harlem
to be more in the thick of things. Baker led the New York City branch
the way she thought all NAACP branches should function. She identified

issues of concern to black people—ordinary working people as well as professionals—and involved as many members as possible in building direct action campaigns to address those issues. She also worked hard to build coalitions with other groups in the city. In New York, unlike many smaller cities where the NAACP was the only civil rights organization in town, the black political scene was eclectic and contentious. But Baker was able to deal with the personalities and navigate the territorial rivalries of various organizations with finesse. Part of the key to her success was that she relished rather than resented other organizational involvement. Every action did not have to be carried out in the NAACP's name. In fact, Baker maintained multiple organizational affiliations even as she presided over the New York branch.

During 1952 and 1953, under Ella Baker's leadership, the New York NAACP branch built coalitions with other groups in the city and carried out aggressive campaigns focused primarily on school reform and desegregation and on police brutality.[1] In the course of these campaigns, Baker employed the whole range of protest tactics she had taught others to utilize: sending public letters of protest, leading noisy street demonstrations, confronting the mayor in front of the news media, and even running for public office, after temporarily taking off her NAACP hat. Baker's photograph and her fiery words appeared regularly in New York City newspapers, as she demanded quality, public education for all New York students, with active parental participation, and called for public accountability and fair treatment for people of color from the police. Often at the head of a crowd of supporters, acting in concert with other groups and individuals, Baker led the New York City NAACP into action alongside progressive whites and Puerto Ricans, the city's second-largest group of people of color.

In her efforts at coalition-building, Baker tried to avoid the divisive Cold War politics that defined the national scene during the early 1950s and threatened to infect the debates over local issues. While Baker continued to have regular contact with Walter White, Roy Wilkins, and Gloster Current, her successor as director of branches, with whom she had a civil but strained relationship, she tried to function as independently as possible. She contacted the executive officers regarding fund-raising efforts, membership strategies, and incidents that occurred in the city that both the New York branch and the national office might respond to. It took a conscious, continuous effort for Baker to carve out her own path in the very backyard of the national office. The personality conflicts and the tension between the national organization and local branches that created long-standing problems in the association were compounded, during the early 1950s, by the growing influence of anticommunism.

The national NAACP asserted its intention to step up the push for racial progress in the wake of World War II when it convened the National Emergency Civil Rights Mobilization in Washington, D.C., in January 1950. The tone and flavor of the event, however, suggested that the organization's national leaders intended to carry out that work safely within the bounds of Cold War rhetoric and ideology. The gathering brought together over 4,000 African American civic, community, and religious leaders in the nation's capital to press President Truman to take stronger action on pending civil rights initiatives. Demands included a permanent Fair Employment Practices Commission and voting rights protection.

The organization wanted to send another message to the Truman administration as well. Roy Wilkins and his colleagues were anxious to defend and reaffirm the NAACP's reputation against allegations of ties with communism. Anticommunist campaigners charged that the NAACP membership included those who presently or formerly belonged to the Communist Party and that communist ideas therefore dominated the association. This was hardly the case, but in the volatile political climate of 1950, and in the wake of the 1947 government decision to require loyalty oaths of federal employees, charges of communist links seemed tantamount to charges of treason. The national NAACP responded by denying the allegations outright, despite the prominent role played by well-known leftists of various ideological bents, including communists, in joint campaigns for racial justice over the previous thirty years.

The conveners of the National Emergency Civil Rights Mobilization went to great lengths formally and publicly to exclude radicals with any hint of communist affiliation. The conference call explicitly declared the mobilization to be a "nonpartisan, non-leftist movement rejecting the persistent proffers of 'cooperation' and 'assistance' made by individuals and organizations long identified as apologists for communist doctrine and Soviet foreign policies." The mobilization in Washington was only the beginning. At its annual convention in Boston in June, the NAACP formally barred communists from membership and following the lead of the CIO—which had recently taken similar steps—proceeded to purge leftists from its ranks.[2] This undemocratic stance was partly a defensive capitulation to the virulent red-baiting that was quickly permeating the political culture. At the same time, it was a continuation and deepening of longstanding tensions between the policies of the dominant leadership and the leftist politics of other antiracist activists, including some who were also NAACP members.

Like most black radicals living in New York City in 1950, Ella Baker had friends and colleagues who were communists. She often disagreed with them but she had worked with them off and on for over twenty years. Baker had managed to stay clear of the debate surrounding the Emergency Mobilization in January, and she had not figured prominently in the arguments that took place at the NAACP's Boston convention. But as head of the New York branch, in a city known for its radical political culture, Ella Baker would not be able to dodge the issues indefinitely.[3]

In the early 1950s in New York and elsewhere, there was a vibrant and multifaceted campaign for quality, integrated public education. Baker brought passion as well as long experience to the issue of educational reform. She was her mother's daughter, so education had always been near and dear to her heart. In contrast to Anna Ross Baker's rather conventional notions of teaching and learning, Ella was eager to explore more creative pathways to knowledge. In the 1930s, she had focused her energies on adult education. In the late 1940s and early 1950s, as the parent of a school-aged child, she turned her attention to elementary and secondary education. Jackie was enrolled in a private Quaker school for most of her time in New York, a sign of Ella's commitment to raising her daughter in an integrated, progressive, and nurturing milieu. But Baker knew that private solutions to public problems were not solutions at all. Her deep interest in public education led Baker to team up with the well-known psychologist and civil rights activist Kenneth Clark and his equally accomplished, less often recognized wife, Mamie Phipps Clark, to push for improved conditions for poor, largely African American and Latino schoolchildren in New York City. Through her relationship with the Clarks, Baker became a strong proponent of "community-based" models of learning in which parents were empowered to help define priorities and design curricula for their children. In this struggle, she also worked alongside Stanley Levison's wife, Bea, who was a reading tutor at the child development center run by the Clarks and a strong supporter of their work.[4]

Ella Baker joined a growing community of education reformers who sought fundamental changes in public education and child welfare policies that went well beyond the simple demand for integration. Milton Galamison, an African American activist in Brooklyn, and Annie Stein, a Jewish communist who was also active in Brooklyn, were pushing the national NAACP leaders as well as city officials to take more aggressive actions.[5]

Baker led her Harlem-based group, Parents in Action, and the citywide NAACP branch into the campaign, and out of that struggle developed a relationship with both Galamison and Stein; the latter became one of Baker's dear friends and close comrades. These were the years in which the NAACP's long-term legal campaign to desegregate public education was about to bear fruit in the landmark Supreme Court decision *Brown v. Board of Education*, and community-based civil rights activists sought to lay the basis for change once litigation had opened the door to desegregation.

Baker officially began working with the Clarks during the early 1950s, although she may have known them earlier through her activities with the NAACP and other organizations in New York. In August 1952, she co-convened a meeting at the Clarks' home in suburban Hastings-on-Hudson, a frequent gathering place for New York's black activist intellectuals, to talk about the issue of segregation in the New York schools. In March 1953, a follow-up meeting was held at the same location. These outreach meetings, directed at activists, educators, and policymakers in the New York area, were an attempt to attract a broad base of support for school desegregation and curricular reform in the city.[6]

Both Kenneth and Mamie Clark were the children of Caribbean-born parents, recipients of Ivy League doctorates in psychology, and staunchly committed social activists. Kenneth was the first African American accepted into Columbia University's graduate program in psychology; in 1942, he became the first black professor on the faculty of the City College of New York.[7] The couple's famous doll studies (which have since been questioned) sought to demonstrate how black children's self-esteem was damaged by racism, as evidenced by their preference for white over black dolls. The Clarks' doll studies were discussed at length in the NAACP's brief in *Brown v. Board of Education*, and the Supreme Court specifically cited the Clarks' work in its historic decision striking down segregated schools as unconstitutional. The Clarks had long careers as scholars and activists before and after the 1954 Brown decision. In 1946 they established the Northside Center for Child Development to provide "social work, psychological evaluation, and remediation services for youth in Harlem since there were virtually no mental health services in the community."[8] They were visible and vocal participants in struggles over housing, health, and poverty, as well as education.

In 1954, Baker agreed to serve as a member of the Intergroup Committee, chaired by Kenneth Clark, which was set up by the New York Board of Education to address some of the problems African American and Latino children encountered in the public schools. On the eve of the *Brown* decision, in April 1954, the committee hosted a conference at the New Lincoln School in Manhattan, titled "Children Apart," which indicted the school system for instilling a sense of inferiority in black children and perpetuating an enormous disparity in the resources allocated to black versus white schools. The meeting drew activists, social workers, educators, and parents from across the city and kicked off several years of intense protests and lobbying for school reform, school desegregation, and increased youth services in New York. Baker was a paid staff person for the conference and devoted several weeks of her time to planning the event, contributing her well-honed organizing skills to ensure its success.[9] She drafted literature and conference documents, lined up speakers, coordinated publicity, met with various participant groups, and strategized with other activists about how to make the event effective in reaching their larger objectives. The conference was perfectly timed: those who attended were primed to act once the imminent legal victory in the *Brown* case created an opening for change.

Ella Baker and the Clarks continued their work with the Intergroup Committee; but, after several years of lobbying and working with city officials, Baker was ready to move from debate to direct action. She feared that her former colleagues at the national NAACP office would either oppose such a step or slow it down with red tape. So, instead of operating exclusively under the banner of the New York City NAACP branch, Baker helped launch Parents in Action against Educational Discrimination, a grassroots coalition composed primarily of African American and Puerto Rican parents that demanded integrated schools and greater parental participation in educational policymaking. Years later, Baker recounted how the organization got started: "New York City didn't act right after the '54 decision. It didn't have any reason to act, so you had to help it to realize it. I was asked to serve on the Mayor's Commission. They finally discovered the city wasn't integrated! And Bob Wagner the second was then Mayor, and we ended up by having several sessions with him. In '57, the entire summer was spent in weekly parent workshops, helping parents become aware that they had certain rights."[10]

In the fall of 1957, the eyes of the nation were focused not on efforts to desegregate public schools in northern cities but rather on the pitched battle being waged in the streets of Little Rock, Arkansas, a confrontation so intense that it led to a standoff between Orval Faubus, the state's segregationist governor, and President Dwight Eisenhower, culminating in the deployment of federal troops. Daisy Bates, Ella Baker's friend and former NAACP colleague, was in the middle of the fray as the leader of the local NAACP branch. Bates negotiated with local school officials and police to try to ensure the protection of the nine brave black teenagers who defied vicious mobs to enroll in Central High School that fall. Bates's home was firebombed, and the newspaper that she and her husband ran was forced to close down because of economic pressures and harassment.[11] In the South in this era, struggles to secure basic legal rights were often met with violent reprisals.

Building on the attention that Little Rock had garnered, New York activists were eager to point out that racial disparities were not unique to the South and that militant challenges to government intransigence would be necessary in New York City as well. As was often the case, Baker found herself trying to push her civil rights colleagues—particularly the national leaders of the NAACP—toward a more militant stance at the same time that she was leading a popular struggle against those in positions of government power. The national NAACP office, afraid of negative publicity and of alienating its moderate, liberal supporters, sought to discourage confrontation and advised the activists to "adopt a less provocative endeavor, pointing out that after all northern school officials, unlike the hostile segregationists of the south, had agreed to integration; it was just a question of how and when," according to Galamison.[12] Baker founded the grassroots parents' group in order to circumvent the NAACP's paralytic bureaucracy and "go slow" politics.[13]

On September 26, 1957, Parents in Action called a rally designed to up the ante and draw greater attention to the campaign. Baker led a spirited picket line of over 500 black and Puerto Rican parents in front of City Hall in Manhattan to protest the beginning of another school year without a serious response to complaints these parents had been making for years. The group was particularly angry with School Superintendent William Jansen, but on this day they took their complaints directly to the mayor. The parents group had planned this confrontation for months. When the day of the scheduled demonstration finally arrived, Baker was one of the angriest and most vocal of the protesters. Although many civil rights activists later described Baker as a quiet, behind-the-scenes organizer, she was by no means hesitant to exert her leadership in this instance. News reports, which quoted Baker extensively, described her as the leader and principal rabble-rouser in the group. Their grievances included overcrowded schools, inappropriate curriculum content, the disproportionate allocation of more experienced teachers away from black and Latino schools, blatant racial segregation throughout the system, and the unresponsiveness of school officials to parents' concerns.

On that Thursday morning, the protesters picketed for nearly two hours demanding an immediate meeting with Mayor Robert Wagner. Finally, when it was apparent that the group would not back down, Wagner was persuaded by one of his colleagues to leave a meeting of the Board of Estimates and see a delegation of twenty-one protesters, many of them local ministers and NAACP activists, led by Ella Baker. Sara Black, a reporter for the Harlem-based *Amsterdam News*, described the meeting as follows: "From 11:55 to 12:12 Mayor Wagner spent an uneasy 17 minutes facing the delegation . . . led by Mrs. Ella J. Baker . . . while the parents leveled their charges. . . . Standing while the Mayor twitched nervously, spokesman Baker said: 'We parents want to know first hand from you just what is, or is not, going to be done for our children. . . . New York City, the world's leading city, should reflect the highest degree of democracy in its public school system.'"[14]

The group demanded a follow-up meeting with the mayor, to which he agreed. Baker then warned Wagner bluntly that he could not afford to alienate black and Puerto Rican voters two months before he would be on the ballot for reelection. After a few more sharp exchanges between Baker and the mayor, the group left City Hall, exhausted and drained after their four-hour-long protest, but claiming a tactical victory.[15]

The campaign for quality integrated schools in New York during the 1950s is historically significant.[16] First, Baker and her allies went beyond the simple demand for racial integration, calling for greater parent and community involvement in running the schools. This campaign was the first stage in the longer-term struggle for community control of the schools, a volatile issue that reemerged during the late 1960s and early 1970s. To insist that parents be empowered to define their children's education was a more substantive and radical demand than simply saying that black and white children should sit next to each other in the classroom. Complaining about distorted media coverage of the New York school struggle in a letter to her friend Ruth Moore, Baker wrote: "The headlines especially are designed to give the impression that the only thing with which we are concerned is integration rather than the fact that integration is desirable because where there is separation, even in New York, the schools are too often inadequate."[17] Second, Baker helped to forge an important biracial alliance between the African American and Puerto Rican communities.

Some of Baker's friends from the school struggles of the 1950s became allies once again in the 1970s, when Baker joined the Puerto Rican Solidarity Committee to push for Puerto Rican independence.

The other major cause that Baker championed during her tenure as New York NAACP branch president was even more volatile: the campaign against police brutality. Police brutality was a problem in black communities throughout the nation, in the North as well as the South. Baker had tackled it in both small towns and big cities during her work as an NAACP field secretary. She was well aware that the issue had larger ramifications. Not only did police brutality against individual black people violate their civil rights, but the intimidation that the entire community faced from local law enforcement was a key way that oppressed communities were discouraged from political protest. From 1950 to 1953, the New York NAACP branch office received nearly 100 complaints about instances of police violence against blacks in the city.[18] The issue came to a head in the summer of 1952 when two men, Jacob Jackson and Samuel Crawford, were brutally beaten by two white officers in the West 54th Street station house. One of the men was so seriously injured that he needed brain surgery.[19]

In February 1953, public anger was fueled by allegations made by the *New York Telegram and Sun* newspaper regarding a secret agreement between the New York Police Department and the U.S. Justice Department that discouraged the FBI from investigating brutality charges leveled against the department and simply allowed the department to handle such complaints as internal matters. The agreement rendered the police department exempt from federal oversight. In March, Attorney General James P. McGranery issued a statement that confirmed the existence of the agreement but claimed it had already been terminated.[20] In response to the initial revelation in the newspaper, Ella Baker issued a sharply worded open letter to the mayor demanding "the immediate resignation" of the police commissioner "to save the City of New York from further disgrace."[21]

The NAACP's national office and the New York City branch co-sponsored a meeting in early February on the subject of police brutality. Representatives from about a dozen other organizations in the city were present. The group formulated a list of demands for the mayor, including the dismissal of all federal and local officials implicated in the secret agreement, an immediate and thorough review of all pending cases, the establishment of a civilian review board, and immediate public disclosure of all allegations of abuse.[22] On February 29, 1953, the New York NAACP sponsored a mass meeting at the Friendship Baptist Church to protest police brutality. The speakers included Baker, police brutality victim Jacob Jackson, Thurgood Marshall, Rev. Thomas Kilgore, and Earl Brown, a progressive member of the New York City Council.[23] Not surprisingly, given his appetite for attention, Adam Clayton Powell, Harlem's flamboyant black congressman, held his own rally against police brutality at the exact same time as the NAACP event. Powell's plan may have been prompted by resentment that he was not offered top billing at the NAACP-sponsored meeting. Such ego rivalries and organizational turf battles were familiar but nonetheless wearying to Baker, and her tolerance for such political theatrics lessened as the years passed.[24]

Later, in March 1953, the Patrolmen's Benevolent Association and other police organizations tried to diffuse mounting criticisms by denouncing the campaign against police brutality as a "Communist plot." The NAACP was one of the main groups attacked, along with councilman Earl Brown. Baker's blunt reply was, "No communist plot can explain away the fact that Jacob Jackson had to undergo two brain operations . . . nor does it explain how other able-bodied persons have walked into police precincts, but had to be carried out as hospital cases."[25]

As a modest concession and half-hearted gesture to the protesters, the police commissioner announced the inauguration of antibias training for officers in order to ease tensions and reduce the chances that police would treat black suspects in a way that might be regarded as using excessive force. The training was to be overseen by a human relations committee that included citizens who were not members of the police force. Ironically, School Superintendent William Jansen, with whom Baker had locked horns over racism in the educational system, headed the police reform committee.[26] Baker was not satisfied with the outcome of the campaign and was determined to keep up the pressure with a vigilant scrutiny of the police. The struggle continued to ebb and flow for some years.

· · · · · ·

Ella Baker experimented with electoral politics in the early 1950s by running unsuccessfully for the New York City Council on the Liberal Party ticket. She first ran for city council in 1951 and lost.[27] In 1953 the slate was led by her friend Rev. James Robinson, an independent candidate for mayor.[28] In the November 1953 poll, Baker was defeated handily by Earl Brown, the incumbent, her adversary in the election but an ally in the NAACP campaign against police brutality.[29] The defeat was probably not unexpected and may have been cushioned a bit by the support of friends like the ever-loyal Pauli Murray, who sent Baker an encouraging note on the eve of the election, "just to wish you good luck at the polls tomorrow . . . affectionately, Pauli."[30]

Ella Baker's 1953 decision to resign temporarily from the NAACP branch presidency in order to run for the New York City Council seems an aberration within a career dedicated to grassroots organizing rather than electoral politics. Later in life, Baker was openly skeptical of electoral politics and career politicians. Within the context of her community-based activism in New York, however, Baker's interest in city politics makes more sense. Not only did the NAACP regularly tangle with elected officials over issues such as school segregation and police brutality, but the broad, popular participation that was characteristic of New York City politics in this period made an electoral campaign seem a logical extension of issue-oriented organizing. Baker may well have realized that she could not win at the polls. The value of the campaign lay not in a vain hope of victory but in the broad-based educational effort that running for office entailed. In the early 1950s, as in later periods, some civil rights activists saw electoral politics as simply another mode of community organizing—a way to get issues in the spotlight. While the Liberal Party's campaign platform focused on the rather tame issues of cleaning up government corruption and inefficiency, the party did include a statement in support of more educational funding (through bond sales), opposition to bigotry and hate groups, and race-relations training for police officers. These may have been some of the issues that attracted Ella Baker to the party. But she was not the only African American activist to work with the Liberal Party in the 1950s. A. Philip Randolph, the socialist labor leader with whom Baker was closely associated in the 1930s, had a brief affiliation with the party, and Pauli Murray had been a Liberal candidate for city council in 1949. Murray's and Baker's willingness to run for office on the Liberal Party ticket suggests that it offered an appealing, although imperfect, alternative to the Democratic and Republican Parties.[31] So, clearly the party embodied some of what independent black activists were looking for in this period.

The Liberal Party was founded in 1944 by David Dubinsky, the leader of the International Ladies Garment Workers Union (ILGWU), as an offshoot of the more left-leaning American Labor Party, which Ella Baker was also briefly aligned with before it split. The Liberal Party drew an odd assortment of characters, a number of whom Baker had worked with before. Jay Lovestone, with whom Baker and Murray had been associated politically during the 1930s, was working with the ILGWU during the early 1940s and was involved in the Liberal Party's formation.[32] Although there is little evidence that the Liberal Party had more than a formal commitment to racial integration, even that was unusual during the 1940s. Running African American women and men for public office represented a clear and appealing departure from politics as usual. Why Baker allied herself more with the Liberal Party than the American Labor Party is unclear. The American Labor Party is better known in progressive circles as a serious third-party experiment that began in 1936 as a way for leftists to back President Franklin D. Roosevelt without supporting the less progressive forces in the Democratic Party. The party, founded by Dubinsky and other socialists including Frank Crosswaith, began to splinter in 1939 over the Hitler-Stalin Pact and the American Communist Party's pragmatic support of that agreement. Crosswaith and others then pushed to expel communists from the American Labor Party, but the anticommunist faction ultimately went its own way and formed the Liberal Party.[33]

Liberal-left coalition work took on new meanings during the postwar period, when virulent anticommunism spread through the organized labor movement, partisan politics, the U.S. government, and even the civil rights movement. At the same time, the move away from inclusive popular front politics and toward a more rigid sectarian agenda on the part of the Communist Party only exacerbated the situation. Comfortable alliances among people on the left who had divergent ideologies and affiliations dissolved under the dual pressures. Some independent socialists stood by current and former Communist Party members who had organized alongside them, while others sought to distance themselves from this increasingly suspect and stigmatized group by denouncing their former co-workers and, in some cases, "naming names" to government investigators to absolve themselves.[34] A few Americans refused to be intimidated, defending civil liberties and deploring McCarthyism. Many progressives, however, were silenced by fear and confusion, failing to fully appreciate the far-reaching dangers of the House Un-American Activities Committee's witch-hunts or, on the other hand, understanding the dangers quite clearly and wanting to spare themselves by pointing a finger at others.[35]

David Dubinsky and the Liberal Party openly espoused anticommunism. According to the historian Paul Buhle, Dubinsky became "fanatically anti-Communist,"[36] and the Liberal Party eventually followed his lead. Some members collaborated with the House Un-American Activities Committee to prosecute their communist counterparts within the United States, while simultaneously working with the CIA to undermine communist influence abroad. Baker would have certainly been aware of these politics, and the fact that she worked closely with the Liberal Party in spite of its undemocratic politics is wholly inconsistent with the views and values she articulated a decade later. It may be that her brief association with the Liberal Party should just be seen as yet another curious example of her eclectic and sometimes unusual political ties.

Although Baker's own relationship with the Communist Party was an ambivalent one, she never collaborated with government agencies to persecute alleged communists. Ironically, throughout the 1950s, even as she positioned herself squarely among the noncommunists, if not the anticommunists, Baker was being kept under heavy surveillance by the FBI as a potential subversive. Informants called her home and office under false pretenses to obtain information. Her apartment was watched, her phone bill intercepted, and her bank account monitored.[37]

In the late 1950s, Baker cooperated, however reluctantly, with NAACP officials when the national organization began to purge communists from the organization. The 1950 decision to exclude communists on the national level was implemented by Baker's old friend J. M. Tinsley, who headed the Committee on Political Domination, the goal of which was to end alleged communist infiltration of the organization.[38] In September 1957, while serving on the executive committee of the New York branch, Baker was asked to serve on the newly established Internal Security Committee, headed by her former Liberal Party running mate, Rev. James Robinson. The committee met on October 14 at Morningside Community Center on West 122d Street and drafted its mission statement and its report to the branch. Although the two-page report began with the unconvincing disclaimer that it was "not a 'witch hunt' committee but a 'watch dog' committee," it proceeded to lay out a rather rigid set of criteria for membership in the branch. "No individual having any affiliation with communists within the past fifteen years should be allowed on the Executive Board," the report stated. Any nominee for the executive board would be required to provide a "written and signed statement listing all past and present affiliations," and if "any officer or member is discovered to have any connection with communism within the past 13 years [15 years stated elsewhere], or to be presently so connected, they shall be expelled from the organization."[39]

The most public ouster was that of former Harlem city councilman Ben Davis Jr., an attorney and a well-known member of the Communist Party who had served time in jail under the Smith Act; his membership fee was returned by the branch president along with a terse letter "condemning atheistic communism."[40] Other New York City branch members were quietly coerced to resign under threat of a possible committee investigation. Baker must have felt enormously torn by this decision since it was at variance with the personal choices she made. Around the time that she served on the NAACP committee to weed out communists, she befriended Anne Braden and Annie Stein, two reputed communists who were also militant antiracist whites and very principled people. In the case of Braden, Baker provided moral and political support, defending Anne and her husband Carl against the kind of persecution that the NAACP itself was replicating on a small scale within the organization. Looking back on her role in the NAACP's Internal Security Committee years later, after the most reactionary implications of McCarthyism had played themselves out, Baker confided to her friend Joanne Grant: "I followed a national office directive to the letter, and I should not have."[41] After her involvement with the Internal Security Committee, political independence became even more critical to Ella Baker.

During the postwar years and after she left the NAACP's national office, Baker was searching for a political home, an organization that embraced a radical and egalitarian practice and vision similar to her own, but she had clearly not yet found it. Finding that political community may have taken on even greater importance to Ella Baker after the death of her beloved mother, Anna Ross Baker, in December 1954. Littleton, North Carolina, the family homestead, and Anna Baker's presence there had been anchoring forces in Ella's otherwise fairly nomadic existence. During her travels for the black cooperative movement in the 1930s and her town-by-town organizing crusades on behalf of the NAACP in the 1940s, her mother's house had been a place for respite and recouping her energy. The house was still there, but gone from it was the woman who had nurtured her early intellectual and political consciousness, toughened her up for the world, and consoled her when that world was unkind. Baker took the long train ride home to attend her mother's funeral and put her affairs in order. She returned north soon thereafter to her second home in Harlem with a renewed resolve to carry on the work that her mother had inspired her to embark on many decades before. A critical component of that work was building political bridges between struggles in the North and the front line struggles in the South. One such bridge was the New York–based fundraising organization, In Friendship.

In Friendship was formed as a way to funnel resources to the activists who had launched and sustained the Montgomery Bus Boycott, which began in December 1955. Only a few months before, the brutal murder of young Emmett Till by white vigilantes in the Mississippi Delta had gal-vanized national attention and black anger. These two events—new forms of resistance coupled with the continuance of racial violence—symbolized the promise and the perils facing southern blacks in the 1950s.

Montgomery activist Joanne Gibson Robinson and the Women's Politi-cal Council, as well as E. D. Nixon and the local NAACP, had been looking for ways to fight back effectively against the humiliating treatment of Mont-gomery's black residents on city busses for some time. On December 5, 1955, NAACP activist Rosa Parks gave them that long-awaited opportunity. In her own personal protest, pregnant with political consequences that she was well aware of, Parks refused to comply with the orders of the white bus driver that she relinquish her seat to a white passenger as required by lo-cal law. Parks' arrest triggered a yearlong boycott of city busses, result-ing in desegregation of those buses and catapulting young Martin Luther King Jr. to national prominence as the eloquent and courageous leader of the protest.

While most eyes were fixed on the emergence of a new leader at the apex of the movement, Baker was more concerned with the base. She viewed the Montgomery boycott as an amazing event, "unpredicted, where thousands of individuals, just black ordinary people, subjected themselves to inconveniences that were certainly beyond the thinking of most folk. . . . This meant you had a momentum that had not been seen, even in the work of the NAACP. And it was something that suggested the potential for wide-spread action throughout the South."[42] This example of commitment and resolve on the part of the rank and file provided an opportunity for progres-sive organizers like Ella Baker.

Baker's close ties with Montgomery's grassroots leaders Parks and Nixon drew her attention to the struggle right from the start. When the implica-tions of the Montgomery Bus Boycott became clear to the nation, Baker quickly began to look for ways she could mobilize support for the protesters and help sustain their militant, direct action movement. In 1956, while still deeply immersed in local issues in New York, Baker and other northern civil rights activists began to discuss the need to establish a northern-based fund-raising organization that would be independent of other organiza-tional agendas and could maximize its aid to those who were hardest hit by reprisals for their civil rights activism. In Friendship was founded as a result.

Ella Baker and two of her closest political allies at the time, Stanley Levison and Bayard Rustin, were the core organizers of In Friendship, which included representatives from various labor, religious, and political groups based in the city.[43] Levison was a wealthy Jewish lawyer and businessman who had been, at one time, affiliated with the Communist Party in New York, which made him a lifelong target of FBI surveillance. He and Baker met while working against the McCarran Act in the early 1950s. In fact, Baker had once shared a platform with Eleanor Roosevelt at an anti-McCarthy program organized by Levison.[44] The McCarran Internal Security Act of 1950 required alleged communists to register with the attorney general, and the McCarran-Walter Immigration Act of 1952 denied entry to the U.S. of any immigrant with communist beliefs or affiliations.[45] W. E. B. Du Bois and Paul Robeson were but two of many prominent activists and dissident intellectuals who were thereby affected. Eleanor Roosevelt and other Cold War liberals saw themselves as both anti-McCarthyites and still devoutly anticommunist. As Carol Polsgrove writes, they hated McCarthy because he "was giving anti-communism a bad name."[46] So, there was no contradiction in their minds between purging communists from their organizations and opposing what they viewed as extremist practices initiated by Senator Joseph McCarthy and continued by the House Un-American Activities Committee after his censure by the Senate in 1954.

Bayard Rustin was a black Quaker from Pennsylvania with an eclectic political past and a passion for social justice. He was also a bit of an eccentric. He joined the Young Communist League briefly during the Great Depression and later broke with the group to work with the more moderate Congress of Racial Equality (CORE) and the Fellowship of Reconciliation (FOR).

Rustin was gay long before there was a gay rights movement, at a time when such sexual choices, if made public, could and often did result in severe personal and political penalties.[47] So, he was not only at risk of attacks from southern segregationists for his antiracism activity, but he was also vulnerable to prejudice from within the movement because of his sexual orientation.

Ella Baker knew Rustin was gay and seemingly accepted him without condition, later reflecting that his homosexuality may have been one of the reasons that he opted to keep a low public profile during his long, active political career in a wide range of organizations and campaigns. This strategy was probably not much of a choice, considering the extent of homophobia and his colleagues' fear that his sexual orientation might draw negative attention and damage their cause. One historian of the civil rights movement describes Rustin this way: "An internationally respected pacifist, as well as a vagabond minstrel, penniless world traveler, sophisticated collector of African and pre-Colombian art, and a bohemian Greenwich Village philosopher. . . . he lived more or less a hobo's life, committed to the ideals of world peace and racial brotherhood. . . . [He was] tall and bony, handsome and conspiratorial, full of ideas that spilled out in a high pitched voice, and a proud but squeaky West Indian accent."[48]

Baker, Levison, and Rustin were an unlikely threesome in many respects, but their ideas and political passions drew them together and enabled them to become comrades and friends. Their close collaboration continued for a number of years, although their friendship was tried, tested, and eventually weakened over the course of the next decade.

Baker was an important catalyst for pulling together the individuals and organizations that comprised the In Friendship coalition in 1956. Among them were dozens of individuals whom Baker had known or worked with in other campaigns and projects over the years. They included Walter Petersen, a leader of the New York chapter of the Liberal Party; Levison, a member of the American Jewish Congress; and Rev. Thomas Kilgore, the minister at Baker's own Friendship Baptist Church in Harlem. Other Baker associates were active in supporting In Friendship: Fay Bennett of the National Sharecroppers Fund; Rae Brandstein of the National Committee for Rural Schools; Cleveland Robinson of the AFL-CIO, District 65; and Norman Thomas, the Socialist Party leader. Ella Baker served as executive secretary of the group, and A. Philip Randolph was persuaded to chair the new coalition for its first two months. The Socialist-affiliated Worker's Defense League, led by Thomas, provided temporary office space. Initially, Baker's position was unpaid, but she managed the office, handled correspondence and bookkeeping, orchestrated publicity and outreach, and did virtually all of the tasks necessary to keep the organization afloat. The group was eventually able to piece together a modest salary for her.

On February 29, 1956, In Friendship launched its inaugural fund-raising campaign with an "Action Conference" held at the McAlpin Hotel on Broadway and 34th Street in Manhattan. Randolph had issued the call for the conference in a letter, dated February 17, that conveyed a sense of urgency about the situation in the South: "Reports from Mississippi indicate that the white Citizens Councils have succeeded in choking off all sources of loans and other credits on which [black] farmers depend. We must show that those who are being attacked do not stand alone in their fight for decency."[49] He noted in passing the occurrence of a similar conference being convened in Washington D.C. by Oscar Lee and Roy Wilkins. Randolph commented casually that the event would "add impetus to our work in this area," glossing over the competition implicit in the simultaneous formation of two organizations to serve the same purpose.[50]

Despite the strong commitment and good intentions of its founders, In Friendship had difficulties getting off the ground. Randolph abruptly resigned as chairman of the organization shortly after its formation and before the New York fund-raiser even took place. He claimed that he was overextended in his obligations and felt it inappropriate that he solicit funds on behalf of In Friendship, since he had already done so recently on behalf of other organizations. It is possible that something else may have prompted Randolph's action, since he was well aware of the existence of competing organizations from the outset, as indicated by his February 17 letter. Perhaps he was persuaded by colleagues in more established organizations to withdraw his support from the nascent group, or perhaps he feared that such an endorsement could become a political liability in his relationships with other groups. Since the initial supporters of In Friendship believed that a roster of prominent sponsors was necessary to give the group credibility, Randolph's resignation came as a particularly sharp blow. In a March 8, 1956, letter to Randolph, Norman Thomas pleaded with him to reconsider his decision, saying that it would "almost wreck a pretty promising beginning at worthwhile work."[51] Randolph resigned anyway. Perhaps in tribute to his long-standing friendship with and respect for Ella Baker, perhaps in order to exert some control over the campaign, he continued to work with the group after he stepped down as chair.

The founders of In Friendship were painfully aware of the competition and tensions with preexisting civil rights organizations, much of which arose from political turf battles and the clash of overinflated egos. Since a number of organizations were already engaged in similar efforts, the founders sought to avoid the appearance of needless duplication. As Fay Bennett of the National Sharecroppers Fund emphasized in a 1956 letter to Norman Thomas: "It should be made clear at the beginning that the contemplated work of the committee [In Friendship] will be handled through existing machinery and that its primary purpose, at least in its initial stages, would be to stimulate efforts on the part of other organizations to help those in the South who need help and in other ways to make an impact on the situation."[52] Despite In Friendship's attempts to avoid rivalry with other organizations, some prominent civil rights figures were still reluctant to view the group as an umbrella fund-raiser for the movement as a whole.

In the spring of 1956, three In Friendship leaders, including Baker, worked nearly full time for six weeks building for a mammoth civil rights rally that was held in Madison Square Garden in May. The other principal sponsor for the event was Randolph's Brotherhood of Sleeping Car Porters. Leaders of In Friendship naturally assumed that they would process all funds raised by the event, since they had formed the umbrella organization meant to pull together everyone else's efforts in civil rights activism. However, A. Philip Randolph had a different idea. As one of the top union officials involved, he opted to set up a separate special committee to direct, monitor, and dispense funds raised by the AFL-CIO. The committee was to have two labor representatives, hand-picked by the head of the AFL-CIO, George Meany; representatives from several other organizations; and a single delegate from In Friendship. Although In Friendship acquiesced to the decision, it was clearly a slap in the face, given the organization's initiative in coordinating precisely the kind of tasks to be handled by the new special committee. Nevertheless, Randolph's powerful stature and the relative newness of In Friendship prompted the group not to openly criticize or oppose the decision. In fact, Ella Baker was at the July 11 meeting in Randolph's office when the new formation was set up. Not wanting to be divisive at the expense of the group's larger goals, she went along with Randolph's move, conceding that it was "understandable that the unions were reluctant to funnel moneys through an organization as young and untested as In Friendship, and In Friendship would willingly participate as one member of the larger committee."[53] The final insult was that the labor representatives on the committee would have veto power over all funding decisions, rendering the In Friendship forces fairly marginal to the whole deliberative process. These events illustrate the internal tensions, hierarchies, and competition for leadership that existed within the early civil rights movement, even among its northern supporters.

The conflict between In Friendship and the union leaders also illustrates the reluctance of established leaders to relinquish any of their power to, or even make room for, upstart organizations. Baker encountered this problem repeatedly over the years. National leaders, in civil rights and other fields, were protective of their prominence and status as the "official" spokespersons for their respective constituencies. Baker was vividly impressed by the deleterious effects of such rivalries and the stifling and coercive nature of the relationship between junior and senior partners in coalitions. She carried these memories with her into the political work she did in subsequent years. In particular, they shaped her desire to be vehemently protective of the independence and autonomy of the Student Non-violent Coordinating Committee when it was founded a few years later. She defended the young militants' right to make their own decisions, despite their youthful inexperience, in the face of annexation attempts by some of Baker's well-established colleagues.

Difficulties and tensions with allies notwithstanding, the small core of In Friendship supporters persevered and made some important contributions. Randolph's resignation and his bid to control fund-raising did not "wreck" the organization, as Thomas had feared. In December 1956, In Friendship hosted its second successful fund-raiser, a major concert at the Manhattan Center featuring Coretta Scott King, Harry Belafonte, Duke Ellington, and others to commemorate the first anniversary of the Montgomery boycott. The event raised $1,800, an appreciable sum at the time. Part of the proceeds went to support the organizing efforts of the Montgomery Improvement Association, the main community group that emerged from the boycott. Funds were also set aside for other grassroots struggles as well. Specifically, In Friendship provided funds to two groups of black tenant farmers who were evicted from their plantations in Clarendon County, South Carolina, and Yazoo, Mississippi, because of their involvement in civil rights activities. The activists in these communities had tried to test the victory of the 1954 *Brown* decision by enrolling their children in previously all-white schools and had suffered harsh economic reprisals as a result.[54]

Civil rights campaigns in places like Yazoo and Clarendon County did not receive the widespread news coverage that the Montgomery campaign did, so the grassroots activists in these rural communities lacked the margin of protection that national media attention and sympathetic support from outsiders might have provided. Throughout the South, civil rights activists who were poor, poorly educated, and economically vulnerable were easy targets for retribution, for which they often had no recourse. In Friendship provided assistance to the grassroots leaders whom Ella Baker saw as the very backbone of the Black Freedom Movement; they were likely, in her view, to be pivotal actors in whatever struggles were to emerge in the years ahead.

Baker's concept of progressive leadership was leadership that helped people to help themselves and allowed ordinary people to feel that they could determine their own future. When she lent her energies to In Friendship, her mission was grassroots empowerment, to tap and build on the activist spirit that the Montgomery boycott had unleashed and to nurture and encourage the emergence of strong indigenous leadership in communities throughout the South. That mission was an extension of the objectives she had worked toward in the NAACP during the 1940s. She not only wanted In Friendship to provide funds to meet the material needs of suffering families; she also wanted it to pay for local leaders to attend conferences, meetings, and workshops, which would boost their confidence as organizers and give them intellectual perspectives and tactical ammunition for the struggles they were engaged in. In other words, Baker believed in the adage that it is more important to teach people to fish and farm than simply to give them food. The funds In Friendship raised were, in Baker's view, leadership development funds, not simply relief funds. For example, in the summer of 1956, while attending the annual NAACP conference in San Francisco, she learned about forty black farmers who were trying to form an agricultural cooperative. Instead of providing a direct grant to the co-op, Baker wanted the farmers to get a better sense of the scope and history of the cooperative movement, so she arranged to have In Friendship pay for a representative of the group, Orsey Malone, to attend a Cooperative Institute being held at Bard College in New York later that year.[55] Such inclusive politics and broad objectives differentiated In Friendship from a number of other support organizations.

In Friendship lasted officially for about three years and provided much-needed resources to sustain activists on the front lines of the southern battle against racism, but ultimately it could not sustain itself. As the civil rights movement grew in visibility and importance, larger organizations stepped in to offer funds, although sometimes with ulterior motives and camouflaged agendas. But the start-up and survival funds that In Friendship provided in the immediate wake of the Montgomery boycott were crucial. Even before its demise, its three founders—Rustin, Levison, and Baker—had begun to redirect their energies from fund-raising to direct consultation with movement leaders in the South, namely, Dr. King and the emergent Southern Christian Leadership Conference.

From the very outset, Baker was thinking of ways she could get closer to the action, confiding to her friend and pastor Rev. Kilgore that she was literally "chafing at the bit to be down there as a part of the struggle."[56] Throughout the late 1940s and early 1950s, Baker was deeply engaged in local political struggles in New York around issues near and dear to her heart, but the new sparks of protest in Montgomery were too important to ignore. That potential ultimately inspired her to return to the South and resume the intense pace of organizing that had characterized her years with the NAACP during the 1940s.

The decade of the 1950s was filled with ambivalence for Ella Baker and many others. She was divided between North and South; between her pragmatic side and her principles; and between her loyalty to old colleagues and her devotion to and empathy with new friends.

THE PREACHER AND THE ORGANIZER

THE POLITICS OF LEADERSHIP IN
THE EARLY CIVIL RIGHTS MOVEMENT

· · · · ·

The Negro must quit looking for a savior, and work to save himself.
Ella Baker, 1947

Leadership never ascends from the pew to the pulpit,
but . . . descends from the pulpit to the pew.
Dr. Martin Luther King Jr., 1954

Ella Baker traveled to the South in January 1957, as a representative of
In Friendship, along with her colleague Bayard Rustin, to help organize
the founding meeting of the Southern Christian Leadership Conference
(SCLC), an organization that sought to spread across the South the seeds of
rebellion that had germinated in Montgomery. Baker was deeply committed to that goal, yet right from the start she had serious reservations
about the way in which SCLC was organized and how it approached the
task of propagating the movement.

Baker welcomed the political developments that occurred in Montgomery in 1955–56 as the beginning of what she hoped would become a new
wave of activism for black freedom based on a strategy of grassroots mass
mobilization. She had learned from her work with the NAACP, both in the
South and in Harlem, that any viable social change organization had to be
built from the bottom up. "Authentic" leadership could not come from the
outside or above; rather, the people who were most oppressed had to take
direct action to change their circumstances. At best, national organizations
could offer activists the resources that they lacked: financial support, media attention, and political education. During her years as a field organizer

for the NAACP, Baker had realized—as the national leadership consistently did not—that the branches were the essence of the organization's strength. Although the NAACP had been founded in the early twentieth century by northern social reformers and intellectuals, since World War II it had been transformed into a membership organization under whose name activists organized locally in cities and small towns across the South, as well as in northern cities whose black populations were swelling as the Great Migration continued. The national NAACP's persistent inability, or determined refusal, to reinvent itself in the image of its changing mass base was at the core of Baker's frustration with the organization throughout the late 1940s and early 1950s.

The new black freedom struggle that had ignited a spark in the South in the mid-1950s had the potential to fulfill Baker's ideal of a truly democratic organization. The Montgomery boycott began not with a convention of prominent race leaders, as the NAACP had, but because masses of ordinary people had gotten in motion. Veteran NAACP organizer Rosa Parks initiated a calculated protest action on her own, and a small network of activists followed up with phone calls and leaflets to publicize what she was doing. Those with official leadership status were then called on to convene a meeting to plan a more organized response. Women, who Baker believed were the "backbone" of the movement, were critical actors. Joanne Gibson Robinson of the Women's Political Council had helped launch the boycott, and black domestic workers, many of whom walked long distances to work to support the protest, had been indispensable. Baker believed that the most effective leaders were ones who emerged directly out of struggle. She was delighted that instead of working through the NAACP, which eschewed mass action, Montgomery's activists formed a new, autonomous, and democratic organization, the Montgomery Improvement Association (MIA).[1]

In 1957 the U.S. Supreme Court declared enforced segregation on public busses to be unconstitutional; it thereby delivered a high-profile victory to the Montgomery struggle and gave high-profile status to its most eloquent spokesman, Dr. Martin Luther King Jr. Ella Baker was most impressed with the rank-and-file activism that had emerged during the bus boycott, and she worked to provide moral support and material assistance to those involved. The eyes of the world, however, were focused on Martin Luther King Jr., the eloquent young minister who had become the leading spokesperson for the campaign. Baker's initial impressions of King were positive. She recounted to an interviewer decades later that the first time she heard King speak, she was literally "carried away."[2] He was earnest and articulate, and he struck Baker as less pompous than some of the ministers she had encountered.[3] Baker knew that King came from a prominent family in Atlanta and could have followed in his father's footsteps rather than taking the risks that political activism entailed. She respected him for choosing a different path and trying to make a contribution to the movement. At the same time, King's sudden fame did not sit right with Baker, especially given his youth and inexperience. Moreover, he did not seem to want to learn about the process of organizing, at least not from her.

Seasoned political veterans like Ella Baker, many of whom moved in and out of organizations and coalitions depending on existing opportunities and pragmatic tactical considerations, were used to navigating personalities and negotiating ideological differences. However, as her relationship with King and SCLC wore on, issues of organization and leadership took on heightened significance in Baker's mind. In the historiography of the modern Black Freedom Movement, scholars have drawn a line between charismatic leadership models and grassroots activist ones, with a parallel distinction made between mobilizing (for big events) and actually organizing communities to feel empowered to assess their own needs and fight their own battles.[4] The tensions between these two models of movement building were apparent in Montgomery during the boycott, and they persisted in SCLC as it evolved. Still, Baker was willing to devote herself to the organization, its limitations notwithstanding, to see what could be accomplished. She was even willing to serve as a provisional, rather than permanent, member of the SCLC staff. Her conflicted relationship with Martin Luther King Jr. turned on such questions as leadership and organization, especially the proper roles of national spokespersons and local participants in mass-based struggles. Baker's involvement in SCLC was, from its inception, shaped by pervasive tensions and fundamental contradictions.

· · · · · ·

FORMING THE SOUTHERN CHRISTIAN LEADERSHIP CONFERENCE

In the wake of the victory in Montgomery, an informal network of activist ministers began to take shape. Some had carried out similar protests on a smaller scale in their home states, such as T. J. Jemison in Baton Rouge, Louisiana. Many others had been in touch with King during and after the boycott, as events in Montgomery attracted media attention. Baker had developed her own contacts with the new crop of southern activists through In Friendship, adding to the independent network of militant NAACP organizers she had maintained since the previous decade. Most of these activists felt greater loyalty to their local struggles and to itinerant organizers like Baker than to any single national or regional organization. The problem facing King, Baker, and other civil rights organizers was that there was no formal organization, national or regional, that could link these various individuals and disparate local groups together and sustain and extend the movement after the Montgomery boycott ended in December 1956.

The idea for a regionwide organization like SCLC germinated in different quarters simultaneously. As Baker herself understood, this idea could not have been traced directly to a single source. Naturally, King and his ministerial colleagues in the South were strategizing about what their next steps should be and how to coordinate their efforts. But they were not the only ones having such conversations. By some accounts, the trio that directed In Friendship laid out a blueprint for SCLC in a series of intense late-night conversations in New York. According to Adam Fairclough, "SCLC might not have come into being but for the political foresight of three northern radicals: Bayard Rustin, Stanley David Levison, and Ella Jo Baker."[5] Baker recalled that she and her two New York colleagues spent many hours discussing ways that movement leaders might "enlarge upon the gains of the Montgomery bus boycott."[6] Rustin and Levison relayed the content of those discussions to King and other ministers involved in the southern civil rights movement, urging them to call a regional meeting to discuss the idea further.[7] These various efforts gave birth to SCLC. Certainly, activists in Alabama and Georgia did not need New York "experts" to tell them how to mobilize a campaign. Nevertheless, these connections underline the fact that the civil rights movement was not organized in isolation from veteran activists such as Baker, Levison, and Rustin, whose long histories in other progressive struggles dated back to the 1930s.

During the months leading up to and following the victory in Montgomery, Bayard Rustin and Stanley David Levison had become two of Martin Luther King Jr.'s closest advisers. They helped garner important resources for MIA and SCLC and offered tactical and strategic advice, earning them King's trust and friendship. Neither Rustin nor Levison played a very public role, but both were in King's inner circle of confidantes. Interestingly, but not surprisingly, their close friend Ella Baker was not. She was certainly as politically sophisticated, articulate, and astute as her male counterparts, and she had twenty years of political experience in the South as well as the North. Yet King kept Baker at arm's length and never treated her as a political or intellectual peer. As Baker later put it: "After all, who was I? I was female, I was old. I didn't have any Ph.D."[8] Furthermore, she explained, she was "not loathe to raise questions. I did not just subscribe to a theory just because it came out of the mouth of the leader."[9] She "was not the kind of person that made special effort to be ingratiating."[10] She was well aware, by the mid-1950s, that her forthrightness in the face of authority carried a certain price, limiting her acceptance by those in positions of official power, but it was a price she was willing to pay in order to think and act according to her conscience.

Baker speculated that Levison's influence over King stemmed from his capacity to raise money and tap resources and that Rustin was most adept at helping King to hone his ideas and garner greater publicity. Baker concluded cynically that "persons who were in a position to provide both financial aid and public relations assistance to the furtherance of the organization or the furtherance of the career of the president [of SCLC] would be certainly high on the list of acceptable advisors."[11] Rustin and Levison were both great admirers of King, and they were as eager to see him ascend as the leader of the movement as they were to see the movement itself grow. They differed with Baker in this respect. In all fairness, King's relationship with Rustin and Levison does not appear to have been as pragmatic and opportunistic as Baker's comments implied. There was an intellectual and philosophical bond and seemingly genuine camaraderie among the three men. Simply put, it was probably King's sexist attitudes toward women, at least in part, that prevented him from having the same kind of collegial relationship with Baker.[12]

The founding meeting of the Southern Christian Leadership Conference took place in Atlanta at Dr. Martin Luther King Sr.'s Ebenezer Baptist Church on January 10, 1957. Ministers from nearly a dozen southern states gathered under the banner of the Southern Leadership Conference on Transportation and Nonviolent Integration. Ella Baker worked with Bayard Rustin to draft statements that framed the issues and set the agenda for the meeting.[13] The new organization was planned from the outset to be a loosely structured coalition linking church-based leaders in civil rights struggles across the South. It was decidedly not a membership organization so as not to appear to compete with the NAACP, which may have initially taken the edge off the rivalry, but did not eliminate it.

Just as the group was convening, the seriousness of their undertaking was driven home by a night of violent attacks in Montgomery, targeting leaders of the new organization. The home of Rev. Ralph Abernathy, a leader of the boycott who was a close colleague of King, was firebombed while his wife, Juanita, and their young daughter were inside; fortunately, no one was seriously hurt. While Abernathy was on the phone with his wife, several other explosions rocked the city, hitting churches and the home of Rev. Robert S. Graetz, a white MIA supporter. Abernathy immediately left Atlanta for Montgomery. A sober determination informed the remainder of the discussions held that weekend.

By the meeting's conclusion, the group decided to emphasize nonviolence as a means of bringing about social progress and racial justice for southern blacks; the new organization would rely on the southern black church for its base of support.[14] The strength of SCLC rested on the political activities of its local church affiliates. By giving church activists a sense of connection to one another and by infusing an explicitly political message into the black theology of the 1950s, SCLC envisioned itself as the "political arm of the black church," according to the sociologist Aldon Morris.[15] However they viewed themselves, King and his colleagues represented an activist minority within the politically heterogeneous black church. The majority of black ministers in the 1950s still opted for a safer, less confrontational political path. This was especially true in the climate of the 1950s when any form of dissent was equated with communism and social, if not legal, sanctions were possible.

Despite their embrace of activism, King and the SCLC ministers still defined their political goals squarely within the respectable American mainstream and were cautious about any leftist associations.[16] This was conscious and strategic. They wanted to pose a challenge to white America: "We are law-abiding, God-fearing citizens, now give us our rights." King's stance would change as he and the movement evolved over the ensuing years.[17]

The Atlanta group met as the Southern Leadership Conference on Transportation and Nonviolent Integration; it later changed its name to the Southern Christian Leadership Conference. The choice of the new organization's name is a subtle indicator of the Cold War ethos that permeated black politics, as it did white society, during the 1950s. The decision to include Christian in the group's name was not simply an affirmation of people's faith that God was on their side but also a conscious effort to deflect any allegations of communist infiltration or influence, since the materialist worldview of communists meant that they were assumed to be atheists.[18]

The cultivated image of a "good citizen"—elegantly clad, well spoken, and generally well educated—was an important marker of respectability for the ministerial leaders that came together to form SCLC. Once it was decided that the new coalition would be an extension of the church, a patriarchal ethos took over. Neither Rosa Parks nor Joanne Gibson Robinson nor any of the women who had sacrificed so much to ensure the Montgomery boycott's success were invited to play a leadership role in the new organization. Daisy Bates was eventually given a nominal seat on the board, but, according to Baker, she never was very active. Baker felt that her own involvement was tolerated more than it was appreciated. "Someone's got to run the mimeographing machine," she later observed, only half-joking.[19]

The founders of SCLC were concerned primarily, but not exclusively, about access to the ballot box and dignified treatment in public accommodations. But theirs was a world apart from the lives of destitute sharecroppers and their families who constituted a considerable portion of the South's black population—people who could barely afford the fare to ride on public transportation even after desegregation. It was this group that Baker worried most about. After she left Atlanta on January 11, she spent the next five days traveling around rural Mississippi meeting and talking with landless and unemployed black farmers about the painful conditions of their lives. She stayed with Amzie and Ruth Moore and kept a careful journal of the families she met, what their names were, how they lived, how many children they had. This heart-wrenching reconnaissance effort was an attempt to identify families in need of In Friendship's support. Baker soon realized that In Friendship would be hard pressed to make a real distinction between families who were victims of political reprisals and those who were victims of economic violence, pure and simple, since such violence saturated the social and political landscape of the rural South.[20] They resigned themselves to provide aid wherever they could without trying to discern whether the need was purely economic or primarily a result of political activity.

The Southern Christian Leadership Conference first stepped on the national political stage as an organization at the Prayer Pilgrimage for Freedom held at the Lincoln Memorial in Washington, D.C., on May 17, 1957, the third anniversary of the *Brown* decision. And Ella Baker was once again instrumental in pulling off a successful large-scale event. Roy Wilkins, Martin Luther King Jr., and A. Philip Randolph were co-chairs of the pilgrimage, which was intended to expose to the nation the crime of racial injustice. Organizers billed it "as a protest to the bombings and violence in the South."[21] As the planning began, there were palpable tensions between the NAACP and the newly formed SCLC, which the association's national leaders saw as a rival attempting to duplicate or interfere with its ongoing, successful work for civil rights. Once again, the esteemed labor leader

A. Philip Randolph served as peacemaker, bringing Wilkins, the head of the NAACP and Ella Baker's longtime friend and former colleague, to join him and King on a three-man leadership committee for the pilgrimage. Ella Baker and Bayard Rustin were the two staff organizers for the event, coordinating communications and doing the day-to-day logistical work necessary to plan the gathering.

The patriotic and religious tenor of the event underscored SCLC's mainstream political orientation. The slogans and statements surrounding the demonstration were carefully selected to present an image of the resurgent civil rights movement as respectable and nonthreatening. Anticommunism was so pervasive that any type of protest was immediately vulnerable to red-baiting. The NAACP had already caved in to these pressures by establishing a formal policy of exclusion. According to an FBI informant who was surreptitiously spying on her, Baker was indeed worried that certain individuals in New York were trying to "stack the delegation with communists."[22] After the event, Rustin and Baker responded defensively to allegations of communist participation. Their response to an *Amsterdam News* article did not even entertain the possibility that such exclusion might be unfair. Rustin and Baker cited a copy of the call for the pilgrimage to the press, tacitly endorsing its Cold War politics: "The Prayer Pilgrimage for Freedom will be a spiritual assembly, primarily by the Negro clergy, and the NAACP. In such an assembly, there will be no place for the irreligious. . . . No communists have been or will be invited to participate in the program either as a speaker, singer, prayer leader, or scripture leader. . . . The Official Call, issued on April 5, 1957, invites all who love justice and dignity and liberty, who love their country, to join in a Prayer Pilgrimage to Washington on May 17, 1957."[23]

The Prayer Pilgrimage for Freedom drew a crowd of between 25,000 and 30,000 to the Lincoln Memorial.[24] It is difficult to quantify the success of such campaigns. However, President Eisenhower did accede to a request that he meet with civil rights leaders soon thereafter, and the rather tepid Civil Rights Act of 1957 was signed into law in August, eventually putting into place a Civil Rights Commission, which was authorized to review and investigate voting rights abuses.

Ella Baker's work as one of the two staff organizers for the pilgrimage is a graphic illustration of her ability to straddle organizational divides, deliberately ignoring and minimizing rivalries and ideological battles that sometimes raged all around her. Even though she was still on the payroll of In Friendship, which had close ties to SCLC, she worked out of the NAACP national office on 40th Street in New York. And while she worked in the same office with her old colleague Roy Wilkins, who could barely contain his hostility and resentment toward King, she would only six months later, without seemingly missing a beat or proffering an explanation, accept an offer to work with King's organization in Atlanta on a full-time basis. Essentially, Baker refused to take sides: when there were no fundamental principles at stake, she did not take territorial claims or ego wounds too seriously—instead she seemed to almost float above it all. She indeed had criticisms of both SCLC and the NAACP and of both King and Wilkins. At any given moment as the flurry of activities in the late 1950s was about to feed into the frenetic pace of the 1960s, Baker's organizational affiliations were often unclear. Having been instrumental in the founding of SCLC in January 1957, Baker remained active in the New York NAACP branch and school reform struggle led by Parents in Action and other New York–based groups unaffiliated with the NAACP like In Friendship. It was all a part of the same drama in Ella Baker's mind, with different characters (all of them slightly flawed) engaged in different plots and subplots, but they were performing on the same political stage and had to coordinate with one another. She was clearly in the mind-set of building a movement rather than any one organization.

After the pilgrimage, Baker returned to New York, where she, Rustin, and Levison continued to discuss ways of sustaining the momentum of protests in the South. Following a few months of floundering, SCLC decided to launch its own independent campaign, the Crusade for Citizenship, a regionwide voting rights project they scheduled to kick off in February 1958. Hoping to capitalize on the passage of the Civil Rights Act of 1957, SCLC leaders planned a sustained mobilization that would gain national attention for voting rights and for the embryonic organization. The goal of the Crusade for Citizenship was to double the number of black voters in the South and to "challenge blacks to take on the responsibilities of fighting for their rights."[25] The campaign's letterhead proclaimed that "the franchise is a citizen's right . . . not a privilege."[26] Designed to put black voter rights on the national political agenda, the campaign was also meant to simultaneously mobilize masses of ordinary African Americans against Jim Crow. For a brand-new civil rights organization, the project was breathtakingly ambitious in its scope, although still relatively moderate in the political tack and tone it took.

The leaders of SCLC had crafted the concept of a new campaign, but the organization had no infrastructure, including the material and human resources necessary to move a campaign forward. By January 1958, Rustin and Levison realized that SCLC's plans for the new crusade were in serious trouble, and they doubted that the group had the personnel and tactical know-how to actually make it happen. The campaign was scheduled to start on February 12, Abraham Lincoln's birthday. The kick-off had already been delayed once because plans were not in place, so this date was firm. But SCLC desperately needed to bring someone on board who had the political sophistication and organizational abilities required to make the necessary arrangements in a very short period of time. Levison and Rustin immediately thought of Ella Baker. Baker certainly had the requisite skills and experience, and she was available. She had separated from her husband, Bob, and her niece, Jackie, was almost nineteen, so, as she later put it, she did not have "any encumbrances" to prevent her from taking on this challenge.[27]

There had been some discussion about the possibility of having Bayard Rustin serve as the executive director of SCLC. After all, he knew the organization, had worked closely with King since the Montgomery bus boycott, could bring considerable organizing experience to the task, and certainly had the commitment. However, given his sexual orientation and the social conservatism and homophobia of the church leaders he would be working closely with, which was compounded by the narrow-minded snobbery of Atlanta's black middle class, he was not a tenable candidate for the job.[28] In retrospect, Baker explained that "Bayard was not prepared, nor could his lifestyle have stood the test of going down there and being the person from up here to stay in Atlanta and help to get things going, because Atlanta had not reached that point where a certain lifestyle was accepted."[29] This remark hints at how Baker may have felt about Rustin's homosexuality. She always chose her words and deployed her language carefully. By describing the attitudes of black Atlantans as not having reached a certain point of acceptance, she implied that she had reached that point and that others should do so as well. She could have described Rustin's behavior in a negative light or as a flaw or weakness in an otherwise good character, as many of his other friends and contemporaries did, but she did not.

Rustin and Levison agreed that Baker would be the ideal person to organize the Crusade for Citizenship. She had built up a network of contacts throughout the South through her work as a field organizer for the NAACP.[30] She had the political know-how and social skills to work with all types of people, from proper, middle-class church members to uneducated sharecroppers. Perhaps most significantly, Baker was a skilled organizer and was well connected. These talents were exactly what SCLC needed to pull off the Crusade for Citizenship within the tight timeline that had been projected.

Levison and Rustin persuaded King to hire Baker as SCLC's first full-time staff member. The three men met at New York's La Guardia Airport while King was on a travel layover.[31] King was initially reluctant to hire Baker, because he had a different profile of the type of person who should share the leadership role with him at the helm of the coalition. King indicated that he did not personally believe that the director had to be a minister, but he recognized that many of his clerical colleagues strongly held that conviction. Of course, choosing a minister also meant that the director must be a man. These preferences notwithstanding, there were few other options at that juncture, and King's two advisers were adamant.

King agreed to hire Baker on a temporary basis, until a more suitable permanent director could be found. She was hired not as a field organizer to work with grassroots activists but as the primary—and sometimes the only—staff member for a fragile and sometimes fractious coalition of clergymen led by Martin Luther King Jr. It was not an ideal arrangement. Still, Rustin and Levison could not imagine that Baker would say no, so they did not bother to discuss the particulars with her before making the pitch to King that she be hired. Ultimately, they were right. But Baker did not like the idea of anyone making decisions for her, even friends who knew her as well as Levison and Rustin did: "To be drafted in the sense of having it be said that I would go when I hadn't been consulted . . . I suppose in that aspect of it, my ego is easily touched; not to ask me what to do but to designate me to do something without even consulting me." The situation, it seemed to her, "was a bit presumptuous" and insulting.[32]

The way in which Baker was recruited to work for SCLC was oddly reminiscent of her sudden and surprising appointment as the NAACP's director of branches in 1943. Nevertheless, she accepted the job with King's organization, just as she had accepted Walter White's unilateral decision to promote her in 1943. She agreed to join the SCLC staff because, for her, politics were more important than protocol. She felt strongly that the movement was at a critical crossroads; there was a lot at stake—or at least great potential. While Baker did not appreciate the way in which she was asked to go to Atlanta, she was thrilled by the opportunity to get closer to the action. So, she packed her bags and headed south for what she thought would be another short-term stint, but which turned out to be a much more extended one.

Ella Baker arrived in Atlanta in mid-January 1958, seven months after the Prayer Pilgrimage, to begin her work at SCLC headquarters. But the organization had a headquarters in name only. When Baker arrived there was no office, no phone, and no other staff. "I had to function out of a telephone booth and my pocketbook," she recalled.[33] "Nobody had made any provisions for space, hadn't even thought about it. . . . I had assumed that certainly we might have been able to function with some degree of sustained effort out of the church office of Ebenezer Baptist Church since the Rev. Dr. King, Sr. was the father of the Rev. Dr. King, Jr., but this was not provided for in the full sense."[34] Baker had to use the mimeograph machine and other office equipment at the church in the evening, after the regular office staff had gone home. It was a frustrating situation, and her ties with other Atlanta activists were all that kept her sane. Eventually, Rev. Samuel Williams, another minister affiliated with SCLC, secured office space on Auburn Avenue, and Baker purchased enough furniture and supplies to set up shop. This modest headquarters became the permanent home of the new organization.

Baker knew her position with SCLC would be a challenge. When she uprooted herself from her home in New York and migrated to the South in the winter of 1958, she was guardedly optimistic about the new organization. Given the broad-based support that had been mobilized around the bus boycott, Baker hoped that SCLC would be able to galvanize the aspirations of the masses of African American people and ignite the kind of movement that would empower them to transform their lives, their communities, and the nation. Yet she knew from the outset that the philosophy, structure, and leadership of SCLC would be problematic for her, and she suspected that ultimately the new organization might itself become a barrier to carrying out the localized, broad-based work that she envisioned.

Baker worked feverishly from mid-January to February 12 to make the ambitiously conceived Crusade for Citizenship a relative success. She tried to infuse it with her own political meanings and recapture the spirit of rank-and-file activism that had defined the earlier boycott. Some time later, in a report to SCLC's Administrative Committee, Baker secularized the term, insisting that "the word crusade connotes, for me, a vigorous movement, with high purpose and involving masses of people."[35]

Events were scheduled to kick off in twenty-one cities on the same day. Baker wrote letters, flyers, and press releases to promote these events. She made extensive phone calls to build support for the campaign, identify and coordinate activities, and make sure all the necessary logistics were in place. Within a few weeks she had a roster of speakers lined up for the rallies, including a few prominent national leaders such as Adam Clayton Powell Jr.[36] Securing Powell's support was particularly important, since some other national leaders were reluctant to affiliate openly with SCLC. Taylor Branch, one of King's biographers, points out that such key national figures as Lester Granger and Ralph Bunche declined to endorse the Crusade for Citizenship campaign because they wanted to remain nonpartisan in what appeared to be, and in fact was, a rivalry between the SCLC and the NAACP.[37]

The Crusade for Citizenship was a pivotal test for the new coalition, the first major regionwide campaign for which it sought to obtain national support and public attention. Initially, SCLC had been very careful to avoid stepping on the political toes of other organizations, most notably the NAACP. The Prayer Pilgrimage was a single event in which SCLC shared the spotlight with the NAACP and organized labor. In contrast, the crusade was being launched by SCLC and its local affiliates and was planned as a sustained mobilization. With this campaign, the embryonic SCLC began to encroach upon the turf of established civil rights groups.

The hard work that went into launching the Crusade for Citizenship paid off, although not to the degree that Baker or her SCLC colleagues had hoped. Ironically, even though the crusade went forward without the NAACP's official endorsement or practical support, it was Ella Baker's NAACP contacts in cities and towns throughout the South who helped her to mobilize a respectable turnout on February 12. The day was marked by church rallies, press conferences, and prayer vigils in nearly two dozen cities. It was a modest beginning that could form the base for future actions. Although King had hired Baker somewhat reluctantly, he had to admit that she worked tirelessly and selflessly on the campaign.[38]

Since Ella Baker's style of political work placed more emphasis on process than on singular, dramatic events, she understood that follow-up activities would be even more important than the kick-off itself. After returning to New York City to get her affairs in order, Baker returned to Atlanta, agreeing to spend some additional time working to build on the contacts she had made and the expectations that had arisen out of the February 12 mobilization. Ever the field organizer, she was not satisfied by her phone contacts with the various SCLC affiliates, so she packed her bags and traveled around the region speaking at local meetings and conferences and conducting workshops to promote and help initiate local civil rights campaigns in the spring and early summer of 1958.[39] The strategy of SCLC was to encourage massive voter registration, working through local affiliate organizations, and to document and report all instances of harassment or interference with blacks attempting to exercise the ballot. The campaign did make some inroads.

Historian Adam Fairclough presents the Crusade for Citizenship campaign as a major shift in the organization's strategy: "No sooner had SCLC formed than it switched its focus [from nonviolent direct action] to voter registration" in an opportunistic response to the passage of the 1957 Civil Rights Act.[40] Perhaps for some neophyte activists the shift from nonviolent direct action for integration to political organizing for voting rights was indeed a major one. For Baker, however, this strategic move was more complex. Drawing on the lessons she had gleaned during her NAACP days, she knew there had to be a catalyst for collective action. The everyday routines of racism inspired spontaneous individual acts of resistance, but these were usually limited responses. Sustained, concerted action required a more proactive stance, grassroots organizing, and a focus. For Baker, legislative victories were opportunities for organizing, not ends unto themselves. She saw the Civil Rights Act of 1957, although pathetically weak in its enforcement capacity, as providing an opportunity to draw national attention to the shame of southern racism and the undemocratic, racial exclusion that dominated the political process. Equally important, the Civil Rights Act could become a focal point for mobilizing local communities. Organizing people to testify at hearings was a way to embolden local leaders and prospective activists; it also served to challenge local elites in a public arena to defend practices that had long been shielded by silence from outside scrutiny and pressure. For Baker, mobilizing for voter registration campaigns, documenting the establishment's corruption that undermined such campaigns, and forcing the hand of the otherwise impotent Civil Rights Commission would inevitably lead to direct action. Given the realities of white vigilante violence in the South at the moment when Jim Crow was facing a major challenge, Baker also recognized that direct action might not always remain nonviolent.

· · · · · ·

GENDER INEQUITY WITHIN THE MOVEMENT

Ella Baker launched SCLC's Crusade for Citizenship with a greater margin of success than one might have expected given the time and resource constraints, demonstrating that she had the skills and commitment the nascent organization required. Yet Baker felt that she was never seriously considered for the job of permanent executive director. At one meeting, a minister from Nashville proposed that Baker be considered as a candidate for the job, but his suggestion fell on deaf ears. "The officialdom didn't take it seriously," Baker recalled.[41] The attitudes that King and other ministerial leaders of the SCLC held toward Baker were not unique to her situation; rather, they were a manifestation of the larger problem of sexism within the church, the organization, and the culture. By this time, Baker was well aware that the SCLC ministers were not ready to welcome her into the organization on an equal footing. That would be to go too far afield from the gender relations they were used to in the church. Baker observed that "the role of women in the southern church . . . was that of doing the things that the minister said he wanted to have done. It was not one in which they were credited with having creativity and initiative and capacity to carry out things."[42] While Baker may have slightly overstated her case—women did have some power and agency—the basic point still had a great deal of merit.

Clearly, women were instrumental forces in the church, but male leaders seldom fully acknowledged women's power and often attempted to limit the authority women exercised.[43] Many of Baker's male colleagues, like their counterparts in white society, viewed women as subordinates and helpmates. Even though African American women have historically worked both inside and outside the home and engaged in public, political activity, the culture that prevailed in the 1950s, especially among the black middle class, as among their white counterparts, emphasized the primacy of women's domestic roles.[44] According to Baker, the majority of the ministers in SCLC wanted to relate to women in this very limited capacity. They were most comfortable talking to women about "how well they cooked, and how beautiful they looked," she complained.[45] Baker's deliberate avoidance of conventional femininity made a number of her male clerical colleagues rather uneasy. "I wasn't a fashion plate," she remarked, "[and] I made no bones about not being a fashion plate."[46] More importantly, "I did not hesitate in voicing my opinion and . . . it was not a comforting sort of presence that I presented."[47] The conditions under which she worked, especially the sexist and often dismissive treatment she endured from her male co-workers, annoyed and offended Baker. Some days she could barely justify persevering in such an adverse situation.[48] "I live to serve" was the tongue-in-cheek way that Baker once described herself to a cousin.[49] This sarcastic statement had a sad ring of truth.

The work that Ella Baker and other women did for SCLC was consistently undervalued. As the organization grew and additional female staffers were hired, Baker protested that these women were taken for granted and treated unfairly as well.[50] A rhetoric of racial equality marked the public pronouncements of SCLC leaders, while old hierarchies based on gender inequities endured within their ranks. Baker refused to accept the situation in silence. She criticized ministerial leaders who came to meetings late and left early, disregarding the inconveniences they caused for the female clerical staff. They expected the women workers to cater to them, Baker complained.[51] Although she never publicly named names, Baker also alluded to unprincipled sexual behavior on the part of some male ministers involved in the movement. She confided to one researcher that certain SCLC ministers would come into the office in the afternoon "after spending the morning at some sister's house doing what they shouldn't have been doing . . . you see, I know too many stories."[52] The ministers' arrogant assumption that they stood above the moral rules they preached to others cost them Baker's respect as ministers and as men.

Despite her frustrations and resentments, Ella Baker assisted SCLC leaders in recruiting, screening, and selecting candidates for the executive director post, which they had tacitly deemed her unqualified to fill. She approached several prospective candidates with whom she had worked in the past. John Tilley, who was hired as executive director, was among them. Tilley was a Shaw alumnus and the pastor of a church in Baltimore.[53] Baker thought he was a good candidate because he "had a clear voice and good thinking" and some political experience in Baltimore.[54] Baker and Stanley Levison met with Tilley at an ice cream parlor in Harlem to discuss the organization and the job.[55] When King met Tilley, he was impressed and agreed to bring him on as the new executive director in May 1958.

The first SCLC meeting after Tilley joined the staff took place in Clarksdale, Mississippi, that same month. The gathering was well attended by some 200 delegates, indicating that in many places the organization's work was gaining support.[56] Convening the group in Mississippi was a bold gesture. Mississippi was so well known for antiblack violence that for many southerners it served as a symbol of the crudest and most brutal brand of white racism. Mississippi continued to hold that distinction as the civil rights movement progressed. It was in Mississippi that young Emmett Till had been murdered only three years earlier. It was in Mississippi that three young civil rights workers—Andrew Goodman, Michael Schwerner, and James Chaney—would be ambushed and murdered in 1964. And it was in Jackson, Mississippi, that Medgar Evers, a state NAACP leader who participated in this SCLC meeting, would be assassinated in his own driveway in 1963. But on the weekend of May 29, 1958, the town of Clarksdale was the site of something hopeful: serious discussions, debates, and strategy sessions about the future direction of the Black Freedom Movement.

Baker went to Clarksdale a few days early to help set up for the meeting.[57] She was optimistic that things were finally coming together for the new coalition. A permanent director was in place; local NAACP leaders such as Evers had agreed to attend the meeting, despite tensions between SCLC and the national NAACP office; and there were sparks of activity in several cities.[58] The participation of Evers and Aaron Henry, a fellow NAACP activist, reflected the willingness of NAACP leaders at the state and local level to work with whatever forces were in motion on the ground, often in direct opposition to national directives.[59] The men and women under attack in the South did not always subscribe to the grandiose objectives and long-term strategies of the national offices and high-level leaders of the organizations with which they worked. Medgar Evers and Aaron Henry never fully agreed with the decision by the NAACP leaders in New York not to form alliances with other civil rights groups, and both men worked closely with SCLC and other groups on particular campaigns.[60] Baker was pleased with the outcome of the 1958 Clarksdale meeting.[61] She hoped Tilley would be a hands-on leader who would expand the base of supporters beyond the church and embrace some of the more militant community-based leaders, both secular and church-related. Toward that end, she invited him to stay on in Mississippi for a few days after the Clarksdale meeting and familiarize himself with the work Amzie and Ruth Moore were doing in Cleveland, Mississippi, which he did. But even putting Tilley in contact with some of the most embattled freedom fighters in the South could not reinvigorate the coalition.[62]

The internal problems of SCLC continued after the meeting in Clarksdale. Tilley did not prove to be the stabilizing force that Baker and King had hoped for. Rev. Tilley continued to head his congregation in Baltimore after assuming his new responsibilities in Atlanta, and he was unable to combine or balance these two demanding positions. His commuting back and forth took its toll on Tilley and on the SCLC's work. In less than a year, King was forced to fire him. Again, by default, Baker was asked to take over as acting or interim director; both titles were used.

Internal problems were compounded by external crises. In September 1958, while Martin Luther King Jr. was on a speaking tour to promote his new book, *Stride toward Freedom*, he was stabbed by a mentally ill woman in Harlem, within walking distance of Baker's apartment on 135th Street. Ella was in town at the time, trying to recover from her own health problems. Suffering from acute back pain, she was stretched out on her living room floor when she heard the shocking news of King's stabbing on the radio.[63] Baker immediately rushed to the hospital to see what she could do to help. King survived the attack, but his recuperation took months. Once again, Baker had to pick up the slack. She filled in for King as a speaker on several occasions, answered his correspondence, explained his incapacitation, and served as publicist and accountant for the sale of his book, a job she did not relish.

After a year of hard labor in the SCLC's trenches, Baker was disappointed that so little had been achieved in terms of regionwide coordinated work. She blamed the clerical leaders. They had not given her the resources necessary to run an office or a campaign efficiently. She had to beg for a working mimeograph machine, an air conditioner in the summer, and secretarial help. She then had to deal with the added frustration of King's veto power within the organization. Nothing could be done, she complained, without his approval.[64] And, to add insult to injury, she was saddled with the responsibility of all promotions of and sales for King's book. Still, Baker did not see too many other political options for herself in 1958–59, especially if she wanted to be based in a black southern community, which she did. So, she persevered.

Baker's 1958 report to the Administrative Committee of SCLC reflected the goals that she would fight to implement throughout her tenure. Baker urged her SCLC colleagues to develop programs for mass action and to target women for activist campaigns. She specifically called for the formation of youth and action teams to help ignite the work. This report was her effort to rally the troops, but the results were modest. Everyone nodded and continued on as they had before. Without support from the principal decision makers in the organization, there was little Baker could do.[65]

On some level, she and the ministers—at least the core of them—were not too far apart in the kind of action they envisioned, but together they could not seem to make it happen. Historian Glenn T. Eskew suggests that Baker was at least in part to blame. He even sees the growing "cult of personality" surrounding King as partly due to the absence of a sustained mass-based campaign, a campaign Baker was responsible for getting off the ground. For Baker, the inverse was true. King's larger-than-life persona inhibited the emergence of local struggles and local leaders.

In December 1958, at the third annual Montgomery Improvement Association Institute on Nonviolence, the program theme was "A Testimonial to Dr. King's Leadership." Taylor Branch maintains that "[t]o Ella Baker, frustrated by SCLC's bare solvency and its paralyzed registration campaign, this sort of activity was not mere froth but a harmful end in itself." She asked King directly why he allowed such hero worship, and he responded simply that it was what people wanted.[66] This answer did not satisfy Baker in the least.

Baker felt that SCLC's increasing reliance on King's celebrity and charisma had all sorts of hidden dangers. Less polished leaders were likely to receive less recognition and might become disaffected from the struggle. For example, E. D. Nixon, the labor and civil rights activist who played a pivotal role in the Montgomery bus boycott, resented the way that an outsider eclipsed local leaders. In a 1958 letter to a friend, Nixon complained bitterly about King's fame and his own diminished stature in the movement. It is disheartening, he explained, "when people give all recognition to one because of his academic training and forge[t] other[s] who do not have that kind of training but are making a worthwhile contribution."[67] Furthermore, no one person could possibly meet the needs of a growing and increasingly complex movement. Even leaders who were motivated by high ideals rather than personal ambition and adopted a humble rather than top-down style had to make way for many others to assume leadership roles. According to Baker, organizations had to alter their very concept of leadership: "Instead of the leader as a person who was supposed to be a magic man, you could develop individuals who were bound together by a concept that benefited the larger number of individuals and provided an opportunity for them to grow into being responsible for carrying out a program."[68]

Ella Baker believed that all their lives poor black people had been spoon-fed the notion that the key to their emancipation was something external to themselves: ostensibly benevolent masters, enlightened legislators, or skillful and highly educated lawyers. Such dependency reinforced poor people's sense of helplessness, Baker felt. Her message was quite the opposite. "Strong people don't need strong leaders," she argued.[69] In Baker's view, oppressed people did not need a messiah to deliver them from oppression; all they needed was themselves, one another, and the will to persevere. The clerical leaders of SCLC, King included, held a very different notion of leadership. As Baker put it, they saw themselves as the new "saviors."[70] As early as 1947, she had insisted that "the Negro must quit looking for a savior and work to save himself."[71] She was even more convinced of this by 1958.

Crisis after crisis and sacrifice after sacrifice, Baker's dissatisfaction with her circumstances grew. She became especially annoyed that many SCLC ministers viewed her as a glorified secretary who was there to simply "carry out King's orders."[72] Although the SCLC needed Baker's skills, it was not willing to recognize or affirm her leadership. As Eugene Walker put it in an interview with Baker, SCLC ministers seemed to "respect your abilities on the one hand, and fear your independence on the other."[73] To be fair, not all of the SCLC board members felt this way, which in part was what kept Baker going. By 1959, she had built strong ties with SCLC activists in Shreveport and Birmingham, and she had alliances with NAACP people in Mississippi. Yet, despite her independent base, Baker felt so suffocated by the magnitude of King's personality and presence that she could not make herself comfortable within the organization.

· · · · · ·

BAKER AND KING

The relationship between Ella Baker and Martin Luther King Jr. is doubly significant. First, the incompatibility between the civil rights movement's most charismatic national spokesperson and one of its most effective grassroots organizers had significant consequences for the development of the movement itself. Baker's decision to leave the SCLC staff in 1960, her choice to support mass-based, grassroots organizations, and her determination to defend the autonomous, democratic decisions made by militant activists changed the course of the Black Freedom Movement, not least by ensuring that the nascent Student Nonviolent Coordinating Committee was not taken over by established civil rights organizations, including SCLC and the NAACP. Second, the conflict between these two civil rights leaders reveals more fundamental conflicts within black politics and African American culture over the meanings of American democracy and the pathways toward social change. If Baker's criticisms of King were overly harsh and unforgiving, that may be because they were intensified by her disappointed hopes in King himself and by her accumulated outrage against the male leaders who had treated her in demeaning ways over many decades.

In some of her harshest, perhaps even gratuitous, criticisms of King, Baker described him as a pampered member of Atlanta's black elite who had the mantle of leadership handed to him rather than having had to earn it, a member of a coddled "silver spoon brigade."[74] He wore silk suits and spoke with a silver tongue. His followers were in awe of him, struggling in vain to imitate him or just seeking to be near him. Young ministers would try to dress like him, even sound like him, Baker observed, and their unsuccessful attempts only reinforced the perception that he deserved the deference and adulation he received. King was, in her words, "the man of the hour . . . [and others] got the reflective glory."[75] In Baker's eyes, King did not identify closely enough with the people he sought to lead. He did not situate himself among them but remained above them. What Baker does not give King credit for is the fact that while he may have allowed others to applaud his leadership skills and oratory talents, he did not hesitate to take risks, putting himself and his family in danger repeatedly for the sake of the cause. So, while attention centered on him, so did the rage of those who, like his assassin, blamed him for the movement's success.

Still, Baker felt the focus on King drained the masses of confidence in themselves. People often marveled at the things King could do that they could not; his eloquent speeches overwhelmed as well as inspired. This disturbed Baker. While she appreciated King's many contributions to the struggle and valued the considerable talents he brought to bear, she was angered and frustrated by the hero worship that surrounded him. Baker challenged King on this matter repeatedly, arguing that he tolerated, even if he did not encourage, such adulation.[76]

In gauging the fairness of Ella Baker's criticisms of King, one should keep in mind that she was known for her patience, tolerance, and willingness to work with individuals of diverse ideologies. She had collaborated with other men who were well known for their inflated egos, from George Schuyler to Walter White. And, as King's biographers have noted, he was in many ways quite humble, given the attention and flattery he received from others. He lived modestly and was initially quite ambivalent about all the attention and accolades that were directed his way.

Why did King provoke Baker so much? Some of her friends and colleagues have asserted that Baker's conflicts within SCLC resulted as much from different personal styles as from political disagreements. Septima Clark, who admired Baker greatly, felt that sometimes she responded too angrily to insults and slights from the male clerics in SCLC, when these situations could have been handled more effectively in a less confrontational manner. There was undoubtedly a subjective component to Baker's criticisms of King and the other SCLC ministers whom she felt did not respect her as an equal. Anne Braden, who was much closer to Baker than to

King personally and politically, admitted that "Ella had a blind spot when it came to King. It was just something about him. She and I differed on this."[77]

It would be misguided to view Baker's analysis of King's political flaws too narrowly, however. She did not see King as unique; rather, she saw what she defined as his weaknesses as reflective of prevalent tendencies in American society. At the same time, she insisted that her criticism never translated into personal animus, as some have alleged. Baker remarked that "some of the King family have said that I hated him, but I didn't."[78] King and Baker were bound together, from the very inception of SCLC, by manifold political ties and real interdependence. Their working relationship was close enough—even with King in Montgomery most of the time and Baker in Atlanta—that their fundamental differences became a recurring source of friction.

Still, King and Baker were more alike than Baker was ever prepared to admit. Both were southerners by birth, and both had grown up in the social and spiritual circles of the southern black Baptist church. Both were college-educated intellectuals, articulate spokespersons for the cause of black freedom and social justice, and eloquent public speakers. And both came from class positions of relative advantage. But Baker and King had made very divergent choices about how to utilize their skills and privileges. They translated religious faith into their political identities in profoundly different ways. Above all, they defined the confluence of their roles as individuals and their roles as participants in a mass movement for social change quite distinctly. Baker was a militant egalitarian, and King was a sophisticated southern Baptist preacher.

In Baker's view, the celebrity status that the movement afforded King was not an aberration but rather a product of a dominant culture that promoted individualism and egocentrism. People "just have to have these high-powered individuals to worship," Baker pointed out.[79] "It's the culture we're in," she insisted. "When the newspaper people come around, what do they look for? They don't look for the solid organizational drive . . . they look for a miracle performer."[80] Baker believed that when ordinary people elevate their leaders above the crowd, they devalue the power within themselves. Her message was that we are all, as individuals, products of the larger society, even as some of us struggle to change it. And all leaders, however well intentioned, are susceptible to the corruption of personal ambition. According to Baker, "We on the outside, we want to be important . . . so we ape the insiders."[81] She argued that activists often unwittingly replicate the values and attributes of those they oppose, which becomes a detriment to the movement. While many black leaders criticized racial hierarchies in the dominant society, they recreated hierarchies based on class, gender, and personality within the movement itself. Baker insisted that leaders live by the principles they espouse. In this sense, she argued, not only is the personal political, but the political is inescapably personal. Transformation has to occur at the societal and institutional level, but also at the local and personal level.

Ironically, Ella Baker could not see in King what other colleagues and his many biographers saw: a young man, talented, brilliant, eager to serve a greater good but reticent about being lionized, and being pushed and pulled in many directions all at once. In Baker's view, he was indeed a talented young man who had been given a precious opportunity to help organize large numbers of people into a fighting force for change, and instead, she lamented, he settled for mesmerizing them.

· · · · · ·

MISSIONARIES AND MESSIAHS

King and Baker had been introduced to politics through the same institution: the southern black Baptist church. Since slavery, the black church had been an influential pillar in the African American community and an important arena for black politics. The church provided blacks with the technical skills to enter the political arena: literacy, fund-raising, public speaking, management, and organization. In addition, the church provided its members with a powerful moral language within which to frame political issues, if they so chose. In a high school essay, Baker wrote eloquently, and uncritically, about the important leadership role played by the black church.[82] Her ideas and analysis of the role of the black church, and of the clergy in particular, had changed considerably over the years, but her understanding of the centrality of the institution in African American life and culture remained intact.

Baker's political awakening began within the black Baptist women's missionary movement in the early 1900s. Her mother was a devoted activist who dragged Ella and her two siblings to missionary meetings throughout their home state of North Carolina. These churchwomen celebrated strength, piety, and quiet, selfless service. Egos and individual accomplishments were downplayed. Humility was a virtue. In contrast, King was groomed from an early age to follow in his father's footsteps into the ministry. Playing a visible leadership role in the church, and thereby occupying a prominent place in the black community, was an honorable career goal for a young man from such a deeply religious family.

King's and Baker's respective orientations within the church could not have been more different. Ministers were trained to be shepherds of their flocks. The metaphor itself suggests the differences between the notions of leadership that ministers practiced and those that missionary women adhered to. Ministers directed their flocks; missionaries gathered people together. In Baker's view, most ministers expected to say their piece and have their congregations obediently carry out their decisions. Baker saw no model for collective or democratic decision making within the mainstream ministerial tradition. The preacher's presumed authority did not trouble men like King, however. As he himself put it, "Leadership never ascends from the pew to the pulpit, but . . . descends from the pulpit to the pew."[83] But Baker saw this flow of authority as a weakness, not a virtue. The socialization of women missionaries meant that they practiced a more democratic and decentralized style of religious service than male ministers did.

Another philosophical position that distinguished Baker from King was the issue of nonviolence. Baker accepted nonviolence as a tactic, but she never internalized the concept as a way of life or made it a defining feature of her worldview. Contrasting herself to her friend Bayard Rustin, Ella Baker remarked: "He had a history of dedication to the concept of nonviolence. I have no such history; I have no such commitment. Not historically or even now can I claim that because that's not my way of functioning."[84] Rustin's pacifism was rooted in his Quakerism, while Baker's Christian faith carried no imperative to turn the other cheek or love your enemies. For her, nonviolence and self-defense were tactical choices, not matters of principle. "Mine was not a choice of non-violence per se," Baker reiterated.[85]

Indeed, Baker questioned the capacity of nonviolence to serve as a philosophical basis on which to build a movement, even while she was working for the SCLC. She later questioned "how far non-violent mass action can go" as a mobilization strategy.[86] Her critique of the limitations of nonviolence was informed by her connections with the militant struggles of the 1930s and the self-defense ethos of those she worked with in the 1940s, and it foreshadowed her support of revolutionary militancy in the late 1960s. Baker consistently gave voice to a radical vision for social transformation and encouraged others to join her in the struggle necessary to realize that vision. The realist in her understood that such a struggle might, at times, become heated and even physical. Engaging in determined conflict entailed utilizing a variety of tactics. Baker felt that oppressed people needed to tap whatever resources they had at their disposal to forge a viable strategy for resistance, especially in the dangerous and violent climate of the Jim Crow South. She was not alone in this view. Some of SCLC's most notable grassroots leaders, including C. O. Simpkins and Daisy Bates, admitted to having firearms for self-defense purposes.[87]

Baker differed with King and other SCLC leaders on questions besides nonviolence and the meaning of leadership in militant mass movements. Bernice Johnson Reagon has suggested that Baker's worldview and political practice can best be defined as a type of radical humanism.[88] It was radical, in that she advocated fundamental social transformation, and it was humanistic, because she envisioned that transformation coming about through a democratic, cooperative, and localized movement that valued the participation of each of its individual members. Baker's unfaltering confidence in the common people was the bedrock of her political vision. It was with them that she felt the locus of power should reside. This confidence was rooted in her understanding of the complex dialectical relationship between deference and defiance in southern black culture. Despite the facade of subservience and acquiescence to white rule and Jim Crow indignities on the part of southern African Americans, many black people embodied a fighting spirit that needed only a viable outlet to demonstrate and to express itself in subtle ways every day. It was important for political organizers to understand and decode the culture of everyday life, and to tap the reservoir of resistance that resided there, in order to pull people into collective action.[89] In Baker's assessment, assuming that people were quiescent was a misreading of southern black culture.

In this respect, Baker's views parallel those of the anthropologist James Scott, who writes eloquently about the "hidden transcript" of opposition within oppressed populations and about the danger of not reading that transcript carefully. Scott warns:

So long as we confine our conception of the political to activity that is openly declared, we are driven to conclude that subordinate groups essentially lack a political life or that what political life they do have is restricted to those exceptional moments of popular explosion. To do so is to miss the immense political terrain that lies between quiescence and revolt and that, for better or worse, is the political environment of subject classes. It is to focus on the visible coastline of politics and miss the continent that lies beyond.[90]

Scott's theoretical work on the nature of popular culture and resistance resembles many aspects of the politics that Ella Baker lived but rarely wrote about. From her point of view, it was a semi-spontaneous action from below—Rosa Parks's reasoned decision to violate a segregation ordinance—that had sparked the Montgomery boycott. It was another semi-spontaneous action—a handful of college students sitting in at a lunch counter in Greensboro, North Carolina, in 1960—that would ignite the next phase of movement activity. These actions were thought through and conscious, but they were both examples of leadership coming from below (the metaphorical pews) rather than from the political pulpits above. These actions also tapped into a subterranean oppositional culture and gave it a political outlet.

Baker's political views were profoundly shaped by her analysis of the complex class dynamics within the black community. As she put it, "There's always a problem in the minority group that's escalating up the ladder in this culture . . . it's a problem of their not understanding the possibility of being divorced from those who are not in their social classification."[91] For this reason, she argued, "I believe firmly in the right of the people who were under the heel to be the ones to decide what action they were going to take to get [out] from under their oppression."[92] She held fast to her conviction that the most oppressed sectors of society had to be in the forefront of the struggle to change society.

Ella Baker's job tenure with SCLC was more frustrating than fruitful. She was unsettled the entire time, politically, physically, and, to a certain extent, emotionally. She had no solid allies in the SCLC office that she could rely on daily as she had done during her years with the NAACP. Her close and increasingly critical view of King put some distance between Baker and her old In Friendship allies, Levison and Rustin, who adored King. Moreover, she had never really settled into her semifurnished apartment in Atlanta and found herself on the road more than she was there. Emotionally, there were some disconnects as well. Jackie was in college. Baker's marriage had ended in divorce in the summer of 1958 while she was in Atlanta.[93] And her health had begun to effect her work. Her eyes were bothering her, as were her back and encroaching arthritis. Still, there were pockets of activity among some SCLC affiliates that persuaded Baker to stay with the organization a little bit longer.

Ella Baker in 1932. (Thanks to The Crisis Publishing Co., Inc.,
publisher of the magazine of the NAACP, *for use of this work,*
first published in The Crisis *magazine, January 1932)*

Ella Baker in suit, ca. 1942. (Library of Congress)

Ella Baker with NAACP colleagues, September 1945.
(From the Gazette and Daily; *photograph Schomburg Center for*
Research in Black Culture, New York Public Library)

Ella Baker with group of girls at NAACP fair, 1950s.
(Schomburg Center for Research in Black Culture,
New York Public Library, Austin Hansen Collection;
courtesy of Joyce Hansen)

Ella Baker with unidentified man in Shreveport, Louisiana, 1959.
(Courtesy of C. O. Simpkins)

*Ella Baker
and Myles
Horton in lawn
chairs at
Highlander
Folk School,
ca. 1960.
(Wisconsin
Historical
Society,
WHi-3236)*

Ella Baker smiling, 1962. (© Danny Lyon/Magnum Photos)

Ella Baker, Fannie Lou Hamer, Eleanor Holmes Norton, Stokely Carmichael, and others at Atlantic City, New Jersey, 1964. (© 1978 George Ballis/Take Stock)

Ella Baker delivering a speech in Atlantic City, New Jersey, 1964.
(© 1978 George Ballis/Take Stock)

Ella Baker at podium, with Charles Evers seated behind her and Ivanhoe Donaldson to her right, delivering a speech in Jackson, Mississippi, 1964.
(© 1976 George Ballis/Take Stock)

Ella Baker singing at SCEF luncheon, 1970s. (© 2002 Charmian Reading)

Ella Baker at Angela Davis rally, 1972. (Photograph by Charley Sands; permission courtesy of the Daily Cavalier, *University of Virginia, Charlottesville)*

Ella Baker with David Dellinger and Marilyn Clement at CCR dinner, May 13, 1980.
(© 2002 Charmian Reading)

Ella Baker with William Kunstler and Marilyn Clement in New York City, 1980.
(© 2002 Charmian Reading)

Ella Baker in her bathrobe in her Harlem apartment, 1984.
(Photograph © Harvey Wang, from Harvey Wang's New York, *1990)*

Ella Baker, Jackie Brockington, and Carolyn Brockington at City College, 1985.
(Courtesy of Jackie Brockington)

NEW BATTLEFIELDS AND NEW ALLIES

SHREVEPORT, BIRMINGHAM, AND THE
SOUTHERN CONFERENCE EDUCATION FUND

. . . . . .

I never worked for an organization but for a cause.
Ella Baker, 1968

In 1959, while continuing to work for the Southern Christian Leadership Conference, Ella Baker devoted her energies to the grassroots struggles that were developing in cities, small towns, and rural counties scattered across the South. Many local civil rights leaders were affiliated with SCLC, but the organizations that conducted mass mobilizations were locally controlled, and their political perspectives and strategies did not always conform to the SCLC's philosophy. That was just fine with Ella Baker. Her main contribution to the civil rights movement during her years with SCLC was not the building of a solid regional coalition, which was what King had hired her to do, but rather the strengthening of several semi-independent local struggles, which were more connected to one another and to itinerant organizers like Baker than they were to the official SCLC leadership in Atlanta. Baker concentrated on those few local SCLC affiliates that were making changes in their communities, not just headlines in the national press.

Two such organizations dear to Baker's heart were the United Christian Movement Inc. (UCMI) in Shreveport, Louisiana, and the Alabama Christian Movement for Human Rights (ACMHR) in Birmingham. Led by committed husband-and-wife teams, these groups seemed to Baker excellent models for sustained, militant democratic organizing. From the winter of 1958 through the summer of 1959, Baker spent a great deal of time shuttling back and forth between Birmingham and Shreveport, punctuated by regular trips to her home base in Harlem. During this period, her sentiments toward SCLC were mixed, but her loyalty to activists in places like Shreveport and Birmingham was unwavering—and she would continue to work with them after she left SCLC. Baker had acted the same way in the 1940s, when she resigned from the national NAACP after serving as its independent-minded director of branches. Baker's fundamental commitment was to grassroots activism, mass mobilization, and democratic change, and wherever she saw signs of movement in that direction she was eager to lend her support, expertise, and passion.

The struggle over racial justice was heating up in 1959. In May, Baker expressed her outrage at the rape of a young black woman in Florida by four white men, adding that "Negroes all over the south would watch developments closely" in the case.[1] Another case, the more widely publicized death of Mack Charles Parker at the hands of a Mississippi lynch mob aroused enormous anger, and the fact that his killers, like so many others before, went free compounded the outrage. The long-standing rule of "Judge Lynch" in the South seemed more than ever a travesty of justice in the late 1950s, and increasing numbers of African Americans refused to back down in the face of vigilante violence or official repression. The militant defiance of Robert Williams, a black activist in North Carolina, and, by the early 1960s, the growing popularity of Malcolm X, the radical minister of the Nation of Islam, signaled a changing mood across the country. Some historians have suggested that established civil rights organizations were paralyzed or weakened during the late 1950s by the conservative and conformist ethos of the Cold War. After all, the *Brown* decision had been followed not by rapid integration of public schools but by a concerted campaign of "massive resistance" across the white South. This view, while not invalid at the national level, is only partly correct; the situation on the ground in some places was quite different. Despite the precarious state of national and regional Black Freedom organizations, there were local pockets of fierce antiracist resistance throughout the South during the late 1950s. Baker's position with SCLC enabled her to jump right into the fray, drawing up battle plans with local leaders and urging other communities to follow their lead.

In 1959, as she traveled the region, Baker searched for political communities where her day-to-day practice could more fully reflect her philosophical principles and political convictions. She concentrated her energies on local sites of struggle that could, she hoped, become launching pads for militant, regionwide mass action and serve as models of a democratic practice. Birmingham, Alabama, and Shreveport, Louisiana, were two such places. Fred and Ruby Shuttlesworth of Birmingham and C. O. and Dorothy Simpkins of Shreveport were effective organizers who shared Baker's commitment to mass mobilization. Baker also began to work very closely with Anne and Carl Braden, radical white activists in the Southern Conference Education Fund (SCEF), an interracial desegregation and human rights group based in the South. With comrades she trusted and close ties to freedom struggles growing up at the grassroots, Ella Baker was slowly creating a more comfortable political home for herself.

· · · · · ·

NOTHING TOO DEAR TO PAY FOR FREEDOM

Baker gave voice to her radical ideas, even when they clashed with SCLC's image and politics, in order to support and educate activists who were organizing mass movements for civil rights in their own communities. On June 5, 1959, in Birmingham, Alabama, she delivered one of the most militant speeches of her political career. She had been invited to deliver the keynote address at the third anniversary celebration for ACMHR. The evening meeting was held at the New Pilgrim Baptist Church, and her friend Ruby Shuttlesworth, a local activist, introduced her. As Baker rose to the podium wearing one of her signature hats and a crisp summer dress, complete with pocketbook and pumps, she must have looked more like a Sunday school teacher or Missionary Society member than the dangerous radical the FBI feared her to be.[2] But when Baker spoke, she expressed radical views that were based on her long experience in organizing for social change and on local activists' long experience of violent repression by the city's white racist officials. Surrounded by a community of people she admired, who had continued their struggle despite beatings, bombings, and economic reprisals, she delivered a provocative address titled "Nothing Is Too Dear to Pay for Freedom."

Baker was unflinching in her indictment of racism and in her call for an intensification of antiracist struggle. Only a few months after King's return from a trip to India, where he reaffirmed his own unfaltering commitment to Gandhian nonviolence, Baker publicly posed the loaded rhetorical question, almost as a gauntlet thrown down for her listeners to pick up: "What is the basic right of the individual to defend himself?"[3]

Ella Baker's speech in Birmingham in 1959, in both tone and substance, exemplified the militancy that predated the 1960s and stretched across regions and generations. Urban black youth in the late 1960s were not the first African Americans to maintain that defending themselves from racist attacks was morally justifiable. Foreshadowing Malcolm X's famous declaration, "by any means necessary," Baker exhorted her audience, "Guideposts to first-class citizenship call for the utilization of all resources at the group's command," and told them that even life itself was not too high a price to pay for freedom. After condemning the "accommodating type Negro leader," Baker questioned the viability of nonviolence in the face of such extreme violence from segregationists. The *Birmingham World*, the city's black paper, described Baker as "calm, analytical, and eloquent" and summarized her remarks at Pilgrim Church that summer evening as follows: "Calling for a re-examination of the doctrine of non-violence, Miss Baker questioned the wisdom of allowing the more favored segment to take violent and unlawful advantage without self-defense. . . . [S]he reminded her listeners that the constitution gives to every citizen the right to defend himself."[4] With clear logic and a direct challenge to her listeners, Baker put her own radical views on the table and took her stand with the emerging militant wing of the civil rights movement.

Baker further reminded her audience that the stakes for freedom were high and applauded militant leaders like Fred Shuttlesworth who were "determined to secure the full loaf of freedom and not just the crumbs."[5] Baker was not calling for guerilla warfare or riots in the streets; she was simply affirming a long-standing black tradition of self-defense against mob violence, which whites had used to enforce the racial and economic hierarchies of the Old South for generations. Undoubtedly fresh in Baker's mind and the minds of her listeners was a vivid example of the long history of vicious antiblack violence that occurred only two months before: the brutal lynching of Mack Charles Parker, a black Mississippian dragged from his jail cell and murdered by a mob, which then threw his body into the Pearl River.[6]

Baker had traveled extensively through Ku Klux Klan territory during the 1940s, and she spent time with people who lived under the constant threat of vigilante violence. In contrast to the predominant, but erroneous, image of southern blacks as passive, foot-shuffling folk who acquiesced to white domination, the southern blacks whom Baker knew and worked with owned guns and were not afraid to use them for personal protection.[7] These were honest, hard-working, God-fearing people, but they were also fighters.

Robert F. Williams, a North Carolina activist to whom Baker alluded in her Birmingham speech, identified with and embodied that tradition of self-defense.[8] As head of the Monroe, North Carolina, branch of the NAACP, Williams became a symbol of southern black militancy and a source of immense controversy within the resurgent Black Freedom Movement. In May 1959, in response to the acquittal of a white man who had assaulted a black woman, the outraged Williams declared that the time had come to "meet violence with violence," since racist courts seemed to place little value on either black rights or black lives.[9] Press across the country picked up the story. The headline of the *New York Times* proclaimed: "NAACP Leader Urges Violence." Roy Wilkins, head of the national association, was furious at Williams, publicly repudiated him, and on May 5 suspended him from his post as president of the Monroe branch. Williams, like Baker, had previously had numerous clashes with the NAACP's national office, and he still claimed many allies and admirers at the branch level. Many North Carolinians wrote to Wilkins to protest Williams's suspension.[10] The Williams controversy was still raging when Baker arrived in Birmingham on June 5. Although she shied away from explicitly endorsing Williams's actions or ideas in her speech, she gave him a favorable nod.[11] Emory O. Jackson, the outspoken editor of the *Birmingham World*, who covered Baker's speech, wrote that after "blistering the accommodating type Negro leader" Baker went on by "citing three instances which reflect the shifting status." One of those examples was "the strike-back declaration of Robert Williams, the unfrocked NAACP branch leader in North Carolina."[12] She then went on to underscore the right to self-defense.

Six months earlier, Ella Baker's old friend Conrad Lynn, a black leftist lawyer she had worked with during the 1930s, had asked her to join the campaign that he and Williams were organizing to defend two black boys, aged eight and ten, who were jailed for allegedly kissing a white girl in Monroe, North Carolina. Although she expressed sympathy for the defendants in the highly publicized "kissing case," Baker declined to become directly involved. Perhaps she anticipated the disapproval of her SCLC colleagues and was playing it safe at that point. Both Williams and Lynn were controversial figures, and the involvement of the Socialist Workers Party in the case had already drawn allegations of communist influence.[13] Avoiding controversy was uncharacteristic for Baker, but she sometimes tempered her inclination to do and say whatever she saw fit with a practical recognition of the possible consequences. By June 1959, she was willing to do so less and less. In her eyes, the mass militancy of the resurgent civil rights movement had the potential of bursting the bounds that regional and national organizations were trying to impose.

Although Baker and Williams never worked together formally in the NAACP or on the "kissing case," there were other political connections between them. One of Baker's dearest friends, the feminist lawyer Pauli Murray, represented Williams at his hearing before the NAACP's national board on June 8, 1959, speaking eloquently, but unsuccessfully, in his defense.[14] Carl and Anne Braden of SCEF also sympathized with Williams, even though they criticized many of his tactics.[15] James Forman, who later worked closely with Baker in the Student Nonviolent Coordinating Committee (SNCC), was beaten and arrested in Monroe in 1961 because of his association with Williams and his supporters. According to Tim Tyson, Williams's biographer, Baker encouraged Forman and his co-worker Paul Brooks to visit Williams's hometown that summer to investigate the situation there.[16] They found the city in flames. Fires of suspicious origins had been set the night before their arrival, igniting accusations and counteraccusations on both sides. Armed groups of white men roamed the streets, and Forman feared for his life. In the heat of one of the nights of turmoil, Williams detained a white couple who had entered a cordoned-off black neighborhood. He claimed that he had kept them indoors to ensure their safety, but the local authorities indicted him on a charge of kidnapping.[17]

In the summer of 1962, just before Williams's trial was scheduled to begin, Baker visited Monroe to check out the situation for herself. The opportunity had presented itself in the most unusual way. Dorothy Dawson (Burlage), a young white civil rights worker originally from Texas, had been sitting in Baker's Atlanta office when she received a phone call telling her that a black teenage volunteer, Raymond Johnson, had died in a suspicious drowning accident in Monroe. Dorothy had befriended the boy's mother, Azalea Johnson, when the two were assigned to room together at an SCLC citizenship school in Dorchester, Georgia, some months earlier. Dorothy had been so impressed with Mrs. Johnson that she drove to Monroe several times over the summer to visit her and soak up some of her wisdom. When the news of Raymond's death came, a distraught Dorothy decided to go to Monroe for the funeral. She was surprised when Baker quickly volunteered to go along. "Miss Baker did not even know Mrs. Johnson at the time; I think she just wanted to comfort her and to be supportive of me. That's how she was."[18] But there was more to it than that. Baker cryptically confided to her friend Anne Braden that the "kidnapping trial was due to be held [in Monroe] on Monday, but I understand it has now been postponed but there are some other developments which bear looking into and this is one of the reasons I am taking this short trip."[19] Yes, Baker was genuinely concerned about Dorothy and the grieving mother, but she was also constantly surveying the political landscape with her fine-tuned political radar, trying to detect signs of activity and to assess their importance. This was an occasion to get a close-up look at what had been brewing, and boiling over, in Monroe. Dorothy and Ella did not arrive in time for the funeral, but they stayed several days with Azalea Johnson, eating, drinking, and talking politics.[20]

Azalea Johnson was not just an ordinary citizen of Monroe, either. She had been the secretary at the Monroe NAACP branch when Williams was expelled and remained in the inner circle of Robert and Mabel Williams. The three of them had founded a newspaper, the *Crusader*, to which Johnson had contributed a regular column. She had traveled to New York with the couple and to Tennessee to the Highlander Folk School with Mabel for a conference. Azalea Johnson was a homegrown intellectual if there ever was one. Not only was she an able writer and political analyst of local race issues, but she was an astute observer of global politics as well. Dorothy was shocked when her plainspoken and unassuming roommate at Dorchester pulled out a book by Mao Zedong and asked if she had ever read it. Dorothy had not even heard of Mao at the time. It was an education on many levels.

Ella and Dorothy got an earful about Williams and Monroe politics during their stay at Johnson's home. The three women sat at Azalea Johnson's kitchen table, Dorothy remembered, drinking Jim Beam bourbon, discussing the political situation in the South and remembering Raymond. Even more memorable than the conversation was the image of black men sitting in the front room and on the front porch with loaded pistols at their sides virtually the whole time they were there. The situation in Monroe was just that volatile.[21]

Fearing a long jail term for what many felt were trumped-up kidnapping charges, Robert Williams ultimately fled the country. He ended up in exile in Cuba, by way of China, while the debate over self-defense within the Black Freedom Movement continued long after his departure.[22] Throughout the Williams ordeal, Baker kept her finger on the pulse of militant upsurges in Monroe and elsewhere.

At the time of her 1959 speech, Baker was not prepared to join forces with Robert Williams and his militant allies. She did not call for the formation of paramilitary groups or for a symbolic public show of armed force; she called, quite simply, for self-defense. At that time, like many black freedom fighters before her, she was unwilling to tolerate enemies of the movement assaulting and murdering leaders with impunity. She had seen too many friends and colleagues victimized by such violence. Moreover, she understood that it was quite commonplace for southern blacks to defend themselves when threatened or attacked, contrary to many northern stereotypes and assumptions. Carrying guns was not a matter of principle or political strategy for most black southerners; it was a means of survival. Baker acknowledged that at times nonviolence was a viable and effective tactic, but she never embraced it as a philosophy. As Baker became more vocal about her radical views in 1959, the FBI became more interested in her.[23]

None of the young militants who led the Black Freedom Movement during the next decade were in the audience to hear Ella Baker's remarks that night at Pilgrim Church in June 1959, but they might as well have been. Her remarks were circulated in the press and echoed through the coming years. Seven months later, young people acted on her call for renewed militancy and direct action by launching the historic desegregation sit-ins in Greensboro, North Carolina. Seven years later, in 1966, others followed Robert Williams's lead by forming the Black Panther Party for Self-Defense in Oakland, California. The young activists of the 1960s did not invent either the radical antiracist ideas they espoused or the confrontational tactics they embraced; rather, they inherited and reconfigured them.

· · · · · ·

BIRMINGHAM

Baker's intimate involvement in the black freedom struggle in Birmingham extended back to the 1940s. Her June 1959 speech on self-defense grew out of the relationship she had developed with local activists and the respect and admiration she had earned. Baker had become comfortable in the "Magic City" during her visits there as a field secretary for the NAACP, when she recruited new members in the city's black barber shops and bars. Birmingham was familiar turf. When Baker returned there during the late 1950s as a staff member of SCLC, she reestablished contact with the old-timers and met younger activists in the Alabama Christian Movement for Human Rights (ACMHR). Baker understood the situation that had shaped the struggles of the city's black residents for more than a generation.

Birmingham was one of the most volatile and racially explosive cities in the entire South, best known for its ruthless chief of police, Eugene "Bull" Connor and his rigid enforcement of the racist hierarchy of the South.[24] For Baker, however, Birmingham's significance came from the fact that it was home to tireless and courageous civil rights activists like Fred and Ruby Shuttlesworth. By the 1950s, the Shuttlesworths were anchors of the local movement there. They had worked with the state NAACP before it was banned and then had helped found the more activist-oriented ACMHR. The Shuttlesworths were no-nonsense fighters who were as bold and determined as they were savvy and pragmatic. Their reputations as local militants were well earned.

Ella Baker's respect for the Birmingham activists was also inspired by what she viewed as their grassroots approach to organizing. Birmingham's leaders, Baker thought, were "much more mass-oriented" in their political work than most organizers she had worked with.[25] Baker felt that Fred Shuttlesworth tried to act in accordance with the wishes of the "masses," even if he did not always poll them to determine what those wishes were. Notably, ACMHR held regular mass meetings to which all were welcome and at which substantive political and strategic discussions could take place.

Baker's assessment of Shuttlesworth's democratic tendencies contrasts with that of some observers, even admiring ones, who described him as more of an authoritarian preacher than an inclusive democrat.[26] Fred Shuttlesworth was indeed a complex character. He was self-confident and aggressive, and he sometimes acted unilaterally. At the same time, he reached out to a wider constituency than most of his peers, and within the movement he fought so that the voices of the poor and the working class, who were frequently marginalized, would be heard. A colorful and charismatic personality, Shuttlesworth was an egalitarian in his principles, if not always a conscientious democrat in his practice. Baker seemed willing to tolerate whatever other shortcomings Fred may have had, praising him as a person of "undaunted courage, even in the face of violence," and applauding his personal integrity and "unselfishness as a leader."[27] She viewed his zeal and charisma as talents applied in the service of the collective interests of the disenfranchised rather than as self-aggrandizing gestures on the part of a single individual, a distinction that, for her, was critical.

The backdrop to Baker's visit to Birmingham in June 1959 was a raging controversy between Fred Shuttlesworth and local attorneys who wanted to charge fees for their civil rights litigation. Shuttlesworth had openly criticized the attorneys' stance as opportunistic and greed-driven, and he characterized many of their middle-class supporters as selfish and elitist.[28]

Over the years, Fred and Ruby Shuttlesworth had numerous run-ins and conflicts with the city's black leaders; many moderates saw them as too brash and militant to be effective. However, under Fred's leadership ACMHR was in closer touch with mass black sentiment in Birmingham than any of its more moderate counterparts. Working-class black youth were in an especially restive, even rebellious mood.[29] By engaging in and encouraging aggressive challenges to Birmingham's white power structure, the ACMHR was responding to a popular mass sentiment. As the historian Robin Kelley has put it, "The Alabama Christian Movement for Human Rights (ACMHR), under the leadership of the Reverend Fred Shuttlesworth, had the largest working poor membership of any of the city's civil rights organizations."[30]

In most southern towns with an active movement in the 1950s and 1960s, the black community had two distinct political factions. There were the deal-makers, who bargained for incremental change, and then there were troublemakers, who raised a ruckus. While the deal-makers complained about the troublemakers' disruptive tactics, the two tendencies were at times complementary; the troublemakers often created the climate in which the deal-makers had greater leverage to negotiate. The problem was that what moderates saw as a victory, militants saw as a token concession. The Shuttlesworths and Ella Baker found themselves more often in the second camp than the first, although they crossed over to play the role of negotiator when the situation required it. Fred Shuttlesworth was a member of the clergy, but he represented a minority tradition of militant social activism within the black church that Baker deeply respected. He embodied what Cornel West refers to as a "combative spirituality," a term that Andrew Manis, Shuttlesworth's biographer, also uses to describe his subject.[31] Shuttlesworth was as critical as Baker was of the self-promoting type of ministers who preached passive compliance with injustice and consolation in better times to come while pumping up their own egos and lining their pockets.

Fred Shuttlesworth came from Oxmoor, Alabama, an impoverished mining community just outside Birmingham.[32] Baker had talked to him about his background and had inquired about, in her typical fashion, who his people were. Unlike Dr. King, Shuttlesworth was not a product of the southern black aristocracy. His parents were never married; he suffered from an abusive stepfather through most of his childhood; and at the age of eighteen he was convicted of illegally distilling whiskey and sentenced to two years probation.[33] Despite this gritty past, or perhaps because of it, Baker concluded with admiration that Fred Shuttlesworth "came out of the masses, . . . [and] he was a part of the masses."[34] Shuttlesworth had broken ranks with the majority of Birmingham's more prominent black clergy over politics and protocol. He was blunt and confrontational, while others were more reticent and cautious. Some viewed him as a hothead and an attention-seeker, but Ella Baker saw something else in him and his wife. Fred and Ruby Shuttlesworth not only engaged in dramatic acts of bravery but worked very hard to build an inclusive, grassroots movement in Birmingham that bridged deep-seated class divisions.

The Alabama Christian Movement for Human Rights consciously defied the social and economic barriers that divided black Birmingham, reaching out to all sectors of the community without privileging local elites with college degrees and social standing.[35] In her travels, Baker found that "in many southern cities, at that stage especially, there were very sharp class lines in terms of what you had and how much education you had."[36] She admired those who rejected this type of class stratification. After Fred Shuttlesworth had obtained an education and attained quasi-middle-class status, he made it his business to reach back across that class divide as a matter of principle. In 1950, before his move to Birmingham, he accepted a job as pastor of the prestigious First Baptist Church of Selma, Alabama. His identification with poor and working-class black folk was a constant source of tension and controversy with the largely middle-class congregation. One of the church elders advised Fred bluntly, "You are pastor of First Baptist now, you don't need to fool around with those little niggers." Fred replied indignantly, "God must have loved those little niggers since he made so many of them."[37] Fred Shuttlesworth's class sensibilities were still firmly in place when he and his family moved to Birmingham some years later.

Ruby L. Keeler Shuttlesworth was as much Fred's colleague and comrade as she was his wife. Her role in the Birmingham movement is often overlooked or underrated. Ruby's adoptive father was a railroad clerk, union official, and part-time undertaker who scraped together enough money so that Ruby could study nursing at Tuskegee Institute in the late 1930s. Not much is known about her mother, who was a homemaker. Ruby left school in 1941 to marry Fred, who was working as a handyman in a local doctor's office where she was employed part-time.[38] Like most men of his generation, and despite his egalitarian tendencies in community organizing, Fred Shuttlesworth held many sexist views about women and marriage. He once commented, only half-jokingly, that no one had the right to tell his wife what to do except him. And while he viewed himself as a political renegade who often disregarded what others thought of him, he pressured Ruby to conform to the expectations of his parishioners—singing in the choir and keeping a spotless home—which is what was expected of a minister's wife. The strong-willed Ruby refused to submit to his wishes on this and many other matters. She had always admired Fred's principled defiance in the face of racism, but when that same bull-headed manner carried over to their domestic life, she resented and resisted it. She was also annoyed by the fact that he was sometimes reckless and irresponsible when it came to family finances. In 1959, she decided to return to school, over Fred's objections, in order to improve her own earnings. Fred's continuing conflicts with Ruby once erupted into a shoving match, and eventually, in 1970, the couple divorced. Years after Ruby's death, Fred admitted remorsefully that he had been too domineering and chauvinistic in his marriage. Personal conflicts and struggles over gender issues were as much a part of the Shuttlesworths' thirty-year relationship as their shared commitment to social justice.[39]

Throughout the 1950s and 1960s, even when they could not reach consensus in their personal lives, Fred and Ruby Shuttlesworth made decisions together to take certain risks for the sake of the civil rights movement. As a result, the entire family was targeted for reprisals, and, as was typical throughout the South, Ruby was not spared because she was a woman and supposedly less threatening. The enemies of the movement knew better than to underestimate her. On Christmas Eve 1956, the Shuttlesworths' home was bombed and two of their children were injured after they announced that ACMHR would launch a desegregation campaign against the city busses, which had become the site of intense confrontations. Two African American men had been shot on the busses not long before.[40] The bombing shook the Shuttlesworths, but they remained undeterred.

The following year, in the spring of 1957, Ruby and Fred together faced down a jeering mob to desegregate the local Greyhound bus station. They sat in the whites-only section and traveled from Birmingham to Atlanta in defiance of public protests by the Ku Klux Klan. Ruby could have stayed at home with the children and allowed Fred to go with one of his male allies, but they chose to take a political stand together.[41] On September 9, 1957, as the school desegregation battle in Little Rock, Arkansas, dominated the headlines, the Shuttlesworths decided to test the *Brown* decision in Birmingham by attempting to enroll their daughters, Ruby Fredericka and Patricia Ann, in one of the city's premier white schools. In correspondence with school officials throughout the month of August, the Shuttlesworths were warned in subtle and not-so-subtle terms that there would likely be retribution if they proceeded with their plans. When Ruby, Fred, and their two daughters, along with two other black students, approached the school on the designated day they were once again confronted by a white mob. Both sides refused to back down. Fred was beaten nearly unconscious with brass knuckles and bicycle chains, and Ruby was stabbed in the hip. One of their daughters was slightly injured as well.[42] That night, ACMHR stationed armed guards outside its meeting, not an uncommon practice in those days.[43]

The Shuttlesworths' home was repeatedly targeted for attack. Despite the danger, Baker maintained a close association with the family, placing her own safety in jeopardy. She visited Birmingham often in the 1950s and early 1960s and always stayed with Ruby and Fred. During one such trip in 1958, Baker's niece, Jackie, happened to be visiting Atlanta from New York and joined Ella for a short trip to Birmingham. This was both a social and political excursion. Jackie slept in the bedroom that had been firebombed not long before. With that knowledge in mind, she slept uneasily. Ella had deliberately kept Jackie safely out of harm's way even as she herself took risks and traveled into volatile situations. That night Jackie fully appreciated just how dangerous her Aunt Ella's work really was. Jackie had known this abstractly before, but as she lay there, feeling her own fear, the magnitude of Ella Baker's courage became apparent to her.[44]

In 1958 and 1959, ACMHR was leading an intense struggle in Birmingham. Fred Shuttlesworth's church was firebombed for a second time in June 1958, and there were cross burnings and firebombings throughout the summer. In October, fourteen people were arrested and held without bail for protesting the revised segregation policy on the city busses. Baker remained in constant contact with the Shuttlesworths throughout this period, as did Anne Braden. Ruby and Fred Shuttlesworth, like Ella Baker, were drawn to the Bradens. They struck up a friendship and began to explore ways that the Southern Conference Education Fund (SCEF) and ACMHR could collaborate. Ignoring red-baiting and the warnings of his ministerial associates, Fred went on a series of highly publicized speaking tours that were jointly sponsored by SCEF and ACMHR. Between 1958 and 1963, Fred Shuttlesworth became more intimately linked to the Bradens and their network of southern white radicals. Many SCLC supporters were dismayed by his open ties with left-wing antiracists.[45] For example, Alice Spearman, a liberal SCLC supporter, confided to Baker that she was concerned about the influence that "radicals" like Shuttlesworth were having on Dr. King. Ironically, the naive Spearman seemed unaware of the fact that Baker shared Shuttlesworth's radical ideas.[46]

· · · · · ·

SHREVEPORT

In 1959, Ella Baker also devoted a considerable amount of her time to aiding the local struggle in Shreveport, Louisiana. The principal organizers in Shreveport, Dorothy Simpkins and C. O. Simpkins, were both militants and democrats, in line with Baker's own politics. She first met C. O. Simpkins at an SCLC meeting in Atlanta in 1956. Simpkins had heard Dr. King speak in Chicago earlier that year, and after the talk he told him what was going on in Louisiana. King invited the young dentist to visit Atlanta and join forces with SCLC. At his first SCLC board meeting, Simpkins was extremely impressed with Baker. She did not talk much, he recalled; but when she did, she was articulate, direct, and insightful. She advocated aggressive actions and placed great emphasis on indigenous leadership. Simpkins liked what he heard.[47] From then on, Baker and Simpkins had regular telephone conversations concerning not only SCLC but also the larger issues related to the movement. In the winter of 1958, when the Shreveport activists were about to launch a major voter registration campaign in preparation for the July hearings of the Commission on Civil Rights, Simpkins appealed to Baker to spend an extended period of time there to oversee the work. At that point, she was eager to get out of Atlanta and away from her ministerial colleagues, so she agreed without hesitation.

Ella Baker had conferred with the activists in both Shreveport and Birmingham about how to take maximum advantage of the Commission on Civil Rights's scheduled hearings on voting discrimination.[48] She saw the hearings as an opportunity to mobilize around citizenship rights and invigorate ongoing local struggles. Baker was well aware of the commission's shortcomings, and she viewed its hearings as a catalyst for organizing local people. As activists put the South's racist and undemocratic electoral practices on trial, they urged disfranchised black citizens to come forward and testify.[49]

The Civil Rights Commission originally scheduled hearings in Shreveport for July 1959, and the Simpkinses' United Christian Movement Inc. (UCMI) was prepared to take full advantage of the opportunity. However, lawsuits by white officials challenging the constitutionality of the commission eventually forced the hearings to be postponed until September 1960.

Baker was well aware of the type of organizing necessary to put teeth into legislative victories. For her, the passage of a law was the beginning rather than the end point of a struggle. Challenging an interviewer in 1968 who invited her to assess the value of such victories, she responded: "As you well know, we had some very fine laws passed prior to the birth of either of us . . . [but] they died as a result of the lack of implementation. Even the recent laws that have been passed are only as valuable as the people you have alerted and [who are] capable of using their combined power to see that they are implemented."[50] Courageous and persistent leaders on the grassroots level were key to creating change: their agitation drew attention to the larger issues at stake and generated the climate for the implementation of old laws and the passage of new ones.

When Baker went to Shreveport for a two-month stay, she was looking forward to the battle that lay ahead. She knew she would be fighting alongside some tough people with whom she had a strong affinity. Like Baker, the Simpkinses—though educated and from middle-class backgrounds— had, as a matter of principle, little use for what historians have termed the "politics of respectability," a strategy of conforming to dominant standards of respectable behavior and appearance in order to prove that oppressed people were worthy of citizenship and economic opportunities. Like his father, C. O. was a dentist, and he had served in the military in Korea. Dorothy had been a teacher in civil rights workshops. Yet the movement they led was inclusive and democratic. The Simpkinses worked closely with poor and working-class people in the Shreveport struggle, making every attempt to blur and downplay the class differences between them. Most importantly, they were rough-and-tumble fighters and had battle scars to prove it.

Dorothy Simpkins had repeatedly challenged segregation ordinances on local trolleys and busses and in the local school system. Early in 1957, she and three others were plaintiffs in a lawsuit against the Shreveport Trade School's policy of excluding black students. In December 1957, she was part of another group that filed suit against the city's policy of segregation on public trolleys and busses. Federal authorities forced the state legislature to repeal the transportation segregation statute in 1958.[51] State lawmakers then passed a series of so-called safety ordinances that allowed drivers full discretion in making seat "assignments" to passengers, supposedly in the interest of safety but in practice enforcing racial segregation. The intrepid Dorothy Simpkins was one of the first to test the new policy. In 1959, when confronted with a trolley driver attempting to enforce the ordinance, Dorothy recognized a prime opportunity to teach the thirty-two young Boy Scouts and Cub Scouts whom she was escorting on a field trip, a lesson in political resistance and personal integrity. When Simpkins was told to move to a segregated section of the trolley, she steadfastly refused. The driver summoned the police, who grabbed her by the arm and arrested her on the spot. Some of the boys were visibly shaken by the incident, but others beamed with pride that Mrs. Simpkins had stood up to the white authorities.[52]

C. O. shared Dorothy's courageous convictions. They were a team, personally and politically, for nearly thirty years. In 1957, after state officials temporarily outlawed the NAACP in Louisiana (as had also occurred in Alabama), C. O. was the only nonminister among the founders of the United Christian Movement Inc. The Simpkinses both suffered extensive harassment, intimidation, and violent attacks for their activism. C. O. Simpkins "was arrested often, and crosses were burned on his lawn; his newly built house was bombed."[53] In the most gruesome harassment of all, dead animals with bullets through their heads were left at the family's front door as a warning of what might happen if they continued their agitation. The couple was forced to leave Shreveport in the early 1960s. Later, they separated and amicably divorced. C. O. Simpkins did not return to Louisiana on a permanent basis until 1987.[54]

For nearly a decade, the Simpkinses spearheaded the civil rights movement in Shreveport. In Baker's view, Shreveport, like Birmingham, served as a model of how a local community could organize itself effectively. C. O. Simpkins, like Fred Shuttlesworth, shared Baker's view of nonviolence as more a limited tactic than a way of life. When white vigilantes shot at Simpkins, he shot back. For example, in 1958, when he was returning from a meeting late one night, racist hoodlums tried to intimidate him by shooting at his car, breaking the passenger window. He had a German Luger pistol in his glove compartment; so, he hit the brakes, reached for his gun, and returned fire. His attackers sped off.[55]

The community elder and local griot known as Papa Tight was another respected figure in the civil rights movement in Shreveport. Papa Tight was a fixture at the town's only barbecue joint, where he held court most afternoons, chatting about politics, people, and current events. Even someone like C. O. Simpkins knew very little about Papa Tight, including his real name, which suggests he was not treated or viewed as a social equal in all respects; but neither was he looked down on. He was recognized as a movement adviser and supporter. Neither educated nor from the middle class, Papa Tight surely gained his nickname from being the quintessential town drunk. He never went to church; he drank too much and too often; and he had frequent run-ins with the law, most of which had nothing to do with politics.[56] Papa Tight was not given to eloquent oratory. He spoke in the plain dialect of the mass of ordinary black southerners who had little formal schooling. In other words, Papa Tight was the antithesis of the model Negro citizen that the national civil rights movement leadership was trying to project to the national media. But he was sympathetic to the movement, and he was well connected among the city's down-and-outers. While established race leaders might have seen Papa Tight as a source of embarrassment, UCMI leaders welcomed him into the movement. "We were not going to close the door on him if he wanted to help," C. O. Simpkins explained. "We needed him and he did good work putting the word out to support the movement."[57] Papa Tight not only served the movement as a recruiter, but he was also sought out for the insight and advice he had to offer.

Ella Baker took a special liking to Papa Tight and enjoyed many long conversations with him during her stay in Shreveport. She was interested in what problems he thought Shreveport blacks were facing and what would motivate ordinary folk to get involved in making a change. Indeed, it would have been out of character for Baker to have shunned Papa Tight in any way.[58] She often railed against the social snobbery and political short-sightedness that led some black leaders not to take seriously the grievances or political insights of those at the bottom of the social and economic ladder and of those who, like Papa Tight, did not conform to bourgeois standards of respectable behavior.[59]

Baker repeatedly recounted the example of how some middle-class Negro leaders distanced themselves from the so-called town drunk to the point of being unwilling to defend him if he were attacked by local racists or beaten by the police. In her experience, "There were those people who, if John Jones was a drinker and not a church goer, they might have had grave doubts about the virtue of going down and . . . getting him out of jail," even if he had been a victim of police brutality.[60] The sinful, hard-drinking, tough-talking fellow with little social standing among the finer families in town was viewed as an embarrassment to the race whose "uncouth" behavior undermined group progress. In the words of Roy Wilkins, Baker's former colleague at the NAACP, "We must clean up and educate and organize our own people, not because they must be perfect in order to be accorded their rights, but they cannot be first-class citizens in truth until they appreciate the responsibilities of that station."[61] Baker's view was quite different. Poor people should not have to be made deserving of their citizenship or their economic claims; such rights were fundamental.

Much of the social and political interaction Baker had witnessed between elite and nonelite black people occurred within the confines of what historians have termed "uplift ideology." These were relationships of unequals, the groomed and educated tutoring and guiding their social subordinates.[62] The obsession with respectability, in Baker's opinion, was a political trap that undermined critical thinking and lessened the ability of activists to be truly radical in their ideas, actions, and alliances. This class-biased ideology also cast middle- and upper-class blacks as the natural leaders and spokespersons for the race, to the exclusion of others.[63] Baker's ideas represented a sharp break with this dominant bourgeois ideology and the political strategies that it spawned, and those ideas opened up the possibility for working-class and poor people to take hold of the mantle of leadership.[64]

In addition to crossing some of the many class barriers that existed within the black community, the leaders of the Shreveport movement made more tepid gestures toward challenging conventional gender roles. The movement boasted a very active core group of women leaders. Many of these women were self-employed, often as beauticians, and thus were less vulnerable to direct economic pressures than domestic workers were. Mamie Love Wallace, Bernice Smith, and Ann Brewster were among the best known.[65] "We had a lot of strong women involved," C. O. Simpkins recalled; "Ella and Dorothy weren't the only ones."[66]

When Baker arrived at the airport in Shreveport in February 1959 with her beat-up suitcase in one hand, her pocketbook in the other, and one of her signature hats perched on her head, she did not look much like the polished political organizer that she was. Her arrival probably went unnoticed by local police officials, but she soon made her presence known. The Simpkinses had arranged for Baker to stay with their neighbor, Willa Bell Clark, a single woman with an extra room. Although Clark was not directly involved in the civil rights struggle, she was one of its many silent supporters. She worked for a wealthy white family in town and was fearful that a more open association with UCMI would jeopardize her job. Letting Baker stay with her was her small, secret way of contributing to the movement. Clark exemplifies the popular support that the Simpkinses had helped to mobilize in Shreveport. Baker appreciated Clark's hospitality and made sure to write her a detailed thank-you note upon her departure, reaffirming that her contribution to the struggle was appreciated.[67]

Baker's routine in Shreveport was to rise early and head over to the UCMI office, situated in a corner of C. O. Simpkins's dental office, to begin a long day of typing, phone calls, visits, and meetings. She often remained there until late into the evening and then joined the Simpkinses for dinner and conversation. Ella had great affection for Dorothy and C. O., and the sentiments were mutual.[68] The three friends sat up late many nights talking about personal and political matters. As close as she felt to her Shreveport friends, Baker kept her secrets. She told them all about Jackie, her pride and joy, but never mentioned that she had been married and was only recently divorced. She was always very private about what she termed her "domestic relationship,"[69] and by 1959 there wasn't much of a relationship left to conceal. She and Roberts had been separated for some time, and her move to Atlanta had put even more distance between them. Their divorce became final in the summer of 1958.

The friendship Baker shared with the Simpkinses helped sustain her throughout the Shreveport campaign. She knew when she went to Caddo Parish that she was entering a volatile and dangerous situation. Shreveport segregationists had made heinous threats and carried out many of them. Churches and homes had been bombed. Activists had been beaten in the street, some of them in broad daylight. Local segregationists were not at all fond of interfering outsiders. In a newspaper report during the voter registration protests, the registrar singled Baker out for particular contempt. "She is not even a Louisianan," he grumbled, indignantly describing her as "that Baker woman from Atlanta." Like many white segregationists who blamed "outside agitators" for stirring up trouble in communities they sought to control, he attributed much of the local unrest to her organizing efforts.[70]

Although Baker reported back to the SCLC office periodically, she functioned in Shreveport as a freelance organizer and political consultant while on SCLC's payroll. Despite some media attention and the Simpkinses' references to her as the coordinator of the Shreveport campaign, she consciously downplayed her role and resisted becoming the primary spokesperson for the group. She directed the day-to-day, behind-the-scenes work related to the campaign, and she served as UCMI's principal strategist, tactician, and staffperson during her seven-week stay. It was the opportunity to dig in and work shoulder-to-shoulder with local activists that most appealed to Baker. She respected the autonomy of the local leadership and resisted any attempts to promote herself as "the" leader or outside expert. Local people would be there long after she had gone. In the final analysis, the major political decisions had to be theirs. She intended to leave behind a more skilled, confident, and emboldened local leadership rather than a singular victory.

Baker worked in Shreveport off and on from early February until late March 1959. She met with local groups and leaders on a weekly basis, worked on the UCMI newsletter, and helped launch and sustain a UCMI youth group.[71] A typical week's schedule for Baker was packed. On February 22, she spoke at the 11:00 A.M. service at Evergreen Baptist Church. The next day she spoke to the Stoner Hill Civic Group in the morning, and at 8:00 P.M. she was standing in the pulpit at Hopewell Baptist Church preaching the virtues of electoral participation. On February 24, she addressed the Shreveport Parent Teacher Association council at the Lakeside Branch Library at 5:30 P.M. and met with the Federated Club Women Presidents group at 8:30 P.M. At 7:30 P.M. the next evening, she gave a talk at Shady Grove Baptist Church. Her schedule often began at 8:00 A.M. and ended well after midnight with a summary report or an informal evaluation meeting reviewing the day's events with Dorothy and C. O.[72]

The citywide voter registration campaign in Shreveport culminated on March 19, which local activists had designated "R-day," or registration day. Activists led a mass attempt to register. They hoped this campaign would either add to the city's black electorate or offer evidence of the obstructionist practices of local officials, which could then be presented to the Commission on Civil Rights. Black Shreveporters who were already registered were asked to gather at 9:30 A.M. on the third floor of the Caddo Parish Courthouse in downtown Shreveport and to bring along at least one friend or family member who was not yet registered.[73]

On R-day, C. O. Simpkins canceled all his dental appointments, closed his office, and encouraged his patients to attend the protest instead. At the crack of dawn, Dorothy and Ella sat sipping coffee at the Simpkinses' kitchen table and going over lists of tasks for the day, including reminder calls that had to be made and people to be picked up. Over 200 people participated in R-day. The organizers had hoped for a bigger crowd, but they were pleased that those who did turn out were steadfast and undaunted by the pouring rain and by the intimidation tactics of the local segregationists.

One of the routine tactics of the registrar of voters was to stall the registration process with unwarranted delays. The protest on March 19 became a "stand-in," as dozens of prospective voters stood for hours in long lines, only to be turned away on an array of technicalities. Some were told they had given the wrong birth date if the date they gave differed by even a day from that recorded by the county. Others were told that the identification they presented was insufficient proof that they resided in the state.[74] Many prospective voters never made it inside the office. At the end of the day, only forty-five of those who stood in line were actually allowed inside, and only a handful of those were actually allowed to register.[75]

Baker had no intention of accepting such treatment silently. When by midday the registration process was creeping along at a snail's pace, she went back to C. O. Simpkins's office and angrily telephoned the Caddo Parish registrar, U. Charles Mitchell, to complain, insisting on more timely and efficient processing of applicants. Mitchell was outraged by her gall and hung up on her.[76] Baker also assiduously detailed every obstructionist tactic in preparation for what she hoped would be public hearings that would put local white political leaders and officials on trial.

The voter registration campaign was countered by intensified opposition from white segregationists. While civil rights activists campaigned to increase black voter registration and to document electoral fraud for the benefit of the Civil Rights Commission, Louisiana segregationists were redoubling their efforts to maintain white control by decertifying black voters who were already registered. State Senator W. M. Rainach, a rabid racist who chaired the joint legislative committee on segregation and was considering a run for governor, was a high-profile spokesman for white supremacy in Louisiana. Milking antiblack fears and hostilities among the white electorate, Rainach toured the state in 1959 "lecturing voter registrars on strict enforcement of voter qualification laws," admitting that, while some of those excluded would be whites, most would be blacks.[77] Rainach worked in open collusion with the Louisiana White Citizens' Councils to purge black voters systematically from the voting rolls. The council members routinely showed up at registrars' offices around the state and insisted on seeing the list of eligible voters. They combed through the list, highlighted black registrants' names with the letter "C" for "colored," and petitioned the registrar to review these voters' eligibility on a variety of flimsy grounds. In the southeastern dairy town of Franklinton, in Washington Parish, the local registrar of voters actually appealed to the courts to impose an injunction blocking the council's campaign because it was interfering with the daily functions of his office. The court refused.

On Friday, March 21, two days after the protest at the Caddo Parish Courthouse, Judge C. A. Barnett threw out the request for an injunction, applauded the segregationists' actions, and called on other white citizens of the state to "stand up and be counted" by joining the crusade to ensure that "unqualified" persons did not exercise the vote. This response reflects the extent of antiblack sentiment and the depth of the commitment to black disfranchisement that permeated all levels of government in the state, as was true across the South during this period.[78]

· · · · · ·

Ella Baker understood that the struggles in Louisiana and Alabama represented only the tip of the iceberg of southern racism and injustice and gave only a hint of black people's willingness to resist oppression. She was committed to the struggle for the long haul, having devoted thirty years to progressive causes. In 1959, she had not yet found the right political organization to serve as her base of operations, but she was finding like-minded allies in the mass movements that were emerging in the South.

One way that she sustained herself physically during times of intense struggle, and psychologically and emotionally during lulls, was by reconnecting with old friends and comrades. They took care of her and provided her with refueling stations and respite from battle as she continued her itinerant insurgency across the South. One such person was Odette Harper Hines, a woman who had overlapped with Baker in Harlem in the 1930s and worked alongside her during her NAACP days in the 1940s. By 1959, Hines had relocated to Alexandria, Louisiana, not far from Shreveport; after several weeks of tireless work in Shreveport, Baker took time out to visit Hines for a few days to relax and regenerate herself. Hines was a true fan of Baker's, describing her as "a person with great integrity . . . very human and warm," with a sharp "clarity of analysis" about political matters—overall, "an extraordinary woman."[79] The two middle-aged activists "talked politics a little," but the purpose of the trip was really to give Ella a break. Hines recalled that when her old friend arrived, "her tongue was hanging out. She was exhausted."[80] So Hines was content to pamper her a bit, make her her favorite shrimp salad, and provide her with some rare moments of solitude and calm. After her stay in Alexandria, Ella Baker went back to the battlefield in Shreveport for a few weeks more and then on to Birmingham, Atlanta, and New York for meetings and mobilizations.

CARL AND ANNE BRADEN AND THE
SOUTHERN CONFERENCE EDUCATION FUND

In the late 1950s, Ella Baker began a relationship with Carl and Anne Braden, two southern white radicals who would over time become two of her closest friends and most trusted allies. Looking back in 1999 at the couple's political contributions, Julian Bond referred to them as "modern abolitionists."[81] In 1957, the Bradens joined the staff of the Southern Conference Education Fund (SCEF), which had grown out of the Southern Conference on Human Welfare (SCHW), a New Deal organization formed in 1938, "based on a vision of a new democratic south that would be built jointly by black and white people."[82] Among SCHW's supporters were Eleanor Roosevelt, Mary McCleod Bethune, and Charlotte Hawkins Brown.[83] In 1946, SCEF was formed as the tax-exempt educational arm of SCHW; and when SCHW folded in 1948, SCEF carried on the work of grassroots organizing. The organization raised funds for embattled black activists, lobbied for implementation of Truman's civil rights proposals, and tried to educate southern whites about the evils of racism. In the 1950s, the members of SCEF lent support to SCLC's efforts as much as it would allow, and in the 1960s they became stalwart supporters of the renewed black protest movement. Fred Shuttlesworth joined SCEF's board in 1958, and Baker accepted a full-time job with the organization in 1962, after serving as a consultant, paid and unpaid, for several years.[84]

The Bradens were part of a small network of progressive white southerners who shared their antiracist views and activist orientation. In their politics, however, they were decidedly to the left of most of their colleagues, both white and black, and the notoriety the Bradens had earned during and after the McCarthy era meant that many civil rights activists were reluctant to work with them.[85] In the context of the Cold War South, where antiracism and communism were virtually synonymous in the segregationist imagination, people committed to equal justice were lumped together regardless of their actual political affiliations; the whole lot of them were labeled subversives and made the targets of reproach, harassment, and reprisals. The Bradens' outspoken advocacy of social justice and racial equality had cost them dearly, although, like Ella Baker, they focused on the struggle rather than the sacrifices it entailed. The couple endured loss of work, death threats, and years of government surveillance and persecution. Carl twice served time in prison for his political work, and Anne was jailed repeatedly for short stints. Throughout these tumultuous years, Anne raised their three children and held the family together.[86] The Bradens' stubborn perseverance endeared them to Baker. Their unflagging allegiance to the cause of racial justice was all the more impressive in comparison to the "ambivalence" expressed and the "moderation" advocated by most white liberals and some leftists during the 1950s.[87]

Anne Gamrell McCarty and Carl Braden, both natives of Louisville, Kentucky, met in 1947 while working as reporters for the *Louisville Times* and married in 1948. From then on, they fought side by side as radicals and social reformers, gaining regional and then national reputations. They were quite a pair. Thin, wiry, and intense, Anne was a keen strategist with an intuitive ability to size people up right away. Carl, a stout, blustery, and sometimes brash working-class union organizer, made up for his lack of finesse with an unconditional commitment to social justice that earned him friends and foes alike. Carl's political passion had won Anne's attention and ultimately her heart. Anne and Carl complemented one another personally and politically, and their mutually supportive relationship sustained their activism over many years.[88]

The Bradens challenged racial injustice in all of its forms, from lynching and segregation to the denial of voting rights. In 1951, Anne went to jail briefly for protesting the unfair prosecution of a black Mississippi man, Willie McGhee, for the alleged rape of a white woman, which evidence suggested he did not commit.[89] In early 1954, the Bradens surreptitiously bought a house in a white section of Louisville on behalf of a black couple, Andrew and Charlotte Wade, deliberately violating the city's segregation laws and triggering a storm of violent protest among whites. Not only were they maligned and hounded for their actions, but Carl Braden was convicted under a World War I–era sedition law and sentenced to eight months in prison.[90] The prosecution argued that the Bradens engaged in a conspiracy to foment chaos by purchasing the house for a black family. In 1958, Carl was targeted again, this time by the Un-American Activities Committee of the U.S. House of Representatives (HUAC). He refused to cooperate with the committee, and in 1961 he spent ten months in prison for contempt of Congress.[91] While the Bradens were not open members of the Communist Party (CP), they believed that socialism represented a more humane way of organizing society than capitalism—a view that Baker had long held—and they refused to countenance the denial of civil liberties to radicals.[92]

Baker was heartened by the moral stamina the Bradens had demonstrated, and she was eager not only to support them but also to find a way to work with them more closely and more consistently. She felt they shared more of her political values than the majority of her SCLC colleagues. In addition to their committed left-wing and antiracist views, the Bradens shared Baker's confidence in the political capacity of ordinary people to change their own lives. According to Anne Braden, one of the most important lessons that she learned during her early political involvement was that poor black people were their own best advocates; while they needed allies and resources, they did not need middle-class whites (or blacks, for that matter) telling them what to do.[93] This is a concept that southern segregationists and the FBI found difficult to grasp. They persisted in the erroneous assumption that southern blacks would simply not stand up for themselves and demand fair treatment unless someone "smarter"—white or northern—put them up to it. Baker and the Bradens vehemently rejected such racist and elitist assumptions.

On the surface, Ella Baker and Anne Braden were very different women. One black, the other white, they were nearly a generation apart. Anne did her political work in tandem with her husband, who was her closest political comrade until his death in 1975. Ella Baker was fiercely independent all of her adult life and consciously disassociated her marriage and family life from the political circles in which she traveled. But in other, more fundamental ways, they were very much alike. Both were women of great principle and integrity. Anne and Ella demonstrated a deep determination to fight injustice that was tempered by patience and generosity toward those alongside whom they fought. Neither was fully recognized or financially recompensed for her achievements and service. Yet each had a major influence on an entire generation of younger activists. Ella Baker and Anne Braden had crafted for themselves identities and work that defied assumptions about what women from middle-class families, black or white, should be and do. Both served as powerful alternative role models for young women who came of age politically during the early 1960s. Bold, confident, and intellectually sophisticated, they were tireless organizers and generous mentors.[94]

Ella Baker met Anne Braden in the winter of 1956, during the campaign to win Carl's release from prison the first time. Anne was traveling around the country desperately trying to drum up support for her husband's case, and in New York a mutual friend who worked with the Emergency Civil Liberties Committee put her in touch with Baker. They got together at a tiny neighborhood restaurant in Harlem. Anne remembered that Ella's immediate response to her request for help was to take out a pen and paper and begin to list the names of other people she could contact in New York. Baker thought it was outrageous that the Bradens would be abandoned by former friends because of their alleged communist affiliation. In February 1956, Baker helped organize a support rally for Carl Braden at the Community Church in Manhattan.[95] At the time, Baker was immersed in the New York City school struggle, but she made the time for a stranger in need. Her unqualified support made a lasting impression on Anne Braden, beginning a close and enduring friendship.

Ella Baker and Anne Braden became reacquainted in the midst of the civil rights campaign in Birmingham in 1958. One chilly fall evening in Ruby and Fred Shuttlesworths' home, Anne recalled, Ella was sitting at a table, "wearing a black pillbox hat pushed to the back of her head," making yet another list—this time a list of what had to be done the next day for the desegregation and voter registration campaign. Anne had driven from Louisville to lend her support. She and Ella chatted, compared observations about civil rights activities in Birmingham and elsewhere throughout the South, and found a bit of humor to share as well.[96] They swapped stories, laughed, and bonded. There was something visceral in the connection.

Anne and Carl Braden became familiar faces to civil rights activists during this period. Like Baker, they gravitated to wherever struggles were taking place. The Bradens crossed paths with Baker and the Shuttlesworths routinely at meetings, late-night strategy sessions, workshops, picket lines, and the homes of mutual friends. Their personal and political bonds deepened as a result. Anne Braden later described Ella Baker as one of her "strong and brave allies" who "never feared association with us and always provided support."[97]

Although Anne Braden appreciated Ella Baker's principled stance in her defense and recognized Baker as one of the most effective opponents of red-baiting within the Black Freedom Movement of the 1960s, she also acknowledged that Baker's position had evolved slowly over time. Like all historical actors, Baker was inescapably influenced by the society and history that she fought so hard to change. During the late 1950s and early 1960s, when American political culture was defined by the ideology and rhetoric of the Cold War, anticommunism was prevalent in the Black Freedom Movement as well. Baker's position on communism and anticommunism was ambivalent at best. She was resolute on most issues, but on this one she vacillated. She worked with Stanley Levison against the anticommunist McCarran Act, then served on the "watchdog" committee to keep communists out of the NAACP, then befriended the Bradens as they were being hounded by HUAC, and then participated in a 1957 mobilization that openly prohibited communist participation.[98]

We can infer a few things from Baker's awkward navigation of this issue. One, she could have been considered a part of what Herbert Hill has described as the anticommunist left of the 1930s, although she would be more aptly characterized as a noncommunist than an anticommunist. She never attacked her communist friends, but she worked with and was surrounded by people who did: A. Philip Randolph, Lester Granger, Pauli Murray, and others. The disagreements were real, but the different sectors of the left—socialists, communists, and other factions—worked together off and on during the 1930s. For some in Baker's circle, they acted principally on their convictions, disagreeing without denouncing their opponents. Others saw Bolshevism and later Stalinism as so detrimental to social progress that they sought to undermine communists at any cost.

When the Cold War and McCarthyism set in, the stakes changed, and old adversaries of the CP had some hard choices to make. Would they join the government crusade against the "reds" or take a stand in defense of the larger principle of civil liberties? Some tried to navigate a position somewhere in between: challenging McCarthyism as the persecution of innocents while implying that the persecution of real communists was justified. Baker seems to have straddled the fence on the question at least for a while, leaning on the pragmatic side of condemning red-baiting without defending the rights of communists. Baker's relationship with the Bradens may have been the critical variable that moved her to a more well defined position. They were closely associated with the left and made no apologies for it, but Baker sided with them anyway, eventually coming to the conclusion that the corrosive effect of anticommunism had to be fought aggressively if any broad-based progressive movement was going to survive. Interestingly, even though Baker sat on a committee that expelled communists from the NAACP's New York branch in the 1950s, she would join the Angela Davis defense committee to win the release of the jailed communist leader in the 1970s. Like Martin Luther King Jr., Malcolm X, and Du Bois, Baker did not hold to static political positions. Her views evolved over the course of her long political career as a result of her engagement with and reassessment of the world and the forces around her. The influence of those she met and respected also had an effect.

• • • • • •

Baker worked directly with the Bradens for the first time in a sustained way when she and Carl joined forces to organize a set of mock civil rights hearings called "The Voteless Speak," which were held in Washington, D.C., in January 1960. Both SCEF and SCLC hoped that the hearings would reactivate the stalled U.S. Civil Rights Commission, which had become dormant soon after its creation under the 1957 Civil Rights Act. In response to the moratorium on official government hearings on civil rights violations, SCEF decided to establish a volunteer commission that would hold its own unofficial hearings on electoral abuses, collect data on voting fraud and discrimination, and use that information to try to resuscitate the official commission.

In order to broaden participation and gain publicity, SCEF invited other groups to cosponsor the hearings. Reactions were mixed. Some of the more mainstream civil rights groups viewed SCEF with suspicion, primarily because of Carl Braden's imprisonment for contempt of HUAC and the couple's openly radical views. There was a debate inside SCLC about whether to even cosponsor the hearings. Baker was a strong proponent of the hearings, and SCLC finally agreed to sign on.

On January 21, 1960, Ella Baker arrived in Washington to join Carl Braden as a co-coordinator of the project.[99] Ella and Carl became close friends during those intense weeks of organizing. While spending long hours arranging conference logistics, they talked about everything from world politics to family life.[100] Few of her close political associates even knew about her private life, but Carl and Anne knew more than most. Although there is no evidence that Baker shared her innermost feelings with Carl or revealed the more personal details of her private life, they talked about what politics, struggle, and sacrifice meant to each of them. Their friendship deepened as a result. Baker commented soon after that "if Carl was a communist, we need more of them."[101] She never asked either Carl or Anne whether they were, in fact, members of the CP. As time went on, it simply did not matter to Baker.

Aaron Henry, a militant Mississippi NAACP leader, came to Washington, D.C., for the hearings, and Braden recruited John McFerren, a representative of the black sharecroppers' struggle in Tennessee, to testify about his experiences. They were also able to involve the veteran activist and educator Nannie Helen Burroughs.[102] Baker held the legendary antiracist and women's rights crusader in high esteem. In their 1959 correspondence, Baker expressed her eagerness to feast on Burroughs's "wit and wisdom" and applauded her "organizational drive and accomplishments."[103] Although Baker could be enormously charming when she chose to be, she never doled out flattery insincerely. When she began doing outreach to

D.C.-area civil rights activists to mobilize local support for the mock hearings, the elderly Burroughs responded enthusiastically, helping Baker and Braden to secure a site for the hearings when the church they had booked canceled at the last minute.[104] This campaign was one of Burroughs's last; she died in 1961.

Ella Baker and Carl Braden were optimistic that the voting rights hearings cosponsored by SCLC and SCEF in Washington, D.C., set to begin on January 31, 1960, had the potential to make a significant impact on national politics and reignite the stalled civil rights movement—or at least light a few sparks. Much to their surprise and delight, the black student sit-in movement began the very next day, entirely independently of their efforts, and immediately overshadowed the hearings.

· · · · · ·

THE ADVENT OF THE SIT-IN MOVEMENT

On February 1, 1960, four black college students sat down at the "whites only" lunch counter at the Woolworth's in Greensboro, North Carolina, and refused to move. After several successive days of sit-ins, the store gave in and served the young black patrons without serious incident. The students' actions ignited a blaze of sit-in demonstrations that spread quickly across the South. By the spring, over 100 cities had been affected, several thousand youthful protesters had been arrested, and violent counter-demonstrations had made headlines across the country. What began as a single protest action had rapidly generated the sparks of a movement, freeing the pent-up political ambitions of students, in particular black students, all over the country.[105]

When the sit-ins erupted seemingly spontaneously, involving clusters of young people throughout the South, they energized and piqued the interest of civil rights activists everywhere, black and white, young and old. The sit-in was a more dramatic and confrontational tactic than the bus boycott of five years before. By doing something, instead of withholding participation, young people put their bodies on the line in order to challenge segregation and second-class citizenship. They steadfastly endured hostility and violence. Lit cigarettes were gouged into some protesters' backs, and food was dumped in their laps. Solidarity demonstrations and picket lines sprang up in cities throughout the North.

When Baker heard about the sit-ins, the protests were still local and small in scale; they had not yet made national headlines. Recognizing the demonstrations' potential to catalyze a mass movement, Baker called her contacts in other cities to find out what was going on. When she returned from Washington to SCLC headquarters in Atlanta, Fred Shuttlesworth called with the news that the sit-ins had just spread to High Point, North Carolina, where he had been visiting. Fred was already excitedly urging students in Birmingham to conduct their own demonstrations. The sit-ins had become contagious. Baker, Shuttlesworth, and the Bradens were all ecstatic.

Baker later recalled that she was not surprised that the initial sit-ins had occurred, since in her view oppressed people had always fought back in one way or another. What did surprise her was how rapidly the protests had caught on in city after city.[106] Baker attributed this chain of events, in part, to social and family networks among southern blacks. When sit-ins occurred at one school, students would call relatives and friends in nearby towns and spread the word in advance of media coverage. Baker knew that organizers had to appreciate and tap into these social and familial networks in order to mobilize southern black communities. During the next few years, with Baker's encouragement, this is precisely what young organizers did under the banner of the Student Nonviolent Coordinating Committee (SNCC), the Mississippi Freedom Democratic Party (MFDP), and their half-dozen or so local organizational affiliates. The sit-in demonstrations and the militant new leadership that emerged from them were the answer to Ella Baker's political prayers.

By the end of 1959, Baker was already preparing to leave SCLC. King invited her to stay on in a diminished capacity once the new director, Wyatt T. Walker, was hired. But there was more promising political work on the horizon, and Baker was ready to go. In 1960, young activists took up the challenge she had laid out in her speech in Birmingham in June 1959. Once again, Baker was invigorated and hopeful about the political possibilities for the South and the nation. "This may only be a dream of mine," she confided to Anne Braden, "but I think it can be made real."[107]

MENTORING A NEW GENERATION
OF ACTIVISTS

THE BIRTH OF THE STUDENT NONVIOLENT
COORDINATING COMMITTEE, 1960–1961

· · · · · ·

Throughout the decade of the sixties, many people helped to ignite or were touched by
the creative fire of SNCC without appreciating the generating force of Ella Jo Baker.
James Forman, 1972

In the young and determined faces of the sit-in leaders, Ella Baker saw the potential for a new type of leadership that could revitalize the Black Freedom Movement and take it in a radically new direction. Baker wanted to bring the sit-in participants together in a way that would sustain the momentum of their actions, provide them with much needed skills and resources, and create space for them to coalesce into a new, more militant, yet democratic political force. Maintaining the neophyte activists' autonomy from established civil rights organizations was one of her key objectives. But she also hoped they would develop their own vision and strategy based on the transformative experience of confronting injustice personally and collectively. The students' direct assaults on Jim Crow had done more to demolish the most ubiquitous and offensive everyday forms of segregation than years of carefully orchestrated national campaigns. While exemplary local movements such as the Montgomery bus boycott seemed difficult to replicate in other locations, the sit-in tactic had spread with startling rapidity. Above all, the young activists themselves seemed transfigured by their success, and their challenge to segregation was reshaping national politics.

After the success at Greensboro and the wave of sit-ins that rippled across the South, Baker took immediate steps to help the students consolidate their initial victories and make linkages with one another, and she set the stage to move them in what she hoped would be a leftward direction. Under the auspices of SCLC, Baker called for a gathering of sit-in leaders to meet one another, assess their respective struggles, and explore the possibilities for future actions. The Southwide Student Leadership Conference on Nonviolent Resistance to Segregation was held on April 16–18 (Easter weekend), 1960, and attracted some 200 participants, more than double the number Baker had anticipated. Many of the young people came out of sheer curiosity, eager to protect their local autonomy but interested to hear what others were doing. The gathering took place at Baker's alma mater, Shaw University, in Raleigh, North Carolina, where she herself had begun her activist career more than forty years earlier. Around the country, a number of similar meetings were convened by various organizations to support the southern students, analyze the significance of their actions, and capitalize on the momentum they had generated. The gathering that Baker convened in Raleigh had the most profound and lasting results.

A month before the Shaw meeting, Baker conducted her own political reconnaissance, contacting friends around the country to collect information on the political mood of the students and others' responses to their actions. She wanted to put her finger on the political pulse and assess the protests' potential before deciding what role she would play at the conference. During the week of March 7–12, Ella Baker met and talked with literally hundreds of students and community leaders about the impact of the sit-ins and potential for future actions. She then wrote up a ten-page report for the Southern Christian Leadership Conference (SCLC) that reflected her findings.[1] Baker also talked the issue over with Doug Moore, a young minister from Durham, who had convened a smaller meeting of sit-in demonstrators in North Carolina in February, and Rev. Glen Smiley, a white official with the Fellowship of Reconciliation, and persuaded them that the students would be better off as a new and independent group.[2] When the Shaw meeting got under way, Baker had already decided to support what she determined was the sit-in leaders' desire for autonomy. Her "basic hope from the beginning was that it would be an independent organization of young people."[3]

A politically shrewd and purposeful organizer, Baker clearly had her own political goals going into the Raleigh meeting, but—ever the democrat—she was careful not to be too presumptuous about what the students themselves did or did not want. She had to strike a balance between putting forward her own very strongly held views and values and being careful not to intimidate, overwhelm, or alienate her prospective allies. After all, in the spring of 1960 there was no basis for them to "embrace me with open arms," as she put it.[4] She had yet to earn their trust. Baker appreciated and encouraged their desire to arrive at their own consensus and even make their own mistakes. She was also a stickler for process. She did not want to rush things; she knew that forming an organization, like building a movement, took time and patience.

Even if Baker had been so inclined, she could not simply have dictated what direction the student movement was going to take. The young activists were inexperienced, but they were not blank slates on which Baker or Martin Luther King Jr. could write a political script. They each brought something with them: ambitions, passions, ideas, and ways of doing things. In the case of the Nashville students, they had already embraced the philosophy of nonviolence as articulated by their mentor, a Vanderbilt seminarian named James Lawson, who was an admirer of Gandhi and a resolute devotee of nonviolence as a philosophy and way of life. The Atlanta students, led by Julian Bond and Lonnie King, had their own ideas as well. They had participated in sit-ins, but they had also drafted a document, the Atlanta Appeal for Human Rights, which had been published in a local paper and which embodied their concept of how the struggle should be framed. So the students had ideas of their own, and no one understood or appreciated this more than Ella Baker.

· · · · · ·

SETTING THE STAGE AND PLANTING THE SEEDS

The atmosphere on Shaw's campus that weekend was electric. The discussions were lively, and the mood was optimistic. For many of the students, it was not until the gathering in Raleigh that they fully appreciated the national significance of their local activities. They felt honored by the presence of Dr. King, whom they had watched on television or read about in the black and mainstream press. He was a hero for most black people in 1960, and his presence gave the neophyte activists a clear sense of their own contribution to the growing civil rights movement. Baker was content to use King's celebrity to attract young people to the meeting, but she was determined that they take away something more substantial. Most of the student activists had never heard of Ella Baker before they arrived. Yet she, more than King, became the decisive force in their collective political future. It was Baker, not King, who nurtured the student movement and helped to launch a new organization. It was Baker, not King, who offered the sit-in leaders a model of organizing and an approach to politics that they found consistent with their own experience and would find invaluable in the months and years to come.

Baker's imprint was all over the Raleigh meeting. She did not make any unilateral decisions, but she handled virtually all of the logistical details.[5] She understood how important details were in shaping the character of an event like this, and she gave every task her utmost attention. She collected news clippings about sit-in protests in various cities and made profiles of the organizations and individuals involved for her own knowledge and for publicity purposes. The group that gathered at Shaw was an amorphous body that, at the outset, had the potential to take any number of political paths. Baker structured the meeting so that those who were politically engaged rather than those who claimed the label of "expert" would be at the center of the deliberations.

The first goal was to provide those who had been directly involved in the protests the opportunity to confer, compare notes, and brainstorm about future possibilities in private. Baker urged those in attendance to give southern students, who were disproportionately black and less politically experienced, the time and space to meet separately, setting the stage for them to be the principal framers of whatever organization might emerge. "The leadership for the South had to be a southern leadership," Baker insisted. In her view, the sit-in leaders were on the front lines. They had taken the initiative and endured the violence. Therefore, they should retain the prerogative to structure and direct whatever organization emerged from the conference. It was a matter of self-determination, defined broadly. Ella Baker was wary of experienced leaders' tendency to move in and take control of locally initiated struggles because they saw themselves as more capable than the local folk. She had seen such dynamics again and again within the NAACP and SCLC. Baker was determined not to let this happen to the nascent sit-in movement.

On the second day of the Raleigh conference, Baker was invited—or, as she described it, she invited herself—to a private meeting at the home of the president of Shaw University, William Russell Strassner. The incoming executive director of SCLC, Rev. Wyatt T. Walker, was there, along with Ralph Abernathy and Dr. King. According to Baker, an effort was made to "capture" the youth movement, an effort to which she refused to be a party.[6] There are different versions of the meeting, and certainly differing views about whether SCLC intended to "capture" and subordinate the emergent student movement. In Baker's account of what occurred, she reprimanded the presumptuous ministers for their territorial ambitions and walked out of the meeting.[7]

Although Baker was generally a sharp judge of character, her suspicions of King's motives may not have been fully warranted in this instance. King's speech to the Raleigh delegates praised the students for having taken initiative and leadership. Yet Baker remained skeptical. Her distrust of SCLC leaders had deepened over the course of her three-year tenure with the organization. In her view, the SCLC ministers had badly mismanaged their own organization, and she wanted to minimize their control over this new crop of activists. She feared their efforts to annex the new group would stifle and suppress the militancy and creativity that the students had displayed. She also understood that since her own troubled relationship with SCLC was about to come to an end, if the students opted to become a part of King's organization, her role would be sorely limited.

While Baker wanted to protect the students' autonomy, she was not the hands-off facilitator that some have made her out to be. She understood that the students needed guidance, direction, and resources from veterans like herself who shared their general political orientation. As she put it at the time, "However hopeful might be the signs in the direction of group-centeredness, the fact that many schools and communities, especially in the South, have not provided adequate experience for young Negroes to assume initiative and think and act independently has accentuated the need for guarding the student movement" against those who might steer them in an undemocratic direction.[8] Simply stated, Baker saw some forms of intervention and influence as empowering and supportive of the students, and others as meddling and self-serving. This may seem like a double standard, but it was a position that grew out of Baker's honest assessment of the political forces at play at the time. She feared that the heavy-handed ministers would usurp the mantle of leadership and the media spotlight. Her own intention was to provide a gentle mentorship that would enable the sit-in movement to develop in a direction that she could influence but would not determine.

Baker's push for the students to remain unaffiliated did not stem primarily from the fact that they were young and the more moderate forces were older, although this was part of the rhetoric that she and others used to make a case for their autonomy. She saw the emergent movement not as a youth-only movement, but as "an opportunity for adults and youth to work together to provide genuine leadership."[9] The fundamental divide was not generational. After all, King, who was only thirty-one years old in 1960, was closer in age to the students than Baker was. The hypothetical case could have been made that SCLC's ministerial leaders, most of whom were some twenty years younger than Baker, were also youthful activists who deserved protection and insulation from the critical interference of old-timers. This was not at all Baker's position. In fact, she argued just as passionately for the autonomy of middle-aged sharecroppers and community activists when student organizers began lending support to their struggles beginning in 1961. In Baker's view, the students who convened at Raleigh needed to be encouraged to take the lead because they were at the forefront of the struggle and represented the greatest hope for a renewed militant, democratic mass movement, not simply because they were young.

For Baker, radical youth did have a unique, although not isolated, role to play in the movement for social change. The energy and passion they brought to bear was a vital resource. Students were less inhibited than adults by concerns about jobs, children, and reputations. Still, Baker was living proof that one did not have to be young to be radical. Her friend Howard Zinn was another example: a white antiracist professor at Spelman College, he became one of the early adult advisers of SNCC. Septima Clark, the civil rights activist who organized Citizenship Schools, first on the Sea Islands, then for SCLC in Georgia, was another middle-aged radical. So were Fred and Ruby Shuttlesworth of Birmingham, Dorothy and C. O. Simpkins of Shreveport, and, of course, Anne and Carl Braden of SCEF. Since young people were less socialized and less indoctrinated with prevailing ideas than their elders, they were generally more rebellious and more open to new ways of thinking. But certainly youth was no guarantee of political radicalism, and age did not always mean moderation.

It was *radical* youth Baker was concerned with. She wanted to preserve the brazen fighting spirit the students had exhibited in their sit-in protests. She did not want them to be shackled by the bureaucracy of existing organizations. At this early stage, the nascent political ideas of the students were not much more radical than those of SCLC's leadership. However, Baker saw enormous promise in their courageous actions, their creativity, and their openness to new forms of struggle, and she wanted to give them the space and freedom for that potential to develop.

Another move Baker made that influenced the climate of the Raleigh meeting was to limit media access to the proceedings. In closed-door strategy sessions, the young people were able to express their views and expectations candidly, without the intrusive presence of reporters. Some of the students had already been captivated by the publicity their actions had garnered, and Baker did not want to encourage any grandstanding or speech making. As she put it, "the step that I took as far as the conference was concerned, was to prevent the press from attending the sessions at which kids were trying to hammer out policy. . . . You see, I've never had any special inclination to being publicized and I also knew that you could not organize in the public press. You might get a lot of lineage, but you really couldn't organize."[10]

The sum of Baker's influence in shaping the outcome of the Raleigh conference was both strategic and ideological. If the group that came together on Easter weekend at Shaw was going to become a permanent organization, a myriad of unanswered questions had to be broached. What type of structure would it adopt, if any? Would the group become a coalition of local chapters or a membership organization? Would it be interracial or all-black? Would it be national or regional? Would it be an explicitly Christian group, or would it be secular? What place would the philosophy of nonviolence have in the group's identity? What tone would the spokespersons set in articulating its politics and purpose? Finally, would the group tackle only the problem of segregation or, as Ella Baker urged, would it take on a more expansive political agenda? All of these were critical questions in the spring of 1960. How they would be answered was not at all clear. In the end, while many factors informed the course of events, Ella Baker had more influence than any other single individual on the development and sustenance of the new organization.

Baker was one of several keynote speakers at the Raleigh conference, and the only woman to address a plenary session. When her opportunity came to speak, she urged the students to see their mission as extending beyond the immediate demand to end segregation. She reiterated this goal in an article published a few weeks later in the *Southern Patriot* summarizing the conference. In her remarks, Baker drew a clear distinction between the "old guard" leadership, which implicitly included the four-year-old SCLC along with the more established NAACP, and the more militant new leadership represented by the students. She warned against having the sparks the students had ignited smothered by bureaucratic organizations. She praised the neophyte activists for their "inclination toward group-centered leadership" rather than toward following a charismatic individual. In a thinly veiled criticism of King, she observed that many had felt "frustrations and the disillusionment that come when the prophetic leader turns out to have heavy feet of clay."[11] In her *Patriot* article, Baker emphasized the students' unwillingness to tolerate any treatment by their elders that "smacked of manipulation or domination." This was as much a warning from Baker as it was an account of the sit-in leaders' sentiments.[12]

In her formal remarks at Shaw and in individual interactions with participants over the ensuing weeks, Baker gave the students an enlarged sense of the importance of their actions. The sit-in movement was part of a worldwide struggle against many forms of injustice and oppression, she insisted. Baker encouraged the participants to see themselves—not their parents, teachers, ministers, or recognized race leaders—as the main catalysts for change. She was trying to pull the student activists beyond the confines of the South and the nation to grapple with, and connect to, a large and complex political world. Her comments made quite an impact on her listeners. Max Heirich, a young white staff person for the American Friends Service Committee working in Chapel Hill, had driven over to attend the conference and was overwhelmed by Ella Baker's presence. "She spoke simply but powerfully. It was as if she was speaking right to you about such large and important issues. She was much more effective than the men," he recalled.[13]

No one was more impressed by Baker's message and the compelling image she projected at the conference than Diane Nash. An idealistic eighteen-year-old, Nash was a native of Chicago and a student at Fisk University. She had become the leader of and principal spokesperson for the sit-in movement in Nashville, Tennessee. Nash looked up to the youthful Reverend James Lawson, who was a political guru for many Nashville students. But, with few female role models, Nash was uncertain of her own abilities as a leader and insecure about the leadership role that she had come to hold. When she went to Raleigh that weekend, she was looking for reassurance and affirmation. Ella Baker provided both.

Diane Nash's involvement in the sit-ins in Nashville was her first taste of politics, and she was both excited and nervous about meeting other students and civil rights leaders. She drove from Nashville to Raleigh with a young seminarian named James Bevel, whom she later married (and divorced), and Marion Barry, soon to be elected the first executive secretary of the new student organization (and, much later, mayor of Washington, D.C.). Articulate, poised, and beautiful by conventional standards, Diane Nash was one of the few young black women leaders who rose to national visibility in the early months of the student sit-in movement. By the time she attended the Raleigh meeting, she had faced down the mayor of Nashville at a press event, braved rowdy mobs, delivered speeches to large crowds, and given interviews to the national press—all bold acts of political leadership she had never dreamed of for herself before February 1960. Yet her sophisticated exterior concealed a scared and naive young woman who was deeply ambivalent about assuming the mantle of leadership. When she saw Ella Baker in action, speaking without a glimmer of self-doubt and exuding confidence with every gesture, Nash's political self-esteem was buoyed. She was struck by Baker's self-possession and eloquent command of language. She recalled thinking to herself, "I'd love to be able to make contributions like that."[14] Ella Baker became a confidence-builder, role model, and adviser for Nash as she evolved into one of the most influential young personalities within the student movement during its first few years.

Raleigh was the launching pad for a new phase of the Black Freedom Movement and a new phase of Ella Baker's career. Northern-based white leftists, southern antiracist liberals, and even anticolonialist leaders abroad followed media coverage of the gathering to see what would come out of it.

At the end of the weekend, the conference participants formed the Student Nonviolent Coordinating Committee (SNCC). Ella Baker, Dr. Martin Luther King, Howard Zinn, Connie Curry, and several other observers at the Raleigh meeting were invited to serve as adult advisers to the new organization. For King, this meant lending his name to the effort and attending its formal gatherings. For Baker, it meant much more: she coordinated the business of the new organization. In her words, "The writing that took place between the conference in April and the activities of the group in the summer came out of the office where I was and much of it I had to do."[15] She typed minutes, drafted internal documents, maintained a mailing list, kept in phone contact with interested students, and recruited new ones. She found meeting sites and office space and secured funds from SCLC and other sympathetic donors. Although Baker was still being paid by SCLC, she was now working for the Student Nonviolent Coordinating Committee.

· · · · · ·

THE SUMMER OF 1960

At Baker's side for most of the summer of 1960 was the hard-working and tenacious Jane Stembridge, who had attended the Shaw meeting and volunteered to take a leave from her studies at Union Theological Seminary in New York to work for the new organization. Stembridge was first moved to act after hearing a speech by King in New York City. His words touched a chord. As a liberal white southerner, she had never felt at ease with the racism that permeated her childhood world, and now she had a way to act on that uneasy feeling. Baker and Stembridge did much of the day-to-day work to hold the embryonic organization together during its first few months of life. Baker's leadership and Stembridge's tireless labor were indispensable at that critical stage. Ella Baker was a heroine for Jane Stembridge, just as she was a model of black female leadership for Diane Nash.

All of the young people who came into Baker's and SNCC's orbits in the 1960s did so at a formative time in their lives, roughly ages eighteen to twenty-four, when they were enormously impressionable. Most were searching. They had been living on their own, away from their parents, for only a short time, if at all. So, they were figuring out their adult identities in a new way in the midst of trying to figure some other very important questions about social change and American society. For Jane Stembridge, coming to grips with her sexuality as a lesbian at a time and place where "absolutely no one talked about such things," as she put it years later, was extremely difficult. In fact, it was "awful" in some ways. Here she was rearranging her life to be a part of a struggle and she could not even reveal to her closest co-workers what she was feeling and going through personally. Like Nash, Stembridge was looking for affirmation and for role models. She turned first to Lillian Smith, the author of *Strange Fruit*, an activist, and a rebel against what it meant to be a southern white woman in those days. Smith was a militant antiracist, an outspoken social critic, and a closeted but suspected middle-aged lesbian. Stembridge visited Smith at her home in Atlanta in search of counsel and support, but she was quickly turned off by Smith's vitriolic anticommunism and her insensitivity to some of the personal dynamics of race. Even though Stembridge never directly came out to Baker and discussed her sexual orientation, she was "open, and didn't hide anything consciously."[16] The perceptive Baker did not miss much. Stembridge found in Baker an accepting mentor whose politics and sensibilities about social change and her personal open-mindedness were in line with her own.

Bob Moses, like Diane Nash and Jane Stembridge, was drawn to Baker's humanistic style of political acumen. A deeply spiritual young man with a sharp intellect and a perceptive ear, Moses read Camus, loved math, and wanted to change the world, especially, but not exclusively, the black world. A resident of New York City, Moses had not participated in the sit-ins and did not attend the Easter weekend meeting. Baker deliberately pulled him into the expanding orbit of SNCC in the summer of 1960, when it was still in the making. From 1961 on, Moses played a critical role in the organization. He and others who made a full-time commitment to activism eventually displaced many of the students who had ignited the sit-in protests in February 1960. Bob Moses, like his mentor Ella Baker, led the group in a radical democratic direction.

In 1960, Moses was working as a math teacher at New York City's prestigious Horace Mann School. He had previously been an undergraduate at Hamilton College and, briefly, a graduate student at Harvard University. During his spring break, in the immediate aftermath of the sit-ins, Moses traveled to Newport News, Virginia, to visit his uncle, a faculty member at Hampton Institute and an activist in the local NAACP. While there, he went to hear Wyatt T. Walker, the incoming director of SCLC, speak about the growing civil rights movement in the South. Moses had already read about the sit-ins in the mainstream and black press. Although the student movement was sweeping the region and plans were already under way to form a southern-based student organization, Walker said little about them. Moses went home energized about the southern struggle—but still unaware that SNCC was in formation.[17]

After returning to New York, Moses immediately went to the Harlem SCLC office and became reacquainted with Bayard Rustin, whom he had met some years before. Rustin, a pacifist, had been a conscientious objector during World War II, and Moses had sought him out for counsel when he was confronted with a similar moral dilemma. Moses hung around SCLC's small Harlem office for a while, where he met and got to know the veteran leftist organizer and former union leader Jack O'Dell and other northern supporters of the movement. But he was still itching to return to the South. So he persuaded Rustin to write a letter of introduction, which was actually addressed to Ella Baker, that would open the door for him to go to Atlanta as an SCLC volunteer.[18]

When Moses arrived in Atlanta in the summer of 1960, he got a room in the Butler YMCA and reported for duty at the SCLC office on Auburn Avenue, letter of introduction in hand, eager to throw himself into the struggle. But, far from feeling he was on the front lines of the resurgent Black Freedom Movement, Moses quickly realized that there was virtually no meaningful work for him to do. He rarely even caught a glimpse of the SCLC leaders. So he spent his time getting acquainted with Jane Stembridge, hearing about SNCC's embryonic campaigns, and learning his way around the city. Stembridge and Moses struck up a friendship right away, talking about religion and philosophy, reminiscing about their common East Coast ties, and sharing their thoughts about the ideals that had brought them both to Atlanta.

They debated the writings of philosophers Paul Tillich and Albert Camus and pondered their relevance to the realities of the agrarian South.

A couple of weeks after Moses arrived, Ella Baker returned to Atlanta from an extended trip, and things began to look up. Baker and Moses developed an immediate rapport, beginning a relationship that changed both of their lives over the coming decades. When Baker first noticed the bespectacled and pensive-looking Moses sitting around the SCLC offices, she took an immediate interest in him. As was her manner, she called him over to her desk one day and began to query him about his life, his family, and his ideas. Who were his people? Where did he attend school? What did he want to accomplish? Ella Baker was always interested in people's life stories, even though she often found it necessary to protect her own privacy. Her personal interest impressed Bob Moses.

Baker's initial response to Moses stood in stark contrast to his first meeting with Dr. King. Moses recalled that one day, after weeks of feeling invisible to the higher-ups in SCLC, King summoned him to his office and grilled him on his participation in a rally that had been sponsored by members of Atlanta's white antiracist left. Moses, who had attended the rally, had been identified in the Atlanta newspapers as an affiliate of SCLC. To King, this meant bad press for the organization. No one in SCLC had endorsed the protest, and Moses had inadvertently linked the group to it. King warned the earnest young student to be more careful. Unlike Baker, he did not bother to find out who Bob Moses was, why he had come to the South, or what he had to offer the movement. His concerns were wholly pragmatic. Moses was sorely disappointed.[19] What King's reaction also illustrated was how strictly SCLC sought to police its public image in 1960, quietly working with leftist allies, like Rustin, Levison, and Baker, but careful not to tarnish its respectability by associating too closely in public with those who may have been labeled subversive by the government.

Baker's and King's differing responses to Moses are telling. King was focused on external perceptions of the movement and how negative publicity might undermine SCLC's efforts. He overlooked what Baker would have regarded as more important: the possible alienation of a talented young recruit. Baker was not worried about bad publicity, especially at that stage. She was more concerned with identifying and developing potential leaders like Moses, who could contribute to the movement's future, than she was about maintaining an organization's public profile.

Moses had been exposed to a brand of politics that predisposed him to progressive ideas and to the direction that the new student movement, under Baker's influence, was headed. He had attended New York's Stuyvesant High School during the 1950s, and many of the young people in his circle had leftist parents. He remembered meeting the radical folk singer Pete Seeger while visiting the apartment of some friends in Greenwich Village. The psychiatrist Alvin Pouissant was a high school classmate of Bob's. According to Moses, Pouissant's father was a black printer who had a number of left-wing clients and customers, which also exposed Bob to these ideas in a roundabout way.[20]

Moses credited his own humble but politically astute father with instilling in him certain values and sensibilities that he later applied in his political work. The senior Moses, an educated blue-collar worker in Harlem for most of his life, always emphasized the integrity of "the common person." Bob Moses recalled that his father "viewed himself as the man on the street . . . and the person at the bottom."[21] The egalitarian values Moses learned in childhood from his father were reinforced during the 1960s by the woman who became his political mother. Baker did not spoon-feed new ideas to Bob or any other young activist. Rather, she looked for and connected with individuals who had a predisposition to the ideas and values she embraced, and she worked with them to deepen and refine those ideas. When Moses entered the movement, he admittedly "hadn't worked out any notions of leadership," but he had an inclination toward "what people later termed grassroots leadership." Baker helped turn that inclination into a conviction.[22]

Bob Moses became Ella Baker's political apprentice. He was one of the young people whom she spent a lot of time talking with and listening to, and he continued in her political tradition—teaching, listening to, and organizing young people—long after her death.[23] Ella and Bob had similar sensibilities. Both were intellectuals, thoughtful and analytical, yet at the same time practical and personable. Both were deeply attentive to ideology and the ideological implications of certain tactical decisions, but both were equally willing to do the messy, hands-on work necessary to implement those ideas. "What is the larger picture we are framing here?" was the implicit, if not explicit, question both of them often asked. Moses absorbed Baker's message that revolution was an ongoing process intimately bound up with one's vision of the future and with how one interacted with others on a daily basis. Moses also shared Baker's confidence and faith in young people. After leaving SNCC in the mid-1960s and living for several years in

Tanzania, he became a radical teacher, in Ella Baker's style and tradition, focused on creative methods of teaching and learning as a strategy for empowerment and social change.[24]

Connie Curry, like Jane Stembridge, immersed herself in the work of the newly formed student wing of the movement during the summer of 1960. A white antiracist southerner, Curry had attended Agnes Scott College, where she was introduced to what was called intergroup work for whites, a euphemism for civil rights and antiracist organizing, through the YWCA. After college she moved to Atlanta to take a job with the National Student Association. Curry often felt quite lonely as a progressive white person in the Jim Crow South, which was nearly as hostile to antiracist whites as it was to all blacks. Curry was ecstatic to meet Ella Baker and the interracial group of young people in the sit-in movement. In 1960–61, Baker used Curry's apartment as a sort of local youth hostel to accommodate the varied assortment of female volunteers who floated through Atlanta. Curry was evicted from one apartment because one of her roommates had entertained a black guest, an act that was viewed as so scandalous she was forced to move out right away. Curry officially became one of SNCC's "adult advisors," but she was not much older than the students themselves were. She was typical of a small minority of white southerners who did not fit into their own communities, and sometimes even their own families, because of their open-mindedness about race issues and sympathy with black aspirations for freedom.[25]

Baker appreciated the importance of progressive white allies like Connie Curry, but she understood the even greater importance of cultivating allies among southern black activists. Baker knew that the students who started the sit-in movement had to move into other areas of political activity and forge a broader base of black support throughout the South if they were going to have a sustained impact. Toward that end, Baker decided to work with Bob Moses to make links and initiate contacts that would pull the students away from the lunch counters and their campuses and into the front lines of the southern battlefields against racism. She wanted to expose them to the kind of grassroots organizers she had worked closely with, most recently the SCLC affiliates in Shreveport and Birmingham and, before that, the activist branches of the NAACP.

The summer of 1960 was filled with hopefulness and newfound camaraderie for Baker as well as for the students. Curry remembers many occasions when the small group of activists deliberated about the possibilities for the resurgent Black Freedom Movement while eating ice cream sundaes in the back room of B. B. Beamon's, Atlanta's legendary black-owned restaurant.[26] Baker's personal regard for them endeared many of the young people in sncc to her. She was clearly not a peer, but she was willing to engage them on their turf, not just intellectually but socially too—over ice cream sundaes, in smoke-filled back rooms, or on long, uncomfortable rides in jalopies of various sorts. Baker was often shuttled back and forth to meetings and conferences in Curry's beloved convertible Karmen Ghia sports car, which Curry emphasized was not a jalopy, holding onto her hat so it wouldn't fly off. Despite her age and encroaching health problems, Baker often rejected anything that could even remotely be construed as special treatment that would put distance between herself and the students. If they sat in uncomfortable chairs for long hours debating this or that, so would she. If they walked long distances, she walked with them at least as far as she could. If they slept in cramped accommodations on road trips, she did the same.[27] Lenora Taitt-Magubane, a Spelman student who became involved in the movement through the ywca and became a dear friend of Ella Baker near the end of her life, remembered one such instance. The two had traveled to Albany, Georgia, in 1961 after there had been numerous arrests of civil rights demonstrators. They were staying at the home of a local activist, Irene Moore, but there were not enough beds to accommodate everyone. Lenora offered to give up her bed, but Baker, then almost sixty, insisted they share the tiny bed since she did not want anyone to have to sleep on the floor, even though Lenora knew Baker "hated sleeping in the bed with someone else."[28] Her example, in this instance and many others, was a lesson in personal egalitarianism that the young people in sncc applied to their own organizing efforts with southern farmers, workers, and youth.

· · · · · ·

PERSONAL MATTERS

July and August 1960 were especially busy months for Ella Baker. She was wrapping up loose ends for sclc, tallying the sales of King's book, *Stride toward Freedom* (a task she did not relish), and getting sclc's files in order. At the same time, she was helping to launch a brand new organization. During these months, Baker departed from her usual pattern by giving greater attention to her own personal affairs. Surgery for cataracts was followed by enforced rest and a brief vacation with Anne Braden and her family. Then, in September, her niece Jackie married Henry Brockington, marking a moment of great fulfillment in Baker's family life.

Her long neglected health concerned her friends and family more than it did Baker herself. Like her mother, Baker was plagued with health problems for her entire life. But she rarely allowed them to slow her down. She sometimes joked with friends that she was entirely too busy to get sick. Baker's chronic asthma was a constant source of discomfort to her. In a period when the health hazards of second-hand smoke were not well known, she often endured long meetings in smoke-filled rooms, sitting patiently with a handkerchief over her mouth and quietly gasping for breath, while impassioned discussions continued on for hours. Baker's vision, which was seriously impaired by cataracts, was the most immediate concern. Years of typing, writing, and reading in poorly lit offices and on trains and busses probably did not help. In the summer of 1960, she finally had the eye surgery she had postponed for months.

Baker took a long overdue vacation while recuperating from her surgery. She had maintained a hectic schedule since the April meeting, and by the middle of the summer she was thoroughly exhausted. Many summers, Baker's only vacation was an extended speaking engagement in one place or another. Her friend Anne Braden, who always took a special interest in Baker's physical and psychological well-being, managed to persuade her to fly to Rhode Island to spend a few days with her at a wooded cabin owned by some movement friends, the O'Connors. Anne and Ella sat on the long front porch of the house in the evenings talking about the direction of the movement and about their own lives and families. Ella enjoyed a glass of expensive Jack Daniels whiskey—one of the very few indulgences she allowed herself—as Anne sat next to her sipping a glass of wine.[29] The two women warriors were refueling themselves physically and emotionally for the battles that lay ahead.

Baker left Rhode Island for a meeting at the Highlander Folk School, made a brief stop in Atlanta, and then flew to New York for the big family event: Jackie's wedding. Ella found herself in the ill-fitting role of the mother of the bride. Her sister Maggie, Jackie's biological mother, was still alive and even attended the wedding, but she had long before relinquished her role as Jackie's primary parent.

Baker had raised Jackie since the age of nine. She had watched Jackie enter high school and excel, experiment with smoking cigarettes, experience her first kiss, and go on to college. Jackie was influenced more by her independent, generous, and strong-willed Aunt Ella than by any other single adult in her life. It was a source of great pride for Ella to see Jackie all grown up and going out on her own to establish a family.

Ella Baker liked and trusted Henry Brockington, the man Jackie had chosen to marry. More importantly, she trusted Jackie to be her own woman and to pursue her own goals in the context of marriage, a balancing act that Baker herself had struggled to manage. So, amid the flurry and excitement of political activity that marked the summer of 1960, Baker took time off to return to New York, shop for a dress and, of course, a hat, and help make catering arrangements. Jackie's wedding took place at St. Mark's Church in Harlem. The reception was held in the legendary Audubon ballroom, where Malcolm X (El Haj Malik El Shabazz) was assassinated four years later while delivering a speech calling for a reinvigorated militant black movement. On September 17, 1960, the Audubon was the site of a happy family occasion. Baker put her political concerns and dilemmas aside to relax and enjoy the celebration. Her family and close personal friends were all there.

It was also good for Ella Baker to see her sister Maggie again. They had not spent much time together since Ella's move to Atlanta, but Jackie's wedding was a happy reunion. In a photograph with Jackie pinning Aunt Ella's corsage on her new suit, Ella is absolutely beaming. Jackie was her personal success story. Although Ella had not had much luck in love and marriage, her relationship with Jackie had met all of her expectations. They remained close until Baker's death a quarter of a century later. Like a good and loving daughter, Jackie nursed Ella during her last years. In 1960, as Jackie and Henry set off on their honeymoon and began a new life together, Ella went back to the love of her life, political work, and to her growing political family in the South.[30]

The wedding was a high point in Ella Baker's personal life, but few of her political associates were invited or even knew about the celebration. She was familiar with some of the most intimate details of the lives of her co-workers, especially her younger comrades, but few of them knew very much about her private side, which she consciously kept separate from the movement. There were rumors of an ex-husband, but Baker refrained from discussing her marriage and divorce even with some of her closest women friends, including Anne Braden. She had a repertoire of family stories that she shared, usually to make a political point, but the messy areas of her personal life were off limits.[31] It is hard to explain why she was so guarded about her private life. Perhaps this was her refuge from the fractious political environment that she inhabited most of the time. Perhaps she did not want her personal choice of a spouse or lover to become a matter of public scrutiny within the movement. Or perhaps she was resisting the ways in which public female figures were so often defined in conjunction with male partners and in terms of their sexual identities. Baker wanted to be respected for her work and her ideas; to open up her personal life to public view might have made her politically vulnerable. Two of her male political colleagues admitted that there were whispers and rumors about Ella Baker's sexuality during the 1930s and 1940s. Her marriage was not a widely known fact. She was "Ella Baker" when she arrived in Harlem as a single woman in 1927, and she remained "Ella Baker" even after her marriage to Roberts; so, many of her associates thought she was single the whole time. "A strong single woman always leads to rumors," remarked John Henrik Clarke, "but none of that stuff was true about Ella."[32]

· · · · · ·

AN ALTERNATIVE MODEL OF WOMANHOOD

Most young women entering the Black Freedom Movement during the early 1960s knew very little about Ella Baker's personal life. Instead, they were awe inspired by her public example as they sought to construct their own identities as independent activist women.[33] Many of them had to contend with circumscribed notions of middle-class black womanhood passed down from their families and teachers. Even those from working-class and poor backgrounds, whose mothers and grandmothers were formidable figures, had been influenced by the socially conservative gender messages from churches and schools. Although some families encouraged their daughters' activism, many young women were told by relatives, ministers, and school officials that protesting and getting arrested were simply "not ladylike" and therefore unacceptable. Fortunately for the movement, many of them did not listen.

Baker offered an alternative image of womanhood that many young women had not previously encountered. As Dorie Ladner, who organized with SNCC in Mississippi, observed, "I never knew anyone quite like Miss Baker."[34] Her external appearance was reserved, even a bit conservative. She was a small, brown-skinned woman with a flawless complexion, sharp features, a commanding voice, and a hearty laugh. Her deep, almost baritone voice belied her diminutive frame. Her hair was generally pulled back, often tucked neatly into a hat. She dressed simply in skirts, suits, or dresses, usually in muted tones, never wearing anything revealing or the least bit flamboyant, and no makeup, save for a scant bit of lipstick now and then. Juanita Abernathy, whose husband Ralph was an SCLC leader, remembered gray suits as Baker's typical uniform during her years on the SCLC staff.

Juanita speculated that "this is how she had to dress to fit in with the men" and perhaps to allay their wives' concerns that she was interested in anything but business.[35]

Baker never developed much of a personal relationship with Coretta Scott King, perhaps because of her deepening criticisms of Martin, but she did with Juanita Abernathy, which was a typical practice of hers. She had made a habit of reaching out to the wives of the male political leaders with whom she worked, even if the woman in the family was not herself explicitly an activist. Juanita played more of a background role in the SCLC, but Baker always acknowledged her presence and welcomed her contributions. Sometimes huddled in the dining room of Juanita's home with the men, Baker would consciously excuse herself and go pay her respects to Juanita. When she was based in Atlanta and Abernathy and King were still in Montgomery, she stayed at the Abernathys' home during visits to the city. This was another opportunity to share her ideas and observations with Juanita. The two women bonded during these visits; and while they were never close friends, there was mutual respect and much cordiality.[36]

Baker situated herself in the dining room debates of the men and kitchen conversations of the women, and through her roles in these often mutually exclusive discussions she came to occupy a category and style all her own. In interviews of any real length, those who knew her well invariably describe Baker as someone with a "presence." "She commanded attention just by the way she came into a room and the way she carried herself," SNCC activist Ivanhoe Donaldson said. According to Lenora Taitt-Magubane, "She just had a certain presence."[37] In Bob Moses's words, "She had this black woman's manner, and she carried that with her into the dangerous arena of radical politics."[38] It was partly the carriage and comportment that Anna had taught her—a reminder to always walk into a room as if you belonged. She retained that confidence of movement and she used it. Baker traveled in all-male circles, and she sometimes found herself in all-white contexts, but she never hesitated. By the 1950s, she maneuvered within these spaces as a middle-aged black woman with her purse tucked under her arm, her hat carefully placed, and her good southern manners. To Moses, a woman taking the dignified and self-respecting manner that was a familiar feature of black family life into the rugged political domain was nothing short of revolutionary.

A white male co-worker found her persona more puzzling. She "was warm" but always had a certain "formality" about her, Howard Zinn observed; "she was friendly enough but you never felt you could go up and give her a hug."[39] Ivanhoe Donaldson agreed: she was "always dignified, never casual," and it was disarming "because physically she was not threatening."[40] Baker kept her boundaries between what was public and private, formal and informal. But she was not rigid about it. Dorothy Dawson (Burlage), a SNCC volunteer and staff member, once "slipped" and called her "Ella" (instead of Miss Baker), a mistake Dawson immediately regretted, feeling she had transgressed a boundary. Baker reassured her, "People know when they are ready to call me Ella. Don't worry about it."[41]

To young women, black and white, Baker embodied the possibility of escaping the restrictions that defined conventional femininity. Authoritative yet unassuming, self-confident and assertive, forcing others to take her seriously simply by presuming that they would, Baker was a revelation. At the time, few of these young women thought they could actually emulate Ella Baker. She was a larger than life figure more than twice their ages. Still, because of her, many young women in the movement did realize that they could define their own identities rather than be defined by others, and in the course of their work with SNCC they developed new ways of interacting with women and men, with other young people and their elders, both in the movement and in the larger black community. Decades after their involvement in the movement, dozens of women remember their lives were touched at a formative stage by a woman who, through her example, showed them a different way of being in the world. Prathia Hall, an African American woman who went south from Philadelphia in 1962 and lived and worked in Terrell County, Georgia, for a year, remembered quite vividly the impact Baker had on her. Qualifying a recollection by saying she did not mean to actually compare herself to Baker, she nevertheless said, "I would see myself in her . . . I was a wandering pilgrim . . . [and] the more I talked to her, the more I understood myself."[42]

Ella Baker was the comforting, nurturing, rock-solid mother to the movement. Yet there was nothing maternal about her in the traditional sense of that term. She was a militant activist, an insurgent intellectual, and a revolutionary, descriptors that are usually associated with men rather than women and with youth rather than the middle-aged. Baker's complex, carefully crafted persona enabled her to cross gender and generational boundaries within the movement. Even in retrospect, she defies categorization.

Baker maintained a dignified public self-presentation partly as a form of camouflage that allowed her to operate in male-dominated and sometimes mainstream political circles. She was a freethinker at heart, accepting of alternative lifestyles, personal eccentricities, and violations of social etiquette.[43] For example, in contrast to her ever-so-sober public posture, Baker frequently enjoyed a stiff shot of bourbon or a glass of red wine at the end of the day. She was not as prim and proper as her conservative gray suits suggested. Baker would talk comfortably about almost any subject, including sex. She often gently teased her young colleagues about their romantic interests or inquired about the lack thereof.[44]

The growing irreverence for conventional standards of morality and respectability among SNCC members disturbed some of their more moderate adult supporters, but it did not bother Baker. Virginia Durr, a white civil rights activist in Montgomery, complimented Baker on her ability to socialize with the young people and tolerate what Durr viewed as their "wild" behavior. Baker responded that she "was prepared to forgo manners" for the sake of the larger politics that were at stake.[45] She was, in fact, prepared to do more than that. She was instrumental in SNCC's rejection of bourgeois respectability as a defensive political strategy, a rejection that opened the organization up to historically marginalized sectors of the black community. When SNCC broke with the largely middle-class, male-centered leadership of existing civil rights organizations, it stripped away the class-based and gender-biased notions of who should and could give leadership to the movement and the black community. Some of the manners and decorum that Durr valued were evident at the Shaw conference in April 1960. Within a year, a visible change was well under way. The young activists' dress, comportment, and language changed considerably, making the organization more welcoming to those traditionally excluded from formal leadership circles. They donned blue jeans and overalls instead of skirts and suits, resembling in their dress workers and peasants of the South rather than preachers and teachers.

Baker encouraged and affirmed the young people's boldness, their growing radicalism, and their risk-taking. Her reasoned approval was important to them. Diane Nash recalls that, as the movement intensified, many of her own relatives were worried about her safety. "Older people would look at you and say you were young and you would calm down when you matured. So, she was the first older person I had known who was so progressive. And I needed that reinforcement. It was important that someone like her thought we were right. It was really important when things got hot and heavy."[46]

MOLDING A NEW ORGANIZATION

Ella Baker gave up her plans to move back to Harlem after leaving SCLC in the fall of 1960, deciding to stay in the South in order to work as closely as possible with the young sit-in activists in SNCC. She still needed a paying position. Although SCEF had offered her a full-time job, which she was tempted to accept, she ultimately declined it because she thought it would demand too much of her time. Aware of Baker's need for autonomy and some flexibility in hours in order to continue her unpaid work with the students, her friend Rosetta Gardner helped her get a job with the YWCA. Gardner was typical of Baker's lesser-known female friends and admirers. She supported the movement but never became a leader herself. As one Atlanta activist who worked alongside the two women remarked, "Rosetta just loved Ella."[47] Women like Gardner admired Baker's competence, her self-possession, her intellect, and her compassion. Above all, they admired her courage to forge another path and assert herself in all kinds of situations. These are the things that most of Baker's close associates loved about her. So, Rosetta did what she could to make it possible for Ella to do the work that was important to her. Ella in turn used her position at the Y to build, nurture, and protect SNCC. Lawrence Guyot recalled that Baker obtained YWCA and YMCA membership cards for young civil rights workers as soon as they came south to give them local identification in case they were stopped by the police and were accused of being outside agitators.[48] More significantly, she traveled around the South conducting workshops for the Y on human relations, which essentially meant trying to foster greater interracial understanding—not as simple a task as one might think given the racially polarized context of the 1960s South. It was through this work that she met and subsequently recruited to SNCC a number of serious, idealistic young women searching for meaningful ways to apply themselves.[49]

In describing her southern-based work with the YWCA in a 1962 report, Baker used the metaphor of planting and cultivation to describe the slow methodical process of bringing young people into political consciousness. She wrote of planting "first the seed," alluding to the outreach recruitment and orientation of new activists, which would nurture their motivation to want to make a difference. Part two of her report, entitled "Then the Blade," described the first rumblings of political activity among "Y women," some of whom had participated in desegregation sit-ins. This was the first visible result of the seeds having been planted. Next, in Baker's narrative of organic leadership development, "the full corn appears." This section describes the need for creating concrete channels for "meaningful social action."[50] The same metaphor could have applied to her work with SNCC.

. . . .

Ella Baker once confided in Vincent Harding, her friend and colleague, that if she ever wrote her memoir, which she never managed to do, she would entitle it "Making a Life, Not Making a Living," because while she did a very good job of the former, she barely accomplished the latter.[51] In the summer of 1960, she made the same choices as before: finding a job that barely paid the bills, she focused instead on creating a meaningful life for herself by building a movement. The movement was more important to Baker than religion, money, or even romantic love; the movement had become her life and her extended family.

Baker was relieved finally to be free from her obligations to SCLC, and she was excited about the emerging student movement. The young people's optimism and sheer energy were uplifting. When Baker was immersed in this kind of struggle, she felt most alive and her creative talents could soar. She had always enjoyed the challenge of building something new: the YNCL in the 1930s, local NAACP branches in the 1940s, even SCLC at the outset. These had been the high points of her political career before 1960. Inherent in Baker's philosophy, however, was the recognition that no organization should last forever. Each must yield to something new as historical circumstances changed. Just as SCLC was yielding, albeit unwillingly, to SNCC, so SNCC would have to be prepared to make room for whatever new, grassroots organizations it might help to create. These politics and sensibilities pervaded SNCC from its inception.

Baker realized that the radical pulse she had detected needed to be sustained, cultivated, and propagated. In the summer of 1960, as several leaders of the emergent organization went off to make speeches to the political elites of the Democratic and Republican Party Conventions in Los Angeles and Chicago, she assigned Bob Moses to meet and speak with an entirely different constituency, one that Baker thought was far more important than national elected officials. She freed Moses up from his mundane clerical duties at SCLC and dispatched him on a bus tour of Alabama, Mississippi, and Louisiana to do outreach for SNCC and to recruit local activists of all ages to attend the group's October conference. Baker had another objective in mind as well. She wanted to put the students in touch as quickly as possible with a set of elders who represented a different class background and political orientation than the ministerial clique heading SCLC.[52] This was her way of planting the seeds.

Ella Baker placed great confidence in the smart and earnest Bob Moses. In him, she saw the makings of the kind of leader she herself had striven to become: modest, principled, and able to empower others through the force of example. Moses did not disappoint her. Baker wrote down the names of contacts in each state, and Moses set off for a monthlong journey with a bus ticket and a list of telephone numbers in his pocket. The contacts he made that summer laid the foundation for some of SNCC's most important community organizing work.

The October conference of SNCC, when it officially formed, was the culmination of Baker's efforts over the spring and summer to help build a permanent organization. Marion Barry, the confident and charismatic young chemistry graduate student from Fisk, stepped down as chair, and Chuck McDew, a stocky, dark-skinned former football player from South Carolina State with a quick wit and disarming sense of humor, was confirmed to replace him. Others were jockeying for the position, but Baker had her eyes on McDew. She had probably been observing him in meetings and recognized his ability to gently but effectively steer the organization forward without indulging his own ego. McDew had to leave the October conference early, so he was not even present when he was nominated and elected as the group's new leader. "Ella Baker made me chairman," McDew later recalled. She persuaded him to accept the nomination and urged others to support it. This was a little behind-the-scenes meddling, but Baker was convinced she was placing the organization in fair and able hands.[53]

Several issues of a newsletter, which Baker suggested they call the *Student Voice*, were published during the spring and summer. The group acquired temporary office space in one corner of the SCLC office on Auburn Avenue and hired one staff person, Jane Stembridge. Representatives made their mark on national electoral politics by testifying before the two major party conventions. Student leaders also met with the nation's top civil rights leaders, from King and the ministers of SCLC to the national officials of the NAACP. Moses established contact with older activists who were conducting their own campaigns and with other students throughout the Deep South who had not been directly involved in the original wave of sit-ins. Already the movement was growing beyond its circumscribed beginnings.

Early on, one of SNCC's difficult decisions concerned the plans for the

October conference and involved Baker's friend Bayard Rustin. The Pack-inghouse Workers Union had pledged some funds to help finance the con-ference. When the union officials learned that Rustin was a scheduled speaker, they threatened to pull the money because of his radical past. Nervous about alienating new allies, especially funders, but not terribly scrupulous about retaining existing ones, SNCC awkwardly disinvited Rus-tin. The details of this decision remain unclear. There is no indication that Baker intervened to question or challenge the decision, and she likely had been instrumental in obtaining the funds since she was handling most of the outreach and fund-raising over the summer. Stembridge, however, was highly upset and feared SNCC was abandoning its principles before it had even gotten off the ground. She abruptly resigned but declined to make a public issue of the matter. Years later, she reasoned that it was probably as much Rustin's sexuality as his leftist past that caused the union to reject him and prompted SNCC not to stand up in his defense. For Baker's part, she was either opting to choose her battles or, in a pragmatic vein, allowing the students to make their own mistakes as they groped to define themselves. Still, Stembridge was "sure" that "Ella would not have approved of this if she had been asked." The SNCC of 1960 took the easy way out. Four years later, the outcome would have likely been quite different.[54] Rustin, used to being mistreated by colleagues, had developed a thick skin. He continued to advise and work with SNCC despite the affront.

Throughout 1960 and early 1961, SNCC staged sit-ins and stand-ins at lunch counters, bus stations, movie theaters, and other segregated public facilities and mounted support campaigns for protesters who were arrested. The group also coordinated Christmas boycotts of segregated businesses in December 1960. Meanwhile, bitter debates and personal power struggles embroiled the more established civil rights leadership, even though they maintained the appearance of unity in public. Baker felt that much of this wrangling was attributable to a kind of egocentrism and organizational competition that she desperately hoped would not infect SNCC, but the young organization was inescapably drawn into the quarrel.

Roy Wilkins of the NAACP was upset that Martin Luther King's supporters were portraying SCLC as the vanguard of the civil rights movement. Wilkins was particularly outraged when Jim Lawson, a sit-in leader and ally of King, was quoted in the New York Times as dismissing the NAACP as "a black bourgeois club."[55] Both SCLC and SNCC tried to distance themselves from these comments, and Lawson claimed that his words were taken out of context. In another political skirmish, Harlem congressman Adam Clayton Powell harshly criticized both Wilkins and King for the protests that occurred outside the Democratic National Convention in August. Powell threatened to spread erroneous rumors about King if he did not sever his ties with Bayard Rustin, whose left-leaning politics Powell objected to. Rustin was a socialist, not a communist, but he was still labeled a "red" by those who did not care about the distinction between one type of leftist and another. However, the nature of Powell's threat, which was that he was going to leak the false rumor that King and Rustin were lovers, suggests that his dislike of Rustin had as much to do with homophobia as with anticommunism, especially since Powell himself had a radical political past. This is what movement infighting had come to.

In the midst of all this animus and rancor, Ella Baker accompanied a small delegation of SNCC leaders and several members of SCLC to a meeting with NAACP officials to try to clear the air. The response was lukewarm, but the fact that the meeting was held signaled the student group's growing reputation as an organization to be reckoned with in national black politics.

Through the summer of 1960 and the winter of 1960–61, a core of about twenty SNCC activists huddled together in a series of meetings to map their future course. While the work in Mississippi was still being contemplated, there were continuing sparks of direct action protest that were inspired by the 1960 sit-ins. One such spark was in Rock Hill, South Carolina, in the early months of 1961. A group of young people had been agitating there for months, picketing, conducting sit-ins, and getting themselves arrested. Finally, they decided to up the ante and refuse bail. They sent out a call to others to join them. The coordinating committee of SNCC was in a meeting at the Butler Y in Atlanta when word of the Rock Hill stance came. A group immediately latched onto the idea and prepared to go. Ella Baker went along to inspect the situation, visit those who had already been arrested, and make sure parents, lawyers, and the media were contacted. She and Connie Curry stayed with a local minister who was supportive of the protests, and the two women drove back to Atlanta two days later to get the word out to allies and the press. Rock Hill was SNCC's first collective protest action after its founding, and Baker was there to urge the students on and help minimize their losses.[56]

· · · · · ·

FREEDOM RIDES

The following spring, SNCC was propelled into a much more visible national spotlight by its involvement in the Freedom Rides. The rides were begun in April 1961 by the Congress of Racial Equality (CORE), a northern-based civil rights group, to desegregate interstate transportation. Still reeling from their stay in the Rock Hill jail, SNCC members looked to the Freedom Rides as their next challenge. Interracial teams of freedom riders took busses from the North to the South and attempted to use waiting rooms and restrooms in violation of the "Whites Only" and "Colored" signs that were posted everywhere. Southern segregationists' response to this campaign was swift and vicious. Vigilantes firebombed busses and angry mobs pummeled the freedom riders, threatening them with death and beating some protesters within inches of their lives. Even the U.S. Justice Department officials who were sent South to observe the civil rights protests and the news reporters who were assigned to cover them were caught up in the violence; some of them were also beaten severely by white mobs. Several freedom riders were hospitalized after an especially bloody melee in Anniston, Alabama. Fearing that the next attack might be fatal, CORE leaders then called off the rides.[57]

So that the protesters would not appear to be caving in to vigilante violence, brazen SNCC activists immediately intervened to continue the Freedom Rides. A determined Diane Nash flew to Birmingham to be part of a team to coordinate a resumption of the rides. SNCC activists, such as John Lewis, a Nashville student who would become SNCC's chairman and later a member of Congress, volunteered for the dangerous assignment. When the rides resumed, so did the violence. The situation provoked a clash between civil rights activists and the new administration in the White House. John F. Kennedy, the son of Irish immigrants and the nation's first Catholic president, had been elected in 1960 with strong African American support by promising to be an ally of civil rights and racial equality. The spectacle of violence in reaction to the Freedom Rides and Kennedy's fairly slow response to the open violation of federal law caused many movement activists to question how strong an ally the young president was really going to be. This distrust of the federal government deepened as the struggle in the South intensified over the next few years.

Ella Baker did not participate directly in the 1961 Freedom Rides. In 1947, she and her close friend Pauli Murray had volunteered to engage in the same kind of action during the Journey of Reconciliation, but they were rebuffed because they were women.[58] This time, even though she was still not a rider, she would not be excluded. In daily contact with Diane Nash, who was on the front lines, Baker dispatched a written critique and analysis to the committee coordinating the rides, raising issues about publicity, future strategies, and what she viewed as bungled negotiations with Attorney General Robert Kennedy.[59] Baker insisted that a better media and outreach strategy had to be crafted: "Although one can understand that the demands upon the committee in recruiting and processing riders would consume a great deal of time and energy, one is, nevertheless, also aware that the full value of the Freedom Rides could only be realized in proportion to the degree to which an aroused and vocal public made its voice felt."[60] She went on to discuss the committee's mistake in its meeting with Robert Kennedy, on which she had been briefed, probably by Nash, after the fact. "It would seem clear to me," she chided, "that the point to have been concentrated on in the conference with the Attorney General was not that of seeking his aid to release persons from jail directly [since they had declined bond already to make a point] but that of urging action in the enforcement of existing laws and regulations which prohibited segregation practices in interstate commerce especially."[61] She pointed out that Robert Kennedy had already noted this contradiction in some of his public comments to the media as a way to get himself off the hook.

It is unclear if Baker ever received a formal reply to her letter, but a three-page typed memo from someone as well connected and influential on the grassroots level as Baker would not have been taken lightly by the committee coordinating the rides. Her motive for such a formal and forceful intervention, as opposed to her preferred mode of communication by telephone, is not fully clear. On the last page of the document, however, there is a hint that this was a gesture to bolster Nash's authority and confidence and to protect SNCC from other organizations that may have wanted to claim the Freedom Rides as their own organizational victory. In this regard, she wrote: "What coordination is to be expected or exacted in connection with public appeals for financial support? All of us, I am confident, will have to agree that the Freedom Rides are the primary basis on which recent contributions to constituent agencies have been made. Therefore, it would appear that the question of stewardship in the handling of public funds is one that deserves more attention than may have been given."[62] She then demanded to know what would happen to "the students who are spending the longest periods in jail [and] will be in need of money for maintaining themselves and for scholarships next school term. Where will this come from?"[63] In other words, since SNCC had salvaged the Freedom Rides and provided most of the courageous volunteers, it deserved its rightful place in the leadership and its share of funds to further advance its work.[64]

Eventually, federal authorities had no choice but to offer some protection to the unflagging freedom riders, whose bloody and bandaged faces appeared on nightly television newscasts across the country. Attorney General Kennedy, brother of the president, cut a deal with local officials in Mississippi, but the deal compromised rather than aided the activists' immediate goals. They were protected, but only by being taken into police custody and charged with violating Mississippi's segregation ordinances, which prevented the protest from continuing. Hundreds of protesters eventually served jail time in Mississippi's notorious Parchman Prison as a result of the so-called protection they were provided. Among those prisoners was Ruby Doris Smith, who later recalled the experience as a transformative moment in her life. It was also a watershed in SNCC's political maturation.[65]

In November 1961, after dozens of freedom riders had been beaten, some nearly to death, and while dozens more were still imprisoned, the Interstate Commerce Commission finally mandated the full desegregation of all interstate travel facilities, implementing a Justice Department ruling made in September. The freedom riders felt at least partly vindicated. Now SNCC had a concrete national victory to its credit. SNCC activists had demonstrated determination and courage under fire. And they had garnered visibility and recognition as a major political force in the growing civil rights movement. After 1961, SNCC members were increasingly viewed as the movement's shock troops. They were able to quickly mobilize people to go to sites of intensified racial conflict: Birmingham in 1963, Selma in 1965, and James Meredith's short-circuited one-man march from Memphis, Tennessee, to Jackson, Mississippi, in the summer of 1966. And the activists were willing to take on difficult and dangerous organizing challenges—such as voter registration in the Mississippi Delta—that other civil rights groups were unwilling to touch.

In the summer of 1961, after a difficult first year, SNCC activists came together to grapple with the question of the political course the organization should take. Smaller groups had met in June in Louisville and in July in Baltimore, but it was the August meeting at the Highlander Folk School in Monteagle, Tennessee, itself an institution under siege and soon to be closed down because of its radical and antiracist politics, that was the most intense. Highlander was the site of many historic meetings. This gathering included new people, discussed new proposals, and faced new political challenges. The political landscape in the country was changing rapidly, and the young people in SNCC were changing as well. One impulse was to do more of the same, to continue nonviolent direct action tactics on an ever more massive scale until the last bastions of segregation fell before the onslaught. After all, the tactic had been successful, although the victories were purchased at a high human cost. Some veterans of the sit-ins and the Freedom Rides wanted to move beyond the demand for desegregation and the tactic of nonviolent direct action. The number of people who were willing to risk their lives to achieve desegregation was limited, and segregated public transportation and accommodations were not the only, or even the most important, forms of oppression that southern blacks faced. The SNCC activists wondered whether they could confront those in power over such issues as citizenship rights and economics.

Layered on top of everything else was the question of allies and affiliations. By attending the national conference of the Students for a Democratic Society (SDS) in June, Chuck McDew, Casey Hayden, and Bob Zellner had linked SNCC to the nascent antiwar movement. Baker was working with Myles Horton to defend the Highlander School against the threat of closure, and in so doing she linked SNCC to the southern white left that had been one of the targets of government red-baiting. Even more significant than the Highlander connection was SNCC's deepening relationship with SCEF, which Baker had largely facilitated and encouraged. Anne Braden had attended most of SNCC's meetings, and SCEF, at Ella Baker's urging, had pledged an annual contribution to SNCC's budget. On the liberal front, politicians attached to foundation funding sources were also vying for SNCC's attention.

As it tried to chart its own course, SNCC was presented with an opportunity to receive funds from several liberal foundations, including the Taconic Foundation, if it joined a Voter Education Project to be administered by the Southern Regional Council. This project was strongly supported by the Kennedy administration. With a hefty residue of suspicion left over from the federal government's response to the Freedom Rides, SNCC activists debated the White House's motives. The Kennedys may well have been sympathetic to civil rights in principle, but they also had a direct interest in promoting voter registration. A campaign that added thousands of new voters to the rolls, most of whom were likely to vote Democratic, would certainly increase the administration's chances of reelection. Some

SNCC members thought that such an intimate involvement with electoral politics would compromise the organization's values and lessen its effectiveness. They felt that the Democrats' obvious opportunism should not be rewarded with cooperation. At one point, the controversy threatened to split the young organization wide open.[66]

Bob Moses had come to the conclusion that the disenfranchisement of poor southern blacks was the cutting-edge issue the movement needed to address. He was not so naive as to think that voting would solve all the problems African Americans faced, but he did become convinced, strongly influenced by Amzie Moore, that their oppression hinged in large part on their total political powerlessness. Moses could not attend the Highlander meeting, but Charles McDew, Charles Sherrod, and Charles Jones were in favor of the voter registration project and argued for that position in the meeting. In contrast, Diane Nash and many of the Nashville activists had retained an almost spiritual investment in the tactic of nonviolent direct action. Becoming involved in the messy business of electoral politics, they concluded, would take the group away from its strength and the moral high ground that they felt the protests embodied. John Lewis feared that the "voter registration push by the government was a trick to take the steam out of the movement, to slow it down."[67] Passions were heated; tensions were high; and some of the participants felt that the only way both factions could remain true to their convictions was to part ways.[68]

Baker vehemently disagreed with the formation of two organizations. And it was her aggressive intervention that calmed the situation, abated the rancor, and preserved unity. "I opposed the split as serving the purpose of the enemy," she recalled years later.[69] The importance of this intervention in SNCC's decision making is generally acknowledged, even by those who remain unaware of the crucial role Baker played at many other moments of decision. She understood that the two approaches being proposed were not mutually exclusive. While she leaned in the direction of expanding the scope of SNCC's work and activities to include voting rights, she knew from her recent experience with SCLC's Crusade for Citizenship and from her years with the NAACP that organizing for voting rights did not preclude direct action. In fact, any attempt to register black voters would precipitate confrontations with white registrars and public officials in small towns and big cities. As both sides stated their case with great fervor, Baker saw that if some compromise were not reached, the group was headed for an even more serious crisis. She stood up and spoke forcefully in the meeting, calling for the formation of two wings of one organization. Rather than two organizations, one wing would focus on direct action and the other on voter education and registration. Nash would head the direct action campaign, and Charles Jones would coordinate the voting rights project.[70] Not everyone was completely won over to the idea, but Baker made a compelling case. No one was prepared to stand up in a meeting and argue vehemently against her.

Although the compromise appeared to give equal weight to both positions, this decision to expand the group's political agenda began the process of redirecting SNCC's energies in significant ways. The shift from transitory, high-profile events like the sit-ins and freedom rides to protracted, day-to-day grassroots organizing in local communities was a significant turning point. Baker insisted that a movement was a web of social relationships. Charismatic leaders could rally an anonymous mass of followers to turn out for a single event or series of events; millions could watch television coverage of heroic actions by a brave few or speeches by mesmerizing orators; but that was mobilization, not organization.[71] In order to be effective organizers in a particular community, Baker argued, activists had to form relationships, build trust, and engage in a democratic process of decision making together with community members. The goal was to politicize the community and empower ordinary people. This was Baker's model, and in 1961 it became SNCC's model.[72]

From the spring of 1960 through the summer of 1961, the new student movement and the group that emerged out of it toughened and matured tactically and ideologically. In the beginning, SNCC was not Baker's ideal organization. As a result of the Rock Hill jail action, the Freedom Rides, and its growing reputation for boldness, SNCC's practices and philosophy became more recognizably similar to Baker's own vision and values. But exactly what were those political values? Dorothy Miller (Zellner), a young white leftist from New York, who worked in SNCC's Atlanta office, admired Ella Baker but always found her politics "a bit of a mystery."[73] What Dorothy really meant by this was that she could not precisely situate Baker within the various ideological tendencies of the left, and Baker was neither a nationalist nor a liberal.[74] She defied orthodoxy, and her views transcended traditional political categories.

Since Baker never wrote an organizing manual or an ideological treatise, her theory was literally inscribed in her daily work—her practice. Some of the most powerful political lessons that she taught were through example, which represented an articulation of her unwritten theory in a conscious set of actions and practices. In no sense an armchair radical, Baker pursued a politics of action more than of words. The concept of political "praxis," meaning the marriage of theory and practice, is a helpful way to try to map Baker's political ideas on the bumpy landscape of her work of more than half a century.[75]

Baker had enormous confidence in the knowledge base of poor and oppressed communities and in the intellectual and analytic capacities of people without formal academic training. This was in part what she modeled in her own exchanges with students, sharecroppers, and movement co-workers. Because she and other women did clerical work, it was assumed that they could not think, analyze, and articulate. Baker rejected the artificial division between mental and manual labor. It was, she said, a problem that "so many people who are 'not educated' always defer to those who have got book learning."[76] She spelled out this problem in the movement's own practice: "The clerical people are the people who take the dictation, . . . put it on paper . . . you don't expect them to be the ones to have the ideas . . . it's not a given."[77] Baker made this observation critically, suggesting that there should be no distinct intellectual leadership; rather, thinking and analysis should be incorporated into all aspects of movement work. She was willing to run the mimeograph machine and type letters, but she was just as determined to offer historical insights and theoretical critiques to the process.

· · · · · · ·

Ella Baker earned the incontestable position of resident elder and intellectual mentor of SNCC during its first six years of existence. Her ideas and teachings permeated the group's discussions, shaped its ethos, and set its tone. She was consulted on issues ranging from strategy and analysis to logistics and fund-raising on an almost daily basis. As Jim Forman, executive secretary of SNCC, later remarked, "Throughout the decade of the sixties, many people helped to ignite or were touched by the creative fire that was SNCC without appreciating the generating force of Ella Jo Baker."[78]

Even though the national media never cast the spotlight on Baker's political career in the 1960s, her colleagues and coworkers fully appreciated the contribution she made. When Howard Zinn, a historian and movement activist, published *SNCC: The New Abolitionists*, the first account of the organization's development, he dedicated the book to Baker. In his words, she was "more responsible than any other single individual for the formation of the new abolitionists [SNCC] as an organized group."[79] In the

1960s, her lifelong friend Pauli Murray, a keen observer of progressive politics, praised Ella Baker as "the gal who I think has done so much for spearheading the revolutionary movement among Negroes in the South."[80] Stokely Carmichael, another SNCC leader, recalled that by the mid-1960s Baker "was just so overwhelming and ubiquitous in SNCC that it seems as if she was always present."[81]

THE EMPOWERMENT OF AN INDIGENOUS
SOUTHERN BLACK LEADERSHIP, 1961–1964

. . . . . .

One of the major emphases of SNCC, from the beginning,
was that of working with indigenous people, not working for them,
but trying to develop their capacity for leadership.
Ella Baker, 1967

Between 1961 and 1964, SNCC launched over a dozen projects in rural and urban communities across the South. Young civil rights activists partici-pated in grassroots struggles in places like Pine Bluff, Arkansas; Danville, Virginia; Albany, Georgia; and, later, Lowndes County, Alabama, and the heart of the Mississippi Delta. In some cases, SNCC supported and helped sustain desegregation and voter rights projects that were already under way. In other places, where protest campaigns had stagnated or had been halted after violent reprisals, SNCC organizers had to start over, identifying people who were ready to take action, helping them select targets and tactics, and offering them whatever resources they could mobilize to con-front their adversaries. Whether SNCC sent activists into a community to support an ongoing campaign or to reinvigorate a local movement, its approach to organizing was a direct outgrowth of Ella Baker's teachings and represented a major shift in the way Black Freedom Movement groups operated in the South.

Ella Baker's unofficial political curriculum was not the only contributing factor to the formation of SNCC's radical democratic approach, but it was a major one. Her message was simple and subtle. She urged SNCC organizers to suppress their own egos and personal and organizational ambitions as much as possible and to approach local communities with deference and humility. She stressed the need to resist organizational chauvinism or any attempts to make proprietary claims on political campaigns that might emerge from their efforts. Finally, she rejected the notion that the black middle class had special claims on leadership of the black community. Even though most of the black youth who were attracted to SNCC in the early 1960s were not wealthy, and some came from very modest means, virtually all of them were college-educated and consequently had social, if not material, capital. Baker appreciated the skills and resources that educated black leaders brought to the movement, but she urged SNCC organizers to look first to the bottom of the class hierarchy in the black community, not the top, for their inspiration, insights, and constituency.[1] Baker influenced SNCC's emergent politics and values primarily by exposing the young activists to people and situations that represented alternative adult leadership— people who would demonstrate to them first-hand the willingness, ability, and determination of oppressed people to resist and overcome their oppression while speaking for themselves: people who were not lawyers or ministers but just as capable as a Martin Luther King or a Thurgood Marshall.[2] Nothing made this point more dramatically than the struggle in Fayette County, Tennessee.

· · · · · ·

SOLIDARITY WITH THE BLACK POOR IN FAYETTE COUNTY

In the fall of 1960, SNCC's national leadership, with Ella Baker's strong encouragement, began building ties to the constituency that soon became the focal point of its southern organizing efforts: the rural and small-town black poor. In August 1959, a group of impoverished black tenant farmers in Fayette County (and later in adjacent Haywood County), a cotton-producing region of southwestern Tennessee, had begun an intense and protracted struggle that was as much about economics as it was about segregation and citizenship. This conflict between black sharecroppers and white landowners was precipitated by black people asserting their right to participate in elections. The response of whites to this political initiative revealed the extent to which land ownership and economic prowess determined the racial hierarchy of the South. White landlords evicted dozens of sharecropping families from the land they had worked and lived on for years because they dared to go down to the county courthouse and attempt to register to vote. Unbowed despite their tactical defeat, the landless farm families had refused to leave the community, opting to stay while they petitioned the federal government for redress. In an unprecedented act of collective resistance, they built makeshift homes on a 200-acre plot of land donated for their use by a sympathetic black landowning farmer, Shepard Towles. The encampment was dubbed "Freedom Tent City."[3]

The struggle in Fayette County received wide coverage in the African American press. The NAACP, CORE, and other civil rights and social justice groups, along with several labor unions, raised funds and collected donations of food and clothing to sustain and support the Tennessee activists. Before he joined SNCC, James Forman helped establish the northern-based Fayette County Emergency Relief Committee and spent many months going back and forth between Chicago and Tennessee with supplies and advice. Forman saw the struggle in Fayette County as a kind of "watershed" in the movement because, in this instance, an indigenous leadership had emerged and was connecting demands for full citizenship and civil rights to economic issues. Forman became so immersed in the Fayette County struggle that at one point he was accused of trying to take it over from the local people. Whether or not this charge was justified, he took it seriously and brought the lessons he had learned in Fayette County with him into SNCC.[4] Ella Baker shared this concern, and from the outset SNCC strove to avoid even the perception of trying to dominate local struggles. SNCC activists publicized the Fayette County struggle through the *Student Voice* and conducted a food drive to provide material aid.[5]

Baker followed the Tennessee story closely, and in the early months of 1961 she urged Ed King, who was then the executive secretary of SNCC, to travel to Tennessee to explore ways in which the young people could lend greater support. The newly formed organization provided both material and moral support to the Fayette County "freedom fighters." For SNCC staff person Jane Stembridge, the struggle graphically illustrated "the connection between poverty and civil rights."[6] In addition to collecting food and clothing, SNCC's leadership cosigned a statement directed at the federal government demanding intervention and relief aid for the embattled former sharecroppers. The significance of this struggle and the heroism of the local people became the topic of many informal discussions around the SNCC office from the fall of 1960 through the summer of 1961.[7] John Lewis recalled that the example of Fayette County was a sobering one for many young SNCC organizers and gave them a glimpse of what lay ahead.[8]

The *Student Voice*, SNCC's newsletter, highlighted the courage and suffering of Fayette County activists and cast them as pivotal forces in the struggle for freedom in the South. The SNCC newsletter covered the issue quite differently from *The Crisis*, the NAACP's journal. Perhaps encouraged by Baker's editorial guidance, the *Student Voice* emphasized the leadership, courage, and oppression of the evicted sharecroppers. Although *The Crisis* also described the desperate conditions of the tent dwellers, it stressed the fact that respectable, middle-class blacks as well as semiliterate sharecroppers had been denied the ballot in Fayette and Haywood Counties. In praising the Justice Department for filing suit in November 1959 against nineteen white Democratic Party officials for excluding blacks from the local primary, Gloster Current, the NAACP's director of branches, pointed out that among those who were denied the right to vote were a "well-to-do grocer," a teacher, and a minister. Current described another would-be voter as a "high school teacher, educated at Iowa State University, and possessor of a master's degree."[9] These four individuals, however, were certainly not representative of the 100 illiterate and semiliterate tenant farmers who were at the center of the struggle in Tennessee.[10]

Ella Baker visited Fayette County in January 1961, met with residents of the tent city, and wrote her own story about the conditions there for the *Southern Patriot*, the newsletter of the Southern Conference Education Fund (SCEF). Baker's report, like the coverage in SNCC's newsletter, differed sharply in tone and emphasis from how the NAACP portrayed the situation. Baker conveyed vividly to her readers the depth of southern black poverty and the harshness of white reprisals against activists. The sharecroppers she visited lived in "olive-drab tents without floors, surrounded by inches of mud and mire: the darkness within these tents that are lighted by kerosene lamps and heated by wood stoves; the not-too-well-clad children crowded into the tents or squashing around in the mud; and the hungry shivering dogs wandering about; all of this painted a picture of anything but hope for the new year."[11]

While *The Crisis* applauded the small steps taken by the U.S. Justice Department, Baker's article in the *Southern Patriot* expressed outrage at how little government intervention there had been. Indicting any notion of American progress that would leave destitute black farmers behind, Baker wrote that "the real tragedy is that in the wealthiest country in the world, in the jet-propelled atomic age of 1961, human beings could honestly say that their mud-floored tents were more comfortable than the shacks they formerly called 'home' for five, ten or 30 years." The material hardships that activists suffered in Freedom Tent City were similar to those they had endured during their entire lives as sharecroppers; and once they had undertaken this act of resistance, their outlook and morale had actually improved. Baker was optimistic that the resolve of the oppressed them-selves, rather than the benevolence of the government, meant "a new dawn of freedom [was] breaking through the age-old social, economic and political discrimination that blighted the lives of both whites and Negroes in the South."[12]

The Tennessee activists founded their own independent group, the Fay-ette County Civic and Welfare League, which was led by John McFerren, a store owner who had become a militant. The McFerrens had a home of their own, so they did not live in the tent city; but they strongly sym-pathized with the evicted families because they had previously been tenant farmers themselves. The White Citizens Council orchestrated a campaign of harassment and intimidation against the league. White merchants re-fused to sell medicine, food, or supplies to tent city residents, and McFerren and his wife, Viola, were subjected to constant surveillance and harass-ment, including many threatening phone calls.[13] Moreover, John McFerren was deliberately run over by a truck and nearly killed. Despite these re-prisals, neither the McFerrens nor the members of the Fayette County Civic and Welfare League gave up their crusade to document and protest politi-cal and economic discrimination against blacks in the county.

Baker had known some of the Fayette County activists before their strug-gle hit the national press. On the eve of the Greensboro sit-ins in January 1960, she and Carl Braden had brought John McFerren to Washington, D.C., to testify at the civil rights hearings cosponsored by SCEF and SCLC. His emotional testimony was one of the most compelling moments of the hearings. As she did with many of the local activists whom she met during her years of organizing, Baker adopted the McFerrens into her political family and kept in touch with them long after the struggle in Fayette County had subsided.[14]

Baker introduced young SNCC activists to the McFerrens so that they could learn from the example, experiences, and perspectives of poor black people.[15] The struggle in Fayette and Haywood Counties was in crucial respects a model of indigenous black defiance and self-defense. The Ten-nessee tenant farmers were the victims of enormously exploitative and repressive conditions. Once moved to act, however, they were not afraid to stand up for themselves with unrelenting courage and defend themselves forcefully if necessary. When shots rang out one night from a passing car-load of white men, a group of armed black men immediately mobilized to defend the tent encampment. Early B. Williams, who had been shot, was transported to a nearby hospital under armed escort.[16] For Ella Baker, this situation underscored not only the terribly oppressive conditions under which so many rural black people suffered but also, perhaps more importantly, the depth of the determination that resided in such communities. Poor black southerners were not downtrodden victims; they were eager to fight to improve their lot.

Baker was rarely surprised by an upsurge of protest in places like Fayette County because, as a keen observer of southern black culture, she could detect rumblings beneath the surface of seemingly calm situations. As she talked with people like Papa Tight in Shreveport and the sharecroppers in Tennessee, they sometimes spoke about things only tangentially related to politics, but she was collecting valuable information all the same. In such seemingly casual conversations, she listened for what historian Earl Lewis calls the "semi-public transcript" of opposition within oppressed communities. Building on the work of political scientist James Scott, historian Robin Kelley, and others, Lewis suggests that what people laugh at, the songs they create and listen to, and the slang they use are all subtle indicators of a nascent political consciousness. A careful, reflective listener can ascertain what those people, if organized, might be prepared to do politically.[17] Ella Baker wanted the young activists in SNCC to hear the stories of Tennessee sharecroppers, to look to them as sources of inspiration, and to extract lessons about the potential, and the dangers, as they could be applied to similar struggles in the future.[18]

· · · · · ·

DEVELOPING A PHILOSOPHY FROM PRACTICE

Between 1960 and 1962, as the historian Clayborne Carson's organizational biography of the group demonstrates, SNCC underwent a dramatic evolution in its politics, culture, and personnel. Many of the students who had attended the Shaw meeting dropped out to pursue other interests or to return to their studies. Those who remained with the organization were augmented by a new cadre of activists who were more determined and more politically savvy than their predecessors. One of them was James Forman. A thirty-three-year-old former teacher from Chicago, Forman joined SNCC's staff in 1961 after he had gained a reputation for his organizing skills in Fayette County. Years later, he recalled that he was told by Charles Jones that he had to meet with Ella Baker's approval before SNCC would make a final decision to hire him. Of course, this practice was entirely unofficial; Baker did not believe that any leader should exercise veto power. But because SNCC staff held her in such high esteem, her opinion was sought on virtually every important decision. Forman made the obligatory pilgrimage to Baker's Harlem apartment to discuss the job, the organization, and politics in general. She sized him up and authorized the hire.[19]

With the skills and passions that Forman and other new recruits brought with them and the help of Ella Baker's subtle, yet powerful guidance, SNCC grew far beyond what its founders had envisioned. Explicit references to religion gradually gave way to a more secular and militant rhetoric, and nonviolence was increasingly viewed as a necessary tactic rather than as a sacred philosophy. Most significantly, the SNCC activists' involvement in struggles like the one in Fayette County directly impacted their class politics, grounding them firmly with black people who were rich in wisdom and courage but poor in terms of economic assets.

When SNCC members went into small towns and cities throughout the South, for example, they first paid their respects to the clergy and to others who might cast themselves as the leaders and representatives of the black community. But then the activists knocked on doors in the most run-down parts of town and in the most remote and impoverished rural areas. Gradually, those doors creaked open. The activists sat down with individuals who had little formal education and asked them to analyze the situation around them and help shape the agenda for change. This was a major departure, both in substance and in style, from the practices of national and regional groups like the NAACP, CORE, and SCLC, which operated on the assumption that leadership came from an educated, professional, or clerical class.[20] Baker understood, however, that small-town black communities were often polarized by class differences, even as they were united by Jim Crow segregation. She had learned from experience that using local elites as conduits to the masses could actually backfire, lessening the credibility of outside organizers who were trying to gain access to a particular community.

In pursuing a more egalitarian political practice, SNCC broke new ground. According to the Mississippi historian John Dittmer, "Not since Reconstruction had anyone seriously proposed that illiterate sharecroppers had the same right to the franchise as did teachers, lawyers and doctors."[21] This radical departure from the approach favored by liberal civil rights groups was heavily influenced by Ella Baker's ideas and organizing style. Through her own life, teaching, and example, she connected the young activists to a tradition of black radicalism that hearkened back to the early twentieth century and before.

In the early 1960s, SNCC organizers were not only challenging white supremacy; they were contributing to the dismantling of the caste system that existed within many black communities.[22] At every opportunity, Baker reiterated the radical idea that educated elites were not the natural leaders of black people. Critically reflecting on her work with the NAACP, she observed, "The leadership was all from the professional class, basically. I think these are the factors that have kept it [the NAACP] from moving to a more militant position." She urged SNCC, as she had urged SCLC and the NAACP, to seek out "indigenous leaders," ordinary people engaged in struggle, regardless of credentials or social class, and to affirm their right to define the politics and direction of the movement.[23]

Local autonomy was the cornerstone of a meaningfully engaged democratic practice. If local people did not have ownership of the struggle they were engaged in, they would be beholden politically to others who would not necessarily experience the consequences of that struggle. Julian Bond observed that the goal of SNCC organizers in local struggles was to help generate "a community movement with local leadership, not a new branch of SNCC."[24] Jane Stembridge, who spent time in the Greenwood office after working closely with Baker in Atlanta, put it this way: "The field staff saw itself as playing a very crucial but temporary role in this whole thing. Go into a community. As soon as local leadership begins to emerge, get out of the community, so that the leadership will take hold and people will not continue to turn to you for guidance. You work yourself out of a job rather than trying to maintain yourself in a position or your organization. It doesn't matter if you go in and call yourself a SNCC worker or a CORE worker or just a person who is there."[25]

The real test of a democratic leadership was whether groups and individuals could downplay their partisan and personal interests for the greater good. Proprietary claims to or by an organization, or to any position within it, were corrupting, Baker believed, arguing instead for placing the ideals and politics of the movement above the interests of any one organization, including SNCC itself. This approach stood in contrast to that of the NAACP, which sought to exert tighter control over its branches despite, and sometimes because of, aggressive local leadership and resistance to centralized authority.

Baker recognized that an organizer's own personal interests and desires might readily become conflated with the larger goals of the group, and the group's partisan interests might get conflated with the goals of a larger movement; so she took deliberate steps to prevent such confusion. Her motto was "I was never working for an organization. I always tried to work for a cause. And that cause was bigger than any organization."[26] Having repeatedly built, let go, and rebuilt movement groups, on some level, Baker considered the process healthy and rejuvenating.

This philosophy accounts, in part, for Baker's rather nomadic political existence and explains why she never stayed with any one organization for very long. Although she maintained a home base in New York City for most of her adult life, she was on the road more often than not. From 1957 on, she had a sparsely furnished apartment in Atlanta's all-black Wallahuje residential hotel. Aside from the family photographs she brought with her from New York, the apartment revealed little about the tastes, preferences, or private life of its occupant. Her interests were revealed primarily by the papers, magazines, books, reports, clippings, and letters that accumulated in piles awaiting her attention. This was a place to read, to catch up on what was happening in other places, and to reflect on the struggle. Except for fixing her signature lamb stew occasionally, she did not cook much, and her refrigerator and cupboards were usually bare. She also paid little attention to other domestic tasks.[27]

Baker's mobility and her belief that organizational loyalties should remain fluid made for a migratory political existence. Before she became involved in SNCC, her political ties were tenuous at best. Because she never stayed in any one organization for very long, she was never able to influence how an organization like the NAACP or SCLC would evolve politically or structurally, as she had once hoped to do. At the NAACP and SCLC, she worked around the centers of power, organizing those who remained on the margins. Yet her identity as a political vagabond helped her because she was always perceived as an independent person without vested interests in one faction or another. This earned her enormous credibility with the young people of SNCC, as it had done with grassroots activists. In the early 1960s, SNCC became the political home and family that she had sought for so long. She was finally settling down—at least temporarily.

· · · · · ·

SOUTHWEST GEORGIA: POLITICAL DIFFERENCES
AND PERSONAL LOYALTIES

As SNCC became a more visible and formidable political force, the more established civil rights groups viewed the upstarts as naive and cocky. They resented SNCC for encroaching on what they regarded as their political turf. These tensions came to a head in the small town of Albany, Georgia ("all benny" as the locals called it), where competing strategies and personalities made national headlines and revealed the growing political rifts within the civil rights movement. The NAACP, SNCC, and SCLC were all involved with local activists in Albany, and they eventually came into conflict over issues of tactics, turf, and leadership. Although Baker dissuaded SNCC from sectarian inclinations, the group had to fight for its autonomy and visibility vis-à-vis other civil rights groups that were throwing their weight around and, in Baker's view, attempting to undermine SNCC's efforts at grassroots organizing.

In November 1961, Charles Sherrod and Cordell Reagon were asked by SNCC's coordinating committee to go to Albany to help bolster the local movement there. Sherrod, whom Baker had recruited as one of SNCC's first field secretaries, placed a high priority on building a strong base with ordinary people in the community.[28] So, the two SNCC activists settled in, got to know community residents, and slowly gained the confidence of a significant number of them, especially the young people. As Cordell Reagon put it, he and Sherrod "acted like neighborhood boys," doing "work with the common people first."[29] This down-to-earth approach became SNCC's trademark. In describing the mode of organizing that the young people in SNCC adopted, John Lewis recalled: "We were meeting people on their terms, not ours. If they were out in the field picking cotton, we would go out in that field and pick with them. . . . Before we ever got around to saying what we had to say, we listened. And in the process we built up both their trust in us and their confidence in themselves."[30]

The Albany Movement, the local umbrella organization, coordinated street demonstrations to protest segregation, organized consumer boycotts against racist businesses, launched a bus boycott, and initiated a campaign to promote black voter registration. As in most other places in the South, Albany's black electorate was virtually immobilized. The NAACP, which had been organizing in the region for years, counseled its local allies to document discrimination and prepare for litigation. The NAACP's national leaders strongly objected to what they viewed as provocative, illegal actions on the part of the "young Turks" in SNCC. Roy Wilkins believed that SNCC had acted irresponsibly in Albany when it pushed for an escalation of protests. Moreover, he resented the young activists' ungrateful attitude. Wilkins felt the NAACP had supported the neophytes, even helping to get some of them out of jail, "only to be insulted for being on the wrong side of the generation gap."[31]

When SCLC came to Albany, the situation became even more complex.

William Anderson, a doctor of osteopathic medicine and a local leader of the Albany Movement, appealed to Martin Luther King to visit the town in order to gain publicity for the struggle and pressure white officials to act on the movement's demands. Many SNCC organizers strongly opposed this move, as did some local activists. Although some early SNCC supporters had tightened their ties to SCLC and some, like James Bevel, had even joined the SCLC payroll, the core leadership of SNCC had grown increasingly skeptical of SCLC's style of organizing and of Dr. King's charismatic style of leadership. Some of the young activists had taken to mockingly calling King "da lawd" behind his back.[32]

On his arrival in Albany in December 1961, King ignited controversy. After being arrested in a protest demonstration, he allowed himself to be bailed out of jail and gave a tacit nod to the city leaders' offer to negotiate an end to the protests. Although recollections vary, there was apparently a breakdown in communication between King and sectors of the Albany Movement. He felt that he was adhering to the consensus of the local leadership, but some local movement participants and SNCC organizers disagreed.[33] Baker saw King's highly publicized visits as undermining local people's confidence and autonomy and lessening the visibility of the Albany Movement's own spokespersons. When he came to town, she complained, "you can imagine who the press looked to."[34] Several SNCC leaders were very vocal about their criticisms of King, making comments to reporters that revealed schisms and tensions within the movement that had not previously been made public.[35]

From the fall of 1961 through the summer of 1962, both Baker and King shuttled in and out of Albany. However, Baker's low-key interventions were in contrast to King's high-profile appearances. Howard Zinn recalled that when he first arrived in Albany in December 1961, Baker was engaged in practical work:

> Hundreds of people were coming out of jail. Many of them had been fired by their white employers, and they gathered in the Shiloh Baptist Church for help. Ella Baker sat in the corner of the church, pen and paper in hand. . . . She was a middle-aged handsome woman with the resonant voice of a stage actress, who moved silently through the protest movements in the South, doing the things the famous men did not have time to do. Now, hour after hour, she sat there as people lined up before her, patiently taking down names, addresses, occupations, immediate money needs.[36]

In addition to her role as an analyst and political strategist, Baker held another job in the movement: attending to the mundane details necessary to keep organizations and individuals going.

The confrontations in Albany were rooted in the political histories of the organizations involved, but personal relationships were entangled in the mesh as well. Vernon Jordan, then a savvy young lawyer, and Ruby Hurley, the tough veteran organizer, were the two top NAACP staffers dispatched from the national office in the fall of 1961 to take charge of the situation in Albany. The NAACP naturally felt it had a proprietary claim to defend, having been active in the area for years; Baker had even spoken there under its auspices. So, the NAACP's national leadership was flustered both by King's appearance and by SNCC's militant activism. Charles Sherrod and other SNCC activists experienced "very sharp confrontations" with Hurley.[37] But while Hurley was one of SNCC's chief adversaries in the Albany struggle, she was not just another NAACP bureaucrat to Ella Baker: she was an old and dear friend.

The two women had significant bonds. Both had worked as field secretaries in the NAACP during the 1940s, and on more than one occasion they had been allies against the top leadership of the organization. They had socialized together too, eating at one another's homes and commiserating about their egotistical male "superiors" in the New York office. Hurley remained part of Baker's extended political family in New York City during the 1950s. In fact, Hurley had taken Ella's niece Jackie shopping to buy her first pair of high-heel shoes, a rite of passage Jackie remembered fondly some forty years later.[38] In Albany, however, Hurley and Baker found themselves on opposite sides of a struggle within the movement. Yet their friendship, even then, survived.

Ella Baker's ability to sustain long-term friendships with other activists when particular political circumstances put them in adversarial positions was one of her most important gifts. Her talent for making and keeping connections, for recognizing in people more than their ideological stance or organizational position, was an important, if sometimes invisible, contribution to the movement. Although she strove to be principled and consistent in her own politics, she allowed for divergent opinions between herself and others, keeping in mind the need for broader networks and coalitions. In turn, people who knew her trusted and respected Ella Baker, even if they did not always agree with her about strategy and tactics.

Baker and Hurley had taken divergent political paths some years before. When Baker decided to break with the national office of the NAACP over questions of democracy and leadership, Hurley opted to stay. The political differences that were reflected in those choices were at the heart of the internal movement struggles that were played out more than a decade later in Albany. Baker had become even more convinced that grassroots activists had to confront their oppression directly, by challenging exploitative land-owners, biased voter registrars, and official and vigilante enforcers of seg-regation. Although she knew full well that racial inequality was structural, to her it was not an abstract system to be tackled indirectly. People them-selves had to make a change by challenging inequality concretely, as they encountered it in their daily lives. From the perspective of Hurley and the NAACP leadership in New York, on the other hand, a nationwide organiza-tion and a centralized, well-coordinated strategy gave coherence and sta-bility to local struggles. In their view, it was ultimately the Congress and the Supreme Court, not protests in the streets, that would determine the outcome of the struggle. What Baker viewed as suffocating interference by outside national leaders, Hurley saw as supportive, expert guidance.

As civil rights struggles sharpened after 1960, militant, confrontational tactics became a key area of disagreement. The NAACP had charted the legal route to political empowerment. This route was not narrow or exclu-sive, but it had to be navigated very carefully to ensure success. The NAACP did engage in protests, and at times its presence elicited violent and repres-sive reactions from southern segregationists. Hurley and her co-workers were certainly experienced and politically sophisticated enough to under-stand this dynamic. Still, the law was the national NAACP's weapon of choice against racism and discrimination, and it had already secured some important victories. Ella Baker, on the other hand, did not have much faith in lawyers, judges, or legislators. In order to shift the political climate and effect real change, the masses had to push against and even disrupt the status quo, and the pressure they applied had to be steady and sustained, not sporadic. In Baker's view, if people did not feel they had taken an active part in their own emancipation, but believed that it had been won for them, then half the battle had already been lost; ordinary people's sense of their own power would be compromised.

The struggle in Albany wore on for nearly eighteen months. Although more than 1,000 activists were arrested, SNCC's participation yielded few tangible concessions from the city government or local businesses. Some observers deemed the Albany struggle a failure, but historians agree that it was an important testing ground for SNCC. Clayborne Carson, Vincent Harding, and Howard Zinn have argued convincingly that SNCC's involvement in the Albany Movement had long-term implications for the organization: the young activists gained greater confidence in their capacity to organize in the face of sustained repression. Carson emphasizes that SNCC was "able to bring previously dormant elements of the black populace into a sustained struggle for civil rights" through the use of militant nonviolent tactics.[39] Because of SNCC's democratic organizing practices, Albany's youth, its poor, and its working class came to be active participants in the movement.

. . . . . .

SCEF

Although Ella Baker devoted most of her political energy in the early 1960s to SNCC, she continued to maintain multiple affiliations, in keeping with her view that one's chief loyalty should be to the movement and not to any one organization. From 1961 to 1963, her income came principally from her involvement in the special human relations project sponsored by the southeastern regional YWCA, but she also had a very close working relationship with her friends in SCEF, including the Bradens, the Shuttlesworths, and black South Carolina radical Modjeska Simkins.[40] As soon as her tenure with SCLC ended in the fall of 1960, Baker embarked on an association with SCEF that eventually led her to join its small staff in the spring of 1963. As rifts developed between various organizations within the movement, she sought to build bridges, in particular between SCEF and SNCC. Each year, SCEF donated several thousand dollars to support SNCC's work, and Anne Braden attended most of SNCC's meetings during its first few years.

In a consulting capacity, Baker attended SCEF board meetings, spoke at SCEF conferences, and documented anti–civil rights activity in the Florida legislature as a part of a monitoring project there. In October 1961, Baker, the Bradens, and allies of theirs, including C. T. Vivien and Myles Horton, formed Operation Freedom, something of a successor to In Friendship, which funneled money to activists "suddenly in dire straits." Their first project was to aid the militant farmers in Fayette County, Tennessee, and they later provided support to Mississippi activists who were victims of economic retaliation by local whites.[41]

One of SCEF's political priorities during the early 1960s was to combat the corrosive effect of anticommunism within the civil rights movement. Toward that end, SCEF launched a concerted effort to link civil rights and civil liberties, pointing out in its literature that the two issues were inseparable; it organized workshops, conferences, and lectures throughout the Southeast to bring attention to the issue. As Ella Baker's respect and admiration for the Bradens strengthened, her ambivalence about the role of suspected communists in the movement seemed to weaken. She became one of the strongest voices within SNCC advocating the principle of free association without any ideological litmus test, the opposite of the NAACP policy she had defended in the 1950s.

In October 1961, Baker helped organize a SCEF-sponsored conference on freedom and the First Amendment in Chapel Hill, North Carolina. Hoping to attract a more mainstream audience, she and Anne Braden went to great lengths to put together a roster of well-respected presenters, such as retired New York City judge Hubert Delany, whom Baker had known in Harlem in the 1930s; Methodist bishop Edgar Love of Baltimore; and SCLC's executive director, Baker's successor, Rev. Wyatt T. Walker. Most of the speakers were ministers, professors, lawyers, or judges; of the nineteen people listed on the program, only three—Baker, Anne Braden, and Casey Hayden—were women.

A lot was riding on this conference for Anne Braden. The explicit harassment and subtle slights that she and Carl had experienced were taking their toll on her emotionally and psychologically, and she simply needed some positive results. She did not mind fighting southern segregationists, the real enemies of racial justice, but, as she would confide to Ella Baker a year later, she was weary at having to "fight for [her] right to fight" alongside supposed allies.[42] The hope was that the 1961 conference would temper some of the anticommunist antagonism within the movement and generate more support for SCEF and other left-wing forces.

The Bradens may have felt shunned by some in liberal circles, but they had won many friends. Some people opposed red-baiting in the southern movement largely out of personal loyalty to Carl and Anne, whose determination, commitment, and courage were admired. They did not operate like party functionaries, if they were indeed members of the Communist Party. They were such staunch antiracist fighters that allowing them to suffer government attacks was deemed by their allies to be indefensible.[43] In Ella Baker's case, friendship may have been the factor that led her to shed her own ambivalent anticommunism, but she quickly developed a more sophisticated and deeply reflective position on civil liberties that extended well beyond her personal relationship with the Bradens.

Around the time of the Chapel Hill conference, Anne and Ella discussed the fact that framing the red-baiting issue in terms of personal friendships and individuals had severe limitations. Anne felt that both Wyatt T. Walker and Fred Shuttlesworth had overemphasized their support of the Bradens as a gesture of personal loyalty rather than as a matter of political principle. She complained, for example, that Shuttlesworth had given a speech in Louisville in which he praised her generously but failed to even mention HUAC's harassment or the issue of civil liberties. Anne explained to Jim Dombrowski that she and Ella had agreed on the need for more internal education and candid private conversations in order to politicize the issue in people's thinking.[44]

Ella Baker and Anne Braden devised a list of people that they thought it important to engage in this process. Among the students they identified were Diane Nash, Bob Moses, Charles Jones, Henry Thomas, and Dion Diamond. Anne commented that Jones had previously testified voluntarily before HUAC but seemed apologetic about it later. Ella had suggested him because she thought he was someone who "responds to his environment and in a civil liberties gathering would be better" than in other settings.[45] Anne also suggested to Baker that she invite her friends John and Viola McFerren from Fayette County to attend.[46]

The daylong conference was held on October 27, 1961, at the Educational Building of the Presbyterian Church in Chapel Hill. As chairperson of the afternoon session, Baker had the difficult task of facilitating an intense, unwieldy, and sometimes fractious discussion involving some fifty people. In her opening remarks, she speculated that "the reason I was asked to preside at this session is because I have had a great deal of experience in being pummeled from both sides [presumably the right and the left] and so I am here to try to keep the session going."[47] She guided and contained the debate with finesse and humor. The audience included some of the most active and engaged intellectuals and organizers on the left, such as Tom Hayden from the Students for a Democratic Society (SDS) and the socialist leader Michael Harrington, and all of them had something to say. Sympathizing with an especially long-winded questioner, but still trying to get him to wrap up his comments, Baker asked him to get to the point, confessing that she was also restraining herself from speaking: "You don't know how I am burning to talk because I love it."[48]

Another person expressed an unpopular opinion about HUAC, eliciting boos and calls of "liar" from the audience before he stormed out of the conference in frustration. After that incident, Baker had to wrestle back control of the floor, chastise the audience, apologize to the speaker for the heckling, and invite him to come back into the room and restate his minority opinion, assuring him he would have the right to do so as long as she was chairing the meeting. Freedom of speech was not only about protesting the government's suppression of dissent but also about insisting that the left not engage in suppression within its own ranks.[49] In terms of the goal of garnering a coalition of forces to challenge political repression and link it to civil rights, this did not occur. What the conference scenes illustrate, however, is how an individual like Ella Baker navigated the ideological minefield that surrounded the burgeoning black freedom struggle where she had located her efforts.

Throughout the early 1960s, Ella Baker worked with SCEF to highlight the principles of civil liberties and freedom of association within the movement and within SNCC in particular. In March 1962, she wrote an article for the *Southern Patriot* titled "Lack of Thought Cripples the South" in which she noted: "Today freedom of speech, association, the right to protest for redress of grievances, and freedom from excessive bails and inhumane punishment are daily being denied in the South under the guise of defending the country against communism, and we should no longer be hoodwinked by that."[50] She put the point more directly in an article in *Liberty Magazine* a few years later: "Man can only be free if he is free to question the postulates of a society. It is the perversion of this position that has given birth to the McCaran Act, HUAC, McCarthyism and the little HUACs of such states as Louisiana, Alabama, and Mississippi."[51] In advance of a workshop on civil liberties in the spring of 1963, and later that year as a follow-up, Baker traveled to communities throughout the South and West to speak at small community gatherings about the need to defend civil liberties as an extension of the goals of the civil rights movement.[52]

In June 1963, some seventy-five people gathered in Atlanta for a three-day workshop titled "How Free Are the 'Free'?" Anne Braden and Ella Baker were again the principal organizers, and once again they were faced with the question of whom to invite. Unlike at the conference in Chapel Hill, no formal presentations were scheduled. The workshop was meant to be an opportunity for key people in the movement to speak candidly about the issue of civil liberties and challenge one another on areas of disagreement. Six months before the event, Anne expressed her frustration with SCLC, feeling that she had to nag them to get their support for anything related to civil liberties, including Carl Braden's clemency petition, which both Wyatt T. Walker and Martin Luther King did endorse. "I am tired" Anne confessed. "I have pursued them [people at SCLC] for almost two years on this civil liberties question (and longer in a sense), and to put it bluntly I have had it."[53] But she had become more optimistic and even argued with Ella about the strategic importance of inviting Walker to be involved in the June workshop. Baker reluctantly conceded after Anne pleaded Walker's case, pointing out that while he was not perfect, she felt he had spoken out more than others had and was worth cultivating as an ally.[54]

The three-day discussion was lively, with Ella Baker and Bob Moses finding themselves sometimes slightly at odds. Moses expressed his concerns frankly. He did not have a gripe with communists; but he was trying to be practical. Fearing the loss of much needed foundation money, he suggested that funders would "pull the rug out from under us if we don't face up to this situation." Baker responded with a warning: "I'm very much afraid of this 'Foundation complex.' We're getting praise from places that worry me."[55] According to Moses, the police were using the charge of communism to attack and undermine the movement; such attacks, he felt, were causing real hardship and undermining the movement's work. Anne Braden challenged Moses to consider whether alleged communists were in fact the cause of the attacks, indicating that she would leave the South immediately if she thought it would further the goal of black freedom. When someone added that organizations like sncc should look at the person and not the ideology, Moses rejected this as an oversimplification of a complex question. "We don't necessarily accept people just because they are helpful," he argued.[56] Moses noted that he had invited Carl Braden to speak on civil liberties in Mississippi the previous summer and had gotten raked over the coals in the local press. "We were tied up in Mississippi" as a result, he concluded.[57] This made him leery. Still, the majority of those in attendance seemed less uncomfortable about communist affiliations, and many spoke of the need to challenge huac more forcibly.

At its December 1963 retreat, sncc took up the issue of civil liberties yet again. The official position was not to exclude anyone based on organizational affiliation but also not to pick a fight with huac by launching a campaign against it. For her part, Ella Baker was not willing to let huac off the hook so easily. She continued to raise concerns about civil liberties in her speeches and writings and at sncc meetings.[58] The issue would haunt sncc for years to come.

In the meantime, Baker had formally joined the scef staff. Jim Dombrowski, scef's executive director, was a Christian socialist and an early supporter of the Highlander Folk School; he had been trying since 1961 to bring Ella Baker on board. Because of his confidence in her good judgment, political instincts, and reputation, he conveyed to Anne Braden his willingness to support unequivocally just about any project that Baker proposed.[59] Once she was on the scef staff, she enjoyed more freedom and flexibility than she had ever previously experienced within an organization. Dombrowski offered her a paycheck along with the autonomy to choose and define her work. During the years that followed, Baker was essentially a free-floating movement consultant, adviser, teacher, and resource person. Not surprisingly, one of her first projects after she joined SCEF's staff was to go on a three-week organizing tour with SCEF field secretary John Salter, a white former Tougaloo College professor, to rally movement support in several western and midwestern states. The pair traveled to Iowa, Nebraska, and Arizona, meeting with church and civic groups and cosponsoring events with local CORE and NAACP people in Des Moines.[60]

· · · · · ·

GENDER POLITICS AND GRASSROOTS ORGANIZING

Bernice Johnson Reagon, who became politicized by the Albany struggle, has pointed out that, although gender politics were not explicitly articulated in the southern-based Black Freedom Movement of the early 1960s, gender was nonetheless deeply implicated in the daily lives and interactions of movement participants. As the young freedom fighters in SNCC set out to dismantle white supremacy in the South, they began, sometimes inadvertently, to challenge and transgress conventional notions of gender. Rather than replicating the patterns of male dominance and female deference that characterized middle-class culture, traditional politics, and certain aspects of working-class culture, the movement created alternatives to them. In Albany and elsewhere, young women who defied segregation inevitably defied the norms that defined middle-class femininity. By being bold, brave, and independent, they stepped out of their "place." The organizational ethos of SNCC also provided a space for older women, who had long worked as rank-and-file troops at the grassroots in local community struggles, to act as leaders and serve as role models for younger people. The emergence of women as indigenous leaders transformed gender relations within the movement. For example, many movement participants recalled seeing more women in the pulpit of the otherwise male-dominated black church during the 1960s than at any time before or after.

In places like Albany, Georgia, and Fayette County, Tennessee, women engaged in acts of protest and suffered arrests and beatings alongside the men. In a sense, this was neither new nor unusual. During the 1940s and 1950s, in places like Birmingham and Shreveport, women had led NAACP branches and local desegregation organizations and had consequently become targets of harassment and violence. In the eyes of many participants and observers, the acts of retribution were regrettable instances of white barbarity, but the role of female militancy remained obscured. What was new about SNCC was its embrace of women as key participants in mass protests and as leaders at the center of the struggle.

Because of its deepening irreverence for conventional standards of authority and respectability, SNCC bestowed credibility and honor on women and girls who protested and fought back in the most unladylike fashion. Young Ola Mae Quarterman drew attention to the Albany bus boycott by confronting a driver who attempted to force her into Jim Crow seating. "I paid my damn twenty cents and I can sit where I want," she proclaimed loudly before being arrested and carted off to jail.[61] Sixteen-year-old Shirley Gaines was arrested and beaten by the police after a protest to desegregate a bowling alley. Glenda Fleming, a rebellious junior high school student, participated in demonstrations in open defiance of her parents' wishes. College students like Bertha Gober and Bernice Johnson risked expulsion from Albany State—and placed their coveted degrees in jeopardy—by continuing their involvement in the protests. Bernice later left school voluntarily in order work in the movement full time.[62] Ella Baker, who summoned Bernice to her apartment to discuss her decision, gave her blessing once she was convinced the young woman had thought through the options carefully.[63] Ignoring the prevailing gender norms, these young women were warmly applauded by SNCC as exemplary militants. Quarterman's language and Gaines's recalcitrance contrasted sharply with the genteel, ladylike demeanor that Rosa Parks exhibited, which had made her an ideal candidate to personify respectable black resistance to segregation in Montgomery in 1955.

Women were also prominent in the struggle in McComb, Mississippi, where SNCC participated in an ongoing desegregation campaign and initiated a voter registration project. Brenda Travis, a tough and tenacious teenager, typified the kind of young women SNCC attracted there. The Travises were not one of town's upstanding families. Brenda's parents were poor and often out of work. In her class origins and defiant demeanor, Brenda resembled Claudette Colvin, the young girl whom the leaders of Montgomery's desegregation movement had deemed unsuitable to represent them in 1955. Colvin, pregnant, poor, and unmarried, had been thrown off a Montgomery bus weeks before Rosa Parks took her now-famous stand, but because Colvin did not fit the image of a respectable, middle-class citizen—because she was not a "lady"—her case was passed over by those who were looking for an opportunity to test the segregation laws and launch a public campaign. In McComb, SNCC welcomed Brenda Travis, even though, or perhaps because, she was labeled a rabble-rouser. She was only fifteen years old, but she was so determined to join the movement that she lied to Bob Moses about her age in order to be accepted as a volunteer.[64]

In August 1961, Brenda Travis and other students from Burgland High School sat in at a Greyhound bus terminal in Pike County, Mississippi. This bold action netted the leaders jail sentences, even though they were minors.[65] After two months in detention, Travis was released on probation, but she was arrested again shortly thereafter for participating in yet another protest. This time, Travis was sent to the Colored Girls Industrial School, a reform school for delinquents in Oaklie, Mississippi. When she was released from custody several months later, her future was uncertain. She was headstrong and stubborn, and her family had problems. Ella Baker quietly intervened and agreed to become Brenda Travis's legal guardian. For several years, Baker arranged for Brenda's care and education.[66]

As her political children entered into more and more dangerous situations, facing formidable enemies at great personal sacrifice, Ella Baker struggled to minimize the casualties of activism. She did not urge vulnerable people to take such risks and then abandon them to the tender mercies of white society. Brenda Travis might have become one of the movement's casualties had Baker not been willing to help out by "accepting a responsibility that [she] had not looked for but consequently [could] not refuse to accept."[67] It was a difficult and frustrating undertaking, and for a time the situation with Brenda put Baker in a state of "constant turmoil." Nevertheless, she saw to it that Brenda had schooling, went to summer camp, and could stay with her in New York for a while. Eventually, Brenda Travis was reunited with her family. Years later, she reflected that her relationship with Baker "changed the direction of my life."[68]

Baker's personal politics and radical humanist philosophy meant that she stayed in touch with local people after the smoke of battle had cleared. She made sure that parents were contacted when their children were arrested, that people going to jail had toothbrushes and hair combs, that those who were expelled from school for their activism found other institutions to accept them and obtained scholarships to support them. She always tried to minimize the emotional and physical hardships experienced by young people like Brenda Travis.

Baker paid particular attention to nurturing the development of young women, whether they had joined local campaigns or had volunteered as field organizers.[69] Ruby Doris Smith, who became one of the more vocal and active members of SNCC in 1961, benefited from Ella Baker's guidance and support.[70] A Georgia native and student at Spelman College, Smith joined the Atlanta Committee of Appeal for Human Rights, a SNCC affiliate, in the fall of 1960 as the group picketed segregated businesses in downtown Atlanta. Her initial foray into politics was modest, and so was her manner; but as she read books about social justice and met more young people involved in the growing movement, her interest and commitment deepened. Along with other SNCC activists, Smith went to Rock Hill, South Carolina, in February 1961 as an act of solidarity with local sit-in leaders who had been jailed and were refusing bail as a matter of principle. This was a bold act for Ruby Doris Smith, but SNCC's Judy Richardson has noted that "it later became a badge of courage."[71]

Smith's brief jail stint in South Carolina was nothing compared to what she and other activists endured a few months later. In May 1961, Smith spent two hellish months in Mississippi's notorious Parchman Prison for her participation in the Freedom Rides. These experiences made Smith more mature politically, more militant tactically, and more determined than ever. Like Ella Baker, she was more inclined toward self-defense than nonviolence. A serious organizer who never hesitated to speak her mind, she became by the fall of 1961 a formidable force within SNCC. According to Cynthia Griggs Fleming, her biographer, Smith had a reputation within the movement as "a savvy veteran . . . who was incredibly brave, as well as politically sophisticated."[72] Five years later, she succeeded Jim Forman as SNCC's executive secretary, becoming the first woman to hold that powerful position.[73]

The relationship between Ruby Doris Smith and Ella Baker was marked by genuine affection and mutual respect. When Smith was in the Hinds County jail in 1961, Baker wrote her a letter to boost her spirits and remind her of the value of her sacrifice: "I hope your present experience has not been too trying for you." Baker spoke of her "continued pride in the courage you have manifested on more than one occasion" and expressed "the hope that your health will not suffer as a result of your stay in Jackson."[74] In seeking to strengthen the resolve and confidence of Smith and other young women, Baker wanted them to rise toward leadership roles in the larger movement.

The transformative process of involvement in a democratically constituted social change movement represented a personal rite of passage for Ruby Doris Smith and the other young activists engaged in the struggle.

Men and women found that, as the meanings of "whiteness" and "blackness" began to change, so too did the meanings of womanhood and manhood. Men were moved to rethink masculinity, questioning the place to which white society had relegated adult black men and, at times, even questioning black men's aspirations to fulfill white norms of manhood. When Charles McLaurin talked about the day he accompanied to the courthouse door three elderly women who were attempting to register to vote in Ruleville, Mississippi, he said that this was "the day I became a man." It was not the day he was jailed or pummeled or delivered his first speech to a large audience or "led" someone from one place to another; it was the day he became the kind of humble warrior whom Baker so often praised. McLaurin's political and personal coming of age was signified by his supporting the political empowerment of a group of poor black women.

Many teenagers became men and women in the dangerous and dynamic context of the evolving civil rights movement. They fell in love, had their first sexual experiences, and defied their parents or allied with them on issues that were more important than doing chores or smoking cigarettes. They experienced local government officials' wrath and vigilantes' violence as adults, not as children. They made life or death choices every day that had consequences not only for themselves but also for people whose trust and confidence they had earned. It was a coming of age like no other. They matured intellectually and emotionally in the Freedom Houses and Freedom Schools that SNCC established in dusty southern towns. In these rural communities, SNCC volunteers taught and learned from black folk who were old enough to be their parents or grandparents. In the process, they forged new identities at the same time that they forged new political ideas and strategies.

As the SNCC activists were tried and tested by the violence that so often met black people's open resistance to white supremacy, it is no wonder that young men in the movement were tempted to reach for the conventional mantle of manhood and act as protectors of "their" women or as the generals and soldiers in a war of liberation. Many of these young men had been socialized into the dominant society's attitudes about gender and behaved in sexist, even macho ways. What is surprising is not the degree of conformity to social norms but rather the extent to which many young men in SNCC began to rethink and reject conventional notions of gender in the process of reconsidering the meanings of race and class and redefining their own identities. For example, reflecting years later on his maturation in the movement, Charles McDew recalled that he embraced his male comrades and told them that he loved them in a way he could not have conceived of doing before he entered the movement. It was not a conscious decision to transgress gender roles; instead, it came somewhat organically out of the situation he found himself in. The ethos of heroism combined with humility bred such displays of warmth and affection. It was a different time, and McDew was consciously becoming a different kind of man.[75]

Lawrence Guyot, a tough, husky Louisianan who attended Tougaloo College and then worked with SNCC in Mississippi, was humbled by his exposure to women like Ella Baker and Pauli Murray, to whom Baker introduced him. He once made what he later admitted was a sexist comment in Baker's presence, and she calmly corrected him with a brief history lesson about women's role in the struggle. "I made one of the most idiotic statements I ever made," he confessed, "and I have never said anything like that since." In his opinion, there was "no one more compassionate or tougher" than Ella Baker; her example inspired him to see differently not only women's role in the movement but his own role as a man as well.[76]

Ivanhoe Donaldson, a New Yorker who attended Michigan State University, was described as a "shrewd and savvy hand at civil rights work" and a "polished pool player."[77] He understood his own transformation in the context of the patriarchal training he and most others had received before coming into the movement. "We came from homes where dinner didn't start until [the father] sat down, and he determined the rules of the house. But then in SNCC you are thrown in with women who are smarter and more talented . . . [and you come to realize] that manhood isn't the ability to knock someone down but finding your own humanity."[78]

What made these alternative practices and philosophies of gender possible within SNCC? In the early 1960s, it was clearly not any explicitly proclaimed feminist principles on the part of the organization. Probably a combination of factors was involved, but Baker's example and influence were crucially important. She was a striking exception to the predominant images that defined black womanhood; her style and demeanor encompassed socially ascribed masculine and feminine qualities—nurturing warmth coupled with a ruggedly unshakable confidence. That made her an inspiration to those who wished to step outside the boundaries of conventional, middle-class gender norms. It is tempting to attribute these norms to the "middle class" because they were certainly embraced more enthusiastically by that sector of the black community. However, through school and church institutions, working-class blacks also adhered to certain patriarchal family practices and restricted gender roles, even when the realities of their everyday lives prevented black women from conforming to the idealized model of homemaker and helpmate. Yet in regard to gender, as in SNCC's alternative approach to class, Baker's indirect influence was even more powerful than her direct presence. In SNCC's grassroots campaigns, young activists met and learned from poor and working-class women who had developed a striking independence of thought and action through years of hard work and repeated confrontations with whites in day-to-day resistance to Jim Crow. As SNCC activists followed these women's examples, they learned other ways of being men and women.

Although women had always been central to community-based campaigns for civil rights, they seldom were accorded recognized leadership roles, and their contributions were often unknown outside the locality and often forgotten after the struggle was over. In the Montgomery bus boycott of 1955–56 and the school desegregation battles in Little Rock and elsewhere, for example, Joanne Gibson Robinson and Daisy Bates played central leadership roles, but in the organizations with which they were affiliated, the Montgomery Improvement Association and the national NAACP, men were the principal spokespersons and decision makers. The MIA and the NAACP were hierarchical in their structures, with the result that gender and class inequities were perpetuated by the overwhelmingly male leadership. The strategy of racial uplift in the early and mid-twentieth century was rooted in the notion that the educated elite would skillfully guide the race toward progress, on the one hand lobbying and litigating for reforms and on the other grooming and socializing the "lower-class" elements to prepare themselves for integration. Restrictive norms of masculinity and femininity were part and parcel of the mainstream, middle-class approach to social change and to leadership roles.[79]

The SNCC activists always had to struggle against the tendencies toward elitism and male domination, but SNCC did enable women, workers, farmers, and youth to emerge as strong, effective, and publicly recognized leaders of the movement. This achievement was in no small measure the result of an active assertion of leadership on the part of SNCC women themselves. As SNCC developed a bold and brazen public image, bold and brazen women were attracted to it; and once they joined, no one sought to constrain them. Ella Baker nudged them along this path and cleared obstacles from their way whenever she could. As architect of SNCC's democratic approach, she in effect widened the space of leadership, so that those most marginalized or excluded from the centers of power in society and in civil rights politics could stand up and be heard. Her fundamental commitment to a democratic vision and inclusive political practice was not based on a feminist perspective per se, but unconsciously, Baker had laid a foundation for subsequent black and white radical feminist work.

MISSISSIPPI GODDAMN

FIGHTING FOR FREEDOM IN THE BELLY
OF THE BEAST OF SOUTHERN RACISM

· · · · · ·

Alabama's gotten me so upset
Tennessee made me lose my rest
And everybody knows about Mississippi Goddamn.
Nina Simone, 1963

During the tumultuous and decisive years of the early 1960s, SNCC played a leading role in the Black Freedom Movement in Mississippi. Young field organizers put the principles that Ella Baker had taught them into practice by working alongside poor and working-class black people in rural communities where white supremacy had seemed impossible to challenge. As a result, the organizers found themselves at the center of a mass uprising that overturned old stereotypes of downtrodden, passive, and terrorized black folk. Americans outside the South, both white and black, became aware of Mississippi Freedom Summer, the grassroots voting rights campaign conducted in 1964, only after the revelation that three young workers had been ambushed and brutally murdered by segregationists. By risking their lives for justice in the face of vigilante violence, SNCC's organizers experienced profound change in their lives, but they were sustained by the example of many black people in Mississippi for whom facing such risks had long been the price of defending their dignity. In Freedom Schools that were founded on the radically democratic pedagogy that Baker espoused and exemplified within SNCC, organizers taught literacy skills and academic subjects to young blacks and, in turn, learned about the underlying economic structures of white supremacy from their students. Discovering the enormous power of people acting together to confront injustice and inequality, SNCC volunteers and staff felt reassured of the vision that had drawn them to the organization.

One of the critical organizing principles that Ella Baker taught, and SNCC absorbed, was the meaning of self-determination in the context of grass-roots organizing in the South. For Baker, this principle was not an exclusively racial proposition, as it was often deployed, but simply the democratic idea that an oppressed group, class, or community had the right to determine the nature of the fight to end its oppression. Such self-control of the movement's leadership by those it purported to represent was essential in Baker's view. Most of SNCC's Mississippi work in the summer of 1964 was carried out under the auspices of a loose coalition called the Council of Federated Organizations (COFO). So, through COFO and the Mississippi Freedom Democratic Party (MFDP), SNCC worked to advance the right of poor black Mississippians to determine their own future.

The decision by SNCC to conduct a major grassroots voting rights campaign in Mississippi in 1961–64 was audacious. From Baker's long experience in the state and from the local activists with whom she had put them in contact, SNCC activists knew that Mississippi's notorious reputation was well earned. Some within the organization dubbed the project the "Move on Mississippi," as if an invasion of enemy territory were being planned. Some of the most brazen and vicious southern segregationists in the South were at the helm of state government there, and Mississippi had a long history of unchecked, often officially sponsored racial violence toward the black population. Many national civil rights leaders had simply written off the state. As Andrew Young, then an SCLC staff person, put it :"We knew the depths of the depravity of southern racism. We knew better than to try to take on Mississippi."[1]

Baker's perspective on Mississippi was precisely the opposite of Young's. She felt that the movement had to organize within the belly of the beast of southern racism rather than on its safer margins. This viewpoint was an expression of her class politics as well. In her words, "If you were supposed to be interested in bettering the lot of the have nots, where . . . [would] be a better start [than] . . . in the rural areas . . . [where] people had the hardest lives?"[2] Baker taught SNCC activists to look to the rural towns and plantations of Mississippi—"areas of greatest direst need . . . where people had [the] least"—as their central organizing challenge.[3] This was not a challenge to be undertaken lightly or quickly. The project that burst on the national stage in 1964 as Mississippi Freedom Summer grew out of years of less publicized, but no less arduous, work throughout the state.

Ella Baker's contacts with grassroots activists in Mississippi stretched back for decades, and she kept in close touch with her friends and allies there even when her work centered on other places. As SNCC sought to extend its organizing efforts into rural and small-town communities across the South, Baker turned to veteran activists in Mississippi to teach a new crop of organizers about mobilizing the masses of people to confront the power of southern elites.

· · · · · ·

AMZIE AND RUTH MOORE

Amzie and Ruth Moore were SNCC's first real contacts in Mississippi in 1960, and Bob Moses returned to the South to reconnect with them in 1961. Ella Baker had known the Moores for years. In many ways, they were exceptional people, but their story was not unlike that of many other militant local activists scattered throughout the region who had long fought racism and repression without much support from outside the South. As Charles Payne put it, they "had been accumulating political capital for a decade, in the form of contacts, networks, knowledge of resources, and personal credibility, capital they were able to transfer to the younger activists" whom Bob Moses and Ella Baker would introduce them to.[4] They were eager to receive the help that SNCC was offering, especially with the understanding that local leadership would remain in charge.

Amzie Moore had grown up dirt poor and left Mississippi for the first time when he was drafted into the military during World War II. He had joined the Black and Tan Party, a group of Negro Republicans active in the South during the 1930s, and later he helped found the Regional Council for Negro Leadership. After the war, Moore served as the head of the Cleveland, Mississippi, chapter of the NAACP. As the owner-operator of a small gas station, he had a greater margin of economic independence from whites than most black people in and around Cleveland. But even independent black business people were hardly immune to racist discrimination. During the 1950s, Amzie and his wife, Ruth, suffered constant harassment and economic reprisals as a result of their activism. Ruth Moore, a beautician whose small business also gave her a certain independence, was as active, committed, and fearless as her husband. Ella Baker and Ruth Moore maintained a close relationship, even when Ruth's and Amzie's marriage fell apart during the early 1960s.[5]

Amzie Moore, like Ella Baker, had numerous run-ins with the national office of the NAACP. He felt that the officers in Washington and New York were sometimes insensitive to the perilous conditions faced by organizers in the Deep South. An outspoken militant, Moore often slept with a gun under his pillow.[6] He was as intolerant of the snobbery of local black elites as he was of the vitriolic racism of Mississippi whites. In 1955, he complained: "The Negroes with money are in a world of their own here in the State of Mississippi. They live to themselves and they don't want things to change . . . they are not interested in the freedom of the common Negro of Mississippi, but they buy their fine cars, furs, homes and stay very much to themselves."[7] Despite their slight degree of economic independence, Ruth and Amzie Moore never enjoyed much financial stability, and by the mid-1950s they had been pushed to the verge of financial ruin. White-owned banks and businesses, in a carefully concerted effort, threatened them with foreclosure and bankruptcy. After Amzie Moore insisted that these problems were the result of his NAACP activities, the national office had offered some help, but the couple's financial situation remained precarious. It was, in part, the desperate plight of organizers like the Moores that had led Baker and her New York allies to form In Friendship in 1956. Amzie and Ruth Moore were among of the first recipients of In Friendship's aid.

Ella Baker made frequent visits to Mississippi during the 1950s and 1960s, often staying at the Moores' home in Cleveland. The bustling household felt more like an office, meeting place, and movement hotel than a private residence. In a letter to Ruth expressing gratitude for her hospitality, Baker joked, "Thank you for the very lovely stay in your home. It meant so much to me to be able to 'rest' for a few days. I say rest advisedly because there is not too much difference between your home and my office [as far as] the number of calls and requests for information and assistance are concerned."[8] The Moores, like the Shuttlesworths in Birmingham and the Simpkinses in Shreveport, were the kind of fervent and unwavering fighters Baker was always drawn to. She wanted the young people in SNCC to meet them and learn from their example.

More than any other person in SNCC, Bob Moses benefited from Amzie Moore's political tutelage. Baker knew that Moore, who had only finished two years of high school, had much to teach the Harvard-trained Moses about the politics and economics of racism in the Delta and how to organize against it. Years later, Bob Moses acknowledged his debt: "Amzie was my father in the movement . . . that was how I learned to organize . . . I heard my way through the world. I listened to Amzie. I just listened and listened. I watched him, how he moved."[9] Moses was immediately convinced that the national movement had to support the kind of work that Amzie and Ruth Moore had been doing in Mississippi. The initial contacts between Moses and the Moores were the organizational beginnings of the efforts that would peak in the summer of 1964 with the national focus on the Mississippi movement, Freedom Summer, and the Mississippi Freedom Democratic Party.

When Bob Moses said, "We did for the people of Mississippi what Ella Baker did for us,"[10] he meant that SNCC field organizers and volunteers tried to absorb the wisdom of indigenous leaders, to build respectfully on the preexisting strength within the communities where they organized, and to provide whatever was lacking—funds, time, youthful energy, and certain skills. In other words, Moses followed the example that Baker had set within SNCC. She never professed to having created SNCC's ideology; rather, she identified and nourished the radical democratic tendencies apparent in the thinking of many of those who were drawn to the organization.

When Bob Moses returned to Mississippi in the summer of 1961 to lend his services to the fledgling movement there, Amzie Moore advised him that conditions were not right for a campaign centered in Cleveland, Mississippi. Moore felt that there was not enough local support there, even though he was personally eager to work with SNCC, having been impressed by what he saw and heard at the newly formed organization's Atlanta conference the previous October. So Moses looked around for another home base from which to launch the Mississippi organizing drive. He settled on McComb, a small town in the hilly southwest corner of the state, to be the headquarters for SNCC's voter registration project. An activist in the town had read about Moses's plans to register voters in Mississippi in *Jet Magazine*; he contacted Amzie Moore, who suggested that Moses look to McComb for a more promising start.[11] Moses enthusiastically agreed. This would be his first real attempt at organizing and the first major community-based campaign for SNCC's voting rights initiative.

The McComb campaign proved to be a baptism by fire. Within a few months of Moses's arrival, there were mass arrests, beatings, expulsions from school, and at least one murder—that of Herbert Lee on September 25, 1961. Lee—an illiterate black dairy farmer, the father of nine children, and a longtime member of the local NAACP—had driven Moses around town to meet local people. According to movement observers, he was singled out for retribution by local racists and was shot dead on a public street by a local white man, allegedly over a personal dispute.[12] After the controversy and violence of those first few months, the people who had initially welcomed Moses with open arms began to pull away. C. C. Bryant, the person who had invited Moses to McComb, was a railroad worker, part-time barber, NAACP branch leader, local bibliophile.[13] But after arrests, beatings, and confrontational protests, especially the unpopular arrest of some 100 high school students, Bryant took a step back and distanced himself from the organization.[14] Moses and the volunteers who came to work with him in McComb nevertheless persevered, even when support from their initial contacts began to wane.

What kept Moses in McComb was the support that SNCC received from groups that had previously been on the margins of the town's black society and had been largely ignored by its civil rights leaders. Perhaps SNCC's greatest accomplishment in McComb was its ability to recruit local young people into its ranks. Brenda Travis, the intrepid teenager whom Baker protected and guided, was a native of McComb and joined the movement there. Hollis Watkins and Curtis Hayes, two teenagers from just outside McComb, also joined forces with SNCC as a result of the 1961 campaign; they eventually became two of the movement's strongest local organizers.[15] Watkins had grown up on a farm in southwest Mississippi, gone off to California after high school, and returned south after witnessing the Freedom Rides on television.[16] The local teenagers participated in desegregation protests at the local Woolworth's drugstore and the Greyhound bus station, leading to their arrest. Brenda Travis was expelled from school for her participation in the movement, an action that triggered a walk-out by sympathetic classmates. Impressed by the boldness and courage that SNCC organizers demonstrated, impatient youths were inspired to join the movement and soon provided inspiration to others.

Another variable that sustained SNCC during its difficult early campaigns was the unwavering moral and material support of Ella Baker. While one-time supporters like C. C. Bryant criticized SNCC for endangering children, Baker obtained financial resources from SCEF, offered strategic advice and encouragement at meetings, and aided individuals whose personal lives were thrown into turmoil because of their involvement. She also reminded SNCC organizers to involve parents and seek parental permission before working with minors in order to minimize opposition. Time and again, Baker expressed her confidence in SNCC's leaders, encouraging them to go forward despite their inevitable mistakes. Such reassurance from the voice of experience was essential to young visionaries just entering the vicious fray of race politics.[17]

According to John Dittmer, one of the lessons SNCC learned from the McComb campaign was that "the black middle class was under severe economic constraints and could not be counted on to support the assault against segregated institutions."[18] This observation points to a pivotal factor in the campaign.[19] Although SNCC was initially welcomed by the local black middle class—the people with education, reputations, and clout—as the struggle intensified that support quickly evaporated.[20] Dittmer concludes that during the course of the McComb campaign SNCC "intuitively grasped a vital part of its future mission in Mississippi: developing a sense of worth and leadership among people who had never been held in high regard in their communities."[21]

The SNCC organizers shook hands with sharecroppers who had dirt under their fingernails and sat at the feet of workers with dust on their boots. They sat on the front porches of ramshackle tenant houses not only to teach but also to learn. Their attitude, like Baker's, was based on the understanding that expertise and wisdom could emanate from outside a formally educated cadre of leaders. According to one SNCC activist, Baker taught the young people in the movement who had achieved some level of formal education that they were no smarter, and certainly no better, than the uneducated farmers and workers in the communities where they were organizing.[22] Barbara Jones (Omolade), a black SNCC worker from New York City, saw in Baker an example of how educated black organizers should comport themselves. "There was no room for talking down to anyone," she recalled. "There was never the expressed attitude that a person who was illiterate had something less to offer." Rather, Baker set a tone that said, "you've got your education, now sit and learn . . . learn what the conditions are that people have around . . . and it was hip to do that at that time."[23]

As she had done in the past, Baker emphasized that when the privileged took it upon themselves to speak for the underprivileged, the whole movement was in danger of losing its direction. Referring to whites with class and racial advantages and to blacks with "good positions," she argued that "those who are well-heeled don't want to get un-well-heeled. . . . If they are acceptable to the Establishment and they're wielding power which serves their interest, they can assume too readily that that also serves the interest of everybody."[24] This perspective on oppression and leadership crystallized during SNCC's early years in Mississippi and became a critical component of SNCC's work from that point on.

. . . . . .

DRIVING DEEPER INTO THE DELTA

The McComb campaign led SNCC organizers to conclude that the struggle had to be intensified if any meaningful change was going to occur. But how that should be done was the subject of ongoing debate. Those who joined Bob Moses in McComb—including Reggie Robinson, John Hardy, Chuck McDew, Charles Sherrod, Ruby Doris Smith, Travis Britt, and Marion Barry—had varying views on what route the Mississippi movement should take. A lingering source of disagreement, which had only been temporarily resolved at the Highlander Folk School meeting on August 11, 1961, was the question of whether SNCC should focus on direct action desegregation campaigns or on the voter registration drive that Bob Moses had initially envisioned. Slowly surfacing was another issue: what should be the future role of northern, mostly white, volunteers? Some SNCC activists reasoned that rural Mississippi's isolation was itself part of the problem of engendering significant change; from their point of view, SNCC needed to draw the glare of media attention to the conditions of disenfranchised blacks in places like McComb and lean on their northern white liberal allies, who professed to be great believers in black freedom, to take a firmer stand in defense of civil rights. One possible scenario was to bring in more outside supporters whose presence would attract such attention. But there was not unanimity on this. Some SNCC staff felt that the initiative should remain with the local people themselves. If SNCC focused on strengthening their skills, confidence, and resolve, they argued, all else would flow from that strength.[25]

SNCC undertook its massive voter registration campaign in Mississippi under the umbrella of the Council of Federated Organizations (COFO), a Mississippi-based coalition that was originally organized by Aaron Henry as an ad hoc group in 1961 and was reconstituted a year later by the new constellation of organizations active in the state. It included SNCC, CORE, a somewhat reluctant NAACP, and an even less active SCLC.[26] Much of the personnel and leadership came from SNCC and CORE. In 1962, COFO received a $14,000 grant through the Voter Education Project (VEP) administered by the Southern Regional Council, with funds provided by the Field and Taconic Foundations. The money helped defray the costs of purchasing supplies, printing literature, and providing subsistence-level stipends (in some cases ten dollars a week) to organizers, who were called field staff.[27] While COFO was most visible to the campaign's northern, white supporters, SNCC and, in some places, CORE represented the campaign to black Mississippians.

Of the nearly two dozen local projects that SNCC initiated in Mississippi during the early 1960s—including ones in Canton, Holly Springs, Natchez, Harmony, Clarksdale, and Jackson—the movement in the Delta community of Greenwood perhaps best reflected the spirit of organizing that Ella Baker advocated. Here, in what would become SNCC's state headquarters, lucrative cotton plantations were thriving while white vigilantes carried out ruthless repression. In the summer of 1962, young Sam Block, a native of Cleveland, Mississippi, and one of Amzie Moore's protégés, arrived on the scene and began the tedious process of meeting people, building relationships, trying to identify local militants, and earning people's trust through his dogged perseverance, thus following Baker's edict that activists meet people where they are. Block walked the streets and met local people. He not only talked to people about SNCC, voting rights, segregation; he also listened to the locals talk about their fears, concerns, and aspirations. Eventually, he asked people to come together in small meetings at the Elks Hall, where at first all they did was sing freedom songs. He gradually introduced political topics to the discussion. The project was slow to gain momentum, but after a while Greenwood would produce some of SNCC's most talented and hard-working local organizers, such as Laura McGhee and June Johnson. Julian Bond, a SNCC leader, described Sam Block's organizing style as essentially the formula for SNCC's day-to-day work: "SNCC organizers spent their first weeks in a new community meeting local leadership, formulating with them an action plan for more aggressive registration efforts, and recruiting new activists through informal conversation, painstaking house to house canvassing, and regular mass meetings."[28]

While Greenwood remained a vital center of movement activity throughout the 1960s, SNCC's work in Ruleville, Mississippi, in adjacent Sunflower County, attracted a middle-aged black woman who would come to personify the heart and soul of the Mississippi movement: Fannie Lou Hamer. One of twenty children born to impoverished sharecroppers in Montgomery County, Mississippi, Hamer never had the opportunity to obtain much formal education, but she was acutely aware of the world around her and the injustices that defined it. A woman of deep religious faith, she once remarked that the civil rights movement appealed to her as much as it did because she was simply "sick and tired of being sick and tired." When in August 1962 SNCC's James Forman and SCLC's James Bevel held a meeting about voter registration in Ruleville, Hamer was in attendance and volunteered, along with seventeen others, to travel to nearby Indianola, the closest courthouse, to register to vote. On her return home, she was fired from the plantation she had worked on for eighteen years; later, she was harassed and shot at by local vigilantes. These attacks only steeled her resolve, she allied herself with SNCC and began to work full time for the movement. In 1963, on her way back from a voter registration workshop in Charleston, South Carolina, Hamer and several others were jailed in Winona County and beaten in retaliation for their activism, an experience that Hamer would never forget and would often talk about. Buoyed by her strong religious faith, she was undeterred. What did she have to lose? she reasoned. "The only thing they could do to me was to kill me and it seemed like they'd been trying to do that a little bit at a time ever since I could remember."[29]

The first statewide campaign that SNCC and COFO carried out in Mississippi, and in which Fannie Lou Hamer and Ella Baker were intimately involved, was Freedom Vote. Held in November 1963, this was a mock election campaign meant to prove that the black electorate would cast their ballots if they were not blocked or intimidated from doing so. The campaign was carried out with the aid of student volunteers, most of whom were white, many of them from elite northern universities. Bob Moses, Ella Baker, and Amzie Moore had long understood that bringing outside resources to bear on the situation in Mississippi was necessary if things were ever going to change. Who, when, and on what terms were always in question. Allard Lowenstein, an eccentric white liberal activist and part-time academic, became the controversial figure at the center of the effort to get some of the attention and human resources the movement so desperately needed. Unfortunately, he made every effort to try to define the terms on which that support would be provided, which meant that he wanted the focus to be on him and his own liberal Cold War agenda. With some reservations, Moses agreed to allow Lowenstein, who had been introduced to SNCC through Clarksdale activist Aaron Henry, to recruit some of his former students from Yale and Stanford to work on the Freedom Vote mock election.[30] The decision to accept the role proposed for Lowenstein and this new cohort of volunteers was not made lightly. It would have far-reaching consequences, both positive and negative, for the evolution of the Mississippi movement.

The plan was to have volunteers travel around the state collecting ballots in an unofficial election process free of intimidating and uncooperative registrars and other deterrents that typically thwarted black participation. A successful turn-out would expose the fact that vigilante violence, economic harassment, and blatant corruption, not apathy, were the obstacles that rendered 98 percent of the state's black electorate voteless.[31] Organizers ran an interracial slate in the November election, in part to demonstrate that the campaign was not solely about race but about building a more inclusive democracy in Mississippi. The gubernatorial candidate was Aaron Henry, the black Clarksdale pharmacist and state NAACP president, and Ed King, the antiracist white chaplain of Tougaloo College, ran for lieutenant governor.[32]

While there may have been some rationale for a biracial gubernatorial ticket in 1963, the reason that two men headed a political campaign in which women formed the largest base of local support is more complex. It foreshadowed the intricate gender politics of the late 1960s.

Some men and women in SNCC felt that black men should be the titular heads of black freedom organizations, thus serving as a counter to the racist culture that sought to systematically relegate them to the denigrated status of boys.[33] Some also felt that black women, long denied the "provisions" and "protection" ostensibly afforded to southern white ladies, deserved to be shielded from the harshest aspects of political combat. These sentiments notwithstanding, there were inclinations and ideological influences pulling SNCC and local activists in another, more egalitarian, direction. Passionate new democratic tendencies pushed hard against old patriarchal habits. The determination to allow each individual to make a contribution and play a role in his or her own emancipation; the emphasis on giving voice and space to those who had previously been excluded from leadership; and the desire to "free men's minds" as Charles Sherrod once put it—all of these sentiments (none of which were articulated specifically in terms of gender) informed the creation of a fluid structure in which women's leadership could and did thrive.[34]

The inclination toward inclusion and a genuinely participatory democracy militated against the tendency to replicate the dominant society's concept of proper gender roles, which most black southern colleges actively encouraged. Even though the violation of dominant gender roles may have seemed an awkward form of racial transgression (black women who challenge sexism to this day are sometimes made to feel like betrayers of black men), it was a violation many women in SNCC made in their actions, if not in their verbal or written expressions. This nonsexist climate was attributable in no small measure to Ella Baker's influence. Writer Carol Mueller argues that Baker actually introduced the concept of participatory democracy to the progressive movements of the 1960s.[35] Others attribute it to Tom Hayden of the Students for a Democratic Society. Whether or not Baker technically introduced the idea, she lived and breathed and modeled it. It was the practice of a new type of inclusive, consensus-oriented democracy, which opened organizational doors to women, young people, and those outside of the cadre of educated elites. Baker helped mold a political environment that did not offer any explicitly feminist rhetoric but in practice countered overt sexist practices and rigidly circumscribed gender roles. This does not mean that sexism did not exist—but it was not institutionally supported or encouraged.

There were chauvinist comments, to be sure. The most often-cited is Stokely Carmichael's off-handed remark in 1964 that the role of women in the struggle was "prone." Even so, there was no serious language, consistent with SNCC's ethos, that allowed Carmichael or anyone else to justifiably exclude women, especially black women, from work they wanted to do.[36] This was one of the points he wanted to make emphatically in an interview in 1995 when he was deathly ill and bedridden. "I would not have been taken seriously as a leader of an organization like SNCC if I had not taken seriously the leadership of women," he insisted. "A woman like Ella Baker would not have tolerated it," he added.[37] Carmichael's actions back up his words to a large extent. He appointed several women to posts as project directors during his tenure as chairman and applauded and occasionally deferred to the leadership of women like Ella Baker and Fannie Lou Hamer.

Some sociologists and some historians argue that as the 1960s wore on and militancy increased, a certain macho rhetoric began to undermine the full participation of women. This is only partly true. There was indeed more macho rhetoric, but militancy and radicalism, if defined broadly, were not masculine domains. In fact, in the latter half of the 1960s more women were in charge of SNCC projects than during the first half. Those sectors of the movement most prone to subjugating and marginalizing women were those individuals and organizations that portrayed women in a "black nation" as supportive complements to male political and decision-making roles. It was this kind of romanticized male dominance that Ella Baker worried about, although this was not a commonly held view in SNCC. Still, she felt it was important enough that she made a public statement about it. In a 1969 speech to the Institute of the Black World in Atlanta, she raised a concern that she discussed more in depth in an interview with John Britton a year earlier. This was the idea that a distorted view of black history led some in the movement to argue that women were beholden to men. Baker argued against the "concept," prevalent after 1965, "that black women had to bolster the ego of the male." In her words, "This implied that the black male had been treated in such a manner as to have been emasculated both by white society and by black women because the female was the head of the household. We began to deal with the question of the need of black women to play the subordinate role. I personally have never thought of this as being valid."

By the late 1960s, SNCC embodied many variations of nationalism, but the more sexist formulations of cultural nationalists that Baker pointed to never materialized. Women like Muriel Tillinghast, Fay Bellamy, and Ruby Doris Smith Robinson were vocal in bringing the organization's popular chairman, Carmichael, down a notch or two when he began to make statements without consulting the organization.[38] From 1960 until the organization's demise, many committed and capable women organizers found the expression of their political ambitions in SNCC, in ways that were simply not possible in SCLC or even the NAACP. As Charles Payne put it: "Women obviously represented an enormous pool of untapped leadership potential. . . . SNCC, despite the traditional expectations of sex roles held by many of its members, was structurally and philosophically open to female participation in a way that many older organizations would not have been."[39] And if any place was fertile ground for the growth of black women's leadership, it was Mississippi.

While the struggle for political power in Mississippi represented a landmark in the southern-based struggle for black freedom, that forward movement came at a hefty price. Violence, harassment, and intimidation escalated, and movement leaders lived with the constant threat of attack.[40] And women were not spared. Homes and offices were routinely firebombed, and arrests, beatings, and death threats were commonplace. Regular acts of violence directed at so-called uppity or dissident black individuals had kept the old order in place. As the black resistance movement grew, violence was increasingly directed at it.

Ella Baker got a first-hand look at the political terrorism that dominated the local scene when she traveled through the state drumming up support for the Freedom Vote campaign in the fall of 1963. On October 31, Halloween night, Baker and two of her young colleagues had a frightening encounter with a gang of local white thugs. Baker had just delivered a speech to a group of black businessmen in Natchez, Mississippi. The engagement had not been a rousing success. Baker was anxious to move on to her next appointment in Port Gibson, some forty miles away. Two volunteers, George Green, a twenty-year-old African American activist from Greenwood, and Bruce Payne, a twenty-one-year-old white political science graduate student from Yale University, were assigned to escort her from Natchez to her next stop. Even though she virtually lived on the road, Baker had never learned to drive; so she often relied on others to help her get from place to place.

When Payne arrived to pick Baker up at the house where she had been staying, he told her he was being followed. In an obvious gesture of intimidation, the two cars that had been following him circled the house while he was inside. After some hesitation, Baker, Payne, and Green decided to take their chances and travel as planned. When they started off, the cars continued to follow them; and when they stopped for directions at a gas station outside of Natchez, Payne was attacked and brutally beaten. As he got out of the car, the men jumped out of their car and punched and kicked him; they banged his head against the gas pumps before jumping back into their car and speeding off. Although Payne suffered facial lacerations and bruises, he did not need to be hospitalized, and the threesome drove on to Port Gibson, where they immediately filed complaints with the U.S. Attorney General's Office and the FBI. Several days later, Green and Payne, who were both warned to stay out of town, had another run-in with the two same men and were shot at and run off the road.[41]

Ella Baker had seen the ugly face of southern vigilantism many times, yet every encounter was horrifying. The beating she witnessed that Halloween proved to be a preview of the even more deadly violence that awaited SNCC activists as their campaign for racial and economic justice in Mississippi shifted into high gear. Baker was both fearful and determined. Despite harassment and intimidation by local officials, between 80,000 and 85,000 Mississippians cast their ballots for Freedom candidates. The mock election contradicted the myth that blacks in the state were politically apathetic and would not vote even if given the opportunity.

Despite the relative success of Freedom Vote that year, 1963 was marked by escalating violence against the southern-based Black Freedom Movement and in the society in general. The type of assault Baker witnessed outside Natchez was not uncommon. Between February and May 1963, SNCC workers and supporters in Greenwood were under constant threat, enduring shootings, firebombings, beatings, and arrests. In June, protesters in Danville were so brutally beaten by local police after a series of desegregation protests that observers labeled the event "Bloody Monday." Medgar Evers, an NAACP organizer, was shot to death in the driveway of his home that same month. His assassination sent anger and fear ricocheting through movement circles and elevated Evers to the status of a national martyr.[42] Headlines across the country blazoned the brutal force that Birmingham's police chief, Eugene "Bull" Connor, unleashed against young civil rights demonstrators and the racist recalcitrance of Alabama's newly elected governor, George Wallace, who made a personal pledge to block school desegregation in the state. The violence in Alabama peaked in September 1963 with the bombing of Birmingham's 16th Street Baptist Church, resulting in the tragic deaths of four young black children. The year was also punctuated by events that put civil rights on the national political agenda. The widely publicized March on Washington was held in August 1963, and President Kennedy met with key black leaders before the march. Some civil rights leaders were optimistic, while others saw the continued violence as the prelude to a second Civil War. The assassination of President Kennedy in November struck many as a culmination of the crescendo of violence that had been building up the whole year. While the nation mourned the death of the president, movement activists mourned the growing number of those wounded and killed within its own ranks. Civil rights advocates wondered whether the new president, Lyndon B. Johnson, a liberal Texan, would be more or less sympathetic to the growing black freedom struggle and willing to defend it against the attacks it was suffering.

· · · · · ·

REFLECTING ON EXPERIENCE AND SETTING A COURSE

In November 1963, a week after the Freedom Vote, COFO leaders, including members of SNCC, came together for a meeting in Greenville to reflect on their experiences in the voter registration campaign and the events of the year and to make plans for the group's future work.[43] One of the most contentious topics of discussion was the role of white students within COFO, particularly the upper-middle-class whites who had been recruited by Lowenstein to work on the November campaign. It was at the Greenville meeting that the idea for Freedom Summer began to percolate. Even though Bob Moses supported the idea of utilizing white volunteers in the project, there was not unanimous support. John Dittmer reported that "many of the veteran organizers favored, at best, a limited future role for white students," and some were opposed even to that. Ivanhoe Donaldson, a SNCC staff person, made his feelings known: "I came into SNCC and saw Negroes running things and I felt good." Inviting an influx of whites, he concluded, would mean that they would be losing "the one thing where the Negro can stand first." The heated discussion included accusations that the presence of rich white students might reinforce a deferential "slavery mentality" in southern blacks. This meeting was the continuation of a long and layered process of grappling with the movement's internal racial dynamics.[44]

At year's end, the SNCC staff met again, this time in Atlanta, in order to revisit some of the issues that had been debated so passionately in Greenville and to confront other dilemmas as well. As was SNCC's practice by 1963, the five-day meeting was divided into two parts. For the first four days, there was open discussion involving staff, ex-staff, and advisers, which presented an opportunity to discuss any issues of concern that people wanted to raise. The final day was "a closed executive committee [meeting] in which final decisions and implementation were decided upon, based on the consensus of the larger meeting."[45] Ella Baker participated actively in both parts of this important gathering.

The marathon meeting in Atlanta proved, if nothing else, that SNCC's members had moved decidedly to the left. While the events of 1964 would further radicalize some individuals within the organization, transforming them from reformists into dedicated revolutionaries, the tone and substance of the discussions at this key meeting indicate that by December 1963 a core element of SNCC's leadership was already there. Those in attendance included Bob Moses, Charles Sherrod, Frank Smith, Gloria Richardson, John Lewis, Courtland Cox, Michael Thelwell, Stokely Carmichael, Jim Forman, Dottie Zellner, Ivanhoe Donaldson, and Joyce Ladner, along with a host of staff and volunteers who floated in and out. Gloria Richardson's presence is particularly significant because she had just led a pitched battle with police in the streets of Cambridge, Maryland, in which shots were fired on both sides, protesters were teargassed, and many feared for their lives. The demands of the Cambridge activists were economic as well as political; the large number of unemployed workers there wanted jobs, as well as elected officials who were accountable to community needs.[46]

The scope of the questions that the group wrestled with over the course of the five-day gathering was posed by Howard Zinn in a presentation on the first day. Having consulted with Baker beforehand about the state of the movement and the proposals that would be considered, Zinn presented their joint views when he spoke. Sounding much like Baker, he posed the questions: "What is our economic and political goal? What kind of revolution do we want?" Pushing SNCC to clarify and more clearly articulate its priorities, Zinn asked, "Do we compromise on some questions to achieve other goals?" He went on to juxtapose long- and short-term goals and suggested the importance of having an organizational structure that could help realize those goals. Baker immediately seconded Zinn's commentary and urged that there be a more in-depth and focused political discussion of some of the points he had raised before any policy decisions were made. This was Freirean teaching by two masters of the technique. Through a series of probing questions, the two veteran activists challenged their young counterparts to tap their own experiences in order to come up with the answers.[47] At the same time, they did not hesitate to put their own views on the table. Zinn was very specific in his attack on "the profit motive"; he emphasized that "the race problem, where SNCC got its start, has emerged into a different and bigger issue." Baker had always believed that the fight against racism was a "bigger issue," with economic, cultural, and international implications that could serve as a catalyst for more comprehensive social change agendas.[48]

Baker reminded those at the Atlanta meeting that the purpose of voter registration efforts was not simply to enable black people to cast a ballot for one political party or the other. For her, voter registration, like integration, was never an end in itself, even if the campaign's outside funders may have thought so. "We got into the Voter Education Project program as a convenient method of organizing and working in the field, knowing we might lose the money because we weren't serving VEP's purpose," she argued.[49]

The role of whites in the upcoming summer project was also taken up again. Moses pointed out that the earlier COFO meeting in Greenville had decided to limit the number of white volunteers to 100, but the plan being "pushed by Al Lowenstein [was to] pour in thousands of students and force a showdown between local and federal governments in an election year."[50] Joyce Ladner then questioned whether "there might be a negative reaction from local Negro leadership because of this outside invasion."[51] Marion Barry "argued in favor of the saturation proposal," insisting it was SNCC's "big chance to force Johnson to commit himself."[52] Moses declined to give a "personal opinion" because it was "a divisive issue," stating he would defer to the will of the group.[53] Ella Baker too was silent at this point, allowing the group to air its feelings; she would weigh in on the issue at a subsequent meeting.

There were disagreements on this and other issues, but what was most palpable in this lengthy discussion was that no one on SNCC's core staff was thinking along the narrow lines of integration and gradual, legal reform, as most had been in 1960. Instead, they were considering broader goals and strategies that would empower the masses of black people. Activists espoused competing visions of the specific goals and objectives of the movement, but all were looking for a longer-term, more radical perspective. Their political ambitions had swelled along with their courage and determination. Frank Smith's comments in the meeting are but one example of the militant positions that were being put forward: "We need to get more hungry people to be massed to turn over the government . . . what we need on February 1 is not a demonstration but a general strike."[54]

As the discussion grew more intense, Moses intervened to suggest that what the group really needed was a systematic program of study to assess the implications of one course of action versus another. Zinn and Baker had hoped that such a program would come out of the meeting, not as a way to delay a move toward greater militancy but rather to ensure that the move was a steady and sober one. Following up on Moses's suggestion, Zinn urged SNCC to "enlist some of the best minds around" to explore ways of transforming or reordering the society. Zinn further pointed out that many academics had historical and theoretical understandings but lacked the close contact with grassroots people and struggles that informed SNCC activists' views. After several hours, "Ella Baker expressed the consensus of the group, that SNCC develop a formal program of economic education for its staff."[55]

Zinn later led a discussion on internal staff education and posed the dilemma of activist-intellectuals: "Education in the classroom tends to be removed from the real problems because educators are by nature removed from where most people live. That is the nature of academic life and why most SNCC workers have left it."[56] Zinn proposed a different type of education and scholarship, one grounded in political struggle and everyday life. A priority for Ella Baker was to ensure that the group was thinking through carefully the political implications of the actions being planned. She gently criticized the group for placing "too much value on action and not enough on planning," strongly supporting the proposal for expanding internal education, and later requesting permission to pull together a broader group of advisers, beyond just herself and Zinn, to help the young activists navigate their way forward. The group agreed.[57]

The December meeting was intense and exhausting. Many sessions lasted well into the night; even on New Year's Eve, the group did not adjourn until 9:30 P.M.[58] The meeting proved to be a pivotal moment in the life of the organization, and Ella Baker was actively engaged in pushing the process along. The leadership group emerged with a deepened commitment to the poor and working class and to the economic issues that plagued their lives; a more open and flexible, although still ill-defined, policy on self-defense, reaffirming the tactical efficacy of nonviolence while factoring in local traditions of self-protection; and finally a reiterated commitment to the importance of education within the movement.

· · · · · ·

FREEDOM DAY, JANUARY 1964

January 22, 1964, was designated Freedom Day in Hattiesburg, Mississippi, and SNCC's leadership convened again, this time for a day of action rather than of talking. Freedom Days were frequently organized as a specific time to orchestrate massive voter registration efforts in a public fashion. Cleveland Sellers remembered these events as affirming and proud moments for the young organizers: "There is nothing so awe-inspiring as a middle aged sharecropper trudging up the steps to the voter registrars office clad in brogans, denim overalls, and a freshly starched white shirt—his only one. I grew to love Freedom Days. More than anything else they provided the motivation that kept me going."[59]

A medium-sized city by Mississippi standards, located in the southwest quadrant of the state, Hattiesburg had a resistance tradition that dated back to the 1940s and before. During the late 1950s, NAACP militants such as Vernon Dahmer and Medgar Evers, two movement martyrs, had worked to build an NAACP youth chapter in the city. Joyce and Dorie Ladner, who became legendary SNCC organizers, grew up in Hattiesburg and were mentored by Dahmer and other local activists. Both women also acknowledged Ella Baker as an empowering role model who inspired, taught, and encouraged them as they matured politically. Despite the efforts at activism, there had not been much progress in Hattiesburg by 1962. So blatant was the disenfranchisement of blacks there that the federal government had indicted the local registrar, Theron Lynd, for his persistent refusal to register qualified black voters. Injunctions notwithstanding, Lynd continued to hold his post in defiance of federal mandates and continued to deny Negro citizens the right to vote.[60]

In the spring of 1962, SNCC workers Curtis Hayes and Hollis Watkins arrived in Forrest County, of which Hattiesburg was a part, and began organizing. In the SNCC tradition, such organizing meant getting rooted and building personal relationships that could be converted into political ones. By November, Hayes and Watkins had built a core of local supporters, rented a house that served as SNCC's headquarters, and held several small informal meetings.[61] SNCC's civil rights organizing focused more attention on the sleepy little town than its residents expected. Bob Moses and Dona Richards, also a dedicated SNCC activist, had just married. They moved into the second floor of the SNCC headquarters and devoted their time and energies to the organizing effort in Hattiesburg. Over many months of agitation and steady, tedious outreach, SNCC developed a base in Hatties-burg that included the likes of the tireless seventy-year-old Mrs. Virgie Robinson and a homemaker and small business person Victoria Gray, who joined SNCC's staff full time in September of 1962.[62]

There was a special emphasis on the 1964 Freedom Day in Hattiesburg. Encouraged by their success in the mock elections in November and eager to keep the momentum going, SNCC members, working within the context of COFO, planned a massive one-day voter registration campaign targeting Hattiesburg. This strategy closely resembled the R-day protests that Baker had organized with the Simpkinses in Shreveport several years earlier. On January 21, new troops arrived in town, including Fannie Lou Hamer, Aaron Henry, and Dave Dennis, CORE's Mississippi director. Ella Baker and John Lewis, who traveled together by train from Atlanta, arrived in the late afternoon. By that time, a serious strategy session was under way at the SNCC headquarters to plan the next day's events. Organizers made detailed contingency plans in case of arrests and the ever-present possibility of police or vigilante violence, which in Mississippi were often one and the same. Since some fifty ministers and rabbis were coming to Hattiesburg from northern cities to act as observers, SNCC planners felt sure that the national media would also be present in force.[63]

As Baker considered the strategies being proposed for Freedom Day, she also mulled over the speech she was scheduled to deliver at the mass meeting later that evening. The strategy session had to be cut short in order for the group to walk over to the church, which was already overflowing with Hattiesburg residents. As one participant described it, "Every seat [was] filled, every aisle packed, the doorways jammed; it was almost impossible to get in."[64] The speakers on the roster had all earned their battle scars in the struggle: John Lewis had been bloodied during the Free-dom Rides; Annelle Ponder had been beaten with Fannie Lou Hamer in the Winona County Jail; and Lawrence Guyot, the young SNCC worker from Louisiana, had done time in the Mississippi's notorious Parchman Prison. All were inspirational. Baker sat patiently nodding and applauding the other speakers' remarks. And then it was her turn.

Aaron Henry, the Freedom gubernatorial candidate, gave his long-time co-worker a special introduction. There was mutual respect between the two veteran activists as they shared the stage that evening. Henry was the son of Mississippi sharecroppers who served in World War II, then went to college on the GI bill, and became active in the NAACP. He had been jailed, harassed, and firebombed.[65] In other words, he had paid his political dues and earned Baker's respect in the process. A reluctant but gifted orator, Baker lived up to the praise Henry had bestowed on her. She began her remarks by reminding the crowd, "We have come here tonight to renew our struggle." Evoking the memory of Medgar Evers, the Mississippi organizer who had been shot dead by Ku Klux Klan assassins when he returned home from a late-night meeting only six months before, Baker roused the crowd. Evers had spent time in Hattiesburg, and the people there knew and loved him. Her remarks were punctuated by applause and shouts of "amen." Evers's murder was a painful and sobering reminder of the risks entailed in the actions they were collectively undertaking that evening. Although the next day's events were on everyone's mind, Baker did not address the immediate questions at hand; rather, she took the opportunity to remind her audience of the movement's larger goals. This was Baker the revolutionary in action, transcending more attendant concerns and reaching for something larger, greater, more inspirational. What was at stake? What were they really fighting for and why? These were the fundamental questions Baker wanted her audience to ponder.[66]

As Howard Zinn's report on Baker's speech attests, she offered her listeners "a vision beyond the immediate." She advised those gathered that evening that, even as they prepared to face hostile crowds and potentially violent police in defense of their right to vote and to use public facilities like any other citizen, these goals alone were not enough. She challenged her listeners to consider the importance of economic and systemic changes, insisting that "even if segregation is gone, we will still need to be free; we will still have to see that everyone has a job. Even if we can all vote, but if people are still hungry, we will not be free . . . Singing alone is not enough; we need schools and learning . . . Remember, we are not fighting for the freedom of the Negro alone, but for the freedom of the human spirit, a larger freedom that encompasses all of mankind."[67] For many people, the movement was about the ballot and defeating Jim Crow, but in Hattiesburg and elsewhere Baker pushed repeatedly, passionately, and irrepressibly against those cramped ambitions to draw people toward a more comprehensive vision. Reiterating the sentiments expressed at the SNCC retreat a month before, she stressed the importance of linking economic justice to racial justice: "People cannot be free until there is enough work in this land to give everybody a job." We are not free, she continued, because "in this country, in a land of great plenty and great wealth, there are millions of people who go to bed hungry every night."[68] As SNCC embarked on another leg of its historic crusade into Mississippi, Ella Baker reminded both young organizers and veteran activists alike that poverty and class inequality and racism were intimately and inextricably bound up together and had to be a part of any truly liberatory freedom agenda.

On Freedom Day, over 150 local black citizens showed up on the steps of the Hattiesburg courthouse to register, in a town where—according to activists' estimates—only a handful of blacks who were eligible to vote were actually registered. Many of them had been in the church meeting the night before. Few were successful in registering, but organizers were pleased with the turnout and with the protesters' determination. Some aspiring black voters stayed on the courthouse steps from 9:30 in the morning until late in the afternoon despite the pouring rain.[69]

Hattiesburg was one of many sites of struggle in the campaign to desegregate and democratize the state of Mississippi during the 1960s, and each one of those sites had battle scars as a result. SNCC offices and the homes where SNCC organizers were staying were firebombed. Felony charges were leveled against organizers, and some did prison time as a result. In this intense and violent time, there was the scent of freedom in the air, and young people flocked to SNCC and its affiliate organizations to be a part of the social revolution that was sweeping the South, the epicenter of which was Mississippi. In a series of long and difficult staff and executive committee meetings, between January and June, Ella Baker assiduously guided, nurtured, and steadied the group as it built up steam going into Freedom Summer.

· · · · · ·

FREEDOM SUMMER

Freedom Summer was the most widely publicized of the SNCC projects in Mississippi, in part because hundreds of student volunteers arrived in Mississippi in several successive waves to aid the ongoing Black Freedom

Movement in the state. After a brief but intense orientation in Oxford, Ohio, the summer volunteers—the overwhelming majority of whom were white—were assigned to projects throughout Mississippi with the expectation that they would assist more experienced field staff in voter education and registration campaigns, staffing freedom schools and keeping the offices up and running.

The concept of Freedom Summer was to draw northern white students directly into the battle for racial democracy in the South and give them, their families, and communities—and hopefully the nation—a greater stake in the outcome. The 1963 Freedom Vote campaign had been the trial run. Charles Payne explains that the unchecked violence against black Mississippians was one of the principal factors that convinced Bob Moses of the need to pull other forces into the fray.[70] There had been five mysterious murders in the state between December 1963 and February 1964, but few people outside the area seemed to notice or to care. As a white SNCC staff member, Mendy Samstein, put it, before 1964 Mississippi organizers often felt isolated without any "relief from the daily and brutal confrontation they had with the whole local state system. There was no relief from that, there was no outrage . . . when Negroes were beaten or killed. Nobody seemed to care about that, nobody seemed to give a damn."[71] Black southerners had been resisting racism, collectively and individually, all along, placing themselves in danger with each challenge to white rule. The new idea was to ask others to take some of the risks and in the process to raise the stakes.

The renewed black freedom struggle had never been a blacks-only affair. Whites had been involved from the beginning. A handful of whites participated in the sit-ins, and a larger number, many of them northerners, had participated in SNCC's founding conference. And Bob Zellner, Bill Hansen, Connie Curry, Jane Stembridge, Mary King, and Casey Hayden had been involved with SNCC for two or three years by 1963. With Charles Sherrod's encouragement, white organizers had begun working in the Southwest Georgia Project in small numbers in the summer of 1963.[72] However, Freedom Summer would bring many unseasoned volunteers into Mississippi to work in communities alongside blacks in all facets of the organizing effort. At the outset, the two principal concerns were whether they would in some way undermine or usurp less confident black leadership and whether their mere presence would provoke local whites to more acts of violence. Baker understood these concerns, but she was a steadfast supporter of the project. In a series of SNCC executive committee meetings, she laid out her reasons.

On June 9–11, 1964, before the summer volunteers descended on Mississippi, SNCC veterans cloistered themselves away for a two-day meeting and retreat to review one last time the politics surrounding the project, examining what they wanted to accomplish and what dangers and obstacles they would likely encounter over the course of the summer. Ella Baker played an active role in the meeting. She began by framing the purpose of the project in this way: "One of the reasons we're going into Mississippi is that the rest of the United States has never felt much responsibility for what happens in the Deep South. The country feels no responsibility and doesn't see that as an indictment. Young people will make the Justice Department move. . . . If we can simply let the concept that the rest of the nation bears responsibility for what happens in Mississippi sink in, then we will have accomplished something."[73]

· · · · · ·

SELF-DEFENSE AND NONVIOLENCE IN THE SUMMER PROJECT

Another key issue taken up at the June meeting was the likelihood of violence against SNCC staff, volunteers, and allies and the implications of any form of self-defense. To some, it already seemed a bit of an oxymoron to call the movement nonviolent when it was under violent assault almost daily. And even though SNCC's name still embodied the concept of nonviolence, four years of vicious assaults, including several murders, had led some activists to reconsider that philosophical stance. For some veterans of the struggle, nonviolence was an ideal whose practical viability had faded over time. There had also been a turnover in SNCC personnel. Some of the more recent recruits had never been invested in the concept of nonviolence, regarding it as a reasonable tactic given the array of firepower amassed against the movement in the South, but never embracing it as a way of life, as most of the Nashville group had. The question of nonviolence was also reconfigured at this point because earlier political activity had been of a mass, public nature. Getting arrested or being beaten when standing with a group of protesters on the courthouse steps was very different from being attacked by vigilantes while driving on lonely roads at night. Doing grassroots work in communities where organizers lived in isolated areas with local families meant that they might encounter a different type of violence altogether.

One sobering factor for the young organizers was the fact that so many of the southern black people with whom they worked in the early 1960s were armed and prepared to shoot if shot at. The nonviolence training that freedom riders had received in 1961 and Freedom Summer volunteers received as a part of their orientation in 1964 emphasized avoiding conflict and deflecting blows if attacked; it did not prepare them to dodge bullets or consider how they might respond to local black traditions of self-defense. Many of the indigenous leaders whom SNCC workers encountered were not disciples of nonviolence at all. For them, being armed and ready to fire if fired on was a more effective deterrent to vigilante attacks than turning the other cheek. As Bob Moses summed up the contradiction, "We were nonviolent, but we were in the houses of people with rifles." He pointed out that Amzie Moore, whom he identified as his political father, sat up at night with a rifle across his lap protecting his home, his family, and the activists who were passing through. Amzie Moore shared Ella Baker's views about the limits of nonviolence.[74]

Baker was generally respectful of the commitment that some young people still had to the concept of nonviolence. Yet, when she was most candid, as she was in a 1980 interview, she acknowledged her inability to be passive in the face of violence: "I frankly could not have sat and let someone put a burning cigarette on the back of my neck as some young people did. Whether this is right or wrong or good or bad, I have already been conditioned, and I have not seen anything in the nonviolent technique that can dissuade me from challenging somebody who wants to step on my neck."[75]

When the issue of nonviolence came up in the June meeting, Baker spoke her mind. Charlie Cobb posed a question about a hypothetical situation in which a SNCC staff member or volunteer would come to the aid of a local person who was fighting back in self-defense. Would SNCC support this person? Baker's response was: "I can't conceive of the SNCC I thought I was associated with not defending Charlie Cobb. What is the basis on which it is now necessary to raise this question? In my book, Charlie would not be operating outside of SNCC if he did what he said."[76] Baker shared her views in other contexts as well. Stokely Carmichael (Kwame Ture) recalled conversations with Baker in which she openly discussed her support of black farmers in the 1940s who carried guns to defend themselves when their NAACP involvement became known and their physical safety was threatened.[77] Judy Richardson recalled that three stalwart local supporters of the Mississippi movement, E. W. Steptoe and Hartman and Sweets Turnbow, were known to have a shotgun nearby in any situation and were also known to profess their intentions to use a gun in self-defense if the need arose.[78] Bob Moses explained to Mary King: "Self-defense is so deeply engrained in rural southern America that we as a small group can't affect it. It's not a contradiction for a farmer to say he's nonviolent and also pledge to shoot a marauder's head off."[79]

The group listened to Baker's admonitions about not carrying their philosophical commitment to nonviolence too far, but for security reasons they decided it was best to avoid associations with weapons of any kind. The group voted officially the next day to bar any summer project participant from carrying a weapon. On a practical level, Baker agreed with this position, pointing out the likelihood that carrying guns would only give local sheriffs an excuse to use even greater force against the movement. How to negotiate this thorny issue in day-to-day situations was in practice left up to each individual's conscience. Some individuals did carry weapons at various times over the course of the summer and thereafter, but this was never a part of SNCC's official policy.[80]

Another equally difficult issue that came up at the June meeting concerned the racial and political implications of allowing so many whites to join the ranks of the southern-based movement. A young volunteer, Willie Blue, questioned whether blacks would let white civil rights workers into their homes. This had been a problem in other projects. Hollis Watkins asked how black activists would deal with their own "hatred of whites." And Don Harris further questioned whether the egos and confidence of local blacks would be diminished by the presence of educated white northerners. Baker cut through the litany of questions with a decisive challenge to the group: "The conversation sounds like this is the first discussion of white involvement. The problem is basically one of insecurity: Perhaps we have an inflated ego. Are we prepared to take the revolution one step further? We can't grow without examining our own [fears and doubts]."[81] Baker's meaning here is best understood by placing her comments in a broader context. The marathon meeting had drifted from discussions of direct action and bond money to "animosity" toward Mississippi staff members "because of the emphasis given to Mississippi."[82] It had ended up considering the problems that white volunteers might present. If SNCC activists were serious, Baker was saying, they would have to stretch beyond their differences, fears, and inhibitions to build a larger movement, forge uncomfortable but principled alliances, and raise the stakes in Mississippi. That is precisely what they did.

The influx of hundreds of young white students into the small towns and cities of Mississippi produced culture shock on both sides. It was not the southern dialect, the pace of life, or the food that represented the biggest challenge for the new arrivals; it was the sobering intensity of the situation the volunteers found themselves in. For those who might not have been fully aware of what could be in store for them as they trekked down to Dixie, June 20 was a baptism by fire. On that day, local authorities arrested three young civil rights workers—Michael Schwerner, James Chaney, and Andrew Goodman—who had been investigating a church bombing. They were reportedly released from jail and then mysteriously disappeared and were never heard from again. Their disappearance—and the eventual discovery of their brutally murdered bodies—brought a huge amount of public attention to the project and had a chilling effect on all those involved, especially SNCC's newest recruits. The case of the three missing civil rights workers, whose fate remained unknown all that summer, offered a graphic illustration of the dangerous ground SNCC veterans and volunteers were traversing. Still, only a handful of the volunteers withdrew from involvement after the disappearance of Schwerner, Chaney, and Goodman. But another critical question arose: was the movement exploiting the naive young volunteers who had ventured south over the summer? At the summer's end, Baker published a column in the *Southern Patriot* in response to that allegation. While she had feared for the lives of all young civil rights workers, she had hoped that Freedom Summer would enhance and transform their lives. So, it was not just a matter of what the volunteers could do for the movement, but also of what the movement might offer them. "We wanted their coming to mean something creative for each of them personally as well as for the movement," Baker wrote.[83] As always, Baker had faith in people's capacities to learn from the situations in which they placed themselves and from the people with whom they undertook to struggle for justice.

For the duration of the summer, Ella Baker played her customary dual role as logistical coordinator and movement philosopher. She helped with such details as funding, housing, and publicity, as well as with finding community contacts for project staffers and volunteers. But her most significant contribution was ideological. Baker wanted to make sure that the core leadership of the project, who would be working within the COFO coalition, had a clarity of purpose and a firm consensus about their politics and priorities for the summer. One priority she emphasized throughout was the need for an agenda and a curriculum for liberatory education.

. . . . . .

FREEDOM SCHOOLS

One of the most visible outcomes of the summer's efforts was the establishment of over fifty Freedom Schools involving hundreds of students and volunteer teachers throughout the state.[84] The first experiment with an alternative classroom as a site for political organizing and popular education
was undertaken during sncc's first few months in McComb, after dozens of
students were suspended from public school for their political activity.
During Freedom Summer, a more ambitious plan was put in place to link
political and practical education to community organizing in Mississippi.
Ella Baker drew on her work with the Worker's Education Project in the
1930s to advise the architects of McComb's Nonviolent High School and the
subsequent Freedom Schools modeled after it. The Freedom Schools were
a welcome supplement to black education in Mississippi, which was in a
desperately impoverished condition because the state government spent
nearly four times as much money per year on white students as it did on
black ones.[85]

In 1964, Charlie Cobb, a student from Howard University and a talented
young writer, was the prime mover behind the Freedom School idea, later
aided by Bob Moses, Freedom School director Staughton Lynd, a phalanx
of volunteers, and a crop of eager students, mostly adolescents and teenagers.[86] Ella Baker's influence in this project, as was the case with most
other sncc efforts, was subtle but palpable. When she taught New York
workers about consumer issues, labor laws, and African history during the
Great Depression, she did so as a way to both bolster their literacy and to
embolden them politically. Similarly, when sncc set up Freedom Schools,
the teacher-organizers fashioned a learning environment and method of
instruction consistent with their evolving political and philosophical beliefs. Rigid hierarchy was abandoned, and the curriculum was designed to
reflect the world and heritage of the schools' students.[87] These were different kinds of classrooms than the Mississippi students had previously
encountered. Nonviolent High and the Freedom Schools that followed
were the first manifestations of a type of "free space" within the movement
for creative and intellectual work.

Coordinated by Staughton Lynd, a white history professor at Spelman,
the first schools opened on July 4, 1964. Lynd ran off the outline on an old
hectograph machine, loaded the copies in the trunk of his car, and delivered them to the Freedom Summer orientation in Oxford, Ohio, in June.

According to Lynd, the curriculum was not a blueprint for the inexperienced young teacher-organizers but "a security blanket," of potential help in case they ran out of things to do.[88] Lynd neither met nor conferred with Ella Baker about how to run the schools. He did not even recall her presence at the New York meeting funded by the National Council of Churches that mapped out the logistics for the schools, but her influence was pervasive and undeniable. The orientation at Oxford, the informal instructions that were given to summer volunteers (some of whom were teachers by profession), and the curriculum itself bore a striking resemblance to everything Baker modeled and advocated with regard to education.

It was almost poetic that radical education had assumed center stage in a movement inspired by the reluctant but relentless teacher Ella Baker. The establishment of the Freedom Schools was an amazing accomplishment. Literacy and an understanding of the Constitution were necessary for black citizens to pass the qualifying test enabling them to vote; so there were practical goals similar to those of the Citizenship Schools, but the Freedom Schools went well beyond the basics. Indeed, they embraced a radical pedagogy and a radical philosophy that were an extension of Baker's teaching style and method, which had been reinforced and popularized through her interactions with SNCC activists every day for four years. Tom Wahman, a twenty-six-year-old teacher from New York, described his understanding of the goals of the Freedom Schools as follows: "We want to bring the student to a point where he questions everything he reads or is taught—the printed word, movies, the 'power structure'—everything." Teachers hoped to encourage students to be more literate and knowledgeable and to apply those intellectual skills to the black freedom struggle.[89]

When the curriculum and structure were still in the planning stages, Baker was called in to help shape the content and philosophy of the project. A SNCC supporter, Lois Chaffee, helped coordinate a major conference on Freedom Schools in March 1964 and invited veteran activists and educators like Baker and Septima Clark to attend and give guidance. When Baker accepted the invitation, Chaffee wrote to her to say that the organizers of the conference were "ecstatic": "We really do want your stamp on the stuff we tell those kids this summer."[90] Ella Baker served as "chairman" at the conference held at the union hall of District 65, located at Astor Place in Greenwich Village, and funded by the National Conference of Churches. The meeting helped lay the groundwork for the Freedom Schools.[91] Baker also consulted with Bob Moses and John O'Neal, a COFO staffer, about the screening and recruitment of prospective teachers.[92] During an all-day conference at Tougaloo College on April 25, Baker met with the summer school administrative committee.[93] The schools were designed as much to build youthful leadership for the movement as they were to facilitate the acquisition and sharing of knowledge.[94] In the Freedom School curriculum, self-knowledge, applied knowledge, and critical thinking were all strongly emphasized as essential components of a participatory democratic process. Although the Freedom School project had a clear approach and definite curriculum, Lynd emphasized that each teacher and class had a great deal of autonomy in deciding what worked best for them. This was an extension of the decentralized structure of SNCC itself.[95] The freedom schools were sites for creative teaching and learning. Judy Richardson, a black New Yorker from working-class roots who had attended Swarthmore College, was impressed with the use of haiku poetry as one of the many innovative teaching devices employed in the schools.[96]

Ella Baker's influence was evident in each Freedom School classroom. When SNCC's core leadership talked about teaching and learning within the context of the Black Freedom Movement, they talked about Ella Baker. "She was a consummate teacher," one SNCC member recalled, "never pounding us, 'You must do this, you must do that,' [but simply] by raising questions."[97] So, what are we trying to accomplish? she would probe. Are we all in agreement? What do we really mean by that? These were her kind of questions. Her method of inquiry often helped anchor or center an unwieldy conversation. Another SNCC activist made similar observations: "Miss Ella would ask key questions, and through the asking of the questions, certain things became revealed."[98] Ella Baker's approach to teaching and learning was the governing ethos of the Freedom School experiment.

Baker's pedagogical style paralleled that of her contemporary, Paulo Freire, the radical Brazilian educator. Three key tenets of Freire's educational philosophy can be found in Baker's practice and in the Freedom Schools themselves. The first is the notion that "to teach is not to transfer knowledge but to create the possibility for the production or construction of knowledge."[99] The second is the idea that teaching and learning should be reciprocal; it would be a contradiction for a teacher who believed in "democracy and freedom" to "at the same time act with arrogance" and be unwilling to listen across boundaries of difference.[100] The final perspective that Freire and Baker shared, one that was manifest in the practices and philosophy of SNCC's Freedom Schools, is skepticism about the conservative impact of traditional ways of teaching and a conviction that a more democratic learning environment has a liberatory potential. Baker had long complained about black female teachers having their freedom of expression "curbed." Freire criticized "the reductionist mentality that talks only of training skills" meant to strengthen "the authoritarian manner of speaking from the top down. In such a situation speaking with, which is part and parcel of any democratic vision of the world, is absent, replaced by the more authoritarian form: speaking 'to.'"[101] These were Baker's sentiments about education as well. Forging an arena for democratic learning and teaching was a critical component of Baker's revolutionary vision of individual, institutional, and societal change.[102]

The final significant feature of the Freedom Schools was the type of student that they targeted. Everyone was welcome, but in their orientation the Freedom School teachers were told to expect the children of SNCC's main constituency, the southern black poor. In an analytical article about the impact of the Freedom Schools written for *Southern Exposure* in 1965, author and attorney Len Holt wrote: "The teachers-to-be had been told that most of their students would be from the 'block,' the 'outs' who were not part of the middle class of Mississippi." He added, "The purpose of the Freedom Schools is to help them begin to question."[103]

In a memo to SNCC's executive committee in January 1964, Charlie Cobb made a strong case for Freedom Schools as a critical component of SNCC's work over the summer. First of all, he indicted Mississippi's schools and then laid out the importance of education as a battlefield of struggle. "Mississippi's impoverished educational system is also burdened with virtually a complete absence of academic freedom, and students are forced to live in an environment that is geared to squash intellectual curiosity and different thinking." He concluded that "[t]he state of Mississippi destroys 'smart niggers' and its classrooms remain intellectual wastelands." The challenge facing SNCC and COFO then was to invigorate the intellectual lives of young black Mississippians, to "fill an intellectual and creative vacuum . . . and get them to articulate their own desires, demands and questions."[104] The next challenge was to help them to act on those desires and demands.

THE MISSISSIPPI FREEDOM DEMOCRATIC PARTY AND THE RADICAL CAMPAIGNS OF THE 1960S AND 1970S

· · · · ·

What Ella Baker did for us, we did for the people of Mississippi.
Bob Moses, 1996

The Mississippi Freedom Democratic Party (MFDP) came into being on April 26, 1964, at a rally of 200 people in the state capital of Jackson. It represented in its humble birth a truly democratic alternative to the whites-only state Democratic Party, and it had a brief moment on the national political stage at the Democratic Party Convention in Atlantic City, New Jersey, in August 1964. The formation of the MFDP was the successful culmination of four years of life-altering, heart-wrenching, awe-inspiring organizing by a determined little band of freedom soldiers advancing county by county throughout the state. Its success was not determined by what would be won at the convention but rather by what had already been achieved by virtue of the delegation's arrival there. The bus and car caravans began to roll into Atlantic City early on the morning of August 21. Some had driven all the way from Jackson; others from different parts of the South and North. Ella Baker had arranged the logistics and planned for delegates to stay at a hotel called the Gem. And a gem it was not, but the rooms there were all Baker could squeeze out of the MFDP's meager budget. Aaron Henry, the leader of the delegation, complained about "the worst accommodations imaginable."[1] However, what MFDP delegates lacked in resources and physical conveniences, they made up for with their righteous determination.

Ella Baker navigated the treacherous, yet familiar waters of national politics with a fierce resolve that made it possible for grassroots activists such as Fannie Lou Hamer to elude politicians' attempts to silence them and speak to a national audience about the oppression they suffered and their hopes for American democracy. The pivotal events of August 1964 not only transformed the national context for the civil rights movement but also reshaped SNCC's political perspective, strategic approach, and evolving identity. Two objectives guided MFDP: affirming black self-determination and challenging northern-based white allies to take a stronger stance in support of the southern-based movement. For some, like Ella Baker, it was a calculated political gamble. It would either win a tactical victory, providing Mississippi activists with another tool with which to push for full freedom, or it would expose the limitations of mainstream party politics and strengthen the resolve of those same activists to find creative and truly democratic methods to realize radical social change.

Mississippi blacks were excluded from participation in Democratic Party precinct meetings—the first phase of the delegate selection process— through a variety of extralegal means: economic threats, physical intimidation, and chicanery. The MFDP delegates and their supporters documented this process of systematic exclusion and moved on to form their own alternative delegate selection process and state party. The MFDP was a grassroots independent initiative, but the goal was to operate sufficiently within Democratic Party rules to be able to demand recognition at the Democratic National Convention.

Freedom Summer volunteers and SNCC and COFO staff circulated literature and canvassed rural and urban communities throughout the state to urge Mississippians to participate in the alternative process of electing their own freedom delegates to go to the Democratic National Convention and hold up two Mississippi alternatives to the nation; one racist and backward-looking, the other democratic and forward-looking. Many activists had decided that black political exclusion was the linchpin holding the entire southern system together. Once that was broken, other possibilities would be created, and black Mississippians would be a force to be reckoned with. Baker was not at all convinced of this, but she thought that any militant mobilization that bolstered local nonelite leadership was a good thing; so she was prepared to support it with all the energy she could muster. The MFDP was another attempt by SNCC to give some of the most oppressed sectors of the black community something of their own, an independent political organization run for and by Mississippi blacks. Once this new political tool was firmly in hand, the idea was that it could be used to extract concessions from northern liberals, to confront them in the most direct way possible to acknowledge the legitimacy of the grievances and claims of Mississippi blacks, and to rally and mobilize the collective strength of black Mississippians. Northern liberal Democrats had taken a hands-off policy while professing support in principle for black political rights. The idea of forming an alternative Democratic Party in the state that was based on inclusion rather than exclusion was designed to force the hand of northern liberals and simultaneously empower local blacks and their allies.

While young SNCC field secretaries donned overalls and boots and traveled the back roads of the state to drum up support, Baker put on her respectable gray suit and knocked on the doors of Congress, labor organizations, and civil rights groups to make sure MFDP delegates had the support they needed when they arrived in Atlantic City. Ella Baker was still on the payroll of SCEF, but Jim Dombrowski and the Bradens shared her assessment about the importance of the MFDP campaign; so the focus of her activity from the summer through the fall of 1964 was the MFDP. She agreed to act as director of the MFDP's Washington, D.C., office. Because the fledgling party had such meager funds, it could not have afforded to pay a full-time staff person, which made Baker's volunteer services all the more welcome.[2]

Much of the struggle to guarantee that the MFDP got a hearing at the Atlantic City convention occurred over the five-month period between the founding conference in April and the national convention in August. The MFDP was founded against the backdrop of African nations declaring their independence from European colonialism. Similarly, black Mississippians declared their independence from the prosegregationist state Democratic Party, which of course they had never really been a part of, and invited any whites bold enough to break ranks to join with them. Few did. But the MFDP was not simply trying to make a symbolic gesture; it wanted to test the resolve of northern Democrats, to have them make good on their promise of inclusion, and ultimately to obtain the power to elect politicians more responsive to their needs. The Democratic Party's convention in Atlantic City would become the place where the gauntlet would be thrown down. The MFDP would demand that the all-white delegation, the state party's so-called regulars, be ousted in favor of a "freedom" delegation.

Baker, the SNCC activists, and the members of the MFDP knew that this was not an effort they could undertake without allies. The new faction had to persuade enough delegates to support them if the issue was going to make it to the convention floor. In March 1964, even before the MFDP's founding convention, Ella Baker and Bob Moses attended the United Auto Workers convention, also in Atlantic City, and met at length with Joseph Rauh, a UAW lawyer who was a leading member of Americans for Democratic Action, a liberal organization. Rauh was eager to get involved in the MFDP campaign, after having talked with Moses earlier that year.[3] Also present was Mildred Jeffrey, a Democratic national committeewoman from Michigan and the mother of a Freedom Summer volunteer. Moses and Baker laid out a convincing case, and Rauh and Jeffrey were on board. On May 20, Moses and Baker went to Washington to again rally support. At a conference that had just ended, the Americans for Democratic Action had passed a resolution supporting the MFDP. Rauh recalls having another meeting with Moses and Baker in a Washington, D.C., park, where they discussed at length various contingencies related to the challenge.[4] Rauh agreed to serve as the MFDP's official legal counsel. Ella Baker then went over to the left-leaning Institute for Policy Studies and solicited white lawyer Bill Higgs to serve as another legal adviser to the campaign. He agreed.[5]

At the outset, and in principle, all the major civil rights leaders and most left-leaning liberals were behind the challenge. But how far would SNCC and the Mississippi delegates be willing to push the issue? What victory meant for them and what victory meant for many of their more moderate supporters was ultimately quite different. In preparing for the convention, SNCC and the MFDP had to chart a rugged political terrain to figure out who could be trusted and who could not. Baker helped them steer the course. For example, when Wiley Branton called a "Meeting of the Council for United Civil Rights Leadership for May 14 [1964] in Atlanta," SNCC staff feared that Branton's group would dilute their plans to orchestrate some type of direct action in Atlantic City; and Baker advised that "it would be important for the militant elements" to meet before the larger Branton meeting in order "to resist the pressure" to conform to a type of "unity" that would compromise SNCC and the MFDP's own agenda.[6]

In the final analysis, what appeared to be SNCC's and the MFDP's plea for inclusion into mainstream politics actually became the watershed that signaled SNCC's departure from the liberal fold toward much more radical directions. As a grassroots organizing strategy, the MFDP was a real success. It politicized many poor black Mississippians, developed new grassroots leaders, and even brought the dire situation of black people in the state to national attention. But the MFDP delegation's experience at the Atlantic City convention was frustrating. Because considerations of partisan politics outweighed those of justice and democracy, even the leaders of national civil rights organizations defected from the MFDP's cause. Ella Baker was not surprised to discover that politicians and the civil rights leaders who looked to them to produce change were reluctant to embrace a grassroots organization when it took an uncompromising stance.

Over the course of the spring and summer, thousands of people joined the MFDP. They were overwhelmingly black. While some of the official party leaders were men, the most visible, vocal, and influential leaders were women: Fannie Lou Hamer, the impoverished sharecropper from Ruleville, Mississippi, who had participated in Freedom Vote and who spoke powerfully about her life in struggle; Annie Devine, a one-time schoolteacher, insurance agent, and CORE organizer from Canton, Mississippi; and Victoria Gray, a young mother of three who ran a small cosmetics business in Hattiesburg and resented the middle-class leaders of the local NAACP because they functioned as a "closed social group."[7] The gender composition and dynamics of the MFDP reflected the characteristics of the grassroots movement of the 1950s and 1960s rather than the male domination that prevailed within more hierarchical organizations. In his book on the movement in Mississippi, Charles Payne asserts that by the early 1960s civil rights activity was defined by a "higher participation of women," in contrast to an earlier period when men, many of them World War II veterans, dominated the movement in the state.[8]

· · · · · ·

Southern black communities were emboldened and empowered as a result of the MFDP mobilization. The stranglehold of fear had been loosened, and the silence had been broken. And once the world saw the ugly reality of Mississippi's racism, some participants believed, it would be unable simply to look the other way. At least in part, they were right. Throughout the summer of 1964, Freedom Summer volunteers and SNCC/COFO volunteers and staff went door to door in small towns and cities throughout the state spreading the gospel about the MFDP and documenting instances of black voter intimidation and outright obstruction. They were joined by local young people who had been angry and dissatisfied with their lot long before the SNCC and COFO organizers arrived and were happy to finally have allies, resources, and a clear outlet for their pent-up political energies.[9] Young Mississippians like Sam Block, Willie Peacock, Curtis Hayes, Hollis Watkins, June Johnson, and Dorie and Joyce Ladner were among them.

When the MFDP held its nominating convention on August 6 in Jackson to select sixty-eight delegates to travel to Atlantic City as representatives of the party, Baker was once again asked to deliver the keynote address. This speech was different. Only two days before, the risks that the struggle for justice entailed had been dramatically revealed by the discovery of the bodies of the three missing civil rights workers. James Chaney, Andrew Goodman, and Michael Schwerner had been brutally murdered, and their mangled bodies had been buried in a dam near Philadelphia, Mississippi. Ella Baker stood before the grief-stricken crowd of 800 that had gathered in Jackson's Masonic Hall on that hot summer night and delivered a political message full of anger and determination. Sensitive to the agony that the families of the victims must have felt at that moment, Baker was both mournful and militant as she eulogized the three young men, and she urged movement activists to carry on where their three brave young comrades had left off. At the same time, she underscored the lesser value that white society placed on black lives: "Until the killing of black mothers' sons is as important as the killing of white mothers' sons, we who believe in freedom cannot rest."[10] And Baker did not rest. From speech making in Mississippi churches and meeting halls to lobbying in Congressional offices, she gave her all to the MFDP campaign.

As director of the Washington, D.C., office of the party, Baker played an important role in coordinating the MFDP's national political strategy and in anchoring its northern-based lobbying effort. Building on the groundwork she and Moses had laid through their spring outreach visits, Baker rallied liberal allies to pledge support for the Freedom Democrats. A white male, Walter Tillow, and a black female, Barbara Jones (Omolade), both New Yorkers and both nineteen years old, were assigned to assist her. They received an apprenticeship like no other. Baker did not relocate to Washington, but she oversaw the business of the office through routine visits and lengthy phone communications. Tillow recalls: "She would take the train from New York and take a cab over to the office. No one went to pick her up. We wouldn't do anything big or do any written stuff without talking to her on the phone. . . . We talked to her a lot on the phone to check with her. Money matters we had to discuss with her. We were supposed to be funded by COFO, but in essence we were funded by SNCC. To rent something, etc., we called her up at her apartment and she would contact Moses or Forman. Even news releases were discussed with Ms. Baker. She played a big role even though she wasn't there each day."[11] Later, after the Atlantic City convention, Lawrence Guyot and Michael Thelwell, who were more seasoned but only slightly older than Jones and Tillow, came on board to coordinate the next phase of the MFDP's challenge, but for much of the summer of 1964 Baker, Tillow, and Jones handled the work to be done in Washington.

Even after she accepted the post as director of the MFDP's Washington office, Baker continued to harbor serious doubts about exactly what the MFDP contingent could manage to accomplish at the convention, and she certainly never expected an all-out victory. Yet she acted as if she were at least guardedly optimistic as plans for Atlantic City moved forward. She hoped for an experience that would mature and radicalize the MFDP's young supporters and give activists from Mississippi a glimpse of the national political stage and their ability to wield some influence on it. So, with these broader goals in mind and her doubts tucked away, Ella Baker worked tirelessly to mobilize support. She called in some favors, utilized contacts with labor and civic leaders who had political clout, and deployed her media connections. She orchestrated mailings to sympathetic delegates, made extensive phone calls, and arranged personal meetings to lobby Democratic Party leaders face to face. Tillow and Jones were in awe of the finesse and savvy Baker exhibited in running the office. She was just as comfortable talking with a senator or a congressman as she was with one of the local activists from Mississippi.[12]

The naive young Walter Tillow remembered being dragged along to a meeting Baker had with Harlem's congressman, Adam Clayton Powell, a longtime associate whom she knew to be more interested in his own career and notoriety than in the democratic principles that SNCC and the MFDP represented. After Powell praised Baker, embraced her, and pledged his loyalty, she quietly told Tillow as they left the meeting, "He's not going to do a thing." The point of the meeting, Tillow later surmised, was to neutralize Powell and make sure he did not oppose the effort—and to demystify the presumed omnipotence of big-shot politicians for a young organizer like Tillow.[13]

· · · · · ·

A POLITICAL GAMBLE IN ATLANTIC CITY

When the weary but determined delegation of Mississippi farmers, beauticians, schoolteachers, and one pharmacist arrived in New Jersey in late August, the outcome of their long, arduous journey was still unclear. Baker had worked long and hard to mobilize support within the Democratic Party's left wing. At least ten state delegations seemed to be on board, and a handful of individuals were resolute advocates, including Edith Greene, a women's rights advocate and strong supporter of the MFDP, whose ideas would take a sharp turn to the right after the convention.[14] The UAW and Americans for Democratic Action had officially endorsed the MFDP delegates, as had Martin Luther King, A. Philip Randolph, and the NAACP. So, on the eve of the convention, many of the Mississippi activists were hopeful.

Two weeks after President Johnson signed the 1964 Civil Rights Act on July 2, an act Baker saw as too little too late, Baker and Fannie Lou Hamer went on a three-week campaign tour punctuated by rallies, press conferences, and meetings with prospective supporters and donors. They stopped in Washington, D.C., Baltimore, Cambridge, and Philadelphia and ended up in New York City on August 5 before heading back to Jackson for the nominating convention.[15] On July 20, Baker sent out a memo to MFDP supporters tying the importance of what was about to take place in Atlantic City to the presumed murder of the three young civil rights workers (which would be confirmed two weeks later): "Three mothers' sons who sought to secure political democracy for the people of Mississippi probably lie buried beneath the murky swamps near Philadelphia, a small town in that state. If they have paid with their lives for believing in the right of the governed to have a voice in the election of those who govern them, all Democrats who can register and vote with freedom are now challenged as never before."[16] The three young men who had come to symbolize the hope of the summer—that good would win out over evil, that hard work would be rewarded with their safe return, that even the brutality of Mississippi racists had its limits—were gone. With large photographs and posters of the three held high, the Mississippians heading off to Atlantic City were all the more determined to make sure the young men had not died in vain.

The first confrontation after they arrived in New Jersey was with the credentials committee of the national convention. Fannie Lou Hamer, the vice chairperson of the MFDP delegation, made an impassioned plea for recognition. All she had to do to make a compelling case against the blatant oppression and disenfranchisement of Mississippi blacks was to tell her own story. She had been threatened, evicted, and beaten by local police for daring to assert her rights as an American citizen. How could northern liberals who professed their commitment to equality and democracy ignore Hamer's ordeal or fail to recognize the challenge it represented for the Democratic Party? But President Johnson was so fearful that Hamer's remarks would upset his electoral ambitions that he called an emergency press conference just as her speech was going to be aired on network television to deflect attention away from the MFDP's most powerful spokesperson.

Protests outside the convention demanding the Democratic leadership take a stand, coupled with the unbending resolve of the Freedom delegates to be seated at the convention, created a series of crises for Johnson and his supporters. They did not want to give any political ammunition to the Republican candidate, Barry Goldwater, by having disruptions or defections in Atlantic City, nor did they want to appear to be callously insensitive to the compelling grievances of black Mississippians. White liberals such as Allard Lowenstein and Joe Rauh, who operated a bit more on the fringes of the Democratic Party mainstream, also faced a crisis. They wanted to please the Mississippi civil rights activists, with whom they had allied themselves going into the convention, but they wanted to do so without alienating the top leadership of the Democratic Party. The crisis spilled over to high-ranking black leaders, such as King, Wilkins, and Rustin. Northern black elected officials and civil rights leaders in attendance at the convention were lobbied hard by supporters of Hubert Humphrey, the aspiring vice presidential nominee, to try to avert a scene; and not wanting to alienate the man who was likely to be vice president, they did.

Much of the drama in Atlantic City was played out behind closed doors. There were numerous late-night strategy sessions in Martin Luther King's hotel suite, in the MFDP's makeshift office, and in the corridors of the convention hall. There were also impromptu vigils and the singing of freedom songs outside the hall. The top Democratic Party leadership sought, above all, to avoid bad publicity and a messy fight on the convention floor. Humphrey, aided by Walter Mondale and a coterie of aides, pushed for some type of compromise short of an all-out concession. The right-wing position at the convention was summed up by Texas governor John Connally, who blurted out in one discussion that he'd walk out if the MFDP "baboons" were seated. In the face of such racist opposition, MFDP sympathizers groped for a solution.[17] Congresswoman Edith Greene proposed one compromise, which would have likely resulted in seating nearly the entire MFDP delegation, but this proposal somehow got lost in the shuffle. The compromise offer that emerged was that the MFDP would be given two symbolic seats on the convention floor alongside the regular all-white delegation. "We didn't come all this way for no two seats," replied an insulted and adamant Fannie Lou Hamer.[18]

A series of confusing and overlapping meetings with a shifting list of participants resulted in the erroneous public perception, fueled by comments made by Joe Rauh, that the MFDP's representatives had accepted the compromise, which put at least two factions within the MFDP coalition sharply at odds. When news of the deal was aired, many of the MFDP delegates, who had not even had a chance to discuss—let alone vote on—the proposal, were outraged. Issues of process melded with debates about the merits of the compromise itself. Through maneuvering and wrangling that no one owned up to after the fact, a "deal" was announced before a full debate and deliberations could occur among the delegates. This put the Freedom Democratic contingent in the awkward position of either going along with a deal that had not actually been negotiated or publicly rejecting it and alienating some of their friends. Baker's old friend Bayard Rustin was a strong proponent of the compromise, insisting that it was a strategic step forward. Baker remained wholly unconvinced. This was not the first time she had principled differences with a friend; still, this was a heartfelt issue, and there must have been some disappointment in Rustin on Baker's part. Rustin's biographer, Jervis Anderson, describes this moment as a watershed in Rustin's career.[19] His defection cost him the respect of the young SNCC activists, some of whom he had developed close ties with over the years. Ever the democrat with a small "d," Baker was more concerned about the closed character of the decision-making process than about the backsliding of individuals, even those she respected. She was furious at how the so-called decision had been made and at the presumptuousness of those who tried to persuade the MFDP delegates to go along with it after the fact.

When it was announced that a compromise had been reached, Baker was in a meeting with the Nebraska delegation, lobbying hard to persuade its sympathetic members to support the MFDP's request to be seated as a group. She was suspicious as the discussion dragged on "that the man who was in charge of the meeting apparently had been alerted to stall until he got some feedback" from another delegate, who Baker realized was governor of the state. When the chairperson interrupted the discussion to make an announcement, Baker "could tell what had taken place." After the compromise was announced, some expected that Baker would bow out gracefully as the chair attempted to end the meeting and declare the issue resolved. They did not know her very well if they did. Baker had no intention of complying. "[H]e acknowledged my presence with the hope that I wouldn't have anything to say. Of course I took the position that the great loss was that of the people who were at the Convention, who had no opportunity to participate in any decision making."[20] Baker was angry and disappointed but not wholly surprised. She had seen political chicanery before, but her a priori doubts about partisan politics did not mute her anger at the final outcome.

In one of the private sessions after the compromise was broadcast as a done deal, Joe Rauh, who claimed to have been misled and misquoted in the original announcement to the press, pleaded with MFDP delegates to support the decision anyway, forgive any insults or injuries that might have been inflicted, and seize the opportunity to make an ally out of Hubert Humphrey. Baker cringed at the duplicitous nature of his appeal, which called on black people's "demonstrated . . . capacity for forgiveness and understanding." A fuming Ella Baker replied with a sharp impatience uncharacteristic of her usual manner of speech, "to call upon us to be understanding of Mr. Humphrey's desire to win, was saying, forget your need, your winning, and support his winning."[21] Baker resented this attempt to manipulate the good will of the delegates and persuade them that someone else's interests were more important than their own. This was the ultimate insult in her opinion. Baker gave Rauh a tongue-lashing that he would never forget. He had made some remarks to the delegates and received polite applause until Baker spoke and the tone of the meeting shifted. "I don't care about traitors like Humphrey," Baker thundered, and then she turned her wrath directly at Rauh. "She just cut me to ribbons," he recalled a few years later, partly offended by the attack but partly impressed by its skillfulness. "If you're going to get it," he remarked, "might as well get it from an expert . . . and I got it from an expert. She just cut me up."[22] Baker viewed Rauh as a power broker attempting to use his knowledge and savvy to coerce inexperienced and idealistic activists into following a political course that was not in their best interest. She found this intolerable, and she was not afraid to say so. Baker made a point of publicly criticizing Rauh because she wanted to make it clear that while she had recruited him to serve as counsel to the MFDP, the partnership was not unconditional.

Another white liberal of dubious motives was Allard Lowenstein, who, after an extended absence from the movement, resurfaced during the Atlantic City convention. Baker was wary of Lowenstein from the start of his involvement in the movement, and the animus between them grew stronger over the years. Much of their antagonism was political, but some of it was attributable to their very different personalities. Lowenstein's overt arrogance, his sense of self-importance as a white person in a predominately black struggle, rubbed Ella Baker the wrong way. He was too impatient, too pragmatic, too eager to place himself at the center of activity and unwilling to wade through the tedious process of democratic decision making that Baker viewed as absolutely essential. Contrasting SNCC's model of organizing with Lowenstein's, biographer Bill Chafe wrote that Lowenstein's "elevated hierarchy and decisiveness; the other [SNCC's] promoted egalitarianism and tolerated ambiguity."[23]

Lowenstein recognized and deplored the vast extent of Baker's influence in SNCC. He saw her as allied with the more radical forces within the larger movement and believed she was the most effective and persistent force in pulling SNCC to the left, which disturbed him greatly. Conversely, Baker was critical of the liberalism that Lowenstein so openly embraced.[24] For Lowenstein, organizing was necessary to make the existing system work for everyone. For Baker, systemic change was necessary. She was as skeptical of career politicians and civilian elites as Lowenstein himself seemed leery of the masses. Much of Baker and Lowenstein's political sparring occurred indirectly. He pushed for a closer alliance with Democratic Party politicians, while she pulled for closer ties to the masses and their radical supporters. Competing worldviews clashed in Atlantic City: a pragmatic liberalism that placed faith in the Democratic politicians versus a principled radical vision that saw a circuitous long-term process of movement building as the salvation for the oppressed.

So, what was the MFDP to do? A handful of the delegates initially wanted to accept the compromise. The two official leaders of the delegation, Aaron Henry and Ed King, even argued its merits. And some of those who had been allies throughout the campaign were also advising moderation, compromise, and cooperation with the Democratic Party, even though establishment party leaders were unwilling to fully support the MFDP. It was the practical thing to do, urged King, Rustin, Wilkins, and Rauh. But the majority of activists who had trekked to Atlantic City on their own political pilgrimage were in no mood to compromise. In an all-night meeting at a local church, speaker after speaker pleaded with the MFDP delegates to be reasonable, to think strategically, to remember who their friends were. Baker said nothing. Her sentiments had already been expressed and were no secret. After the speech making, the delegates met alone to confer and opted to reject the compromise. Later that night, there was a vigil on the boardwalk where the group sang freedom songs; some cried, and others expressed anger and disbelief at what had happened—all against the backdrop of three haunting images, those of Chaney, Goodman, and Schwerner. The next day, the MFDP again captured media attention and disrupted the convention by forcibly occupying a row of seats with false credentials given to them by sympathetic delegates from other states. They had no intention of retreating quietly.[25]

The showdown in Atlantic City was a turning point in the movement. Many hopes had been riding on the outcome of the convention. Those hopes had been dashed. Time, energy, dollars, and lives had been invested to obtain this small slice of freedom. Many MFDP activists went away from the 1964 convention feeling cheated and betrayed. Baker had been less optimistic at the outset; so she was less disappointed in the end. She did not view the MFDP campaign as a defeat. Rather, she saw it as a "testing force" and an "alerting process." It had not wrested political power from the hands of the Democratic Party elites, but it had successfully mobilized a solid core of Mississippi activists. The experience had provided a set of political lessons for organizers, as she hoped it would, lessons that could not have been obtained from any book, lecture, or workshop. In Baker's mind, the MFDP experiment had "settled any debate" about "the possibility of functioning through the mainstream of the Democratic Party."[26] It also stiffened the resolve and determination of those who were not wholly alienated and disheartened to fight harder and to fight for more radical kinds of changes.

· · · · · ·

Shortly after the ordeal in Atlantic City, SNCC members gathered in October at the Gammon Seminary in Atlanta and the following month at Gulfside Church in Waveland, Mississippi, to map out what they would do next. Disappointed at the way things had unfolded in New Jersey and confused about who were and were not reliable allies, SNCC pondered its future. At the Gammon meeting, Ella Baker tried to negotiate with both sides of the growing rift between those who wanted SNCC to become a more disciplined organization (Forman) and those who wanted it to remain loose, informal, and familial (Moses). These two factions eventually referred to one another as the hard-liners and the floaters, respectively. In the meeting, Baker supported the idea that more power should be given to local people, as Moses did, but still felt that veteran SNCC organizers had a role to play and that more accountability was needed. She urged SNCC to consolidate, evaluate, and clarify its existing problems before it ambitiously took on new projects. She was trying to anchor the group as it grew, expanded its mission, and grappled with internal tensions and external attacks and criticisms.[27]

At the Waveland retreat, which Baker did not attend, fundamental questions were put on the table in over thirty position papers. The group debated issues of race, class, ideology, structure, and strategy. Some questioned again whether whites should play as major a role as they had in Freedom Summer. Since over seventy volunteers, most of them white, had requested to stay on and work with SNCC after the summer, the implications were considerable. Forman proposed a tighter structure and more discipline for the organization, while others complained that the spontaneous and decentralized character of SNCC would be lost.

A paper on sexism in SNCC emerged from a workshop on women's concerns. Crafted largely by two white women, Casey Hayden, a staff member in the Jackson office, and Mary King, who worked closely with Julian Bond on communications in Atlanta, the paper compared the treatment of women in the movement with the condition of blacks in the society. Those who might have been receptive at another moment were not terribly receptive then, when the organization was facing what they viewed as more pressing crises. It was also a time of heightened tensions about the growing number of whites in SNCC; since the paper originated from two white women, it was more readily dismissed by blacks in the organization, men and women, who felt it did not represent their gender experiences in SNCC. Many issues were aired at Waveland, but few were resolved.[28]

Overwhelmed and frustrated by the magnitude of the work, the decisions that had to be made, and the internal rifts that were brewing within the once harmonious family of freedom fighters, some SNCC veterans pulled back from the movement. Sherrod went back to school; Forman took a brief medical leave; and in December Moses dropped out and eventually traveled to Tanzania, where he lived for several years. For those who remained, there were enormous organizational challenges to overcome.

The year after the confrontation in Atlantic City SNCC took increasingly militant positions and came under increasingly bitter attacks from the media and mainstream politicians. Immediately after the Democratic Party convention, the NAACP held a meeting of liberal forces in New York at which Gloster Current attacked SNCC and its emphasis on grassroots democracy, as did Allard Lowenstein. Rustin would later concur, arguing that one of SNCC's problems was that it believed it could win a struggle relying solely on poor people. The principal targets of the attacks were those whom the FBI, liberals, and conservatives saw as radicalizing influences and, for very different reasons, wanted to undermine. Bob Moses was denounced as a draft dodger by Mississippi senator James Eastland because of his conscientious objector status in opposition to the war in Vietnam.[29] And Ella Baker was singled out for ruthless attack by conservative columnists Rowland Evans and Robert Novak in the *New York Herald Tribune* from September 3, 1964 to April 9, 1965.[30] The columnists excoriated SNCC as communist-dominated and raked Ella Baker over the coals as one of the "unquestioned leaders" of the MFDP, saying that her involvement was "cause . . . for concern."[31] One of Baker's allegedly sinister acts was her effort, according to Evans and Novak, to link the MFDP to SCEF and the Highlander Folk School. Another of their columns linked Baker and the MFDP to the *National Guardian* (a left-wing publication), the National Lawyers Guild (a radical association of lawyers and legal professionals), and leftist trade unions, such as the United Electrical Workers (to which Russell Nixon, general manager of the *Guardian* was formerly affiliated). When Baker addressed the annual convention of the United Electrical Workers in September 1964, calling for a greater alliance between the civil rights and labor movements, Evans and Novak characterized her as a "veteran leftist."[32] Conservative criticism was to be expected, but as Baker became more openly allied with the left wing of the movement, supporting SNCC even as it became more militant and agreeing to work for the HUAC-labeled subversives in SCEF, liberals also attacked her.[33]

. . . . . .

COMING TO GRIPS WITH BLACK POWER

Between the events in Atlantic City and the summer of 1966, both the movement and the nation underwent convulsive changes. Accelerating anti–Vietnam War protests melded with black uprisings in the streets of nearly a dozen cities. Ella Baker's beloved Harlem erupted in 1964, followed by Watts in 1965 and dozens of urban areas in the years thereafter. These tumultuous times tested even Baker's characteristic calm. After 1966, SNCC went through a profound transformation, not simply an escalation in militancy but also a shift in vision, philosophy, and structure. The demand for inclusion into mainstream institutions gave way, by the late 1960s, to the goal of revolutionary social transformation, and the goal of an interracial beloved community gave way to the call for black power, which for some—not all—meant black nationalism and racial separatism of some type. Baker thought that some aspects of that shift were progressive, while others were wholly counterproductive.

Ella Baker did not let her differences with the new tendencies within SNCC get in the way of her continued support for the original ideals of the organization as she understood them or her love and affection for the individuals involved, some of whom she had nurtured to political adulthood. After all, if she had sustained her relationship with the NAACP and SCLC, despite some very fundamental differences, why should she sever her relationship with SNCC because it had departed from the path she had envisioned for it? Baker's personal investment in the group was much deeper. So she continued to aid and defend SNCC even as many of its positions deviated from her own. At the same time, she began to devote her energies and attentions to other related organizations and causes.

The transition from the politics, personalities, and tactics of the early 1960s to those of the late 1960s has been analyzed as a shift from nonviolence to self-defense, from a southern focus to a northern one, and from interracial solidarity to black nationalism and separatism. The shorthand version of the polar vision of the early versus the late sixties is often summed up in the personas of the moderate and peace-loving ministers of SCLC, on the one hand, and the militant, angry warriors of the Black Panther Party, with whom SNCC briefly affiliated, on the other. As with all simple bifurcations, this one does not hold up, especially when one factors Ella Baker into the mix. She was a militant and a democrat, a Harlemite born in the South, who in many ways considered both places home. She was an internationalist who grounded herself unapologetically in black communities and working-class black culture, at the same time that she forged strong and enduring ties with white radicals and liberals and other peoples of color.

The years between 1964 and 1966 were intense, hectic, and confusing. The early consensus within SNCC had begun to unravel, an unraveling precipitated by internal and external factors. A spiral of unsettling and debilitating events hit the movement hard. Malcolm X, whom some in SNCC had come to admire, was assassinated in Harlem in February 1965. In Alabama, SNCC member Jimmy Lee Jackson was killed that February after a demonstration, and Sammy Younge was shot in January 1966. With great hopes for building an oasis of black political empowerment in the Deep South, SNCC helped launch the Lowndes County Freedom Organization in Alabama, using the black panther as its symbol. Those hopes quickly faded. And headlines and television newscasts across the country blazoned the images of civil rights workers brutally attacked by policemen on horseback on the Edmund Pettus Bridge outside Selma in March 1965. That event, termed "Bloody Sunday," further aggravated growing fissures within the movement over strategy and leadership. Some were disappointed with King's leadership, viewing it as vacillating and unresponsive to local desires. Prathia Hall, the former director of SNCC's project in Terrell County,

Georgia, and a devout apostle of nonviolence herself, was so upset by the way nonviolence was preached so rigidly by SCLC forces after the Selma attack that she left the movement entirely, exhausted and disillusioned.[34]

In a June 1966 protest march across the state of Mississippi, Stokely Carmichael, the newly elected, charismatic, and controversial head of SNCC, began to popularize the slogan "Black Power," with militant SNCC staffer Willie Ricks leading the chants as they caravanned from town to town. The march had been hastily convened by Martin Luther King in an effort to resume a one-man protest march initiated by James Meredith, who had been shot soon after he had started on it. Both the nonviolent and more militant factions of the rapidly evolving Black Freedom Movement were involved. King led the marchers, and the paramilitary group, Deacons for Defense, provided security, something to which King had reluctantly conceded.

Carmichael had defeated John Lewis for the chairmanship of SNCC in a close vote that some felt was less than fair. But once the organizational reins were in his hands, Carmichael was determined to steer the group in a more militant and nationalist direction. "Black power" as he conceived it was a part of that vision. The very tone of it made some of the movement's more mainstream supporters nervous. "Power"—as opposed to "rights"— was a scary proposition to white liberals and to many black liberals as well. It was not a term that scared Ella Baker, but she wanted to know whom this power was for and how it would be exercised.

Even though Baker was still held in high regard by Carmichael and others who had grown up politically within the environs of SNCC, she recognized that the organization had changed in fundamental ways, as had her relationship to it. The distance that developed between Baker and SNCC gave her a sense of loss. After all, SNCC had been her political family; the group made her feel at home more than any other organization with which she had been affiliated. Throughout her political life before 1960, she was in a constant struggle to be heard and listened to. As a SNCC adviser, she was revered, and she accepted that status with great humility. In the end, there was not a sharp break but a gradual drift and erosion of the relationship. She attended fewer and fewer meetings and was called less and less for consultation. Still, she spoke supportively of the new SNCC leadership, explaining that people held down so long would naturally be angry and impatient.

A sign of Baker's eroding relationship with SNCC was her low visibility in an organization in which she was once a ubiquitous presence. When Kathleen Cleaver joined SNCC's New York staff in 1967, she never saw Ella Baker come into the office, even though she sat at the front desk and greeted all visitors and Baker was frequently in the neighborhood. But Cleaver's recollections are a bit misleading. Ivanhoe Donaldson, who was in charge of the New York office at that time, recounted that he visited Baker regularly at her apartment on 135th Street to talk things over and solicit her advice. "Ella didn't come to the office," Donaldson said; "the office came to her."[35] Baker was still a valued adviser and sounding board for those who, like Donaldson, had come up through the ranks of SNCC in the early 1960s. Yet she was not the fixture that she had once been. Baker's involvement was diminishing, as was her health. She was no longer able to keep up physically with a hectic pace of activity.

Ella Baker never broke with SNCC emotionally, despite her political differences. The organization and the group of people in it were the political love of her life. In Baker's view, even the expulsion of whites from the organization was not a reason to condemn it or write off its remaining leaders, although this action clearly did not please her. Among her closest political allies in the 1960s were white radicals like the Bradens. At the same time, Baker had a keen sense of the cultural and psychological character of racism and the importance of black self-determination. In a cultural context in which whites were generally more educated, more privileged, and often more self-assured because of conditioning, it was easy for black leadership, especially the leadership of poor black southerners, to get displaced. Baker saw black power as a response to that fear. It was not her response, but it was one she understood. Baker had worked in all types of organizations, including all-black ones. In the 1930s, she and George Schuyler had made the tactical decision, based on the realities of segregation at the time, to organize all-black cooperatives and buying clubs while maintaining an affiliate relationship with the predominately white cooperative movement. And Baker's work with the NAACP branches had been, for all intents and purposes, black community organizing. Even when SNCC was formed, Baker understood and insisted on the importance of black leadership. But she never argued for a separatist/nationalist agenda. In her words: "The logical groups for blacks to coalesce with would be the impoverished white, the misrepresented and impoverished Indians . . . or the alienated Mexican-American. These are the natural allies in my book." However, she added the caveat that groups had to be united before they tried to forge coalitions with other groups: "You've got to coalesce from a position of power, not just for the sake of saying 'we're together.'"[36]

It should be noted that by 1966 there were several cleavages within SNCC, and those advocating black power were by no means homogeneous. Stokely Carmichael and Cleveland Sellers called for black power while asserting they were never antiwhite. However, the Atlanta SNCC group, which had undergone an enormous transformation from the early days when Julian Bond and Lonnie King had been involved, made no such professions. The members of the Chicago SNCC affiliate went so far as to call on blacks to "fill ourselves with hate for all things white."[37] It was Carmichael's more thoughtful advocacy of black power to which Baker was sympathetic. In an interview with John Britton in 1967, Baker explained that if one really listened to Carmichael, there was nothing offensive in his explication of the concept. From her point of view, he was talking about what SNCC had talked about for years: self-determination for oppressed people, namely, black people.[38]

Still, Baker felt the organization getting away from itself, as well as from her. She wanted to re-anchor it. She wanted to sit people down and push them to think through the issues they were taking on, sometimes without much thought or deliberation. As an almost last ditch effort, she proposed at a May SNCC retreat in Kingston Springs, Tennessee, that the organization consider a series of seminars on "revolutionary ethics," to be led by third world revolutionaries. The idea never bore fruit, but it seems as though Baker may have been groping for a way to challenge ideologically the direction she perceived the group was headed in. And since a delegation of SNCC people had just traveled to Africa and many were hungrily devouring *The Wretched of the Earth* by Franz Fanon, along with works by the Ghanaian leader Kwame Nkrumah and the Guinean revolutionary Amilcar Cabral, perhaps Baker hoped that bringing in third world revolutionaries could be a unifying force.[39]

From the summer of 1966 until December of that year, SNCC was moving more and more toward a black nationalist position. Carmichael had popularized the slogan "Black Power," but black power was not the same thing as black separatism. White and black antiracists could still work together in Carmichael's scenario, but whites needed to take up the task of working in white communities to combat racism there. As their roles became increasingly circumscribed and some slogans and attitudes turned explicitly antiwhite, many whites voluntarily left SNCC. Stalwarts like Bob and Dottie Zellner stayed the longest. In December 1966, SNCC met at the summer home of a black entertainer, Peg Leg Bates, in upstate New York. The secluded setting was chosen so that the group could focus on some of the internal tensions that were plaguing it and hopefully achieve a greater degree of peace in the large and fractious family. This was not to be. A general call went out that everyone should try to attend this meeting. So, even people who were no longer on SNCC's payroll or actively working in a project came to see whether fences could be mended and what could be salvaged of the organization they so deeply loved. The Atlanta office headed by Bill Ware was advocating a rigid nationalist agenda and came to the meeting to argue that whites should be expelled from SNCC altogether. Judy Richardson recalls that tempers were so inflamed that it was the first SNCC gathering—which were known for their passionate debates—where she actually feared for her physical safety.

Ella Baker was there, too. She drove up from New York City with Joanne Grant and Bob Zellner, a white southerner who began working with SNCC in the fall of 1961 after a summer internship at the Highlander Folk School. He had been arrested, beaten, and tortured in a Louisiana prison and had proven himself time and again as one of SNCC's most loyal members. His wife Dorothy had made similar sacrifices. Zellner did not know quite what to expect at the meeting, but it was an emotionally charged moment in his political and personal life. Ella Baker softened the blow he was about to be dealt. During the hour-long ride to the meeting site, "she prepared me for what was going to happen," Bob recalled. "She told me that she had been talking to people and that there was a strong move to make the organization a black organization so that it could be more effective in the north. She told me that Stokely and others intended to support the idea that we [Bob and Dorothy] be made exceptions because we had been with SNCC from the beginning and there would be a place for us. It was not cut and dry," he recalled her telling him. She did not advise him what to do but had likely arranged the car ride as a time to raise the issue and give Zellner a chance to reflect on the situation he was walking into. It was at this meeting that Zellner proposed a SNCC-sponsored project focused on building support for SNCC's agenda in the white community, which he and Dorothy would run and raise funds for. The idea was rejected because, as he put it, he was unwilling to be a second-class member of the organization; even though he supported black power, he felt strongly about the principle of black and white together in a single movement organization. He and Dorothy reluctantly parted ways with SNCC at that point.[40]

Three weeks later, despite palpable tensions and outright animus between certain factions of SNCC, Baker still retained confidence in the group's larger humanitarian mission, explaining to an interviewer that

"SNCC defines itself in terms of the blacks, but is concerned with all excluded people."[41] The group's deepening interest in and ties to revolutionary movements in other parts of the world bore her out on that point. But she was stretching it. Clearly, not everyone in SNCC, particularly the group in Atlanta, felt that way. When asked during the same interview, "What is the basic goal of SNCC?," Baker replied, "To change society so that the have-nots can share in it."[42] This had been her basic goal for some thirty-five years. After the upstate New York meeting, she had her doubts about the group's sustainability, but publicly she still wanted to put the best face on things.

For its first four years of existence as a collective, SNCC functioned like a political family. When the family broke up in the late 1960s, the results were traumatic for many. There were bitter debates, resignations, self-imposed exiles, and the severance of longstanding friendships. It was unclear to many exactly where Baker stood in all of the conflict. Perhaps most saw her as standing above it. Each side claimed her as its own. She never supported black separatism or the macho posturing that sometimes accompanied it, but Carmichael still held her in the highest esteem and vice versa. When he was asked to pay tribute to her at a SCEF fund-raiser in 1968, even though it meant sharing the stage with white SNCC members whom he had done battle with not long before, he "simply could not say, no."[43] His loyalty to and reverence for Baker outweighed any negative feelings he might have had toward former comrades.

In April 1968, at one of the most critical and confusing moments in the movement's evolution, Carmichael appeared at the Roosevelt Hotel in New York City to speak at the dinner for Baker, flanked by bodyguards and accompanied by an entourage. The atmosphere at the hotel that evening was palpably tense. It was an extension of the tension that was in the air throughout the nation. Only three weeks before, Martin Luther King had been assassinated while visiting Memphis, Tennessee, in support of a black sanitation workers' strike. Black urban neighborhoods across the country had erupted in violent protest at the news of his murder. The rubble was still smoldering when the interracial audience gathered on April 24 to honor Ella Baker. Rosa Parks had been scheduled to appear, but she was still too distraught over King's death to even make the trip. The gathering had been conceived of as a tribute, a fund-raiser, and a unity dinner. Anne Braden, who coordinated the event on behalf of SCEF, asked Carmichael if in his speech he might try to be conciliatory, to use the opportunity to bridge some of the gulfs and schisms that had been growing within the movement. He refused. "I was not there to gloss over serious political differences. I was there to honor Miss Baker plain and simple."[44] Although SCEF raised some $30,000 that evening, no political bridges were built.

In Ella Baker's view, "black power" was a misunderstood and sometimes misappropriated term. When it was framed as self-determination, she could identify with the concept to some extent. Referring to Carmichael, Baker observed, "I've seen him make some very profound developments from this whole concept of black power. I've seen him do it at a level that there is nothing irritating about it for anybody who is willing to have sense enough to deal with the facts at all." Her concern about the excesses and reckless use of black power rhetoric can be partly attributed to the fact that "black power" became, in some cases, an empty slogan taken up by young people "who had not gone through any experiences or steps of thinking" that Carmichael had.[45] For the inexperienced, it simply meant "give us what we are demanding now." But SNCC members who had marched, picketed, petitioned, and pleaded had, in Baker's view, earned the right to be impatient. They had also earned the consent of poor black southerners to speak in tandem with them and at times on their behalf.

Baker was supportive of intensified struggle, increased confrontation, and even sharper, more revolutionary rhetoric. She viewed explicitly anti-white sentiments, however, as counterproductive, misguided, and shortsighted. She saw some SNCC members' use of the term "honky," for example, as unfortunate and born of frustration and anger rather than a calculated political gesture.[46]

Baker compared the appeal of the new revolutionary rhetoric to the stale and unmoving demands and language of the more mainstream civil rights organizations and leaders at the time. Referring to a leaflet for "Solidarity Day," drafted by her friend Bayard Rustin, Baker confessed, "This doesn't touch me"; it "leaves me cold." She concluded: "I would think it would leave people who are closest to the activist movement, the younger people, even more chilled—so, I don't think it's unnatural for them [young black activists in SNCC] to feel the need for the more revolutionary method."[47] When she tried to explain to an interviewer in 1968 why she thought white liberals had such a hard time understanding the urgent demand for black power, she recited some lines of verse: "The frog beneath the harrow knows, where the nail point goes, while the butterfly upon the road, preaches contentment to the toad."[48] In other words, those with privilege and insulation from certain abuses have the luxury to insist on patience and moderation. Those experiencing the painful results of injustice, and those who identify with them and try to see the world through their eyes, have a different perspective altogether. For most of her adult political life, Baker's perspective was that of the frog beneath the harrow.

Baker worked as a paid member of SCEF until 1967 and functioned as consultant and board member after that. She continued to lend her name and waning energies to other campaigns and causes as well. The two principal areas of political work Baker focused on in the 1970s were opposition to political repression and persecution at home and to war, imperialism, and colonialism abroad. She also accepted an increasing number of invitations from women's organizations and participated in several of the founding meetings of the Third World Women's Alliance and the Women's Emergency Committee.[49] In 1969, Ella Baker went to Atlanta to deliver a talk at the Institute for the Black World titled "The Black Woman in the Civil Rights Struggle." There, she criticized sexist practices and attitudes within the civil rights movement and went on to describe women as the "backbone" of the movement, explaining that "[w]hen demonstrations took place and when the community acted, usually it was some women who came to the fore."[50]

· · · · · ·

FREE ANGELA, FREE OURSELVES

One campaign around a prominent woman activist that Baker took special interest in was the "Free Angela" campaign. A Communist Party member and Black Panther Party supporter, Angela Y. Davis had been implicated in a failed prisoner rescue attempt in California in which several people were killed. Davis was not directly involved, but a gun registered to her was found at the scene, and she was closely associated with two of the men involved, prisoner-activist George Jackson and his younger brother, Jonathan. This provided enough of a reason for the authorities to issue a warrant for her arrest and, when she fled, for the FBI to declare her one of its ten most wanted persons. Davis was eventually captured, and an international campaign was mounted to win her release, with her supporters arguing that putting her in jail was an attempt by the government to silence a radical black voice for change.

At one of its regular board meetings held in Birmingham, Baker proposed that SCEF should get involved in the National Free Angela Coalition. Anne Braden recalled years later that she was not altogether convinced that Angela's campaign was where SCEF should place its limited energies, or that it could make a difference, but Baker was adamant.[51] Feeling respect and sympathy for Davis's plight, she understood all too well how government persecution targeted outspoken political activists. Other SCEF board members were sympathetic, too, having had their own run-ins with the FBI and HUAC. Baker's specific suggestion was that the group contact Davis's mother, Sallye Davis, herself a veteran civil rights activist and former member of the Southern Negro Youth Congress, and look into the idea of having some type of support rally in the family's hometown of Birmingham.[52] When SCEF accepted Baker's proposal, she called up Sallye Davis, who came over right away to where the group was meeting. After all, Baker knew the landscape in Birmingham. She also knew Sallye Davis by reputation and thought they would have no trouble pulling off a successful event there. In December 1970, a citywide Committee to Defend Angela Davis was formed in Birmingham, and on Monday, January 11, 1971, Baker flew into town to deliver the keynote address at the city's first "Free Angela" rally, held at the First Congregational Church. Baker's FBI file, which had been fairly dormant for several years, was reactivated as she began speaking across the country on behalf of Communist Party member Davis.[53]

For Baker, Angela Davis's imprisonment had concrete and symbolic significance. As a young black woman and a radical intellectual who had refused to be intimidated or silenced by harassment (she had been fired as a professor in the California state university system by Governor Ronald Reagan for her political views), Davis represented, Baker felt, a spirit of resistance that had to be defended. Although different in style, age, and demeanor, Baker may have identified with Davis on some level. She immediately felt protective. She claimed Davis as one of her own, praising her "strength and moral courage," even though the two women had never met. Davis had been jailed in October 1970, and the campaign for her release was growing. Baker contacted friends around the country to ask them to support the campaign. On February 24, 1971, Baker spoke on the University of Virginia campus in Richmond in a call for Angela Davis's release from prison, saying that "we have rights only as long as we are willing to struggle for them."[54]

By the 1970s, when she was in her seventies and suffering from a variety of physical ailments, Ella Baker was no longer able to maintain the rigorous day-to-day organizer's regimen that had characterized most of her adult life, yet she remained as engaged as health and stamina would allow— giving speeches, offering counsel, lending her name to petitions, and helping to raise funds for a variety of campaigns and organizations.

During the 1970s, Baker became deeply involved in an effort to organize a viable left-wing political party; the Mass Party Organizing Committee (MPOC) was an exploratory committee that lasted nearly seven years but never actually formed a party. Some of her former SNCC colleagues were also involved. In 1977, Baker served as co-chairperson of MPOC, along with a leftist lawyer, Arthur Kinoy.[55] The MPOC experiment was an attempt to transcend the painful limitations of the two-party system that the MFDP had encountered in 1964 and create a truly progressive alternative. A paper that Kinoy wrote in 1974, "Toward a Mass Party of the People," served as a call to action and as the group's founding document. The group articulated a progressive and far-reaching platform that encompassed many of the goals the MFDP had aspired to in terms of the democratic representation of the disenfranchised, but it went further. Based in New York City with affiliates throughout the country, the MPOC hoped to solidify an interracial antiracist constituency.[56] The group also embraced an explicitly socialist vision and took strong positions against the War in Vietnam and on behalf of Puerto Rican independence. Poverty and racism, as well as the plight of workers, were critical domestic issues highlighted by the MPOC. Baker participated in several workshops, retreats, and administrative meetings in 1976 and 1977 trying to consolidate the MPOC's eclectic base of supporters. Unfortunately, it never bore the fruit that its founders had hoped for.[57]

More than ever, Ella Baker identified closely with leftist and radical forces on the international scene. The issue of Puerto Rican independence was especially relevant to her internationalist vision. Her treasured clippings file was full of news articles and literature on Puerto Rico. For someone who had lived in New York City over many decades, the Puerto Rican community was a large and politically vibrant presence. In the 1950s, Baker worked closely with Puerto Rican community activists in the school reform struggle. So, when her friend Annie Stein, who had been involved in the same struggle and many other progressive causes thereafter, got involved with the Puerto Rican Solidarity Organization (PRSO), Baker did, too.[58]

By the time she became active in PRSO in the 1970s, Baker's asthma had worsened, and arthritis slowed her down even more. She did attend meetings, write letters of support, and speak at rallies, but her ability to travel was limited. In 1974, along with Noam Chomsky, Fran Beal, Dave Dellinger, and Jim Forman, she lent her name to the roster of the planning committee for the National Puerto Rican Independence rally.[59] In 1978, she agreed to serve as "spokesperson for the 'U.S. People's Delegation'" to the United

Nations Special Committee on Decolonization.[60] She delivered an eloquent keynote address to an overflow crowd at a Puerto Rican Independence rally in Madison Square Garden—featured in the final frame of Joanne Grant's film documentary *Fundi*—that reflected the passion and insights that Baker brought to the the issue.[61]

Even though she could not be as active as she would have liked, Baker encouraged her younger SNCC comrades, whom she still kept in touch with and advised when they would listen, to take a wider interest in global politics and to travel and meet revolutionaries from other parts of the world. She did not have to do too much persuading because this was the direction SNCC was headed in anyway. A delegation had visited Africa, and Carmichael toured a half-dozen countries in the late 1960s, meeting with radical and revolutionary leaders. Puerto Rico, because of its proximity and colonial relationship to the United States, was of particular significance, Baker argued. She made arrangements for Carmichael and Ivanhoe Donaldson to visit the island and participate in a conference on the Independista movement. "Her contacts were so extensive," Ivanhoe marveled. "She knew what had gone on [in Puerto Rico] by the time we got back because she had talked to people down there. Her connections were amazing." Even though she did not travel internationally, her vision and her network did.[62]

Ella Baker maintained international connections by building personal relationships with people from around the world who were visitors to the United States. In 1976, in the immediate wake of the historic Soweto youth uprising against South African apartheid, Baker befriended Violet Cherry, a South African living temporarily in the United States. The woman's son had been arrested for political activism in the South African city of Durban, and she was trying to publicize his case and garner support. Baker agreed to host a meeting of New York activists to talk about the case of twenty-two-year-old Lloyd Padayachi. Baker extended herself to his mother as she had done with so many other mothers of young activists over the years. National boundaries were not relevant.[63]

Ella Baker maintained a myriad of political affiliations in the 1970s, most of which involved more than simply lending her name to a letterhead; she was engaged in real consultation and strategizing. She attended several antiwar rallies, spoke twice at International Women's Day activities in New York, and signed numerous letters and petitions for various progressive and left-wing causes. She had always been politically promiscuous in this way, insisting that no one organization could ever claim her full loyalty, which she reserved for the larger movement and its larger goals. However, in the early 1970s, it was not the survival of any single organization that worried Baker; rather, it was the survival of the movement to which she had devoted her life. Ultimately, she remained convinced that the protracted democratic revolution that she believed in so fiercely, that awkward circuitous process of generation after generation of people striving to push the world toward a greater justice and humanity would continue. But the question was, In what form? Would external repression or internal divisions undo what she had watched a generation of activists build? At age seventy-six, she mused, "I don't claim to have any corner on an answer, but I believe that the struggle is eternal. Someone else carries on."[64]

Even as SNCC began to unravel organizationally, Baker looked for promise and hope in the plethora of local, national, and international struggles that blossomed in the 1960s and 1970s. They were sometimes poorly organized or short-lived, but they were cause for optimism that a spirit of resistance was alive. The extensive clippings file that Baker kept in the 1970s carefully followed the plight of the Soledad prison activists in California, the Attica prison uprising in New York, the Native American struggle at Wounded Knee, as well as events in Puerto Rico, South Africa, and Vietnam.[65]

In her thinking and in the way she lived her life, Baker was much more of a materialist (in the sense of being proactive) than an idealist. That is, she was a practical, action-oriented kind of person. Exploring how ideas were relevant and linked to concrete experiences was her approach. Yet, despite the importance of her deeds, perhaps her most lasting contribution to social justice movements of the late twentieth century was in the form of her ideas. She provided movement activists in the 1960s and 1970s with a philosophy, a worldview, an approach to social change that they took with them into cultural, political and global arenas and into their personal lives, careers and relationships. Baker's radical democratic humanism was the core philosophy that gave meaning to her personal and political practice for over a half century. In her role as a movement teacher and insurgent intellectual, she sparked new ideas, both reaffirmed and rejected old ones, and gave a new generation the intellectual, political, and, at times, material wherewithal to carry on.

A FREIRIAN TEACHER, A GRAMSCIAN INTELLECTUAL, AND A RADICAL HUMANIST

ELLA BAKER'S LEGACY

• • • • • •

Intellectual work for radical democrats must always link the visionary to the practical.
Cornel West, 1990

If there is any philosophy, it's that those who have walked a certain path
should know some things, should remember some things that they can pass on,
that others can use to walk the path a little better.
Ella Baker, 1980

Ella Baker performed her share of menial movement chores over the years, from typing leaflets to licking stamps to buying toiletries for jailed protesters. She assumed multiple and fluctuating titles and identities, but her most enduring role in the Black Freedom Movement of the 1960s and early 1970s was that of "master teacher" and resident griot.[1] This role was most pronounced during her work with SNCC from 1960 to 1966. Baker was a powerful intellectual presence within the organization and a moral and ethical compass for the young activists with whom she worked so intimately and intensely. Her young protégés went from their classrooms at Spelman, Howard, Fisk, and Tougaloo Colleges to Ella Baker's classroom without walls. It was a very different kind of classroom, indeed, one infused with a radical pedagogy, epistemology, and worldview. In an article about the influence that Baker and her friend and colleague Septima Clark, both "activist community educators," had on the radical curricula of the Citizenship and Freedom Schools of the 1960s, the scholar-activist Bill

Ayers writes: "This kind of education opposes fear, ignorance, and helplessness by strengthening knowledge and ability. It enables people to question, to wonder, and to look critically . . . it is an education for freedom."[2]

. . . . . .

TEACHER AND PRACTITIONER OF A
RADICAL DEMOCRATIC PEDAGOGY

Baker had insisted all her life that she would never become a teacher because of the restrictive social role it represented for women and because of the class and gender expectation that all capable black girls of her generation were obliged to become teachers. She saw the teaching profession as an elite and conservative one, for the most part, requiring women to be prim and proper and to follow the dominant protocol for ladylike behavior. In describing early-twentieth-century uplift ideology, the historian Kevin Gaines writes, "The bourgeois morality of their cultural mentors was drummed into black students: piety, thrift, self-control and the work ethic," as well as a "Victorian sexual morality" and a sense of bourgeois etiquette.[3] Teachers collaborated in this socialization and were victims of it at the same time, in Baker's view. She noticed, for example, that when "progressive" and open-minded young women who were sent off for teacher training returned, they were frequently "no longer that type of person. . . . [A]nyone with spirit would be curbed."[4] This was not what Baker wanted for herself, and so she declined to pursue a traditional teaching career, in spite of or perhaps because of her mother's wishes, and turned down a relatively prestigious offer from the president of Bennet College.[5] She was stubbornly determined to be her own woman, and she would encourage the young women of SNCC to do the same. As SNCC activist Barbara Jones (Omolade) observed, Baker "was really . . . able to disavow all those other kinds of womanhood that were offered to black women" and to carve out her own identity as a radical, an intellectual, and, ultimately, a teacher.[6]

In the context of SNCC, much of Ella Baker's leadership was didactic. She was the teacher-activist in every sense. Joyce Ladner described Baker's teaching style this way: she "was a quiet presence in a way. What she did was to distill, sum up and take [discussions] to the next level, point out gaps in your own information, enlighten you in some broader sense, bring information to you about what other people were doing and voids that you could fill."[7] In Baker's view, people had many of the answers within themselves; teachers and leaders simply had to facilitate the process of tapping and framing that knowledge, of drawing it out. Given this view, debate and the open exchange of ideas were critically important. Ladner continued: "You see, Miss Baker's presence was felt at meetings even when we stood there and talked and screamed, with her tacit approval, and she just stood there but she always knew that we would at some point have to stake an opinion about it."[8] This description of Ella Baker's subtle teaching style is reminiscent of Gerald Graff's creative pedagogical theory, which advocates using conflict itself as a teaching tool.[9]

Ella Baker's early reservations about traditional methods of teaching came in part from the conservatizing impact she felt teacher training had on the young women of her generation and her mother's generation. She objected not only to how most schools taught but also to what they taught: conformity and obedience. In contrast, Baker's pedagogy was democratic and reciprocal. Although they never met, and there is no evidence that she was familiar with his writings, Baker's teaching style very much resembled that of the Latin American educator and activist Paulo Freire. Within the circle of inexperienced but courageous young activists who became Baker's students, she challenged the conventional meanings of both education and leadership. Building on the progressive philosophy of education she had embraced during her time as a teacher for the Workers' Education Project, and augmented by her own political experiences and personal sensibilities, Baker concluded that curricula had to be socially relevant and that learning needed to be based on a fluid and interactive relationship between student and teacher.[10]

Baker's approach to learning and teaching was consistent with that of Italian Marxist and theorist Antonio Gramsci. "Every teacher," he said, "is always a pupil and every pupil is always a teacher."[11] Baker tried to build camaraderie with her young allies because it was her belief that young people should be able to "feel a sort of communion and friendship with their teachers."[12] Moreover, her view of teaching for liberation was based on the need to empower ordinary people to dig within themselves and their collective experiences for the answers to social and political questions. She did not want her students to see her as the repository of all knowledge but to discover their own insights and knowledge base.[13] As the sociologist and movement historian Charles Payne put it, "Miss Baker was reluctant to see people entrust too many of their dreams to individual leaders," or teachers.[14] They had to rely on their own judgments.

According to SNCC member Prathia Hall, Baker's style of teaching was a lesson in itself. She "was a consummate teacher, always opening us to new understandings," Hall remembered. "It was never the pounding, 'you must do this, you must do that,' but by raising a question and then raising another question and then helping us to see what was being revealed through the answer was her mode of leadership. She was the one who taught us how to organize . . . to organize in such a way that when we left, the people were fully capable of carrying on the movement themselves."[15] Baker taught by inquiry and by example. She did not tell people what to do or think; she guided them toward answers and solutions by teasing out the ideas and knowledge that already existed within the group, and within individuals, and then by encouraging people to express that information in their own words. She was also patient enough to allow this process to unfold.

Echoing Hall's and Ladner's observations, a former Spelman College activist, Lenora Taitt-Magubane, recalled, "Miss Ella would ask questions, key questions . . . and sometimes people don't recognize or appreciate this as leadership. . . . She would sit there and she would literally almost let a meeting fall apart. People were at each other before she would intervene, because she wanted the decision to come out of the group and not be hers. She would say: 'Well, what about so and so?' or 'Well, have you thought through this or that?' She was always pushing people to think and challenging you."[16] Mary King, a young white woman whom Baker recruited to SNCC through her YWCA work and who worked closely with Baker in Atlanta, remembers her mentor as a powerfully effective teacher. "With Socratic persistence, in her resonant and commanding voice, she would query, 'Now let me ask this again, what is our purpose here? What are we trying to accomplish?' Again and again she would force us to articulate our assumptions. . . . She encouraged me to avoid being doctrinaire. 'Ask questions, Mary,' she would say."[17]

Ella Baker also pushed Eleanor Holmes Norton, a young African American law graduate from Yale, to think for herself and to ask questions: "Miss Baker's presence and her contributions were different than telling us what to do. Which was one of her gifts, real gifts—such that the intervention always seemed to be, 'Wow, isn't that exactly right? Why didn't we think of that?'" At the same time, she adds, Baker brought seriousness, sobriety and maturity to SNCC's deliberations. "What professionalized the meetings was Ella Baker," Holmes Norton concluded.[18] Baker's powerful moral and intellectual presence and the confidence she exuded were critical in inspiring Holmes Norton to configure her own identity as a politician and a feminist.

Ella Baker taught, but she rarely lectured. Part of her criticism of southern preachers was that they constituted what she termed "a verbal society" and did little more than verbalize.[19] As a young child, Baker had been an eloquent public speaker; tutored in diction, grammar, and presentation by her mother, she competed in oratory contests around the South and often spoke at church and school events. However, she was turned off by certain types of speech making early on. When she was about seven or eight years old, her parents took her to hear a public lecture by Charles Sachel Morris Jr. Baker was initially impressed by his "flowery speech" and "good articulation"; but when she heard him another time deliver the exact same speech, she realized it was more performance than substance. So, when one of her professors suggested she might consider going on the lecture circuit after graduation, she "was saved from that" by the negative encounters she had had with disingenuous orators who had turned her off entirely.[20]

Baker's feeling was that even though "I had the oratorical chords, I resented oratory. You should be able to have some speech making that has some purpose," rather than simply dazzling an audience to boost your ego.[21] Again, Baker's views on social action and the formulation and exchange of ideas were consistent with Gramsci's. He wrote: "The mode of being of the new intellectual can no longer consist in eloquence, which is an exterior and momentary mover of feelings and passions, but in active participation in practical life, as constructor, organizer, 'permanent persuader' not just a simple orator."[22] Baker expanded on this notion, insisting that one's words are important "only as they help people to do things that are of value to themselves. And we've had too much of the mesmerizing type of talking."[23] Catherine Orr has characterized Baker's rhetorical style as a conscious reflection of her egalitarian and democratic politics and as being deliberately engaging rather than mesmerizing. According to Orr, the way she spoke, her choice of pronouns, where she stood relative to her audience, and the cadence of her voice all conveyed a message about who she was and what kind of political vision she wanted to project to her listeners.[24]

Baker had a talent for making complex ideas simple. This was another carryover from her experience with the Worker's Education Project, in which it was stressed that teachers should "use words workers can understand."[25] Her teaching method resembled a conversation more than a tutorial. SNCC activist Joyce Ladner attested to this: "I don't remember her citing works of particular authors that we should read. I think what she did more of was instill information and put it in a form that would be palatable to us. . . . [S]he may have mentioned Garvey or mentioned someone else, but she used that as a launching pad more than anything else. She was a practitioner, . . . for her it was always getting back to the practical aspects of how do you go about changing things."[26]

Ella Baker, like Paulo Freire, viewed education as a collective and creative enterprise requiring collaboration and exchange at every stage. She would have likely agreed with Freire's statement that "to teach is not to transfer knowledge but to create the possibilities for the production or construction of knowledge."[27] A part of that process, both Freire and Baker insisted, was the ability to humble oneself and to simply listen. This was also a part of the process of taming the ego, in Baker's opinion. She repeatedly criticized unchecked, inflated egos and excessive individualism as obstacles to social change. "The importance of silence in the context of communication is fundamental," Freire wrote. He went on: "It is intolerable to see teachers who give themselves the right to behave as if they own the truth. . . . [T]he democratic-minded teacher who learns to speak by listening is interrupted by the intermittent silence of his or her own capacity to listen, waiting for that voice that may desire to speak from the depths of its own silent listening."[28] Baker spent many hours sitting silently through long and cumbersome SNCC discussions, making her interventions often at the very end of the meeting. She interrupted only to make sure that others were allowed to speak and that the more confident speakers were made to listen. This was the pattern she established early on in her relationship with the youth activists in SNCC, and it was a practice that became characteristic of SNCC's deliberations and Baker's role in them. Prathia Hall took the lessons seriously when she began organizing in small communities in Georgia: "We'd sit sometimes and rock on the porch for hours. Our intention was to finally convince a person to go and register. But we'd sit and we'd listen, and we'd listen to the person talk about survival and talk about families . . . I think some of the most important lessons I learned were on the porches of people who couldn't read or write their names."[29]

Baker's political philosophy emphasized the importance of tapping oppressed communities for their own knowledge, strength, and leadership in constructing models for social change. She took seriously and tried to understand seriously the ways in which poor black people saw and analyzed the world. And her own base of knowledge came primarily from those same communities. In many respects, Baker was what Gramscian theorists refer to as an "organic intellectual."[30] Part of her work as a writer, orator, and analyst was not to invent or impose ideas on the masses but rather to help them, as she put it, "see their own ideas."[31]

Baker functioned as an organic intellectual to the extent that she validated and relied on the collective wisdom that resided in poor and oppressed communities and to the extent that she respected and affirmed the intellectual capacity and political astuteness of individuals who had no formal academic training or credentials. "I have never been diploma conscious," Baker once remarked.[32] For her, wisdom came from many sources and was transmitted via many different languages, including the language of action. Academic credentials alone did not impress Baker, especially when such training was used to advance individual careers rather than for some greater good. From her point of view, her own political education was derived not only from her formal training at Shaw University but also from what she learned on the streets and in meeting places and union halls of New York City, as well as at rural and urban churches, barber shops, and kitchen tables throughout the South. This type of popular education she saw as vital.

Radical black women intellectuals who have tried to function in this same tradition have articulated Baker's epistemological stance in their writings. The historian and political activist Elsa Barkley Brown, for example, has identified her mother and the larger southern black community of which she was a part as her primary intellectual mentors while she was growing up. They taught her the indispensable lessons of "how to ask the right questions" and of having respect "for people's abilities to understand their own lives."[33] Ella Baker learned the same lessons from her childhood community and from the people she worked with in New York and throughout the South.

Ella Baker was Edward Said's kind of intellectual. For Said, a Palestinian activist and literary scholar, being an intellectual means, as Baker herself once wrote, "to think in radical terms."[34] Said elaborates, explaining that the role of a radical intellectual is "to confront orthodoxy and dogma (rather than reproduce them), to be someone who cannot easily be co-opted by governments or corporations, and whose raison d'être is to represent all those people and issues that are routinely forgotten or swept under the rug."[35] Said uses the compelling metaphor of the exile to further amplify his point:

Even if one is not an actual immigrant or expatriate, it is still possible to think as one, to imagine and investigate in spite of barriers, and always to move away from the centralizing authorities towards the margins, where you see things that are usually lost on minds that have never traveled beyond the conventional and comfortable. . . . [T]o be as marginal and undomesticated as someone who is in real exile is for an intellectual to be unusually responsive to the traveler rather than the potentate, to the provisional and risky rather than the habitual, to innovation and experiment rather than the authoritatively given status quo. The exilic intellectual does not respond to the logic of the conventional but to the audacity of daring, and to representing change, to moving on, not standing still."[36]

The content of Ella Baker's teachings and her style of "renegade intellectual" work, as Robin Kelley might describe it, was a powerful force in the Black Freedom Movement of the 1960s and beyond.[37] But what was the substance of her ideas and her worldview? Her political and moral influence on SNCC from 1960 to 1966 can be divided into several areas. First, she encouraged a democratic practice and an egalitarian structure as an alternative to the normative presence of many undemocratic traditions in both the black and the white American institutions that the young people had been a part of, mainly schools and churches. Second, she gently nudged the students in the direction of embracing a class analysis of racism and injustice that allied them with those at the bottom of the social and economic hierarchy—those who were sometimes at the margins of mainstream societies, black and white, but who were central to resistance efforts.

Third, Ella Baker affirmed in her practice and her teachings a style of personal grassroots organizing that, while more common among women than men, was a part of a radical democratic humanist tradition that both men and women could lay claim to. With the subtle power of her presence, Baker offered a different model of gender relations and a broader spectrum of gender identities. Her own transgressive female identity was represented by her uninhibited occupation of predominately male political spaces, her refusal to be a conventional teacher, and her rejection of a social identification as someone's wife. Her way of being a black woman challenged men in SNCC to rethink manhood and masculinity, just as it gave women in the movement a widened sense of their own possibilities as doers, thinkers, and powerful social change agents.

In essence, Baker's leadership from 1960 to 1966 helped create within SNCC the space where traditional hierarchies of race, class, and, to a lesser extent, gender could be turned on their heads.[38] As the progenitor and presiding elder of SNCC for the better part of the decade, Baker helped set the terms for an interracial and interclass organization of men and women to function in a principled and nontraditional manner, reinforcing a new set of social and interpersonal relations in the process. To say this is not to portray SNCC as an egalitarian utopia; it was not. However, Ella Baker's leadership and presence helped fashion the practice and philosophy of the group in such a way that traditional norms of male dominance, white privilege, and class elitism were overturned in much of the day-to-day functioning of the group and in the public image it projected. In the Jim Crow South, in an America still unready to afford black citizens the most basic civil rights, a small cadre of whites were persuaded (at least in principle and to a large extent in practice) to accept a secondary, supportive role in a black-led organization.[39] And, in a society and culture whose main institutions still accorded women a subordinate status, men were persuaded to accept an organization whose intellectual, spiritual, and political guide was—rather than a towering male patriarch or a messiah of some kind—an unassuming middle-aged woman. This was radical indeed.

By rejecting the dominant values of society and the elitist markers of supposed success, Baker encouraged young people to wrap themselves in a different culture, not as an escape but as part of their re-envisioning and redefining a new form of social relations that prioritized cooperation and collectivism over competition and individualism.

The inversion of conventional class hierarchies within SNCC was most pronounced. Talented and educated young black people were persuaded to forfeit their privileged claim to leadership of the race, a status that would naturally have been afforded them according to pre–World War II uplift ideology, and instead to defer to the collective wisdom of sharecroppers, maids, and manual laborers, many of whom lacked even a high school education. White activists were encouraged to reject existing race and class hierarchies and do the same. This was a fundamental break with black politics as usual. Poor southern black people were not merely SNCC's constituency; they were revered for their knowledge, commitment, and sacrifice. Women like Fannie Lou Hamer and others became the heroines of the movement. Biographer Chana Kai Lee points out that Fannie Lou Hamer was a serious movement strategist and analyst and that those who worked closely with her understood this quite clearly and valued it.[40]

SNCC's decidedly open and fluid structure, especially during the first few years, made it possible for those who were poor and working-class, women, youths, and political novices to exercise enormous influence within the group and play central roles. Structurally, SNCC had a chairperson and an executive secretary, but when asked who the leader of the group was, SNCC members would often reply, "We all are." Even with strong personalities like Jim Forman and later Ruby Doris Smith Robinson and Stokely Carmichael in official leadership positions, there was a rambunctious confidence among the rank and file that militated against heavy-handed top-down leadership, something that Ella Baker applauded and encouraged.

· · · · · ·

A DIFFERENT CONSTRUCTION OF GENDER IDENTITY

Baker was much more explicit in the expression of her ideas about social class and race than she was when it came to gender. Diane Nash once observed, "Ella Baker was a feminist more in what she did than what she said."[41] Her views and lessons about gender politics and identities were deeply embedded in her daily work and in the public image she cultivated. Through private advice and public example, Baker helped young women activists navigate the minefield of gender and sexual politics within the movement and within their own lives. For example, Casey Hayden, a young white field secretary from Texas, consulted Baker about whether she should apply for a job as a full-time organizer given her impending marriage to Tom Hayden, leader of the Students for a Democratic Society (SDS). Baker's answer was an unfaltering yes. Years later, after Hayden's marriage had ended and other problems set in, Ella was there for Casey once again, bolstering her confidence that she could make it on her own. "Ella got me through that period" with many late-night conversations, Casey recalled years later with great emotion and affection.[42]

Similarly, Prathia Hall, a seminary student and Southwest Georgia field secretary for SNCC, confided her marriage plans to Baker and worried about how her independence might be compromised if she were to become someone's wife. In turn, Baker shared with Hall something she shared with very few people: her own difficulties with juggling marriage and politics. Baker did not, however, encourage Hall to follow the path she herself had taken—ultimately choosing politics over domesticity—but simply warned her about what problems she might anticipate.[43]

Some young women did not fully appreciate the impact Baker had on their lives in these formative years until much later. When Barbara Jones (Omolade)—now a successful teacher, writer, and feminist activist—began to analyze the gender politics within the movement twenty years after

SNCC's demise, she immediately thought of Ella Baker as a radical model of black womanhood.[44] Baker was independent, a "social theorist and an intellectual," a no-nonsense person who could hold her own in any situation and commanded respect from those around her. This model of a confidant, committed, and savvy black woman was one that many of the young women whose lives Baker touched would strive to emulate.[45]

Eleanor Holmes Norton, who met Baker when she was in her early twenties and fresh out of Yale law school, remembered Baker as "a woman who seemed unintimidated by the fact that she was a woman in a movement led by men. She was just very smart. And she wasn't afraid to be a smart woman." Baker never called herself a feminist. She could not have, Norton insists—"there wasn't any such animal then." At the same time, "Ella Baker performed and acted as a feminist." She operated with confidence, intelligence, and authority, and consequently "she was not treated as a woman. She was treated as one of the most talented people in the room." Ella Baker was not a feminist per se. That is, she did not use or embrace the term. But, through her actions and what her work represented, she could safely be called what Joy James refers to as "profeminist," someone who is a strong advocate of gender equality and liberatory concepts of manhood and womanhood, without a self-conscious investment in the term "feminist" or its attendant theories.[46]

In a sense, Ella Baker simply ignored conventional gender mandates. As a result, in some contexts, she was not treated the way other women were treated, even by men who held sexist views on the proper place of women. She was so savvy and had so many of the skills and insights the movement needed that her gender was sometimes "overlooked," if only to exploit her talents. She was at certain moments seemingly able to negotiate an exemption from the existing confines of patriarchal gender roles. But there was also a limit to the sexual neutrality she was afforded. There were many times when her gender became quite important and she was reminded that she had overstepped the bounds. Baker's role was somewhat unique: because of her skills, experience, and knowledge of an organization's inner workings—as in the case of the NAACP or SCLC—she was allowed to sit at the table but was rarely dealt into the game. As her friend Septima Clark observed, these insulting reminders infuriated Baker.[47] Most of the time, however, Baker was able to navigate the bumpy gender terrain of the Black Freedom Movement and make significant contributions anyway. She developed strategies to insulate herself and minimize the psychological damage. Such strategies understandably took a toll.[48]

SITUATIONAL DEMOCRACY AND HUMANISTIC PRACTICE

Baker's emphasis on grassroots participatory democracy stemmed from her realization that the forces being mobilized by SNCC in the 1960s were potentially some of the most radical in the nation. Her philosophy was not simply to "let the people decide," as the popular SNCC and SDS slogan suggested. Rather, it was to let the disenfranchised vote, let the silenced be heard, let the oppressed be empowered, and let the marginalized move to the center.[49] The distinction is an important one. In other words, she was not advocating a simple populist formula of majority rule or "one person, one vote," a paradigm that, as the work of the legal scholar Lani Guinier illustrates, is sorely limiting and essentially unfair in certain situations. Democracy, for Ella Baker, was about fairness and inclusion, not sheer numbers. Therefore, democratic practice could never be formulaic but rather had to revolve around real participation and deliberation. It was given meaning by the specific situation or historical moment in which it was tested. In their book on race and democracy, *The Miner's Canary*, Guinier and Gerald Torres argue that in order to realize a more meaningful and inclusive democracy we must "disrupt certain habits of individual thought or self-defeating rituals, while introducing new possibilities for reciprocity, collaboration, problem solving, networking and innovation. To do this, [a] community needs the capacity to confront embedded hierarchies and to engage with the untidiness of conflict over time."[50] Such a view very closely resembles Baker's.

Embracing this radical approach of situational democracy meant Baker had to constantly assess and reassess the power dynamics in any given situation and then tilt the leadership scales in the direction of the least powerful. For example, Baker's shifting posture within the movement reflected her understanding of the power dynamics in each new organizational setting she found herself in. She had a greater degree of authority and influence in SNCC than she had ever had before, but, instead of exercising it forcefully, she relented and exercised her power lightly and subtly. She could have intimidated and dominated, as certain leaders had attempted to overpower and dominate her, but she did not. She took precisely the opposite approach.

Ella Baker's vision of radical democracy was a profoundly historical concept, based on the idea that in order to achieve democratic ideals one first had to assess the specific historical parameters of exclusion, especially racism, sexism, and class exploitation. It is important to note that Baker would have been the last to argue the conservative colorblind argument with regard to race and inequality.[51] Her conviction was that previously oppressive practices had to be radically reversed, not simply halted—those with racial, class, and gender privileges had to relinquish them, and corrective measures had to be put into place. This was as true within the movement as it was in the larger society. And this explains what may have appeared to be an inverted social hierarchy within SNCC. Black leadership had to be emphasized and poor people's voices amplified because in absolutely every other facet of social life the opposite pressures and privileges were in force.

The challenge of a radical democratic practice was both a personal and an organizational one. Group relations had to be reorganized, but individuals had to grapple with personal changes as well. The process of building a movement for social transformation had to allow for, encourage, and nurture the transformation of the human beings involved. Individuals had to rethink and redefine their most intimate personal relations and their identities. Activists could not simply "ape the insiders," Baker insisted.[52] Social change organizations could not replicate the cold impersonalism of the market-driven dominant culture. Personal relations were key building blocks for a new, more humane social order and for a successful revolutionary movement. It is in this sense that Ella Baker was a humanist. While she bemoaned the fact that "our whole society has been built to a large extent upon the ascendancy of the individual, of individual leadership," she also celebrated the importance and dignity of each person.[53] She saw value and a complex beauty in human beings, despite all their imperfections. She embraced "the concept that . . . all contacts with people, if you are interested in people, can be valuable."[54]

It was her contention that the political was inherently personal long before it was a slogan for Second Wave feminism. Just as teachers had to know their students, organizers had to know their communities, and comrades had to know one another and treat one another decently. Movement leaders could not condemn hierarchy, elitism, and impersonalism in the society and emulate those same values in their own work and personal interactions. "Anytime you continue to carry on the same kind of organization that you say you are fighting against, you can't prove to me that you have made any change in your thinking," Baker observed in an interview in the 1970s.[55] Activists could not make themselves feel more important by disparaging and "tyrannizing over others." Baker went on to explain: "As we begin to grow in our own strength and as we flex our muscles of leadership, we can begin to feel that the other fellow should come through us. But this is not the way to create a new world . . . [which] requires understanding that human beings are human beings."[56]

Ella Baker's political praxis—the combination of her theory and practice—reflected what political scientists describe as a deliberative model. Interaction, discussion, debate, and consensus building were key components of that praxis. In contrast, voting, lobbying the corridors of power, and getting favored candidates elected were secondary considerations. Once people were in motion in a committed and sustained mass struggle, Baker felt that access to legislators and media would follow. "If you are involved with people and organizing them as a force, you didn't have to go and seek out the establishment people. They would seek you out," she insisted, explaining that politicians had passed numerous laws over time with little impact on people's daily lives until the people themselves decided to make implementation of those laws real and meaningful.[57] Southern black youth could have petitioned the president and the attorney general ad nauseam without a reply before February 1, 1960. But once they were engaged in a set of protests that disrupted business as usual, government officials in Washington were ready to listen.[58] For Baker, elections, court decisions, and even legislative victories were the events that punctuated the real ongoing political process, which consisted of a discursive exchange, the building of a set of trusting relationships, individual and organizational, the transmission of skills and confidence, and the forging of a shared democratic vision for the future. That was the meat of political work for Ella Baker. The rest was extra.[59] This political orientation put Baker on the ideological margins of the predominantly male black political leadership circle and mainstream civil rights organizations. Still she located herself at the center of grassroots struggles.

· · · · · ·

THE OUTSIDER WITHIN

The concept of the "outsider within," a person who functions in close proximity to those in power but who is never given official recognition as a member of the club, is a useful way to understand one aspect of Ella Baker's complex and unique political career.[60] The "outsider within" has the benefit of observation up close, but she is still not an authentic member of the inner circle in terms of actual power, access to resources, or social status within the group. Baker knew and worked with some of the most powerful black male political leaders of the twentieth century: A. Philip Randolph, W. E. B. Du Bois, Walter White, Thurgood Marshall, and Martin Luther King Jr. She knew them all, but she was never really what SCLC minister Ralph Abernathy's wife, Juanita, perceived her as being, which was "one of the boys."[61] In contrast, Baker consistently described herself as operating on the periphery of respected black leadership circles.

Baker was an "outsider within" the national leadership of several major civil rights organizations, with direct access to a host of powerful male leaders, yet she consciously compromised her insider status by speaking her mind forcefully, because in her words, she had "no capacity for worshipping the leader."[62] The inescapable fact that she was a woman amid a decidedly male political elite only compounded her difficulties. She was not a team player because she often contested the rules of the game, which angered and annoyed many male organizers and some women. Still, it would be wrong to assume that this status rendered her powerless. She had real power and real influence, largely because she secured it for herself. She insinuated herself into situations where others thought she did not belong, speaking out in a way that some thought she should not. She built up a loyal network of local allies that gave her some protection from possible capricious actions on the part of her "superiors." Baker was an outsider, in part, because of circumstance and in part because of her own political choice and agency. She knew that sexist traditions limited her ability to function as a top leader. However, her own political views, as they evolved, brought her to the conclusion that she did not want to function in that capacity, as it was construed, and she was critical of those who did. At the same time that Baker developed a strategy for navigating the undemocratic structures and practices that threatened to keep her and others at the margins of national black political leadership, she fought to transform the structural pillars of elitism within the Black Freedom Movement into something more democratic. Historian Darlene Clark Hine observes that "African American women had to create a patchwork of identities just to get through most days."[63] Baker certainly had to maintain a variety of public and private identities in order to carry out the work that she did in different venues and in disparate political and social climates. There were times when she was a quiet, dutiful "worker in the vineyards," as her mother's missionary group would have said. At other times, she was a bold and formidable presence, motivating some and challenging and confronting others.

For much of her adult political life, Ella Baker was a socialist without a party or a party line. As a friend of hers, the author and filmmaker Joanne Grant, observed, Baker was not often explicit about her socialist beliefs, but there were times when she was as straightforward as one could be. "The only society that can serve the needs of large masses of poor people is a Socialist society," she declared in a 1977 interview.[64] She was a harsh critic of capitalism, but resisted any hints of sectarianism or ideological orthodoxy. She loathed dogma of any kind and was openly critical when she observed this kind of rigid thinking on the part of friends and colleagues. Her own worldview was constructed from an amalgam of different ideologies and traditions, combining the black Baptist missionary values of charity, humility, and service with the economic theories of Marxists and socialists of various stripes who advocated a redistribution of wealth. She also embraced the militant self-defense tradition of the black South. Her affiliation with the openly socialist Mass Party Organizing Committee (MPOC) and her defense of Communist Party member Angela Davis are further indicators of her unequivocal identification with the left by the 1970s. She had become her own unique kind of revolutionary.

For Baker, revolution was above all about a protracted and layered democratic process. The journey was as important as the destination. In the final analysis, Baker's political philosophy was undergirded by a deep and profound sense of connection to and love of humanity. This spirit of radical humanism, with its embedded understanding and appreciation of the human process of struggle, is also reflected in the life and writings of the Caribbean-born socialist C. L. R. James.[65] In the following words, James summed up much of his view of revolutionary transformation and his sensitivity to the human characters that are the agents of that change: "A revolution is first and foremost a movement from the old to the new, and needs above all new words, new verse, new passwords—all the symbols in which ideas and feelings are made tangible. The mass creation and appropriation of what is needed is a revealing picture of a whole people on their journey into the modern world, sometimes pathetic, sometimes vastly comic, ranging from the sublime to the ridiculous, but always vibrant with the life that only a mass of ordinary people can give."[66] Baker lived her life engaged in political struggle and forged relationships and sustained organizations as if she believed precisely what James's statement conveys.

· · · · · ·

In trying to delineate Ella Baker's life and harness and distill it in well-ordered chapters, I felt her resistance. There was an elegant fluidity about her life that proved to be both the source of her amazing "presence" and, at times, a biographer's nightmare. In looking back on the semi-coherence of a life lived, one is humbly reminded that life is an art and not a science. In eavesdropping on Ella Baker's life story, I found parts of it that made a visceral impact and simply could not be poured adequately into words. As I sought advice from friends, relatives, and colleagues who knew Ella Baker or had themselves researched her life, I was repeatedly reminded that "she was bigger than that" and that no term or label quite captured her. She was forever shrugging off every definitional shawl I tried to gently drape over her shoulders. She really lived outside categories and labels, as difficult as that is for some academics to accept. And yet she was still an intellectual with a very coherent, although dynamic, worldview. As my jazz-aficionado husband would say, like Duke Ellington she was "beyond category." Still, going back to the beginning of my story of her life, she was both a self-made woman and a product of the world, country, culture, and ideas that surrounded her. In celebrating her life, I do not want to mystify or circumscribe it. While, as my son constantly reminds me, we are all products of the multitude of experiences, influences, and stimuli that touch us as we struggle to formulate ideas and identities, those experiences are the raw material we then mold into our own unique form. So, trying to sum up and repackage a life full of detours, depth, and contradictions is like trying to hold water in your hands. You can feel it, but you can't quite contain it.

Some metaphors and comparisons are better than others for trying to convey a sense of what Ella Baker's life was all about. In an eloquent eulogy given at a SNCC reunion in 2000 in Raleigh, North Carolina, Timothy Jenkins, a former SNCC member and a national student leader in the 1960s, described Ella Baker as the "mortar between the bricks" holding different sectors of the movement together with a tacit strength that was indispensable but almost invisible. I love Timothy Jenkins's metaphor, but for me it is still not quite right—too hard, too harsh, perhaps. For me, in looking back at Baker's life in all of its rich complexity, I am reminded of the eclectic crazy quilt that has hung on my wall since I began this project and is of the same generation as Ella Baker. It reminds me of how she patched together her worldview from the ideological fragments in her repertoire, binding together seemingly mismatched theories and traditions, stitching it all together into something both functional and utterly amazing. The patchwork quilt reminds me of how Baker served the movement: identifying the value in people who were raggedy, worn, and a little bit tattered—people who were seen by some as the scraps, the remnants, the discarded ones. In each one, as in each strip of fabric, Ella Baker saw enormous beauty and potential. And, like the quilting tradition itself, her life's work was collective work. She understood the labor-intensive process required to stitch together all the tiny pieces and hold them in place. She knew it could not be done alone and required the skill, trust, and commitment of a team of quilters. Ella Baker's legacy then is a collective legacy, bound up with the work of the Pauli Murrays, the Lucille Blacks, the Septima Clarks, the Fannie Lou Hamers, the Amzie Moores, the Bob Moseses, and the Anne Bradens of the world and many more. She has not left us a manifesto, perhaps quite deliberately so. Manifestos make us lazy. Rather, she has left us a warm and complex work of art, a reminder of a process, a way of working and living, a way of looking at that which may seem of little value and finding its enormous transformative power.

APPENDIX

ELLA BAKER'S ORGANIZATIONAL AFFILIATIONS, 1927–1986

(A Partial List)

Ad Hoc Committee on the Sunflower (County) Elections, 1960s

American Labor Party, 1930s

American League against War and Fascism, 1930s

Americans for Traditional Liberties, 1950s

Angela Davis Defense Committee, 1970s

Aubrey Williams Foundation, 1968

Charter Group for a Pledge of Conscience, 1970s

Coalition of Concerned Black Americans, 1970s

Committee to Defend the Harlem Five, 1970s

Fund for Educational and Legal Defense, 1960s–1970s

Harlem Branch Library, Young People's Forum, 1930s

Harlem's Own Cooperative Inc., 1930s

Highlander Folk School, 1950s–1960s

Independent Black Voters' League, 1970s

In Friendship, 1950s

Jeannette Rankin Brigade, 1968–1969

Liberal Party, 1950s

Mass Party Organizing Committee, 1970s

Mississippi Freedom Democratic Party, 1960s

National Association for the Advancement of Colored People, 1940s–1950s

National Association of Consumers, 1940s

National Committee to Abolish HUAC, 1950s

National Sharecroppers Fund, 1960s–1970s

National Urban League, 1930s

New York Public Schools Intergroup Committee, 1950s

Operation Freedom, 1960s

Parents in Action, 1950s

Prayer Pilgrimage for Freedom, 1957

Puerto Rican Solidarity Committee, 1970s

Rand School, 1930s

Southern Christian Leadership Conference, 1950s
Southern Conference Education Fund, 1960s
Student Nonviolent Coordinating Committee, 1960s
Third World Women's Alliance, 1970s
Volunteer Civil Rights Commissions, 1950s
We Care, 1960s
Women's Emergency Coalition, 1960s
Works Progress Administration Workers Education Project, 1930s
World Fair Boosters and Friends of Africa, 1934
Young Negroes' Cooperative League, 1930s
Young Women's Christian Association, Harlem Branch, 1930s
Youth Committee of One Hundred against Lynching, 1930s
YWCA Regional Committee on Human Relations, 1960s

NOTES

NOTE ON PRIMARY SOURCES

The Ella Baker Papers (EBP) cited here are housed at the Schomburg Center for Research in Black Culture, which is part of the New York Public Library system, Harlem, New York. It consists of nine boxes of documents and correspondence. Unfortunately, at the time this book is going to press, the papers are still being processed and cataloged, and are not open to the public. I have viewed these papers in their entirety and consulted with the curator of the collection about how they will be organized for purposes of citation. I have indicated as clearly as possible where other researchers can find the documents referenced here. The collection will be organized chronologically, with a separate correspondence file that will contain letters not directly associated with a major organization or campaign. There will also likely be two separate files, one of Ella Baker's writings (which will be small) and another miscellaneous file containing documents and newspaper clippings that Baker collected pertaining to events and activities that she herself was not directly involved in. In addition, my own collection of approximately ten boxes of materials pertaining to Ella Baker's life and collected during the course of my research—some of which overlaps with the contents of the EBP—will be cataloged and deposited at the Schomburg for reference by other researchers.

Through the Freedom of Information Act (FOIA), I petitioned the U.S. Department of Justice to obtain Ella Baker's FBI files, which date from the 1940s through the 1970s. There are three distinct files: Atlanta (file no. 100-5837), New York (file no. 100-136886), and Headquarters (file no. HQ 100-430167). In the notes they will simply be referred to as "Ella Baker's FBI files" with the relevant location. Unfortunately, these files are not a reliable source of empirical information. There are numerous factual inaccuracies in them, ranging from the wrong birthdate to a misidentification by one agent of Ella Baker's husband as her cousin. The most useful function these declassified government documents seem to serve is as a convenient file of clippings showing the coverage of Baker's various affiliations and speaking appearances. I have not relied on this material for any information that is not verifiable elsewhere without offering qualifiers or disclaimers.

INTRODUCTION

The epigraph introducing this book appears as an addendum to Joanne Grant's *Ella Baker*. As it happens, Robert Moses and Charles Cobb chose the same epigraph to introduce their book *Radical Equations*. Initially, I worried about using the very same words for an introductory statement. But then I realized that Moses, Cobb, and Grant, all of whom worked closely with Ella Baker in the heyday of SNCC, had selected a quotation that best represented her philosophy and politics. That being the case, it seemed altogether appropriate to highlight again the remarks about radicalism that Baker made in 1969.

1. Evans, *Personal Politics*; Mueller, "Ella Baker and the Origins of 'Participatory Democracy'"; Omolade, interview by author; Holmes Norton, interview by author.

2. Darlene Clark Hine, "Rape and the Inner Lives of Black Women: Thoughts on the Culture of Dissemblance," in *Hine Sight*, 37.

3. Ibid., 43.

4. Kochiyama, telephone interview by author.

5. Joyce Ladner made this observation about Baker at the SNCC reunion at Shaw University, Raleigh, N.C, Apr. 2000.

CHAPTER ONE

1. Giddings, interview by author.

2. Census records and transcribed interviews vary in the spelling of Ella Baker's paternal grandfather's name, with some identifying him as "Teemer" and others "Teema."

3. Baker, interview by Hayden and Thrasher, 13.

4. Minutes of the Thirteenth Annual Session of the Women's Auxiliary Progressive Baptist Convention of North Carolina, Elizabeth City, N.C., Oct. 29–Nov. 1, 1931, North Carolina Collection (NC Collection), Wilson Library, University of North Carolina at Chapel Hill, 5.

5. Gilmore, *Gender and Jim Crow*. For more discussion of how black women negotiated race, class, and gender identities in this period, see Perkins, "The Impact of the 'Culture of True Womanhood' on the Education of Black Women"; Gaines, *Uplifting the Race*; and Shaw, *What a Woman Ought to Be and to Do*.

6. Shaw, *What a Woman Ought to Be and to Do*, 91. Shaw argues that, despite some elitist underpinnings, black middle-class women formed an identity that included service to those less fortunate, even when providing such service involved some seemingly unfeminine behavior by conventional standards. She further argues that the black community's expectation of public works by women undermined the cult of true womanhood's emphasis on domesticity. The emphasis on humility undermined class snobbery toward the black poor.

7. Baker, interview by Hogan, 15.

8. Minutes of the Thirteenth Annual Session of the Woman's Auxiliary Progressive Baptist Convention, 7.

9. Eric Anderson, *Race and Politics in North Carolina*, 12.

10. Baker, interview by Hayden and Thrasher, 26, 28.

11. U.S. Census Population Schedule, North Carolina, 1870 and 1880.

12. Warren County Sunday School Convention proceedings, July 14, 1926, bulletin no. 82, NC Collection.

13. Baker, interview by Hogan, 14.

14. Ibid., 14–15.

15. Minutes of the Thirteenth Annual Session of the Woman's Auxiliary Progressive Baptist Convention, 4. These were the only extant minutes I could locate with Anna Ross Baker's name in them. Even though Baker was a young adult in 1931, all of her interview accounts suggest that the missionary work her mother did in the 1930s was a continuation of the same kind of work she had done when Ella Baker was a child. So, I am inferring that these service projects are representative examples of earlier work. Note that on p. 5 of the minutes the session is described as the fourteenth annual session. It is unclear whether the gathering was the thirteenth or the fourteenth, but all other information is consistent.

16. Baker, interview by Hogan, 15.

17. See Salem, *To Better Our World*, and Bekeley, "'Colored Ladies Also Contributed.'"

18. See Higginbotham, *Righteous Discontent*, 13–18, 221–229; and Gilmore, *Gender*

and Jim Crow, for further discussion of the political and community service intervention of middle-class black women in the South in the early 1900s.

19. Minutes of the Thirteenth Annual Session of the Women's Auxiliary Progressive Baptist Convention, 13.

20. Higginbotham, *Righteous Discontent*, 120–21.

21. "Lifting as we climb" was the motto of the National Association of Colored Women, formed in 1896. See Giddings, *When and Where I Enter*, 93–98.

22. There is a very lively debate in the literature about the nature of class, leadership, and respectability among African Americans in the early 1900s. Shaw argues for the sense of obligation black middle class women felt for the masses of black folk. Despite some elitism, she contends, social status was actually dependent on social responsibility to the community. This relationship was underwritten by the close proximity and shared racial discrimination faced by all blacks regardless of class. Gaines and Higginbotham place greater emphasis on the ways in which the black middle class policed the moral behavior of the poor and earned benefits as a result. Gilmore sees the politics of respectability as a shrewd strategy by middle-class blacks to win reform victories for the entire community.

23. See Gaines, *Uplifting the Race*, for further discussion of the limits and contradictions of "uplift" ideology that privileged black middle-class male leadership and inadvertently reinforced antiblack racism. Also see Frankel and Dye, *Gender, Class, Race, and Reform*.

24. Burroughs quoted in Higginbotham, *Righteous Discontent*, 208.

25. Cantarow and O'Malley, "Ella Baker," 59.

26. Ibid.

27. Ibid., 60.

28. For more evidence of middle-class black women's belief in the compatibility of successful private and public lives in the first quarter of the twentieth century, see Shaw, *What a Woman Ought to Be and To Do*, and Gilmore, *Gender and Jim Crow*.

29. Minutes of the Thirteenth Annual Session of the Woman's Auxiliary Progressive Baptist Convention, 7.

30. Cantarow and O'Malley, "Ella Baker," 59.

31. Collins, *Black Feminist Thought*, 119.

32. Baker, interview by Hayden and Thrasher, 26.

33. Baker, interview by Hogan, 86.

34. Ibid.

35. Ibid., 82, 85. The term "precise-spoken" is from Baker, interview by Hayden and Thrasher, 9.

36. Baker, interview by Boyte, 4.

37. Baker, interview by Hogan, 86.

38. Baker, interview by Hayden and Thrasher, 22.

39. Ibid., 22.

40. Ibid., 23.

41. Ibid., 22.

42. Ibid., 22–23.

43. U.S. Census Population Schedule, Norfolk City, Virginia, 1900, Norfolk Public Library, Norfolk, Va. This census schedule lists the year of marriage.

44. Du Bois, "Forethought," in *The Souls of Black Folk*, 34. Du Bois first made this famous statement in his address to the first Pan-African conference, held in London in July 1900.

45. Ella Baker's maternal family was from Littleton, N.C., which is now a part of Warren County; however, Littleton was formerly a part of both Warren and adjacent Halifax Counties.

46. U.S. Census Population Schedule, North Carolina, 1900 and 1910. This census listed whether respondents could read or write and whether they owned or rented land.

47. Black sociologist E. Franklin Frazier's *Black Bourgeoisie* attacked the snobbery and selfish attitudes of privileged African Americans. However, Baker's family does not fit his profile.

48. Geospatial and Statistical Data Center, University of Virginia Library. Richmond City had a larger population, with 85,050. U.S. Historical Census Data Browser, ⟨http://fisher.lib.virginia.edu/census⟩.

49. Earl Lewis, *In Their Own Interest*, 10.

50. Ibid., 22–23.

51. "Judge Fines Insolent Negro $25," *Norfolk Landmark*, July 8, 1910, 2.

52. For more information on Jim Crow and segregation, see Chafe et al., *Remembering Jim Crow*; Dailey et al., *Jumpin' Jim Crow*; and Perman, *Struggle for Mastery*.

53. Earl Lewis, *In Their Own Interest*, 21–22. Black disenfranchisement was not the sole intent of the redistricting in Norfolk, but it was the net result.

54. "Fourth Ends in Turmoil of Riot," *Norfolk Landmark*, July 5, 1910, 1. For details on antiblack violence after the Jack Johnson fight, see Roberts, *Papa Jack*.

55. Norfolk City Directory, 1895–96, Norfolk Collection, Norfolk Public Library, Norfolk, Va., 93.

56. Norfolk City Directory, 1897, 565.

57. Baker, interview by Hayden and Thrasher, 6.

58. Norfolk City Directory, 1897, 565, and 1900, 749.

59. Norfolk City Directory, 1910, 740.

60. Ibid.

61. Baker, interview by Hayden and Thrasher, 11.

62. Baker, interview by Hogan, 11. The transcript says, "I don't think it was Dennis Austin—was tall and very black . . ." I think there was an error in the transcription from the audio, since census records indicate that Dennis Alston of North Carolina was a neighbor of the Bakers in Norfolk and otherwise fits Ella Baker's description. He is likely the person she is referring to as the Black Money King. See also Norfolk City Directory, 1910, 740, and Baker, interview by Hayden and Thrasher, 14.

63. Baker, interview by Hayden and Thrasher, 14.

64. Baker, interview by Hogan, 10–11.

65. Baker, interview by Hayden and Thrasher, 2.

66. Baker, interview by Hogan, 81.

67. Ibid., 81–82.

68. Baker, interview by Hayden and Thrasher, 8.

69. Ibid., 12.

70. Ibid., 11.

71. Ibid., 16.

72. Ibid., 12.

73. Ibid., 21.

74. Norfolk City Directory, 1908, 1217.

75. "Fourth Ends in Turmoil of Riot," *Norfolk Landmark*, July 5, 1910, 1.

76. Baker, interview by Hayden and Thrasher, 21.

77. Cantarow and O'Malley, "Ella Baker," 58–60; Baker, interview by Hogan, 14–16, 86–89; Baker, interviewer not known, Duke University Oral History Program (DUOHP), Durham, N.C., 8.

78. Warren County Register of Deeds, Warrenton, N.C., 1888; and Baker, interview by Hayden and Thrasher, 19.

79. Baker, interview by Britton, 2–3; Warren Co. Register of Deeds, 1888.

80. Baker, interview by Hayden and Thrasher, 2, 24.

81. Cantarow and O'Malley, "Ella Baker," 57.

82. Baker, interviewer not known, DUOHP, 4–9.

83. Newell, interview by author; "Our Colored People," *Littleton News Reporter*, June 18, 1897, 5.

84. Newell, interview by author. Jenny Newell was a classmate and neighbor of Ella Baker in the 1910s.

85. Baker, interview by Hayden and Thrasher, 21.

86. On Maggie, see Solomon, interview by author. On Blake Curtis, see U.S. Census Population Schedule, North Carolina Census, 1920, v. 42, ED 138, sheet 19, line 11.

87. Solomon, interview by author. Maude Solomon was a neighbor of the Baker family and a friend of Ella Baker's younger sister in the 1910s and 1920s.

88. Newell, interview by author.

89. Johnson, *Shadow of the Plantation*, 129; also Jaynes, *Branches without Roots*.

90. Ella Baker, interview by Morris, 17A.

91. Baker, interview by Hayden and Thrasher, 16–17.

92. Baker, interview by Morris, 13A; the "tomboy" reference is from Baker, interview by Hogan, 89.

93. Baker, interview by Hayden and Thrasher, 11–13, 16; Baker, interviewer not known, DUOHP, 1.

94. Baker, interview by Hogan, 86.

95. Baker, interview by Hayden and Thrasher, 16.

96. Baker, interview by Hogan, 86.

97. Baker, interview by Hayden and Thrasher, 8.

98. Cantarow and O'Malley, "Ella Baker," 73.

99. Baker, interview by Morris, 12A.

100. Baker, interview by Hayden and Thrasher, 15.

101. Ibid., 25. For more on class and preaching styles see, Wheeler, *Uplifting the Race*.

102. Baker, interview by Hayden and Thrasher, 14.

103. Baker, interview by Morris, 12A.

104. Cantarow and O'Malley, "Ella Baker," 57.

105. Ibid., 5, 61; Gilchrist, interview by author.

106. Warren County Register of Deeds, 1888.

107. North Carolina Real Estate Index for Warren County, 1888, book 53, 625, N.C. State Archives, Raleigh, N.C.; 1889, book 54, 156; 1890, book 54, 848.

108. Baker, interview by Hayden and Thrasher, 61.

109. Cantarow and O'Malley, "Ella Baker," 61.

110. Baker, interview by Hogan, 74.

111. Charles Payne, "Ella Baker and Models of Social Change."

112. Eric Anderson, *Race and Politics in North Carolina*, 2–5.

113. Ibid., 5. For more on African Americans in North Carolina politics during this period, see Helen Edmonds, *The Negro and Fusion Politics in North Carolina*; Ray Gavins, "Black Leadership in North Carolina to 1900."

114. Baker's childhood memories are documented in nine in-depth personal interviews conducted with her by various researchers between 1968 and 1981.

115. Baker, interview by Boyte, 3.

116. Ibid., 3–4.

117. Newell, interview by author; Solomon, interview by author.

118. Escott, "White Republicanism and Ku Klux Klan Terror," 29; Williamson, *A Rage for Order*, 128–33.

119. *Littleton Courier*, Sept. 1, 1892, 4.

120. *Littleton News Reporter*, Aug. 16, 1897, 2, column by Bill Arp.

121. *Littleton News Reporter*, June 4, 1897, 5. The mid-1890s were marked by widespread economic hardship.

122. Cantarow and O'Malley, "Ella Baker," 60.

123. Solomon, interview by author.

124. Baker, interview by Hayden and Thrasher, 20.

125. Ibid., 10.

126. Solomon, interview by author.

127. Ibid.

128. For discussions on the class politics within the African American community in the South in the early 1900s, see Gatewood, *Aristocrats of Color*.

129. Baker, interview by Hogan, 79–80.

130. Blake Baker's Estate, Warren County Estates Records, 1831. Blake Baker's will lists Temer Baker as property to be distributed to his heirs.

131. Cantarow and O'Malley, "Ella Baker," 60.

132. Ibid., 58.

133. Baker, interview by Hayden and Thrasher, 25.

134. Cantarow and O'Malley, "Ella Baker," 73.

135. Gilchrist, interview by author.

CHAPTER TWO

1. Baker, interviewer not known, Duke University Oral History Program (DUOHP), Durham, N.C., 5.

2. Baker, interview by Britton, 1–2. This additional year of schooling explains why Ella Baker was slightly older than her classmates upon graduation in 1927.

3. Baker, interviewer not known, DUOHP, 5.

4. Ibid., 4; Baker, interview by Hogan, 14.

5. Nash, interview by author, Oct. 1990.

6. Baker, interview by Hogan, 14.

7. James D. Anderson, *The Education of Blacks in the South*.

8. Carter, *Shaw's Universe*, 223.

9. Gutman, "Schools for Freedom," 260–61.

10. Minutes of the Thirteenth Annual Session of the Women's Auxiliary Progressive Baptist Convention of North Carolina, Elizabeth City, N.C., Oct. 29–Nov. 1, 1931, North Carolina Collection, Wilson Library, University of North Carolina.

11. Baker, interview by Hogan, 82.

12. Carter, *Shaw's Universe*, 5, 225.

13. Ibid., iv.

14. James D. Anderson, *The Education of Blacks in the South*, 240–42; Goggin, *Carter G. Woodson*.

15. Higginbotham, *Righteous Discontent*, 187.

16. Catalogue and Announcements of Shaw University, session of 1927–1928, North Carolina Collection (NC Collection), Wilson Library, University of North Carolina, Chapel Hill. Absences from religious services could result in loss of scholarships and honors.

17. "Shaw University," pamphlet, 1945, Shaw University Archives (SUA), Raleigh, N.C., 6.

18. Baker, interview by Hogan, 76.

19. Ibid., 85.

20. Ibid., 82.

21. *Shaw University Journal*, Nov. 1925, box 59, 4, SUA.

22. Higginbotham, *Righteous Discontent*, 24–28.

23. David Levering Lewis, *W. E. B. Du Bois: Biography of a Race*, 549. Also see Abrahams, "Negotiating Respect." Although Du Bois popularized the phrase "the talented tenth" beginning in 1903, it was coined by Henry Morehouse, executive secretary of the American Baptist Home Mission Society from 1897 to 1893 and from 1902 to 1917. See Higginbotham, *Righteous Discontent*, 20, 25.

24. Higginbotham, *Righteous Discontent*, 25–27.

25. Ibid., 20.

26. Sundquist, *The Oxford W. E. B. Du Bois Reader*, 10.

27. Carter, *Shaw's Universe*, 139.

28. Catalogue and Announcements of Shaw University, session of 1926–1927, 16, NC Collection.

29. Carter, *Shaw's Universe*, 49.

30. Shaw University Faculty Council Minutes, Jan. 26, 1925, and Apr. 22, 1925, box 146, SUA.

31. Carter, *Shaw's Universe*, 139–40.

32. *Shaw University Bulletin*, 1922, 14, NC Collection.

33. Catalogue and Announcements of Shaw University, session of 1926–1927, 16. This training might have prepared young women to work as domestic servants. However, Shaw apparently presumed that women would perform such work on behalf of their own families. Similar work requirements were common at elite private colleges for white women during this time. Of course, having students do this work also saved money.

34. For further discussion of contemporary ideas regarding black women's domestic responsibilities and their professional and public roles, see Shaw, *What a Woman Ought to Be and to Do*.

35. Yergan, interview by author. Effie Yergen is a cousin of Max Yergan, the famous Shaw alumnus, missionary, and later political associate of Paul Robeson.

36. Ibid., 3.

37. Shaw University Faculty Council Minutes, Feb. 12, 1925, box 22, 5, SUA.

38. Carter, *Shaw's Universe*, 139–40.

39. Catalogue and Announcements of Shaw University, session of 1927–1928, 16.

40. Carter, *Shaw's Universe*, 139–40. For a discussion of how black urban working-class leisure activities were negatively viewed by middle-class black leaders, see Hunter, *To 'Joy My Freedom*, chaps. titled "Dancing and Carousing the Night Away" and "Wholesome and Hurtful Amusements."

41. Franklin and Moss, *From Slavery to Freedom*, 294.

42. For more information on black politics during and after World War I, see Ellis, *Race, War, and Surveillance*.

43. Delany and Delany, *Having Our Say*, 99.

44. See Ella Baker, "Shaw Valedictorian Speech," 1927, Ella Baker Papers (EBP), Schomburg Center for Research in Black Culture, New York, N.Y.; and Ella Baker's high school transcripts, 1918–1923, Shaw University Registrar, SUA. Copy of transcript in author's possession.

45. Yergan, interview by author.

46. Benjamin Brawley (1882–1939) was the author of ten scholarly books including *A Short History of the American Negro* (New York: Macmillan, 1913); *Women of Achievement* (Chicago: Woman's American Baptist Home Mission Society, 1919; *Early American Negro Writers* (Chapel Hill: University of North Carolina Press, 1935); *Paul Lawrence Dunbar, Poet of His People* (Chapel Hill: University of North Carolina Press, 1936); *A New Survey of English Literature: A Text Book for Colleges* (New York: Knopf, 1925); and *The Negro in Literature and Art in the United States* (New York: Duffield, 1930).

47. Carter, *Shaw's Universe*, 216.

48. Ibid., 111.

49. Ibid., 217.

50. Yergan, interview by author.

51. Cantarow and O'Malley, "Ella Baker," 64.

52. Baker, interview by Hayden and Thrasher, 217; Ella Baker to Brawley, circa 1931, EBP, correspondence files (1930s).

53. *Shaw University Journal*, Jan. 1924, box 59, SUA.

54. *Shaw University Journal*, Nov. 1925, box 59, SUA.

55. Ella Baker's Shaw University transcript, Shaw University Registrar, SUA.

56. Ella Baker's résumé, NAACP Papers, group II, box A572, Library of Congress, Washington, D.C.

57. Baker, interview by Hayden and Thrasher, 45.

58. Brockington, interview by author, Feb. 1990.

59. See Grant, *Ella Baker*, 21. Roberts was also known by the name Robinson.

60. Yergan, interview by author.

61. Carter, *Shaw's Universe*, 49.

62. Lynch, *Black American Radicals and the Liberation of Africa*, 17–18.

63. Yergan ultimately moved to the far right and repudiated the left-wing ideas he had once embraced; see ibid., 51.

64. *Shaw University Bulletin*, 1922.

65. Baker, interviewer not known, DUOHP, 5.

66. Cantarow and O'Malley, "Ella Baker," 55.

67. *Shaw University Journal*, Mar. 1925, 5, box 59, SUA.

68. Ibid.

69. Baker, interview by Hayden and Thrasher, 35.

70. Ibid.

71. Baker, "The Negro Church, the Nucleus of the Negroes' Cultural Development," EBP.

72. Ibid.

73. Ibid.

74. Protests against rigid, conservative policies occurred on a number of southern black college campuses during the decade following World War I. Shaw experienced comparatively little of this turmoil. See Wolters, *The New Negro on Campus*.

75. Baker, interview by Walker, 8.

76. *Shaw University Bulletin*, 1923, 3.

77. Baker, interview by Hogan, 82.

78. Ibid.

79. Ibid., 83.

80. Baker, interview by Hayden and Thrasher, 31.

81. Baker, interview by Hogan, 83.

82. Baker, interview by Hayden and Thrasher, 30.

83. Catalogue and Announcements of Shaw University, session of 1927–1928.

84. Baker, interview by Hayden and Thrasher, 31.

85. Ibid.

86. Shaw University Faculty Council minutes, Feb. 1, 1926, box 146, SUA.

87. Ibid.

88. Ella Baker's Shaw University transcript, Shaw University Registrar, SUA.

89. Yergan, interview by author, 2.

90. For "inevitable," see Baker, interview by Hayden and Thrasher, 37; for "rebellious streak," see Baker, interviewer not known, DUOHP, 11.

91. Baker, interviewer not known, DUOHP, 12.

92. Ibid., 11.

93. Baker, interview by Hayden and Thrasher, 37–38.

94. Baker, interview by Britton, 4.

95. "Our Heritage and Its Challenge," Ella Baker's valedictorian speech, EBP.

CHAPTER THREE

1. This description of Harlem streets and of Ella Baker's reaction is drawn from several sources: Baker, interview by Scott; *Amsterdam News*, issues from Sept. through Nov. 1927; Naison, *Communists in Harlem*; and David Levering Lewis, *When Harlem Was in Vogue*.

2. Cantarow and O'Malley, "Ella Baker," 72.

3. Ibid.

4. Baker, interviewer not known, Duke University Oral History Program (DUOHP), Durham, N.C., 17.

5. Ibid., 5.

6. Telegrams from Roberts (aka Robinson) to Ella Baker, Mar. 6, 1928, June 15, 1936, July 14, 1929, Ella Baker Papers (EBP), correspondence folder, Schomburg Center for Research in Black Culture, New York, N.Y. No explanation of why Roberts/Robinson was known by two different surnames can be found.

7. Ibid.

8. Murray, *Autobiography of a Black Activist*, 75.

9. For studies with a focus on the Great Migration, see Sernett, *Bound for the Promised Land*; Trotter, *The Great Migration in Historical Perspective*; and Adero, *Up South*.

10. See Naison, *Communists in Harlem*, and Turner and Turner, *Richard B. Moore*.

11. Cantarow and O'Malley, "Ella Baker," 64.

12. Naison, *Communists in Harlem*, 67–72.

13. Cantarow and O'Malley, "Ella Baker," 64. Books that capture some of the flavor and culture of Harlem in this period include Huggins, *Harlem Renaissance*; David Levering Lewis, *When Harlem Was in Vogue*; Clarke, *Harlem*; Jervis Anderson, *This Was Harlem*; Kirby, *Black Americans in the Roosevelt Era*; Weiss, *Farewell to the Party of Lincoln*; Naison, *Communists in Harlem*; Watkins-Owens, *Blood Relations*; and Greenberg, "Or Does It Explode?"

14. Baker, interview by Morris, 10A.

15. Baker, interview by Hayden and Thrasher, 33.

16. Greenberg, "Or Does it Explode?" 76.

17. Ella Baker's valedictorian speech, "Our Heritage and Its Challenge," 1927, EBP.

18. Baker, interview by Hayden and Thrasher, 35.

19. Baker, interview by Scott, 4.

20. Ibid., 5.

21. Lynn, interview by author. This is not to imply that Ella Baker was a Marxist per se. She was not. However, she functioned at a time and in a political milieu in which Marxism and other socialist ideas were taken seriously.

22. Hughes, "My Early Days in Harlem," 62.

23. Betty Jenkins, "A White Librarian in Black Harlem."

24. Watkins-Owens, *Blood Relations*, 93.

25. Baker, interview by Morris, 17A.

26. Ella Baker to Columbus Alston, Young People's Protective League, Apr. 17, 1936, EBP; and Ella Baker to Columbus Alston, May 10, 1936, EBP.

27. Ella Baker, letter of application to Walter White, Sept. 26, 1938, NAACP Papers, group II, box A572, folder: Staff, Ella Baker, Library of Congress, Washington, D.C.

28. Sinnette, *Arthur Alfonso Schomburg*, 170.

29. Ella Baker's Experience Sheet, NAACP Papers, group II, box A572.

30. Ernestine Rose to "Dear Sirs," June 11, 1940, NAACP Papers, group II, box A572.

31. Ibid.

32. Murray, *Autobiography of a Black Activist*, 74–75.

33. Ibid., 75.

34. The descriptions of women in Harlem are drawn from Marvel Cooke, interview by author; Weisenfeld, *African American Women and Christian Activism*; and Greenberg, "Or Does it Explode?" For an analysis of black women and the YWCA, see Adrienne Lash Jones, "The Struggle among Saints," and Hedgeman, *The Trumpet Sounds*.

35. Deborah Gray White, *Too Heavy a Load*, 17.

36. Pauli Murray to Ella Baker, Dec. 1945; and Pauli Murray to Ella Baker, Feb. 11, 1961, EBP.

37. Cantarow and O'Malley, "Ella Baker," 64.

38. George S. Schuyler, "The Young Negro Co-operative League," 472.

39. Watkins-Owens, *Blood Relations*, 92.

40. Ibid.

41. Lynn, interview with author. For more on Brookwood, see Aktenbaugh, *Education for Struggle*; Kates, *Activist Rhetorics and American Higher Education*; Howlett, *Brookwood Labor College*; Murray, *Autobiography of a Black Activist*, 105–6.

42. Kates, *Activist Rhetorics and American Higher Education*, front jacket flap.

43. Lipsitz, *A Life in the Struggle*, 10. Joy James, a feminist scholar-activist, has questioned the use of Gramsci's writings on organic intellectuals to describe Ella Baker. She sees such comparisons as serving to "deradicalize" Baker and erroneously casting her as a proponent of vanguard politics rather than of popular democratic politics. Joy James, *Transcending the Talented Tenth*, 86. My reading of both Gramsci's work and Baker's life leads me to different conclusions. Gramsci is useful for understanding Baker because he distinguishes between those who see the source of their knowledge as formal academic training and those who see their knowledge as arising from practice and engagement with a community, which is itself seen as a reservoir of knowledge and analytic insights. In his detailed glossary to his edited collection of Gramsci's writings, David Forgacs offers the following useful summary of Gramsci's democratic and nonelitist view of

intellectual work as a part of a revolutionary process: "Gramsci is thus able to envisage a situation in which, as part of the revolutionary transformation of society, the intellectual function is massively expanded—in other words more and more people share the tasks of mental activity, of organizing, deliberating and leading, both politically and within the sphere of economic production. For Gramsci, this would also be a process of democratization and would inhibit the formation of bureaucracies, which arise precisely where decision-making is monopolized by a specialized elite of intellectuals." This description is consistent with my own reading of Gramsci's writings and with my understanding of Ella Baker's practice as a nonuniversity-based public intellectual—and, indeed, with Joy James's description of nonelite intellectuals. See Forgacs, *The Antonio Gramsci Reader*, 425.

44. Hedgeman, *The Trumpet Sounds*, 56–57.

45. Baker and Cooke, "The Bronx Slave Market," 330.

46. The author's interview with Marvel Cooke confirmed that she and Baker did not have any significant disagreements about the final article. There were apparently some political disagreements about language and details that Cooke declined to comment on; it is likely she did not even remember them after fifty years. Therefore, this article can be analyzed as an expression of Baker's views without in any way diminishing Cooke's contribution.

47. See Crenshaw, "Mapping the Margins"; hooks, *Feminist Theory from Margin to Center*; and Guy-Sheftall, *Words of Fire*, introduction.

48. Cooke, interview by author.

49. Baker, interview by Scott, 8.

50. See David Levering Lewis, *W. E. B. Du Bois: The Fight for Equality*, 539.

51. Floyd J. Calvin, "Schuyler Launches Program to Awaken Race Consciousness," *Pittsburgh Courier*, Feb. 7, 1931, 1, 4.

52. Cooke, interview by author.

53. Lynn, interview by author.

54. Baker, interview by Morris, 56A.

55. Baker, interview by Hayden and Thrasher, 39.

56. Cooke, interview by author.

57. Baker, interview by Hayden and Thrasher, 40.

58. For discussions of black intellectuals' responses to Jürgen Habermas's concept of the public sphere, see Black Public Sphere Collective, *The Black Public Sphere*, especially the afterword, "Mapping the Black Public Sphere," by Thomas C. Holt; also see Banks, *Black Intellectuals*.

59. Cooke, interview by author.

60. Calvin, "Schuyler Launches Program," 1, 4.

61. Schuyler, a onetime socialist turned anarchist, became a staunch conservative by the end of his life. A rabid anticommunist during the McCarthy era, he even maintained friendly relations with the racist John Birch Society, opposed the awarding of the Nobel Prize to Martin Luther King Jr., and condemned Malcolm X as a "pixilated criminal." See Peplow, *George S. Schuyler*. Also see Schuyler, *Black Empire*, and Schuyler, *Rac(e)ing to the Right*, ed. Leak. The Leak collection covers Schuyler's conservative views but does not mention much about the YNCL.

62. Jervis Anderson, *A. Philip Randolph*, 143–44. See also Chateauvert, *Marching Together*; Harris, *Keeping the Faith*; Arnesen, *Brotherhoods of Color*; Pfeffer, *A. Philip Randolph*.

63. Jervis Anderson, *A. Philip Randolph*, 141.

64. Baker, interview by Hayden and Thrasher, 39.

65. Jervis Anderson, *A. Philip Randolph*, 144.

66. Lynn, interview by author.

67. Ibid. Lynn indicated that he never knew Baker to attend church "or express much interest in religion. She was interested in other ideas."

68. George Schuyler, "Views and Reviews," *Pittsburgh Courier*, May 24, 1930, Nov. 8, 1930.

69. Baker, interview by Hayden and Thrasher, 40.

70. Baker, interview by Morris, 22A.

71. Baker, interview by Hayden and Thrasher, 40.

72. I argue elsewhere in the book that Baker supported the idea that how one behaves as a civilian, so to speak, was related to how one conducts political organizing work. It was important to be principled and fair in personal relations as an extension of re-creating social relations in the public sphere.

73. There is a lively ongoing debate among contemporary feminists and historians about the politics and significance of marital infidelity on the part of public figures. Baker seems to have viewed Schuyler's sexual behavior as unprincipled but private. This stance is at variance with much of her work, which sees the cultivation of personal relationships and the private behavior of political organizers as critical to their effectiveness as leaders and their ability to construct a vision of a transformed society based on a different set of personal values as well as public policies.

74. Baker, interviewer not known, DUOHP, 29.

75. George Schuyler, "Views and Reviews," *Pittsburgh Courier*, Nov. 15, 1930.

76. Ibid.

77. George Schuyler, "The Young Negro Cooperative League," *Crisis*, Jan. 1932, 456.

78. "Schuyler Heads Up League," *Pittsburgh Courier*, Oct. 24, 1931, 1, 4.

79. Report of First Conference of YNCL held at Center Avenue Branch of YMCA in Pittsburgh, Oct. 18, 1931, EBP, YNCL files.

80. Ella Baker, form letter, ca. 1931, EBP, YNCL files.

81. Open letter from Ella Baker to membership of YNCL, Sept. 26. 1932, EBP.

82. George Schuyler, "An Appeal to Young Negroes" (pamphlet issued by the Young Negroes' Cooperative League), 10, EBP, YNCL files.

83. Schuyler, "The Young Negro Cooperative League," 456.

84. Ibid.

85. Ibid., 472.

86. Ibid., 456.

87. George Schuyler to Mordecai Johnson, Dec. 18, 1931, EBP.

88. Schuyler, "The Young Negro Cooperative League," 456.

89. Ella Baker, letter to "Irvena," EBP. The content of the letter suggests that the date is roughly Dec. 1931. The letter mentions the Urban League meeting site. A receipt for $2.00, Mar. 2, 1932, from Urban League for YNCL use of meeting room. EBP.

90. Ella Baker, acting secretary treasurer of YNCL, memo, n.d., EBP, YNCL files.

91. Ella Baker, letter to John M. Gray, chairman of Committee for International Negro Youth Conference in Chicago, May 19, 1933, EBP, YNCL files, correspondence folder.

92. Sam Cantrell, "Consumer Coops," unpublished article, EBP, YNCL files.

93. Payne, "Ella Baker and Models of Social Change," 884.

94. Schuyler, "An Appeal to Young Negroes," 10.

95. Ella Baker, "Youthful City Workers Turning to Cooperative Farming," *Amsterdam News*, May 11, 1935, 2.

96. George Schuyler, *Pittsburgh Courier*, Nov. 22, 1930.

97. George Schuyler, *Pittsburgh Courier*, Nov. 15, 1930.

98. Ella Baker, untitled article written in Philadelphia, circa Feb. 12, 1940, EBP, Ella Baker Writings file.

99. Ella Baker, interview by *Urban Review* editors, 23.

100. Marable, *W. E. B. Du Bois*, 147–48.

101. Ibid., 148.

102. Ibid., 147–49.

103. For biographical information on Divine, see Weisbrot, *Father Divine and the Struggle for Racial Equality*, and Watts, *God, Harlem, U.S.A.*

104. Peplow, *George S. Schuyler*, 27.

105. Ibid., 117 n. 25.

106. The caption under a front-page photo of Schuyler in the *Pittsburgh Courier*, Oct. 17, 1931, reads: "He recently returned from a six month visit in Europe where he studied intensively the fundamental principles of the Consumer's Co-operative Societies of Great Britain."

107. "A Century of Progress" (1932; brochure announcing Chicago World's Fair), EBP. Baker, interview by Scott, 2, 4–9, 11–13, 19; Clarke, interview by author; Ella Baker's résumé, NAACP Papers, group II, box A572; Harlem's Own Cooperative letterhead (blank), EBP, 1930s folder.

108. Baker, interview by Hayden and Thrasher, 35.

109. Ibid., 55.

110. For information on African Americans and the WPA, see Sitkoff, *A New Deal for Blacks*; Sullivan, *Days of Hope*; Ferguson, *Black Politics in New Deal Atlanta*.

111. Murray, *Autobiography of a Black Activist*, 104.

112. Ibid., 104.

113. Ibid., 90.

114. Lynn, interview by author.

115. Ibid. The Triangle Shirtwaist fire occurred in New York City in 1911 and took the lives of more than 100 immigrant workers, mostly women, who were trapped in the unsafe building. The tragedy galvanized public support for safer working conditions.

116. Pauli Murray, to Miss (Isabel) Taylor and Miss (Floria) Pickney, "Recruiting and Promotion," Oct. 28, 1938, Murray Papers, WPA files, box 72, Schlesinger Library, Radcliffe College, Cambridge, Mass.

117. Works Progress Administration, Workers Services Division, NYC reports, 1938–39, Works Progress Administration (WPA) Papers, box 19, National Archives, Washington, D.C.

118. Ibid.

119. Ella Baker, "A Course in Consumer Education," prepared for Worker's Education Project of WPA, WPA Papers, box 18, folder: "New York, Programs Miscellaneous, 1936–1939."

120. Works Progress Administration, NYC reports, report for Feb. 1938, WPA Papers, box 19.

121. Pauli Murray, "Report on Worker's Education Exhibit," Oct. 13, 1938, to Mr. E. Rosenberg, (no title given), 1–3, Murray Papers, WPA files, box 72.

122. Murray, *Autobiography of a Black Activist*, 104.

123. Conrad Lynn, *There Is a Fountain*, 66.

124. Cantarow and O'Malley, "Ella Baker," 64.

125. On Oct. 11, 1936, Baker writes D. Mines, stating that she will meet him at Rand School where she will be attending a lecture. Also, see letter from Julia Primoff of Women's Afternoon Classes, Rand School, to Baker, Apr. 30, 1937, EBP, asking her to lecture at the school.

126. Swanson, "Rand School of Social Science." For more information, see Cornell, "A History of the Rand School."

127. Baker, interview by Hayden and Thrasher, 51–52.

128. Conrad Lynn, *There Is a Fountain*, 66.

129. Ella Baker, "A Course in Consumer Education," prepared for Workers Education Project of WPA, WPA Papers, box 18, folder: "New York, Programs Miscellaneous, 1936–1939."

130. Ibid.

131. Ibid.

132. Ibid.

133. Ibid.

134. Baker, interview by Hayden and Thrasher, 51.

135. A "cell" is a small, tightly knit working group within the larger pyramid structure of a "democratic centralist" organization like the Communist Party and many other Communist organizations throughout the world. What the "cell" does and organizes around could vary depending on the analysis, "line," or politics of the larger organization at any given time. Given the anticommunism of Baker's later political career, which did not preclude personal relationships or even political collaborations with Communists, she was likely applauding the form of the "cell" rather than the content of the CP's political ideology.

136. Lynn, interview by author.

137. Ibid., and Conrad Lynn, *There Is a Fountain*, 66.

138. Naison, *Communists in Harlem*, 309.

139. On Lovestone and his faction, see Alexander, *The Right Opposition*; Morgan, *A Covert Life*; and Wald, *The New York Intellectuals*, 153–54. The Lovestonites were followers of Russian socialist Nikolai Bukharin. Later, the faction underwent a major internal split, and the remaining leadership moved considerably to the right by the 1950s. Jay Lovestone eventually became a strong CIA supporter and rabid anticommunist within the right wing of the American labor movement.

140. Lynn, interview by author; and Clarke, interview by author.

141. Murray, *Autobiography of a Black Activist*, 103.

142. Solomon, *The Cry Was Unity*.

143. Ibid., 64–65.

144. Ibid., 75.

145. The Workers (Communist) Party changed its name to the Communist Party USA in 1929. Bertram Wolfe was a Marxist during the 1930s, but he moved steadily to the right along with Jay Lovestone and ultimately helped found the Hoover Institute, a conservative think tank. Details taken from Buhle et al., *The Encyclopedia of the American Left*, 435–37. See also Alexander, *The Right Opposition*, and Morgan, *A Covert Life*.

146. Buhle et al., *The Encyclopedia of the American Left*, 435–37.

147. Clarke, interview by author.

148. Baker, interview by Morris, 8A.

149. Clarke, interview by author.

150. Lynn, interview by author.

151. Ibid., and Conrad Lynn, *There is a Fountain*, 68.

152. Lynn, interview by author.

153. Naison, *Communists in Harlem*, 16.

154. Ibid., 157. See also Winston James, *Holding Aloft the Banner of Ethiopia*, and Solomon, *The Cry Was Unity*.

155. Baker and Imes collaborated on a number of projects during these years. See Ella Baker's résumé, NAACP Papers, group II, box A572, listing Imes as a reference. Invitation to a meeting, June 25, 1935, co-sponsored by Dunbar Housewives League and Citizens for Fair Play, listing Imes as a convener, EBP. Also, Baker was in charge of education and publicity for the Harlem's Own Cooperative, Inc., of which William Imes was president; there is a letterhead in her papers with her name on it, EPB.

156. Ella Baker, "Light on a Dark Continent," EBP, Ella Baker's Writings file.

157. Marable, *W. E. B. Du Bois*, 147.

158. Typed essay by Ella Baker, no title, circa Feb. 12, 1940, written in Philadelphia, Pa., EBP, Ella Baker's Writings file. This essay reads as if written for a publication, but no published version was located.

159. Baker, interview by Britton, 68.

160. Baker, interview by Hayden and Thrasher, 12.

161. Ibid., 36–37; Baker, interviewer not known, DUOHP, 19.

162. Ibid.

163. Emma Lance, letter to Ella Baker, circa 1930s, EBP, correspondence files.

164. Freeman H. Hubbard, letter to Ella Baker, June 8, 1934, EBP, correspondence files.

165. A series of telegrams from Roberts to Baker dated Oct. 25, 1927, and Mar. 6, 1928–June 14, 1929, EBP, correspondence files.

166. No record of the marriage could be located, probably because of the confusion regarding T. J. Roberts/Robinson's last name. Marriage registries were checked in all of the boroughs of New York, in Warrenton and Halifax Counties in North Carolina, and in Newark, N.J. It is clear that Baker and Roberts were legally married, however, because divorce papers (1958) were located in the Office of the City Clerk in New York.

167. Gilchrist, interview by author.

168. Ella Baker Files, FBI, Department of Justice, Washington, D.C., NY file, misc. report, Sept. 10, 1941.

169. Baker, interview by Hayden and Thrasher, 57–58.

170. Bernice Johnson Reagon, telephone interview by author. Jackie Brockington declined to discuss Bob or the marriage in much detail because, in her words, "Aunt Ella never wanted to talk about it."

171. Joyce Ladner, interview with author.

172. Baker, interview by Hayden and Thrasher, 58.

173. Prathia Hall (Wynn), interview by author.

174. T. J. Roberts, letter to a railway express agency's complaint department, EBP, correspondence files.

175. Ella Baker, letter to D. J. Philips, President, Consolidated Tenants League, Inc., Sept. 21, 1945, EBP, correspondence files.

176. In her correspondence with her landlord, Baker uncharacteristically used her married name, referring to herself as Ella Roberts, perhaps to avoid complications or questions of marital legitimacy. See letter from Ella Baker (Roberts) to Roy Zisser, Dophen Realty Co., Dec. 7, 1955, EBP, correspondence files.

177. Clarke, interview by author.

178. Taitt-Magubane, interview by author.

179. Ibid.

180. Brockington, interview by author.

181. T. J. Roberts, letter in response to a *New York Times* classified job advertisement, Jan. 8, 1939, EBP.

182. Ella Baker, letter to League for Mutual Aid, 104 5th Ave., NYC, Jan. 24, 1940, EBP.

183. Clarke, interview by author.

184. Baker, interview by Britton, 4.

CHAPTER FOUR

1. Baker, interview Hayden and Thrasher, 56.

2. Hill, interview by author.

3. For background information on the NAACP, see Tushnet, *The NAACP's Legal Strategy against Segregated Education*; Ware, *William Hastie*; Zangrando, *The NAACP Crusade against Lynching*; David Levering Lewis, *W. E. B. Du Bois: Biography of a Race* and *W. E. B. DuBois: The Fight for Equality and the American Century*; Kellogg, *NAACP*; B. Joyce Ross, *J. E. Spingarn and the Rise of the NAACP*; and Walter Francis White, *A Man Called White*.

4. See Kellogg, *NAACP*, and Zangrando, *The NAACP Crusade against Lynching*. See also Hine et al., *The African American Odyssey*, 2:484.

5. Baker, interview by Hogan, 27.

6. Rudwick and Meier, "The Rise of the Black Secretariat in the NAACP."

7. David Levering Lewis, *W. E. B. Du Bois: Biography of a Race*; Marable, *W. E. B. Du Bois*; and Rampersad, *The Art and Imagination of W. E. B. Du Bois*. Du Bois later abandoned his talented tenth formula, embraced Marxism, joined the Communist Party, and died in exile in Ghana in 1963 at the age of ninety-five.

8. Baker, interview by Britton, 7.

9. Horne, *Race Woman*.

10. Walter White, letter to "CH," Feb. 8, 1941, NAACP Papers, group II, box A572, folder: Ella Baker, staff, 1940–1942, Library of Congress, Washington, D.C.

11. For information on Daisy Lampkin, see Edna Chappell McKenzie, "Daisy Lampkin," in Hine et al., *Black Women in America*, 1:690–93.

12. C. Herbert Marshall Jr., letter to Walter White, Mar. 24, 1941, NAACP Papers, group II, box A572, folder: Ella Baker, staff, 1940–1942.

13. E. Frederic Morrow, branch coordinator, letter to Jerry Gilliam, Norfolk, Va., Sept. 22, 1941, NAACP Papers, group II, box C307. For more biographical background on Morrow, see Branch, *Parting the Waters*, 180–81.

14. Ella Baker, letters to Roy Wilkins, Mar. 10, 1941; Mar. 21, 1941; Apr. 11, 1941, NAACP Papers, group II, box A572, folder: Ella Baker, staff, 1940–1942.

15. Braden, interview by author, Apr. 13, 1991.

16. Williams, *Eyes on the Prize*, 180.

17. A state law required the group to turn over its membership lists to authorities and banned it for refusing to do so. NAACP leaders rightly feared reprisals against its membership if such a list were made public and did not want to set a precedent for cooperating with this type of harassment.

18. Ella Baker, letter to Mr. and Mrs. J. J. Green, Apr. 15, 1941, NAACP Papers, group II, box C307.

19. Baker, interviewer not known, Duke University Oral History Program (DUOHP), Durham, N.C., 33.

20. Louise B. Gibbs, letter to Ella Baker, July 25, 1944; Baker, letter to Gibbs, July 27,

1944; Baker, letter to station manager, Union Station, Washington, D.C., July 27, 1944; NAACP Papers, group II, box A573, folder: Staff, Ella Baker, 1943–1944.

21. Ella Baker, letter to Roy Wilkins, Mar. 20, 1941, NAACP Papers, group II, box A572, folder: Staff, Ella Baker, 1940–1955.

22. Ibid.

23. Ella Baker, letter to Roy Wilkins, Mar. 11, 1942, NAACP Papers, group II, box A572, folder: Staff, Ella Baker, 1940–1955.

24. Ibid.

25. Baker, interview by Scott, 13.

26. Cantarow and O'Malley, "Ella Baker," 72.

27. Ibid., 70.

28. Sacks, *Caring By the Hour*, 3.

29. Ella Baker to J. M. Tinsley, Apr. 3, 1941, NAACP Papers, group II, box C301.

30. J. M. Tinsley, letter to Walter White, Apr. 7, 1941, NAACP Papers, group II, box C210.

31. Baker, interview by Hogan, 43.

32. Ibid., 38–39.

33. J. M. Tinsley, letter to Walter White, June 3, 1941, NAACP Papers, II, box C210, folder: Virginia State Conference.

34. Report of Dept. of Branches to Board of Directors, May 1941 meeting (n. 6), NAACP Papers, group II, box C390, folder: Monthly Reports, 1940–1942.

35. Ibid.

36. Baker, interview by Hogan, 21; Baker, interviewer not known, DUOHP, 19; Baker, interview by Hayden and Thrasher, 49–50.

37. Ella Baker, "Report of Dept. of Branches," May 1941, Board of Directors Meeting, NAACP Papers, group II, box C390, folder: Monthly Reports, 1940–1942.

38. Baker, interview by Hogan, 39.

39. Ella Baker, letter to Ruth Tinsley, Richmond, Va., ca. Dec. 1942 or 1943, EBP, NAACP files. The content of the letter suggests it was written in December of either 1941 or 1942, when Baker was still a field staff member of the NAACP.

40. Baker, interview by Hogan, 23.

41. Ella Baker, "Report of Dept. of Branches" (report no. 6), Dec. 1941 Board of Directors Meeting, NAACP Papers, group II, box C390, folder: Monthly Reports, 1940–1942.

42. Ibid.

43. Ibid.

44. Ibid.

45. Ella Baker, letter to Walter White, Oct. 4, 1941, NAACP Papers, group II, box C307, General Branch Files.

46. Ella Baker, letter to Walter White, Feb. 18, 1943, NAACP Papers, group II, box B98.

47. NAACP Papers, group II, box C307, General Branch Files. Letters throughout the file illustrate this pattern.

48. Lynn, interview by author. The comment was made to Lynn by Baker, and he recalled it in precise and convincing detail fifty years later.

49. Ella Baker to "Mr. Green," Feb. 13, 1948, EBP, mentions that her husband is hospitalized in North Carolina. Also, see Ella Baker to Lester Granger, July 10, 1947, EBP.

50. Hill, interview by author.

51. Ibid.

52. Ella Baker, letter to Lucille Black, May 4, 1942, NAACP Papers, group II, box A572, folder: Ella Baker, staff, 1940–1942.

53. Ella Baker, letter to Lucille Black, May 25, 1942, NAACP Papers, group II, box C307, General Branch Files.

54. Ella Baker, letter to Lucille Black, May 4, 1942, NAACP Papers, group II, box A572, folder: Ella Baker, staff, 1940–1942.

55. Ella Baker to Lucille Black, Mar. 11, 1942, NAACP Papers, group II, box A572, folder: Ella Baker, staff, 1940–1942.

56. Baker, interview by Walker, 6.

57. For more information on the politics of respectability in the black community, see Gaines, *Uplifting the Race*; Higginbotham, *Righteous Discontent*; and Gilmore, *Gender and Jim Crow*.

58. Charlotte Crump, letter to Ella Baker, Oct. 9, 1941, NAACP Papers, group II, box A572, folder: Ella Baker, staff, 1940–1942.

59. Memos to Charlotte Crump from Walter White, Dec. 19, 1941, and Jan. 22, 1942, reprimanding her for her performance; memo to Charlotte Crump from Roy Wilkins, Jan. 10, 1942, also reprimanding her. NAACP Papers, group II, box A579, folder: Staff, Charlotte Crump.

60. Ella Baker, letter to Roy Wilkins, Apr. 1, 1942, NAACP Papers, group II, box A572, folder: Staff, Ella Baker, 1940–1955. "Into Fifth" refers to the building where the NAACP offices were located.

61. Charlotte Crump, letter to Ella Baker, Mar. 2, 1942; Baker, letter to Wilkins, Apr. 1, 1942; and Walter White, memo to Ella Baker, Oct. 18, 1941; NAACP Papers, group II, box A572, folder: Staff, Ella Baker, 1940–1955.

62. Ella Baker to Ruby Hurley, June 7, 1944, NAACP Papers, pt. 10, series B, 1940–1955, reel 16 (microfilm).

63. Ibid.

64. Ruby Hurley to Pauli Murray, July 11, 1945, NAACP Papers, reel 16 (microfilm).

65. One measure of Jackson's elitism and snobbery is the ostentatious wedding she hosted for her daughter, Juanita, when she married Clarence Mitchell Jr., a lawyer with the National Urban League. For a detailed description of the elaborate gala, see Denton L. Watson, *Lion in the Lobby*, 117–19.

66. Watson, *Lion in the Lobby*, 117.

67. Carl Murphy to Walter White, Aug. 9, 1944, and Ella Baker to Walter White, Oct. 4, 1941, NAACP Papers, group II, box C76; Lillie Jackson, letter to Walter White, Oct. 19, 1941, NAACP Papers, group II, box C76.

68. Hill, interview by author.

69. Lillie Jackson, letter to Walter White, Oct. 19, 1941, NAACP Papers, group II, box C76.

70. Ibid.

71. Roy Wilkins, letter to Walter White, Oct. 21, 1941, NAACP Papers, group II, box C76.

72. Assistant field secretary report, in Report of the Dept. of Branches, NAACP Papers, group II, box C390, Monthly Reports folder.

73. Roy Wilkins, letter to Walter White, Oct. 21, 1941, NAACP Papers, group II, box C76.

74. Ibid.

75. Walter White, letter to Lillie Jackson, Oct. 21, 1941, NAACP Papers, group II, box C76.

76. Baker, interviewer not known, Duke University Oral History Program (DUOHP), 33–34. This incident probably took place in 1942, in either Savannah or New Brunswick, Ga.

77. Ibid., 34.

78. Ibid., 33.

79. Ella Baker, memo to Roy Wilkins, June 1, 1943, NAACP Papers, group II, B184. See C. E. Bell (Seaboard Railway Company) to W. P. Bartel (Interstate Commerce Commission), Sept. 14, 1943. Copy in this file is a carbon sent to Thurgood Marshall (NAACP Legal Defense and Education Fund), NAACP Papers, group II, B184.

80. Ibid.

81. Ibid.

82. Ibid.

83. G. W. Laird (Interstate Commerce Commission) to Thurgood Marshall, July 28, 1943, NAACP Papers, group II, 184.

84. See Duster, *Crusade for Justice*, and Giddings, *When and Where I Enter*, 22. See also McMurry, *To Keep the Waters Troubled*.

85. EBP, NAACP folder.

86. In his biography of Harry Moore, *Before His Time*, Ben Green argues that Moore was too independent and militant for the New York office and was nudged out of leadership shortly before he was killed.

87. Ella Baker files, FBI, Washington, D.C.

88. Ella Baker Files, FBI, Washington, D.C., "Correlation Summary," July 19, 1965, 17. This summary cites the speculation about her instability.

89. Ella Baker, letter to Lucille Black, May 25, 1942, NAACP Papers, group II, box A572.

90. Baker, interview by Hayden and Thrasher, 46.

91. Mable Davis of Wise, N.C., letter to Ella Baker, n.d., NAACP Papers, group II, box C307, General Branch Files, folder: Letters and Memos, 1940–1942.

92. Gilchrist, interview by author.

93. Ella Baker to Madison Jones, Apr. 1942, NAACP Papers, group II, A572, 1940–1942, folder: Staff, Ella Baker, 1941–42; Brockington, interview with author, Feb. 1990.

94. Rollins, *All Is Never Said*, 76–77.

95. Ella Baker, memo to Committee on Branches, July 6, 1943, NAACP Papers, group II, box C307, General Branch Files.

96. Brier et al., *Who Built America?*, 2:408, 453.

97. Ella Baker, letter to Lucille Black in N.Y., Nov. 2, 1942, NAACP Papers, group II, box C307, General Branch Files.

98. Ibid.

99. Ella Baker, letter to Walter White, Feb. 18, 1943, NAACP Papers, group II, box B98.

100. Ella Baker, letter to Walter White, Dec. 3, 1942, NAACP Papers, group II, box B98; and Ella Baker, letter to Walter White, Feb. 18, 1943, NAACP Papers, group II, box B98.

101. Ella Baker, letter to Walter White, Dec. 3, 1942, NAACP Papers, group II, box B98, 1–2.

102. Ibid.

103. Ibid.

104. Ibid.

105. Ibid.; and Ella Baker, letter to Walter White, 3 Dec. 1942, NAACP Papers, group II, box B98, 1–2, and Dec. 18, 1943, NAACP Papers, group II, box B98.

106. William A. Fowlkes, "U.S. Warned to Make Democracy Work at Home: Miss Ella Baker Electrifies Jan. 1 Bethel Audience," *Atlanta Daily World*, Jan. 2, 1947, 1.

107. Ella Baker, letter to Lillian Coleman in Fairfield, Ala., Apr. 16, 1941, NAACP Papers, group II, box C307, General Branch Files.

108. Ella Baker, letter to Mr. Robert H. McLaskey, Apr. 18, 1945, NAACP Papers, group II, box C66.

109. Campaign Manual for Branches, n.d., EBP; and NAACP Papers, group II, box C307, General Branch Files.

110. Ella Baker to Mr. and Mrs. J. J. Green, Apr. 14, 1941, NAACP Papers, group II, box C307, General Branch Files.

111. Ella Baker, memo to Walter White, May 3, 1946, NAACP Papers, group II, box C307, General Branch Files.

112. Ella Baker, memo to Walter White, June 4, 1942, NAACP Papers, group II, box A572, folder: Staff, Ella Baker, 1940–1945.

113. Ella Baker, letter to Roy Wilkins, Mar. 11, 1942, NAACP Papers, group II, box A572, folder: Staff, Ella Baker, 1940–1950.

114. Ella Baker, letter to Walter White, May 14, 1946, NAACP Papers, group II, box A573, folder: Staff, Ella Baker, 2.

115. Ibid.

116. Baker, interview by Hogan, 32.

117. Green's biography of Harry Moore, *Before His Time*, gives more background on tensions between the national office and militant local branches.

118. Ella Baker, letter to Roy Wilkins, Mar. 11, 1942, NAACP Papers, group II, box A572, folder: Staff, Ella Baker, 1940–1950.

119. Ella Baker, "Conducting Membership Campaigns," a document prepared for the 33d Annual NAACP Convention in Los Angeles, 1942, NAACP Papers (microfilm), 4, reel 11. The document consists of reports from three field secretaries; the quotation is taken from the section authored by Ella Baker.

120. Ella Baker, memo to Walter White, May 3, 1946, NAACP Papers, group II, box C307, General Branch Files.

121. Ella Baker, "Conducting Membership Campaigns," presented at 33rd annual NAACP conference, Los Angeles, 1942, NAACP Papers (microfilm), reel 11.

122. Ibid.

123. Marable, *W. E. B. Du Bois*, 168–69.

124. Ella Baker, letter to Lucille Black, May 4, 1942, NAACP Papers, group II, box A572, 1940–42.

125. Ella Baker, memo to the Branch Officers, Oct. 2, 1944, NAACP Papers, group II, box C376, folder: Leadership Training Conference, National Office, Oct. 1944.

126. Ella Baker, memo to the Branch Officers, Oct. 2, 1944, NAACP Papers, group II, box C376, folder: Leadership Training Conference, National Office, Oct. 1944.

127. Baker, interview by Hayden and Thrasher, 50.

128. Pauli Murray, letter to Walter White, July 23, 1944, NAACP Papers, group II, box A426, folder: Pauli Murray.

129. Pauli Murray, letter to Roy Wilkins, Aug. 2, 1944, NAACP Papers, group II, box A426, folder: Pauli Murray.

130. Pauli Murray, letter to Walter White, July 23, 1944, NAACP Papers, group II, box A426, folder: Pauli Murray.

131. Roy Wilkins, letter to Ella Baker, July 3, 1946, NAACP Papers, group II, box A573, folder: Staff, Ella Baker.

132. Ella Baker, memo to the Branch Officers, Oct. 2, 1944, NAACP Papers, group II, box C376, folder: Leadership Training Conference, National Office, Oct. 1944.

133. Ibid.

134. Tulsa Leadership Conference, 1946, NAACP Papers, group II, box C376, folder:

Leadership Training Conference, Nov. 1944; and Report of the Dept. of Branches for Feb. 11, 1946 Board of Directors Meeting, NAACP Papers, group II, box C390, Monthly reports, 1945–46.

135. Ella Baker, memo to the Branch Officers, Oct. 2, 1944, NAACP Papers, group II, box C376, folder: Leadership Training Conference, National Office, Oct. 1944.

136. Ibid.

137. Ibid.

138. Ibid.

139. Baker, interview by Hogan, 45–49.

140. Braden, interview by author, Jan. 3, 1997.

141. Parks, telephone interview by author.

142. Hill, interview by author; Current, telephone interview by author.

143. Hill, interview by author.

144. Baker, interview by Britton, 5–6.

145. Hill, interview by author.

146. The specific nature of the issue at Sydenham hospital remains unclear. The tenor of Walter White's memo suggested that he was more concerned with the recalcitrant behavior of two female staff members than with the actual substance of the issue itself. He described their dissension as "embarassing"—presumably to him. Memo from Walter White to Ella Baker and Ruby Hurley, May 17, 1944, NAACP Papers, group II, box A573, folder: Staff, Ella Baker, 1943–44; Baker, interview by Hogan, 30; Ella Baker, letter to Walter White, May 14, 1946, NAACP Papers, group II, box A573, folder: Staff, Ella Baker, 2.

147. Ella Baker, memo to Walter White and Thurgood Marshall, Nov. 5, 1945, NAACP Papers, group II, box A573, folder: Staff, Ella Baker, 1945.

148. Walter White, letter to Ella Baker, Nov. 13, 1945, NAACP Papers, group II, box A573, folder: Staff, Ella Baker, 1945. Also see Ella Baker, memo to Walter White in which Ella Baker rebuffs criticisms for violating procedures, ca. 1945, EBP.

149. Ella Baker, letters to Walter White, Feb. 23, 1943 and Dec. 27, 1943, NAACP Papers, group II, box A573, folder: Staff, Ella Baker, 1943–44. These memos indicate specific health problems and doctor's visits.

150. Ella Baker, letter to Miss Freeland, Aug. 11, 1945, NAACP Papers, group II, box A573, folder: Staff, Ella Baker, 1945.

151. Walter White, telegram to Ella Baker, Oct. 18, 1945, NAACP Papers, group II, box A573, folder: Staff, Ella Baker, 1945. The staff was small and spent long hours working in close proximity. It would have seemed appropriate for the executive officer to attend the funeral of a close family member of one of his staff. In his telegram, White acknowledged Martha as Ella Baker's sister, indicating that he realized she was an immediate family member.

152. Letter to Ella Baker, signed "your brother," Jan. 3, 1946, EBP.

153. Solomon, interview by author.

154. Baker, interview by Hayden and Thrasher, 56.

155. Brockington, interview by author.

156. Baker, interview by Hayden and Thrasher, 58.

157. Clarke, interview by author.

158. For biographical information on Bethune, see Ross, "Mary McLeod Bethune and the National Youth Administration; Hine et al., eds., *Black Women in America*, vol. 1 (Bethune entry by Elaine M. Smith).

159. Ella Baker, letter to Mary McLeod Bethune, Nov. 18, 1945, NAACP Papers, group

II, box A573, folder: Staff, Ella Baker, 1945; and see Bethune, letter to Ella Baker, Nov. 27, 1945, EBP.

160. Ella Baker, letter to Walter White, May 14, 1946, NAACP Papers, group II, box A573, folder: Staff, Ella Baker, 2 (resignation letter); also see Shirley Graham Du Bois, "Why Du Bois Was Fired in 1948," *Masses and Mainstream* 1, no. 9 (November 1948): 15–26.

161. Current, interview by author.

162. John L. Leflore, letter to Ella Baker, July 12, 1946, NAACP Papers, group II, box A573, folder: Staff, Ella Baker. Leflore was an especially good friend of Baker's, since the two of them had worked together through the YNCL during the 1930s. He was listed as council chairman of the YNCL in Mobile, Ala., on the Young Negroes Cooperative League stationery of around 1932. See EBP, YNCL files.

163. William A. Fowlkes, "U.S. Warned To Make Democracy Work at Home: Miss Ella Baker Electrifies Jan. 1 Bethel Audience," *Atlanta Daily World*, Jan. 2, 1947, 1.

CHAPTER FIVE

The epigraph is from Braden, *The Wall Between*, 341.

1. On Baker's involvement in the New York City NAACP branch, see NAACP Papers, group II, series C, B127, branch file, New York, Library of Congress.

2. Ella Baker to "Dear Sir," n.d., EBP, cites the 1950 call for the Emergency Mobilization. Horne, *Black and Red*; Gloster Current, memo to Thurgood Marshall, Nov. 7, 1952, NAACP Papers, group II, box A128, folder: Committee on Political Domination. Current's memo, which outlines the NAACP's stance on the exclusion of communists, reads: "The 41st Annual Convention in Boston adopted an anti-communist resolution on June 23, 1950." That resolution (which was attached to the memo) empowered the Board of Directors "to take the necessary action to eradicate such infiltration [by communists] and if necessary to suspend and reorganize or lift the charter and expel any unit, which . . . comes under Communist or other political control or domination." Current went on to cite a January 2, 1951, recommendation from the board of the NAACP that required branch officials to report "communistic or other political infiltration or domination." Similar resolutions were passed in 1956 at the San Francisco annual convention.

3. Baker acknowledged that Communists and socialists of various stripes had been some of the most militant fighters against racial discrimination and economic injustice.

4. Baker, interview by *Urban Review* editors, 10. For information on Bea Levison, see Markowitz and Rosner, *Children, Race, and Power*, 46, 111, 147.

5. See Clarence Taylor, *Knocking at Our Own Door*. In Baker, interview by Hayden and Thrasher, 59, mention is made of Galamison and Stein.

6. Ella Baker to Mamie and Kenneth Clark, July 28, 1952, Kenneth B. Clark Papers, Library of Congress, Washington, D.C., box 60, folder 7; Kenneth Clark to "Dear Friend," ca. 1953, letter on Intergroup Committee on New York Public Schools letterhead (Ella Baker is listed on the letterhead as a member of the steering committee), Clark Papers, box 56, folder 2.

7. Markowitz and Rosner, *Children, Race and Power*, 24, 27, 32–33.

8. Ibid., 18.

9. "Harlem Students Learn Inferiority," *Amsterdam News*, May 1, 1954, 1. "Dear Friends" letter from Kenneth Clark, June 14, 1954; press release regarding "Children Apart" conference, Apr. 23, 1954; Clark Papers, box 56, folder 2. Ella Baker to Kenneth Clark, July 18, 1953, Clark Papers, box 93, folder 10.

10. Cantarow and O'Malley, "Ella Baker," 68.

11. See Bates, *The Long Shadow of Little Rock*, for a vivid, first-person account.

12. Clarence Taylor, *Knocking at Our Own Door*, 67–69.

13. Ibid., 70.

14. Sara Black, "Don't Forget N.Y. Has Its Own School Problem," *Amsterdam News*, Sept. 28, 1957, 1.

15. Ibid.

16. See Markowitz and Rosner, *Children, Race and Power*; Biondi, *To Stand and Fight*.

17. Letter to Ruth Moore from Ella Baker, Feb. 25, 1957, on In Friendship letterhead, Amzie Moore Papers, box 2, folder: Correspondence, 2, State Historical Society of Wisconsin (SHSW), Madison.

18. NAACP Papers, group II, box A456, folder: New York City police brutality, 1953–54; and "Law Which Police Flaunted," *Amsterdam News*, Feb. 21, 1953, 2.

19. "Resignation Urged of 2 Top Officials," *Amsterdam News*, Feb. 21, 1953, 2.

20. "Two Public Protests Set for Sunday," *Amsterdam News*, Feb. 28, 1953, 3. See Feb. 19, 1953, press release from NAACP national office, "Civic groups demand action against secret rights pact," NAACP Papers, group II, box A456, folder: New York City police brutality.

21. Telegram to Mayor Vincent R. Impellitteri from Ella Baker, Feb. 16, 1953, NAACP Papers, group II, box A456, New York City police brutality folder, 1953–54.

22. NAACP Papers, group II, box A456, folder: New York City police brutality, 1953–54.

23. Telegram to Mayor Vincent R. Impellitteri from Ella Baker, Feb. 16, 1953, NAACP Papers, group II, box A456, folder: New York City police brutality, 1953–54; "Two Public Protests Set for Sunday," *Amsterdam News*, Feb. 28, 1953, 3.

24. "Two Public Protests Set for Sunday."

25. "A 'Red' Plot Says Police Assn.—NAACP Leaders Answer Charges," *Amsterdam News*, Mar. 21, 1953, 2.

26. "Monaghan Starts Anti-Bias Training," *Amsterdam News*, Mar. 28, 1953.

27. "Ella Baker Liberal Party Candidate" (flyer), EBP, 1950s files, Liberal Party or New York Politics folder.

28. By 1951 Baker had known Robinson for at least three years. She had proposed to work with him in garnering support for the Morningside Community Center, but these plans did not materialize. Ella Baker to James Robinson, Jan. 26, 1948, EBP.

29. For information on Baker's city council candidacy, see "Ella Baker Resigns to Run for Council," *Amsterdam News*, Sept. 12, 1953.

30. Pauli Murray to Ella Baker, Nov. 2, 1953, EBP.

31. See also Murray, *Autobiography of a Black Activist*, and Pauli Murray Papers, "Liberal Party," box 73h, Schlesinger Library, Radcliffe College, Cambridge, Mass.

32. Yevette Richards, *Maida Springer*, 71.

33. Naison, *Communists in Harlem*, 232–47; and Yevette Richards, *Maida Springer*, 71.

34. The House Un-American Activities Committee (HUAC) became a permanent standing committee of the U.S. House of Representatives in 1946, after two previous incarnations.The committee then zealously took up the task of ferreting out alleged Communists and subversives ostensibly to protect U.S. national security from pro-Soviet spies and enemies of the government. The commmittee's hearings, held around the country, put dissidents of all sorts on trial to prove they were not Communists. Many were blacklisted; careers were destroyed; and several people went to jail for refusing on prinicpal to cooperate with such an undemocratic body.

35. For more on anticommunism and the American left, including African American

progressives and organized labor, see Polsgrove, *Divided Minds*, and Dudziak, *Cold War, Civil Rights*.

36. "Lovestonites," in *Encyclopedia of the American Left*, ed. Buhle et al., 436.

37. FBI report, Ella Baker files, New York. There are numerous unsigned reports throughout Baker's file. My conclusions are drawn from extracting information from nearly a dozen short, unsigned reports.

38. NAACP Papers, group II, box A128, folder: Committee on Political Domination, 1952.

39. "Report" of the New York Branch of the NAACP, Internal Security Committee, Oct. 14, 1957, submitted by Aloncita J. Flood; and James Robinson to Roy Wilkins, letter with committee report attached, Nov. 18, 1957, NAACP Papers, group III, box C102, folder: "Internal Security Committee."

40. Russell Crawford to Benjamin J. Davis Jr., Nov. 9, 1957, ibid.

41. Grant, *Ella Baker*, 99.

42. Baker, interview by Walker, 29.

43. Garrow, *Bearing the Cross*, 84.

44. Baker, interview by Hayden and Thrasher, 61.

45. Moss, *Moving On*, 79–80.

46. Polsgrove, *Divided Minds*, 43.

47. Branch, *Parting the Waters*, 168–72. For more information on Rustin, see Jervis Anderson, *Bayard Rustin*, which deals very little with Rustin's sexuality. A forthcoming biography by John D'Emilio promises to take up the issue in greater depth. Homosexuality and Communism were closely related offenses in the twisted minds of McCarthyites, giving Rustin good reason to be doubly cautious.

48. Branch, *Parting the Waters*, 168.

49. A. Philip Randolph to "Dear Friends," Feb. 17, 1956, A. Philip Randolph Papers, box 23, In Friendship folder, 1956, Library of Congress, Washington, D.C.

50. A. Philip Randolph, letter to In Friendship, Feb. 17, 1956, Norman Thomas Papers (microfilm), reel 30, General Correspondence folder, New York Public Library.

51. Norman Thomas, letter to A. Philip Randolph, Mar. 8, 1956, Randolph Papers, box 23, In Friendship folder, 1956.

52. J. Oscar Lee, letter to Norman Thomas, Jan. 30, 1956, outlines other activities under way; Fay Bennett, letter to Norman Thomas, Jan. 19, 1956, Norman Thomas Papers (microfilm), reel 30.

53. Minutes of the Executive Committee of "In Friendship," June 20, 1956, New York City, A. Philip Randolph Papers, LC, box 23, "In Friendship" folder, 1956, 2.

54. Baker, interview by Walker, 7.

55. Ella J. Baker, memo to Executive Committee of In Friendship, July 26, 1956, NAACP Papers, group III, box A177.

56. Ella Baker to Rev. Kilgore, Feb. 26, 1956, EBP.

CHAPTER SIX

1. For an account of the participation of women in the initiation of the boycott, see Jo Anne Gibson Robinson, *The Montgomery Bus Boycott and the Women Who Started It*.

2. Baker, interview by Morris, 24A.

3. Brockington, interview by author, includes an assessment of Baker's views about King.

4. See Morris, *Origins of the Civil Rights Movement*; and Payne, *I've Got the Light of Freedom*.

5. Fairclough, *To Redeem the Soul of America*, 38.

6. Baker, interview by Walker, 10.

7. Ibid., 9–10.

8. Ibid., 91.

9. Ibid., 19.

10. Ibid., 20.

11. Ibid., 27.

12. Ling, "Gender and Generation."

13. Baker, interview by Britton, 10.

14. Morris, *Origins of the Civil Rights Movement*, 83–86.

15. Ibid., 99.

16. Fairclough and others point out that King was never openly anticommunist, as some of his NAACP colleagues were, but he was at times politically pragmatic and at other times ambivalent when it came to this question. For example, he continued his association with Stanley Levison despite the latter's Communist past, but he rebuked Bob Moses for participating in a demonstration organized by white leftists in Atlanta.

17. Garrow, "From Reformer to Revolutionary," 427; see also Harding, *Martin Luther King*, 58–81.

18. Baker, interview by Britton, 23.

19. Baker, interview by Hayden and Thrasher, 63.

20. Ella Baker to Bayard Rustin, Jan. 30, 1957, Southern Christian Leadership Conference (SCLC) Papers (microfilm), reel 20, King Center, Atlanta, Ga.

21. Thomas Kilgore Jr., Bayard Rustin, and Ella Baker to James Hicks, June 4, 1957, EBP, SCLC files, Prayer Pilgrimage folder.

22. Ella Baker's FBI files, New York.

23. Thomas Kilgore Jr., Bayard Rustin, and Ella Baker to James Hicks, June 4, 1957, EBP.

24. Branch, *Parting the Waters*, 217; see also Garrow, *Bearing the Cross*, 92.

25. Morris, *Origins of the Civil Rights Movement*, 106.

26. Correspondence on Crusade for Citizenship letterhead is represented throughout the Southern Christian Leadership Conference (SCLC) Papers, King Center, Atlanta, Ga.

27. Baker, interview by Morris, 31B.

28. Branch, *Parting the Waters*, 172. Rustin had been arrested on "morals charges" for allegedly having sex in public in a car with another man. Rustin's sexual orientation, in the context of a homophobic culture, meant he was always vulnerable to a potential scandal.

29. Baker, interview by Hogan, 60.

30. Ibid., 62.

31. Branch, *Parting the Waters*, 231.

32. Baker, interview by Walker, 5.

33. Ibid., 1.

34. Ibid., 2.

35. Memo, "SCLC as a Crusade," Oct. 23, 1958, EBP, SCLC files.

36. Martin Luther King Jr. to Hon. A. Clayton Powell, Feb. 7, 1958, SCLC Papers, box 32, folder 7; Baker, interview by Walker, 2.

37. Branch, *Parting the Waters*, 231.

38. See Ella Baker correspondence, SCLC Papers, Jan.–June 1958, regarding details of the Crusade.

39. Flyers announcing Ella Baker as a speaker in Apr. 1958, EBP, SCLC files, flyers and announcements folder.

40. Fairclough, *Martin Luther King, Jr.*, 53.

41. Baker, interview by Walker, 17–18.

42. Ibid., 18.

43. Higginbotham, *Righteous Discontent*, 3, writes: "Male-biased traditions and rules of decorum sought to mute women's voices and accentuate their subordinate status vis-à-vis men. Thus, tainted by the values of the larger society, the black church sought to provide men with full manhood rights, while offering women a separate and unequal status."

44. See Shaw, *What a Woman Ought to Be and To Do*, and Kevin Gaines, *Uplifting the Race*, for more discussion of the politics of respectability as they relate to gender and black protest and activism in the early twentieth century. See also May, *Homeward Bound*, for a discussion of gender and the Cold War.

45. Baker, interview by Walker, 20.

46. Ibid., 19.

47. Ibid., 15–16.

48. Ella Baker, letter to "Dear Mattie," June 3, 1958, EBP.

49. Ella Baker, letter to Vincent (Baker), Mar. 22, 1960, EBP. He appears to have been a cousin of Baker's with whom she had not been in close touch.

50. Ella Baker, memo to SCLC Administrative Committee on office procedures and personnel, June 2, 1960, EBP, SCLC files.

51. Baker, interview by Morris, 31B. A call for democratizing the movement's clerical work was analogous to women's demand that men share in household chores. Baker was critical of the gendered division of labor between primarily female clerical staff and primarily male "professional" staff. This issue recurred in SNCC in 1964 when female staffers—half serious and half teasing—"called a strike in the Atlanta [SNCC] office to protest always being asked to take minutes." Richardson, interview by author.

52. Baker, interview by Morris, 31B. King's alleged extramarital affairs are discussed by Garrow in his biography of King, *Bearing the Cross*, and by Abernathy in his autobiography, *And the Walls Came Tumbling Down*.

53. Baker, interview by Walker, 11–12.

54. Ibid., 11, 14.

55. Ibid., 12.

56. Branch, *Parting the Waters*, 233.

57. Alethea Wyatt, letter to Ella Baker, May 27, 1958, SCLC Papers, King Center, box 32, folder 7.

58. SCLC Papers, box 32, folder 7.

59. See Green, *Before His Time*.

60. See Dittmer, *Local People*, 76–78, for details on Evers and the NAACP-SCLC rivalry in Mississippi.

61. Baker, interview by Walker, 13.

62. John Tilley to Amzie Moore, Oct. 30, 1958, Amzie Moore Papers, box 1, folder: 1958 Correspondence, State Historical Society of Wisconsin, Madison.

63. Baker, interview by Morris, 81A.

64. Ibid., 83A.

65. SCLC Administrative Report, July 3, 1958, EBP, SCLC files.

66. Eskew, *But for Birmingham*, 28; Branch, *Parting the Waters*, 247.

67. Quoted in Tyson, *Radio Free Dixie*, 117.

68. Baker, interview by Morris, 42A.

69. Cantarow and O'Malley, "Ella Baker," 53.

70. See Morris, *Origins of the Civil Rights Movement*, 115.

71. "U.S. Warned to Make Democracy Work at Home," *Atlanta Daily World*, Jan. 2, 1947, 1.

72. Baker, interview by Walker, 5.

73. Ibid., 19.

74. Baker, interview by Morris, 65A.

75. Ibid., 80A.

76. Branch, *Parting the Waters*, 247.

77. Clark, interview by Hall, 87; Braden, interview by author, June 1991

78. Baker, interview by Britton, 36.

79. Baker, interview by Morris, 39A.

80. Ibid., 55A.

81. Ibid., 48A.

82. Ella Baker, "The Negro Church, the Nucleus of the Negroes Cultural Development," unpublished high school paper (circa 1923), EBP.

83. Fairclough, *Martin Luther King, Jr.*, 19.

84. Baker, interview by Walker, 32.

85. Ibid., 24.

86. Baker, interview by Walker, 32.

87. Tyson, *Radio Free Dixie*, 153; Simpkins, interview by author.

88. Bernice Johnson Reagon, interview by author.

89. Ella Baker, letter to Ruth Tinsley, Richmond, Va., ca. Dec. 1942 or 1943, EBP, NAACP files.

90. Scott, *Domination and the Arts of Resistance*, 199.

91. Cantarow and O'Malley, "Ella Baker," 70.

92. Ibid., 84.

93. Divorce decree, City Clerk's Office for the Borough of Manhattan, N.Y., file number 30849-1958.

CHAPTER SEVEN

1. "Four To Be Charged in Negro Co-eds Rape," *Washington Evening Star*, May 4, 1959.

2. Ella Baker was under FBI surveillance off and on from the 1940s through the 1970s. She was heavily monitored in 1959, and even though, at certain points, agents reported her to be a "non-threat," her files were repeatedly closed only to be reopened. The FBI was especially interested in Baker's connections to Stanley Levison, Anne and Carl Braden, and Bayard Rustin. Ella Baker FBI Files, New York and Atlanta.

3. Note that I use the term "militancy" to refer specifically to the willingness to justify physical force as an act of self-defense. This position was directly contrary to pacifism and to King's philosophical convictions. King would have argued, some years later, that he too was a militant, although a nonviolent one; he was prepared to be confrontational but was not prepared to strike a physical blow or resort to the use of arms. Baker was not willing to rule these tactics out. Emory O. Jackson, "'Nothing Is Too Dear to Pay for Freedom,' Miss Baker," *Birmingham World*, June 10, 1959, 1.

4. Ibid., 6. She did not publicly criticize the politics of SCLC very often. In fact, a month after her fiery speech in Birmingham, Baker was on a panel at the Institute on Nonviolent Resistance to Segregation, held at Spelman College, in which her copanelists championed nonviolence. Baker talked about the importance of local grassroots struggle

and the pivotal moment of history that the movement was witnessing, but in this context she declined to tackle the issue of nonviolence head on.

5. Manis, *A Fire You Can't Put Out*, 217.

6. For more information on the Mack Parker lynching, see Smead, *Blood Justice*.

7. For examples of activists possessing guns for protection, see Daisy Bates quoted in Tyson, *Radio Free Dixie*, 165; Simpkins, interview by author; Payne, *I've Got the Light of Freedom*, 204.

8. Tyson, *Radio Free Dixie*.

9. Ibid., 149.

10. Ibid., 51–58.

11. Emory O. Jackson, "'Nothing Is to Dear to Pay for Freedom,' Miss Baker," *Birmingham World*, June 10, 1959, 1, 6.

12. Ibid., 6.

13. Tyson, *Radio Free Dixie*, 116.

14. Ibid., 159.

15. Ibid., 216–17. For nuances of Braden's support and Forman and Brooks's visit, see Anne Braden to Jim Dombrowski, July 27, 1961, 2, Carl and Anne Braden Papers, "White SCEF Student Project," folder 1, State Historical Society of Wisconsin, Madison, Wis.

16. Tyson, *Radio Free Dixie*, 262.

17. Ibid., 279–82.

18. Burlage, telephone interview by author.

19. Ella Baker to Anne Braden, Aug. 16, 1962, 1, Braden Papers, 38:5, Southern Patriot and Field Organizers files, correspondence, Apr.–Aug. 1962, SHSW.

20. Burlage, telephone interview with author. See also Tyson, *Radio Free Dixie*, 81, 193–207.

21. Burlage, telephone interview by author.

22. Tyson, *Radio Free Dixie*, 248–308. After living in Cuba and spending time in North Vietnam and China, Williams returned to the United States in 1969.

23. On Jan. 26, 1959, the FBI was contacting the Department of Motor Vehicles for information on Baker; since she never had a driver's license, this was of no use. On Jan. 29, 1959, a special agent for the FBI called Baker under pretext of wanting information about getting involved. Ella Baker FBI Files, Atlanta and New York.

24. Eskew, *But for Birmingham*, 124–50.

25. Baker, interview by Britton, 28.

26. Manis, *A Fire You Can't Put Out*, 72, 329.

27. Ella Baker to Fred Shuttlesworth, n.d. [circa Apr. 1960], EBP, correspondence file (1960s).

28. Manis, *A Fire You Can't Put Out*, 215.

29. See Kelley, "Birmingham's Untouchables," 77–100. The ACMHR's orientation toward its mass base was a matter of conscious policy; this point is underlined by the fact that, as in most civil rights organizations, its paid membership was predominantly middle class, but it retained a large following among the poor.

30. Kelly, "Birmingham's Untouchables," 84. See also, Manis, *A Fire you Can't Put Out*, 329.

31. Manis, *A Fire You Can't Put Out*, 8.

32. Ibid., xvi, 13.

33. Ibid., 11–17.

34. Baker, interview by Morris, 37A.

35. Eskew, *But for Birmingham*, 122–25.

36. Baker, interview by Hogan, 20.

37. Eskew, *But for Birmingham*, 123.

38. Manis, *A Fire You Can't Put Out*, 36.

39. Ibid., 100, 224–25, 256, 436–39.

40. Eskew, *But for Birmingham*, 31.

41. Ibid., 135.

42. Ibid., 140–41.

43. Ibid.

44. Brockington, telephone interview by author, May 1994.

45. Braden, interview by author, April 13, 1991. See also Linda Reed, *Simple Decency and Common Sense*, 177.

46. Alice Spearman to Ella Baker, Dec. 1959, Ella Baker Papers (EBP), SCLC files, correspondence, Schomburg Center for Research in Black Culture, New York, N.Y. Pete Daniel, *Lost Revolutions*, 229–34, gives more biographical information on Spearman's politics.

47. Simpkins, interview by author.

48. Branch, *Parting the Waters*, 221. King and Baker both saw the bill as limited.

49. Proviser and Pederson, *Grassroots Constitutionalism*, 147.

50. Baker, interview by Britton, 38.

51. Burton, *On the Black Side of Shreveport*, 95.

52. Ibid., 95–96.

53. Ibid., 95–96.

54. Ibid., 96–97.

55. Simpkins, interview by author.

56. Ibid.

57. Ibid.

58. Ibid.

59. The standard of conduct embraced by working-class and nonelite blacks did not endorse excessive drinking either. However, the middle-class leaders who sought to police black behavior not only targeted alcohol, dancing, gambling, and other "vices" but attempted to regulate speech, dress, and comportment as well, and they linked all of these standards to the requirements and expectations of citizenship.

60. Baker, interview by Hogan, 25.

61. Roy Wilkins, speech before National Negro Publishers Association meeting, May 18, 1958, reprinted in Wilson, ed., *In Search of Democracy*, 384.

62. Baker, interview by Hogan, 35.

63. See Gaines, *Uplifting the Race*, which stresses the connections between uplift ideology and a conservative, patriarchal view of family and gender. Also see Cohen, *Boundaries of Blackness*, for a late-twentieth-century version of the politics of respectability as it applies to the AIDS crisis and the response of traditional black leaders. Cohen, a political scientist, argues that in order to project an image of black respectability many leaders initially distanced themselves from the AIDS issue, even as it ravaged black communities, to avoid the stigma of homosexuality and drug use that were associated with the disease.

64. See also Joy James, *Transcending the Talented Tenth*; and Shaw, *What a Woman Ought to Be and Do*.

65. Burton, *On the Black Side of Shreveport*, 104. Tragically, Brewster became a local movement martyr. After many years of open civil rights agitation, including hosting meetings at her home and experiencing several arrests and routine harassment by the

Shreveport police, she died in 1963 under suspicious circumstances. Although her death was ascribed to suicide, some speculated that she may have been killed; no indictments were ever made.

66. Simpkins, interview by author.

67. Ibid.

68. Ibid. Years later, when the Simpkinses were living in New Jersey and Baker was back in Harlem, they rekindled their friendship and spent many hours together.

69. Baker, interview by Hayden and Thrasher, 57.

70. "200 Negroes Appear, 14 Register in Drive." *Shreveport Times*, Mar. 20, 1959.

71. Simpkins, interview by author.

72. Shreveport folder, 1950s, EBP. Composite sketch of activities drawn from extensive memos and clippings throughout this folder.

73. Ibid.

74. "Negro Voter Purge Aided by Decision," *Shreveport Times*, Mar. 21, 1959.

75. Shreveport folder, 1950s, EBP. Composite sketch of activities drawn from extensive memos and clippings throughout this folder.

76. "Negro Voter Purge Aided by Decision," *Shreveport Times*, Mar. 21, 1959.

77. Ibid.

78. Ibid.

79. Rollins, *All Is Never Said*, 76–77.

80. Ibid.

81. Julian Bond, foreword to Braden, *The Wall Between*, xiii.

82. Braden, *The Wall Between*, 322. See also Linda Reed, *Simple Decency and Common Sense*, 33.

83. Linda Reed, *Simple Decency and Common Sense*, 31–32.

84. Ibid., 102, 128–29, 176; Klibaner, *Conscience of a Troubled South*; Klibaner, "The Travail of Southern Radicals"; and Braden, telephone interview by author, Jan. 3, 1997.

85. See Linda Reed, *Simple Decency and Common Sense*, on SCHW; and Sullivan, *Days of Hope*, for more details on SCEF, SCHW, and white southern liberals and antiracists before and during the civil rights movement era.

86. See Braden, *The Wall Between*.

87. See Polsgrove, *Divided Minds*.

88. For more biographical information, see Fosl, *Subversive Southerner*.

89. Braden, telephone interview by author, Jan. 3, 1997.

90. Ibid.

91. The House Un-American Activities Committee emerged out of a Cold War political climate in which anyone who challenged any government policy was labeled a Communist. People who were subpoenaed by HUAC were required to testify before the committee, which asked them whether they and others were then or had ever been members of the Communist Party or various "front" organizations. Some "took the Fifth," refusing to answer on the grounds that they might incriminate themselves, but that was generally regarded as a confession of Communist affiliation. Others refused to testify on the grounds that the First Amendment protected free speech and free association. Imprisonment for contempt of Congress was one possible consequence of refusing to testify. For information on HUAC during the late 1950s, see Shrecker, *Many Are the Crimes*. For details of the Bradens' political careers before 1958, see Braden, *The Wall Between*.

92. Braden, telephone interview by author, June 2002. See Linda Reed, *Simple Decency and Common Sense*, 161–62, and Braden, *The Wall Between*. As late as 2002, over a generation after the end of the 1960s phase of the Black Freedom Movement, Anne

Braden still declined to say definitively whether she and Carl were or were not members of the CP, even to her own biographer, Catherine Fosl, or me. In her view, whether one is a Communist is still wrongly used as a litmus test of political respectability, and it should not matter. My view is that it matters if in fact some of the most stalwart antiracist whites in the movement were Communists. It potentially deflates, rather than fuels, anti-Communist stereotypes.

93. Braden, *The Wall Between*, 32.

94. See Evans, *Personal Politics*; and Omolade, *The Rising Song of African American Women*.

95. Anne Braden to Ella Baker, ca. Feb. 1956, EBP; Braden, interview by author, June 1991.

96. Braden, interview by author, Apr. 13, 1991.

97. Braden, *The Wall Between*, 325. Anne Braden also lists Vincent Harding, Martin Luther King Jr., James Forman, and Fred Shuttlesworth in this category of brave allies.

98. Braden, telephone interview by author, June 2002. When Anne Braden asked for Baker's help in 1965, Baker explained her position to her this way. "She did not think Communists should be allowed to be members of the NAACP because it put the organization at risk" of persecution by the government, which was not an unfounded fear. At the same time, she disagreed with her NAACP cohorts that the organization should not aid or defend those who were the objects of persecution. This was a fine line indeed. Such a position had the potential of going either way "to challenge or reinforce anti-Communist sentiments."

99. Braden, interview by author, Apr. 13, 1991. Anne was nearly nine months pregnant at the time and unable to make the trip. The Bradens' baby was born on Feb. 7, one week after the hearings and one week after the student desegregation sit-ins began in Greensboro, North Carolina. Anne and Carl jokingly referred to their daughter as their "sit-in baby."

100. Braden interview by author, Jan. 3, 1997.

101. Braden, interview by author, June 1991.

102. The opportunity to work alongside Nannie Helen Burroughs was a special honor for Ella Baker, since Burroughs had been an inspiration for the Baptist women's movement that Georgianna Ross Baker had been so devoted to. Baker and Burroughs had met on at least one previous occasion.

103. Baker to Nannie H. Burroughs, Jan. 8, 1959, Southern Christian Leadership Conference (SCLC) Papers, Ella Baker correspondence, Jan. 1959–Jan. 1960, King Center, Atlanta, Ga.

104. Braden Papers, SCEF files, SHSW.

105. In places like Nashville and Atlanta, groups of black students had been plotting, planning, and praying for an opportunity to strike back at Jim Crow indignities.

106. Baker, interview by Carson, 4–5. The sparks ignited by the Greensboro students set off a "wildfire" of protest.

107. Ella Baker to Anne Braden, Mar. 21, 1960, SCLC Papers, box 32, folder 18.

CHAPTER EIGHT

1. "Report," 10-page handwritten report from Ella Baker (on SCLC letterhead), Mar. 12, 1960, EBP, SCLC files; Ella Baker to "Students" requesting biographical information, Apr. 8, 1960, SNCC Papers (microfilm), reel 11.

2. Garrow, *Bearing the Cross*, 68, 131.

3. Baker, interview by Carson, 8.

4. Baker, interview by Hogan, 6.

5. Baker met with and consulted King, but she sent out the actual correspondence and made most of the final decisions about logistics, program, structure, and precisely who would be invited. This authority was not bestowed on Baker; rather, it was a byproduct of her location within the organization. She did most of the planning and outreach; so the details were left to her. The details in shaping the Raleigh meeting were important and ultimately politically significant.

6. Baker, interview by Carson, 9. According to Garrow, *Bearing the Cross*, 132–33, King was receiving pressure from advisers to push for an affiliation with the new sit-in movement without getting into an all-out fight with Ella Baker. King relented and never made an effort to "capture" the group, as Baker feared he would.

7. Forman, *The Making of Black Revolutionaries*, 217. See also Robnett, *How Long? How Long?*, 99, for a portion of Ella Baker's comments about her walkout at the SNCC conference.

8. Baker, "Bigger than a Hamburger," 4.

9. Ibid.

10. Baker, interview by Britton, 43–44.

11. Baker, "Bigger than a Hamburger," 4.

12. Ibid.

13. Hierich, interview by author.

14. Nash, interview by author, Sept. 1997.

15. Baker, interview by Carson, 12.

16. Stembridge, interview by author.

17. Moses and Cobb, *Radical Equations*, 28.

18. Moses, interview by author.

19. Ibid.

20. Moses, interview by author; Moses and Cobb, *Radical Equations*, 108.

21. Moses and Cobb, *Radical Equations*, 8.

22. Moses, interview by Carson, 3.

23. Baker's influence on Moses is evident in his writings. A larger-than-life poster of Baker greets visitors as they walk into the offices of the Algebra Project in Cambridge, Mass., which Moses heads. His book, with Cobb, quotes and pays homage to Baker throughout. The Algebra Project is a math literacy project based on Moses's view that unequal access to mathematical knowledge perpetuates social, racial, and economic inequities.

24. See Moses and Cobb, *Radical Equations*.

25. See the personal accounts of white women in the movement in Constance Curry et. al., *Deep in Our Hearts*.

26. Curry, interview by author.

27. Taitt-Magubane, interview by author. Taitt-Magubane would later become one of Ella Baker's closest friends in New York City, hosting annual birthday parties in her friend's honor.

28. Ibid.

29. Braden, interview by author, June 1991.

30. Brockington, interview by author, Feb. 1990.

31. Reagon, interview by author; and Joyce Ladner, interview by author.

32. Clarke, interview by author.

33. In 1960 most young women activists admired Ella Baker and saw her level of political savvy as being far out of their reach; but, as they matured, many of them found

they had modeled their identities as politically active adult women after Baker. See author's interviews with Diane Nash, Eleanor Holmes Norton, Bernice Johnson Reagon, and Dorie Ladner. See also Evans, *Personal Politics*.

34. Dorie Ladner, interview by author.

35. Abernathy, interview by author.

36. Ibid.

37. Author's interviews with Donaldson, Taitt-Magubane, Dorothy Miller Zellner, and Nash.

38. Moses, interview by author.

39. Zinn, interview by author.

40. Donaldson, interview by author.

41. Burlage, interview by author.

42. Hall (Wynn), interview by author, 1–2.

43. Author's interviews with Curry and Taitt-Magubane.

44. Curry, interview by author.

45. Grant, *Fundi*.

46. Nash, interview by author, Sept. 1997.

47. Curry, interview by author.

48. Guyot, interview by author.

49. Mary King and Casey Hayden both entered SNCC via the YWCA, and Connie Curry had Y affiliations, as did Lenore Taitt-Magubane and Bobby Yancy, all of whom would remain a part of Baker's life until the end.

50. Baker, "Report for the Southeastern Region, 9/1/61–8/31/62," YWCA Files, YWCA New York Branch Collection, YWCA National Headquarters, New York.

51. Harding, interview by author.

52. It would be inaccurate to characterize all SCLC ministers as privileged. But even though these ministers comprised the more activist wing of the black church, Baker felt they were resistant to grassroots leadership, democratic organiztion, and militant tactics.

53. Grant, *Ella Baker*, 144.

54. Stembridge, interview by author; Carson, *In Struggle*, 29.

55. Claude Sitton, "Negro Criticizes N.A.A.C.P. Tactics," *New York Times*, Apr. 17, 1960, 32.

56. *Student Voice* 2, no. 2 (Feb. 1961): 1; Curry, interview by author; Coordinating Committee meetings, Feb. 3–5, 1961, Student Nonviolent Coordinating Committee (SNCC) Papers. For Powell controversy, see Branch, *Parting the Waters*, 847.

57. Farmer, *Lay Bare the Heart*, 195–203.

58. For information on 1961 freedom rides, see Branch, *Parting the Waters*; for 1947 rides, see Grant, *Ella Baker*, 91–92.

59. Nash, interview by author, Sept. 1997; and Branch, *Parting the Waters*, 466.

60. Ella Baker, memo to "Coordinating Committee of the Freedom Rides," n.d. [ca. May 1961], 1, SNCC files, EBP.

61. Ibid., 2.

62. Ibid., 3.

63. Ibid.

64. Baker's partisan intervention on behalf of SNCC during the Freedom Rides reflects the tension embedded in her advice that organizational affiliation and loyalty should not matter. In the context of competing organizations, the group that is least selfish or self-promoting is likely to get the least attention and resources, which then has a negative bearing on its practical ability to continue and expand its work.

65. Fleming, *Soon We Will Not Cry*.

66. Dittmer, *Local People*, 119–20; Carson, *In Struggle*, 70; and Lewis, *Walking with the Wind*, 178–81.

67. Lewis, *Walking with the Wind*, 180; and Carson, *Struggle*, 41–42.

68. Minutes for Meeting of Co.-Committee, August 11, Highlander Research and Education Center Papers, box 71, folder 16, State Historical Society of Wisconsin (SHSW), Madison, are handwritten and incomplete. The tone of the meeting and the debate about splitting the organization are recounted in numerous SNCC interviews and chronicled in secondary sources.

69. Baker, interview by Emily Stoper, in Stoper, *The Student Nonviolent Coordinating Committee*, 269.

70. Ibid.

71. This is a distinction that sociologists Aldon Morris and Charles Payne elaborate on in their works on the movement.

72. Payne, "Ella Baker and Models of Social Change."

73. Dorothy Miller Zellner, interview by author.

74. Ibid.

75. The best definition of praxis, a term introduced by theorist Antonio Gramsci, is "a philosophy which is also politics." The function of praxis "draws out and elaborates that which people already 'feel' but do not 'know,' in other words that which is present in nascent or inchoate form in their consciousness but which is contradicted and immobilized by other conceptions." In discussing the idea of praxis, Gramsci describes the work of revolutionary intellectuals as that of "drawing out and elaborating elements of critical awareness and good sense." Forgacs, *The Antonio Gramsci Reader*, 323.

76. Baker, interview by Morris, 69A.

77. Ibid., 29A.

78. Forman, *The Making of a Black Revolutionary*, 215.

79. Zinn, *SNCC, the New Abolitionists*, dedication and acknowledgements.

80. Murray, interview by Martin.

81. Ture (Carmichael), interview by author.

CHAPTER NINE

1. Although SNCC staff and volunteers came from varied backgrounds, most of them were college students when they joined the movement. In 1960 only a small percentage of African Americans had ever attended college. Still, education was a critical marker of class status and a criterion for leadership posts in traditional civic and social organizations. Therefore, even those who were not from well-off families had a certain social capital as a result of their access to education. Cleveland Sellers illustrated the point in his movement biography, *River of No Return*. His family was not rich, but it was better off than most.

2. Payne, in *I've Got the Light of Freedom*, and Moses and Cobb, in *Radical Equations*, reiterate the point that small-business owners, landowners, and those with a source of income independent of whites were key in the support they offered to the movement. Two other factors should be noted with regard to these individuals. First, they often also found themselves economically threatened because of their political stances despite their semi-independent circumstances; and second, even though they had some financial security that others did not, most were rebels against certain middle-class values, especially snobbery and exclusivity. While they enjoyed certain advantages, they identified with the poor as social if not economic peers.

3. "Freedom Village Tennessee," *Student Voice* 2, no. 1 (Jan. 1961); Forman, *The Making of Black Revolutionaries*, 114–45.

4. Forman, *The Making of Black Revolutionaries*; Forman, interview by author; Sellers, *River of No Return*.

5. "Let's Help Fayette County Fight for Free Rights," *Student Voice* 1, no. 4 (Nov. 1960): 2.

6. Stembridge, interview by author.

7. Curry, interview by author, and Sherrod, interview by author.

8. John Lewis, *Walking with the Wind*, 180.

9. Gloster Current, "Which Way Out?" *Crisis*, Mar. 1961.

10. Curry, interview by author, and Sherrod, interview by author.

11. Baker, "Tent City: Freedom's Front Line."

12. Ibid.

13. See Forman, *The Making of Black Revolutionaries*, 137–45, for a detailed description of Fayette Tent City.

14. See "The Fight for the Vote—Fayette County," testimony of John McFerren, Jan. 31, 1960, in Grant, ed., *Black Protest*, 274–77; Brockington, interview by author.

15. Anne Braden to Ella Baker, June 20, 1963, Carl and Anne Braden Papers, box 41, folder 1, State Historical Society of Wisconsin (SHSW), Madison, Wis.

16. Forman, *The Making of Black Revolutionaries*, 116–17.

17. Lewis is both borrowing from and expanding on James Scott's notion of the "hidden transcript," that is, the covert messages in which oppressed communities express how they really feel about the society and their condition in it. See "Race, Equity and Democracy."

18. Ed King, "SNCC Visits Fayette," *Student Voice* 2, no. 1 (Jan. 1961): 1.

19. Forman, interview by author.

20. Patterson, *Brown v. Board of Education*, mentions a number of grassroots community activists who were instrumental in building support and recruiting litigants for the NAACP's legal cases during the 1950s. See references to Gardiner Bishop, Barbara Johns, and Albert DeLaine.

21. Dittmer, *Local People*.

22. For an interesting comparison of the U.S.-based Black Freedom Movement's internal class politics and the Dalit Movement of the so-called untouchable caste in India, see Rajshekar, *Dalit*.

23. Baker, interview by Britton, 76.

24. Carson, *In Struggle*, 62.

25. Jane Stembridge, interview by Emily Stoper, in Stoper, *The Student Nonviolent Coordinating Committee*, 248.

26. "Ella Baker's Hattiesburg Speech," Jan. 21, 1964, Hattiesburg, Miss. Speech transcribed by and provided courtesy of Catherine Orr.

27. This composite sketch of Baker's apartment is drawn from author's interviews with Mary King, Connie Curry, and Casey Hayden.

28. Sherrod, interview by author.

29. Carson, *In Struggle*, 57.

30. John Lewis, *Walking with the Wind*, 187.

31. Wilkins, *Standing Fast*, 286.

32. See Carson, *In Struggle*, 63.

33. In some ways the movement in Albany, Georgia, in 1962 signaled the beginning of open tensions between the SCLC and SNCC. However, it would be wrong to assume that,

from that time on, hostilities necessarily dominated the relationships between individuals in the two organizations. Most SNCC people respected Martin Luther King Jr. even though they might disagree with him politically. Many of them continued to maintain cordial personal relationships with him until his death in April 1968. Stokely Carmichael enjoyed occasional dinners at the King home in Atlanta as late as 1967. For details, see Carson, *In Struggle*, 56–65; Garrow, *Bearing the Cross*, 173–230; and Ricks, "'De Lawd' Descends and Is Crucified," 5–12.

34. Baker, interview by Morris, 70A.

35. Carson, *In Struggle*, 63; Forman, *The Making of Black Revolutionaries*, 256; Ricks, "'De Lawd' Descends and Is Crucified."

36. Zinn, *You Can't Be Neutral*, 51.

37. Sherrod, interview by Britton, 26.

38. Brockington, interview by author.

39. Carson, *In Struggle*, 56–57.

40. Based in Columbia, South Carolina, Simkins had been active in the NAACP in the 1940s and 1950s; she had also been loosely associated with the Communist Party and communist popular front organizations like the Southern Negro Youth Congress. See Woods, "Modjeska Simkins."

41. "Operation Freedom" (flyer), 1961, EBP, Operation Freedom folder, 1960s files.

42. Anne Braden to Ella Baker, Oct. 4, 1962, Braden Papers, box 39, folder 2, Southern Patriot and Field Organizers Files, Correspondence, Sept.–Dec. 1962, SHSW.

43. In the minutes of a workshop two years after the Chapel Hill conference, Septima Clark and Charles Girard still spoke about how their confidence in interracial work and opposition to anticommunism were influenced by their personal relationships with the Bradens. Minutes/Summary of Civil Liberties–Civil Rights Conference, June 28–30, 1963, Atlanta, Ga., Braden Papers, box 47, folder 9, SHSW.

44. Anne Braden to Jim (Dombrowski), June 20, 1961, Braden Papers, box 35, folder 5, SHSW.

45. Anne Braden to Jim (Dombrowski), Oct. 4, 1961, Braden Papers, box 36, folder 5, SHSW.

46. Braden, interview by author, June 1991.

47. "Freedom and the First Amendment," Oct. 27, 1961, conference transcript, Braden Papers, box 48, folder 8, panel 3, p. 1, SHSW.

48. Ibid., 3.

49. Ibid., 3–11.

50. Baker, "Lack of Thought Cripples South."

51. Baker, "Great Society or Grim Society."

52. Anne Braden to Victor Rabinowitz, Apr. 13, 1963, Braden Papers, box 47, folder 9, SHSW.

53. Anne Braden to James Dombrowski, Dec. 24, 1962, Braden Papers, box 47, folder 9, SHSW.

54. Anne Braden to Ella Baker, Apr. 18, 1963, Braden Papers, box 47, folder 9, SHSW.

55. Minutes/Summary of Civil Liberties–Civil Rights Conference, June 28–30, 1963, Atlanta, Ga., Braden Papers, box 47, folder 9, p. 6, SHSW.

56. Ibid.

57. Dittmer, *Local People*, 231; Moses, interview by author. A newspaper headline in the *Daily News* of Jackson, Miss., blazoned: "Red Crusader Active in Jackson Mixed Race Drive."

58. The issue of association with reputed Communists came up again for SNCC when

the leftist National Lawyers Guild offered legal assistance to southern civil rights workers. SNCC accepted the aid. Dorothy Miller Zellner, interview by author.

59. James Dombrowski to Anne Braden, June 21, 1961, Braden Papers, box 35, folder 5, SHSW.

60. John Salter to Anne and Carl (Braden), Oct. 25, 1963, Braden Papers, box 41, folder 8; John Salter to Jim (Dombrowski), Nov. 20, 1963, Braden Papers, box 41, folder 8; Ella Baker to Anne Braden, n.d. (in June–Nov. 1963 folder), and Salter letter dated Nov. 20, 1963, Braden Papers, box 41, folder 8, SHSW.

61. Zinn, *Albany*, 5.

62. See Reagon, interview by author; Ricks, "'De Lawd' Descends and Is Crucified"; and Zinn, *Albany*. Reagon eventually returned to school, obtaining a Ph.D. from Howard University and developing a successful career as a cultural worker with the women's a capella group, Sweet Honey in the Rock, and as a historian at the Smithsonian Institution.

63. Reagon, interview by author.

64. Payne, *I've Got the Light of Freedom*, 120.

65. Carson, *In Struggle*, 48.

66. Ella Baker to Anne Braden, Aug. 16, 1962, Braden Papers, box 38, folder 5; Braden Papers, Southern Patriot and Field Organizers Files, Correspondence, Apr.–Aug. 1962, SHSW.

67. Ella Baker to Anne Braden, Aug. 16, 1962, Braden Papers, box 38, folder 5, Correspondence, Apr.–Aug. 1962, SHSW.

68. Brenda Travis, conversation with author at Shaw SNCC Reunion, Apr. 2000, Raleigh, N.C.

Baker aided young men as well as young women. Travis Britt was another troubled teenager whom she took under her wing and tried to help. A native of North Carolina, Britt was expelled from Albany State as a result of his involvement in the 1961 Freedom Rides and then spent time organizing in McComb. According to Baker, he had also "seen too much of the seamy side of life" and did not have many resources to help him get back on his feet. When he turned up jobless and needy in New York, Baker referred him to her friend Rev. Thomas Kilgore, asking that he try to help the young man get counseling and a job. Ella Baker to Thomas Kilgore, ca. 1963, EBP.

In the case of Elroy Embery, a sit-in participant expelled from Alabama State College, Baker appealed to Rev. John Marion of the United Presbyterian Church in New York, asking for a scholarship contribution. If Baker could not meet a need or resolve a problem herself, then she found someone else who could. Ella Baker to Rev. John Marion, ca. 1965, EBP.

69. Nash, interview by author; Omolade, interview by author; King, interview by author; Reagon, interview by author; Burlage, interview by author.

70. Ruby Doris Smith married Clifford Robinson in 1963 and changed her name to Ruby Doris Smith Robinson. However, she was Ruby Doris Smith when she joined the movement in 1960.

71. Richardson, interview by author.

72. Fleming, *Soon We Will Not Cry*, 90. For general biographical information on Robinson, including her views on self-defense, see ibid., 82–88.

73. Jane Stembridge's brief tenure as secretary was in 1960, when SNCC was still forming as an organization. The role of secretary was quite different in subsequent years. Smith Robinson's position, following Forman's lead, held a great deal of power.

74. Ella Baker to Ruby Doris Smith, EBP, correspondence folder. Baker was concerned about the health of all those who served time in prison. Although Baker had no particu-

lar reason at that time to be especially concerned about Ruby Doris Smith's health, Smith died of cancer before she was thirty.

75. Charles McDew's comments at Shaw University conference on Ella Baker, Apr. 1960, Raleigh, N.C. For McLaurin quote, see Dittmer, *Local People*, 136.

76. Guyot, interview by author.

77. Neary, *Julian Bond*, 76.

78. Donaldson, interview by author, Jan. 18, 2002.

79. See Gaines, *Uplifting the Race*; Higginbotham, *Righteous Discontent*.

CHAPTER TEN

1. Quoted in Payne, *I've Got the Light of Freedom*, 103.

2. Baker, interview by Carson, 15.

3. Ibid., 11.

4. Payne, *I've Got the Light of Freedom*, 176.

5. Moses, interview by author; "Amzie Moore," the biographical statement that precedes the "Guide to the Amzie Moore Papers," Amzie Moore Papers, State Historical Society of Wisconsin (SHSW), Madison, Wis. (bio of Moore in inventory).

6. "You don't know what it's like to have to sleep with your gun in your hand, where every passing car might bring Death!" Amzie Moore to Roy Wilkins, June 21, 1955, 2, NAACP Papers, group II, box A422, Amzie Moore folder, Library of Congress, Washington, D.C.

7. Ibid. The preceding information on Moore is drawn from the same source.

8. Ella Baker to Ruth Moore, Feb. 6, 1957, Amzie Moore Papers, SHSW.

9. Comments from Robert Moses at the Conference on Ethics and Morality: Voices of the Civil Rights Movement, National Museum of American History, Washington, D.C., Feb. 3, 1980, 5 (transcript courtesy of the Martin Luther King Papers Project, Stanford University).

10. Moses, interview by author. Moses repeated this statement quite often to interviewers and in speeches and publications.

11. Moses, "Comments of Robert Moses," Conference on Ethics and Morality: Voices of the Civil Rights Movement.

12. Payne, *I've Got the Light of Freedom*, 121–124; Dittmer, *Local People*, 109.

13. Payne, *I've Got the Light of Freedom*, 113; Dittmer, *Local People*, 73, 106.

14. Dittmer, *Local People*, 109, 111.

15. Ibid., 106, 113.

16. Payne, *I've Got the Light of Freedom*, 118–119.

17. Dittmer, *Local People*, 111. Nash, interview by author. Nash reiterates how important Baker's encouragement was because other adults were critical.

18. Dittmer, *Local People*, 115.

19. Also see Clyde Woods, *Development Arrested*, for an economic and cultural analysis of the racial and class politics in the region.

20. Dittmer, *Local People*, 104, 111–15.

21. Ibid., 113.

22. Hall (Wynn), interview by author.

23. Omolade, interview by author.

24. Baker, interview by Britton, 82.

25. Dittmer, *Local People*, 105–7; Payne, *I've Got the Light of Freedom*, 117.

26. Dittmer, *Local People*, 118–19. The NAACP eventually withdrew from COFO. The

national NAACP was hostile to the COFO project from the outset. It was the state NAACP that worked with COFO for a while.

27. Ibid., 119–20.

28. Bond, "SNCC: What We Did," 19.

29. Hamer, *To Praise Our Bridges*, 12. For a fuller discussion of Hamer's life, see Lee, *For Freedom's Sake*, and Kay Mills, *This Little Light of Mine*.

30. This involvement was the stepping stone to Freedom Summer. See Moses reference to Lowenstein in Minutes of the Meeting of the SNCC Executive Committee, Dec. 27–31, 1963, SNCC Papers (microfilm), reel 3, 28–29, subgroup A, series II, Executive and Central Committees 1961–1967 files, King Center, Atlanta, Ga.

31. Payne, *I've Got the Light of Freedom*, 1. Payne calculates that in 1960 98 percent of black Mississippians eligible to vote were not even registered.

32. See Henry and Curry, *Aaron Henry*.

33. See Hall (Wynn), interview by author; Robnett, *How Long? How Long?*; Olson, *Freedom's Daughters*; and Moses, interview by author.

34. Sherrod comment in SNCC, "Southwest Georgia Report," Dec. 27, 1963, EBP.

35. Mueller, "Ella Baker and the Origins of Participatory Democracy."

36. White women may have been excluded from certain roles because they were white and the priority within a self-consciously Black Freedom Movement was on black leadership.

37. Ture (Carmichael), interview by author.

38. Ruby Doris Smith Robinson memo to Executive Committee, July 2, 1966, EBP, SNCC files; "A Little Old Statement from Fay Bellamy," Sept. 1, 1966, EBP, SNCC files.

39. For 1969 Ella Baker speech, see Grant, *Ella Baker*, 229; for Payne quote, see Payne, *I've Got the Light of Freedom*, 268.

40. In *I've Got the Light of Freedom*, Payne documents gruesome acts of violence, but he argues that some of the worst forms of violence actually abated when local blacks fought back. Violence directed at SNCC remained considerable, however.

41. "Statement on Events in Natchez, Miss.—November 1 and 2, 1963," MFDP Papers, Appendix A to SNCC Papers, reel 69, frame 504. Ella Baker's FBI files also indicate that Payne reported to the FBI. Whether he did so as an individual or whether he was reporting the incident in hopes of receiving protection for the group is unclear.

42. See Vollers, *Ghosts of Mississippi*.

43. Dittmer, *Local People*, 207.

44. Ibid., 208–9, 210, 211.

45. Minutes of the Meeting of the SNCC Executive Committee, Dec. 27–31, 1963, SNCC Papers, reel 3. It should be noted that the minutes from SNCC meetings are fairly inconsistent in depth and quality. Some are handwritten, some partially in shorthand, and some illegible. A few are not dated. In at least one instance, there are two sets of slightly different handwritten minutes, obviously taken by different note takers, for the same meeting. Neither is signed. The Dec. 27–31, 1963, minutes are exceptionally precise and extensive. The document is thirty-two pages long, typed single-space. There are also detailed quotes from individual participants in the minutes.

46. Ibid.

47. Ibid., 2.

48. Ibid.

49. Ibid., 8.

50. Ibid., 28.

51. Ibid.

52. Ibid., 29.

53. Ibid., 28.

54. Ibid., 5.

55. Ibid., 6.

56. Ibid., 16.

57. Ibid., 3, 9, 26.

58. Ibid., 32.

59. Sellers, *The River of No Return*, 100.

60. Dittmer, *Local People*, 180.

61. Ibid., 178–83.

62. Ibid., 181–83.

63. Zinn, *SNCC*, 105–6.

64. Ibid., 105.

65. Henry and Curry, *Aaron Henry*, xii, 65.

66. Zinn, *SNCC*, 105.

67. Ibid., 106.

68. Ibid.

69. *Student Voice*, Jan. 27, 1964, 2; Zinn, *SNCC*, 105–6.

70. Payne, *I've Got the Light of Freedom*, 299.

71. Mendy Samstein, interview by Romaine, 138–39.

72. Minutes of the Meeting of the SNCC Executive Committee, Dec. 27–31, 1963, SNCC Papers, reel 3.

73. Quoted in Mary King, *Freedom Song*, 319.

74. Discussion of black self-defense among local people in SNCC Executive Committee minutes, June 11, 1964, in Howard Zinn Papers, box 2, folder 7, State Historical Society of Wisconsin, Madison, Wis. See also Moses, "Comments of Robert Moses," 6.

75. Cantarow and O'Malley, "Ella Baker," 82.

76. Quoted in Mary King, *Freedom Song*, 324.

77. Ture (Carmichael), interview by author.

78. Richardson, interview by author. See also Dittmer, *Local People*, 106, 191, 285; McDew, interview by Shannon.

79. Payne, *I've Got the Light of Freedom*, 204.

80. SNCC minutes indicate that the group decided that no SNCC staff or volunteer should carry weapons. However, in a 1966 interview with Emily Stoper, Baker interpreted the decision to mean that whether to aid a local person in defending his home if it came under attack was "left to the individual." Baker, interview by Emily Stoper, in Stoper, *Student Nonviolent Coordinating Committee*, 269; Grant, *Ella Baker*, 196.

81. Minutes of the Meeting of the SNCC Executive Committee, June 9–11, 1964, 30–31, EBP.

82. Ibid., 12, reel 47.

83. Untitled article by Ella Baker, *Southern Patriot* 22, no. 8 (Oct. 1964): 3.

84. These figures are an estimated rounding off of several sets of figures with overlapping discrepancies. See *Student Voice* 5, no. 17 (July 22, 1964): 1; Dittmer, *Local People*, 259; *Student Voice* 5, no. 19 (Aug. 5, 1964): 2–3.

85. McAdam, *Freedom Summer*, 24.

86. Description of Cobb from Holt, "Freedom Schools," 42.

87. Perlstein, "Teaching Freedom"; Rothschild, "The Volunteers and the Freedom Schools."

88. Lynd, interview by author.

89. "Volunteers to Open Freedom Schools," *Washington Post*, July 5, 1964, A11.

90. Lois Chaffee to Ella Baker, Mar. 10, 1964, MFDP Papers, in SNCC Papers (microfilm), reel 64, 90.

91. Ibid.; "Dear Friends" letter from Lois Chaffee about logistics of curriculum meeting, n.d., MFDP Papers, in SNCC Papers (microfilm), reel 64, 90.

92. John O'Neal to Ella Baker, Apr. 13, 1964, MFDP Papers, in SNCC Papers (microfilm), reel 67.

93. Ibid. O'Neal's letter refers to conversations between Moses and Baker regarding assignments and hires for the Freedom Schools project; he is also soliciting advice. See also *Freedom Now Newsletter*, May 4, 1964, in SNCC Papers (microfilm), reel 42.

94. Lois Chaffee to Ella Baker, Mar. 10, 1964, SNCC papers (microfilm), reel 64.

95. Teodori, *The New Left*, 103.

96. Richardson, interview by author.

97. Hall (Wynn), interview by author.

98. Taitt-Magubane, interview by author.

99. Freire, *Pedagogy of Freedom*, 30.

100. Ibid., 61.

101. Ibid., 103.

102. The Italian theorist Antonio Gramsci spelled out an approach to education that Ella Baker embodied in her daily work. He distinguished between "instruction (imparting of knowledge)" and "education (drawing out of the pupils' capacities)." He further emphasized the importance of "the truly active participation of the pupil in the school, which could only exist if the school is related to life." See Forgacs, *The Antonio Gramsci Reader*, 314, 416 n. 3.

103. Holt "Freedom Schools."

104. Memo, Charles Cobb to SNCC Executive Committee, COFO Summer Program Committee, Jan. 14, 1964, SNCC Papers (microfilm), reel 68.

CHAPTER ELEVEN

1. Henry and Curry, *Aaron Henry*, 180.

2. Ibid., 166.

3. Rauh, interview by Romaine, 302–6.

4. Ibid., 302–3.

5. Higgs, interview by Romaine.

6. Minutes of meeting on the challenge to the Democratic National Convention (only 6 persons attending), May 5, 1964, SNCC Papers (microfilm), reel 47.

7. Gray quoted in Dittmer, *Local People*, 182.

8. Payne, "Men Led, but Women Organized," 2.

9. I conflate SNCC and COFO because many volunteers identified with both.

10. Quoted by Orr, "'The Struggle Is Eternal,'" 1. The speech was delivered on Aug. 6, 1964 in Jackson, Miss. See also *Student Voice* 5, no. 20 (Aug. 12, 1964): 1, 4; *Student Voice* 5, no. 21 (Aug. 19, 1964): 1; Grant, *Ella Baker*, 163–64.

11. Tillow, interview by author; Anderson, *Bayard Rustin*, 277.

12. Ibid.; Omolade, interview by author.

13. Ibid.

14. John Painter Jr., "A Synonym for Oregon: Congresswoman Green Focused on Education," *Oregonian Weekly*, Apr. 22, 1987, B8.

15. "Mississippi Freedom Rally Series . . . ," *Amsterdam News*, July 25, 1964, 35.

16. Ella Baker to "Dear Convention Delegate," July 20, 1964, SNCC Papers (microfilm), reel 41.

17. Lee, *For Freedom's Sake*, 85. Dittmer, *Local People*, 290, has a slightly different version of the quote: "If you seat those black buggers, the whole South will walk out." We can infer that some variation on these comments was what was said. The venomous tone and meaning of the message is the same.

18. Lee, *For Freedom's Sake*, 99.

19. Rustin, *Strategies for Freedom*, 51–54. Rustin had felt that the compromise was the best deal MFDP could get at that particular juncture and that to reject it would be a "strategic error." In *Strategies*, he points out that, although a few years later SNCC "collapsed," the MFDP challenge was the impetus for a democratization and diversification of the delegate selection process within the Democratic Party.

20. Baker, interview by Romaine, 369.

21. Ibid., 382.

22. Rauh, interview by Romaine, 340.

23. Chafe, *Never Stop Running*, 205.

24. Ibid., 198.

25. Mary King, *Freedom Song*, p. 343–49; Lee, *For Freedom's Sake*, 86–101; Dittmer, *Local People*, 272–302; Payne, *I've Got the Light of Freedom*, 340–41.

26. Baker, interview by Romaine, 382–83.

27. Staff meeting, Oct. 11, 1964, SNCC Papers (microfilm), reel 3.

28. Carson, *In Struggle*, 145–48; Ture (Carmichael), interview by author; Mary King, *Freedom Song*, 465.

29. Carson, *In Struggle*, 181; Anderson, *Bayard Rustin*, 280.

30. Rowland Evans and Robert Novak, "Inside Report: Freedom Party Postscript," *New York Herald Tribune*, Sept. 3, 1964.

31. Ibid.

32. Rowland Evans and Robert Novak, "Inside Report: A Longer Look at Snick," *New York Herald Tribune*, Apr. 9, 1965.

33. John Dittmer points out that Curtis Gans of the Americans for Democratic Action, the group Joe Rauh is most closely associated with, expressed concern about Baker's influence in the MFDP. Dittmer, *Local People*, 317.

34. Hall (Wynn), interview by author.

35. Donaldson, interview by author, Jan. 18, 2002.

36. Baker, interview by Britton, 68.

37. "We Want Black Power," Chicago SNCC leaflet reprinted, in section titled "We Must Fill Ourselves with Hate for All Things White," in *Black Protest Thought in the Twentieth Century*, ed. Meier et al., 487.

38. Baker, interview by Britton, 67.

39. Carson, *In Struggle*, 201–4.

40. For Zellner quotes, see Robert Zellner, interview by author; for Richardson's views, see Richardson, interview by author.

41. Baker, interview by Stoper, 268.

42. Ibid., 265.

43. Ture (Carmichael), interview by author.

44. Ibid.; Braden, interview by author, Apr. 13, 1991.

45. Baker, interview by Britton, 67.

46. Ibid., 66.

47. Ibid., 68.

48. Ibid., 88–89.

49. Beal, interview by author; also see Ella Baker, letter to "dear friends" mentioning the Emergency Women's Committee, n.d. [circa 1970s], Ella Baker Papers (EBP), correspondence files (1970s), Schomburg Center for Research in Black Culture, New York, N.Y.

50. Grant, *Ella Baker*, 230.

51. Braden, interview by author, June 1991.

52. Ibid. For more information on Sallye Davis's interesting political background, see Davis, interview by Painter.

53. "Ella Baker to Speak on Angela's Defense Here January Eleventh," *Birmingham Times*, Jan. 7, 1971. This clipping included in the FBI's Ella Baker files, New York.

54. *Richmond Times Dispatch*, Mar. 17, 1971. A reference to this same article can be found in an internal FBI memo dated Apr. 7, 1971, to "Director, FBI," from "SAC 100-136886," in the FBI's Ella Baker files, New York file. The memo does not mention the article's title. See also Brian Siegle, "Baker Attacks Public Complacency," *Daily Cavalier* (University of Virginia), Feb. 26, 1971.

55. For more information, see EBP, Mass Party folder, 1970s file; general Mass Party literature in Arthur Kinoy Papers, State Historical Society of Wisconsin (SHSW), Madison, Wis.; and Saltzman, interview by author.

56. EBP, Mass Party folder and correspondence; Glick, interview by author.

57. EBP, Mass Party folder and correspondence.

58. Baker, interview by Britton, 56, Paul Horowitz to Ella Baker, Aug. 2, 1978, and Annette Rubinstein to Ella Baker, June 24, 1974, EBP, correspondence files (1970s); Baker, interview by Allen, 2; Baker, interview by Hayden and Thrasher, 59.

59. Puerto Rico Solidarity Organization, statement in support of Puerto Rican independence, n.d. [ca. 1974], with list of names of supporters including Ella Baker, EBP, 1970s Puerto Rico Solidarity files.

60. Paul Horowitz of Puerto Rico Solidarity Organization to Ella Baker, Aug. 2, 1978, EBP, Puerto Rican Solidarity Organization folder.

61. EBP, Puerto Rican Solidarity Organization folder.

62. Donaldson, interview by author, Apr. 23, 2002.

63. Violet Cherry to Ella Baker, Sept. 7, 1976, EBP, correspondence folder (1970s).

64. Cantarow and O'Malley, "Ella Baker," 93.

65. Political clippings folder, EBP.

CHAPTER TWELVE

In comparing Ella Baker to Gramsci and Freire—two men, one a European and the other a Latin American—I am reminded of radical philosopher Lewis Gordon's powerful critique of the way in which Eurocentric intellectual traditions push scholars to subsume black thinkers and theorists beneath white ones in order to somehow legitimate them. This is a danger, but the other danger is to essentialize and isolate black thought from parallel ideologies. I have not asserted that Baker learned from, borrowed from, or imitated these two well-known theorists; instead, I contend that through her own process of political evolution she arrived at a very similar place. In distinct cultural and historical contexts, those struggling to analyze injustice and realize a more humane alternative can and do arrive at similar conclusions without one being a derivative of the other. See Gordon, *Existentia Africana*.

1. This is a point illustrated effectively in Grant's documentary film *Fundi* when Bob Moses refers to Baker as a master teacher, "mfundi or fundi" in Swahili. It is a point

reiterated in Ayers, "'We Who Believe in Freedom,'" 54, and in Moses and Cobb, *Radical Equations*, 23–57.

2. Ayers, "'We Who Believe in Freedom,'" 524. The term *griot* refers to a story-teller/teacher and in some cases to a visionary and adviser.

3. Gaines, *Uplifting the Race*, 33, 35.

4. Baker, interview by Hayden and Thrasher, 37.

5. Ibid., 38. Other scholarship suggests that while many teachers erred on the side of avoiding political controversies to keep their jobs and make a difference that way, others did in fact reject their socialization and engage in protest politics. See Fairclough, "'Being in the Field of Education,'" 75 ("the image of the black teacher as Uncle Tom or race traitor is a grotesque stereotype"). See also Gilmore, *Gender and Jim Crow*, regarding teachers and political leadership. John Dittmer asserts that there were few places where teachers got involved in movement activity in significant numbers before 1965. Dittmer, *Local People*, 75.

6. Omolade, interview by author.

7. Joyce Ladner, interview by author.

8. Ibid.

9. Graff, *Beyond the Culture Wars*.

10. See Baker, interview by *Urban Review* editors; and "The Workers Education Project," n.d., Works Progress Administration (WPA) Papers, Workers Service Division, New York City Reports, National Archives, Washington, D.C.

11. Cited in Morera, "Gramsci and Democracy," 26.

12. Baker, interview by *Urban Review* editors, 20.

13. An illustration of this methodology and approach to teaching in action is reflected in an account written by Jane Stembridge as an observer in a Freedom School class taught by SNCC activist Stokely Carmichael, "Notes on Class," in Carmichael, ed., *Stokely Speaks*, 3–4.

14. Payne, *I've Got the Light of Freedom*, 409.

15. Hall (Wynn), interview by author.

16. Taitt-Magubane, interview by author. See author's interviews with Hall (Wynn), Moses, Reagon, and King for the same sentiment.

17. Mary King, *Freedom Song*, 60. Baker's students went on to enjoy illustrious careers, likely attributable, at least in part, to her encouragement and tutelage. Joyce Ladner became a sociologist, author, and interim president of Howard University. Mary King served in the administration of President Jimmy Carter. Eleanor Holmes Norton is a congresswoman from the District of Columbia.

18. Holmes Norton, interview by author.

19. Baker, interviewer not known, Duke University Oral History Program (DUOHP), 13.

20. Ibid., 21.

21. Ibid.

22. Gramsci, *Selections from Prison Notebooks*, 9, 10. Citation from Lipsitz, *A Life in the Struggle*, 9.

23. Baker, interview by Morris, 55A.

24. Orr, "'The Struggle Is Eternal.'"

25. "Report of Conference of Educational Directors and Educational Committee Members of Labor Organizations Cooperating with the Workers Education Project: Methods of Promoting Educational Programs," Jan. 22, 1938, 2, Pauli Murray Papers, WPA files, box 72, Schlesinger Library, Radcliffe College, Boston, Mass.

26. Joyce Ladner, interview by author.

27. Freire, *Pedagogy of Freedom*, 30.

28. Ibid., 104.

29. Hall (Wynn), interview by author.

30. Radical black intellectual Cornel West also identifies Martin Luther King Jr. as an "organic intellectual." See "Martin Luther King Jr: Prophetic Christian as Organic Intellectual," in West, *The Cornel West Reader*, 424–34.

31. Baker, interview by Morris, 89A.

32. Baker, interviewer not known, DUOHP, 14.

33. Elsa Barkley Brown, "Mothers of Mind," 8–9.

34. Ella Baker, "The Black Woman in the Civil Rights Struggle," a speech delivered in Atlanta, Ga., in 1969. Reprinted in Grant, *Ella Baker*, 230.

35. Said, *Representations of the Intellectual*," 11.

36. Ibid., 63–64.

37. Kelley, *Freedom Dreams*.

38. In interviews later in her life, Baker insisted she was not a leader but a facilitator. I respectfully disagree with her humble self-portrait. She was a leader in that she had a profound, conscious, and defining impact on the politics and culture of the campaigns and organizations with which she was affiliated. She was indeed a leader if we can conceive of leadership in horizontal as well as vertical terms. She led and was led by the masses and her comrades. She was, however, not a traditional leader and did not exhibit the characteristics of self-promotion sometimes associated with individual leadership.

39. See Curry et al., *Deep in Our Hearts*, for discussion of white women activists' varied views of their necessarily supportive role as whites.

40. Lee, *For Freedom's Sake*.

41. Nash, interview by author.

42. Hayden in Browning, Curry, and Hayden, group interview by author.

43. Hall waited awhile, but ultimately did marry. Hall (Wynn), interview by author.

44. Omolade, *The Rising Song of African American Women*, has a chapter devoted to Ella Baker's legacy.

45. Omolade, interview by author.

46. Holmes Norton, interview by author; James, *Transcending the Talented Tenth*.

47. Clark, interview by Hall, 81, 87.

48. Baker, interview by Morris, 56A.

49. See hooks, *Feminist Theory from Margin to Center*, for an elaboration of the notion of bringing the marginal sectors of the community to the center as an empowerment strategy and also as a means of enriching a movement's theoretical understanding of oppression and liberation.

50. Guinier and Torres, *The Miner's Canary*, 159.

51. For example, Baker's views are inconsistent with those of black conservatives like Shelby Steele who argue that colorblindness was the goal of the civil rights movement, that it has been achieved, and that now we need a raceless political agenda. Baker felt that differences had to be acknowledged and debated and that marginality could actually be harnessed as a resource rather than treated as simply a liability. Unlike Steele, her goal was not simply assimilation.

52. Baker, interview by Morris, 48A.

53. Baker, interview by Carson, 10–11.

54. Baker, interview by Britton, 75.

55. Baker, interview by Morris, 49A.

56. Ibid., 52A. Anthropologist Karen Brodkin Sacks, in her research on the Duke University Hospital Workers struggle in Durham, N.C., documents a style and method of political organizing that revolved around a set of personal and political relationships sustained largely by women workers, who on the surface might not have appeared to be leaders in any traditional sense. The socially connected women who were key in holding these networks together and putting them to political use were in Sacks's terminology "centerwomen." Sociologist Belinda Robnett has borrowed that concept and expanded on it in her formulation of female "bridge organizers," who, she points out, connected grassroots networks and everyday acts of resistance to the formal campaigns and national organizations during the civil rights movement. Chana Kai Lee's biography of Fannie Lou Hamer further exemplifies these theories of black women's leadership. All of these approaches to leadership and political community are variations and reformulations of an understanding that Ella Baker incorporated tacitly into her own political practices as early as the 1940s. See Sacks, *Caring by the Hour*; Robnett, *How Long? How Long?*; and Lee, *For Freedom's Sake*.

57. Baker, interview by Britton, 6, 38.

58. SNCC leaders were able to obtain access to members of the Justice Department and the president's staff during the Freedom Rides and Freedom Summer in a way that they would not have been able to if not for the grassroots organizing and mobilizing and visible campaigns in the streets. Of course, the reality was that access still did not translate into the physical protection that movement workers so desperately needed or into all of the rights and reforms that were being demanded.

59. Ella Baker's view of situational or contextual democracy is effectively articulated, in part, by political scientist and philosopher Iris Marion Young, who argues for what she terms the "deepening of democracy," an inclusive, historical concept of democratic practice, which takes into account group differences and inequalities. For Young, as for Baker, simple inclusion is not enough; the terms of that inclusion are key. Every citizen or participant does not come to the table with the same resources and privileges, so the differences and inequalities have to be a part of the democratic equation. Like legal scholar Lani Guinier, Baker never bought into artificially simplistic notions of democracy as defined by an aggregate model of calculated group interests. See Iris Marion Young, *Democracy and Inclusion*, and Guinier, *Tyranny of the Majority*.

60. The notion of a conditional insider, as conceptualized by black feminist sociologist Patricia Hill Collins, describes the positionality of black women domestics who on the one hand worked, and often lived, in intimate proximity to their "white family" but who simultaneously understood they would never be full-fledged members of such a family. Yet their exploited labor ensured the family's day-to-day survival, and their location allowed them to wield subtle power and provided them with unique social and political insights that whites did not have. Collins, *Black Feminist Thought*, 11.

61. Abernathy, interview by author. Abernathy made this observation because of Baker's relative insider status versus her own feelings of exclusion as the wife of a prominent male leader. She watched Ella Baker sit in the living room with the men while the wives were attending to household matters. What she did not fully appreciate from her vantage point was that Baker was an "outsider within." She was close to the center of political power within civil rights groups but was never fully welcomed into the club because of her gender, her politics, and at times her age and personality.

62. Baker, interview by Britton, 40.

63. Hine, *Speak Truth to Power*, 41.

64. Grant, *Ella Baker*, 218, citing an interview with Ella Baker by Wesley Brown and Arverna Adams, New York, N.Y., 1977.

65. Ella Baker shared some of C. L. R. James's views but by no means all of them. She was never a Trotskyist and never as absorbed as James in the internal ideological feuds within the organized left. This comparison does not mean to locate Baker in one particular political camp. As has been emphasized throughout the book, she was a very independent thinker, who nevertheless valued lessons learned from myriad theories and traditions.

66. Untitled essay by C. L. R. James, *Race Today* 6, no. 5 (1974): 144.

BIBLIOGRAPHY

ARCHIVAL MATERIALS

Ann Arbor, Michigan
Hatcher Library, University of Michigan
  Joseph Labadie Collection

Atlanta, Georgia
Archives, Martin Luther King Jr. Center for Nonviolent Social Change, Inc.
  Anne Romaine Oral History Collection (interviews from Romaine, "The Mississippi
    Freedom Democratic Party through August 1964," are on deposit in the King
    Center)
  Fred Shuttlesworth Papers
  Southern Christian Leadership Conference Papers
  Student Nonviolent Coordinating Committee Papers, 1959–1972 (microfilm)
    MFDP Papers

Birmingham, Alabama
Birmingham Public Library
  Birmingham Collection

Boston, Massachusetts
Mugar Library, Boston University
  Martin Luther King Papers

Cambridge, Massachusetts
Schlesinger Library, Radcliffe College
  Virginia Foster Durr Papers
  Pauli Murray Papers

Chapel Hill, North Carolina
Wilson Library, University of North Carolina
  North Carolina Collection (Baptist Missionary Pamphlets)
  Southern Oral History Project

Chicago, Illinois
Chicago Historical Society
  Claude Barnet Papers (Associated Negro Press)
National Archives Regional Center
  U.S. Census Population Schedules for Virginia and North Carolina (microfilm)

Detroit, Michigan
Walter P. Reuther Library, Wayne State University
  Rosa Parks Papers

Durham, North Carolina
Duke University Oral History Program

Ithaca, New York
M. P. Catherwood Library, Cornell University
   International Ladies Garment Workers Union Papers
   Charles S. Zimmerman Papers

Madison, Wisconsin
State Historical Society of Wisconsin
   Carl and Anne Braden Papers
   Highlander Research and Education Center Papers
   Myles Horton Papers
   Arthur Kinoy Papers
   Staughton Lynd Papers
   "Mississippi's 'Freedom Summer' Revisited" (1979)
   Amzie Moore Papers
   Charles Sherrod Papers
   Southern Conference Education Fund Papers
   Howard Zinn Papers

New Orleans, Louisiana
Tulane University
   Amistad Collection
      Fannie Lou Hamer Papers (microfilm)

New York, New York
New York Public Library
   Division of Rare Books and Manuscripts
      Norman Thomas Papers (microfilm)
   Schomburg Center for Research in Black Culture
      Ella Baker Papers
      William Pickens Papers, NAACP Files
      Bayard Rustin Papers (microfilm)
Teachers College, Columbia University
   New York Public School Papers—Mayor's Committee on Schools
Young Women's Christian Association National Headquarters
   YWCA New York Branch Collection (Harlem Y)

Norfolk, Virginia
Norfolk Public Library
   Norfolk Collection

Raleigh, North Carolina
North Carolina State Archives
   U.S. Census Population Schedule, Raleigh, North Carolina
Shaw University Archives
   Shaw University Journal

Stanford, California
Martin Luther King Jr. Papers Project, Stanford University

Syracuse, New York
Syracuse University
   George Schuyler Papers, Arents Collection

Warrenton, North Carolina
Warren County Estate Records
Warren County Register of Deeds

Washington, D.C.
Federal Bureau of Investigation, U.S. Department of Justice
    Ella Baker Files
    Student Nonviolent Coordinating Committee Files
Library of Congress
    Nannie H. Burroughs Papers
    Kenneth B. Clark Papers
    NAACP Papers
    A. Philip Randolph Papers
    Joseph Rauh Papers
    Bayard Rustin Papers (microfilm)
Moorland-Spingarn Research Center, Howard University
    Benjamin Griffith Brawley Papers
    Civil Rights Documentation/Ralph Bunche Collection
    Pauli Murray Papers
National Archives
    Works Progress Administration Papers

Winston-Salem, North Carolina
Wake Forest University Library
    Black Baptist Collection

INTERVIEWS BY AUTHOR

Abernathy, Juanita. Interview by author. Atlanta, Ga., September 1998.
Beal, Frances. Interview by author. Oakland, Calif., February 12, 1991.
Braden, Anne. Interview by author. Louisville, Ky., April 13, 1991.
——. Interview by author. Chapel Hill, N.C., June 1991.
——. Telephone interview by author. January 3, 1997.
——. Telephone interview by author. June 2002.
Brockington, Jackie. Interview by author. New York, N.Y., February 1990.
——. Telephone interview by author. May 1994.
Browning, Joan, Connie Curry, and Casey Hayden. Group interview by author. Atlanta,
    Ga., November 8, 1997.
Burlage, Dorothy (Dawson). Telephone interview by author. May 13, 2002.
Clarke, John Henrik. Interview by author. Harlem, N.Y., September 12, 1993.
Cooke, Marvel (Jackson). Interview by author. Harlem, N.Y., April 14, 1996.
Current, Gloster. Telephone interview by author. September 3, 1996.
Curry, Connie. Telephone interview by author. November 3, 1997.
Donaldson, Ivanhoe. Telephone interview by author. January 18, 2002.
——. Telephone interview by author. April 23, 2002.
Forman, James. Interview by author. Ann Arbor, Mich., January 22, 1991.
Giddings, Paula. Interview by author. Chapel Hill, N.C., June 10, 1996.
Gilchrist, Helen. Interview by author. Littleton, N.C., June 10, 1991.
Glick, Ted. Telephone interview by author. May 2002.
Grant, Joanne. Interview by author. New York, N.Y., October 4, 1989.
——. Interview by author. New York, N.Y., October 5, 1989.

Guyot, Lawrence. Interview by author. Washington, D.C., March 26, 1990.
Hall, Prathia (also known as Prathia Hall Wynn). Interview by author. Denver, Colo., June 25, 1997.
Harding, Vincent. Interview by author. Denver, Colo., June 26, 1997.
Harris, Doug. Interview by author. New York, N.Y., November, 1990.
Heirich, Max. Interview by author. Ann Arbor, Mich., September 5, 1996.
Hill, Herbert. Interview by author. Madison, Wis., May 24, 1996.
Holmes Norton, Eleanor. Telephone interview by author. March 1997.
King, Mary. Interview by author. Washington D.C., October 30, 1997.
Kochiyama, Yuri. Telephone interview by author. May 2002.
Ladner, Dorie. Interview by author. Washington, D.C., March 24, 1990.
Ladner, Joyce. Interview by author. Washington, D.C., March 23, 1990.
Lynd, Staughton. Telephone interview by author. April 11, 2002.
Lynn, Conrad. Interview by author. Nanuet, N.Y., February 6, 1990.
Moses, Robert. Interview by author. Cambridge, Mass., July 9, 1996.
Nash, Diane. Telephone interview by author. October 1990.
———. Interview by author. Chicago, Ill., September 4, 1997.
Newell, Jenny. Interview by author. Littleton, N.C., June 10, 1991.
Omolade, Barbara (Jones). Telephone interview by author. February 5, 1997.
Parks, Rosa. Telephone interview by author. July 5, 1990.
Reagon, Bernice Johnson. Telephone interview by author. April 9, 1991.
Richardson, Judy. Telephone interview by author. April 25, 2002.
Saltzman, Steven. Interview by author. Chicago, Ill., April 18, 2002.
Sherrod, Charles. Interview by author. Denver, Colo., June 24, 1997.
Simpkins, C. O. Telephone interview by author. August 27, 1997.
Solomon, Maude. Interview by author. Littleton, N.C., June 10, 1991.
Stembridge, Jane. Telephone interview by author. April 13, 2002.
Taitt-Magubane, Lenora. Interview by author. New York, N.Y., February 6, 1990.
Tillow, Walter. Telephone interview by author. August 19, 1997.
Ture, Kwame (Stokely Carmichael). Interview by author, Chicago, Ill., June 1997.
Yergan, Effie. Interview by author. Raleigh, N.C., June 11, 1991.
Zinn, Howard. Interview by author. Cambridge, Mass., July 8, 1996.
Zellner, Dorothy (Miller). Telephone interview by author. April 28, 2002.
Zellner, Robert. Telephone interview by author. April 2002.

INTERVIEWS BY OTHERS
Baker, Ella. Interview by Archie E. Allen. November 7, 1968. Private papers of Archie E. Allen, Santa Barbara, Calif.
———. Interview by Harry G. Boyte. January 15, 1977. Boyte Family Papers, 1941–81, Special Collections, Duke University, Durham, N.C. (Hard copy of interview in author's possession.)
———. Interview by John Britton. June 19, 1968. Civil Rights Oral History Project, Moorland-Spingarn Research Center, Howard University, Washington, D.C.
———. Interview by Clayborne Carson. New York, N.Y., May 5, 1972. Martin Luther King Jr. Papers Project, Stanford University, Stanford, Calif.
———. Interview by Casey Hayden and Sue Thrasher. New York, N.Y., April 19, 1977. Southern Oral History Program, University of North Carolina, Chapel Hill.
———. Interview by Lenore Bredeson Hogan. New York, N.Y., March 4, 1979. Highlander Research and Education Center, New Market, Tenn.

——. Interview by Aldon Morris. New York, N.Y., August 28, 1978. (In author's possession.)

——. Interview by Anne Cooke Romaine. New York, N.Y., 1967. Martin Luther King Jr. Center Archives, Atlanta, Ga.

——. Interview by Julius Scott. New York, N.Y., n.d. (circa 1974). Permission to use interview tape courtesy of Julius Scott; transcribed by Sarah Wood.

——. Interview by *Urban Review* editors. *Urban Review* 4, no. 3 (May 1970): 19–23.

——. Interview by Eugene Walker. September 4, 1974. Southern Oral History Project, University of North Carolina, Chapel Hill.

——. Interviewer not known. N.d. (circa 1980). Duke University Oral History Program, Durham, N.C.

Clark, Septima. Interview by Jacquelyn Dowd Hall. July 25, 1976. Southern Oral History Project, Wilson Library, University of North Carolina, Chapel Hill.

Davis, Sallye. Interview by Nell Irvin Painter. Birmingham, Ala., Oct. 17, 1976. Southern Oral History Project, Wilson Library, University of North Carolina, Chapel Hill.

Higgs, Bill. Interview by Anne Cooke Romaine. January 1967. In Romaine, "The Mississippi Freedom Democratic Party through August 1964," 280–300.

Lawson, James. Interview by Milton Viorst. Los Angeles, January 1978. Moorland-Spingarn Research Center, Howard University, Washington, D.C.

Levison, Stanley. Interview by James Mosby. New York, N.Y., February 14, 1970. Moorland-Spingarn Research Center, Howard University, Washington, D.C.

Lewis, John. Interview by Milton Viorst. Washington, D.C., June 1978. Moorland-Spingarn Research Center, Howard University, Washington, D.C.

McDew, Charles. Interview by Katherine Shannon. Washington, D.C. August 24, 1967. Moorland-Spingarn Research Center, Howard University, Washington, D.C.

Murray, Pauli. Interview by Robert Martin. New York, N.Y., August 15, 1968. Moorland-Spingarn Research Center, Howard University, Washington, D.C.

Rauh, Joseph. Interview by Anne Cooke Romaine. Washington, D.C., June 1967. Romaine, "The Mississippi Freedom Democratic Party through August 1964," 302–6.

Samstein, Mendy. Interview by Anne Cooke Romaine. Knoxville, Tenn., September 1966. Romaine, "The Mississippi Freedom Democratic Party through August 1964," 136–82.

Sherrod, Charles. Interview by John Britton. June 19, 1968. Civil Rights Oral History Project, Moorland-Spingarn Research Center, Howard University, Washington, D.C.

NEWSPAPERS AND PERIODICALS

Amsterdam News
Atlanta Constitution
Atlanta Daily World
Baltimore Afro-American
Birmingham World
Chicago Defender
Crisis
Liberty
Littleton Courier
Littleton News Reporter
Nashville Banner
National News
New York Times

Norfolk Journal and Guide
Norfolk Landmark
Pittsburgh Courier
Richmond Times Dispatch
Shreveport Times
Southern Patriot
Student Voice
Washington Evening Star
West Indian News

PUBLISHED SOURCES, DISSERTATIONS, THESES, AND UNPUBLISHED COMMENTS

Abernathy, Ralph David. *And the Walls Came Tumbling Down*. New York: Harper and Row, 1989.

Abrahams, Roger D. "Negotiating Respect: Patterns of Presentation among Black Women." *Journal of American Folklore* 88 (1975): 58–80.

Adams, Frank, with Myles Horton. *Unearthing Seeds of Fire: The Idea of Highlander*. Winston-Salem, N.C.: John F. Blair, 1975.

Adelson, Alan. *SDS*. New York: Scribner, 1972.

Adero, Malaika, ed. *Up South: Stories, Studies, and Letters of This Century's African American Migrations*. New York: New Press, 1992.

Aktenbaugh, Richard J. *Education for Struggle: The American Labor Colleges of the 1920s and 1930s*. Philadelphia: Temple University Press, 1990.

Alexander, Robert Jackson. *The Right Opposition: The Lovestonites and the International Communist Opposition of the 1930's*. Westport, Conn.: Greenwood Press, 1981.

Anderson, Carol Elaine. "Eyes off the Prize: African-Americans, the United Nations, and the Struggle for Human Rights, 1944–1952." Ph.D. diss., Ohio State University, 1995.

Anderson, Eric. *Race and Politics in North Carolina, 1972–1901: The "Black Second" Congressional District*. Baton Rouge: Louisiana State University Press, 1981.

Anderson, James D. *The Education of Blacks in the South, 1860–1935*. Chapel Hill: University of North Carolina Press, 1988.

Anderson, Jervis. *A. Philip Randolph: A Biographical Portrait*. New York: Harcourt Brace Jovanovich, 1972.

——. *Bayard Rustin: Troubles I've Seen*. New York: HarperCollins, 1997.

——. *This Was Harlem: A Cultural Portrait, 1900–1950*. New York: Farrar Straus Giroux, 1982.

Anderson, William G. "The Spirit of Albany." *Labor Today* 3 (Winter 1962–63).

Arnesen, Eric J. *Brotherhoods of Color: Black Railroad Workers and the Struggle for Equality*. Cambridge, Mass.: Harvard University Press, 2001.

Avery, Sheldon. *Up from Washington: William Pickens and the Negro Struggle for Equality, 1900–1954*. Newark, Del.: University of Delaware Press, 1989.

Ayers, William. " 'We Who Believe in Freedom Cannot Rest until It's Done': Two Dauntless Women of the Civil Rights Movement and the Education of a People." *Harvard Educational Review* 59, no. 4, (November 1989): 520–28.

Baker, Ella. "Bigger Than a Hamburger." *Southern Patriot* 18, no. 5 (June 1960): 4.

——. "The Black Woman in the Civil Rights Struggle." In *Ella Baker: Freedom Bound*, by Joanne Grant, 227–31. New York: Wiley, 1998.

——. "Developing Community Leadership." In *Black Women in White America*, ed. Gerda Lerner, 345–52. New York: Random House, 1972.

——. "Great Society or the Grim Society." *Liberty* (June 1965): 3.

——. "Lack of Thought Cripples South." *Southern Patriot* 20 (March 1962).

——. "Tent City: Freedom's Front Line." *Southern Patriot* 19 (February 1961): 1.

Baker, Ella, and Marvel Cooke. "The Bronx Slave Market." *Crisis* 42 (November 1935): 330–331, 340.

Bambara, Toni Cade, ed. *The Black Woman: An Anthology*. New York: Signet, 1970.

Banks, William M. *Black Intellectuals: Race and Responsibility in American Life*. New York: Norton, 1996.

Barnard, Hollinger F., ed. *Outside the Magic Circle: The Autobiography of Virginia Foster Durr*. Tuscaloosa: University of Alabama Press, 1985.

Barnes, Catherine A. *Journey from Jim Crow: The Desegregation of Southern Transit*. New York: Columbia University Press, 1983.

Barnett, Bernice McNair. "Invisible Southern Black Women Leaders in the Civil Rights Movement: The Triple Constraints of Gender, Class, and Race." *Gender and Society* 7, no. 2 (June 1993): 162–82.

——. *Sisters in Struggle: Invisible Black Women in the Civil Rights Movement 1945–1970*. New York: Routledge, 1996.

Bartley, Numan V. *The New South, 1945–1980*. Baton Rouge: Louisiana State University Press, 1995.

Bass, Jack. *Unlikely Heroes*. New York: Simon and Schuster, 1981.

Bates, Daisy. *The Long Shadow of Little Rock*. New York: David McKay, 1962.

Bekeley, Kathleen. " 'Colored Ladies Also Contributed': Black Women's Activities from Benevolence to Social Welfare, 1866–1896." In *The Web of Southern Social Relations*, ed. Walter J. Fraser Jr. et al., 181–203. Athens: University of Georgia Press, 1985.

Belfrage, Sally. *Freedom Summer*. New York: Viking, 1965.

Bell, Inge Powell. *CORE and the Strategy of Nonviolence*. New York: Random House, 1968.

Bennett, Lerone, Jr. "SNCC: Rebels with a Cause." *Ebony*, July 1965, 146–53.

Bianchi, Eugene C. *The Religious Experience of Revolutionaries*. Garden City, N.Y.: Doubleday, 1972.

Biondi, Martha. *To Stand and Fight: The Civil Rights Movement in Postwar New York City*. Cambridge, Mass.: Harvard University Press, 2003.

Black Public Sphere Collective, ed. *The Black Public Sphere: A Public Culture Book*. Chicago: University of Chicago Press, 1995.

Bloom, Jack M. *Class, Race, and the Civil Rights Movement*. Bloomington: Indiana University Press, 1987.

Blumberg, Rhoda L. *Civil Rights: The 1960s Freedom Struggle*. Boston: Twayne Publishers, 1984.

Bond, Julian. "SNCC: What We Did." *Monthly Review*, October 2000, 14–28.

——. *A Time to Speak, a Time to Act: The Movement In Politics*. New York: Simon and Schuster, 1972.

Bosmajian, Haig A., and Hamida Bosmajian, eds. *The Rhetoric of the Civil Rights Movement*. New York: Random House, 1969.

Boynton, Amelia P. *Bridge across Jordan*. New York: Carlton Press, 1979.

Bracey, John, August Meier, and Elliot Rudwick, eds. *Black Protest in the 1960's*. New York: M. Wiener, 1990.

——, eds. *Conflict and Competition: Studies in the Recent Black Protest Movement*. Belmont, Calif.: Wadsworth Publishing Co., 1971.

——, eds. *The Rise of the Ghetto*. Belmont, Calif.: Wadsworth Publishing Co., 1971.

Braden, Anne. "The Southern Freedom Movement in Perspective." *Monthly Review*, July–August 1965, 1–93.

——. *The Wall Between*. New York: Monthly Review Press, 1958.

Branch, Taylor. *Parting the Waters: America in the King Years, 1954–1963*. New York: Simon and Schuster, 1988.

Breines, Wini. *Community and Organization in the New Left, 1962–1968: The Great Refusal*. South Hadley, Mass.: J. F. Bergin, 1982.

Brier, Stephen, et al. *Who Built America?: Working People and the Nation's Economy, Politics, Culture, and Society*. 2 vols. New York: Pantheon, 1992.

Brown, Cynthia Stokes, ed. *Ready from Within: Septima Clark and the Civil Rights Movement*. Trenton, N.J.: Africa World Press, 1980.

Brown, Elsa Barkley. "Mothers of Mind." *Sage* 6 (Summer 1989): 4–11.

Browning, Joan C. "Invisible Revolutionaries: White Women in Civil Rights Historiography." *Journal of Women's History* 8 (Fall 1996): 186–204.

Buhle, Mari Jo, Paul Buhle, and Dan Georgakas, eds. *The Encyclopedia of the American Left*. Urbana: University of Illinois Press, 1992

Burner, Eric. *And Gently He Shall Lead Them: Robert Parris Moses and the Civil Rights Movement in Mississippi*. New York: New York University Press, 1994.

Burns, Stewart. *Social Movements of the 1960s: Searching for Democracy*. Boston: Twayne Publishers, 1990.

——, ed. *Daybreak of Freedom: The Montgomery Bus Boycott*. Chapel Hill: University of North Carolina Press, 1997.

Burran, James Albert. "Racial Violence in the South during World War II." Ph.D. diss., University of Tennessee, 1977.

Burton, Willie. *On the Black Side of Shreveport*. Self-published, circa 1979. Courtesy of Shreveport, La., Public Library, Special Collections.

Button, James. *Blacks and Social Change: The Impact of the Civil Rights Movement in Southern Communities*. Princeton: Princeton University Press, 1989.

Cabral, Amilcar. *Unity and Struggle: Speeches and Writings of Amilcar Cabral*. New York: Monthy Review Press, 1979.

Cagin, Seth, and Philip Dray. *We are Not Afraid: The Story of Goodman, Schwerner, and Chaney and the Civil Rights Campaign for Mississippi*. New York: Macmillan, 1988.

Campbell, Clarice. *Civil Rights Chronicle: Letters from the South*. Jackson: University Press of Mississippi, 1997.

Cantarow, Ellen, and Susan Gushee O'Malley. "Ella Baker: Organizing for Civil Rights." In *Moving the Mountain: Women Working for Social Change*, ed. Ellen Cantarow, Susan Gushee O'Malley, and Sharon Hartman Strom, 53–93. New York: Feminist Press, 1980.

——. "NAACP, SCLC, and SNCC—Ella Baker Got Them Moving." *MS. Magazine*, June 1980, 56–58, 79–80, 82.

Carmichael, Stokely. *Stokely Speaks: Black Power Back to Pan-Africanism*. New York: Vintage Books, 1971.

Carmichael, Stokely, and Charles V. Hamilton. *Black Power: The Politics of Liberation in America*. New York: Random House, 1967.

Carson, Clayborne. *In Struggle: SNCC and the Black Awakening of the 1960s*. Cambridge, Mass.: Harvard University Press, 1981.

——. "Martin Luther King, Jr.: Charismatic Leadership in Mass Struggle." *Journal of American History* 74 (September 1987): 448–54.

——, ed. *The Student Voice: Periodical of the Student Nonviolent Coordinating Committee.* Westport, Conn.: Meckler, 1990.

Carson, Clayborne, Ralph E. Luker, and Penny A. Russell, eds. *The Papers of Martin Luther King, Jr.* 4 vols. Berkeley: University of California Press, 1992–.

Carter, Wilmoth. *Shaw's Universe.* Rockville: D.C. National Publishing, Inc., 1973.

Chafe, William H. *Civilities and Civil Rights: Greensboro, North Carolina, and the Black Struggle for Freedom.* New York: Oxford University Press, 1980.

——. "The Greensboro Sit-Ins." *Southern Exposure* 6 (Fall 1978): 78–87.

——. *Never Stop Running: Allard Lowenstein and the Struggle to Save American Liberalism.* New York: Basic Books, 1993.

Chafe, William H., et al., eds. *Remembering Jim Crow: African Americans Tell about Life in the Segregated South.* New York: New Press, 2001.

Chappell, David. *Inside Agitators: White Southern Women in the Civil Rights Movement.* Baltimore: John Hopkins University Press, 1994.

Charity, Ruth H., Christiana Davis, and Arthur Kinoy. "Danville Movement." *Southern Exposure* 10 (July–August 1982): 35–45.

Chateauvert, Melinda. *Marching Together: Women of the Brotherhood of Sleeping Car Porters.* Urbana: University of Illinois Press, 1998.

Clark, Septima B. *Echo in My Soul.* New York: Dutton, 1962.

Clark, Wayne Addison. "Analysis of the Relationship between Anti-Communism and Segregationist Thought in the South, 1948–1964." Ph.D. diss., University of Wisconsin, Madison, 1976.

Clarke, John Henrik, ed. *Harlem: A Community in Transition.* New York: Citadel, 1964.

Cluster, Dick, ed. *They Should Have Served That Cup of Coffee.* Boston: South End Press, 1979.

Cobb, Charles. "Prospectus for a Summer Freedom School Program." *Radical Teacher,* Fall 1991, 36.

Cobb, James. " 'Somebody Done Nailed Us to the Cross': Federal Farm and Welfare Policy and the Civil Rights Movement in the Mississippi Delta." *Journal of American History* 75 (December 1990): 912–36.

Cohen, Cathy J. *The Boundaries of Blackness: AIDS and the Breakdown of Black Politics.* Chicago: University of Chicago Press, 1999.

Collier-Thomas, Bettye, and V. P. Franklin, eds. *Sisters in the Struggle: African-American Women in the Civil Rights–Black Power Movement.* New York: New York University Press, 2001.

Collins, Patricia Hill. *Black Feminist Thought: Knowledge, Consciousness, and the Politics of Empowerment.* Boston: Unwin Hyman, 1990.

——. *Fighting Words: Black Women and the Search for Justice.* Minneapolis: University of Minnesota Press, 1998.

Cone, James. *For My People: Black Theology and the Black Church.* Maryknoll, N.Y.: Orbis Books, 1984.

Cooke, Michael. Review of *Memories of the Southern Civil Rights Movement,* by Danny Lyon. *Mississippi Quarterly* 47 (Spring 1994): 353–55.

Cornell, Frederick. "A History of the Rand School of Social Science, 1906–1956." Ph.D. diss., Columbia University, 1976.

Crawford, Vicki L., Jacqueline Anne Rouse, and Barbara Woods, eds. *Women in the Civil Rights Movement: Trailblazers and Torchbearers, 1941–1965.* Bloomington: Indiana University Press, 1993.

Crenshaw, Kimberle. "Mapping the Margins: Intersectionality, Identity Politics, and Violence against Women of Color." *Stanford Law Review* 43 (1991): 1241–99.

Cross, Theodore. *The Black Power Imperative: Racial Inequality and the Politics of Nonviolence*. New York: Faulkner, 1986.

Crowe, Jeffrey, and Robert E. Winters Jr., eds. *The Black Presence in North Carolina*. Raleigh: North Carolina Museum of History, 1978.

Cruse, Harold. *The Crisis of the Negro Intellectual*. New York: William Morrow, 1967.

Curry, Constance. *Silver Rights*. New York: Harvest/Harcourt, 1996.

Curry, Constance, et al. *Deep in Our Hearts: Nine White Women in the Southern Civil Rights Movement*. Athens: University of Georgia Press, 2000.

Dailey, Jane, et al., eds. *Jumpin' Jim Crow: Southern Politics from Civil War to Civil Rights*. Princeton: Princeton University Press, 2000.

D'Angelo, Raymond N. *The American Civil Rights Movement: Readings and Interpretations*. Guilford, Conn.: McGraw-Hill/Dushkin, 2000.

Daniel, Pete. *Lost Revolutions: The South in the 1950s*. Chapel Hill: University of North Carolina Press, 2001.

Davidson, Osha Gray. *The Best of Enemies: Race and Redemption in the New South*. New York: Scribner, 1996.

Davis, Benjamin J. *Communist Councilman from Harlem*. New York: International Publishers, 1969.

Davis, Vanessa Lynn. "Midwifery and Grassroots Politics: Ella Jo Baker and Her Philosophy of Community Development." M.A. thesis, Vanderbilt University, 1992.

Dawson, Michael C. *Black Visions: The Roots of Contemporary African-American Political Ideologies*. Chicago: University of Chicago Press, 2001.

Delany, Sarah L., and A. Elizabeth Delany. *Having Our Say: The Delany Sisters' First 100 Years*. New York: Bantam, 1993.

Demuth, Jerry. "Tired of Being Sick and Tired." *Nation*, 1 June 1964, 548–51.

———. "The Movement as History." *Reviews in American History* 18 (December 1990): 562–67.

Dent, Thomas C. *Southern Journey: A Return to the Civil Rights Movement*. New York: William Morrow, 1997.

Dittmer, John. *Local People: The Struggle for Civil Rights in Mississippi*. Urbana: University of Illinois Press, 1994.

———. "The Movement as History." *Reviews in American History* 18 (December 1990): 562–67.

Draper, Alan. *Conflict of Interests: Organized Labor and the Civil Rights Movement in the South, 1954–68*. Ithaca: ILR Press, 1994.

Duberman, Martin B. *Paul Robeson*. New York: Knopf, 1988.

Du Bois, W. E. B. *The Autobiography of W. E. B. Du Bois*. New York: International Publishers, 1968.

———. *The Souls of Black Folk*. Chicago: A. C. McClurg and Co., 1903.

Dudziak, Mary. *Cold War, Civil Rights: Race and the Image of American Democracy*. Princeton: Princeton University Press, 2000.

Dulaney, W. Marvin, and Kathleen Underwood, eds. *Essays on the American Civil Rights Movement by John Dittmer, George C. Wright, and W. Marvin Dulaney*. College Station: Texas A&M University Press, 1993.

Duster, Alfreda M., ed. *Crusade for Justice: The Autobiography of Ida B. Wells Barnett*. Chicago: University of Chicago Press, 1970.

Eagles, Charles. Review of *Inside Agitators: White Southern Women in the Civil Rights*

Movement, by David Chappel. *Journal of Interdisciplinary History* 27 (Summer 1996): 171–72.

———, ed. *The Civil Rights Movement in America*. Jackson: University Press of Mississippi, 1986.

Edelman, Marion Wright. *Lanterns: A Memoir of Mentors*. Boston: Beacon Press, 1999.

Edmonds, Helen. *The Negro and Fusion Politics in North Carolina, 1894–1901*. Chapel Hill: University of North Carolina Press, 1951.

Egerton, John. *Speak Now against the Day: The Generation before the Civil Rights Movement in the South*. New York: Knopf, 1994.

Elliot, Aprele. "Ella Baker: Free Agent in the Civil Rights Movement." *Journal of Black Studies* 26 (May 1996): 593–603.

Ellis, Mark. *Race, War, and Surveillance: African Americans and the United States Government during World War I*. Bloomington: Indiana University Press, 2001)

Erenrich, Susie, ed. *Freedom Is a Constant Struggle: An Anthology of the Mississippi Civil Rights Movement*. Montgomery, Ala.: Black Belt Press, 1999.

Escott, Paul. "White Republicanism and Ku Klux Klan Terror: The North Carolina Piedmont during Reconstruction." In *Race, Class, and Politics in Southern History*, ed. Jeffrey J. Crow, Paul Escott, and Charles Flynn Jr. Baton Rouge: Louisiana State University Press, 1989.

Eskew, Glenn T. *But for Birmingham: The Local and National Movements in the Civil Rights Struggle*. Chapel Hill: University of North Carolina Press, 1985.

Evans, Sara. *Personal Politics: The Root of Women's Liberation in the Civil Rights Movement and the New Left*. New York: Vintage Books, 1980.

Evers, Charles, and Andrew Szanton. *Have No Fear: The Charles Evers Story*. New York: J. Wiley and Sons, 1997.

Evers-Williams, Myrlee, and William Peters. *For Us, the Living*. Jackson: University Press of Mississippi, 1996.

Eynon, Bret. "Cast upon the Shore: Oral Histories and New Scholarship on the Movements of the 60's." *Journal of American History* 62 (September 1996): 560–70.

Fairclough, Adam. "'Being in the Field of Education and Also Being a Negro . . . Seems . . . Tragic': Black Teachers in the Jim Crow South." *Journal of American History* 87 (June 2000): 65–91.

———. *Martin Luther King, Jr*. Athens: University of Georgia Press, 1995.

———. *Race and Democracy: The Civil Rights Struggle in Louisiana, 1915–1972*. Athens: University of Georgia Press, 1995.

———. *To Redeem the Soul of America: The Southern Christian Leadership Conference and Martin Luther King Jr*. Athens: University of Georgia Press, 1978.

———. "The Southern Christian Leadership Conference and the Second Reconstruction, 1957–1973." *South Atlantic Quarterly* 80 (Spring 1981): 177–94.

Farmer, James. *Lay Bare the Heart: An Autobiography of the Civil Rights Movement*. New York: Arbor House, 1985.

Ferguson, Karen J. *Black Politics in New Deal Atlanta*. Chapel Hill: University of North Carolina Press, 2002.

Finch, Minnie. *The NAACP: Its Fight for Justice*. Metuchen, N.J.: Scarecrow Press, 1981.

Findlay, James F., Jr. *Church People in the Struggle: The National Council of Churches and the Black Freedom Movement, 1950–1970*. New York: Oxford University Press, 1997.

Fleming, Cynthia Griggs. *Soon We Will Not Cry: The Liberation of Ruby Doris Smith Robinson*. Lanham, Md.: Rowman and Littlefield, 1998.

Forgacs, David, ed. *The Antonio Gramsci Reader*. New York: New York University Press, 2000.

Forman, James. *The Making of Black Revolutionaries: A Personal Account*. Washington, D.C.: Open Hand, 1985.

Fosl, Catherine. *Subversive Southerner: Anne Braden and the Struggle for Racial Justice in the Cold War South*. New York: Palgrave, 2002.

Frankel, Nora Lee, and Nancy Dye. *Gender, Class, Race, and Reform in the Progressive Era*. Lexington: University of Kentucky Press, 1991.

Franklin, John Hope, and Alfred Moss Jr. *From Slavery to Freedom*. 7th ed. New York: Knopf, 1988.

Frazier, E. Franklin. *Black Bourgeoisie*. New York: Free Press, 1957.

Freire, Paulo. *Pedagogy of Freedom: Ethics, Democracy and Civic Courage*. Lanham, Md.: Rowman and Littlefield, 1998.

——. *Pedagogy of the Oppressed*. Trans. Myra Bergman Ramos. New York: Continuum, 1989.

Friedman, Leon, ed. *The Civil Rights Reader: Basic Documents of the Civil Rights Movement*. New York: Walker, 1967.

Gaillard, Frye. *The Dream Long Deferred*. Chapel Hill: University of North Carolina Press, 1988.

Gaines, Kevin K. *Uplifting the Race: Black Leadership, Politics, and Culture in the Twentieth Century*. Chapel Hill: University of North Carolina Press, 1996.

Garfinkel, Herbert. *When Negroes March: The March on Washington Movement in the Organizational Politics of the FEPC*. Glencoe, Ill.: Free Press, 1959.

Garrow, David J. *Bearing the Cross: Martin Luther King Jr. and the Southern Christian Leadership Conference*. New York: William Morrow, 1986.

——. "Black Ministerial Protest Leadership, 1955–1970." In *Encyclopedia of Religion in the South*, ed. Samuel S. Hill, 106–8. Macon, Ga.: Mercer University Press, 1984.

——. *The FBI and Martin Luther King Jr.* New York: Norton, 1981.

——. "From Reformer to Revolutionary." In *Martin Luther King Jr.: Civil Rights Leader, Theologian, Orator*, ed. David Garrow, 2:427–36. Brooklyn, N.Y.: Carlson Publishing, 1989.

——. *Protest at Selma: Martin Luther King Jr. and the Voting Rights Act of 1965*. New Haven: Yale University Press, 1978.

Gatewood, Willard. *Aristocrats of Color: The Black Elite, 1880–1920*. Bloomington: Indiana University Press, 1990.

Gavins, Raymond. "Black Leadership in North Carolina to 1900," in *The Black Presence in North Carolina*, ed. Jeffrey Crowe and Robert E. Winter Jr. Raleigh: North Carolina Museum of History, 1978.

——. "The NAACP in North Carolina during the Age of Segregation." In *New Directions in Civil Rights Studies*, ed. Armstead Robinson and Patricia Sullivan, 105–25. Charlottesville: University Press of Virginia, 1991.

Geschwender, James A., ed. *The Black Revolt: The Civil Rights Movement, Ghetto Uprisings, and Separatism*. Englewood Cliffs, N.J.: Prentice-Hall, 1971.

Giddings, Paula. *When and Where I Enter: The Impact of Black Women on Race and Sex in America*. New York: William Morrow, 1984.

Gilkes, Cheryl. "Building in Many Places: Multiple Commitments and Ideologies in Black Women's Contemporary Work." In *Women and the Politics of Empowerment*, ed. Ann Bookman and Sandra Morgen, 53–76. Philadelphia: Temple University Press, 1988.

Gilmore, Glenda Elizabeth. *Gender and Jim Crow: Women and the Politics of White Supremacy in North Carolina, 1896–1920*. Chapel Hill: University of North Carolina Press, 1996.

Gitlin, Todd. *The Whole World Is Watching: Mass Media in the Making and Unmaking of The New Left*. Berkeley: University of California Press, 1980.

Goggin, Jacqueline. *Carter G. Woodson: A Life in Black History*. Baton Rouge: Louisiana State University Press, 1993.

Goings, Kenneth W. *The NAACP Comes of Age: The Defeat of Judge John Parker*. Bloomington: Indiana University Press, 1990.

Gordon, Lewis. *Existentia Africana: Understanding Africana Existential Thought*. New York: Routledge, 2000.

Graff, Gerald. *Beyond the Culture Wars: How Teaching the Conflicts Can Revitalize American Education*. New York: Norton, 1992.

Gramsci, Antonio. *Selections from Prison Notebooks*. Edited by Quintin Hoare and Geoffrey Nowell Smith. New York: International Publishers, 1971.

Grant, Joanne. *Ella Baker: Freedom Bound*. New York: Wiley, 1998.

——. *Fundi: The Story of Ella Baker*. Film documentary. New York: First Run/Icarus Films, 1986.

——. "Mississippi Politics—A Day in the Life of Ella Baker." In *The Black Woman*, ed. Toni Cade, 55–62. New York: Signet, 1970.

——. "Political Mama." In *The American Civil Rights Movement: Readings and Interpretations*, ed. Raymond D'Angelo, 290–302. Guilford, Conn.: McGraw-Hill/Dushkin, 2001.

——, ed. *Black Protest: 350 Years of History, Documents, and Analyses*. 1968. Reprint, New York: Ballantine, 1996.

Green, Ben. *Before His Time: The Untold Story of Harry T. Moore* (New York: Free Press, 1999).

Greenberg, Cheryl Lynn. *"Or Does It Explode?": Black Harlem in the Great Depression*. New York: Oxford University Press, 1991.

Grossman, James R. *Land of Hope: Chicago, Black Southerners, and the Great Migration*. Chicago: University of Chicago Press, 1991.

Guinier, Lani. *Tyranny of the Majority: Fundamental Fairness in Representative Democracy*. New York: Free Press, 1994.

Guinier, Lani, and Gerald Torres. *The Miner's Canary: Enlisting Race, Resisting Power, Transforming Democracy*. Cambridge, Mass.: Harvard University Press, 2002.

Gutman, Herbert. "Schools for Freedom: The Post-Emancipation Origins of Afro-American Education." In *Power and Culture: Essays on the American Working Class*, by Herbert Gutman, 260–61. New York: Pantheon Books, 1987.

Guy-Sheftall, Beverly, ed. *Words of Fire: An Anthology of African American Feminist Thought*. New York: New Press, 1995.

Haines, Herbert H. *Black Radicals and the Civil Rights Mainstream, 1954–1970*. Knoxville: University of Tennessee, 1988.

Halberstam, David. *The Children*. New York: Random House, 1998.

Hall, Jacquelyn Dowd. "The Mind That Burns in Each Body." *Southern Exposure* 12 (November-December 1984): 64–69.

Halpern, Rick. "Organized Labor, Black Workers, and the Twentieth Century South: The Emerging Revision." *Social History* 19 (October 1994): 359–83.

Hamer, Fannie Lou. *To Praise My Bridges: An Autobiography*. Jackson, Miss.: KIPCO, 1967.

Hamilton, Charles V. *Adam Clayton Powell Jr.: The Political Biography of an American Dilemma*. New York: Macmillan, 1991.

Hampton, Henry, Steve Fayer, and Sarah Flynn, eds. *Voices of Freedom: An Oral History of the Civil Rights Movement from the 1950s through the 1980s*. New York: Bantam Books, 1990.

Hansberry, Lorraine. *The Movement: Documentary of a Struggle for Equality*. New York: Simon and Schuster, 1964.

Harding, Vincent. *Martin Luther King: The Inconvenient Hero*. Maryknoll, N.Y.: Orbis Books, 1996.

——. *There Is a River: The Black Struggle for Freedom in America*. New York: Vintage Books, 1981.

——. "Where Have All the Lovers Gone?" *New South* 21 (Winter 1966): 27–38.

Harris, William H. *Keeping the Faith: A. Philip Randolph, Milton P. Webster, and the Brotherhood of Sleeping Car Porters, 1925–37*. Urbana: University of Illinois Press, 1991.

Haygood, Will. *King of the Cats: The Life and Times of Adam Clayton Powell*. Boston: Houghton Mifflin, 1993.

Hedgeman, Anna Arnold. *The Trumpet Sounds: A Memoir of Negro Leadership*. New York: Holt, Rinehart and Winston, 1964.

Henry, Aaron, and Constance Curry. *Aaron Henry: The Fire Ever Burning*. Jackson: University Press of Mississippi, 2000.

Higginbotham, Evelyn Brooks. *Righteous Discontent: The Women's Movement in the Black Baptist Church, 1880–1920*. Cambridge, Mass.: Harvard University Press, 1993.

Hill, Lance E. "The Deacons for Defense and Justice: Armed Self-Defense and the Civil Rights Movement." Ph.D. diss., Tulane University, 1997.

Hill, Robert A., ed. *The FBI's RACON: Racial Conditions in the United States during World War II*. Boston: Northeastern University Press, 1995.

Hine, Darlene Clark. *Hine Sight: Black Women and the Re-construction of American History*. Bloomington: Indiana University Press, 1997.

——. *Speak Truth to Power: Black Professional Class in United States History*. Brooklyn, N.Y.: Carlson Publishing, 1996.

Hine, Darlene Clark, Elsa Barkley Brown, and Rosalyn Terborg-Penn, eds. *Black Women in America: An Historical Encyclopedia*. 2 vols. Brooklyn, N.Y.: Carlson Publishing, 1993.

Hine, Darlene Clark, William C. Hine, and Stanley Harrold. *The African American Odyssey*. 2 vols. Upper Saddle River, N.J.: Prentice-Hall, 2002.

Holt, Len. "Freedom Schools." 1965. Reprint, *Southern Exposure* 9, no. 1 (Spring 1981): 42.

——. *The Summer That Didn't End*. London: Heinemann, 1965.

Honey, Michael. *Black Workers Remember: An Oral History of Segregation, Unionism, and the Freedom Struggle*. Berkeley: University of California Press, 2000.

hooks, bell. *Feminist Theory from Margin to Center*. Boston: South End Press, 1984.

Horne, Gerald. *Black and Red: W. E. B. Du Bois and the Afro-American Response to the Cold War*. Albany: State University of New York Press, 1986.

——. *Race Woman: The Lives of Shirley Graham Du Bois*. New York: New York University Press, 2000.

Horton, Aimee Isgrig. *The Highlander Folk School: A History of Its Major Programs, 1932–1961*. Brooklyn, N.Y.: Carlson Publishing, 1989.

Horton, John B. *Not without Struggle*. New York: Vantage Press, 1979.

Howlett, Charles F. *Brookwood Labor College and the Struggle for Peace and Social Justice in America*. Lewiston, N.Y.: Edwin Mellen Press, 1993.

Huggins, Nathan Irvin. *Harlem Renaissance*. New York: Oxford University Press, 1971.
——. "Martin Luther King Jr.: Charisma and Leadership." *Journal of American History* 74 (September 1987): 477–81.
Hughes, Langston. "My Early Days in Harlem." In *Harlem, a Community in Transition*, ed. John Henrik Clarke, 62–64. New York: Citadel Press, 1964.
Hunter, Tera. *To 'Joy My Freedom: Southern Black Women's Lives and Labors after the Civil War*. Cambridge, Mass.: Harvard University Press, 1997.
Jackson, James E. "Democratic Uprising of the Negro People." *Political Affairs* 42 (October 1963): 17–21.
James, Joy. *Transcending the Talented Tenth: Black Leaders and American Intellectuals*. New York: Routledge, 1997.
James, Winston. *Holding Aloft the Banner of Ethiopia: Caribbean Radicalism in Early Twentieth Century America*. New York: Verso, 1998.
Jaynes, Gerald. *Branches without Roots: Genesis of the Black Working Class*. New York: Oxford University Press, 1986.
Jenkins, Betty. "A White Librarian in Black Harlem." *Library Quarterly* 60 (July 1990): 216–31.
Johnson, Charles S. *Shadow of the Plantation*. 1934. Reprint, New Brunswick, N.J.: Transaction Press, 1996.
Jones, Adrienne Lash. "The Struggle among Saints: African American Women and the YWCA, 1870–1920." In *Men and Women Adrift: The YMCA and the YWCA in the City*, ed. Nina Mjagkij and Margaret Spratt, 160–87. New York: New York University Press, 1997.
Jones, Jacqueline. *Labor of Love, Labor of Sorrow: Black Women, Work, and the Family from Slavery to the Present*. New York: Basic Books, 1985.
Kapur, Sudarshan. *Raising Up a Prophet: The African American Encounter With Gandhi*. Boston: Beacon Press, 1992.
Kates, Susan. *Activist Rhetorics and American Higher Education, 1885–1937*. Carbondale: Southern Illinois University Press, 2000.
Katz, Milton S. "Peace Liberals and Vietnam: SANE and the Politics of 'Responsible' Protest." *Peace and Change* 9 (Summer 1983): 21–39.
Kelley, Robin D. G. "Birmingham's Untouchables: The Black Poor in the Age of Civil Rights." In *Race Rebels: Culture, Politics, and the Black Working Class*, by Robin D. G. Kelley. New York: Free Press, 1994.
——. *Freedom Dreams: The Black Radical Imagination*. Boston: Beacon Press, 2002.
——. *Hammer and Hoe: Alabama Communists during the Great Depression*. Chapel Hill: University of North Carolina Press, 1990.
Kellogg, Charles Flint. *NAACP: A History of the National Association for the Advancement of Colored People*. Baltimore: Johns Hopkins University Press, 1973.
Kenzer, Robert C. *Enterprising Southerners: Black Economic Success in North Carolina, 1865–1915*. Charlottesville: University Press of Virginia, 1997.
King, Coretta Scott. *My Life with Martin Luther King, Jr*. New York: Holt, Rinehart and Winston, 1969.
King, Martin Luther, Jr. *Stride toward Freedom: The Montgomery Story*. New York: Harper and Brothers, 1958.
——. *The Trumpet of Conscience*. New York: Harper and Row, 1964.
——. *Where Do We Go from Here: Chaos or Community?* New York: Harper and Row, 1967.
——. *Why We Can't Wait*. New York: New American Library, 1964.

King, Mary. *Freedom Song: A Personal Story of the 1960s Civil Rights Movement.* New York: William Morrow, 1987.

King, Robert Thomas, ed. *Fighting Back: A Life in the Struggle for Civil Rights, from Oral History Interviews with James B. McMillan Conducted by Gary E. Elliott.* Reno: University of Nevada Oral History Program, 1997.

King, Slater. "The Bloody Battleground of Albany." *Freedomways* 4 (Winter 1964): 93–101.

Kirby, John. *Black Americans in the Roosevelt Era.* Knoxville: University of Tennessee Press, 1980.

Klibaner, Irwin. *Conscience of a Troubled South: The Southern Conference Educational Fund, 1946–1966.* Brooklyn, N.Y.: Carlson Publishing, 1989.

——. "The Travail of Southern Radicals: The Southern Conference Education Fund, 1946–1976," *Journal of Southern History* 49 (May 1983): 179–202.

Korstad, Robert, and Nelson Lichtenstein. "Opportunities Found and Lost: Labor, Radicals and the Early Civil Rights Movement." *Journal of American History* 75 (December 1988): 786–811.

Kotz, Nick, and Mary Lynn Kotz. *A Passion for Equality: George A. Wiley and the Movement.* New York: Norton, 1997.

Krueger, Thomas A. *And Promises to Keep: The Southern Conference for Human Welfare, 1938–1948.* Nashville, Tenn.: Vanderbilt University Press, 1967.

Kunstler, William M. *Deep in My Heart.* New York: William Morrow, 1966.

Laue, James H. *Direct Action and Desegregation, 1960–1962: Toward a Theory of the Rationalization of Protest.* Brooklyn, N.Y.: Carlson Publishing, 1989.

Lawrence, Ken. "Mississippi Spies." *Southern Exposure* 9 (Fall 1981): 8–86.

Lawson, Steven F. *Black Ballots: Voting Rights in the South, 1944–1969.* New York: Columbia University Press, 1976.

——. "Freedom Then, Freedom Now: The Historiography of the Civil Rights Movement." *American Historical Review* 96 (April 1991): 456–71.

——. *In Pursuit of Power: Southern Blacks and Electoral Politics, 1965–1982.* New York: Columbia University Press, 1985.

Lawson, Steven F., and Charles Payne. *Debating the Civil Rights Movement, 1945–1968.* Lanham, Md.: Rowman and Littlefield, 1998.

Lee, Chana Kai. *For Freedom's Sake: The Life of Fannie Lou Hamer.* Urbana: University of Illinois Press, 1999.

Lerner, Gerda, ed. *Black Women in White America.* New York: Random House, 1972.

Levine, Daniel. *Bayard Rustin and the Civil Rights Movement.* New Brunswick, N.J.: Rutgers University Press, 2000.

Levine, Lawrence. *Black Culture and Black Consciousness.* New York: Oxford University Press, 1977.

Levy, Charles J. *Voluntary Servitude: Whites in the Negro Movement.* New York: Appleton-Century-Crofts, 1968.

Levy, Peter B., ed. *Documentary History of the Modern Civil Rights Movement.* Westport, Conn.: Greenwood Press, 1992.

Lewis, David Levering. *King: A Critical Biography.* Urbana: University of Illinois Press, 1970.

——. *W. E. B. Du Bois: Biography of a Race, 1868–1919.* New York: Henry Holt, 1993.

——. *W. E. B. Du Bois: The Fight for Equality and the American Century, 1919–1963.* New York: Henry Holt, 2000.

——. *When Harlem Was in Vogue.* New York: Random House, 1979.

Lewis, Earl. *In Their Own Interest: Race, Class, and Power in Twentieth-Century Norfolk, Virginia*. Berkeley: University of California Press, 1991.

———. "Race, Equity and Democracy: African Americans and the Struggle for Civil Rights." In *The Social Construction of Democracy, 1870–1990*, ed. George Reid Andrews and Herrick Chapman, 193–217. New York: New York University Press, 1995.

Lewis, John, with Michael D'Orso. *Walking with the Wind: A Memoir of the Movement*. New York: Simon and Schuster, 1998.

Ling, Peter. "Gender and Generation: Manhood at the Southern Christian Leadership Conference." In *Gender in the Civil Rights Movement*, ed. Peter J. Ling and Sharon Monteith, 101–6. New York: Garland Publishers, 1999.

———. "Local Leadership in the Early Civil Rights Movement: The South Carolina Citizenship Education Program of the Highlander Folk School." *Journal of American Studies* 29 (December 1995): 399–422.

Ling, Peter J., and Sharon Monteith, eds. *Gender in the Civil Rights Movement*. New York: Garland Publishers, 1999.

Lipsitz, George. *A Life in the Struggle: Ivory Perry and the Culture of Opposition*. Philadelphia: Temple University Press, 1988.

Litwack, Leon. *Trouble in Mind: Black Southerners in the Age of Jim Crow*. New York: Knopf, 1998.

Logan, Rayford Whittingham, ed. *What the Negro Wants*. Chapel Hill: University of North Carolina Press, 1944.

Lomax, Louis. *The Negro Revolt*. New York: Signet, 1962.

Lowen, James W., and Charles Sallis. *Mississippi: Conflict and Change*. New York: Pantheon Books, 1974.

Lowery, John. "Should Violence Be Met With Violence?" *Realist* 32 (March 1962): 7–9.

Luker, Ralph. *A Historical Dictionary of the Civil Rights Movement*. Lanham, Md.: Scarecrow Press, 1992.

———. "Racial Matters: Civil Rights and Civil Wrongs." *American Quarterly* 43 (March 1991): 165–71.

Lynch, Hollis. *Black American Radicals and the Liberation of Africa: The Council on African Affairs, 1937–1955*. Ithaca: Cornell University Monograph Series, 1978.

Lynd, Staughton. "The New Negro Radicalism." *Commentary* 36 (September 1963): 252–56.

Lynn, Conrad. *There Is A Fountain: The Autobiography of a Civil Rights Lawyer*. Westport, Conn.: Lawrence and Hill, 1979.

Lynn, Susan. *Progressive Women in Conservative Times: Racial Justice, Peace, and Feminism, 1945 to the 1960s*. New Brunswick, N.J.: Rutgers University Press, 1992.

Lyon, Danny. *Memories of the Southern Civil Rights Movement*. Chapel Hill: University of North Carolina Press, 1992.

Macedo, Stephen, ed. *Reassessing the Sixties: Debating the Political and Cultural Legacy*. New York: Norton, 1997.

MacNair, Ray H. "Social Distance among Kin Organizations: Civil Rights Networks in Cleveland and Birmingham." Ph.D. diss., University of Michigan, 1970.

Manis, Andrew M. *A Fire You Can't Put Out: The Civil Rights Life of Birmingham's Reverend Fred Shuttlesworth*. Tuscaloosa: University of Alabama Press, 1999.

Marable, Manning. *From the Grassroots*. Boston: South End Press, 1980.

———. *Race, Reform, and Rebellion: The Second Reconstruction in Black America, 1945–1982*. Jackson: University Press of Mississippi, 1991.

———. *W. E. B. Du Bois: Black Radical Democrat*. Boston: Twayne Publishers, 1986.

Marable, Manning, and Leith Mullings. "The Divided Mind of Black America: Race, Ideology and Politics in the Post Civil Rights Era." *Race and Class* 36 (July–September 1994).

Markowitz, Gerald, and David Rosner. *Children, Race, and Power: Kenneth and Mamie Clark's Northside Center*. Charlottesville: University of Virginia Press, 1996.

Marsh, Charles. *God's Long Summer: Stories of Faith and Civil Rights*. Princeton: Princeton University Press, 1997.

Martin Luther King Jr. Papers Project Staff, eds. *The Student Voice, 1960–1965: Periodical of the Student Nonviolent Coordinating Committee*. Westport, Conn.: Meckler, 1990.

Marx, Gary, and Michael Useem. "Majority Involvement in Minority Movements: Civil Rights, Abolition, and Untouchability." *Journal of Social Issues* 27 (1971): 81–104.

Matusow, Allen J. "From Civil Rights to Black Power: The Case of SNCC, 1960–1966." In *Twentieth Century America*, ed. Barton J. Bernstein and Allen J. Matusow, 494–520. New York: Harcourt Brace Jovanovich, 1972.

May, Elaine Tyler. *Homeward Bound: American Families in the Cold War Era*. New York: Basic Books, 1988.

McAdam, Doug. "The Decline of the Civil Rights Movement." In *Social Movements of the Sixties and Seventies: How Women Entered Party Politics*, ed. Jo Freeman, 279–319. New York: Longman, 1983.

———. *Freedom Summer*. New York: Oxford University Press, 1988.

———. "Gender as a Mediator of the Activist Experience: The Case of Freedom Summer." *American Journal of Sociology* 97 (March 1992): 1211–40.

———. *Political Process and the Development of Black Insurgency, 1930–1970*. Chicago: University of Chicago Press, 1982.

McCord, William. *Mississippi: The Long, Hot, Summer*. New York: Norton, 1965.

McClain, Paula D. "Black Politics at the Crossroads? Or in the Cross-Hairs?" *American Political Science Review* 90 (December 1996): 867–73.

McFadden, Grace Jordan. "Septima P. Clark and the Struggle for Human Rights." In *Women in the Civil Rights Movement: Trailblazers and Torchbearers, 1941–1965*, ed. Vicki L. Crawford, Jacqueline Rouse, and Barbara Woods, 85–97. Bloomington: Indiana University Press, 1990.

McKenzie, Edna B. "Daisy Lampkin: A Life of Love and Service," *Pennsylvania Heritage*, Summer 1983.

McLemore, Leslie B. "The Mississippi Freedom Democratic Party: A Case Study of Grassroots Politics." Ph.D. diss., University of Massachusetts, Amherst, 1971.

McMillen, Neil, ed. *Remaking Dixie: The Impact of World War II on the American South*. Jackson: University Press of Mississippi, 1997.

McMurry, Linda O. *To Keep the Waters Troubled: The Life of Ida B. Wells*. New York: Oxford University Press, 1999.

McWhorter, Diane. *Carry Me Home: Birmingham, Alabama: The Climactic Battle of the Civil Rights Revolution*. New York: Simon and Schuster, 2001.

Meier, August. *CORE: A Study in the Civil Rights Movement, 1942–1968*. Urbana: University of Illinois Press, 1974.

———. "The Dilemmas of Negro Protest Strategy." *New South* 21 (Spring 1966): 1–18.

———. "New Currents in the Civil Rights Movement." *New Politics* 2 (Summer 1963): 7–32.

———. "On the Role of Martin Luther King." *New Politics* 4 (Winter 1965): 52–59.

——. "The Revolution against the NAACP." *Journal of Negro Education* 32 (Spring 1963): 146–52.

Meier, August, Elliott Rudwick, and Francis L. Broderick, eds. *Black Protest Thought in the Twentieth Century*. 2d ed. Indianapolis: Bobbs-Merrill, 1971.

Meyers, David R., ed. *Toward a History of the New Left: Essays from Within the Movement*. Brooklyn, N.Y.: Carlson Publishing, 1989.

Miller, James. *Democracy Is in the Streets: From Port Huron to the Siege of Chicago*. New York: Simon and Schuster, 1987.

Mills, Kay. *This Little Light of Mine: The Life of Fannie Lou Hamer*. New York: Dutton, 1993.

Mills, Nicholas. *Like a Holy Crusade: Mississippi '64, the Turning Point of the Civil Rights Movement in America*. Chicago: I. R. Dee Publishing: 1992.

Mjagkij, Nina, and Margaret Spratt, eds. *Men and Women Adrift: The YMCA and the YWCA in the City*. New York: New York University Press, 1997.

Moody, Anne. *Coming of Age in Mississippi*. New York: Dell, 1968.

Morera, Esteve. "Gramsci and Democracy." *Canadian Journal of Political Science* 23, no. 1 (March 1990): 28–37.

Morgan, Ted. *A Covert Life: Jay Lovestone, Communist, Anti-Communist, and Spy*. New York: Random House, 1999.

Morris, Aldon. "The Black Southern Student Sit-in Movement: An Analysis of Internal Organization." *American Sociological Review* 46 (1981): 744–67.

——. *Origins of the Civil Rights Movement*. New York: Free Press, 1984.

Moses, Bob. "Mississippi: 1961–1962." *Liberation* 14 (January 1970): 7–17.

Moses, Robert. "Comments of Robert Moses." Conference on Ethics and Morality: Voices of the Civil Rights Movement. National Museum of History, Washington, D.C., February 3, 1980. Transcript courtesy of Clayborne Carson.

Moses, Robert, and Charles Cobb Jr. *Radical Equations: Math Literacy and Civil Rights*. Boston: Beacon Press, 2001.

Moss, George Donelson. *Moving On: The American People since 1945*. Englewood Cliffs, N.J.: Prentice-Hall, 1994.

Mueller, Carol. "Ella Baker and the Origins of 'Participatory Democracy.'" In *Women in the Civil Rights Movement: Trailblazers and Torchbearers, 1941–1965*, ed. Vicki L. Crawford, Jacqueline Anne Rouse, and Barbara Woods, 51–70. Bloomington: Indiana University Press, 1993.

Murray, Pauli. *The Autobiography of a Black Activist, Feminist, Lawyer, Priest, and Poet*. Knoxville: University of Tennessee Press, 1987.

Myrdal, Gunnar, Richard Sterner, and Arnold Rose. *An American Dilemma: The Negro Problem and Modern Democracy*. New York: Harper and Brothers, 1944.

Naison, Mark. *Communists in Harlem during the Depression*. New York: Grove Press, 1984.

Nash, Diane. "Inside the Sit-ins and Freedom Rides." In *The New Negro*, ed. Mathew Ahmann, 43–60. Notre Dame, Ind.: Fides Publishers, 1961.

Nash, Gary B. "Free People of Color: Inside the African-American Community." *African American Review* 5 (Summer 1996): 285–86.

Neary, John. *Julian Bond: Black Rebel*. New York: Morrow, 1971.

Norrell, Robert J. *Reaping the Whirlwind: The Civil Rights Movement in Tuskegee*. New York: Knopf, 1985.

Oates, Stephen. *Let the Trumpet Sound: The Life of Martin Luther King, Jr*. New York: Harper and Row, 1982.

Oberschall, Anthony. "The Decline of the 1960s Social Movements." In *Research in*

Social Movements, Conflicts and Change, ed. Louis Kriesberg, 1:257–89. Greenwich, Conn.: JAI Press, 1978.

O'Dell, J. H. "Climbin' Jacob's Ladder: The Life and Times of the Freedom Movement." *Freedomway* 9 (Winter 1969): 7–23.

Olson, Lynne. *Freedom's Daughters: The Unsung Heroines of the Civil Rights Movement from 1830 to 1970*. New York: Scribner, 2001.

Omolade, Barbara. *The Rising Song of African American Women*. New York: Routledge, 1994.

Orange, James. "With the People." *Southern Exposure* 9 (Spring 1981): 110–14.

O'Reilly, Kenneth. *Racial Matters: The FBI's Secret File on Black America, 1960–1972*. New York: Free Press, 1989.

Orr, Catherine M. " 'The Struggle Is Eternal': A Rhetorical Biography of Ella Baker." M.A. thesis, University of North Carolina, Chapel Hill, 1991.

Osofsky, Gilbert. *Harlem: The Making of a Ghetto*. New York: Harper and Row, 1966.

Patterson, James. *Brown v. Board of Education: A Civil Rights Milestone and Its Troubled Legacy*. New York: Oxford University Press, 2001.

Paul, Ellen Frankel, Fred D. Miller Jr., and Jeffrey Paul. *Reassessing Civil Rights*. Cambridge, Mass.: Blackwell Publishers, 1991.

Payne, Charles. "Ella Baker and Models of Social Change." *Signs: Journal of Women in Culture and Society* 14, no. 4 (Summer 1989): 885–99.

———. *I've Got the Light of Freedom: The Organizing Tradition and the Mississippi Freedom Struggle*. Berkeley: University of California Press, 1995.

———. "Men Led, but Women Organized: Movement Participation by Women in the Mississippi Delta." In *Women in the Civil Rights Movement: Trailblazers and Torchbearers, 1941–1965*, ed. Vicki L. Crawford, Jacqueline Anne Rouse, and Barbara Woods, 1–12. Brooklyn, N.Y.: Carlson Publishing, 1990.

Peake, Thomas R. *Keeping the Dream Alive: A History of the Southern Christian Leadership Conference from King to the 1980s*. New York: P. Lang, 1987.

Peck, James. *Freedom Ride*. New York: Simon and Schuster, 1962.

Peek, Edward. *The Long Struggle for Black Power*. New York: Scribner, 1971.

Peplow, Michael W. *George S. Schuyler*. Boston: Twayne Publishers, 1980.

Perkins, Linda. "The Impact of the 'Culture of True Womanhood' on the Education of Black Women." *Journal of Social Issues* 39 (1983): 17–28.

Perkins, Margo V. *Autobiography as Activism: Three Black Women of the Sixties*. Jackson: University Press of Mississippi, 1998.

Perlstein, Daniel. "Teaching Freedom: SNCC and the Creation of the Mississippi Freedom Schools." *History of Education Quarterly* 30, no. 3 (Fall 1990): 297–324.

Perman, Michael. *Struggle for Mastery: Disenfranchisement in the South, 1888–1908*. Chapel Hill: University of North Carolina Press, 2001.

Petty, Pamela. "Non-positional Leadership: The Case of Ella Baker and the Student Nonviolent Coordinating Committee." Ph.D. diss., University of Michigan, 1997.

Pfeffer, Paula. *A. Philip Randolph: Pioneer of the Civil Rights Movement*. Baton Rouge: Louisiana State University Press, 1990.

Piven, Frances Fox. *Poor People's Movements: Why They Succeed, How They Fail*. New York: Vintage Books, 1979.

Plumer, Brenda Gayle. *Rising Wind: Black Americans and U.S. Foreign Affairs, 1935–1960*. Chapel Hill: University of North Carolina Press, 1996.

Polsgrove, Carol. *Divided Minds: Intellectuals and the Civil Rights Movement*. New York: Norton, 2001.

Posnock, Ross. "How It Feels to Be a Problem: Du Bois, Fanon, and the 'Impossible Life' of the Black Intellectual." *Critical Inquiry* 23 (Winter 1997): 323–49.

Powlege, Fred. *Free at Last?: The Civil Rights Movement and the People Who Made It.* Boston: Little, Brown, 1991.

Proviser, Norman W., and William D. Pederson, eds. *Grassroots Constitutionalism: Shreveport, the South, and the Supreme Law of the Land.* Lanham, Md.: University Press of America, 1988.

Raines, Howell. *My Soul Is Rested: The Story of the Civil Rights Movement in the Deep South.* New York: Putnam, 1977.

Rajshekar, V. T. *Dalit: The Black Untouchables of India.* Atlanta: Clarity Press, 1987.

Ralph, James, Jr. *Northern Protest: Martin Luther King, Chicago, and the Civil Rights Movement.* Cambridge, Mass.: Harvard University Press, 1993.

Rampersad, Arnold. *The Art and Imagination of W. E. B. Du Bois.* Cambridge, Mass.: Harvard University Press, 1976.

———. *The Life of Langston Hughes.* Vol. 1: *1902–1941, I Too, Sing America.* New York: Oxford University Press, 1986.

Ransby, Barbara. "Ella J. Baker and the Black Radical Tradition." Ph.D. diss., University of Michigan, 1996.

Reagon, Bernice J. "Songs of the Civil Rights Movement, 1955–1965: A Study in Culture History." Ph.D. diss., Howard University, 1975.

Reddick, L. D. "The State vs. the Student." *Dissent* 7 (Summer 1960): 219–28.

Reed, Adolph. *Class Notes: Posing as Politics and Other Thoughts on the American Scene.* New York: New Press, 2000.

Reed, Christopher R. *The Chicago NAACP and the Rise of Black Professional Leadership, 1910–1966.* Bloomington: Indiana University Press, 1997.

Reed, Linda. Review of *Women in the Civil Rights Movement: Trailblazers and Torchbearers, 1941–65,* ed. Vicki L. Crawford, et al. *Journal of Southern History* 58 (May 1992): 384–86.

———. *Simple Decency and Common Sense: The Southern Conference Movement, 1938–1963.* Bloomington: Indiana University Press, 1991.

Richards, Johnetta. "The Southern Negro Youth Congress: A History." Ph.D. diss., University of Cincinnati, 1987.

Richards, Yevette. *Maida Springer: Pan-Africanist and International Labor Leader.* Pittsburgh: University of Pittsburgh Press, 2000.

Ricks, John A. "'De Lawd' Descends and Is Crucified: Martin Luther King, Jr., in Albany, Georgia." *Journal of Southwest Georgia History* 2 (Fall 1984): 3–14.

Riggs, Marcia Y., ed. *Can I Get a Witness?: Prophetic Religious Voices of African American Women, an Anthology.* Maryknoll, N.Y.: Orbis Books, 1997.

Roberts, Randy. *Papa Jack: Jack Johnson and the Era of White Hopes.* New York: Free Press, 1983.

Robinson, Armstead, and Patricia Sullivan, eds. *New Directions in Civil Rights Studies.* Charlottesville: University Press of Virginia, 1991.

Robinson, Cedric. *Black Movements in America.* New York: Routledge, 1997.

———. *Black Marxism: The Making of the Black Radical Tradition.* Chapel Hill: University of North Carolina Press, 1983.

Robinson, Jo Anne Gibson. *The Montgomery Bus Boycott and the Women Who Started It.* Knoxville: University of Tennessee Press, 1987.

Robnett, Belinda. *How Long? How Long?: African-American Women in the Struggle for Civil Rights.* New York: Oxford University Press, 1997.

Rollins, Judith. *All Is Never Said: The Narrative of Odette Harper Hines*. Philadelphia: Temple University Press, 1995.

Romaine, Anne Cooke. "The Mississippi Freedom Democratic Party through August 1964." M.A. thesis, University of Virginia, 1970.

Ross, B. Joyce. *J. E. Spingarn and the Rise of the NAACP, 1911–1939*. New York: Atheneum, 1972.

———. "Mary McLeod Bethune and the National Youth Administration: A Case Study of Power Relationships in the Black Cabinet of Franklin D. Roosevelt." In *Black Leaders of the Twentieth Century*, ed. John Hope Franklin and August Meier, 191–219. Urbana: University of Illinois Press, 1982.

Ross, Kenneth. Review of *Free At Last?: The Civil Rights Movement and the People Who Made It*, by Fred Powledge. *Journal of Southern History* 59 (February 1993): 171–72.

Rothschild, Mary Aiken. *A Case of Black and White: Northern Volunteers and the Southern Freedom Summers, 1964–65*. Westport, Conn.: Greenwood Press: 1982.

———. "The Volunteers and the Freedom Schools: Education for Social Change in Mississippi." *History of Education Quarterly* 22, no. 4 (Winter 1982): 401–20.

Rudwick, Elliot, and August Meier. "The Rise of the Black Secreteriat in the NAACP, 1909–1935." In *Along the Color Line: Explorations in the Black Experience*, ed. Elliot Rudwick and August Meier, 94–127. Urbana: University of Illinois Press, 1976.

Rustin, Bayard. *Down the Line: The Collected Writings of Bayard Rustin*. Chicago: Quadrangle Books, 1971.

———. *Report on Montgomery, Alabama*. New York: War Resisters League, 1956.

———. *Strategies for Freedom: The Changing Patterns of Black Protest*. New York: Columbia University Press, 1976.

Sacks, Karen Brodkin. *Caring by the Hour: Women, Work, and Organizing at Duke Medical Center*. Urbana: University of Illinois Press, 1988.

Said, Edward. *Representations of the Intellectual*. New York: Pantheon Books, 1994.

Sale, Kirkpatrick. *SDS*. New York: Random House, 1973.

Salem, Dorothy. *To Better Our World: Black Women in Organized Reform, 1890–1920*. New York: Carlson Publishing, 1990.

Sales, William W., Jr. *From Civil Rights to Black Liberation: Malcolm X and the Organization of Afro-American Unity*. Boston: South End Press, 1994.

Schmeidler, Emilie. "Shaping Ideas and Actions: CORE, SCLC, and SNCC in the Struggle for Equality, 1960–1966." Ph.D. diss., University of Michigan, 1980.

Schulke, Flip. *He Had a Dream: Martin Luther King and the Civil Rights Movement*. New York: Norton, 1995.

Schuyler, George. *Black and Conservative*. New Rochelle, N.Y.: Arlington House, 1966.

———. *Black Empire*. Edited by Robert A. Hill and R. Kent Rasmussen. Boston: Northeastern University Press, 1991.

———. *Rac(e)ing to the Right: Selected Essays of George S. Schuyler*. Edited by Jeffrey B. Leak. Knoxville: University of Tennessee Press, 2001.

———. "The Young Negro Cooperative League." *Crisis* 38 (January 1932): 456, 472.

Scott, James C. *Domination and the Arts of Resistance: Hidden Transcripts*. New Haven: Yale University Press, 1990.

Sellers, Cleveland, with Robert Terrell. *The River of No Return: The Autobiography of a Black Militant and the Life and Death of SNCC*. New York: Morrow, 1973.

Sernett, Milton C. *Bound for the Promised Land: African American Religion and the Great Migration*. Durham: Duke University Press, 1997.

Sessions, Jim, and Sue Thrasher. "A New Day Begun: An Interview with John Lewis." *Southern Exposure* 4 (Fall 1976): 14–21.

Shapiro, Herbert. *White Violence and Black Response: From Reconstruction to Montgomery*. Amherst: University of Massachusetts Press, 1988.

Shaw, Stephanie. *What a Woman Ought to Be and to Do: Black Professional Women Workers during the Jim Crow Era*. Chicago: University of Chicago Press, 1996.

Shrecker, Ellen. *Many Are the Crimes: McCarthyism in America*. Boston: Little, Brown, 1998.

Shultz, Debra. *Going South: Jewish Women in the Civil Rights Movement*. New York: New York University Press, 2001.

Silver, James. *Mississippi: The Closed Society*. New York: Harcourt, Brace and World, 1966.

Sinnette, Elinor Des Verney. *Arthur Alfonso Schomburg: Black Bibliophile and Collector*. Detroit, Mich.: New York Public Library and Wayne State University Press, 1989.

Sinsheimer, Joseph A. "The Freedom Vote of 1963: New Strategies of Racial Protest in Mississippi." *Journal of Southern History* 55, no. 2 (May 1989): 217–44.

Sitkoff, Harvard. "African American Militancy in the World War II South: Another Perspective." In *Remaking Dixie: the Impact of World War II on the American South*, ed. Neil McMillen, 70–92. Jackson: University Press of Mississippi, 1997.

——. *A New Deal for Blacks: The Emergence of Civil Rights as a National Issue: The Depression Decade*. New York: Oxford University Press, 1978.

——. "Racial Militancy and Interracial Violence in the Second World War." *Journal of American History* 58 (1971): 663–83.

——. *The Struggle for Black Equality, 1954–1980*. New York: Hill and Wang, 1981.

Smead, Howard. *Blood Justice: The Lynching of Mack Charles Parker*. New York: Oxford University Press, 1986.

Solomon, Mark I. *The Cry Was Unity: Communists and African Americans, 1917–1936*. Jackson: University Press of Mississippi, 1998.

Southern Exposure, editors of. "The Mississippi Movement: Interviews with Ella Jo Baker and Fannie Lou Hammer." *Southern Exposure* 9 (Spring 1981): 40–41.

Southern Regional Council. *The Freedom Ride*. Atlanta: Southern Regional Council, 1961.

Spivey, Donald. *Schooling for the New Slavery: Black Industrial Education, 1868–1915*. Westport, Conn.: Greenwood Press, 1978.

Stoper, Emily. *The Student Nonviolent Coordinating Committee: The Growth of Radicalism in a Civil Rights Organization*. Brooklyn, N.Y.: Carlson Publishing, 1989.

——. "The Student Nonviolent Coordinating Committee: Rise and Fall of a Redemptive Organization." *Journal of Black Studies* 8 (September 1977): 13–34.

Sugarman, Tracy. *Strangers at the Gates: A Summer in Mississippi*. New York: Hill and Wang, 1966.

Suggs, Henry Lewis. *P. B. Young, Newspaperman: Race, Politics and Journalism in the New South*. Charlottesville: University Press of Virginia, 1988.

Sullivan, Patricia. *Days of Hope: Race and Democracy in the New Deal Era*. Chapel Hill: University of North Carolina Press, 1996.

Sundquist, Eric J., ed. *The Oxford W. E. B. Du Bois Reader*. New York: Oxford University Press, 1996.

Sutherland, Elizabeth ed. *Letters from Mississippi*. New York: McGraw-Hill, 1965.

Swanson, Dorothy. "Rand School of Social Science." In *The Encyclopedia of the*

American Left, ed. Mari Jo Buhle, Paul Buhle, and Dan Georgakas, 640–42. Urbana: University of Illinois Press, 1992.

Tanksley, Amma. "Ella Josephine Baker: An Analysis of Liberatory Leadership." M.A. thesis, Cornell University, 1997.

Taylor, Clarence. *Knocking at Our Own Door: Milton A. Galamison and the Struggle to Integrate New York City Schools* (New York: Columbia University Press, 1997).

Taylor, Ula. "The Historical Evolution of Black Feminist Theory and Praxis." *Journal of Black Studies* 29, no. 2 (November 1998): 234–53.

Taylor, Verta. "Social Movement Continuity: The Women's Movement in Abeyance." *American Journal of Sociology* 54 (October 1987): 761–75.

Teodori, Massimo, ed. *The New Left: A Documentary History*. Indianapolis: Bobbs-Merrill, 1969.

Thelwell, Michael, ed. *Duties, Pleasures, and Conflicts*. Amherst: University of Massachusetts Press, 1987.

Trotter, Joe William, ed. *The Great Migration in Historical Perspective: New Dimensions of Race, Class, and Gender*. Bloomington: Indiana University Press, 1991.

Turmos, Allen. Review of *Speak Now against the Day: The Generation before the Civil Rights Movement in the South*, by John Egerton. *Virginia Quarterly Review* 73 (Winter 1997): 179–83.

Turner, W. B., and Joyce Moore Turner, eds. *Richard B. Moore: Caribbean Militant in Harlem: Collected Writings, 1920–1972*. Bloomington: Indiana University Press, 1988.

Tushnet, Mark V. *The NAACP's Legal Strategy against Segregated Education, 1925–1950*. Chapel Hill: University of North Carolina Press, 1987.

Tyson, Timothy B. *Radio Free Dixie: Robert F. Williams and the Roots of Black Power*. Chapel Hill: University of North Carolina Press, 1999.

Unger, Irwin. *The Movement: A History of the American New Left, 1959–1972*. New York: Harper and Row, 1974.

U.S. Congress. Senate. Select Committee to Study Governmental Operations with Respect to Intelligence Activities [Church Committee]. *Hearings: Federal Bureau of Investigation*. Vol. 6. 94th Cong., 1st sess., 1976. Washington, D.C.: Government Printing Office, 1976.

Van Deburg, William L. *New Day in Babylon: The Black Power Movement and American Culture, 1965–1975*. Chicago: University of Chicago Press, 1992.

Vincent, Theodore G., ed. *Voices of a Black Nation: Political Journalism in the Harlem Renaissance*. Trenton, N.J.: Africa World Press, 1990.

Vollers, Maryanne. *Ghosts of Mississippi: The Murder of Medgar Evers, the Trials of Byron de la Beckwith, and the Haunting of the New South*. Boston: Little, Brown, 1996.

Wald, Alan. *The New York Intellectuals: The Rise and Decline of the Anti-Stalinist Left from the 1930s to the 1980s*. Chapel Hill: University of North Carolina Press, 1987.

Walker, Eugene P. "A History of the Southern Christian Leadership Conference, 1955–1965." Ph.D. diss., Duke University, 1978.

Walker, Jack L. "Protests and Negotiation: A Case Study of Negro Leadership in Atlanta, Georgia." *Midwest Journal of Political Science* 7 (May 1963): 99–124.

Ward, Brian, and Tony Badger, eds. *The Making of Martin Luther King and the Civil Rights Movement*. New York: New York University Press, 1996.

Ware, Gilbert. *William Hastie: Grace under Pressure*. New York: Oxford University Press, 1984.

Warren, Robert Penn. "Two for SNCC." *Commentary*, July 1965, 38.

Watkins-Owens, Irma. *Blood Relations: Caribbean Immigrants and the Harlem Community, 1900–1930*. Bloomington: Indiana University Press, 1996.

Watson, Denton L. *Lion in the Lobby: Clarence Mitchell Jr.'s Struggle for the Passage of Civil Rights Laws*. New York: Morrow, 1990.

Watson, Steven. *The Harlem Renaissance: Hub of African-American Culture, 1920–1930*. New York: Pantheon Books, 1995.

Watters, Pat. *Down to Now: Reflections on the Southern Civil Rights Movement*. New York: Random House, 1971.

Watters, Pat, and Reese Cleghorn. *Climbing Jacob's Ladder*. New York: Harcourt, Brace and World, 1967.

Watts, Jill. *God, Harlem, U.S.A.: The Father Divine Story*. Berkeley: University of California Press, 1995.

Webb, Sheyann, and Rachel West Nelson. *Selma, Lord, Selma*. Tuscaloosa: University of Alabama Press, 1980.

Wedin, Carolyn. *Mary White Ovington and the Founding of the NAACP*. New York: John Wiley and Sons, 1997.

Weisbrot, Robert. *Father Divine and the Struggle for Racial Equality*. Urbana: University of Illinois Press, 1983.

——. *Freedom Bound: A History of America's Civil Rights Movement*. New York: Norton, 1990.

Weisenfeld, Judith. *African American Women and Christian Activism: New York's Black YWCA, 1905–1945*. Cambridge, Mass.: Harvard University Press, 1998.

Weiss, Nancy. *Farewell to the Party of Lincoln*. Princeton: Princeton University Press, 1983.

West, Cornel. *The Cornel West Reader*. New York: Basic Books, 1999.

——. *Race Matters*. Boston: Beacon Press, 1993.

West, Guida, and Rhoda Lois Blumberg, eds. *Women and Social Protest*. New York: Oxford University Press, 1990.

Wheeler, Edward L. *Uplifting the Race: The Black Minister in the New South, 1985–1902*. Lanham, Md.: University Press of America, 1986.

White, Deborah Gray. *Too Heavy a Load: Black Women in Defense of Themselves, 1894–1994*. New York: Norton, 1999.

White, Walter Francis. *The Fire in the Flint*. 1924. Reprint, Athens: University of Georgia Press, 1996.

——. *A Man Called White*. New York: Viking, 1948.

Whorley, Tywanna. "Harry Tyson Moore: A Soldier for Freedom." *Journal of Negro History* 79 (Spring 1994): 197–211.

Wigginton, Eliot, and Sue Thrasher. "To Make the World We Want: An Interview with Dorothy Cotton." *Southern Exposure* 10 (September 1982): 25–31.

Wilkins, Roy. *40 Years of the NAACP*. New York: NAACP, 1949.

——. *Standing Fast: The Autobiography of Roy Wilkins*. New York: Viking Press, 1982.

Williams, Juan. *Eyes on the Prize: America's Civil Rights Years, 1954–1965*. New York: Viking, 1987.

Williamson, Joel. *A Rage for Order: Black-White Relations in the American South since Emancipation*. New York: Oxford University Press, 1986.

Wilson, Sondra Kathryn, ed. *In Search of Democracy: The NAACP Writings of James Weldon Johnson, Walter White, and Roy Wilkins, 1920–1977*. New York: Oxford University Press, 1999.

Wolters, Raymond. *The New Negro on Campus: Black College Rebellions of the 1920s*. Princeton: Princeton University Press, 1975.

Woods, Barbara. "Modjeska Simkins and the South Carolina Conference of the NAACP, 1939–1957." In *Women in the Civil Rights Movement: Trailblazers and Torchbearers, 1941–1965*, ed. Vicki L. Crawford, Jacqueline Anne Rouse, and Barbara Woods, 99–120. Bloomington: Indiana University Press, 1993).

Woods, Clyde. *Development Arrested: Race, Power and the Blues in the Mississippi Delta*. London: Verso, 1998.

Woodward, C. Vann. *The Strange Career of Jim Crow*. 2d ed. New York: Oxford University Press, 1966.

Woodward, C. Vann, Paul Feldman, and Bayard Rustin. *Civil Rights: The Movement Re-examined*. New York: A. Philip Randolph Educational Fund, 1967.

Young, Andrew. *An Easy Burden: The Civil Rights Movement and the Transformation Of America*. New York: HarperCollins, 1986.

Young, Iris Marion. *Democracy and Inclusion*. New York: Oxford University Press, 2000.

Young, Richard P. *The Roots of Rebellion: The Evolution of Black Politics and Protest since World War II*. New York: Harper and Row, 1970.

Youngblood, Susan. "Testing the Current: The Formative Years of Ella J. Baker's Development as an Organizational Leader in the Modern Civil Rights Movement." M.A. thesis, University of Texas, Austin, 1983.

Zangrando, Robert I. *The NAACP Crusade against Lynching, 1909–1950*. Philadelphia: Temple University Press, 1980.

Zieger, Robert. *CIO, 1935–1955*. Chapel Hill: University of North Carolina Press, 1995.

Zinn, Howard. *Albany: A Study in National Responsibility*. Atlanta: Southern Regional Council, 1962.

——. *SNCC, the New Abolitionists*. 1964. Reprint, Westport, Conn.: Greenwood Press, 1985.

——. *You Can't Be Neutral on a Moving Train: A Personal History of Our Times*. Boston: Beacon Press, 1994.

INDEX

Community-based schools, 151, 153, 154–55

Community movements. *See* Grassroots organizing

Community service, 18, 44, 50, 153

Congress of Industrial Organizations (CIO), 80, 92, 132–35, 150

Congress of Racial Equality (CORE), 163, 265, 279, 306, 307

Connally, John, 338

Connor, Eugene ("Bull"), 111, 129, 217, 313

Consumer education, 91–98

Cooke, Marvel Jackson, 76–78, 79

Cooperative movement, 5, 13, 37–38, 82–91, 99, 168, 347

CORE. *See* Congress of Racial Equality

Council of Federated Organizations (COFO), 300, 306–7, 308, 313, 315, 318; and Freedom Summer, 320–25; and Freedom Schools, 327; and Mississippi Freedom Democratic Party, 331, 334, 335

Council on African Affairs, 57

Cox, Courtland, 314

Crisis, 56, 72, 77, 109, 112, 276

Crosswaith, Frank, 73, 80, 159

Crump, Charlotte, 110, 120–21

Crusade for Citizenship, 179–83, 269

Crusader, 215

"Culture of dissemblance," 8

Current, Gloster, 141, 146, 149, 276, 343

Curry, Connie, 252–53, 264, 321, 409 (n. 49)

Dahmer, Vernon, 317

Danville, Va., 116, 117, 273, 313

Davis, Angela, 10, 235, 352–53, 372

Davis, Ben, Jr., 160

Davis, Sallye, 353

Dawson (Burlage), Dorothy, 214, 215, 258

Deacons for Defense, 346

Delany, Hubert, 54, 287

Delany, Sarah and Elizabeth, 54

Dellinger, David, 354

Democratic humanism, 356, 364

Democratic National Convention (1960), 261–62, 264

Democratic National Convention (1964), 330, 331, 332, 336–42, 343

Democratic Party, 159, 268–69

Democratic processes, 189; Baker's commitment to, 139, 310, 364; and local autonomy, 280; and SNCC, 309–10; Baker's definition of, 368–69; and parameters of exclusion, 369

Dempsey, J. W., 41

Dennis, Dave, 318

Depression era. *See* Great Depression

Desegregation: as NAACP agenda, 107, 109; of public transportation, 171; of interstate travel, 267. *See also* School desegregation

Desegregation protests. *See* Freedom Rides; Sit-in movement

Devine, Annie, 334

Diamond, Dion, 288

Diaspora, African, 99

Dittmer, John, 279, 305, 313–14, 420 (n. 5)

Dombrowski, Jim, 288, 291, 332

Domestic workers, 76–77, 171, 226, 365; as conditional insiders, 422 (n. 60)

Domingo, W. A., 67

Donaldson, Ivanhoe, 257, 258, 296, 314, 347, 355

Douglass, Margaret, 71

Dubinsky, David, 158, 159

Du Bois, W. E. B., 3, 4, 77, 100, 109, 235, 371; on color line, 23; on Talented Tenth, 51–52; on all-black cooperatives, 88; and pan-Africanism, 99; and NAACP, 107–10, 139; background and personality of, 109; and communism, 163, 392 (n. 7)

Durr, Virginia, 5, 259

Eastland, James, 343

Ebenezer Baptist Church (Atlanta, Ga.), 174, 181

Education: Baker's approach to, 6, 151–56, 328–29, 357–64; and New York City reform movement, 10, 149, 151–56, 178, 354; black Baptist women's fostering of, 15; Jim Crow limitations on, 29–30; as Ross-Baker family focus, 29–30, 32, 37, 44, 47; black church sponsors of, 48–49; Workers Education Project, 72, 75, 91–98, 132, 326, 359, 361; community-based school models, 151, 153, 154; and Freedom Schools, 295, 299–300, 326–29; and restrictions of traditional teacher training, 359. *See also* School desegregation

Eisenhower, Dwight, 153, 177

Elams, N.C., 24, 31, 37, 38

Elitism: and black Baptist women's movement, 19; and Shaw Academy, 56; and NAACP local members, 120; and King family, 189–90; and "uplift ideology," 226, 297; and Baker's view of teaching profession, 358; intellectual, 387 (n. 43). *See also* Social class

Ella Baker (Grant), 377

Ellington, Duke, 167, 373

Embery, Elroy, 413 (n. 68)

Emergency Civil Liberties Committee, 233

Escott, Paul, 40

Eskew, Glenn T., 187

Ethiopia, Italian invasion of, 98–99

Evans, Rowland, 344

Evers, Medgar, 185–86, 317; assassination of, 313, 319

Fairclough, Adam, 173, 183

Fair Employment Practices Commission, 150

Fanon, Franz, 348

Farmville, Va., 116, 117

Fascism, 3, 92, 94, 98, 105

Father Divine, 88–89

Faubus, Orval, 153

Fayette County, Tenn., 274–78, 279, 286, 291

Fayette County Civic and Welfare League, 277

Fayette County Emergency Relief Committee, 275

Federal Bureau of Investigation (FBI), 156, 163, 233, 352; surveillance of Baker by, 102, 129–30, 160, 177, 216, 353, 403 (n. 2), 404 (n. 23)

Fellowship of Reconciliation (FOR), 163, 240

Feminism, 4–5, 21, 66, 71, 77, 114, 366, 367

Feminist Theory from Margin to Center (hooks), 421 (n. 49)

Field Foundation, 306

Fifth Amendment, 406 (n. 91)

First Amendment, 406 (n. 91)

Fleming, Cynthia Griggs, 294

Fleming, Glenda, 292

Forman, James (Jim), 214, 335, 407 (n. 97); appreciation of Baker by, 239, 271; and SNCC, 275, 278–79, 294, 308, 314, 342, 343, 366, 413 (n. 73); and Puerto Rican independence, 354

Forrest County, Miss., 318

Fort-Whiteman, Lovett, 97

Fosl, Catherine, 407 (n. 92)

Frazier, E. Franklin, 23, 108, 380 (n. 47)

Frederickson, Elizabeth, 73

"Free Angela" campaign, 10, 352–53, 372

Freedom Day (Hattiesburg, Miss.), 317–20

Freedom Houses, 295

Freedom of association, 287–89

Freedom of speech, 288–89, 406 (n. 91)

Freedom Rides, 265–68, 294, 304, 325, 422 (n. 58)

Freedom Schools, 295, 299–300, 326–29, 420 (n. 13); Baker's influence on, 327–29, 357–58; goals of, 327

Freedom Summer (1964), 299, 301, 303, 320–25, 326, 422 (n. 58); and murder of three volunteers, 299, 325, 335, 337, 341; inception of, 313–14; and white student volunteers, 313–14, 321, 343; and Mississippi Freedom Democratic Party delegates, 331, 334

Freedom Tent City (Fayette County, Tenn.), 275–78, 286

Freedom Vote campaign, 308, 311–12, 313–14, 321

Freire, Paulo, 328–29, 359, 362

Friendship Baptist Church (Harlem), 156, 164

Friends of Negro Freedom, 80

Fundi (Grant), 355, 419 (n. 1)

Gaines, Kevin, 358

Gaines, Shirley, 292

354; and Baker's friendships, 81, 148, 161, 211, 221, 231, 233–34, 347; and labor organizing, 132; and SCEF, 211, 231, 350–51; and SNCC policy changes, 247–48, 252–53, 306, 315–16, 321, 347–48; and white northern student volunteers, 308–9, 313–16, 321, 324–25; and Mississippi Freedom Democratic Party, 338–41; and black nationalist rhetoric, 348, 351; and white liberals, 351–52

Interstate Commerce Commission, 267

Jackson, Elijah, 134
Jackson, Emory O., 213
Jackson, George, 352
Jackson, Jacob, 156, 157
Jackson, Jimmy Lee, 345
Jackson, Juanita, 122, 394 (n. 65)
Jackson, Lillie, 122–24
Jackson, Marvel. *See* Cooke, Marvel Jackson
Jackson, Miss., 185–86, 307, 330, 343
James, C. L. R., 372
James, Joy, 367, 386–87 (n. 43)
Jansen, William, 154, 157
Jeffrey, Mildred, 333
Jemison, T. J., 172
Jenkins, Timothy, 373
Jet Magazine, 303
Jim Crow segregation. *See* Racial segregation
John Birch Society, 387 (n. 61)
Johnson, Azalea, 214, 215
Johnson (Reagon), Bernice. *See* Reagon, Bernice Johnson
Johnson, Jack, 25
Johnson, James Weldon, 107
Johnson, June, 307, 334
Johnson, Lyndon B., 313, 315, 337, 338
Jones (Omolade), Barbara, 305, 335, 336, 358, 366–67
Jones, Charles, 269–70, 278, 288
Jones, Claudia, 67
Jones, Donald, 141
Jones, Madison, 110
Jordan, Vernon, 284
Justice Department, U.S., 156, 265, 267, 276, 422 (n. 58)

Kaplan, Temma, 114
Kates, Susan, 74
Kelley, Robin, 218, 278, 364
Kennedy, John F., 265, 268, 313
Kennedy, Robert, 266, 267, 268
Kenyatta, Jomo, 27
Kilgore, Thomas, 157, 164, 168, 413 (n. 68)
King, Coretta Scott, 167, 257
King, Ed, 275, 309, 341
King, Lonnie, 241, 346, 348
King, Martin Luther, Jr., 235, 264, 289–90, 407 (n. 97); and Baker, 4, 10, 13, 34–35, 171–74, 187, 188–95, 238, 243, 245, 253, 257, 371; on Birmingham's racism, 111; and Montgomery bus boycott, 162, 171; and SCLC, 168, 176–77, 180, 185, 222; leadership philosophy of, 170, 188–89; charisma of, 171, 187–89, 191, 241, 245, 247, 283; inner circle of, 173, 174; sexism of, 174; and Prayer Pilgrimage for Freedom, 176, 177; Wilkins's resentment of, 178; stabbing of, 186–87; privileged background of, 189–90; and black Baptist church, 191, 192–93; and nonviolence, 211, 403 (n. 3); and civil rights radicals, 222; and Southwide Student Leadership Conference, 241, 242, 243; and student activists, 243–44, 283; and Albany Movement, 283, 411–12 (n. 33); and SNCC leadership, 283; and NAACP, 284; and Mississippi Freedom Democratic Party, 337, 338, 341; critics of, 345–46; Mississippi protest march by, 346; assassination of, 350; and anticommunism, 401 (n. 16); as organic intellectual, 421 (n. 30)
King, Martin Luther, Sr., 174, 181, 192
King, Mary, 321, 323, 343, 360, 409 (n. 49), 420 (n. 17)
Kinoy, Arthur, 354
"Kissing case," 213, 214
Kochiyama, Yori and Billy, 11
Ku Klux Klan, 129, 212, 220, 319

Labor movement, 158–59, 166, 263, 333; Baker's work with, 5, 132–35, 344; and

Mutual aid tradition, 37–38, 43, 86, 88, 89

NAACP. *See* National Association for the Advancement of Colored People
Naison, Mark, 98
Nash, Diane, 4, 246–47, 248, 259, 265, 266, 269, 270, 288, 366
Nashville, Tenn., student activists, 241, 246–47, 269
Natchez, Miss., 307, 312
National Association for the Advancement of Colored People (NAACP), 4, 9–10, 105–47, 306; and Baker as field organizer, 13, 72, 102–37, 171, 261, 347; and status of women staff members, 106–7, 110, 121, 137, 297; first black head of, 107; founding and growth of, 107–8; legal-political agenda of, 107, 127, 280, 285; racial equality agenda of, 107, 109; dominant personalities of, 108–10; internal conflicts of, 108, 110, 138, 143; Baker's grievances with, 110, 122–24, 142–47, 171; popular participation in, 116; anticommunism of, 134, 150–51, 157, 160–61, 177, 234, 235, 287, 407 (n. 98); women's contribution to, 135–37, 297; and Baker as director of branches, 137–47, 180; and branches vs. national office, 139–40, 149–50, 171, 280, 285; leadership training conferences, 140–42; and Baker as New York City branch president, 148–69, 177–78, 235; and leftist politics, 150–51; and National Emergency Civil Rights Mobilization, 150, 151; moderate stance of, 154; and New York City police brutality charges, 156–57; SCLC rivalry with, 174, 176–77, 182, 186, 263–64; and black militancy advocates, 213; and Robert Williams case, 213–15; and SNCC, 264, 282, 343; and Fayette Freedom Tent City, 276; and social class, 279; and Albany Movement, 282, 284; civil rights philosophy of, 285; hierarchal structure of, 297; male leadership of, 297, 311; and Mississippi branch office, 301,

302; and Mississippi Freedom Democratic Party, 337; Baker's status with, 367, 370
National Association of Colored Women's Clubs, 18
National (Black Baptist) Women's Convention, 18
National Committee for Rural Schools, 164
National Council of Churches, 327
National Council of Negro Women, 71, 111
National Emergency Civil Rights Mobilization, 150, 151
National Free Angela Coalition, 352
National Guardian, 344
National Lawyers Guild, 344, 413 (n. 58)
National Negro Business League, 89
National News, 56, 91, 92
National Puerto Rican Independence rally, 354
National Sharecroppers Fund, 164, 165
National Student Association, 252
Nation of Islam, 210
"The Negro Church, the Nucleus of the Negroes' Cultural Development" (Baker), 58–59
Negro History Club, 69
New Deal, 91–92, 231
Newell, Jenny, 32
New Pilgrim Baptist Church (Birmingham, Ala.), 211, 212, 216
Newport News, Va., 133–34, 137
New York, N.Y.: Baker's reform activities in, 10, 148–61, 178; Baker's first visit to, 58; NAACP branch in, 141, 148–69, 177–78, 235; school reform movement, 149, 151–56, 354; and Liberal Party politics, 157–58. *See also* Harlem
New York Board of Education, 152–53
New York Cancer Committee, 147
New York City Council, 157–60
New York Herald Tribune, 344
New York Police Department, 156
New York Public Library, 69
New York Telegram and Sun, 156
New York Times, 104, 213, 263
New York Urban League, 91
Niagara Movement, 107
Nixon, E. D., 142, 162, 188

Profeminists, 367

Public schools. *See* Education; School desegregation

Public sphere concept, 387 (n. 58)

Public transportation: and Jim Crow situations, 124–27; Supreme Court desegregation ruling on, 171; and segregation challenges, 220, 221, 223–24, 263, 265–71, 292, 293; interstate desegregation of, 267. *See also* Montgomery bus boycott

Puerto Rican independence movement, 6, 10, 100, 156, 354–55, 356

Puerto Ricans, 149, 151–56, 354

Puerto Rican Solidarity Committee, 156

Puerto Rican Solidarity Organization (PRSO), 354

Quarterman, Ola Mae, 292

Race riots, 25, 29, 30, 67, 121, 133, 340

Racial segregation: effects on black life, 16, 24–25, 40; and "separate but equal" ruling, 23; and poor public schools, 29–30; and black colleges, 49; and black accommodationism, 51, 107, 120; in armed forces, 53–54, 107; in World War I era, 53–54; and black cooperatives, 88; and all-black self-help needs, 99; and Baker's NAACP organizing work, 106, 124–31; Birmingham as apotheosis of, 111, 216–17; and physical dangers, 124–29, 185–86, 194, 212; U.S. Supreme Court rulings against, 152, 153, 167, 171; student challenges to, 195, 216, 237–38, 239; activist challenges to, 223–24, 265–71. *See also* Civil rights movement

Racism: historical significance of, 3, 4; in multiracial coalitions, 6, 324–25; Baker's childhood insulation from, 22–23, 39–40; post–World War I, 54; and capitalism, 88; and Communist Party, 97, 287; NAACP's founding as challenge to, 107; charges of against AFL, 134; and Clarks' doll studies, 152; militant response to, 211–16; and red-baiting, 287; Mississippi's reputation for, 298, 300; class analysis of, 364; democratic process and, 369. *See also* Racial segregation; Vigilante violence

Radical democracy, 368–69

Radical Equations (Moses and Cobb), 377, 408 (n. 23), 410 (n. 2)

Radical humanism, 194, 293, 369, 372

Radical intellectual, 363–64

Radicalism: and Baker, 63, 66, 68, 75, 216, 222, 244, 363–64; in 1930s Harlem, 67, 71, 73, 84; spectrum of in Workers Education Program, 93–94; national NAACP dissociation from, 150; of SNCC activists, 244, 259, 265, 314, 333

Rainach, W. M., 229

Raleigh, N.C., 9, 14, 46, 244, 373; racial climate of, 54

Rand, Carrie Sherfey, 94

Randolph, A. Philip, 4, 80, 96, 158, 176–77, 235, 337, 371; and In Friendship, 164–65, 166, 167

Rand School for Social Science, 94

Rape, 8, 210

Rauh, Joseph, 333, 338, 339, 340, 341, 418 (n. 33)

Reagan, Ronald, 353

Reagon, Bernice Johnson, 8–9, 12, 102, 114, 194, 413 (n. 62)

Reagon, Cordell, 282

Reconstruction era, 48–49

Red-baiting. *See* Anticommunism

Regional Council for Negro Leadership, 301

Republican Party, 261–62, 338

Richards, Dona, 318

Richardson, Gloria, 314

Richardson, Judy, 294, 323, 328, 349

Richmond, Va., 114–16

Ricks, Willie, 346

Roberts (Robinson), T. J. (Bob) (Ella Baker's husband), 57, 66, 101–4, 118, 119, 145, 179, 195, 227

Robeson, Essie, 57, 77

Robeson, Paul, 57, 77, 163

Robinson, Cleveland, 164

Robinson, James, 157, 160

Robinson, Joanne Gibson, 127, 162, 171, 175, 176, 297

GENDER AND AMERICAN CULTURE

Rank Ladies: Gender and Cultural Hierarchy in American Vaudeville
by M. Alison Kibler (1999)

Strangers and Pilgrims: Female Preaching in America, 1740–1845
by Catherine A. Brekus (1998)

Sex and Citizenship in Antebellum America
by Nancy Isenberg (1998)

Yours in Sisterhood: Ms. Magazine and the Promise of Popular Feminism
by Amy Erdman Farrell (1998)

We Mean to Be Counted: White Women and Politics in Antebellum Virginia
by Elizabeth R. Varon (1998)

*Women Against the Good War: Conscientious Objection and Gender on
the American Home Front, 1941–1947*
by Rachel Waltner Goossen (1997)

Toward an Intellectual History of Women: Essays by Linda K. Kerber
(1997)

*Gender and Jim Crow: Women and the Politics of White Supremacy in North Carolina,
1896–1920*
by Glenda Elizabeth Gilmore (1996)

*Delinquent Daughters: Protecting and Policing Adolescent Female Sexuality
in the United States, 1885–1920*
by Mary E. Odem (1995)

U.S. History as Women's History: New Feminist Essays
edited by Linda K. Kerber, Alice Kessler-Harris, and Kathryn Kish Sklar (1995)

*Common Sense and a Little Fire: Women and Working-Class Politics in the United States,
1900–1965*
by Annelise Orleck (1995)

How Am I to Be Heard?: Letters of Lillian Smith
edited by Margaret Rose Gladney (1993)

Entitled to Power: Farm Women and Technology, 1913–1963
by Katherine Jellison (1993)

Revising Life: Sylvia Plath's Ariel Poems
by Susan R. Van Dyne (1993)

Made From This Earth: American Women and Nature
by Vera Norwood (1993)

Unruly Women: The Politics of Social and Sexual Control in the Old South
by Victoria E. Bynum (1992)

The Work of Self-Representation: Lyric Poetry in Colonial New England
by Ivy Schweitzer (1991)

Labor and Desire: Women's Revolutionary Fiction in Depression America
by Paula Rabinowitz (1991)